The Presence of Others

Voices and Images That Call for Response

THIRD EDITION

The Presence of Others

Voices and Images
That Call for Response

ANDREA A. LUNSFORD
The Ohio State University

JOHN J. RUSZKIEWICZ
The University of Texas at Austin

BEDFORD/ST. MARTIN'S
Boston ◆ New York

For Bedford/St. Martin's

Executive Editor: Marilyn Moller
Developmental Editor: John Elliott
Senior Production Editor: Shuli Traub
Senior Production Supervisor: Dennis J. Conroy
Marketing Manager: Brian Wheel
Art Director: Lucy Krikorian
Text and Cover Design: Anna George
Copy Editor: Wendy Polhemus-Annibell
Photo Research: Rose Corbett Gordon/Inge King
Composition: Pine Tree Composition, Inc.
Printing and Binding: RR Donnelley & Sons Company

President: Charles H. Christensen
Editorial Director: Joan E. Feinberg
Editor in Chief: Nancy Perry
Director of Editing, Design, and Production: Marcia Cohen
Managing Editor: Erica T. Appel

Library of Congress Catalog Card Number: 99-62177

Manufactured in the United States of America.

5   4   3   2   1   0
f   e   d   c   b   a

For information, write: Bedford/St. Martin's, 75 Arlington Street, Boston, MA 02116   (617-399-4000)

ISBN: 0-312-20172-9

Acknowledgments

Acknowledgments and copyrights appear at the back of the book on pages 733–736, which constitute an extension of the copyright page. It is a violation of the law to reproduce these selections by any means whatsoever without the written permission of the copyright holder.

Preface

"For excellence," writes philosopher Hannah Arendt, "the presence of others is always required." Not genius, she tells us, not divine inspiration, not even good old-fashioned hard work, but *others*. In choosing a title for this text, we thought of Arendt's statement, because this book aims to lead students toward excellence in reading and writing, toward excellence in thinking through difficult ideas and topics, toward excellence in articulating their own positions on issues and providing good reasons for supporting those positions, always in relation to other people's thoughts, words, and images.

Given these aims, we have been delighted at the response from those using the first two editions of *The Presence of Others:* teachers and students report that they have indeed been spurred to react to the many perspectives presented in the text, saying "yes" to some, and "no" or even "maybe" to others. They have been moved to think hard about these differing viewpoints and about their own positions. Equally important, they tell us that the multiple (and often competing) voices and views in this text call out for response, leading from reading and thinking to writing and often back again.

Two of the voices calling out for response in this book belong to us, the editors, Andrea Lunsford and John Ruszkiewicz. Longtime friends, we take very different views on most issues, and we make many of those views and opinions known in *The Presence of Others*. But disagreement, conflict, and agonism are not guiding principles of this book. It is not a tennis match of ideas, one that will yield winners and losers. Rather, we are interested in how we all come to know and to take positions on various issues, how we can nurture productive exchanges of ideas. These are the kinds of open discussions the readings from *The Presence of Others* have generated in our own classes.

So we invite readers to join the conversation yet again, to question, challenge, and delight in many points of view, including our own. For this third edition, we've tried our best to provide a balanced set of readings that represent widely varying opinions on topics ranging from education to ethics, from science and technology to the world of work. Many of these readings will likely surprise anyone who believes that attitudes can be predicted by labels as equivocal as "liberal" or "conservative"—just as we have been surprised by the complex positions students have taken in our classes.

The Presence of Others thus aims to open and sustain animated conversation among the 69 readings, the editors and students whose commentaries accompany the readings, and the teachers and students we hope will put forth their own ideas and responses. To encourage this engagement, we offer a variety of pedagogical features.

NOTABLE FEATURES

A *balance of viewpoints* gives every student ideas to support and to dispute. Readings represent many genres as well—stories, speeches, sermons, prayers, poems, personal memoirs, interviews, Web pages, photographs, and advertisements, as well as essays and articles—and they take a wide range of varying and sometimes opposing perspectives. In Chapter 3, for instance, John Henry Newman rubs conversational shoulders with bell hooks, Mike Rose, and Gwendolyn Brooks. Cross-references throughout lead readers back and forth among the readings, drawing them deeper into the discussion.

The *editorial apparatus* encourages students to join the conversation as well. Each chapter opens with a series of *brief quotations* from the readings and a visual text, giving a glimpse of what's to come. *Headnotes* to each reading provide background information and offer some explanation for our editorial choices. Because these introductions often offer our own strong opinions about the selection, each one is signed. The selections are followed by sequences of *questions* that ask students to challenge the text (and sometimes the headnote), to make connections with other readings, and to join the conversation by writing. One or more of the questions in each reading is designed for group work, which we hope will encourage further dialogue and make the presence of others evident right there in the classroom. A *list of other readings and Web resources* concludes each chapter.

An *annotated reading* in each chapter includes commentary by the editors and student commentators, demonstrating how to ask critical questions and read with a critical eye.

Chapters 1 and 2 provide strategies on *reading and thinking critically* and on moving *from reading to writing.* In addition, *guidelines for writing a critical response essay* and *a sample student essay* appear in Chapter 2, showing students how they might respond in writing to what they have read.

The accompanying *Guide for Teachers,* by Melissa Goldthwaite, provides detailed advice for teaching this book, including commentary on each selection, sequenced reading and writing assignments, and a selection of essays and articles regarding current controversies over the college curriculum.

NEW TO THIS EDITION

- **Forty new readings.** The fresh selections generally offer more pragmatic, broader-based views than the ones they replace. Among the authors newly represented are Peter Gomes, Barbara Dafoe Whitehead, Kenneth Brower, James Q. Wilson, Ron Suskind, Sherry Turkle, and Henry Louis Gates Jr. We looked particularly for new pieces dealing with issues college students will recognize—for example, dorm life conflicts and scholastic dishonesty. We also include pieces by three writers still very close to their college experiences: Wendy Shalit, James Prosek, and Reilly Brennan.

- **A new chapter on moralities.** Our previous chapter on faith has now become a broader exploration of ethical issues, a timely subject, we think, at the beginning of the new millennium. The chapter not only raises fundamental questions about definitions of morality but also addresses specific issues as diverse as cheating in college, the righteousness of civil disobedience, and the ethics of consumption.

- **A new chapter on identities.** We learned from reviewers and our own experiences teaching *The Presence of Others* that students wanted a richer, more dynamic invitation to topics of gender and difference. We have responded by merging these important concerns and others into a single chapter that explores the multiple influences that help to create a sense of self.

- **A new chapter on images.** In this challenging section, we encourage readers to consider how images today shape their thinking and enhance their powers of expression. We include selections on advertising, photography, cartooning, and much more. This chapter also incorporates a new eight-page color insert of "images that call for response." For this grouping, we have chosen images that speak to major cultural, moral, economic, and/or political issues, and we ask students to explore what responses the images provoke and how they achieve their power.

- **A strong emphasis on reading images.** The new images chapter is the centerpiece of a new focus on visual rhetoric that extends throughout *The Presence of Others*. As in the last edition, each thematic chapter opens with a visual text—a photo, a magazine illustration, a brochure—accompanied by questions to help students read images critically. In addition, at least one selection in each chapter includes its original illustration(s), enabling students to consider how written and visual texts work together. To help students think critically, we provide detailed guidelines in Chapter 1 for reading and responding to images.

- **New coverage of online rhetoric.** Because more and more of the voices and images that students encounter come to them in electronic form, we've expanded our treatment of computer-related issues. New readings include a group of mission statements from the Web sites of five colleges and universities, which encourage students to analyze how schools seek to create distinctive online images. To aid in such assignments, Chapters 1 and 2 incorporate new material on the special challenges of reading online texts critically and writing online.

ACKNOWLEDGMENTS

This anthology has changed considerably in the nine years since we first began exploring its possibilities, primarily because of the presence of many, many others whose perspectives and voices echo in these pages. Of great importance have been the extensive support and ongoing spirited conversation we have received from the Bedford/St. Martin's staff, and particularly from John Elliott, who has cheerfully and carefully guided the development of this third edition. We also thank Jessica Zorn and Shuli Traub, who managed this complex project with aplomb, and designer Anna George, whose visual literacy knows no bounds. And we have once again enjoyed the extraordinary energy of Marilyn Moller's editorial acumen. For this edition, we are especially grateful for the insights and extensive legwork of photo researchers Rose Corbett Gordon and Inge King and art director Lucy Krikorian.

In addition to these friends at Bedford/St. Martin's, we are indebted to many colleagues at our home institutions: first and especially to Melissa Goldthwaite of The Ohio State University, who assisted in the search for the best possible readings and prepared the Guide for Teachers. This manual we believe to be thoroughly informed by contemporary writing and reading theories as well as by Melissa's practical experience from having taught the materials in the text. We owe sincere thanks as well to Maureen Stanton, Jennifer Cognard-Black, Carrie LaManna, and Vic Mortimer for helping us to answer many obscure questions and identify references.

We are particularly grateful to the students who agreed to add their voices to this text: Heather Ricker, Jennifer Smith, and Teresa Essman from The Ohio State University and Joshua G. Rushing from the University of Texas. At the University of Texas at Austin, one group of students in John Ruszkiewicz's spring 1999 Critical Reading and Persuasive Writing class were so influential in shaping the third edition that we'd like to thank them individually: Cory Berendzen, Kari Braband, Elaina Breitling, Sir Robert Burbridge, Shelley Callahan, Aaron Cervantes, Kris Copeland, Matt Entsminger, Jason Jankovic, Brandi Jones, Sarah Colley Jones, Alan Laughlin, Doug Martin, Lindsay Naccarato, Zach Neeley, Rita Sanders, Polo Santos, Dana Swanson, Michael Wacher, Anna Waitt, and Marques White. And we salute as well the many other students who have taught us over the years how to be better classroom colleagues. In many subtle ways, their voices are everywhere present in this text.

Finally, we have been instructed and guided by extraordinarily astute reviewers, with whom we have been in conversation throughout this project. We thank Kathleen Bottaro, Manchester Community Technical College; Deborah Coxwell-Teague, Florida State University; Elizabeth H. Curtin, Salsbury State University; Kitty Chen Dean, Nassau Community College; Katherine Ellis, Ph.D., Mesa State College; Gregory R. Glau, Arizona State University; Margaret Graham, Iowa State University; Kay Halasek, Ohio State University; Paul Heilker, Virginia Tech; Andrew J. Hoffman, San Diego Mesa College; Kathy M. Houff, University of Georgia; Deborah L. Kirkman, University of Kentucky; Matthew Kozusko, University of Georgia; Nancy Lippert, Scottsdale Community College; Stephen Metzger, California State University–Chico; Ken Smith, Indiana University–South Bend; Toby Sonneman, Western Washington University; Linda Spain, Linn–Benton Community College; H. W. Spradley II, University of Texas–San Antonio; and Anne E. Wallace, John Jay College.

Andrea A. Lunsford
John J. Ruszkiewicz

Contents

Preface   *v*

Profiles of the Editors and Student Commentators   *xxi*

....

PART ONE HOW WE LEARN

1. **On Reading and Thinking Critically**   *1*

What Is Critical Reading?   *1*
  Saying Yes, No, *and* Maybe   *2*
Why Become a Critical Reader?   *2*
Are You a Critical Reader?   *3*
  Do You Read Online Materials Critically?   *4*
How Can You Become a More Critical Reader?   *5*
  Previewing   *5*
  Annotating   *6*
  Summarizing   *6*
  Analyzing   *6*
  Rereading   *7*
  Responding   *7*
How Can You Read Visual Texts Critically?   *8*
  For Charts, Graphs, and Tables   *8*
  For Photographs, Drawings, and Advertisements   *8*
How Can You Read Online Texts Critically?   *9*
What Does Reading Have to Do with Writing?   *10*

2. **From Reading to Writing**   *13*

Writing to Learn   *13*
Learning to Write Effectively   *14*
  Considering the Assignment   *14*

Considering Purpose and Audience   *14*
Generating Ideas and Making Plans   *15*
Drafting   16
Getting—and Giving—Feedback   *17*
Revising   *17*
Editing   *18*
Preparing the Final Version   *18*
An Alphabetical Catalog of the Writing Assignments
in This Book   *19*
Analyzing   *19*
Arguing   *21*
Brainstorming   *22*
Comparing and Contrasting   *22*
Defining   *23*
Describing   *24*
Writing a Dialogue   *24*
Evaluating   *25*
Exploring   *25*
Freewriting   *26*
Interviewing   *27*
Writing a Letter to the Editor   *27*
Narrating   *28*
Writing to an Online Forum or Listserv   *28*
Parodying   *29*
Writing a Position Paper   *30*
Proposing Solutions   *31*
Keeping a Reading Log   *31*
Reporting   *32*
Working with Sources   *32*
Evaluating Sources   *32*
Quoting   *33*
Paraphrasing   *33*
Summarizing   *34*
Deciding Whether to Quote, Paraphrase, or Summarize   *34*
Incorporating Sources   *35*
Acknowledging Sources   *35*
Working with Others   *35*
A Sample Critical Response Essay   *37*

3.   **Education: The Idea of a University**   *43*

JOHN HENRY NEWMAN   *The Idea of a University*   *46*
"If then a practical end must be assigned to a University course, I say it is that
of training good members of society."

Mission Statements from The University of Minnesota; Morehouse College; The Evergreen State College; California State University, Monterey Bay; and Thomas Aquinas College   *51*

"Our graduates will have an understanding of interdependence and global competence, distinctive technical and educational skills, the experience and abilities to contribute to California's high-quality workforce, the critical thinking abilities to be productive citizens, and the social responsibility and skills to be community builders."

JON SPAYDE   *Learning in the Key of Life*   *58*

"The American tradition, in learning as well as jazz and activism, is improvisatory. There are as many ways to become an educated American as there are Americans."

ADRIENNE RICH   *What Does a Woman Need to Know?*   *65*

"What does a woman need to know to become a self-conscious, self-defining human being?"

SHELBY STEELE   *The Recoloring of Campus Life*   *72*

"What has emerged on campus in recent years . . . is a *politics of difference,* a troubling, volatile politics in which each group justifies itself, its sense of worth and its pursuit of power, through difference alone." [**annotated and with readers' response**]

BELL HOOKS   *Keeping Close to Home: Class and Education*   *93*

"Studying at Stanford, I began to think seriously about class differences. To be materially underprivileged at a university where most folks . . . are materially privileged provokes such thought."

MIKE ROSE   *Lives on the Boundary*   *105*

"If the canon itself is the answer to our educational inequities, why has it historically invited few and denied many?"

DAVID THOMAS   *The Mind of Man*   *120*

"The issue here is not just favoritism that teachers may show to pupils of their own sex, but the instinctive understanding that an adult will enjoy with a child who is going through a process which he or she went through too."

JEFFREY HART   *How to Get a College Education*   *126*

"What is the liberal-arts education supposed to produce? Once you have the answer to this question, course selection becomes easy."

GWENDOLYN BROOKS   *We Real Cool*   *133*

"We real cool. We / left school."

PART TWO   WHAT WE BELIEVE

4.   Moralities: Most Sacred Values   *139*

MARTIN LUTHER KING JR.   *Letter from Birmingham Jail*   142
"I have tried to make clear that it is wrong to use immoral means to attain
moral ends. But now I must affirm that it is just as wrong, or perhaps even
more so, to use moral means to preserve immoral ends."

STEPHEN L. CARTER   *The Rules about the Rules*   157
"We, the People of the United States, who a little over two hundred years ago
ordained and established the Constitution, have a serious problem: too many of
us nowadays neither mean what we say nor say what we mean."

CAROL GILLIGAN   *Concepts of Self and Morality*   169
"If you had to say what morality meant to you, how would you
sum it up?"

JOAN DIDION   *On Morality*   179
"You see I want to be quite obstinate about insisting that we have no way
of knowing . . . what is 'right' and what is 'wrong', what is 'good' and what
'evil.'"

MARK CLAYTON   *A Whole Lot of Cheatin' Going On*   185
"Cheating *is* an answer . . . It might not be a good answer, but none the less it
is an answer."

ANTHONY BRANDT   *Do Kids Need Religion?*   191
"Morality can survive without religion, it appears; children can be taught the
importance of right versus wrong without benefit of religious training."
[annotated and with readers' response]

DAVID BROOKS   *Conscientious Consumption*   200
"Remember, if your furniture is distressed your conscience needn't be."

PETER J. GOMES   *Civic Virtue and the Character of Followership:
A New Take on an Old Hope*   205
"We need passionate followers of an ideal of civic virtue, an ideal that does not
conform, as St. Paul says in Romans 12: 1&2, but is transformed by the renewing of one's mind and one's soul."

WENDY SHALIT   *The Future of Modesty*   214
"I don't want to have sex because 'I guess' I want it. I want to wait for something more exciting than that, and modesty helps me understand why."

KATHLEEN NORRIS   *Little Girls in Church*   222
"I had not yet done the things / that would need forgiving."

5. Science and Technology: O Brave New World   229

MARY SHELLEY   *Frankenstein*   231
"Learn from me . . . how dangerous is the acquirement of knowledge and how much happier that man is who believes his native town to be the world, than he who aspires to become greater than his nature will allow."

J. MICHAEL BISHOP   *Enemies of Promise*   237
"Resistance to science is born of fear. Fear, in turn, is bred by ignorance. And it is ignorance that is our deepest malady."

JEREMY RIFKIN   *Biotech Century: Playing Ecological Roulette with Mother Nature's Designs*   244
"Genetically engineered insects, fish and domesticated animals have also been introduced, like the sheep/goat hybrid 'geep.'"

TODD OPPENHEIMER   *The Computer Delusion*   255
"[T]he battle over computers . . . is not just the future versus the past, uncertainty versus nostalgia; it is about encouraging a fundamental shift in personal priorities—a minimizing of the real, physical world in favor of an unreal 'virtual' world." [**annotated and with readers' response**]

EMILY MARTIN   *The Body at War: Media Views of the Immune System*   286
"The portrait of the body conveyed most often and most vividly in the mass media shows it as a defended nation-state, organized around a hierarchy of gender, race, and class."

JAMES Q. WILSON   *Cars and Their Enemies*   303
"Imagine the country we now inhabit—big, urban, prosperous—with one exception: the automobile has not been invented."

PAMELA SAMUELSON   *The Digital Rights War*   315
"Why shouldn't recording companies issue CDs that are coded to self-destruct or lock up after 15 plays, forcing those who want to hear more to pay more?"

EDWARD O. WILSON   *The Biological Basis of Morality*   322
"Ethics and religion are still too complex for present-day science to explain in depth. They are, however, far more a product of autonomous evolution than has hitherto been conceded by most theologians."

PART THREE   WHO WE ARE

6. **Identities: The One in Many/The Many in One**   *345*

SOJOURNER TRUTH   *Ain't I a Woman?*   *348*

"If the first woman God ever made was strong enough to turn the world upside down all alone, these women together ought to be able to turn it back. . . ."

ANDREW SULLIVAN   *What Are Homosexuals For?*   *350*

"Growing up homosexual was to grow up normally but displaced; to experience romantic love, but with the wrong person; to entertain grand ambitions, but of the unacceptable sort; to seek a gradual self-awakening, but in secret, not in public."

MAXINE HONG KINGSTON   *No Name Woman*   *361*

"She obeyed him; she always did as she was told."

DAVE BARRY   *Guys vs. Men*   *372*

". . . if God did not want us to make gender-based generalizations, She would not have given us genders." [*annotated and with readers' response*]

ZORA NEALE HURSTON   *How It Feels to Be Colored Me*   *384*

"I remember the very day that I became colored."

GEORGINA KLEEGE   *Call It Blindness*   *389*

"Of the students who drop my class after the first meeting, there may be some who find the idea of a blind professor ludicrous, aggravating, or frightening. But I will never know."

ROBERT D. KING   *Should English Be the Law?*   *409*

"I suggest that we relax and luxuriate in our linguistic richness and our traditional tolerance of language differences."

BRUCE FEILER   *Gone Country*   *422*

"Just as rock-and-roll foreshadowed many of the changes in gender and race relations that followed in the 1960s, country music today—with it's suburban, middle-aged themes of family and renewal—may be the clearest reflection of many of the anxieties and aspirations that have just begun to bubble to the surface in American political life."

ALEX SHOUMATOFF   *The Navajo Way*   *433*

"For us, every day is a thanksgiving day, a prayer in the cycle of life. . . . But for you whites, every day is a slogan."

SHERRY TURKLE   *Who Am We?*   *442*

"A MUD can become context for discovering who one is and wishes to be. In this way, the games are laboratories for the construction of identity."

LANGSTON HUGHES   *Theme for English B*   *459*

"I guess being colored doesn't make me not like
the same things other folks like who are other races.
So will my page be colored that I write?
Being me, it will not be white."

7.   **Images: Mirror, Mirror on the Wall**   *465*

PLATO   *Allegory of the Cave*   *467*

". . . [T]he prison-house is the world of sight, the light of the fire is the sun, and you will not misapprehend me if you interpret the journey upwards to be the ascent of the soul into the intellectual world. . . ."

MITCHELL STEPHENS   *"By Means of the Visible":*
A Picture's Worth   *473*

"There was fear too of the magic that seems to lurk in images. They steal likenesses. They do what only gods should be able to do: They re-create the living and preserve the dead."

JOHN UPDIKE   *The Mystery of Mickey Mouse*   *489*

"Like yin and yang, like the Christian cross and the star of Israel, Mickey can be seen everywhere—a sign, a rune, a hieroglyphic trace of a secret power, an electricity we want to plug into."

WARD CHURCHILL   *Crimes against Humanity*   *497*

"Think about why Land-o-Lakes finds it appropriate to market its butter with the stereotyped image of an 'Indian princess' on the wrapper."

JAMES PROSEK   *Introduction to* Trout   *506*

"For me, the trout in its stream is the essence of life—encompassing survival and beauty, death and birth."

NEIL POSTMAN   *The Great Symbol Drain*   513

"One picture, we are told, is worth a thousand words. But a thousand pictures, especially if they are of the same object, may not be worth anything at all." [*annotated and with readers' response*]

HENRY LOUIS GATES JR.   *Net Worth*   532

"Michael Jordan has become the greatest corporate pitchman of all time. As a twentieth-century sports hero, he has plausible competition from Babe Ruth and Muhammad Ali; as an agent of brand equity, he is without peer."

KENNETH BROWER   *Photography in the Age of Falsification*   554

"Our own time is, as much as anything else, the Age of Falsification. The nip, the tuck, the face-lift, the silicone implant."

LINDA S. WATTS   *Review of* Inside the Mouse   575

"If you have ever visited one of the Disney theme parks, . . . you have likely wondered at the labor—both seen and unseen—necessary to maintain these fanciful environments. . . . What keeps employees ('cast members') so poised, meticulously groomed, and endlessly cheerful?"

PART FOUR   HOW WE LIVE

8.   At Home: The Places I Come From   *585*

RON SUSKIND   *A Hope in the Unseen*   588

"Well, college is supposed to be broadening, he muses, and there's no doubt he'll get broadened this year with a roommate like Cedric."

ALICE WALKER   *The Place Where I Was Born*   596

"I remember early morning fogs in Georgia, not so dramatic as California ones, but magical too because out of the Southern fog of memory tramps my dark father, smiling and large, glowing with rootedness, and talking of hound dogs, biscuits and coons."

BARBARA SMITH   *Home*   601

"Sometimes I feel like I'm frozen in time, caught in a nightmare of a hot October afternoon when everything changed because my mother stopped living."

TERRY TEMPEST WILLIAMS   *The Clan of One-Breasted Women*   607

"Most statistics tell us breast cancer is genetic, hereditary, with rising percentages attached to fatty diets, childlessness, or becoming pregnant after thirty.

What they don't say is that living in Utah may be the greatest hazard of all."
[*annotated and with readers' response*]

BARBARA DAFOE WHITEHEAD *The Making of a Divorce Culture* *619*

"Just as no patient would have designed today's system of health care, so no child would have chosen today's culture of divorce."

STEPHANIE COONTZ *The Way We Wish We Were* *628*

"In a 1990 *Newsweek* poll, 42 percent predicted that the family would be worse in ten years and exactly the same percentage predicted that it would be better."

JILL FRAWLEY *Inside the Home* *645*

"The long-term-care facility . . . I work for is owned by a corporation that owns nursing homes throughout the country. Giving corporations like this control over the quality of medical care is handing over control to the fox."

FRED BARNES *Quantity Time* *649*

"Fatherhood isn't brain surgery. I say this in defiance of the new conventional wisdom that being a father is breathtakingly difficult. . . ."

Ask Martha: Guest Towels *654*

"If you're expecting overnight guests, tie a bath towel, hand towel, and wash-cloth together with a ribbon and set it at the end of each guest's bed."

TOM CONNOR and JIM DOWNEY *Well-Stacked Logs* *656*

"The idea is to impress others, not warm the house."

MARGARET TALBOT *Les Très Riches Heures de Martha Stewart* *657*

"To read Martha Stewart is to know that there is no corner of your domestic life that cannot be beautified or improved under careful tutelage, none that should not be colonized by the rhetoric and the discipline of quality control."

ED MADDEN *Family Cemetery, near Hickory Ridge, Arkansas* *668*

"Grandpa's flowers are scattered
down the line of tombstones, decorating
the graves of his wife, his children"

9. Work: As Poor Richard Says . . . *675*

BENJAMIN FRANKLIN *The Way to Wealth* *678*

"We are taxed twice as much by our idleness, three times as much by our pride, and four times as much by our folly; and from these taxes the commissioners cannot ease or deliver us by allowing an abatement."

MERIDEL LESUEUR   *Women and Work*   687
"My first job was to jump off a burning ship into salt water with dangerous tides. I lived."

JULIA CARLISLE and FLORENCE HOFF
Young, Privileged, and Unemployed   691
"'We want to work. We are trying hard to work. . . .' We are worth something even if our ships have come in and set sail again without us." [**with readers' response**]

ARTHUR KRYSTAL   *Who Speaks for the Lazy?*   697
"I was materialistic to the core: I loved money; I loved the idea of money; I even liked novels about the rich and movies about how the poor became rich. I liked everything about money except the prospect of buckling down and making it."

REILLY BRENNAN   *Would You Buy a Car
from This Man?*   706
"More lectures eventually lead us to the 'sales orientation,' a frighteningly brief twenty-five minutes in length, nearly devoid of specifics. . . . I go to sleep at night wondering when we will receive instructions on how to sell these cars."

ROBERT A. LUTZ   *The Primary Purpose of Business
Is Not to Make Money*   712
"Do they go to work each morning because they love the challenge of creation and wouldn't switch vocations even if they were offered marginally higher pay?"

BELL HOOKS   *Work Makes Life Sweet*   717
". . . southern black work traditions taught us the importance of working with integrity irrespective of the task."

WALTER S. MINOT   *Students Who Push Burgers*   726
". . . in all the lengthy analyses of what's wrong with American education, I have not heard employment by students being blamed."

MARGE PIERCY   *To Be of Use*   730
"The work of the world is common as mud."

Acknowledgments   **733**

Index   **737**

Profiles of the Editors
and Student Commentators

Throughout *The Presence of Others,* you will read the comments of the editors who chose the selections and wrote the introductions. You will also meet three student editors—two from The Ohio State University, the other from The University of Texas at Austin—and learn their opinions. To give perspective to their sometimes strong, sometimes controversial remarks, we include the following brief self-portraits of Andrea A. Lunsford (A.L.), John J. Ruszkiewicz (J.R.), Teresa Essman (T.E.), Joshua G. Rushing (J.G.R.), and Heather Ricker (H.R.). Use these biographies to help you read particular introductions, commentaries, or afterwords with more awareness of the editors' experiences, sensitivities, and blind spots. Think, too, about how your own ideas and beliefs have been shaped by your upbringing, communities, and education.

ANDREA ABERNETHY LUNSFORD   I was born in Oklahoma and have lived in Maryland, Florida, Texas, Washington, Ohio, and British Columbia, yet when I think of "home" I think of the soft rolling foothills of the Smoky Mountains in eastern Tennessee. The hills there are full of Cunninghams, and my granny, Rosa Mae Iowa Brewer Cunningham, and her husband, William Franklin, seemed to know all of them. Like many people in this region, my mother's folks claimed Scottish descent. Indeed, when I later traveled to Scotland, I discovered that many of the songs we sang on my grandparents' big porch were Scottish.

The only one of her large family to enjoy postsecondary education, my Mama graduated with training in teaching and in French from Maryville College in Tennessee. An uncle helped pay her way to school, and it was on a visit to see him that she met my father, another Scottish descendant, Gordon Grady Abernethy. His college education cut short by World War II, Dad gave up his goal of following his father into dentistry and instead took examinations to become a certified public accountant. In hard times, he and my mother left Oklahoma and settled near her family, where Dad got a job with a defense contractor at Oak Ridge. Mama taught briefly and then stayed home with me and, later, with my two sisters and brother. I played in a special playhouse I built in the woods, spent weekends with my grandparents and dozens of Cunningham cousins, and alternated attending my grandparents' Baptist church (where they baptized my cousins by plunging them into a river) and my parents' Presbyterian church, where baptisms seemed like a snap. On occasional Sundays, I got to visit a sister church whose congregation was black, where the music was mesmerizing, and where I first began to recognize this country's legacy of segregation and racism. My family, I learned, was proud to have fought for the North, although supporting the Union's cause did not exempt them—or me—from that legacy.

We read a lot in Sunday School and at Summer Bible School, and at home as well. There I had the luxury of receiving books as gifts, especially from my father's sister, and of being read to often: *Gulliver's Travels* as it appeared in *The Book of Knowledge* (our family's one encyclopedia), Joseph and His Coat of Many Colors from Hurlbut's *Stories of the Bible,* Tigger and Roo and Christopher Robin from A. A. Milne, and poems from *A Child's Garden of Verses* are among my earliest memories of texts that grew, over the years, into an animated chorus of voices I still carry with me. Later, I read all of the Nancy Drew, Hardy Boys, and Cherry Ames Senior Nurse series, to be regularly punished for reading in school when I should have been doing something else. Like many young women, I was often "lost in a book," living in a world of heroines and heroes and happy endings. Only slowly and painfully did I come to question the master plot most of these stories reproduced, to realize that endings are never altogether happy and that the roles I play in my own story have been in some important senses scripted by systems beyond my control.

My father wanted me to begin secretarial work after high school, but when I won a small scholarship and got a student job, he and my mother agreed to help me attend our state school, the University of Florida. I graduated with honors but was encouraged by my (male) advisor not to pursue graduate school but rather to "go home and have babies." Instead, I became a teacher, a reasonable job for a woman to aspire to in 1965. Only seven years later did I gather my courage to apply to graduate school after all—and to pursue a Ph.D. Teaching in high school, at a two-year college (Hillsborough Community College in Tampa), and as a graduate assistant helped me reaffirm my commitment to a career in education and introduced me to the concerns that have occupied my professional life ever since: What can I know and learn through my relationships with others? How do people develop as readers and writers? What is the connection between teaching and learning? What does it mean, as the twentieth century draws to a close, to be fully literate?

I pursued these questions in graduate school at Ohio State and beyond, all the while trying to live through two marriages and the loss of my granny; of both my parents; of my brother, Gordon Abernethy; of a much-loved aunt, Elizabeth McKinsey; and, most recently, of my sister Kerry Abernethy. Such experiences have led me to think hard not only about the burdens and hard sorrows every human life entails but also about the privileges my status as a white, relatively middle class woman has afforded me. These privileges are considerable, and I do not wish to forget them. In addition, I have enjoyed the support of a vital network of women friends and colleagues. Thanks in large measure to them, I am now a professor in a large research university, can savor the time I can spend with those I love (especially Lisa Ede, my sisters Ellen and Liz, and their children), and am somewhat able to indulge my desire to experience as much of the world as possible. I even have season tickets to basketball and football games (no mean feat these days), which I attend regularly with my colleague and friend Beverly Moss. These relationships—and my very special relationship with my students—have added to the chorus of animated voices I carry with me always.

These and other formative relationships and experiences have helped me learn a lesson that informs my teaching, my life, and my work on this book: that where you stand influences in great measure what you can see. My college advisor, standing as he did in an all-white male professoriate, couldn't quite "see" a young woman joining this elite group, even as a student. My parents, standing as they did in a lower middle class, single-income family with vivid memories of the depression, couldn't easily "see" beyond the desire for their oldest daughter to get a good, steady job as soon as possible. And I, standing where *I* do now, am not able to "see" through my students' eyes, to experience the world as they experience it.

Keeping this point in mind leads me to two acts that are by now habitual: examining where I stand, with all that implies about inevitable partial vision and perspective; and asking myself where others stand as well. So I came to this textbook project with John, my friend of more than 25 years now, with at least one specific agenda item: to look as carefully and respectfully as I could at his perspective, at where he stands, and to do the same thing for myself and for every voice included in this text. Such acts are necessary, I believe, before I can say that my opinions are fully considered. My view will always be heavily informed by where I stand. But insofar as I am able to entertain other points of view, I have a chance to understand my own better and to broaden my point of view as well.

JOHN J. RUSZKIEWICZ   My grandparents never spoke much about their reasons for emigrating from eastern Europe early in the twentieth century; their grounds for starting new lives in the United States must have seemed self-evident. Only rarely did I hear them talk nostalgically about the lands left behind. So I'm a second-generation American with roots in, but no strong ties to, Slovakia, Poland, and Ukraine.

My father and mother were both born in rural Pennsylvania, my dad with five brothers and sisters, my mom with seven—eight if you count the infant boy who died of measles. Both my grandfathers mined coal in western Pennsylvania, as did several uncles—a dangerous and difficult living. After World War II, my parents moved to Cleveland, where jobs were more plentiful, and my Dad began a thirty-year stretch on the loading dock at Carling's Brewery. I did my share of manual labor, too, for a short time working in a tool-and-die factory, even paying dues to the Teamsters.

But my blue-collar stints were merely summer jobs between college semesters. Education would be my generation's ticket to the American dream. My parents never allowed my brother (who became a physician) or me to think we had any choice but college. We attended parochial schools, where headstrong nuns and priests introduced us to learning, moral responsibility, and culture. (By eighth grade, students at Saint Benedict's elementary school could sing three High Masses and two Requiems, one of those services in Gregorian chant. We knew what most of the Latin words meant, too.) As grade-schoolers, we had homework—hours of it—every night.

High school was the same, only tougher. I didn't have a free period in high school until the semester I graduated. I spent what little extracurricular time I had in the offices of the school paper—where I eventually became editor. It wasn't a prestigious position in a school that specialized (to this day) in accumulating state football titles. But I saw to it that we ran a respectable sports page.

The ethnic neighborhood in Cleveland where I grew up in the 1950s is now considered inner-city. It was very much *in the city* when I lived there too, but a nine- or ten-year-old could safely bicycle to church alone at 6:00 A.M. to serve Mass or ride the rapid transit downtown to watch a baseball game. I did so often enough, suffering through season after losing season with the then-hapless Indians. But Cleveland was a divided place too, and in the long, hot summer of 1966, inner-city neighborhoods erupted in race riots. From my front porch, I could watch the fires that would change the civic landscape, leading to the election of the first black mayor of a major American city—Carl Stokes—in 1967.

Politically, I come from a family of Democrats—my gregarious mother, far more interested in people than issues, was a party worker in Cleveland's 29th Ward. One of my earliest memories is watching John F. Kennedy parade down Euclid Avenue in 1960 during his presidential campaign. But frankly, I was more interested in the bright red Chrysler convertible ferrying the portly governor of Ohio. I have retained my fondness for old Chryslers—and just about anything with four wheels.

The first president I voted for was George McGovern, about what you'd expect from a baby boomer who spent high school listening to Bob Dylan and who went to college deep in the heart of the sixties. I turned seventeen during the "summer of love" (1967), drove a VW Beetle, missed the draft thanks to a high lottery number, and spent hours shooting Super 8 movies that had some connection to my major in English for film classes. St. Vincent College and Latrobe, Pennsylvania, were a long way from Haight-Ashbury. But like most college kids then, my friends and I read Marcuse, thumbed *Ramparts,* and recited mantras of peace and revolution. Rock 'n' roll thundered from our dorms, and when the karma was right, we'd wander as far as Pittsburgh for a peace demonstration. One balmy autumn evening, Joan Baez sang at a gathering in a riverside park, and I thought then that I understood what Wordsworth had meant when he wrote at a more authentic revolutionary moment: "Bliss was it in that dawn to be alive, / But to be young was very Heaven!"

Yet it was during an anti-Vietnam War rally at St. Vincent College that my drift to the political right began. I had read enough history of the war to know that the communist Viet Cong involved in the struggle were not without sin, but the people at the demonstration acted as though they were. A professor of physics delivered an impassioned anti-American speech filled with what I recognized as falsehoods, but no one seemed to care. That moment resonates, after all these years.

Despite the activist times, my college days remained focused mostly on academic subjects—philosophy, history, literature. St. Vincent was small enough to nurture easy commerce among disciplines, so I met faculty from every field, and my roommates were all science majors with views of the world different from my own. Debate was intense, frequent, and good-natured. Emotionally I leaned left, but intellectually I found, time and again, that conservative writers described the world more accurately for me. They still do.

National politics didn't matter much in graduate school at Ohio State in the mid 1970s—where I was the only Ph.D. candidate in English who would admit to voting for Gerald Ford. My interests then were mainly Shakespeare, and rhetoric. I met my coeditor, Andrea Lunsford, during our first term at Ohio State in an Old English class; we graduated on the same day five years later. We also shared a common interest in both literature and literacy. Yet even such an enthusiasm would prove political, for the teaching of writing in most American colleges and universities, graduate students quickly learn, is held in less esteem than the study of literature.

In different ways, both Andrea and I have spent much of our subsequent professional careers working to alter that perception. As a result, I've been drawn into academic brawls that, if not exactly the revolutionary struggles I'd imagined in college, have had their moments of smoke and thunder. One such conflict led to the establishment of a Division of Rhetoric and Composition (DRC) at the University of Texas at Austin, where I have been teaching for almost a quarter of a century.

In the DRC, I think we are doing a good job fulfilling our mission to teach undergraduates how to write at the same time that we're exploring new technologies and theories of composing. We've made a substantial commitment to electronic literacy both in our classrooms and in our research. Yet I wonder about the powerful machines that sit on every desk. I know computers have altered the way I write and teach, but I'm not yet sure they always enrich our lives—and they sure don't make our jobs simpler. And there are other issues as well, including the matter of access to technology. Will electronic literacy bring our fractured society closer together or crack open new fault lines, dividing those at home in cyberspace from people who can't afford or don't want to travel there? We'll need to find out—and soon.

For now, the traditional ideologies seem to offer few satisfactory answers. I do still consider myself an academic and political conservative and enjoy playing that countercultural role on a predominantly liberal campus. Yet I'd rather ride a mountain bike these days than watch C-SPAN, and my daydreams waft me to the canyons and deserts of the west, where the wide open spaces have a way of putting problems into perspective. (My biggest professional regret is deciding not to pursue a teaching position in Wyoming.) Like any good conservative, I'd prefer to keep my life simple—I could be content with a good car, a sensible dog, and a dependable racquetball partner. But life is rarely simple. (One of my dogs has grown neurotic, and my racquetball game is not what it used to be.)

What does endure is the pleasure of teaching and learning. And it's on classroom matters that my coeditor Andrea and I are most likely to agree—even if, on most other issues, our political stands differ with a predictability that confounds us and amuses our editors. So when I first proposed an anthology for writing classes that would broaden the range of readings available to students and make the political persuasion of the editors a part of the package, Andrea agreed to the project. She said it embodied the feminist concept of "situated knowledge." Well, sure, if that thought makes her happy. I'm no theorist. I'm just glad to have the privilege and pleasure, once again, of working on this third edition of the book with my good friend and political *other*.

TERESA ESSMAN   Born and raised in central Ohio, I am a country girl through and through. I hate shoes, love fresh vegetables, and live for the smell of autumn when my family presses and cans fresh apple cider.

My family has had an enormous impact on who I have become. My parents encouraged me to form my own opinions, rarely pushing their own views on me. Perhaps it is because of this upbringing that I have little patience with people who cling self-righteously to ideas but are unable to back them up. One of my pet peeves has always been people who believe in something simply because they think they should, or because their parents believed it.

My family has had an indirect influence on me, as well. As the youngest of four kids and one of seventeen grandchildren on my mom's side, I have had ample opportunities to watch people. You can learn a great deal about how you want to run your own life that way. Don't get me wrong; I don't imply passivity. I like to watch how people live and then decide if those are things I want to do. The misfortunes and triumphs of others can be learning tools, if you choose to pay attention.

In my four years at Ohio State, I have learned two very important things: never stop questioning, and never give up on yourself. I firmly believe

I can never stop learning, because there will always be people who know more than I do about an issue or hold a perspective I have yet to consider. By questioning those people, I can only broaden my views and understanding.

I am currently studying to become a physical therapist, a career path that marks a great achievement for me. At Ohio State, admission into the physical therapy program is intensely competitive. I made it past the first cuts the first year I applied, but was turned down for admission. I was crushed, because for years I had been determined I was going to become a pediatric physical therapist. I was bombarded with pamphlets from well-meaning people about finding another course for my life, changing my major, and moving on. I just couldn't do it; I knew I could not be as happy in another profession, so I steeled myself, buckled down for another year, and reapplied. Happily, I received notice of my admission. (Later I found out that less than 15% of the applicants had been offered positions that year.) Now, in the first two years of professional training, I couldn't be happier with my decision not to give up on my dream. My father told me that if I wanted it badly enough, I would get in. Well, Daddy, I wanted it. So there!

After graduation, I would like to travel to another country, possibly Honduras, and work in the orphanages there for a year or so. So many of the children there are physically handicapped and just left in cribs because the facilities don't have the funding to care for them properly. I would like to change that somehow. Ultimately, I want to have my own pediatric physical therapy practice in the United States, incorporating the use of animals in therapy. I plan to have a few llamas (another one of my life passions) from my llama ranch included, along with dogs and miniature horses. It may sound a bit strange, but I can think of no better way to combine my love of kids, animals, and the country.

JOSHUA G. RUSHING   Although I was made in Japan (conceived on a parental vacation), I cannot claim to be anything other than a pure Texan — as well as a father, husband, marine, and full-time college student. That may sound like a great deal for a twenty-four-year-old to bear, but the truth is I don't bear the load at all — *they,* my family and corps, carry me. During my short time in the corps, six years, I have been fortunate to be granted extended visits to exotic locations such as Europe, the Middle East, and the Arctic Circle. In addition to getting to see the world, I have enjoyed long stays in coastal North Carolina, where I was stationed for almost four years, and New Orleans, my last duty station before I moved to Austin. But no matter where I am, in my soul a neon Lone Star perpetually flashes to the rhythm of a Willie Nelson tune.

That I refer to my "soul" seems strange, considering my pragmatic agnosticism. Having previously staked claims on both sides of the divine fence (for which I wish there were a saddle), I have been forced between a rock (the lack of empirical evidence for the existence of God, hence the need for faith) and a hard place (the same void of conclusive proof that there is not a God, hence the same need for faith).

Although I do not necessarily believe in a God, I do believe that I have been blessed with a fabulous family. My wife makes me look forward to waking up in the morning next to her, and my four-year-old son is a wellspring of new ideas and perspectives (for example: "What kind of animal is Gumby?"). Speaking of animals, our family also includes a yellow Labrador puppy named Cuervo.

I tend to be no more polar in politics than I am in religion. My centrist beliefs might make it seem as though I lead a fairly dull life when it comes to opinions, but, on the contrary, I have found that practicing the fine and delicate art of fence-riding allows me to take sides in more arguments than William F. Buckley Jr. My niche affords me the freedom to play the incessant devil's advocate. One would be hard pressed to find an issue on which I could not disagree with people—no matter what side of the argument they're on. Much to my wife's frustration, daily debating has become my mental aerobics. Having said that, I must admit that the inevitable responsibilities of life have been swaying me from my well-worn tracks down the middle. As I grow older, my political views are starting to lean to the right—a predictable trend that, in my experience, affects most people.

Glancing to the future, I still wonder what I will be when I grow up. I have no clue and, truthfully, not even a desire for a particular profession. I have always been envious of peers who have known since they were four that they wanted to be doctors and at my age are now graduating from medical school. My strongest hopes are to be a good father and husband; besides that I think I will abide by the old Scottish proverb: "Be happy while you're living for you're a long while dead."

HEATHER RICKER   As a third-year undergraduate student and someone who delayed declaring a major in English as long as I could, I'm the kind of person who thinks over most decisions a long time. When I come across new ideas I let them percolate in my head, asking myself questions before coming to a conclusion. My academic interests hover around the humanities, fueled by the fascination with literature I've had since I first felt the thrill of entering the fictional worlds of Laura Ingalls Wilder and Cam Jansen. Music is another of my passions. Listening to Sarah Brightman sing in the Phantom and Louis Armstrong's version of *What a Wonderful World* on my CD player is one of my favorite pastimes. I also enjoy playing the piano to relax when school gets hectic, as well as skiing and swimming. As a little girl, I plastered my bedroom walls and ceiling with maps; I still have an endless fascination with other cultures and have the traveling bug.

Nevertheless, there's no place like home. As I've grown up, this phrase has taken on more meaning for me. Like many other American families, my family made a big move in the middle of my childhood. It took us from the front range of the Rocky Mountains, which I tenaciously loved with my ten-year-old heart, to the heart of the Midwest. This unknown, not very exciting place had little to recommend itself. Coming from the diversity of Denver, I considered myself a city girl and therefore an expert judge of the merits of city life. This move also took me away from one set of grandparents.

But this loss was balanced by being closer to the other side of the family, who live on the East Coast. From then on, our family summer vacations alternated between one side of the family and the country and the other. The relationships I developed with grandparents, aunts, uncles, and cousins by these visits, phone calls, and letters reinforced my identity and definition of home. I learned about who they were, unconsciously knowing this was a part of me. Now I realize how much their ideas and values have affected me. I'm glad to have these reference points as I sort out life's challenges, and think my knowledge of my relatives' experience benefits me by giving me a starting point from which to explore other viewpoints. The ideas that have influenced me include the political liberalism, Catholicism, and working-class values of my Irish grandparents as well as the feminism and nontraditional religious views held by my other grandparents. My parents have influenced me by their own search for spiritual truth, which has introduced me to the teachings of various churches. A strong faith in God and family is important to me and influences the way I look at life and issues. Nevertheless, my own views in many specific areas are not yet set. I want to be able to adapt my views when there are good arguments for doing so.

The Presence of Others

Voices and Images That Call for Response

On Reading
and Thinking Critically

Introduction

THIS IS A BOOK for and about reading. Its pages contain voices joined in conversation and debate over issues important to all of us: What, how, and under what circumstances should we learn and become educated? Who are we as individuals and as members of various groups and cultures? What do we believe? How do we choose to live? In the conversations surrounding these issues, the editors of this book have joined in, and you will find our reasons for choosing particular selections and our thoughts about these selections running throughout this text. The primary aim of the book, however, is to invite *you* to join in this conversation, to add your voice to the discussion in these pages. Doing so invites you to assume the perspective of a critical reader.

•   •   •

WHAT IS CRITICAL READING?

If you've been wondering what critical reading is, you're already demonstrating one of the hallmarks of a critical reader: a questioning attitude, one that probes for definitions, explanations, proofs, and assumptions. Perhaps we can further clarify what we mean by critical reading by focusing on two everyday uses of the word *critical*. In its most common usage, *critical* means acting like a critic, as in "many voters have been highly critical of Clinton's personal behavior," or "some members of the African American community have been critical of what they see as Terry McMillan's negative treatment of men in her novels." In this sense of the word, *critical* suggests that you have explored an issue and are ready to evaluate it, to see whether and how it meets your standards. But *critical* is also used to denote something of singular importance, as in "critical care unit" or "a critical point in negotiations." In this sense of the word, *critical* suggests that you attach importance to what you are examining and to your own critical responses to it. For the purposes of this text, then, critical readers are those who bring all their powers to bear on understanding, analyzing, and evaluating some important question, issue, or perspective contained in a piece of writing. Critical readers, in other words, do not accept things blindly or at face value, but instead look at them from a variety of perspectives, saying both *yes* and *no* to them until they are ready to take their own stance on the issues.

Saying *Yes, No,* and *Maybe*

The chapters of this text will allow you many chances to practice saying *yes* and *no*—and sometimes *maybe*—to ideas. As you read the selections in Chapter 3, Education, for example, you will encounter widely varying perspectives on whom and what higher education is for as well as what its content should be. When you read Adrienne Rich's "What Does a Woman Need to Know?" her answers to this question may seem perfectly reasonable to you; you find you can understand her point of view and say *yes* to her ideas. But then you begin to wonder about them and to say, well, *maybe,* or even to say *no.* Are Rich's ideas appropriate today, and do they respond to the problems you think women need to confront? Are the charges she brings fair and accurate? All of these acts—saying *yes, maybe,* and/or *no*—are necessary for critical reading, for the kind of reading that is open to new ideas but that insists on thinking them through from every perspective.

Thus, critical reading is what you do when you need to understand the terms of a contract you are about to sign, decide which of several automobile financing plans will be best for you, master the material necessary to shine on an important examination, evaluate the arguments for or against a political proposal or candidate, or compare doctors' opinions about whether you should undergo surgery. It is the kind of reading Mortimer Adler is talking about when he says, "When [people] are in love and are reading a love letter, they read for all they are worth. They read every word three ways; they read between the lines and in the margins; they read the whole in terms of the parts, and each part in terms of the whole."

WHY BECOME A CRITICAL READER?

Given our definition of critical reading, the answer to this question is probably already obvious to you. Critical readers are "in on" the conversation surrounding any issue. They resist ready-made or hand-me-down opinions whenever they can. Much in our society makes such critical reading difficult; we are, after all, inundated with ready-made opinions on television and in other mass media as well as in educational, religious, political, and even family institutions. In fact, so many forces are at work to make up our minds for us that many people question whether we aren't fooling ourselves to think that we can control and use language at all, rather than the other way around.

You can probably think of instances in your own life that support this view. The bombardment of commercials at the movies, for example, tempts you to buy popcorn and Coca-Cola. Or you may be aware that educational labels like *honors* or *remedial* have dramatically affected your life. Many studies suggest that we tend to live up (or down) to such labels—for better or worse. This fact of modern life led one theorist of language to say that words we try to use or control are already "half-way in someone else's mouth," meaning that the words we use are already so weighed down with the meanings our society has given them that it is hard to do anything other than accept those meanings. It's hard, that is, for any one person to resist the lure of advertising or to reject the power of educational or social labels.

To some extent, this theory clearly rings true: we do not absolutely control the language we use or read. But the result of such a position is to give up trying to make your voice heard or to bring about any change. Why become a critical reader, then? To resist being controlled by other people's language, to exert some control of your own, to test your wits, to define for yourself your perspective on any issue, to contribute to the thoughts and actions related to those issues. You become a critical reader, in short, **to get involved in the conversation and to make your voice count.**

ARE YOU A CRITICAL READER?

Our guess is that you are already a critical reader when you need to be. You may want to take stock of your general reading habits, however, by answering the following questions. As a rule, when you are reading important material, do you

1. Read carefully, either with or without skimming first?
2. "Talk back" to what you are reading, noting what does or doesn't make sense, what seems right or wrong?
3. Ask questions as you read?
4. Take notes in the margins or on a separate sheet of paper?
5. Ask yourself why the writer takes the position he or she does?
6. Think about the writer's perspective—what his or her interests are in writing the piece?
7. Ask what larger social, economic, political, or other conditions may have influenced the creation of the piece of writing?

8. Consider what in your experience and background leads you to agree with or like, or to disagree with or dislike, the piece of writing?

9. Imagine other ways of looking at the subjects or ideas presented?

10. Summarize the gist of what you have read?

11. Compare what you're reading with other things you have read about the subject?

Do You Read Online Materials Critically?

Being a strong critical reader is increasingly important in this age of information, particularly since so much of that information exists in the fluid, ever-changing world of the Internet and World Wide Web. Things you read online one day may change dramatically—or disappear—the next day. In addition, since anyone can create a Web site or contribute to an online discussion group without having to go through an editor or a publisher, you need to bring specific critical scrutiny to reading online. When you are reading online, do you

1. Check to find out who is responsible for a document, a posting, or a Web site? Is it, for example, a commercial site whose main goal is to sell, rather than to evaluate, a particular product?

2. Check to see when the item was put on the Net, or when it was last updated?

3. Ask what the item's "credentials" are? Is it, for example, a research report that carries the authority of a respected group such as the Linguistics Society of America or the Association of Consulting Engineers?

4. Check any links to see what they might reveal about the credibility and trustworthiness of the item?

5. Ask how the use of graphics, color, visual images, and so on affect the message of the item?

Examining Your Reading Habits   If you answered *yes* to most of the questions in the two preceding lists, you are already reading with a critical eye, and you will understand what we mean when we say reading is a partnership: the text in front of you has words and images set down, but you are the one who realizes the ideas in those words and images, tests them against what you know, and puts them to use in your life.

Take five or ten minutes to write a description of yourself as a reader. How do you usually approach a text that you want or need to understand? Do you usually practice critical reading habits? Why, or why not? Bring your description to class for discussion. Compare your description with those of two or three other students in your class, noting the ways in which your reading strategies are similar and/or different.

HOW CAN YOU BECOME A MORE CRITICAL READER?

If you have compared your notes on how you typically read with those of friends or classmates, you have probably noticed some differences. Indeed, reading practices vary widely, and even highly skilled readers may differ dramatically in the approaches they take. The most effective and satisfying critical reading strategies for you may differ from those for your friends. In particular, your reading strategies are undoubtedly related to who you are, to your gender, age, cultural background, life experiences, prior reading experiences, even your eyesight. In addition, strategies for reading vary widely depending on purpose and situation: you might skim the ingredients listed on a food package just to check that it doesn't contain something you are allergic to, or you might pore slowly over the directions for connecting a modem to make sure that you don't make a mistake.

Thus, part of your job as a critical reader is to get to know your own preferred strategies, your own strengths and weaknesses, and to build on your strengths. While we can't know exactly what will be most effective for any one individual reader, we can offer some general guidelines you can experiment with. From them you should be able to design an individual blueprint for reading. We hope that these guidelines will help you when you tackle difficult reading material or material for which you have almost no background. In the annotated essays in Chapters 3 through 9 of this book, you will find examples of most of these guidelines, written in the margins as responses to those essays.

Previewing

- Determine your purpose for reading. Is it to gather information for a writing assignment? To determine whether a source will be useful for a research project? To study for an examination? To prepare for class discussion? To determine your own stance toward the topic—and what in your experience and background leads you to take that stance?

- Consider the title and subtitle, if there is one. What do they tell you about what is to come?

- Think about what you already know about the subject. What opinions do you hold on this subject? What major topics do you anticipate?

What do you hope to learn? What other things about this topic have you read?

- What do you know about the author? What expertise does he or she have in the subject? What particular perspective on the subject might he or she hold?
- What does the headnote or opening of the reading tell you?
- Look at how the text is structured. Are there subdivisions? Read over any headings. Skim the opening sentences of each paragraph.
- Decide what you think the main point or theme of the text will be.
- Check to see if the conclusion contains a summary of the main point or a statement of its significance. If so, previewing that can help you read more efficiently and critically.

Annotating

- Read carefully, marking places that are confusing or that you want to reread.
- Identify key points or arguments, important terms, recurring images, and interesting ideas, either by underlining them in the text or by making notes in the margin.
- Note any statements you question or disagree with and any counter-evidence or counterarguments that occur to you.
- Note any sources used in the text.

Summarizing

- Summarize the main points. Do they match your expectations? Why, or why not?
- Jot down any points you want to remember, questions you want to raise, and ideas for how you may use this material.

Analyzing

- Identify evidence that supports the main argument or illustrates the main point. Is it sufficient to convince you? Is there any evidence that seems to contradict the author's point?
- Identify the writer's underlying assumptions about the subject, where he or she is "coming from" on this issue.

- Ask what may have led the author to this position.
- How does the writer's stance affect his or her presentation of the material or argument?
- Describe the writer's tone. Is it cautious? Angry? Insulting? Serious or amusing? How is the tone created, and what effects does it strive to achieve?
- Question the sources used. Ask yourself whether each source is relevant to the topic, whether it is timely, whether it carries sufficient expertise, and whether its perspective or position on the subject is different from yours or from others you know and respect. If so, why?
- Think of other points of view on this topic, perhaps from other things you have read or seen. Is the author's perspective the most persuasive — and why?

Rereading

- Reread quickly to be sure you have understood the reading.
- Identify the author's purpose(s). Were those purposes accomplished?
- Determine whether the questions you had during the first reading have been answered.

Responding

- What one question would you like to ask the writer? How do you think the writer might respond?
- Think about the reading as a whole. What did you like best about it? What puzzled or irritated you? What caused you to like or dislike the piece? Were your expectations met? If not, why not? What more would you like to know about the subject?
- Note what you have learned about effective writing from this reading.
- If you keep a reading log, record these notes there. (For three example reading log entries, see the Afterwords on pp. 89 and 197.)

Examining Your Critical Literacy   To practice reading a text critically, turn to one of the texts in this book that is *not* annotated and analyze the piece using the guidelines for thinking and reading critically. For an example of one student's critical response to a reading, see pp. 37–40.

HOW CAN YOU READ VISUAL TEXTS CRITICALLY?

Some have labeled the late twentieth century as the "age of the image," and it's not hard to understand why. Today, images crowd in from all directions, not only from television, video, film, and the Web, but from traditional print texts as well—from the graphs and charts in a financial report to the daily newspaper to the textbook you hold in your hand. And far from being mere decoration, these images carry part or most of the message readers are intended to receive. As a result, critical readers pay very careful attention to the visuals in any text they read, understanding that these have a significant impact on how readers interpret and respond to those texts. If a picture *is* sometimes worth a thousand words, it pays to spend some time thinking about what makes that picture so valuable.

The following questions can help you shape your critical reading of visual texts—whether they stand on their own, as in a photograph or painting, or are combined with print—beginning with those you find throughout this book. To get started, take a close look at the front cover to see what it may tell you about the content of the book, the goals of the editors, and the overall message it sends. You will see only a few words on this cover: the title, subtitle, names of editors, and notice of "Third Edition." What effect do size and placement have on the meaning and emphasis these words convey? Note also the background of the cover and its use of color. What does the color add or suggest? Take a close look at the images on the cover: how many can you identify?

The following questions will help you read the images in this text, and those all around you, with a critical eye.

For Charts, Graphs, and Tables

1. What information does the chart, graph, or table convey?

2. Does it present numbers or statistics? How does the visual representation affect your understanding of the information? Does it emphasize or downplay, or even exaggerate or understate, anything?

3. Does it illustrate a trend or change? If so, does it emphasize the change fairly—or not?

4. Does it highlight anything (a particular year? a topic?) to attract your attention?

For Photographs, Drawings, and Advertisements

1. Why was the visual created? What does its main meaning or message seem to be? How does the visual make you notice and perhaps remember this message?

2. What in the visual is your eye drawn to, and why?

3. What is in the foreground? In the background? What is in focus or out of focus? Is the most important part of the visual blended into the rest, or is it contrasted somehow? What details are included or emphasized? What is omitted or de-emphasized, and why?

4. What is placed high in the visual? What is placed low? To the left? To the right?

5. How are light and color used? How do they affect your reading of the visual?

6. Is anything in the visual repeated, intensified, or exaggerated? Look for anything that is made to seem "supernormal" or idealized (by airbrushing or computer manipulation, for example). What effect does the exaggeration or repetition have on you as a reader?

7. Is anything downplayed? Ambiguous? Confusing or distracting? If so, what effect does this have on your reading of the visual? Does any ambiguity call on you as a reader to fill in some gaps? If so, to what effect?

8. What values or ideals does the visual convey or allude to? Family values? The good life? Harmony? Success? Beauty? Power? Pleasure? Sex appeal? Youth? Wisdom? Adventure? Is the visual text reinforcing or questioning these values? How does it do so?

9. Does the visual include imagery or people that carry very positive—or very negative—associations? If so, how do such images or people affect your response? (Think of ads that use celebrities to make readers notice—and buy!—the product.)

10. Does the image use humor? If so, how does it affect your reading?

11. How does the visual relate to any written text that accompanies it? Do the two reinforce each other, or does one undermine the other?

HOW CAN YOU READ ONLINE TEXTS CRITICALLY?

Texts you encounter online, especially pages on the World Wide Web, require new reading skills because they combine many different elements—including headlines, printed words, static images, moving images, sounds, and even film clips. Chances are you picked up the skills so quickly for navigating these electronic texts that you barely realized how many new conventions you were absorbing, from scrolling pages (rather than turning them) to clicking items to move to new places or to open email messages. But you need to do more than just explore online texts; you need to appreciate how they work to attract and direct your attention.

In many cases, the visual and, to a lesser extent, aural items on a Web page are designed to move you to select specific menus or links. But commercial pages usually offer many more options than you need just to keep you browsing and looking. More and more, Web pages are also interrupted by pop-up advertisements, obviously designed to get you to move to more sites. The visual clutter of many commercial pages, especially those for Web search engines, may even surprise you. The box for typing in a search term is often obscured by blinking images and clusters of links, all competing for your attention and, often, your money.

So you have to learn to filter out the clutter on electronic pages and evaluate their overall design to determine what information is being offered to you and in what order. The way that information is presented usually tells you what the site designers or owners value. They may use colors or images to highlight ideas they want you to encounter and bury less important material deep in a site or omit it entirely.

You should be especially careful with online texts that fail to identify themselves clearly. Look for information about identity, authorship, sponsorship, and currency. If an online text resists even your basic attempts to read it critically, you should perhaps move on to another. There are likely to be dozens of additional choices, whatever the subject you are exploring.

1. How does the online text combine visual and written material? Which dominates, and to what effect?

2. What perspective is represented in text? What group or individual is responsible for the information provided? What is the credibility or reputation of the author or sponsor? Is the text sponsored by or linked to a commercial enterprise? For Web sites, be sure to check out the domain name: *.com* indicates a commercial site. Is there an email address you can use to contact those responsible for the text?

3. Does the text include links to other online texts? If so, what do the links tell you about the credibility and usefulness of the text you are reading?

4. How current is the text? When was it last updated?

5. How easy is it to find information in this text? Does it have a search function and/or a site map that will help you read it?

6. What about this text makes it worth bookmarking (or not)?

WHAT DOES READING HAVE TO DO WITH WRITING?

In one sense, critical reading *is* writing. That is, as you read carefully, asking questions and talking back to a text, you inevitably create your own version of the text. Even if that interpretation is not written down on paper, it is "written" in your mind, composed and put into words you can understand and remember. And if you add some of your own ideas—or those you and classmates develop together—to what you read, you can build a new text altogether, one you may later write down.

As our society uses electronic texts more often, in fact, reading and writing will almost certainly become even more intertwined. The "reader" of interactive fiction or a hypertext, for instance, may write part of the text. Those on electronic bulletin boards or conferences may write their own ideas and responses into what they are reading on the screen, something first written by another reader.

But critical reading is also closely related to your own writing, because it enables you to assess what you have written, to say *yes* and *no* and *maybe* to your own ideas—to evaluate the logic of your prose, the effectiveness of your word choice, the degree to which you have gotten your points across. In short, you can apply these same reading strategies to your own writing, to see your own words with a critical eye. Thus, reading critically and writing effectively become reciprocal activities, strengthening each other as you learn to use language more powerfully.

Because we are convinced that reading and writing are closely related, we want this text to offer you many opportunities for moving back and forth from reading to writing to reading. We will, in fact, invite you to experiment with a number of kinds of writing as you read your way into the conversations taking place in the chapters that follow. We turn now, therefore, to Chapter 2, From Reading to Writing, for an overview of the writing practices this book invites you to experience.

From Reading to Writing

Introduction

No ONE CAN PREDICT how you will respond to what you read, but the act of reading does often lead to action. Maybe reading a pamphlet handed to you on campus will convince you to vote for a student government candidate. Or a slick brochure arriving in the mail could lead you to buy apartment insurance—or to complain about false advertising to a state regulatory agency. Gaudy graphics on a Web page might entice you to click for more information, or maybe all that design clutter offends you so much that you remove the annoying site from your "favorites" list. A dull book could make you reconsider your major; a great book might change your life.

One action that reading often provokes is writing. You preserve and extend your ideas whenever you write about what you have read or seen. In effect, you enter a conversation someone else has started and invite still others to join you. Sometimes these conversations will be simple and immediate, as when you respond quickly to email requests from people you know. At other times, your reading and writing will bridge wider gaps, perhaps even between different cultures or eras, and then you'll need to respond much more deliberately.

• • •

WRITING TO LEARN

Most classes in college will require some written work. Although these tasks may seem too routine to think of as actual "writing," don't underestimate them. Writing of almost any kind can fix ideas in your mind and stimulate your thinking. Following are some types of college writing that may help you learn better: class notes, lab notes, reading notes and annotations, listserv messages, comments on other students' writing, research log entries, abstracts of articles, summaries, outlines,

13

essay examinations, and class presentations. Consider such writing assignments as opportunities to learn.

LEARNING TO WRITE EFFECTIVELY

Many of your college courses will ask you to prepare formal essays or other extended pieces of writing related to what you read, hear, or learn. The following guidelines are designed to help you respond effectively to such assignments.

Considering the Assignment

Find out as much as you can about an assignment before starting to write.

- Analyze a writing project carefully. Look for key words in the assignment, such as *analyze, summarize, compare, contrast, illustrate, argue, defend, refute, persuade, respond,* and so on.
- If you don't understand an assignment, ask your instructor for clarification.
- Pay attention to limits on length and time. The length of an assignment will surely influence the focus and thesis of any essay. In general, the shorter the piece, the narrower its focus will need to be.
- Plan your time to allow for all necessary reading, thinking, drafting, and editing.

Considering Purpose and Audience

Beyond what the assignment itself dictates, consider the larger purpose of the writing. A piece that is largely informative (such as a report) will be somewhat different from one that takes an argumentative stance (such as an editorial). What does the writing have to accomplish to be successful? Your responses to that question will help determine the form, organization, tone, style, and length of your writing. Here are some other questions to help you think about purpose:

- Does the assignment itself specify a purpose?
- What does your instructor expect you to do in this assignment? What do you need to do to meet those expectations?

- How do you want readers to react to your writing? Do you want them to be entertained? Should they learn something? Should they be moved to action?
- Where might you like to have this piece read? Will it appear in print or online?

Consider also who will read your piece. The primary audience for your college writing may be instructors, but *they* may have in mind some other specific audience—your classmates, for example, or the general public.

Following are some questions that can help identify key characteristics of your audience:

- Do your readers belong to some identifiable group: college students, Democrats, women, parents, sociologists?
- How would you characterize your readers? What values and principles do you hold in common with them? What differences are there between you?
- Are your readers likely to know more or less than you do about your subject? What background information do you need to provide?
- Are your readers likely to be engaged by your subject, or do you have to win their attention?
- Are your readers likely to be favorable, neutral, or hostile to your positions?
- Should you use simple, general language, or technical language? Should you use images?
- Are you addressing more than one audience? If so, do any of the audiences seem incompatible?
- Is your writing going online where it can be read by the general public?

Generating Ideas and Making Plans

You don't need to know what you are going to say before you begin writing. Even so, all writers must start somewhere. You may find the following techniques helpful in discovering ideas:

- Read any assigned material carefully, annotating key information, summarizing main points, and noting connections among readings.
- Try specific techniques for developing ideas, such as freewriting, brainstorming, or journal writing. (Consult a writing handbook for more about these techniques.)

- Get more information—from the library, from the World Wide Web, from professional organizations, from friends or instructors, and so on.
- Do field research. Conduct a survey or some interviews.
- Get involved in discussions about your subject. Talk to people. Listen to their ideas and opinions. Read a newsgroup or join a listserv.
- Draw on your personal experiences, especially when dealing with social, cultural, and political issues. *Your* experience counts.

Once you have ideas, sketch out a plan, a scheme to make a project manageable. Here are some ways of working out a plan:

- Fix on a tentative thesis statement or main point you want to prove, defend, or illustrate. Think of it as a commitment to your readers.
- Prepare a scratch outline by listing the major ideas you want to cover and then arranging them in an order that makes sense to you.
- Construct a formal outline if you find such devices useful.
- Try a "zero draft"—a quick, discardable version of an essay to help you focus on the major issues.

DRAFTING

Drafting is the point in the writing process when words are put down on the page or up on the screen. The cold swimming hole approach works best for some writers: just plunge in. After all, you can't do much as a writer until you produce some words. In case you don't much like cold water, however, here's some other advice for getting started on a first draft:

- Control your expectations. No one expects a first draft to be perfect. In fact, no one expects a final draft to be the last word on any subject. So take it easy.
- Skip the introduction if you find yourself stuck on the opening sentences. Start somewhere else, perhaps with an idea you are especially eager to develop. Then write another portion of the essay, and then another. You can put all the parts together later; if you are working on a computer, you'll need only a few keystrokes.
- Set some reasonable goals, especially for longer projects. Commit yourself to writing one or two pages before getting up from your desk, and try to stop at a point where you feel confident about what comes next. That way, beginning again will be easier. Reward yourself when you meet your goal.
- Try a quick draft: sketch out the full essay without stopping.

Getting—and Giving—Feedback

Seek responses from other readers. Within whatever guidelines your instructor establishes, ask classmates, friends, or any potential readers to read and react to your drafts. Here are some guidelines for your readers to use in reviewing your draft:

- Begin by describing what you think the draft is saying. That description might prove enlightening to the author.
- Point out any word, phrase, or sentence that is confusing or unclear.
- Describe what is most memorable in the draft.
- List the strengths of the draft. How can they be enhanced?
- List the weaknesses. How might they be eliminated or minimized?
- Suggest specific revisions. What more do you as one reader want or need to know? Which other arguments or ideas should be considered?

Revising

Respond to comments on a first draft by looking at the entire assignment anew. Reshape the essay as much as necessary to serve your purpose, your subject matter, and your readers. Here are some specific suggestions for revising:

- To gain perspective, put a printed draft aside for a day or two.
- Be as tough minded as you can about the condition of a draft. Discard whole paragraphs or pages when they simply don't work. Don't just tinker or look for the easiest way of salvaging weak material. You may need a new thesis or a completely different structure.
- Consider very carefully any responses you've received. But don't overreact to criticism.
- Consider alternative plans for organization. Be flexible.
- Consider the overall strategy of the essay. Might a different point of view or tone make it more effective?
- Review your thesis or main idea. Is the thesis fully explained and supported?
- Reconsider whether you know enough about your subject to write about it with authority. If not, go back to your sources or do more reading.
- Pay attention to transitions. You can help your readers with a few careful phrases that point to where you're going—or where you've been.

- Pay attention to visual details—to any images you are using and the design of the text. Test them with readers to make sure they are appropriate and effective.

Editing

Once you've revised your draft, it's time to edit your work by attending carefully to the structure of paragraphs, the shape of sentences, the choice of words, the presentation of illustrations and images, and the conventions of punctuation and mechanics.

- Reconsider openings and closings. In academic writing, openings should capture the reader's attention and identify key points, while conclusions should summarize ideas and draw implications.
- Read your draft aloud, paying attention to the length, variety, rhythm, and coherence of sentences.
- Look for wordiness. Stylistically, nothing hurts an essay more than empty phrases.
- Consider your vocabulary for appropriateness. Is it appropriate to use contractions or slang or dialect? Do any technical terms need defining?
- Check any documentation of sources for the correct form. Reconsider also the way you incorporate sources—do you quote, paraphrase, and summarize appropriately? Do you weave quotations smoothly into your own text? Do your Web links make sense?
- Check for problems of grammar and usage, particularly any that have caused you problems in the past.
- For detailed examples and answers to questions of grammar, usage, and style, check a handbook.
- Find a suitable title. For most academic work, titles should provide clear descriptions of the contents. Titles are also important for online documents.

Preparing the Final Version

Now is the time to assemble and check your final version.

- Review the assignment to be sure you have met all requirements of form. Does your instructor want a title page? An outline? A Web page?
- Be sure your name appears in the proper place(s).
- Paginate, and clip printed pages together. (Do not staple them.)

- Proofread one last time for typographical errors, spelling errors, and other slips. If you have a spell checker, run it for a final check.

- Make sure the final version is presented professionally, whether a printed text or an electronic document.

AN ALPHABETICAL CATALOG OF THE WRITING ASSIGNMENTS IN THIS BOOK

Throughout *The Presence of Others* we invite you to respond to the readings we've selected, to join in conversation with all the people who've collaborated to write this book—writers, editors, reviewers, and students. Following is an alphabetical catalog of guidelines to the writing assignments you may be asked to do as you use this book. As you read and use these guidelines, remember that a *text* can be an article, an image, a Web site—anything that you "read."

Analyzing

Analytical writing puts ideas under scrutiny. To analyze a text—whether a print, visual, or electronic one—question the validity of arguments, the accuracy of facts, the logical relationship of ideas, the fairness of conclusions, and the assumptions underlying them. Here are some suggestions for analyzing a text:

- To begin, identify exactly what you want to analyze, from a paragraph to a full work.

- Note any preconceptions or assumptions you bring to the topic of your analysis. Think about how they may affect your analysis.

- Mark the text and any images you are analyzing thoroughly. Annotate in the margins, highlight key quotations, and circle terms or features you think are especially important.

- Divide the text into its main ideas, and look at each one carefully. What support exists for each idea?

- Look for connections between ideas. Are these connections clear and logical to you? Do you see the point of intriguing juxtapositions of ideas or images?

- Try to think of opposing points of view or alternative perspectives on the topic. Does the writer consider them fairly?

For an example of analysis, see the essay by Adrienne Rich (p. 65).

Writing a Rhetorical Analysis   In its simplest form, a rhetorical analysis explores two basic questions: What is the writer's purpose? How is that purpose presented to an intended audience? Answers to these important questions help readers appreciate the options that writers face and the possible reasons behind particular choices of language, image, genre, and so on. A rhetorical analysis looks at the particular strategies a writer uses and gauges their success. A rhetorical analysis can also consider how a writer's cultural, economic, social, or political contexts affect the reading and writing of the text.

Here are tips for examining a text rhetorically:

- Try to define the major purpose of the text, but understand that it may be composed for more than one reason. Identify these multiple purposes when you can, pointing out in your analysis where they may conflict. When possible, show where such conflicts may have affected the writer's choice of arguments, evidence, vocabulary, examples, and so on.

- Try to identify a primary audience and describe its expectations. What do members of the primary audience know about the subject and what do they need to know? How does the text address their expectations or needs?

- Identify any secondary audiences. How do their needs differ from those of the primary audience?

- Explore the author's attitude toward the topic or issue. What is the author's stake in the subject?

- Explore the relationship of the author to the audience. Does he or she maintain a position of distance and authority or seek to "come close to" readers?

- Explain how the text has been shaped by rhetorical concerns, including the complexity of the discussion, the detail, the author's tone and voice, the vocabulary choices, and the kinds of sentences.

For an example of a rhetorical analysis, see the essay by John Updike (p. 489).

Writing a Critical Analysis   A critical analysis may examine many of the same issues as those in a rhetorical analysis. But a critical analysis usually makes more value judgments about the integrity of a text—its power and its reach.

A critical analysis looks carefully at the logic of a text, identifying its claims and assessing the premises and evidence that support those claims. Critical analysis seeks to answer questions such as these: Does the author make a coherent claim? Are the assumptions behind the claim defensible? Are the connections among assumptions, claims, and evidence logical? Is the evidence presented sufficient and reliable? Is the text fair or is the author biased in a way that undermines the credibility of the piece?

A critical analysis also looks at the *success* of a text—at how persuasive it is, how well it makes emotional or ethical appeals, how successfully it moves or delights readers.

Here are some tips for examining a text critically:

- Understand the intended audience(s) and purpose(s). Consider the work's historical, social, and political contexts in some detail.
- Identify the claims, both stated and implied.
- Identify the premises behind the claims, and determine how those assumptions would be received by the intended reader(s).
- Examine the evidence for each claim. What are the sources of information? Study any statistics and how they are used. Consider the sources and reliability of polls and surveys.
- Explore the logic of the argument. Does the writer use any logical fallacies? Consider, too, the rhetorical force of the evidence. Is it sufficient? Overwhelming?
- Consider the way the writer presents himself or herself. Does the author make a persuasive, appealing case? Is he or she appropriately engaged in or deliberately removed from the text?
- Consider the way the text makes its overall appeal. Is the format appropriate to its audience? Is it appropriately serious? Humorous? Academic? Colloquial?

For an example of critical analysis, see the essay by Pamela Samuelson (p. 315).

Arguing

Among a writer's toughest jobs is making a persuasive argument, one that moves readers to reaffirm a commitment—or to consider changing their minds or taking action. Almost all the readings and images in this book contain arguments. As you work at reading these texts, you may want to construct arguments of your own. Here are some suggestions for writing an effective academic argument:

- Develop a clear, carefully limited thesis to defend. This thesis will often evolve gradually as you learn about your subject.
- Find various good reasons for someone to agree with the thesis. Support all statements with specific and appropriate evidence, including images if appropriate.
- Show that any evidence you have gathered is fair, appropriate, and accurate; that your various arguments support one another; and that they outweigh possible counterarguments.

- When building an argument from something you've read, regard the text and everything connected with it as potential evidence. This would include the language and style of the writer, his or her background and reputation, the time and place of publication, the reputation of the publisher, images that accompany the written text, and so on.
- Quote from the piece carefully to demonstrate the points you are making. Bring the writer's voice into your side of the conversation.
- Appeal to the readers you are trying to convince by connecting your argument to subjects they are likely to know and care about. An effective argument stimulates thinking and conversation. It doesn't close off discussion or create enemies.

For examples of effective arguments, see the essays by J. Michael Bishop (p. 237) and Barbara Dafoe Whitehead (p. 619).

Brainstorming

Brainstorming is an activity that can jump-start your thinking. It consists simply of putting down ideas—about a reading, a writing topic, a problem to solve, whatever—just as they come to mind.

You can certainly brainstorm alone, although it often works better in a group. If you are working with a group, assign one person to jot down notes. You can brainstorm either as you read or immediately afterward. Here are some specific tips for brainstorming:

- List your thoughts as they occur. Put down whatever comes; let your ideas flow. Prune and reorder ideas *later.*
- Don't judge the quality of your brainstorming prematurely. Record your intuitions. Give yourself slack to explore ideas—even silly or outlandish ones.
- Once you've written all your thoughts down, look for connections among them. What conclusions can you draw about your position on the subject by looking at these connections?

Comparing and Contrasting

Strictly speaking, when you compare things, you are looking for similarities; when you contrast them, you are pointing out differences. Here are some suggestions for comparing and contrasting:

- Break your subject into parts or aspects that can be studied profitably. As the old saying goes, you don't want to compare apples and oranges.

- Pursue your comparison or contrast analysis systematically, point by point, using images as well as words if they are appropriate. Group the comparisons or contrasts purposefully so that they make or support a point about your subject.

- Use appropriate transitional words and phrases. Readers can easily get lost if you jump from one point of comparison or contrast to another without providing the necessary bridges.

- Be fair. Even when you are inclined to favor one side over another, be sure to consider the other side fairly.

The selections by Shelby Steele (p. 72) and Ron Suskind (p. 588) provide examples of comparing and contrasting.

Defining

When asked to define a word or concept in a paragraph, you're usually expected to write an extended explanation of the term, accompanied by illustrations and examples. Terms can also be defined through descriptions of their components, descriptions of processes (how something works), or any appropriate combination of these methods. Here are some suggestions for defining:

- To define a term, place it within a larger category and then list features or characteristics that distinguish it from other items in that category: "A skyscraper is a building of unusual height."

- Then expand the simple definition by providing additional distinguishing details: "A skyscraper is a building of unusual height, most often supported by a steel skeleton and having many stories. The earliest skyscrapers appeared in American cities, especially Chicago and New York, late in the nineteenth century. The height of buildings was confined at first by construction techniques that required massive masonry walls and by the limits of elevator technology. The invention of steel skeletons that supported both floors and walls and the development of high-speed elevators made much taller buildings possible. Among the most famous skyscrapers are the Empire State Building in New York and the Sears Tower in Chicago."

- In most cases, try to keep the tone of a formal definition factual and impersonal. An extended definition, however, can be composed in many different registers, from the serious to the satiric.

Differences over definitions often give rise to the disagreements that people have about important political and social issues. Therefore, always be sensitive to the key words in a text. Quite often, while you and other readers agree on the core meanings of such important terms (their denotations), you may not share the feelings, images, and associations that these words evoke (their connotations). For examples of definition, see the essays by Joan Didion (p. 179), Peter J. Gomes (p. 205), and Dave Barry (p. 372).

Describing

A description provides a snapshot of something—explaining what it looks like at a particular moment. You can describe things through words or images.

- Consider your perspective on the item you want to describe. From what angle are you observing it? Share this point of view with readers.
- Record the most distinctive features and details, those that will enable readers to visualize what you are describing. In most types of writing, your goal is to convey an accurate *impression* of what you have seen, be it person, thing, or even idea.
- Written descriptions depend heavily on modifiers—words that specify shape, size, color, smell, and so on. Modifiers should be chosen very deliberately—and used sparingly.

For an effective example of description, see the selection by Terry Tempest Williams (p. 607).

Writing a Dialogue

A dialogue is a conversation between two or more people—as in an interview, where ideas and opinions are exchanged, or in fiction or nonfiction writing, where a conversation is reproduced or imagined. To write such a conversation, you need to know something about the way the participants think, how they view the world, even the way they speak. Writing a fictional dialogue thus requires—and allows—imaginative role playing. Here are some suggestions for creating one:

- Try to put yourself within the minds of the characters and consider how they might respond to each other. Look closely at the typical attitudes, interests, habits, and expressions used by your characters. Try to reproduce them.
- It's not enough just to have characters "talk"; you have to figure out a subject for them to talk about. The liveliest dialogues usually feature some exchange of ideas or opinions.
- Set the dialogue in a particular place and time.

- A dialogue can be a stimulating way to respond to a reading. Imagine a dialogue among yourself and some friends on the reading—or place yourself in conversation with the writer. What would you like to say to bell hooks (p. 93), Mary Shelley (p. 231), or Robert A. Lutz (p. 712)? What might they say to you?

Evaluating

Writing an evaluation involves making and justifying judgments. First, you need to determine the appropriate criteria for the evaluation. Obviously, you wouldn't use the same standards in evaluating an elementary school play that you would in reviewing a Broadway production. In most cases, it is best to take a clear position in a review. Don't make your evaluation so subtle that no one can tell what your stance is. Here are some suggestions for writing an evaluation:

- Determine the appropriate criteria for the evaluation. Sometimes these standards will be obvious or given. In other cases, you will have to establish and define them. Readers will want to know why you are applying certain measures so that they can determine whether to trust your opinions.
- Measure your subject according to these standards.
- Base your evaluation on clear and sufficient evidence. A good evaluation is based on tangible facts and compelling arguments.
- Let readers see how you arrived at your judgment. For example, if you are raising doubts about the competence of an author, make clear what led you to that conclusion. If you are evaluating something visual, include illustrations if possible.
- Arrange your arguments in logical order—perhaps in order of increasing importance. Sometimes you can bolster your argument by comparing and contrasting your subject with objects or ideas already familiar to your readers.

For examples of evaluation, see the selections by Todd Oppenheimer (p. 255) and Linda S. Watts (p. 575).

Exploring

The point of exploratory writing is to examine subjects imaginatively, so such pieces are often more tentative than reports or more purely argumentative writing. Exploratory pieces allow you to take risks, to jump into controversies too complex to be resolved easily. So when you want to explore an issue in writing, try to go beyond predictable and safe positions. Following are some strategies for doing so:

- Read a series of provocative articles from various perspectives. Talk with friends or classmates. Reach for dialogue, discussion, and debate.

- Be prepared for multiple drafts. Your best ideas are likely to emerge during the composing process.

- Be open to alternative views and voices not always listened to. Bring other writers into the discussion.

- As the piece evolves, show it to interested readers and ask for their frank response. Incorporate questions, debates, or other material into the discussion. Dialogue can be a particularly stimulating technique for exploration.

- Don't expect to wrap up this kind of writing with a neat bow. Be prepared for gaps and gaffes. Exploratory writing often produces more questions than answers.

For examples of exploratory writing, see the essays by Wendy Shalit (p. 214), Andrew Sullivan (p. 350), and Zora Neale Hurston (p. 384).

Freewriting

Freewriting is a technique for generating ideas. When you freewrite about something, you follow ideas to see where they lead. Freewriting in response to reading might be prompted by particular words, phrases, passages, or images that you have highlighted while reading. It can also be useful for exploring connections between two or three different selections. Here are some specific tips for freewriting:

- One way to get started is by answering a question—for instance, "This topic makes me think of . . ." or "When I think of this topic, I feel . . ."

- Write nonstop for a fixed period of time—five or ten minutes, perhaps. Don't stop during that time; the point is to generate as much material as you can.

- If you can't think of anything to write, put down a nonsense phrase or repeat a key word just to keep your pen or cursor moving.

- Don't stop to question or correct your work while freewriting. Forget about style and correctness. Get the intellectual juices flowing.

- After freewriting, read the words you have produced to recover the ideas you may have generated. If you have come up with observations worthy of more exploration, make those ideas the focus of more freewriting.

Interviewing

We routinely ask people questions to satisfy our curiosity, but to turn a conversation with an interesting and knowledgeable person into a useful interview, you need to do your homework. The first step is to decide who you wish to interview—and you don't have to limit yourself to experts only. Friends and classmates have knowledge and opinions you might tap by interviewing them. Think of an interview as a high-powered conversation, a new way to learn. Here are some suggestions for arranging, conducting, and recording an interview:

- Call or write ahead for an appointment.
- Prepare your questions in advance, perhaps brainstorming a preliminary list, then augmenting it with who-what-where-when-why-how items. Arrange your queries in a sensible order, perhaps beginning with more factual questions and then moving to more complex questions of opinion.
- Prepare some open-ended questions—the kind that can't be answered in a word or phrase. Give yourself leeway to take the conversation down any paths that open up.
- Record your subject's responses carefully, later double-checking with him or her any direct quotations you might want to use. Use a tape recorder if your subject approves.
- Record time, date, place, and other pertinent information about the conversation for your records.
- After an interview, summarize the information briefly in your own words.

Writing a Letter to the Editor

A familiar kind of persuasive writing is the letter to the editor, in which writers explain why they agree or disagree with something they've read. Such letters are typically composed in response to positions taken by newspapers, magazines, or journals. In most cases, letters to the editor are spirited arguments, somewhat personal, and carefully targeted.

Letters to the editor follow the conventions of business letters and should be dated and signed. Here are some suggestions for writing one:

- Think about who reads the periodical to which the letter will be sent. Because such a letter is intended for publication, it is usually written more to win the support of other readers than to influence editors or publishers.

- Identify your target article within the first line or two. Let readers know exactly what piece provoked your ire or admiration.

- Make your case quickly. Since space for letters is very limited in most publications, expect to make only one or two points. Execute them powerfully and memorably, using the best examples and reasons you can.

- When appropriate, use irony, satire, or humor.

For an example, see the letter to the editor written by Florence Hoff (p. 691).

Narrating

Whereas descriptions usually refer to stationary things, narratives depict motion, whether it be the action of a single person or the unfurling of a complex historical event, such as a war or social movement. When you narrate, you usually tell a story of some kind. But a narrative may also explain *how something occurred* (analyzing a process) or *why something happened* (tracing cause and effect). Here are some suggestions for narrating:

- Place the events you are discussing in a meaningful order, usually chronological—first this happened, then this, then this, and so on.

- Provide necessary background information by answering the questions who, what, where, when, why, and how the events occurred.

- Most narrative calls for some description. Flesh out any characters and describe any scenic details necessary to the narrative. Consider using appropriate images.

- Use transitional phrases (*then, next, on the following day*) or series (*in the spring, during the summer, later in the year*) to keep the sequence of the narrative clear. Remember, however, that the sequence doesn't always have to be chronological (you've certainly seen flashbacks in movies).

For examples of narration, see the selections by Mary Shelley (p. 231) and Maxine Hong Kingston (p. 361).

Writing to an Online Forum or Listserv

In some courses, you may be expected to write about a topic or reading in an online forum or on a listserv. In a topic forum, you typically respond to a prompt on a Web page and read what your classmates have to say there; postings to and from a listserv are exchanged as email messages. Whichever technology is used, electronic discussions provide instantaneous communication and rapid response—which are both their strength and their weakness. But you can learn to write effectively in these environments with just a little practice.

- If you are the first to post a response to a prompt from an instructor or classmate, address the question directly and thoughtfully: you may be setting the tone for an entire discussion.

- When you join a discussion already in progress, get a feel for the conversation before posting a message. Pay attention to both the content and the tone of the forum. Let your message suggest that you have given due consideration to the thoughts of others who have already contributed to the discussion. Avoid the temptation to fire off just a few quick words in response to a classmate's posting. No one wants to open a message that says simply *You're wrong!* or *I agree.*

- Be sure your message places your ideas in context. Quite often, you'll be responding to a specific question or to messages others have already sent. So sometimes it helps to repeat portions of previous messages in your posting, but don't copy long strings of text. All the repetition may clutter your own message and even make it hard to find.

- Consider how the title of your posting might convey both your context and your point. In most forums, the responses to an original posting will be linked by the familiar abbreviation for "with reference to," *Re:.* You can keep a string going, but vary the title of your message slightly to indicate your own slant.

> Newman's THE IDEA OF A UNIVERSITY
>> Re: Newman's THE IDEA OF A UNIVERSITY — Still relevant?
>> Re: Newman's THE IDEA OF A UNIVERSITY — Who cares?
>> Re: Newman's THE IDEA OF A UNIVERSITY — I care.
>> Re: Newman's THE IDEA OF A UNIVERSITY — Hart cares too.

- Edit your posting before you send it. Online communications tend to be less formal than other kinds of writing. But show respect for your classmates by editing messages before you send them into the public square. Remember that you won't be able to recall or correct your blunders once you send a posting electronically.

Parodying

Your appreciation of a written work can't be tested better than by parody. A *parody* is an imitation of an author, a work, or an attitude written with a humorous and sometimes critical edge. Parody succeeds when readers recognize both your target and your criticism; they should laugh at the wit in your mimicking something they too have experienced.

When you write a parody, you are in certain ways collaborating with other writers. You will necessarily learn much about the way they think and use language. Here are some suggestions for writing a parody:

- Choose a distinctive idea or work to parody. The more recognizable an attitude or famous a work is, the easier it will be to poke fun at. But even the most vapid work can be mocked for its dullness.

- Look for familiar subjects, motifs, images, or opinions, and distort them enough to be funny but not so much that the original idea becomes unrecognizable.

- When parodying a well-known work or writer, try shifting from a serious theme to a frivolous one; for example, imagine a pompous opera critic reviewing 'N Sync's latest video or a dour news commentator interviewing the ghost of Elvis.

- Pinpoint the habits of language ordinarily used to discuss your subject—typical sentence openers, preferred jargon, distinctive patterns of repetition, favorite sentence patterns, unusual punctuation. Then exaggerate those habits.

- Don't make your parody too long. Parody is a form of wit, and brevity is its soul.

- Above all, have fun. When a parody ceases being funny, it becomes simply tedious imitation.

For an example of parody, see the selection by Tom Connor and Jim Downey (p. 656).

Writing a Position Paper

A position paper is a short (often one-page or one-screen) argument that can sometimes be exploratory. In it, you will usually present a thesis—a statement that needs to be proved or defended. But such a paper is often assigned to jump-start discussions or to get various points of view on the table, so feel free to take risks and examine new approaches. A position paper need not have the gloss of a polished argument, and its language can be livelier than that of more formal academic arguments. It should stimulate your readers—often your classmates—to respond actively to your ideas. Here are some suggestions for writing a position paper:

- Begin by taking a stand on a subject. Find a statement you can defend reasonably well.

- Support your thesis with various kinds of evidence—arguments, examples, statistics, illustrations, expert opinions, and so on.

- If the position paper is very brief, suggest the direction a fuller argument might take.

- Write an open-ended conclusion, qualifying your original thesis or pointing to avenues for further study.

For an example of a position paper, see the selection by Ward Churchill (p. 497).

Proposing Solutions

Proposals identify a problem and suggest action that will remedy the problem. You need to convince readers first that a problem exists and is serious, then that your solution is a feasible remedy. Often you will try as well to inspire your readers to take some action.

- To demonstrate that the problem exists, give examples and cite evidence such as statistics or the testimony of experts. Use photographs or other images if appropriate.
- Consider your audience. Are readers likely to be aware of the problem? Try to connect the problem to concerns they might have.
- To convince readers to accept your solution, you need to show that it is feasible—and that it is better than other solutions that might reasonably be proposed. Again, images may help here.

For examples of essays that propose solutions, see the selections by Adrienne Rich (p. 65) and Jeffrey Hart (p. 126).

Keeping a Reading Log

Many writers use reading logs to record their feelings and detailed impressions about what they're reading and thinking. Your instructor may ask you to keep one and turn it in as part of your work for a course. Here are some suggestions for keeping a reading log:

- If you want to remember what you've read, take time to summarize the text or list its main ideas.
- Write out your immediate reactions to the text. These may include memorable lines; things that made you angry, sad, puzzled, or delighted; or things that you want to know more about. Later, in a more extended comment, summarize your thoughts about the text. Reflect on what in the piece and in your experience may have shaped your reactions.
- Make some notes about the author's perspective, where he or she seems to be coming from, noting places in the text that provide clues to the perspective.
- Write in an informal, exploratory style, almost as if you were talking to yourself.

- Date your entries, and be sure to identify the text.
- Look at your commentary in the context of your notes on other readings. Do you see any useful or interesting connections?

For examples of writing similar to reading log entries, see the editors' responses to Anthony Brandt's essay (p. 191).

Reporting

Doing a report is one of the most common academic assignments. Reports are explanations that transfer information from writers to readers. That information may come directly from the writers' minds or from other sources of information—from traditional libraries to field research to computer networks.

- Focus a report around a thesis, a clear statement of purpose. The thesis is the point or controlling idea of a piece. A thesis statement makes a promise to readers, telling them what to expect, and it limits the subject matter and scope of your report.
- Acknowledge any sources you use.
- Define any terms your readers may not know.
- Arrange information according to a plan your readers can easily follow. For example, a report on the major events of the Cold War could follow a chronological organization: first, second, third. A report on the Cold War policies of Joseph Stalin and Harry Truman might use a structure comparing and contrasting the two leaders.
- Use images if they will help readers follow your points.
- Conclude by summarizing your work and exploring its implications.
- Give the report a concise, factual, and descriptive title.

For an example of a report, see the selection by Mark Clayton (p. 185).

WORKING WITH SOURCES

Much of the college writing you will do will involve the use of source materials. Following are guidelines for evaluating, quoting, paraphrasing, and summarizing sources.

Evaluating Sources

Not all sources are equally authoritative or useful. Here are some general tips for evaluating sources; consult your instructor, librarian, or writing handbook for further advice.

- Note whether a source is a primary or secondary one.

- Learn the differences between scholarly and trade books, and choose sources appropriate to your work. The claims in scholarly books are systematically documented and carefully reviewed; trade books may be just as factual and reliable, but they typically lack formal documentation.

- Understand the differences between scholarly journals and popular magazines. Both may serve your research needs, but in different ways. Journals written for specialists will often be highly technical and, consequently, difficult for people outside a profession to read; popular magazines serve wider audiences and present more accessible — if less authoritative — information.

- Understand the limits of online sources. World Wide Web sites, for example, vary enormously in quality, from those carefully maintained by institutions and professional organizations to playful home pages posted by individuals. Be especially careful with sites associated with familiar figures or institutions but not actually maintained or authorized by them.

Quoting

Quoting involves noting down a source's *exact words*. You will have many occasions in working with the readings in this book to use direct quotation. Many of the headnotes that introduce each reading show examples of direct quotation.

- Copy quotations *carefully,* with punctuation, capitalization, and spelling exactly as in the original.

- Use ellipses to indicate any omitted words, and enclose the ellipses in square brackets if you are using MLA (Modern Language Association) documentation style.

- Bracket any words you need to add to the quotation.

- Enclose the quotation in quotation marks.

Paraphrasing

A paraphrase accurately states all the relevant information from a passage *in your own words and phrasing,* without any additional comment or elaboration. Use paraphrases when you want to cite ideas from a source but have no need to quote exact words.

- Include the main points and some important details from the original, in the same order in which they are presented in the source.
- Use your own words and sentence structures. If you want to include especially memorable language from the original, enclose it in quotation marks.
- Leave out your own comments and reactions.
- Recheck the paraphrase against the original to be sure that the words and structures are your own and that they express the author's meaning accurately.

Summarizing

A summary concisely restates key ideas *in your own words*. Sometimes you may need to summarize something in a sentence or two: "In *The Culture of Disbelief,* Stephen L. Carter argues that American culture pressures people with strong religious beliefs not to act on their principles." Often a more detailed synopsis is necessary. Preparing such a summary takes some planning. Here are some suggestions:

- Outline the text you are summarizing. Identify its main points, subpoints, and key bits of supporting evidence.
- Flesh out the outline with necessary details, taking care to show the connections between key ideas.
- Check that your concise version of a longer work can stand on its own. Remember that your readers may not have access to the original piece, so all references need to be clear.
- Double-check against the piece you are summarizing to make sure the wording in your summary is your own.

For an example of summary, see portions of Barbara Dafoe Whitehead's essay (p. 619).

Deciding Whether to Quote, Paraphrase, or Summarize

- *Quote*
  Wording that expresses a point so perfectly that you cannot improve or shorten it without weakening the meaning you need
  Authors' opinions you wish to emphasize
  Respected authorities whose opinions support your own ideas
  Authors whose opinions challenge or vary from others in the field

- *Paraphrase*
  Passages that you do not wish to quote but whose details you wish to note *fully*
- *Summarize*
  Long passages whose *main points* you wish to record *selectively*

Incorporating Sources

Incorporate quotations, paraphrases, and summaries into your own writing carefully, often by using a signal phrase such as *he said* or *she remarks*. Choose the verbs you use to introduce source material carefully; be sure they express your thoughts accurately. Notice, for instance, the difference between saying someone "said," "claimed," or "asserted." For effective incorporation of sources, see the many quotations in Robert D. King's essay (p. 409).

Acknowledging Sources

When quoting, paraphrasing, or summarizing sources in formal essays, reports, or research projects, be sure to acknowledge all sources according to the conventions required by your field or instructor.

WORKING WITH OTHERS

The title for this text recalls a remark by philosopher Hannah Arendt that "for excellence, the presence of others is always required." Nowhere is Arendt's observation more accurate than in the college community. Your college coursework will call on you to read, write, and research a vast amount of material. But you will not—or need not—do all that reading, writing, and researching alone. Far from it. Instead, you can be part of a broad conversation that includes all the texts you read; all the writing you produce; all the discussions you have with teachers, friends, family members, and classmates; all the observations and interviews you conduct. Throughout this book, we draw on Arendt's concept—from our title to the way we group readings in conversation with one another to the many assignments that ask you to work with others.

Collaboration can play an important part in all the writing you do, first if you talk with others about your topic and your plans for approaching it, then if you seek responses to your draft and gather suggestions for improving it. In much the same way, reading can be done "with others"—first by entering into mental conversation with the author and with the social and historical forces at work shaping the author's text, then by comparing your understanding of the text with that of other readers and using points of agreement or disagreement as the basis for further analysis.

As you read this book, the most immediate and valuable of your collaborators may be your classmates. Indeed, you can learn a great deal by listening carefully both to them and to your instructor. You can profit even more by talking over issues with them, by comparing notes and ideas with them, and by using them as a first and very important audience for your writing. They will inevitably offer you new perspectives, new ways of seeing and knowing.

- Once you establish a group, be sure to trade phone numbers, email addresses, and schedules, and set a time to meet.

- Set an agenda for each meeting. If you intend to study or compare certain readings, be sure everyone knows in advance and brings the essay or book to the meeting. Perhaps begin by brainstorming major questions you have about the reading.

- Use the group to work through difficult readings. If a reading is especially long, have each member take one section to explain and "teach" to the others.

- If the group corresponds via email, be sure to create a mailbox for the project where you can collect and keep all correspondence.

- If you need to prepare something as a group, decide on a fair and effective means of dividing the task. Assign each group member specific duties. Arrange for a time to meet when those individual duties will have been accomplished. At the meeting, work to review the various parts and put them together.

- If a project involves a group presentation or report, figure out what each member will contribute. Plan all the work that is to be done and schedule any necessary meetings. For the presentation, make sure every group member is involved in some way. Decide on any visual aids or handouts in advance and prepare them carefully. Finally, *practice the presentation*. Everyone will benefit from a "dress rehearsal."

- Most important, listen to every member of the group carefully and respectfully; everyone's ideas must be taken into consideration. If conflict arises—and in any lively and healthy collaboration, it will—explore all areas of the conflict openly and fairly before seeking resolution.

- Take time each meeting to assess the effectiveness of the group. Consider these questions: What has the group accomplished so far? With what has it been most helpful? With what has it been least helpful? What have you contributed? What has each of the others contributed? How can you all make the group more effective?

A SAMPLE CRITICAL RESPONSE ESSAY

We have outlined in this chapter some of the ways you may be asked to respond to selected readings in your writing classes. A type of response you are most likely to be asked to do is a critical response essay (guidelines for writing a critical analysis begin on p. 20.) Read the following critical response essay by Jennifer E. Smith to see how one student responds to the selection in this book by J. Michael Bishop, "Enemies of Promise" (p. 237).

JENNIFER E. SMITH
Questioning the Promises of Science

JENNIFER E. SMITH, a first-year student at The Ohio State University, wrote "Questioning the Promises of Science" after her instructor asked the class to choose one essay from the chapter on science and technology in this text and respond critically to it. Smith chose the piece by J. Michael Bishop, "Enemies of Promise."

It is overwhelming to think of the number of questions that science seeks to answer. Science tries to explain how every aspect of the universe works; it is indeed a broad topic. For this reason, as J. Michael Bishop concludes in his essay "Enemies of Promise," educating the public about the advancements, or even general knowledge, of science is difficult. Thus, Bishop points out, the scientific ignorance of the public leads to a fear of science, and "[r]esistance to science is born of fear." Though Bishop, on behalf of the scientific community, takes responsibility for neglecting public scientific education, he seems to accuse all those who question science of suffering from ignorance. Though I agree with Bishop's point about the lack of education in the sciences, I disagree with his approach. Bishop does not prove his point well in "Enemies of Promise"; he does not offer sufficient counterarguments to his postmodern detractors, nor does he offer any solutions to the problems with education, which he claims are the cause of postmodern critiques.

Bishop begins "Enemies of Promise" by marveling over the "fruits of scientific inquiry" and questioning why "science today is increasingly mistrusted and under attack." Throughout the essay, Bishop seems too proud of the scientific field to admit that current scientific methods are less than perfect. Even in the age of computer technology, scientists, *humans,* still perform the research. When humans are involved, there will always be some degree of bias; business and politics will have their influence. Though these biases may be minimal and are usually unintended, they still exist; science is not immune to human nature. Bishop does not recognize this and angrily dismisses the postmodern view, which calls science on its biases, as "arrant nonsense." The postmodern view may be an exaggerated response to the frustration associated with the politics of science, but these critics do raise some valid points and should not be dismissed. It is ironic that the scientific community, which was born out of questioning that which was assumed to be known, is now angered when its own knowledge is questioned. Bishop shows this anger throughout the essay when he responds to his critics. He refers to postmodernism as "either a strategy for advancement in parochial precincts . . . or a display of ignorance." Instead of debating Václav

Havel's remarks on science, Bishop accuses him of using "angry words" whose "precise meaning is elusive." Bishop also refers to all questioners of science as a "chorus of criticism and doubt."

While his easy dismissal of some critics is troubling, Bishop does offer a good response to the criticisms of Brown and Lamm. Brown is frustrated by the "'knowledge paradox,'" which Bishop paraphrases as "an expansion of fundamental knowledge accompanied by an increase in social problems." Lamm no longer believes "that biomedical research contributes to the improvement of human health" because of the lack of access in the United States to these health care advancements as well as the abundance of social diseases in today's society. Bishop points out that Brown and Lamm are placing blame on science for "the failures of individuals or society to use the knowledge that science has provided." He also notes that critics often expect too much, too soon, from science and fail to realize that scientific study is dependent on feasibility and that results are often unpredictable.

Bishop continues "Enemies of Promise" by noting the stereotypes that the public has about scientists themselves and how these stereotypes contribute to the general mistrust of science. According to him, the public has "exaggerated expectations about what science can accomplish" because of the rapid successes of science in the past. Bishop then attacks the 1992 film *Lorenzo's Oil,* equating it with some sort of anti-science propaganda. The movie does portray scientists according to common stereotypes; as Bishop points out, it shows them as "insensitive, close-minded, and self-serving." However, Bishop does little to disprove this stereotype; in fact, throughout the essay he shows signs of possessing all of these characteristics. He is obviously close-minded in response to his critics, especially postmodernists. He seems insensitive in his discussion of the true life story behind *Lorenzo's Oil* and in the way he discusses other people's scientific ignorance. Though Bishop is not obviously "self-serving," he does seem overly proud of his role as a scientist and of the role of science in general. Describing our age as one "of scientific triumph," he sees science as "one of the great, ennobling tasks of humankind" and biomedical research as "one of the great triumphs of human endeavor."

Bishop begins his conclusion to "Enemies of Promise" well with his discussion of the difficulties in educating people about science. He admits how far behind the United States is in the process and notes that most scientists specialize and are often ignorant about fields of science outside their own. Bishop correctly places blame for this lack of education with the scientific community. However, as soon as he notes this problem, instead of offering a solution, he returns to praising science with flowery language: "We of science have begun the quest well, by building a method of ever-increasing power, a method that can illuminate all that is in the natural world." The concluding paragraph is consistent with the rest of the essay in that it focuses too much on building up science as the quintessence of human reason rather than addressing the real problems of educating others about science.

Bishop's pride seems to have prevented him from giving proper focus in his essay. For his argument to be a convincing one, the focus should have been directed toward the education problem. Bishop concludes that those who question science do so out of ignorance, yet he offers no suggestions for how to diminish this ignorance. Instead, the whole essay seems to focus on asserting how great science is, not with evidence but with catchy phrases. As a result, this essay only seems to support the stereotypes that the public has about scientists and their egocentricity.

Chicago will put
you in the
company
of some of the best
students anywhere.

They come to
this campus
from 50
states and
33 countries.

They have
excelled
and they have
achieved
in the classroom.

They are accomplished
and creative, with
interests that
transcend
the merely academic.

Here, they occupy
and **shape**
a bigger,
broader, more
challenging world.

Look carefully at the brochure on the preceding page. What in this picture first draws your eye, and where does that part of the image lead you next? ■ Why do you think the name of the school (the University of Chicago) is not featured more prominently? ■ To whom do you think the creators of the brochure are appealing as a primary audience—and how do you know? ■ After studying the verbal and visual elements carefully, try your hand at paraphrasing the major message this brochure seeks to send.

Education: 3
The Idea of a University

If then a practical end must be assigned to a University course, I say it is that of training good members of society.

JOHN HENRY NEWMAN, *The Idea of a University*

Our graduates will have an understanding of interdependence and global competence, distinctive technical and educational skills, the experience and abilities to contribute to California's high-quality workforce, the critical thinking abilities to be productive citizens, and the social responsibility and skills to be community builders.   CALIFORNIA STATE UNIVERSITY, MONTEREY BAY, *Vision Statement*

The American tradition, in learning as well as jazz and activism, is improvisatory. There are as many ways to become an educated American as there are Americans.   JON SPAYDE, *Learning in the Key of Life*

What does a woman need to know to become a self-conscious, self-defining human being?   ADRIENNE RICH, *What Does a Woman Need to Know?*

What has emerged on campus in recent years . . . is a *politics of difference,* a troubling, volatile politics in which each group justifies itself, its sense of worth and its pursuit of power, through difference alone.

SHELBY STEELE, *The Recoloring of Campus Life*

Studying at Stanford, I began to think seriously about class differences. To be materially underprivileged at a university where most folks . . . are materially privileged provokes such thought.

BELL HOOKS, *Keeping Close to Home: Class and Education*

If the canon itself is the answer to our educational inequities, why has it historically invited few and denied many?   MIKE ROSE, *Lives on the Boundary*

The issue here is not just the favoritism that teachers may show to pupils of their own sex, but the instinctive understanding that an adult will enjoy with a child who is going through a process which he or she went through too.

DAVID THOMAS, *The Mind of Man*   43

What is the liberal-arts education supposed to produce? Once you have the answer to this question, course selection becomes easy.

JEFFREY HART, *How to Get a College Education*

We real cool. We / Left school.   GWENDOLYN BROOKS, *We Real Cool*

Introduction

YOU MAY BE SURPRISED to learn that until fairly recently in the United States most people either did not have the resources to attend college or were excluded from the majority of colleges for other reasons (such as race or gender). Today, however, nearly half of all high school graduates extend their education at a two-year or four-year college or university. And many older individuals who had never pursued higher education or had left college for some reason are now returning to the classroom. More and more people are attending college these days—but what kind of education are they receiving?

In fact, questions about the purpose of education have been under scrutiny at least since Socrates was put on trial in 399 B.C. on charges of corrupting the youth of Athens by his teaching of philosophy. But no one seems to agree these days in the United States, any more than in ancient Greece, about what the role of higher education should be. Who should be encouraged to attend colleges and universities—and who should not be? Should education be a mechanism for advancing the welfare of the nation—augmenting its productivity, management skills, and technology and preserving the quality of its workforce? Should it be an instrument of social change—teaching ideas of social justice, adjusting to new demographics in the population it serves, and providing the rationale for radical reforms of the economic order? Should it exist primarily to stimulate the intellect and the imagination of students? Or should schooling serve other or multiple purposes?

In this chapter, we have selected readings that bring different perspectives—and offer very different answers—to these central questions about the purposes of higher education. We hope these readings will lead you to consider such questions yourself, to think hard and long about what higher education is for and what it *should* be for in the future. Before you begin reading, however, you may want to think over some of the issues raised in this chapter. Here are some questions to get you started thinking:

- What are your reasons for coming to college? Do you think your reasons correspond to your college's or university's goals for its students?

- In what ways was your decision to attend college shaped or influenced by factors outside your control?
- What should be the goals of higher education? If you were president of your college or university, what would you list as the school's aims? What would be your top priorities?

• • •

JOHN HENRY NEWMAN
The Idea of a University

*J*OHN *H*ENRY *N*EWMAN's The Idea of a University *is among the most famous at-tempts to define a liberal arts education. Originally written in 1852 in response to a papal proposal for a Roman Catholic university in Ireland,* The Idea of a University *served as an intellectual manifesto for Catholics, who had long been an oppressed mi-nority in the British Isles. Full emancipation occurred for them only in 1829; prior to that date, Catholics had been denied political rights in England and Ireland as well as admission to the great British universities, Oxford and Cambridge.*

Newman (1801–90), a well-known Anglican priest who had converted to the Roman church, wrote The Idea of a University *to explore what a Catholic university would be like—how it might merge religious and secular concerns. He was also re-sponding to a world growing ever more secular in its interests, more scientific in its methods, more utilitarian in its philosophy. Revolutions in technology and industrial organization seemed to be reshaping every human endeavor, including the academy.*

Newman had reservations about these changes, many of which we take for granted today, such as the division of universities into various "schools" (arts, sciences, professional schools), the selection by students of their own programs of study, and the establishment of areas of specialization (what we would call majors*). His aim in this essay is to defend the value of learning for its own sake.*

The Idea of a University *is an example of deliberative rhetoric: Newman is both recommending and defending the proposal for a Catholic university. He faces both an entrenched Anglican tradition and a scholarly community leaning in the direction of what is today called secular humanism. The following excerpts from this book-length work do not focus on religious issues, however. Instead, they explain several of New-man's goals for the liberal arts university.*

—J.R.

DISCOURSE V
KNOWLEDGE ITS OWN END

1

I have said that all branches of knowledge are connected together, be-cause the subject-matter of knowledge is intimately united in itself, as being the acts and the work of the Creator. Hence it is that the Sciences, into which our knowledge may be said to be cast, have multiplied bearings one on an-other, and an internal sympathy, and admit, or rather demand, comparison and adjustment. They complete, correct, balance each other. This considera-tion, if well-founded, must be taken into account, not only as regards the at-

46

tainment of truth, which is their common end, but as regards the influence which they exercise upon those whose education consists in the study of them. I have said already, that to give undue prominence to one is to be unjust to another; to neglect or supersede these is to divert those from their proper object. It is to unsettle the boundary lines between science and science, to disturb their action, to destroy the harmony which binds them together. Such a proceeding will have a corresponding effect when introduced into a place of education. There is no science but tells a different tale, when viewed as a portion of a whole, from what it is likely to suggest when taken by itself, without the safeguard, as I may call it, of others.

Let me make use of an illustration. In the combination of colors, very different effects are produced by a difference in their selection and juxtaposition; red, green, and white, change their shades, according to the contrast to which they are submitted. And, in like manner, the drift and meaning of a branch of knowledge varies with the company in which it is introduced to the student. If his reading is confined simply to one subject, however such division of labor may favor the advancement of a particular pursuit, a point into which I do not here enter, certainly it has a tendency to contract his mind. If it is incorporated with others, it depends on those others as to the kind of influence which it exerts upon him. Thus the Classics, which in England are the means of refining the taste, have in France subserved the spread of revolutionary and deistical doctrines. In Metaphysics, again, *Butler's Analogy of Religion** which has had so much to do with the conversion to the Catholic faith of members of the University of Oxford, appeared to Pitt* and others, who had received a different training, to operate only in the direction of infidelity. And so again, Watson, Bishop of Llandaff,* as I think he tells us in the narrative of his life, felt the science of Mathematics to indispose the mind to religious belief, while others see in its investigations the best parallel, and thereby defense, of the Christian Mysteries. In like manner, I suppose, Arcesilas* would not have handled logic as Aristotle, nor Aristotle have criticized poets as Plato; yet reasoning and poetry are subject to scientific rules.

It is a great point then to enlarge the range of studies which a University professes, even for the sake of the students; and, though they cannot pursue every subject which is open to them, they will be the gainers by living among those and under those who represent the whole circle. This I conceive to be the advantage of a seat of universal learning, considered as a place of education. An assemblage of learned men, zealous for their own sciences, and rivals

---

Butler's Analogy of Religion: a defense of Christian revelation (1736) by Joseph Butler (1692–1752)

Pitt: William Pitt (1708–78), British parliamentarian and orator

Watson, Bishop of Llandaff: Richard Watson (1737–1816), a professor of chemistry and divinity

Arcesilas: Greek philosopher (c. 316–241 B.C.) who advocated rational skepticism

of each other, are brought, by familiar intercourse and for the sake of intellectual peace, to adjust together the claims and relations of their respective subjects of investigation. They learn to respect, to consult, to aid each other. Thus is created a pure and clear atmosphere of thought, which the student also breathes, though in his own case he only pursues a few sciences out of the multitude. He profits by an intellectual tradition, which is independent of particular teachers, which guides him in his choice of subjects, and duly interprets for him those which he chooses. He apprehends the great outlines of knowledge, the principles on which it rests, the scale of its parts, its lights and its shades, its great points and its little, as he otherwise cannot apprehend them. Hence it is that his education is called "Liberal." A habit of mind is formed which lasts through life, of which the attributes are, freedom, equitableness, calmness, moderation, and wisdom; or what in a former Discourse I have ventured to call a philosophical habit. This then I would assign as the special fruit of the education furnished at a University, as contrasted with other places of teaching or modes of teaching. This is the main purpose of a University in its treatment of its students.

And now the question is asked me, What is the *use* of it? and my answer will constitute the main subject of the Discourses which are to follow.

• • •

DISCOURSE VII
KNOWLEDGE VIEWED IN RELATION TO PROFESSIONAL SKILL

10

But I must bring these extracts to an end. Today I have confined myself   5
to saying that that training of the intellect, which is best for the individual himself, best enables him to discharge his duties to society. The Philosopher, indeed, and the man of the world differ in their very notion, but the methods, by which they are respectively formed, are pretty much the same. The Philosopher has the same command of matters of thought, which the true citizen and gentleman has of matters of business and conduct. If then a practical end must be assigned to a University course, I say it is that of training good members of society. Its art is the art of social life, and its end is fitness for the world. It neither confines its views to particular professions on the one hand, nor creates heroes or inspires genius on the other. Works indeed of genius fall under no art; heroic minds come under no rule; a University is not a birthplace of poets or of immortal authors, of founders of schools, leaders of colonies, or conquerors of nations. It does not promise a generation of Aristotles or Newtons, of Napoleons or Washingtons, of Raphaels or Shakespeares,

though such miracles of nature it has before now contained within its precincts. Nor is it content on the other hand with forming the critic or the experimentalist, the economist or the engineer, though such too it includes within its scope. But a University training is the great ordinary means to a great but ordinary end; it aims at raising the intellectual tone of society, at cultivating the public mind, at purifying the national taste, at supplying true principles to popular enthusiasm and fixed aims to popular aspiration, at giving enlargement and sobriety to the ideas of the age, at facilitating the exercise of political power, and refining the intercourse of private life. It is the education which gives a man a clear conscious view of his own opinions and judgments, a truth in developing them, an eloquence in expressing them, and a force in urging them. It teaches him to see things as they are, to go right to the point, to disentangle a skein of thought, to detect what is sophistical, and to discard what is irrelevant. It prepares him to fill any post with credit, and to master any subject with facility. It shows him how to accommodate himself to others, how to throw himself into their state of mind, how to bring before them his own, how to influence them, how to come to an understanding with them, how to bear with them. He is at home in any society, he has common ground with every class; he knows when to speak and when to be silent; he is able to converse, he is able to listen; he can ask a question pertinently, and gain a lesson seasonably, when he has nothing to impart himself; he is ever ready, yet never in the way; he is a pleasant companion, and a comrade you can depend upon; he knows when to be serious and when to trifle, and he has a sure tact which enables him to trifle with gracefulness and to be serious with effect. He has the repose of a mind which lives in itself, while it lives in the world, and which has resources for its happiness at home when it cannot go abroad. He has a gift which serves him in public, and supports him in retirement, without which good fortune is but vulgar, and with which failure and disappointment have a charm. The art which tends to make a man all this, is in the object which it pursues as useful as the art of wealth or the art of health, though it is less susceptible of method, and less tangible, less certain, less complete in its result.

QUESTIONING THE TEXT

1. Examine the goals Newman explicitly provides for the university in the passage from Discourse VII. Do these goals still seem relevant today? Why, or why not? If you keep a reading log, answer this question there.

2. As you reread Newman's essay, record your reactions to his style in the margins. Does it feel stuffy or solemn? Does it move you or impress you? When you are finished, draw some conclusions from your comments.

3. The introduction emphasizes that Newman's *The Idea of a University* was written in response to changes occurring in the United Kingdom in the nineteenth century. Do any of these changes seem relevant to events in the United States in the twenty-first century?

MAKING CONNECTIONS

4. Would Mike Rose or the students he describes in "Lives on the Boundary" (p. 105) fit into the university Newman describes? Write a two- to three-page essay exploring this issue.

5. One of the major complaints made against contemporary universities by Jeffrey Hart (p. 126) is that they give students too little guidance through the curriculum. Discuss the underlying principle in Newman and Hart that a good liberal arts education approaches knowledge as a whole, not as a collection of separate courses, fields, or career paths.

JOINING THE CONVERSATION

6. Can Newman's concept of *liberal arts* survive in our world today? Does it deserve to? Why, or why not? Write a position paper on this subject.

7. For a national newsmagazine, write an evaluation of American higher education as you imagine Newman might regard it if he were living today. What might he admire? What would he criticize?

8. With a group of classmates, discuss the usefulness of the education you have had in high school and college. Which courses of study seem to have the most direct application to daily life? Which, if any, seem designed primarily as learning for its own sake?

THE UNIVERSITY OF MINNESOTA; MOREHOUSE COLLEGE; THE EVERGREEN STATE COLLEGE; CALIFORNIA STATE UNIVERSITY, MONTEREY BAY; and THOMAS AQUINAS COLLEGE
Mission Statements

If John Henry Newman had been able to build a Web site for his ideal university, what might it have looked like and how would it have represented his goals for the institution? These are questions we had in mind as we set out to browse contemporary college and university Web sites, much as you may have done as you began thinking about which schools you might prefer or be able to attend. Of special interest to us are the ways in which various institutions describe their goals within the confines of a computer screen, where space is limited and readers are often impatient. So we decided to take a closer look at these representations, and to choose several for you to examine in the context of this chapter's discussion of education.

The five statements we have chosen represent different kinds of schools in different areas of the country. The University of Minnesota, in Minneapolis, is one of the country's largest research universities; it has extensive undergraduate and graduate curricula. In contrast, California State University at Monterey Bay is a new and as yet small school that focuses primarily on undergraduates. Morehouse College (in Atlanta, Georgia), the Evergreen State College (in Olympia, Washington), and Thomas Aquinas College (in Santa Paula, California) are all liberal arts colleges. Morehouse is one of the country's most distinguished historically black colleges and admits only male students; Evergreen State, a coeducational school, is equally well known for its emphasis on experimentation and innovation. And Thomas Aquinas is distinctive in its own way, with a curriculum focused on the Great Books and a religious (Roman Catholic) orientation.

You may want to visit the Web sites of these five schools to discover more about their campuses, students, faculty, and staff. Or you may decide to visit your own campus Web site, seeking out its statement of mission, vision, or belief in order to compare it to the ones offered here. If you do visit, be sure to note the use of color and visual images, which often carry a good part of the messages the schools wish to convey. Which school's mission most appeals to your own goals and values? —A.L. and J.R.

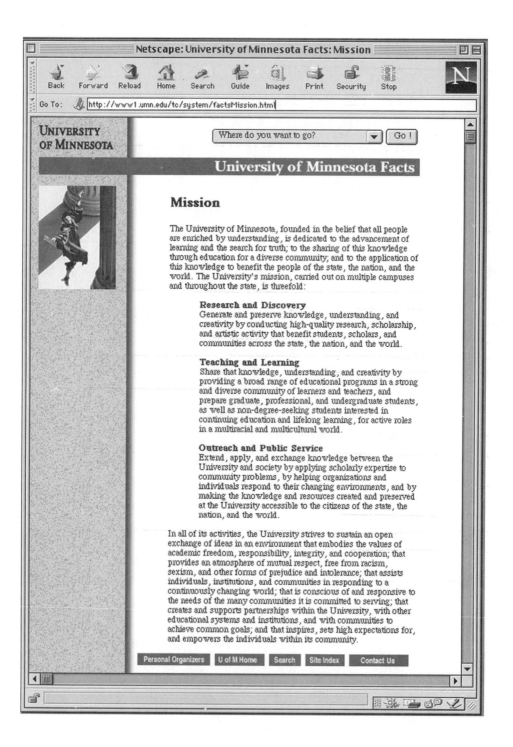

Netscape: University of Minnesota Facts: Mission

Back Forward Reload Home Search Guide Images Print Security Stop

Go To: http://www1.umn.edu/tc/system/factsMission.html

UNIVERSITY OF MINNESOTA

Where do you want to go?   Go !

University of Minnesota Facts

Mission

The University of Minnesota, founded in the belief that all people are enriched by understanding, is dedicated to the advancement of learning and the search for truth; to the sharing of this knowledge through education for a diverse community; and to the application of this knowledge to benefit the people of the state, the nation, and the world. The University's mission, carried out on multiple campuses and throughout the state, is threefold:

Research and Discovery
Generate and preserve knowledge, understanding, and creativity by conducting high-quality research, scholarship, and artistic activity that benefit students, scholars, and communities across the state, the nation, and the world.

Teaching and Learning
Share that knowledge, understanding, and creativity by providing a broad range of educational programs in a strong and diverse community of learners and teachers, and prepare graduate, professional, and undergraduate students, as well as non-degree-seeking students interested in continuing education and lifelong learning, for active roles in a multiracial and multicultural world.

Outreach and Public Service
Extend, apply, and exchange knowledge between the University and society by applying scholarly expertise to community problems, by helping organizations and individuals respond to their changing environments, and by making the knowledge and resources created and preserved at the University accessible to the citizens of the state, the nation, and the world.

In all of its activities, the University strives to sustain an open exchange of ideas in an environment that embodies the values of academic freedom, responsibility, integrity, and cooperation; that provides an atmosphere of mutual respect, free from racism, sexism, and other forms of prejudice and intolerance; that assists individuals, institutions, and communities in responding to a continuously changing world; that is conscious of and responsive to the needs of the many communities it is committed to serving; that creates and supports partnerships within the University, with other educational systems and institutions, and with communities to achieve common goals; and that inspires, sets high expectations for, and empowers the individuals within its community.

Personal Organizers   U of M Home   Search   Site Index   Contact Us

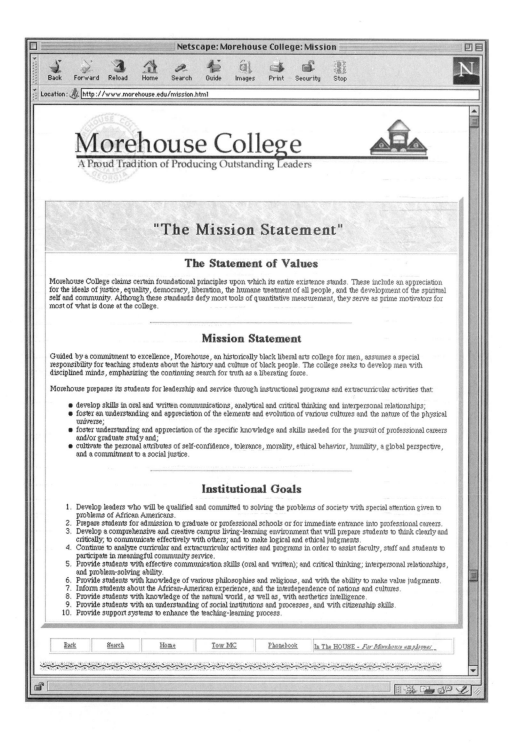

Netscape: Morehouse College: Mission

Back Forward Reload Home Search Guide Images Print Security Stop

Location: http://www.morehouse.edu/mission.html

Morehouse College
A Proud Tradition of Producing Outstanding Leaders

"The Mission Statement"

The Statement of Values

Morehouse College claims certain foundational principles upon which its entire existence stands. These include an appreciation for the ideals of justice, equality, democracy, liberation, the humane treatment of all people, and the development of the spiritual self and community. Although these standards defy most tools of quantitative measurement, they serve as prime motivators for most of what is done at the college.

Mission Statement

Guided by a commitment to excellence, Morehouse, an historically black liberal arts college for men, assumes a special responsibility for teaching students about the history and culture of black people. The college seeks to develop men with disciplined minds, emphasizing the continuing search for truth as a liberating force.

Morehouse prepares its students for leadership and service through instructional programs and extracurricular activities that:

- develop skills in oral and written communications, analytical and critical thinking and interpersonal relationships;
- foster an understanding and appreciation of the elements and evolution of various cultures and the nature of the physical universe;
- foster understanding and appreciation of the specific knowledge and skills needed for the pursuit of professional careers and/or graduate study and;
- cultivate the personal attributes of self-confidence, tolerance, morality, ethical behavior, humility, a global perspective, and a commitment to a social justice.

Institutional Goals

1. Develop leaders who will be qualified and committed to solving the problems of society with special attention given to problems of African Americans.
2. Prepare students for admission to graduate or professional schools or for immediate entrance into professional careers.
3. Develop a comprehensive and creative campus living-learning environment that will prepare students to think clearly and critically; to communicate effectively with others; and to make logical and ethical judgments.
4. Continue to analyze curricular and extracurricular activities and programs in order to assist faculty, staff and students to participate in meaningful community service.
5. Provide students with effective communication skills (oral and written); and critical thinking; interpersonal relationships, and problem-solving ability.
6. Provide students with knowledge of various philosophies and religions, and with the ability to make value judgments.
7. Inform students about the African-American experience, and the interdependence of nations and cultures.
8. Provide students with knowledge of the natural world, as well as, with aesthetics intelligence.
9. Provide students with an understanding of social institutions and processes, and with citizenship skills.
10. Provide support systems to enhance the teaching-learning process.

Back   Search   Home   Tour MC   Phonebook   In The HOUSE - For Morehouse employees

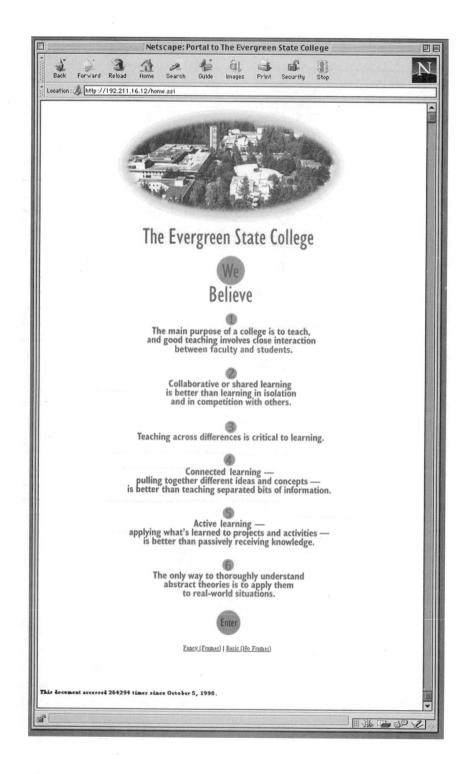

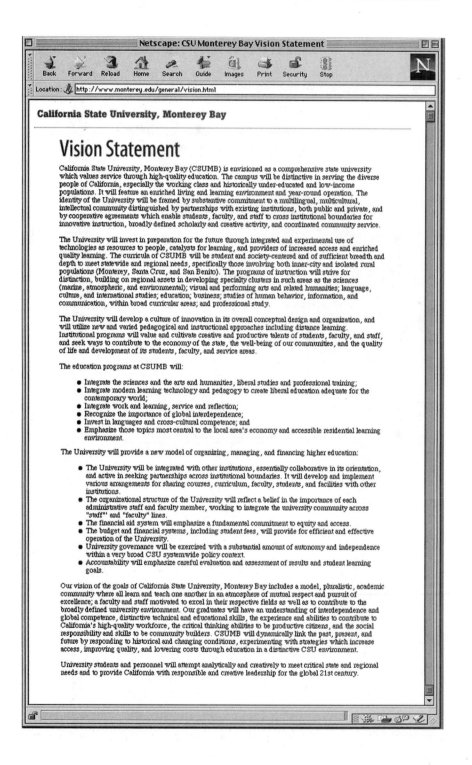

Netscape: CSU Monterey Bay Vision Statement

Back   Forward   Reload   Home   Search   Guide   Images   Print   Security   Stop

Location: http://www.monterey.edu/general/vision.html

California State University, Monterey Bay

Vision Statement

California State University, Monterey Bay (CSUMB) is envisioned as a comprehensive state university which values service through high-quality education. The campus will be distinctive in serving the diverse people of California, especially the working class and historically under-educated and low-income populations. It will feature an enriched living and learning environment and year-round operation. The identity of the University will be framed by substantive commitment to a multilingual, multicultural, intellectual community distinguished by partnerships with existing institutions, both public and private, and by cooperative agreements which enable students, faculty, and staff to cross institutional boundaries for innovative instruction, broadly defined scholarly and creative activity, and coordinated community service.

The University will invest in preparation for the future through integrated and experimental use of technologies as resources to people, catalysts for learning, and providers of increased access and enriched quality learning. The curricula of CSUMB will be student and society-centered and of sufficient breadth and depth to meet statewide and regional needs, specifically those involving both inner-city and isolated rural populations (Monterey, Santa Cruz, and San Benito). The programs of instruction will strive for distinction, building on regional assets in developing specialty clusters in such areas as the sciences (marine, atmospheric, and environmental); visual and performing arts and related humanities; language, culture, and international studies; education; business; studies of human behavior, information, and communication, within broad curricular areas; and professional study.

The University will develop a culture of innovation in its overall conceptual design and organization, and will utilize new and varied pedagogical and instructional approaches including distance learning. Institutional programs will value and cultivate creative and productive talents of students, faculty, and staff, and seek ways to contribute to the economy of the state, the well-being of our communities, and the quality of life and development of its students, faculty, and service areas.

The education programs at CSUMB will:

- Integrate the sciences and the arts and humanities, liberal studies and professional training;
- Integrate modern learning technology and pedagogy to create liberal education adequate for the contemporary world;
- Integrate work and learning, service and reflection;
- Recognize the importance of global interdependence;
- Invest in languages and cross-cultural competence; and
- Emphasize those topics most central to the local area's economy and accessible residential learning environment.

The University will provide a new model of organizing, managing, and financing higher education:

- The University will be integrated with other institutions, essentially collaborative in its orientation, and active in seeking partnerships across institutional boundaries. It will develop and implement various arrangements for sharing courses, curriculum, faculty, students, and facilities with other institutions.
- The organizational structure of the University will reflect a belief in the importance of each administrative staff and faculty member, working to integrate the university community across "staff" and "faculty" lines.
- The financial aid system will emphasize a fundamental commitment to equity and access.
- The budget and financial systems, including student fees, will provide for efficient and effective operation of the University.
- University governance will be exercised with a substantial amount of autonomy and independence within a very broad CSU systemwide policy context.
- Accountability will emphasize careful evaluation and assessment of results and student learning goals.

Our vision of the goals of California State University, Monterey Bay includes a model, pluralistic, academic community where all learn and teach one another in an atmosphere of mutual respect and pursuit of excellence; a faculty and staff motivated to excel in their respective fields as well as to contribute to the broadly defined university environment. Our graduates will have an understanding of interdependence and global competence, distinctive technical and educational skills, the experience and abilities to contribute to California's high-quality workforce, the critical thinking abilities to be productive citizens, and the social responsibility and skills to be community builders. CSUMB will dynamically link the past, present, and future by responding to historical and changing conditions, experimenting with strategies which increase access, improving quality, and lowering costs through education in a distinctive CSU environment.

University students and personnel will attempt analytically and creatively to meet critical state and regional needs and to provide California with responsible and creative leadership for the global 21st century.

QUESTIONING THE TEXT

1. Four of the five statements use different terms to describe what we had been thinking of as *goals statements:* two use the word *mission,* while the others refer to *beliefs* or *vision.* Three head their pages with a noun or noun phrase—"Mission"; "'The Mission Statement'"; "Vision Statement"— while one leads off with a noun-verb combination—"We Believe." Think carefully about these differing terms and phrases and spend five or ten minutes brainstorming with your classmates about the effect these choices have on readers. What differing messages do they send?

2. Examine the format and organizing principles of each mission statement. Include all aspects of the Web page in your analysis, including any use of columns, varying fonts or type sizes, illustrations, headings, buttons, and so on. Which statement do you find most effective in terms of organization, and why?

3. Are any aspects of college life as you know it absent from these mission statements? Identify some of those components and then, in a group, discuss possible explanations for the omissions.

MAKING CONNECTIONS

4. Choose another reading from this chapter and use it as the basis for inferring a "mission statement" that the author might write for his or her ideal university. Which one of the mission statements reproduced here would this inferred statement most resemble, and why?

5. In "How to Get a College Education" (p. 126), Jeffrey Hart asks whether we are getting the education we deserve. His question suggests that many colleges and universities may not be living up to their own missions. How might Hart respond to the mission statement for the Evergreen State College? For Thomas Aquinas College?

JOINING THE CONVERSATION

6. Working with two classmates, draft a mission statement that you think reflects the goals of your college or university. You may need to gather some data from the college catalog, student newspaper, and so on to complete this assignment.

7. Write a parody of a college mission statement. Use the parody as a way to explore problems in education today rather than just to poke fun at an institution.

JON SPAYDE
Learning in the Key of Life

"The whole world's a classroom," says Jon Spayde, a concept he much prefers to narrower definitions of education that limit it to what takes place in school, where it is too often equated with technical competence or "training for competitiveness." Noting that training is often a code word for the education of poor Americans, Spayde rejects these narrow utilitarian goals in favor of enriched study of the humanities in the context of everyday life. This "in-the-streets definition of education" assumes that learning takes place across the span of a lifetime, not just in sixteen years of formal schooling, and that what is being learned takes root and life through connections we make in contact with "the real world." A truly good education, Spayde argues, may well be one "carpentered out of the best combination we can make of school, salon, reading, online exploration, walking the streets, hiking in the woods, museums, poetry classes at the Y, and friendship. . . ."

Spayde's definition of education is perhaps particularly appealing at a time when change is so swift that the shelf life of technical knowledge is six months (at best). In addition, his definition appeals to my own sense that much of our most important and lasting education has always taken place outside of—or on the periphery of—school. In this brief essay, however, Spayde is short on specifics. Although he offers several examples of "in-the-streets education," he hasn't the time or space to set forth any concrete proposals for change. As a result, I would like to hear much more about how ordinary citizens and students might take up this new definition of education in their own lives. Perhaps Spayde, well-known interviewer, editor, and longtime contributor to the Utne Reader *(where this essay first appeared in May–June 1998), will oblige.*

—A.L.

What does it mean—and more important, what *should* it mean—to be educated?

This is a surprisingly tricky and two-sided question. Masquerading as simple problem-solving, it raises a whole laundry list of philosophical conundrums: What sort of society do we want? What is the nature of humankind? How do we learn best? And—most challenging of all—what is the Good? Talking about the meaning of education inevitably leads to the question of what a culture considers most important.

Yikes! No wonder answers don't come easily in 1998, in a multiethnic, corporation-heavy democracy that dominates the globe without having much of a sense of its own soul. For our policyheads, education equals something called "training for competitiveness" (which often boils down to the mantra

**Left to right from top: Lao Tzu   Toni Morrison   Black Elk   Anaïs Nin
Henry David Thoreau   Orson Welles   Thelonious Monk   Groucho Marx
Leo Tolstoy   Miles Davis   Jane Austen   Johann Sebastian Bach   Billie
Holiday   Jalal ad-Din ar-Rumi   Bart Simpson   Gabriel Garcia Marquez
Mohandas Gandhi   Simone de Beauvoir**

of "more computers, more computers"). For multiculturalists of various stripes, education has become a battle line where they must duke it out regularly with incensed neo-traditionalists. Organized religion and the various "alternative spiritualities"—from 12-step groups to Buddhism, American style—contribute their own kinds of education.

Given all these pushes and pulls, is it any wonder that many of us are beginning to feel that we didn't get the whole story in school, that our educations didn't prepare us for the world we're living in today?

We didn't; we couldn't have. So what do we do about it?   5

The first thing, I firmly believe, is to take a deep, calm breath. After all, we're not the first American generation to have doubts about these matters. One of the great ages of American intellectual achievement, the period just before the Civil War, was ruled by educational misfits. Henry David Thoreau was fond of saying, "I am self-educated; that is, I attended Harvard College," and indeed Harvard in the early 19th century excelled mainly in the extent and violence of its food fights.

Don't get me wrong: Formal education is serious stuff. There is no divide in American life that hurts more than the one between those we consider well educated and those who are poorly or inadequately schooled. Talking about education is usually the closest we get to talking about class; and no wonder— education, like class, is about power. Not just the power that Harvard- and Stanford-trained elites have to dictate our workweeks, plan our communities, and fiddle with world financial markets, but the extra power that a grad school dropout who, let's say, embraces voluntary simplicity and makes $14,000 a year, has over a high school dropout single mom pulling down $18,000. That kind of power has everything to do with attitude and access: an attitude of empowerment, even entitlement, and access to tools, people, and ideas that make living—at any income level—easier, and its crises easier to bear.

That's something Earl Shorris understands. A novelist and journalist, Shorris started an Ivy League–level adult education course in humanities for low-income New Yorkers at the Roberto Clemente Family Guidance Center on the Lower East Side, which he described in his book *New American Blues* (Norton, 1997). On the first day of class, Shorris said this to the students, who were Asians, whites, blacks, and Hispanics at or near the poverty line: "You've been cheated. Rich people learn the humanities; you didn't. The humanities are a foundation for getting along in the world, for thinking, for learning to reflect on the world instead of just reacting to whatever force is turned against you. . . . Do all rich people, or people who are in the middle, know the humanities? Not a chance. But some do. And it helps. It helps to live better and enjoy life more. Will the humanities make you rich? Absolutely. But not in terms of money. In terms of life." And the Clemente course graduates did get rich in this way. Most of them went on to further higher education, and even the hard-luck Abel Lomas (not his real name), who got mixed up in a drug bust after he graduated, dumbfounded the classics-innocent prosecutor with arguments drawn from Plato and Sophocles.

By deliberately refusing to define poor Americans as nothing more than economic units whose best hope is "training" at fly-by-night computer schools, Shorris reminds us all that genuine education is a discourse—a dialogue—carried on within the context of the society around us, as well as with the mighty dead. School helps, but it's just the beginning of the engagement between ideas and reality—as Abel Lomas can attest.

Shorris' radical idea—more controversial even than expecting working-class students to tackle a serious college curriculum—was to emphasize the humanities, those subtle subjects that infuse our minds with great, gushing ideas but also equip us to think and to argue. As more and more colleges, goaded by demands for "global competitiveness" from government officials and business leaders, turn themselves into glorified trade schools churning out graduates with highly specialized skills but little intellectual breadth, you might think humanities would go the way of the horse and buggy.

"It's an enormous error to believe that technology can somehow be the content of education," says John Ralston Saul, a Canadian historian and critic with years of experience in the business world. "We insist that everyone has to learn computer technology, but when printing came in with Gutenberg and changed the production and distribution of knowledge profoundly, nobody said that everyone should learn to be a printer. Technical training is training in what is sure to be obsolete soon anyway; it's self-defeating, and it won't get you through the next 60 years of your life." Training, says Saul, is simply "learning to fit in as a passive member of a structure. And that's the worst thing for an uncertain, changing time."

Oberlin College environmental studies professor David Orr poses an even fiercer challenge to the argument that education in the 21st century should focus primarily on high-tech training. In a recent article in the British magazine *Resurgence* (No. 179), he defines something he calls "slow knowledge": It is knowledge "shaped and calibrated to fit a particular ecological and cultural context," he writes, distinguishing it from the "fast knowledge" that zips through the terminals of the information society. "It does not imply lethargy, but rather thoroughness and patience. The aim of slow knowledge is resilience, harmony, and the preservation of long-standing patterns that give our lives aesthetic, spiritual, and social meaning." Orr says that we are focusing far too much of our energy and resources on fast knowledge, ignoring all the richness and meaning slow knowledge adds to our lives. Indeed, slow knowledge is what's needed to save the planet from ecological disaster and other threats posed by technological, millennial society.

"Culturally, we just are slow learners, no matter how fast individuals can process raw data," he says. "There's a long time gap between original insights and the cultural practices that come from them. You can figure out what you *can* do pretty quickly, but the ethical understanding of what you *ought* to do comes very slowly."

Miles Harvey, a Chicago journalist who assembled a list of environmental classics for *Outside* magazine (May 1996), reminds us that much of the divisiveness in contemporary debates on education boils down to a time issue. "The canon makers say you've only got so much time, so you have to choose between, say, Shakespeare and Toni Morrison, on the assumption that you can't get to both," he says. "Well, it is hard. The level of creativity and intellectual activity in this country would jump up if we had a four-day work-week."

But suppose we redefined this issue from the very beginning. Suppose   15
we abandoned the notion that learning is a time-consuming and obligatory filling of our heads, and replaced it with the idea, courtesy of Goethe, that "people cannot learn what they do not love"—the idea of learning as an encounter infused with eros. We always find time for what we truly love, one way or another. Suppose further that love, being an inclusive spirit, refused to choose between Shakespeare and Toni Morrison (or Tony Bennett, for that matter), and we located our bliss in the unstable relationship between the two, rattling from book to book, looking for connections and grandly unconcerned about whether we've read "enough," as long as we read what we read with love.

And we wouldn't just read. We would reflect deeply on the relationship between our everyday lives and big philosophical questions—for, as Nietzsche memorably said, "Metaphysics are in the street." The Argentine novelist Ernesto Sabato glosses him this way: "[By metaphysics Nietzsche means] those final problems of the human condition: death, loneliness, the meaning of existence, the desire for power, hope, and despair." The whole world's a classroom, and to really make it one, the first thing is to believe it is. We need to take seriously the proposition that reflection and knowledge born out of contact with the real world, an education carpentered out of the best combination we can make of school, salon, reading, online exploration, walking the streets, hiking in the woods, museums, poetry classes at the Y, and friendship, may be the best education of all—not a makeshift substitute that must apologize for itself in the shadow of academe.

One of the things I like about this in-the-streets definition of education is how classical it is. In what's still one of the best concise summaries of classical education, Elizabeth Sutton Lawrence notes in *The Growth of Modern Education* (1971), that ancient Greek education "came largely from firsthand experience, in the marketplace, in the Assembly, in the theater, and in the religious celebration; through what the Greek youth saw and heard." Socrates met and challenged his adult "pupils" in the street, at dinner parties, after festivals, not at some Athenian Princeton.

Educational reactionaries want to convince us that the Western classical tradition is a carefully honed reading list. But as the dynamic classicist and philosopher Martha Nussbaum, who teaches at the University of Chicago Law School, insists, "The very idea that we should have a list of Great Books would have horrified the ancients. If you take to heart what the classical philosophers had to say, you'll never turn them into monuments. Their goal was to enliven the mind, and they knew that to enliven the mind you need to be very alert to what is in the world around you."

To really believe this casts a new light, to say the least, on the question of what the content of our learning ought to be. In her latest book, *Cultivating Humanity: A Classical Defense of Reform in Liberal Education* (Harvard University Press, 1997), Nussbaum argues compellingly that study of the non-Western world, of women's issues, of alternative sexuality, and of minority cultures is completely in line with classical principles, in particular the Stoic ideal of the "world citizen" with a cultivated ability to put her- or himself into the minds and lives of the members of divergent groups and cultures.

And New York jazz and rock writer Gene Santoro—trained in the   20 classics and Dante studies—points out there's nothing frivolous about paying attention to popular culture: "Popular culture, and particularly popular music, is the place where the dominant culture is most heavily affected by marginal cultures. Jazz, for example, became wide enough to take in much of the range of American reality, from the African American experience to the European classical tradition to the Latin and Caribbean spirit. It's the artistic version of the American social experience, and if you care about this culture, you'll look at it." And, he adds in a Socratic vein, "Jazz can help you think. It's both disciplined and unpredictable. It gives you tradition but doesn't let you settle into preconceived notions."

Colin Greer—co-editor of *The Call to Character* and *The Plain Truth of Things,* progressive responses to William Bennett's *Book of Virtues*—suggests further ways to make the most of the relationship between books and what's going on in the streets. "You could study the moments of major change in the world," he proposes. "The end of slavery. The early struggle against child labor. Woman suffrage. The organization of labor. People have forgotten what it really took to accomplish these things: What pragmatic things were done and how people learned to be generous and decent to their opponents. It's important to know the real story of how change works, and recognize that to fall short of your highest goals is OK as long as you stick to the struggle."

You get the idea. The American tradition, in learning as well as jazz and activism, is improvisatory. There are as many ways to become an educated American as there are Americans. To fall short of your highest goals—mastering that imaginary "complete" reading list, say—is OK as long as you stuck to the struggle. And the joy.

QUESTIONING THE TEXT

1. Spayde opens his essay with a question: "What does it mean—and more important, what *should* it mean—to be educated?" After reading the essay carefully with this question in mind, identify the answers

Spayde provides. Do his answers fulfill the implicit promise he makes in the opening—to tell readers what it means to be educated? Why, or why not?

2. Look carefully at the illustration that accompanies this essay (you might review the discussion of reading visual texts on p. 8 before doing so). In what ways does this illustration add evidence or proof for the argument Spayde is making?

3. Spayde uses first-person plural forms (especially *we* and *our*) often in his essay. Why do you think Spayde made this choice? What is its effect on you as a reader? Are you included in this *we*—and why, or why not?

MAKING CONNECTIONS

4. Which of the writers in this chapter would be most likely to approve of what Spayde calls "in-the-streets education?" Choose one writer who would likely *not* approve of Spayde's definition of education and write a one-page criticism of Spayde from that writer's point of view.

5. Look back at the five college mission statements (pp. 52–56). Which mission fits best with the kind of education Spayde advocates? Which fits least well—and why?

JOINING THE CONVERSATION

6. Working with two classmates, come up with a name for a hypothetical college that will promote Spayde's vision of education. Then create a home page for that college.

7. Working on your own or with a classmate, try writing your own extended definition of what it means to be educated. (For guidelines on writing definitions, see p. 23.)

ADRIENNE RICH
What Does a Woman Need to Know?

Adrienne Rich (b. 1929) has been a writer and a teacher all her life. Winner of the Yale Series of Younger Poets Award in 1951 for her first volume of poems, A Change of World, *and of the National Book Award for Poetry in 1974 (for* Diving into the Wreck*), she has also written novels, plays, essays, and speeches, including the one you are about to read.*

If John Henry Newman describes the university as "an assemblage of learned men," Rich looks at college from a slightly different perspective, noting the "changing landscape of knowledge itself" and asking "what does a woman need to know?" to negotiate such a landscape. Rich's question is particularly appropriate in context, for she delivered this speech as a commencement address to the graduates of a women's college, Smith, in 1979. Speaking directly to her audience, Rich pulls no punches; she is not sanguine about the state of women's education. In fact, she finds that "there is no women's college today which is providing young women with the education they need for survival as whole persons in a world which denies women wholeness. . . ." In the face of what she sees as a fact of life in the academy, Rich argues that women should gain all the knowledge they can from their university educations and from the professions they enter. But they should also realize that what they most need to know will have to be self-taught.

Rich challenges women students to take control of their own learning experience, to find out what they need to know, and to take responsibility for seeing that they learn it. Although she does not say so directly, the substance and site of this commencement address suggest an implicit argument for attending same-sex institutions, a topic of considerable interest to the first-year college students I am teaching, more than two decades after Rich's address. I chose this speech not only because it raises the issue of all-female or all-male schools, however, but because I wish I had heard such a commencement address when I graduated from college. In the thirty-something years since my graduation day, I have come to recognize how much my own career has been influenced by the kinds of schools I attended, by the kinds of teachers I had (no women in my college experience!), and by the kinds of models I emulated (all of them male/masculine). While I still value some of those teachers and models, Rich suggests that I might profit from asking what they did not teach me—and how I might have taught myself better.

—A.L.

I have been very much moved that you, the class of 1979, chose me for your commencement speaker. It is important to me to be here, in part because Smith is one of the original colleges for women, but also because she has chosen to continue identifying herself as a women's college. We are at a point in history where this fact has enormous potential, even if that potential is as yet unrealized.

The possibilities for the future education of women that haunt these buildings and grounds are enormous, when we think of what an independent women's college might be: a college dedicated both to teaching women what women need to know and, by the same token, to changing the landscape of knowledge itself. The germ of those possibilities lies symbolically in The Sophia Smith Collection, an archive much in need of expansion and increase, but which by its very existence makes the statement that women's lives and work are valued here and that our foresisters, buried and diminished in male-centered scholarship, are a living presence, necessary and precious to us.

Suppose we were to ask ourselves simply: What does a woman need to know to become a self-conscious, self-defining human being? Doesn't she need a knowledge of her own history, of her much-politicized female body, of the creative genius of women of the past—the skills and crafts and techniques and visions possessed by women in other times and cultures, and how they have been rendered anonymous, censored, interrupted, devalued? Doesn't she, as one of that majority who are still denied equal rights as citizens, enslaved as sexual prey, unpaid or underpaid as workers, withheld from her own power— doesn't she need an analysis of her condition, a knowledge of the women thinkers of the past who have reflected on it, a knowledge, too, of women's world-wide individual rebellions and organized movements against economic and social injustice, and how these have been fragmented and silenced?

Doesn't she need to know how seemingly natural states of being, like heterosexuality, like motherhood, have been enforced and institutionalized to deprive her of power? Without such education, women have lived and continue to live in ignorance of our collective context, vulnerable to the projections of men's fantasies about us as they appear in art, in literature, in the sciences, in the media, in the so-called humanistic studies. I suggest that not anatomy, but enforced ignorance, has been a crucial key to our powerlessness.

There is—and I say this with sorrow—there is no women's college today which is providing young women with the education they need for survival as whole persons in a world which denies women wholeness—that knowledge which, in the words of Coleridge, "returns again as power." The existence of Women's Studies courses offers at least some kind of life line. But even Women's Studies can amount simply to compensatory history; too often they fail to challenge the intellectual and political structures that must be challenged if women as a group are ever to come into collective, nonexclusionary freedom. The belief that established science and scholarship—which have so relentlessly excluded women from their making—are "objective" and "value-free" and that feminist studies are "unscholarly," "biased," and "ideological" dies hard. Yet the fact is that all science, and all scholarship, and all art are ideological; there is no neutrality in culture. And the ideology of the education you have just spent four years acquiring in a women's college has been largely, if not entirely, the ideology of white male supremacy, a construct of male subjectivity. The silences, the empty spaces, the language itself, with its excision of the female, the methods of discourse tell us as much as the content, once we learn to watch for what is left out, to listen for the unspoken, to study the patterns of established science and scholarship with an outsider's eye. One of the dangers of a privileged education for women is that we may lose the eye of the outsider and come to believe that those patterns hold for humanity, for the universal, and that they include us.

And so I want to talk today about privilege and about tokenism and   5 about power. Everything I can say to you on this subject comes hard-won, from the lips of a woman privileged by class and skin color, a father's favorite daughter, educated at Radcliffe, which was then casually referred to as the Harvard "Annex." Much of the first four decades of my life was spent in a continuous tension between the world the Fathers taught me to see, and had rewarded me for seeing, and the flashes of insight that came through the eye of the outsider. Gradually those flashes of insight, which at times could seem like brushes with madness, began to demand that I struggle to connect them with each other, to insist that I take them seriously. It was only when I could finally affirm the outsider's eye as the source of a legitimate and coherent vision, that I began to be able to do the work I truly wanted to do, live the kind of life I truly wanted to live, instead of carrying out the assignments I had been given as a privileged woman and a token.

For women, all privilege is relative. Some of you were not born with class or skin-color privilege; but you all have the privilege of education, even if it is an education which has largely denied you knowledge of yourselves as women. You have, to begin with, the privilege of literacy; and it is well for us to re-member that, in an age of increasing illiteracy, 60 percent of the world's illiter-ates are women. Between 1960 and 1970, the number of illiterate men in the world rose by 8 million, while the number of illiterate women rose by 40 mil-lion.[1] And the number of illiterate women is increasing. Beyond literacy, you have the privilege of training and tools which can allow you to go beyond the content of your education and re-educate yourselves—to debrief yourselves, we might call it, of the false messages of your education in this culture, the mes-sages telling you that women have not really cared about power or learning or creative opportunities because of a psychobiological need to serve men and pro-duce children; that only a few atypical women have been exceptions to this rule; the messages telling you that woman's experience is neither normative nor cen-tral to human experience. You have the training and the tools to do indepen-dent research, to evaluate data, to criticize, and to express in language and visual forms what you discover. This is a privilege, yes, but only if you do not give up in exchange for it the deep knowledge of the unprivileged, the knowledge that, as a woman, you have historically been viewed and still are viewed as existing, not in your own right, but in the service of men. And only if you refuse to give up your capacity to think as a woman, even though in the graduate schools and

---

[1]United Nations, Department of International Economic and Social Affairs, Statistical Office, *1977 Compendium of Social Statistics* (New York: United Nations, 1980).

professions to which many of you will be going you will be praised and rewarded for "thinking like a man."

The word *power* is highly charged for women. It has been long associated
for us with the use of force, with rape, with the stockpiling of weapons, with the
ruthless accrual of wealth and the hoarding of resources, with the power that acts
only in its own interest, despising and exploiting the powerless—including
women and children. The effects of this kind of power are all around us, even
literally in the water we drink and the air we breathe, in the form of carcinogens
and radioactive wastes. But for a long time now, feminists have been talking
about redefining power, about that meaning of power which returns to the
root—*posse, potere, pouvoir:* to be able, to have the potential, to possess and use
one's energy of creation—*transforming power.* An early objection to feminism—
in both the nineteenth and twentieth centuries—was that it would make
women behave like men—ruthlessly, exploitatively, oppressively. In fact, radical feminism looks to a transformation of human relationships and structures in
which power, instead of a thing to be hoarded by a few, would be released to
and from within the many, shared in the form of knowledge, expertise, decision
making, access to tools, as well as in the basic forms of food and shelter and
health care and literacy. Feminists—and many nonfeminists—are, and rightly
so, still concerned with what power would mean in such a society, and with the
relative differences in power among and between women here and now.

Which brings me to a third meaning of power where women are concerned: the false power which masculine society offers to a few women, on
condition that they use it to maintain things as they are, and that they essentially "think like men." This is the meaning of female tokenism: that power
withheld from the vast majority of women is offered to a few, so that it appears that any "truly qualified" woman can gain access to leadership, recognition, and reward; hence, that justice based on merit actually prevails. The
token woman is encouraged to see herself as different from most other
women, as exceptionally talented and deserving, and to separate herself from
the wider female condition; and she is perceived by "ordinary" women as
separate also, perhaps even as stronger than themselves.

Because you are, within the limits of all women's ultimate outsider-
hood, a privileged group of women, it is extremely important for your future
sanity that you understand the way tokenism functions. Its most immediate
contradiction is that, while it seems to offer the individual token woman a
means to realize her creativity, to influence the course of events, it also, by
exacting of her certain kinds of behavior and style, acts to blur her outsider's
eye, which could be her real source of power and vision. Losing her outsider's vision, she loses the insight which both binds her to other women and
affirms her in herself. Tokenism essentially demands that the token deny her
identification with women as a group, especially with women less privileged
than she: if she is a lesbian, that she deny her relationships with individual
women; that she perpetuate rules and structures and criteria and methodolo-
gies which have functioned to exclude women; that she renounce or leave

undeveloped the critical perspective of her female consciousness. Women un-like herself—poor women, women of color, waitresses, secretaries, house-wives in the supermarket, prostitutes, old women—become invisible to her; they may represent too acutely what she has escaped or wished to flee.

President Conway tells me that ever-increasing numbers of you are   10
going on from Smith to medical and law schools. The news, on the face of it, is good: that, thanks to the feminist struggle of the past decade, more doors into these two powerful professions are open to women. I would like to be-lieve that any profession would be better for having more women practicing it, and that any woman practicing law or medicine would use her knowledge and skill to work to transform the realm of health care and the interpretations of the law, to make them responsive to the needs of all those—women, people of color, children, the aged, the dispossessed—for whom they func-tion today as repressive controls. I would like to believe this, but it will not happen even if 50 percent of the members of these professions are women, unless those women refuse to be made into token insiders, unless they zeal-ously preserve the outsider's view and the outsider's consciousness.

For no woman is really an insider in the institutions fathered by masculine consciousness. When we allow ourselves to believe we are, we lose touch with parts of ourselves defined as unacceptable by that consciousness; with the vital toughness and visionary strength of the angry grandmothers, the shamanesses, the fierce marketwomen of the Ibo Women's War, the marriage-resisting women silkworkers of prerevolutionary China, the millions of widows, mid-wives, and women healers tortured and burned as witches for three centuries in Europe, the Beguines of the twelfth century, who formed independent women's orders outside the domination of the Church, the women of the Paris Commune who marched on Versailles, the uneducated housewives of the Women's Cooperative Guild in England who memorized poetry over the washtub and organized against their oppression as mothers, the women thinkers discredited as "strident," "shrill," "crazy," or "deviant" whose courage to be heretical, to speak their truths, we so badly need to draw upon in our own lives. I believe that every woman's soul is haunted by the spirits of earlier women who fought for their unmet needs and those of their children and their tribes and their peoples, who refused to accept the prescriptions of a male church and state, who took risks and resisted, as women today—like Inez Garcia, Yvonne Wan-row, Joan Little, Cassandra Peten—are fighting their rapists and batterers. Those spirits dwell in us, trying to speak to us. But we can choose to be deaf; and tokenism, the myth of the "special" woman, the unmothered Athena sprung from her father's brow, can deafen us to their voices.

In this decade now ending, as more women are entering the professions (though still suffering sexual harassment in the workplace, though still, if they have children, carrying two full-time jobs, though still vastly outnumbered by men in upper-level and decision-making jobs), we need most profoundly to re-member that early insight of the feminist movements as it evolved in the late sixties: *that no woman is liberated until we all are liberated.* The media flood us with messages to the contrary, telling us that we live in an era when "alternate life styles" are freely accepted, when "marriage contracts" and "the new intimacy" are revolutionizing heterosexual relationships, that shared parenting and the "new fatherhood" will change the world. And we live in a society leeched upon by the "personal growth" and "human potential" industry, by the delusion that individual self-fulfillment can be found in thirteen weeks or a weekend, that the alienation and injustice experienced by women, by Black and Third World people, by the poor, in a world ruled by white males, in a society which fails to meet the most basic needs and which is slowly poisoning itself, can be mitigated or dispersed by Transcendental Meditation. Perhaps the most succinct expression of this message I have seen is the appearance of a magazine for women called *Self*. The insistence of the feminist movement, that each woman's selfhood is precious, that the feminine ethic of self-denial and self-sacrifice must give way to a true woman identification, which would affirm our connectedness with all women, is perverted into a commercially profitable and politically debilitating narcissism. It is important for each of you, toward whom many of these messages are especially directed, to discriminate clearly between "liberated life style" and feminist struggle, and to make a conscious choice.

It's a cliché of commencement speeches that the speaker ends with a peroration telling the new graduates that however badly past generations have behaved, their generation must save the world. I would rather say to you, women of the class of 1979: Try to be worthy of your foresisters, learn from your history, look for inspiration to your ancestresses. If this history has been poorly taught to you, if you do not know it, then use your educational privilege to learn it. Learn how some women of privilege have compromised the greater liberation of women, how others have risked their privileges to further it; learn how brilliant and successful women have failed to create a more just and caring society, precisely because they have tried to do so on terms that the powerful men around them would accept and tolerate. Learn to be worthy of the women of every class, culture, and historical age who did otherwise, who spoke boldly when women were jeered and physically harassed for speaking in public, who—like Anne Hutchinson, Mary Wollstonecraft, the Grimké sisters, Abby Kelley, Ida B. Wells-Barnett, Susan B. Anthony, Lillian Smith, Fannie Lou Hamer—broke taboos, who resisted slavery—their own and other people's. To become a token woman—whether you win the Nobel prize or merely get tenure at the cost of denying your sisters—is to become something less than a man indeed, since men are loyal at least to their own world view, their laws of brotherhood and male self-interest. I am not suggesting that you imitate male loyalties; with the philosopher Mary Daly, I believe that the bonding of women must be utterly different and for an utterly different end: not the misering of resources and power, but the release, in each other, of the yet unexplored resources and transformative power of women, so long despised, confined, and wasted. Get all the knowledge and skill you can in whatever professions you enter; but remember that most of your education must be self-education, in learning the things women need to know and in calling up the voices we need to hear within ourselves.

QUESTIONING THE TEXT

1. Rich says that the term *power* is "highly charged for women," and she uses it in several different senses in this essay. Look carefully at these different meanings of *power*. Which meaning fits best with your own understanding—and would you agree that *power* is "highly charged for women"?

2. Rich lists three broad areas of knowledge that, she argues, women most need. What reasons and evidence does she offer to explain why women need such knowledge?

3. How does A.L.'s reference to her own school experience affect your reading of Rich's essay, if at all? Why do you think A.L. included this information in the introduction?

MAKING CONNECTIONS

4. Do you agree with Rich that women's educational needs are different from men's? Why, or why not? In "The Idea of a University" (p. 46), John Henry Newman seems to suggest that all students have the same basic needs. How might Rich respond to him on this point?

5. Writing about seventeen years after Rich, Jeffrey Hart, in "How to Get a College Education" (p. 126), has a very different perspective on the ways in which colleges do not teach students what they most need to know. Would Rich be likely to agree with Hart? Write a one-page dialogue between the two authors on the subject of what a university should teach its students.

JOINING THE CONVERSATION

6. What, if any, changes has your school made in the last twenty-five years or so to accommodate the needs and interests of women students? Consider such factors as increased hiring of women faculty, the opening of a women's student center or a women's studies program or department, speakers on women's issues, improvements in campus safety. Write a brief editorial intended for your campus newspaper in which you reflect on the extent to which your school is "user-friendly" for women and whether women at your school can learn what they most "need to know."

7. Try your own hand at writing a brief essay answering the question "What Does a Woman [or Man] Need to Know?" You may want to compare your essay with those of other classmates, noting points of agreement and disagreement—particularly among women and men.

SHELBY STEELE
The Recoloring of Campus Life

SHELBY STEELE'S BOOK *on race relations in the United States,* The Content of Our Character *(1990), takes its title from Martin Luther King Jr.'s "I Have a Dream" speech, delivered at a civil rights demonstration in Washington, D.C., in 1963. In that address, King called for the eradication of racial prejudices: "I have a dream my four little children will one day live in a nation where they will not be judged by the color of their skin but by the content of their character." More than a generation later, Steele (b. 1946) poses the painful question of whether the civil rights establishment has abandoned King's dream. Has the goal of desegregation, he asks, been supplanted by ethnic and racial separation? Has the ideal of equal opportunity been tainted by quotas?*

The lengthy chapter of the book reprinted here examines the sensitive subject of race relations on campus frankly and openly. Steele, a professor of English at San Jose State University in California, is a controversial figure, a black man whose views, like those of Supreme Court Justice Clarence Thomas, affirmative action opponent Ward Connerly, and economist Thomas Sowell, challenge the agenda of many civil rights organizations. Steele confronts the anxieties of both blacks and whites with uncommon directness. It is a measure of the national discomfort we feel in talking about race and racism that some people regard views like Steele's as politically "incorrect." Judge for yourself whether he is raising issues that ought not to be matters of debate. —J.R.

> The U.S. has about 3,000 colleges and universities. Do 80 incidents a year—most involving ethnic "insensitivity"—really constitute an increase in racial tensions? Was there a time when such incidents were fewer? —J.R.

In the past few years, we have witnessed what the National Institute Against Prejudice and Violence calls a "proliferation" of racial incidents on college campuses around the country. Incidents of on-campus "intergroup conflict" have occurred at more than 160 colleges in the last two years, according to the institute. The nature of these incidents has ranged from open racial violence—most notoriously, the October 1986 beating of a black student at the University of Massachusetts at Amherst after an argument about the World Series turned into a racial bashing, with a crowd of up to three thousand whites chasing twenty blacks—to the harassment of minority students and acts of racial or ethnic insensitivity, with by far the greatest number of episodes falling in the last two categories. At Yale last year, a swastika and the words "white power" were painted on the university's Afro-American cultural center. Racist jokes

> What is this institute—and what is its agenda? —A.L.

*Are such anony-
mous acts the re-
sult of true hatred
for other races or
are they simply
immature behav-
ior?* —T.E.

were aired not long ago on a campus radio station at
the University of Michigan. And at the University of
Wisconsin at Madison, members of the Zeta Beta
Tau fraternity held a mock slave auction in which
pledges painted their faces black and wore Afro wigs.
Two weeks after the president of Stanford University
informed the incoming freshman class last fall that
"bigotry is out, and I mean it," two freshmen defaced
a poster of Beethoven — gave the image thick lips —
and hung it on a black student's door.

*These examples
make me think of
racist acts on my
own campus — but
also of attempts
to counter those
acts with acts of
respect and gen-
erosity for all
people.* —A.L.

*Why do racial in-
cidents proliferate
on campuses usu-
ally regarded as
"progressive" —
Stanford, Berke-
ley, Wisconsin, U
Mass?* —J.R.

In response, black students around the country
have rediscovered the militant protest strategies of
the sixties. At the University of Massachusetts at
Amherst, Williams College, Penn State University,
University of California–Berkeley, UCLA, Stanford
University, and countless other campuses, black
students have sat in, marched, and rallied. But
much of what they were marching and rallying
about seemed less a response to specific racial incidents than a call for broader action on the part of
the colleges and universities they were attending.
Black students have demanded everything from
more black faculty members and new courses on
racism to the addition of "ethnic" foods in the cafeteria. There is the sense in these demands that

*Are they imply-
ing whites and
blacks teach differ-
ently based on
skin color? Isn't
this racism,
too?* —T.E.

racism runs deep. Is the campus becoming the battleground for a renewed war between the races? I
don't think so, not really. But if it is not a war, the
problem of campus racism does represent a new and
surprising hardening of racial lines within the most
traditionally liberal and tolerant of America's institutions — its universities.

*Is he suggesting
that racism doesn't
run deep? If so, I'll
need a lot of evi-
dence to be con-
vinced.* — A.L.

As a black who has spent his entire adult life on
predominantly white campuses, I found it hard to believe that the problem of campus racism was as dramatic as some of the incidents seemed to make it.
The incidents I read or heard about often seemed

*Steele must never
have been the tar-
get of any of these
types of racist acts.
He would view
them more harshly
if he had.* —T.E.

prankish and adolescent, though not necessarily
harmless. There is a meanness in them but not much
menace; no one is proposing to reinstitute Jim Crow
on campus. On the California campus where I now
teach, there have been few signs of racial tension.

And, of course, universities are not where racial
problems tend to arise. When I went to college in

*Interesting that he
presents his own
perspective ("not
much menace") as
the only one.
Other African
Americans may
not have this per-
spective.* —A.L.

the mid-sixties, colleges were oases of calm and understanding in a racially tense society; campus life—with its traditions of tolerance and fairness, its very distance from the "real" world—imposed a degree of broad-mindedness on even the most provincial students. If I met whites who were not anxious to be friends with blacks, most were at least vaguely friendly to the cause of our freedom. In any case, there was no guerrilla activity against our presence, no "mine field of racism" (as one black student at Berkeley recently put it to me) to negotiate. I wouldn't say that the phrase "campus racism" is a contradiction in terms, but until recently it certainly seemed an incongruence.

I was in college at this same time and this does not describe my experience on a very racist and often hostile campus. —A.L.

But a greater incongruence is the generational timing of this new problem on the campuses. Today's undergraduates were born after the passage of the 1964 Civil Rights Act. They grew up in an age when racial equality was for the first time enforceable by law. This too was a time when blacks suddenly appeared on television, as mayors of big cities, as icons of popular culture, as teachers, and in some cases even as neighbors. Today's black and white college students, veterans of "Sesame Street" and often of integrated grammar and high schools, have had more opportunities to know each other than any previous generation in American history. Not enough opportunities, perhaps, but enough to make the notion of racial tension on campus something of a mystery, at least to me.

He's now assuming it's a "new" problem, but he hasn't proven it. —A.L.

To look at this mystery, I left my own campus with its burden of familiarity and talked with black and white students at California schools where racial incidents had occurred: Stanford, UCLA, and Berkeley. I spoke with black and white students—not with Asians and Hispanics—because, as always, blacks and whites represent the deepest lines of division, and because I hesitate to wander onto the complex territory of other minority groups. A phrase by William H. Gass—"the hidden internality of things"—describes, with maybe a little too much grandeur, what I hoped to find. But it is what I wanted to find, for this is the kind of problem that makes a black person nervous, which

I don't follow him here. What does he mean by "hidden internality"? —A.L.

is not to say that it doesn't unnerve whites as well. Once every six months or so someone yells "nigger" at me from a passing car. I don't like to think that these solo artists might soon make up a chorus, or worse, that this chorus might one day soon sing to me from the paths of my own campus.

I have long believed that the trouble between the races is seldom what it appears to be. It was not hard to see after my first talks with students that racial tension on campus is a problem that misrepresents itself. It has the same look, the archetypal pattern, of America's timeless racial conflict—white racism and black protest. And I think part of our concern over it comes from the fact that it has the feel of a relapse, illness gone and come again. But if we are seeing the same symptoms, I don't believe we are dealing with the same illness. For one thing, I think racial tension on campus is more the result of racial equality than inequality.

How to live with racial difference has been America's profound social problem. For the first hundred years or so following emancipation it was controlled by a legally sanctioned inequality that kept the races from each other. No longer is this the case. On campuses today, as throughout society, blacks enjoy equality under the law—a profound social advancement. No student may be kept out of a class or a dormitory or an extracurricular activity because of his or her race. But there is a paradox here: on a campus where members of all races are gathered, mixed together in the classroom as well as socially, differences are more exposed than ever. And this is where the trouble starts. For members of each race—young adults coming into their own, often away from home for the first time—bring to this site of freedom, exploration, and (now, today) equality, very deep fears, anxieties, inchoate feelings of racial shame, anger, and guilt. These feelings could lie dormant in the home, in familiar neighborhoods, in simpler days of childhood. But the college campus, with its structures of interaction and adult-level competition—the big exam, the dorm, the mixer—is another matter. I think campus racism is born of the rub between racial difference and a setting, the campus itself, devoted to interaction and

Maybe this is what he means—the old appearance/reality binary. —A.L.

Has racism ever really "gone"? —T.E.

Is this the main point he is arguing? —A.L.

He's right: higher education challenges the comfortable assumptions most students bring to campus. —J.R.

I've never experienced such feelings where race is concerned, and I come from a predominantly white community. —T.E.

equality. On our campuses, such concentrated micro-societies, all that remains unresolved between blacks and whites, all the old wounds and shames that have never been addressed, present themselves for attention—and present our youth with pressures they cannot always handle.

I have mentioned one paradox: racial fears and anxieties among blacks and whites, bubbling up in an era of racial equality under the law, in settings that are among the freest and fairest in society. But there is another, related paradox, stemming from the notion of—and practice of—affirmative action. Under the provisions of the Equal Employment Opportunity Act of 1972, all state governments and institutions (including universities) were forced to initiate plans to increase the proportion of minority and women employees and, in the case of universities, of students too. Affirmative action plans that establish racial quotas were ruled unconstitutional more than ten years ago in *University of California* v. *Bakke,* but such plans are still thought by some to secretly exist, and lawsuits having to do with alleged quotas are still very much with us. But quotas are only the most controversial aspect of affirmative action; the principle of affirmative action is reflected in various university programs aimed at redressing and overcoming past patterns of discrimination. Of course, to be conscious of past patterns of discrimination—the fact, say, that public schools in the black inner cities are more crowded and employ fewer top-notch teachers than a white suburban public school, and that this is a factor in student performance—is only reasonable. But in doing this we also call attention quite obviously to difference: in the case of blacks and whites, racial difference. What has emerged on campus in recent years—as a result of the new equality and of affirmative action and, in a sense, as a result of progress—is a *politics of difference,* a troubling, volatile politics in which each group justifies itself, its sense of worth and its pursuit of power, through difference alone.

In this context, racial, ethnic, and gender differences become forms of sovereignty, campuses become balkanized, and each group fights with whatever means are available. No doubt there are many

This idealistic view of a university as "free and fair" would be contested by many. —A.L.

The beneficiaries of affirmative action are usually middle-class students—not poor minority youth from inner cities. Do middle-class whites resent that fact? —J.R.

Identity politics (I get my identity solely and only through one characteristic, such as race) to me is different from politics of difference, which seeks to honor differences among all people while not ignoring commonalities. —A.L.

factors that have contributed to the rise of racial tension on campus: What has been the role of fraternities, which have returned to campus with their inclusions and exclusions? What role has the heightened notion of college as some first step to personal, financial success played in increasing competition, and thus tension? But mostly, what I sense is that in interactive settings, fighting the fights of "difference," old ghosts are stirred and haunt again. Black and white Americans simply have the power to make each other feel shame and guilt. In most situations, we may be able to deny these feelings, keep them at bay. But these feelings are likely to surface on college campuses, where young people are groping for identity and power, and where difference is made to matter so greatly. In a way, racial tension on campus in the eighties might have been inevitable.

I would like, first, to discuss black students, their anxieties and vulnerabilities. The accusation black Americans have always lived with is that they are inferior—inferior simply because they are black. And this accusation has been too uniform, too ingrained in cultural imagery, too enforced by law, custom, and every form of power not to have left a mark. Black inferiority was a precept accepted by the founders of this nation; it was a principle of social organization that relegated blacks to the sidelines of American life. So when young black students find themselves on white campuses surrounded by those who have historically claimed superiority, they are also surrounded by the myth of their inferiority.

Of course, it is true that many young people come to college with some anxiety about not being good enough. But only blacks come wearing a color that is still, in the minds of some, a sign of inferiority. Poles, Jews, Hispanics, and other groups also endure degrading stereotypes. But two things make the myth of black inferiority a far heavier burden—the broadness of its scope and its incarnation in color. There are not only more stereotypes of blacks than of other groups, but these stereotypes are also more dehumanizing, more focused on the most despised human traits: stupidity, laziness, sexual immorality, dirtiness, and so on. In America's racial and ethnic hierarchy,

Black shame and white guilt? Steele's analysis looks simplistic. Can he sustain it? —J.R.

Steele implies that college students are shallow, that they would immediately focus on race if any problem arose. This is not my experience. —T.E.

When he uses "of course" I always wonder whether I'll agree with what comes next! —A.L.

blacks have clearly been relegated to the lowest level—have been burdened with an ambiguous, animalistic humanity. Moreover, this is made unavoidable for blacks by sheer visibility of black skin, a skin that evokes the myth of inferiority on sight. Today this myth is sadly reinforced for many black students by affirmative action programs, under which blacks may often enter college with lower test scores and high school grade point averages than whites. "They see me as an affirmative action case," one black student told me at UCLA. This reinforces the myth of inferiority by implying that blacks are not good enough to make it into college on their own.

Test scores reflect biased test designs, and grades can too. I don't buy this argument. —A.L.

I have often wondered if any blacks felt affirmative action projects were just racist and belittling. —T.E.

So when a black student enters college, the myth of inferiority compounds the normal anxiousness over whether he or she will be good enough. This anxiety is not only personal but also racial. The families of these students will have pounded into them the fact that blacks are not inferior. And probably more than anything it is this pounding that finally leaves the mark. If I am not inferior, why the need to say so?

This myth of inferiority constitutes a very sharp and ongoing anxiety for young blacks, the nature of which is very precise: it is the terror that somehow, through one's actions or by virtue of some "proof" (a poor grade, a flubbed response in class), one's fear of inferiority—inculcated in ways large and small by society—will be confirmed as real. On a university campus where intelligence itself is the ultimate measure, this anxiety is bound to be triggered.

A black student I met at UCLA was disturbed a little when I asked him if he ever felt vulnerable—anxious about "black inferiority"—as a black student. But after a long pause, he finally said, "I think I do." The example he gave was of a large lecture class he'd taken with over three hundred students. Fifty or so black students sat in the back of the lecture hall and "acted out every stereotype in the book." They were loud, ate food, came in late—and generally got lower grades than whites in the class. "I knew I would be seen like them, and I didn't like it. I never sat by them." Seen like what, I asked, though we both knew the answer. "As lazy, ignorant, and stupid," he said sadly.

Or smart but bored? —A.L.

Steele makes a
convincing distinc-
tion here. Grow-
ing up, I heard
Polish jokes and
slurs, but not
often enough to
think that society
really believed
the stereotype.
That makes a
difference.   —J.R.

Had the group at the back been white fraternity brothers, they would not have been seen as
dumb whites, of course. And a frat brother who
worried about his grades would not worry that he
[had] been seen "like them." The terror in this situation for the black student I spoke with was that his
own deeply buried anxiety would be given credence, that the myth would be verified, and that he
would feel shame and humiliation not because of
who he was but simply because he was black. In
this lecture hall his race, quite apart from his performance, might subject him to four unendurable feelings—diminishment, accountability to the preconceptions of whites, a powerlessness to change those
preconceptions, and finally, shame. These are the
feelings that make up his racial anxiety, and that of
all blacks on any campus. On a white campus a
black is never far from these feelings, and even his
unconscious knowledge that he is subject to them
can undermine his self-esteem. There are blacks on
any campus who are not up to doing good college-
level work. Certain black students may not be
happy or motivated or in the appropriate field of
study—*just like whites.* (Let us not forget that many
white students get poor grades, fail, drop out.)
Moreover, many more blacks than whites are not
quite prepared for college, may have to catch up,
owing to factors beyond their control: poor previous schooling, for example. But the white who has
to catch up will not be anxious that his being behind is a matter of his whiteness, of his being
racially inferior. The black student may well have
such a fear.

This, I believe, is one reason why black colleges in America turn out 37 percent of all black
college graduates though they enroll only 16 percent of black college students. Without whites
around on campus, the myth of inferiority is in
abeyance and, along with it, a great reservoir of culturally imposed self-doubt. On black campuses,
feelings of inferiority are personal; on campuses
with a white majority, a black's problems have a
way of becoming a "black" problem.

But this feeling of vulnerability a black may
feel, in itself, is not as serious a problem as what he

I don't buy this—
the fraternity stereo-
type is quite strong,
too. Why wouldn't
a frat brother be
disturbed?   —T.E.

I'm irritated by
his continued at-
tempts to speak for
all African Ameri-
cans.   —A.L.

Do Asian Ameri-
can students feel
similarly pressured
by a stereotype
that marks them
all as diligent,
hard-working, and
extraordinarily
smart?   —J.R.

Going to an all-
black college doesn't
shut out the rest of
the world. I don't
buy this.   —T.E.

Do all blacks feel this way? Steele is generalizing. —T.E.

or she does with it. To admit that one is made anxious in integrated situations about the myth of racial inferiority is difficult for young blacks. It seems like admitting that one is racially inferior. And so, most often, the student will deny harboring the feelings. This is where some of the pangs of racial tension begin, because denial always involves distortion.

In order to deny a problem we must tell ourselves that the problem is something different from what it really is. A black student at Berkeley told me that he felt defensive every time he walked into a classroom of white faces. When I asked why, he said, "Because I know they're all racists. They think blacks are stupid." Of course it may be true that some whites feel this way, but the singular focus on white racism allows this student to obscure his own underlying racial anxiety. He can now say that his problem—facing a classroom of white faces, *fearing* that they think he is dumb—is entirely the result of certifiable white racism and has nothing to do with his own anxieties, or even that this particular academic subject may not be his best. Now all the terror of his anxiety, its powerful energy, is devoted to simply *seeing* racism. Whatever evidence of racism he finds—and looking this hard, he will no doubt find some—can be brought in to buttress his distorted view of the problem while his actual deepseated anxiety goes unseen.

This helps explain the dilemma of many black students on mainly white campuses. —J.R.

This seems a kind of false either/or argument to me. Either the problem is all external (white racists) or all internal (deepseated anxieties). —A.L.

Denial, and the distortion that results, places the problem *outside* the self and in the world. It is not that I have any inferiority anxiety because of my race; it is that I am going to school with people who don't like blacks. This is the shift in thinking that allows black students to reenact the protest pattern of the sixties. *Denied racial anxiety—distortion—reenactment* is the process by which feelings of inferiority are transformed into an exaggerated white menace—which is then protested against with the techniques of the past. Under the sway of this process, black students believe that history is repeating itself, that it's just like the sixties, or fifties. In fact, it is not-yet-healed wounds from the past, rather than the inequality that created the wounds, that is the real problem.

Obsessive attention to race can breed racist feelings. That's one reason I'm uneasy with multicultural curriculums that emphasize difference. —J.R.

This process generated an unconscious need to exaggerate the level of racism on campus—to make it a matter of the system, not just a handful of students. Racism is the avenue away from the true inner anxiety. How many students demonstrating for black theme dorms—demonstrating in the style of the sixties, when the battle was to win for blacks a place on campus—might be better off spending their time reading and studying? Black students have the highest dropout rate and the lowest grade point average of any group in American universities. This need not be so. And it is not the result of not having black theme dorms.

People said the same thing to the '60s civil rights protesters. —A.L.

It was my very good fortune to go to college in 1964, when the question of black "inferiority" was openly talked about among blacks. The summer before I left for college, I heard Martin Luther King speak in Chicago, and he laid it on the line for black students everywhere: "When you are behind in a footrace, the only way to get ahead is to run faster than the man in front of you. So when your white roommate says he's tired and goes to sleep, you stay up and burn the midnight oil." His statement that we were "behind in a footrace" acknowledged that, because of history, of few opportunities, of racism, we were, in a sense, "inferior." But this had to do with what had been done to our parents and their parents, not with inherent inferiority. And because it was acknowledged, it was presented to us as a challenge rather than a mark of shame.

Of the eighteen black students (in a student body of one thousand) who were on campus in my freshman year, all graduated, though a number of us were not from the middle class. At the university where I currently teach, the dropout rate for black students is 72 percent, despite the presence of several academic support programs, a counseling center with black counselors, an Afro-American studies department, black faculty, administrators, and staff, a general education curriculum that emphasizes "cultural pluralism," an Educational Opportunities Program, a mentor program, a black faculty and staff association, and an administration and faculty that often announce the need to do more for black students.

At my university, these programs are tiny and underfunded. At Ohio State, only 3.2% of faculty are African American. —A.L.

It may be unfair to compare my generation with the current one. Parents do this compulsively and to little end but self-congratulation. But I don't congratulate my generation. I think we were advantaged. We came along at a time when racial integration was held in high esteem. And integration was a very challenging social concept for both blacks and whites. We were remaking ourselves—that's what one did at college—and making history. We had something to prove. This was a profound advantage; it gave us clarity and a challenge. Achievement in the American mainstream was the goal of integration, and the best thing about this challenge was its secondary message—that we *could* achieve.

Integration is a goal rarely mentioned in campus discussions of racial problems these days.   —J.R.

Is "achievement in the American mainstream" another way of saying "being like white people"?   —A.L.

There is much irony in the fact that black power would come along in the late sixties and change all this. Black power was a movement of uplift and pride, and yet it also delivered the weight of pride—a weight that would burden black students from then on. Black power "nationalized" the black identity, made blackness itself an object of celebration, an allegiance. But if it transformed a mark of shame into a mark of pride, it also, in the name of pride, required the denial of racial anxiety. Without a frank account of one's anxieties, there is no clear direction, no concrete challenge. Black students today do not get as clear a message from their racial identity as my generation got. They are not filled with the same urgency to prove themselves because black pride has said, *You're already proven, already equal, as good as anybody.*

This may be true, but it's another one of those either/or arguments I'm always leery of.   —A.L.

The "black identity" shaped by black power most forcefully contributes to racial tensions on campuses by basing entitlement more on race than on constitutional rights and standards of merit. With integration, black entitlement derived from constitutional principles of fairness. Black power changed this by skewing the formula from rights to color—if you were black, you were entitled. Thus the United Coalition Against Racism (UCAR) at the University of Michigan could "demand" two years ago that all black professors be given immediate tenure, that there [be] a special pay incentive for black professors, and that money be provided for an all-black student union. In this formula, black becomes the very color of entitlement, an extra right in itself, and a very dangerous grandiosity is promoted in which blackness amounts to specialness.

Race is, by any standard, an unprincipled source of power. And on campuses the use of racial power by one group makes racial, ethnic, or gender difference a currency of power for all groups. When I make my *difference* into power, other groups must seize upon their difference to contain my power and maintain their position relative to me. Very quickly a kind of politics of difference emerges in which racial, ethnic, and gender groups are forced to assert their entitlement and vie for power based on the single quality that makes them different from one another.

On many campuses today academic departments and programs are established on the basis of difference—black studies, women's studies, Asian studies, and so on—despite the fact that there is nothing in these "difference" departments that cannot be studied within traditional academic disciplines. If their rationale is truly past exclusion from the mainstream curriculum, shouldn't the goal now be complete inclusion rather than separateness? I think this logic is overlooked because those groups are too interested in the power their difference can bring, and they insist on separate departments and programs as tribute to that power.

This politics of difference makes everyone on campus a member of a minority group. It also makes racial tension inevitable. To highlight one's difference as a source of advantage is also, indirectly, to inspire the enemies of that difference. When blackness (and femaleness) become power, then white maleness is also sanctioned as power. A white male student I spoke with at Stanford said, "One of my friends said the other day that we should get together and start up a white student union and come up with a list of demands."

It is certainly true that white maleness has long been an unfair source of power. But the sin of white male power is precisely its use of race and gender as a source of entitlement. When minorities and women use their race, ethnicity, and gender in the same way, they not only commit the same sin

I agree. It's just as racist (and negative) to have all-black unions as it is to have all-white ones. —T.E.

I agree. Balkanization can present a danger, but that doesn't mean we should reject difference. —A.L.

Quite true—but does one lead to the other? —T.E.

but also, indirectly, sanction the very form of power that oppressed them in the first place. The politics of difference is based on a tit-for-tat sort of logic in which every victory only calls one's enemies to arms.

This elevation of difference undermines the communal impulse by making each group foreign and inaccessible to others. When difference is celebrated rather than remarked, people must think in terms of difference, they must find meaning in difference, and this meaning comes from an endless process of contrasting one's group with other groups. Blacks use whites to define themselves as different, women use men, Hispanics use whites and blacks, and on it goes. And in the process each group mythologizes and mystifies its difference, puts it beyond the full comprehension of outsiders. Difference becomes inaccessible preciousness toward which outsiders are expected to be simply and uncomprehendingly reverential. But beware: in this world, even the insulated world of the college campus, preciousness is a balloon asking for a needle. At Smith College graffiti appears: "Niggers, spics, and chinks. Quit complaining or get out."

Another either/or. I don't accept the notion that we must honor only one or the other— difference or community. —A.L.

I think that those who run our colleges and universities are every bit as responsible for the politics of difference as are minority students. To correct the exclusions once caused by race and gender, universities—under the banner of affirmative action—have relied too heavily on race and gender as criteria. So rather than break the link between difference and power, they have reinforced it. On most campuses today, a well-to-do black student with two professional parents is qualified by his race for scholarship monies that are not available to a lower-middle-class white student. A white female with a private school education and every form of cultural advantage comes under the affirmative action umbrella. This kind of inequity is an invitation to backlash.

In a decision startling to many, a federal court has ruled that affirmative action programs at my school based on race and ethnicity are unconstitutional. —J.R.

These generalizations simply are not true. Affirmative action at my school does nothing to advantage the students described here. —A.L.

What universities are quite rightly trying to do is compensate people for past discrimination and the deprivations that followed from it. But race and gender alone offer only the grossest measure of this. And the failure of universities has been their back-

ing away from the challenge of identifying principles of fairness and merit that make finer and
more equitable distinctions. The real challenge is
not simply to include a certain number of blacks,
but to end discrimination against all blacks and to
offer special help to those with talent who have also
been economically deprived.

I agree.   —A.L.

    With regard to black students, affirmative ac-
tion has led universities to correlate color with
poverty and disadvantage in so absolute a way as to
encourage the politics of difference. But why have
they gone along with this? My belief is that it is due
to the specific form of racial anxiety to which
whites are most subject.

*I agree. These
special funds make
me uncomfortable.*
    —T.E.

    Most of the white students I talked with
spoke as if from under a faint cloud of accusation.
There was always a ring of defensiveness in their
complaints about blacks. A white student I spoke to
at UCLA told me: "Most white students on this campus think the black student leadership here is made
up of oversensitive crybabies who spend all their
time looking for things to kick up a ruckus about."
A white student at Stanford said, "Blacks do nothing but complain and ask for sympathy when
everyone really knows that they don't do well because they don't try. If they worked harder, they
could do as well as everyone else."

    That these students felt accused was most ob-
vious in their compulsion to assure me that they
were not racist. Oblique versions of some-of-my-
best-friends-are stories came ritualistically before or
after critiques of black students. Some said flatly, "I
am not a racist, but . . ." Of course, we all deny
being racist, but we only do this compulsively, I
think, when we are working against an accusation
of bias. I think it was the color of my skin itself that
accused them.

*Too bad Steele
deliberately
avoided talking
with Hispanic and
Asian minorities.
Their perspectives
on the matter of
"guilt" would have
enriched the discus-
sion here.*   —J.R.

    This was the meta-message that surrounded
these conversations like an aura, and it is, I believe,
the core of white American racial anxiety. My skin
not only accused them; it judged them. And this
judgment was a sad gift of history that brought them
to account whether they deserved such accountability or not. It said that wherever and whenever blacks

were concerned, they had reason to feel guilt. And whether it was earned or unearned, I think it was guilt that set off the compulsion in these students to disclaim. I believe it is true that, in America, black people make white people feel guilty.

Guilt is the essence of white anxiety just as inferiority is the essence of black anxiety. And the terror that it carries for whites is the terror of discovering that one has réason to feel guilt where blacks are concerned—not so much because of what blacks might think but because of what guilt can say about oneself. If the darkest fear of blacks is inferiority, the darkest fear of whites is that their better lot in life is at least partially the result of their capacity for evil— their capacity to dehumanize an entire people for their own benefit and then to be indifferent to the devastation their dehumanization has wrought on successive generations of their victims. This is the terror that whites are vulnerable to regarding blacks. And the mere fact of being white is sufficient to feel it, since even whites with hearts clean of racism benefit from being white—benefit at the expense of blacks. This is a conditional guilt having nothing to do with individual intentions or actions. And it makes for a very powerful anxiety because it threatens whites with a view of themselves as inhuman, just as inferiority threatens blacks with a similar view of themselves. At the dark core of both anxieties is a suspicion of incomplete humanity.

So, the white students I met were not just meeting me; they were also meeting the possibility of their own inhumanity. And this, I think, is what explains how some young white college students in the late eighties could so frankly take part in racially insensitive and outright racist acts. They were expected to be cleaner of racism than any previous generation—they were born into the Great Society. But this expectation overlooks the fact that, for them, color is still an accusation and judgment. In black faces there is a discomforting reflection of white collective shame. Blacks remind them that their racial innocence is questionable, that they are the beneficiaries of past and present racism, and the sins of the father may well have been visited on the children.

Steele overgeneral-izes. All whites are not racists.   —T.E.

And yet young whites tell themselves that they had nothing to do with the oppression of black people. They have a stronger belief in their racial innocence than any previous generation of whites and a natural hostility toward anyone who would challenge that innocence. So (with a great deal of individual variation) they can end up in the para-doxical position of being hostile to blacks as a way of defending their own racial innocence.

I think this is what the young white editors of the *Dartmouth Review* were doing when they harassed black music professor William Cole. Weren't they saying, in effect, I am so free of racial guilt that I can afford to attack blacks ruthlessly and still be racially innocent? The ruthlessness of these attacks was a form of denial, a badge of innocence. The more they were charged with racism, the more ugly and con-frontational their harassment became (an escalation unexplained even by the serious charges against Pro-fessor Cole). Racism became a means of rejecting racial guilt, a way of showing that they were not, ul-timately, racists.

The politics of difference sets up a struggle for innocence among all groups. When difference is the currency of power, each group must fight for the in-nocence that entitles it to power. To gain this inno-cence, blacks sting whites with guilt, remind them of their racial past, accuse them of new and more subtle forms of racism. One way whites retrieve their inno-cence is to discredit blacks and deny their difficulties, for in this denial is the denial of their own guilt. To blacks this denial looks like racism, a racism that feeds black innocence and encourages them to throw more guilt at whites. And so the cycle continues. The pol-itics of difference leads each group to pick at the vul-nerabilities of the other.

Steele is lumping all administrators together; this makes me skeptical of the following argument.
—T.E.

Men and women who run universities—whites, mostly—participate in the politics of differ-ence because they handle their guilt differently than do many of their students. They don't deny it, but still they don't want to *feel* it. And to avoid this feeling of guilt they have tended to go along with whatever blacks put on the table rather than work with them to assess their real needs. University administrators have

too often been afraid of guilt and have relied on negotiation and capitulation more to appease their own
guilt than to help blacks and other minorities. Administrators would never give white students a racial
theme dorm where they could be "more comfortable
with people of their own kind," yet more and more
universities are doing this for black students, thus fostering a kind of voluntary segregation. To avoid the
anxieties of integrated situations blacks ask for theme
dorms; to avoid guilt, white administrators give
theme dorms.

*This is undoubt-
edly often true.
—A.L.*

When everyone is on the run from their anxieties about race, race relations on campus can be reduced to the negotiation of avoidances. A pattern
of demand and concession develops in which both
sides use the other to escape themselves. Black studies departments, black deans of student affairs, black
counseling programs, Afro houses, black theme
dorms, black homecoming dances and graduation
ceremonies—black students and white administrators have slowly engineered a machinery of sepa-
ratism that, in the name of sacred difference, re-
draws the ugly lines of segregation.

*White professors
who make compa-
rable observations
are sometimes
charged with
racism. What does
such an accusation
reveal about the
advocates of a
campus "politics
of difference"?
—J.R.*

Black students have not sufficiently helped
themselves, and universities, despite all their concessions, have not really done much for blacks. If
both faced their anxieties, I think they would see
the same thing: academic parity with all other
groups should be the overriding mission of black
students, and it should also be the first goal that universities have for their black students. Blacks can
only *know* they are as good as others when they are,
in fact, as good—when their grades are higher and
their dropout rate lower. Nothing under the sun
will substitute for this, and no amount of concessions will bring it about.

Universities can never be free of guilt until
they truly help black students, which means leading
and challenging them rather than negotiating and
capitulating. It means inspiring them to achieve
academic parity, nothing less, and helping them to
see their own weaknesses as their greatest challenge.
It also means dismantling the machinery of sepa-
ratism, breaking the link between difference and
power, and skewing the formula for entitlement

away from race and gender and back to constitutional rights.

As for the young white students who have rediscovered swastikas and the word "nigger," I think that they suffer from an exaggerated sense of their own innocence, as if they were incapable of evil and beyond the reach of guilt. But it is also true that the politics of difference creates an environment that threatens their innocence and makes them defensive. White students are not invited to the negotiating table from which they see blacks and others walk away with concessions. The presumption is that they do not deserve to be there because they are white. So they can only be defensive, and the less mature among them will be aggressive. Guerrilla activity will ensue. Of course this is wrong, but it is also a reflection of an environment where difference carries power and where whites have the wrong "difference."

I think universities should emphasize commonality as a higher value than "diversity" and "pluralism"—buzzwords for the politics of difference. Difference that does not rest on a clearly delineated foundation of commonality is not only inaccessible to those who are not part of the ethnic or racial group, but also antagonistic to them. Difference can enrich only the common ground.

Integration has become an abstract term today, having to do with little more than numbers and racial balances. But it once stood for a high and admirable set of values. It made difference second to commonality, and it asked members of all races to face whatever fears they inspired in each other. I doubt the word will have a new vogue, but the values, under whatever name, are worth working for.

Not an exaggerated sense of their own importance and power? —A.L.

Basing affirmative action programs (if we must have them) on economic need, not race and gender, would do more to ease tensions on campus than most current solutions. —J.R

I want to value commonality and diversity without establishing a hierarchy where one must always be on top. —A.L.

Afterwords

The most striking line to me in this selection is Steele's almost casual observation that "every six months or so someone yells 'nigger' at me from a passing car." I admire the courageous way he reacts to such racist acts, refusing to dwell on the pain and insult he must certainly feel. Taking no pleasure in the convincing evidence he has that racism endures in the United States, Steele patiently searches for solutions to the problem, exempting no one from scrutiny, treating no one with contempt. That search is what "The Recoloring of Campus Life" is all about.

In the years since Steele wrote "The Recoloring of Campus Life," the racial issues he explores have been debated intensely in the United States—especially the fairness of affirmative action policies, which had been imposed chiefly by executive order and judicial fiat without the deliberative scrutiny of the legislative process. Despite demagoguery on both sides, the debate has at least made it possible to talk more openly about the enmities Steele records in his groundbreaking chapter. Such honesty will be required in order to open up American education to once-excluded groups without discriminating and segregating anew. The key to success may well be keeping bureaucrats and politicians, especially those in Washington, out of the loop when it comes to decisions about college admissions and enrollment.   —J.R.

While I agree with many individual points Steele makes (all students should be challenged to achieve their full potential; commonalities among us are important and should be nurtured), I came away disappointed in this article for several reasons. First, Steele seems too glib in his dismissal of affirmative action, which for all its flaws helped him to achieve and to prosper. In addition, his tendency to locate the source of racial tension in individual anxieties—inferiority for African Americans, guilt for Caucasians—tends to put the blame for problems on campus on individuals or on "a handful of students." In doing so, Steele ignores the degree to which the system of higher education and much else in American society—with its hypercompetition, rank-ordering, and glorification of the kind of extreme individualism that breeds alienation—work to fuel racism that ends up harming all students. Finally, I find that Steele thinks, ironically, in black-and-white terms: either commonality or difference; either affirmative action or equality for all; either black studies, women's studies, and so on or a fair and "common" core. My own experience tells me that such polarized thinking is usually oversimplified and that "both/and" is preferable to "either/or." I want to celebrate and value and understand differences among people and those common ties that bind us together. I want to know and appreciate what makes me unique, as well as what makes me like other folks, including Shelby Steele. The college campus, I believe, is just the place to enact such a "both/and" philosophy. That's why I like being there. And that's why I have a more hopeful reading of "the recoloring of campus life" than does Steele.   —A.L.

As a college student reading Steele's article, I believe that many of his points make sense. I agree that many affirmative action programs lead some whites to resent the extra aid given to black students. It is difficult to see someone who is not as qualified receive special benefits based on an externality, especially with financial aid, when money matters are often a determining factor in the ability to attend college. However, these special programs never led me to believe black students were unqualified or could not earn scholarships any other way.

Steele overgeneralizes. I do not like to be told, as a Caucasian student, the way in which my race affects how I view my African American classmates. I am sure that some students feel the way Steele believes I should, but to imply that all white students feel guilt seems ludicrous to me. I think, in most cases, generalizations are harmful to the proposed argument; they force readers like me to be skeptical of the arguments.

I personally feel very boxed in by Steele's argument. Blacks think one way, whites think another, according to him. We either have affirmative action or complete equality (if such a thing is possible). This mode of thinking bothers me, because the world operates in such vast terms that gray areas are unavoidable. Such polar arguments make it seem as if all campuses are alive with inescapable racial tensions and that noticing differences brings out the racist in everyone. I disagree: college is a place of learning and discovery. It is possible to see differences in background (or color) and understand that those differences do not have to alienate us from others. All people possess qualities that are innately different from or the same as those of others. We can recognize and appreciate these differences without considering them obstacles to be overcome before any similarities can be discovered. —T.E.

QUESTIONING THE TEXT

1. "The Recoloring of Campus Life" contains a great number of "cause and effect" analyses. Identify one example of an effect that Steele traces to its root causes, and then write a paragraph assessing the persuasiveness of his reasoning.

2. Steele notes that about once every six months, someone yells a racial epithet at him from a passing car. Freewrite about such an incident, perhaps describing a similar experience and/or considering how it would feel to be a victim of one.

3. Look at the use of quotation marks in the annotations next to Steele's text. Which ones are used to mark direct quotations, and which ones are used for some other purpose? What other purposes do A.L., T.E., and J.R. have for placing certain words in quotes?

MAKING CONNECTIONS

4. Compare the perspectives on education offered by Steele and by bell hooks in "Keeping Close to Home" (p. 93) and the language they use to make their cases. How do they differ in tone and language? What audience do you believe each is trying to reach? Do you find one author more successful than the other? Why, or why not?

5. Would John Henry Newman's concept of the university, as described starting on p. 46, be able to accommodate the kinds of problems with "difference" that Steele describes? Explore the question in a brief essay.

JOINING THE CONVERSATION

6. Steele seems to blame affirmative action programs for many of the racial problems on campuses. Talk to officials on your campus or use the library to augment your understanding of such programs. How do they operate? What is their relationship to the sensitive issue of quotas? Bring your findings to class for discussion.

7. Steele inveighs against the establishment of black "theme" dorms. In a brief column such as might appear in a student newspaper, argue for or against the establishment of dormitories, student unions, or campus cultural programs designed to serve particular ethnic or racial groups.

8. Steele deliberately does not explore the status of other minorities on campus—notably Hispanic and Asian students. With a group of classmates, discuss the problems faced by these groups or others on your campus, such as women, homosexuals, older students, men, Christians, Jews, and so on. Then write a report applying what Steele observes about black-white relationships to the relationship between one of these groups and other students.

BELL HOOKS
Keeping Close to Home: Class and Education

BELL HOOKS *(b. 1952), like Adrienne Rich and Mike Rose, gives us ways to know what it means to see education as the practice of exclusion. Her own education was both difficult and hard won. As she says, "To a southern black girl from a working-class background who had never been on a city bus, who had never stepped on an escalator, who had never travelled by plane, leaving the comfortable confines of a small town Kentucky life to attend Stanford University was not just frightening; it was utterly painful."*

In fact, hooks drafted her first book, Ain't I a Woman: Black Women and Feminism, *when she was an undergraduate at Stanford. She has since written many other volumes:* Feminist Theory: From Margin to Center *(1984);* Talking Back *(1989), from which the following selection is taken;* Teaching to Transgress: Education as the Practice of Freedom *(1994); and* Remembered Rapture: The Writer at Work *(1999). In "Keeping Close to Home," hooks talks about her experiences as an undergraduate and offers an implicit argument for the role a university should play in the life of a nation. She also offers an implicit response to Shelby Steele by explaining why she wanted to acquire the "mainstream" education Stanford had to offer and to retain her own separate background and values as well. "Both/and," hooks says, in response to Steele's "either/or."*

A few years ago I heard hooks speak about her experiences as a teacher in largely white universities. I was struck by how open and responsive hooks was to her again almost all-white audience, and I particularly noted a gesture that she made. In signaling to one questioner after another, hooks never once pointed her finger. Instead, she extended an open palm, issuing an invitation rather than a command (or an accusation). I've never forgotten that gesture, or her passion as she spoke about her own need for an education and her determination to gain that education without giving up her own voice and style. Thus, I jumped at the chance to include her voice in these pages. —A.L.

We are both awake in the almost dark of 5 A.M. Everyone else is sound asleep. Mama asks the usual questions. Telling me to look around, make sure I have everything, scolding me because I am uncertain about the actual time the bus arrives. By 5:30 we are waiting outside the closed station. Alone together, we have a chance to really talk. Mama begins. Angry with her children, especially the ones who whisper behind her back, she says bitterly, "Your childhood could not have been that bad. You were fed and clothed. You did not have to do without—that's more than a lot of folks have and I just can't stand the way y'all go on." The hurt in her voice saddens me. I have always wanted to protect mama from hurt, to ease her burdens. Now I am part of what troubles. Confronting me, she says accusingly, "It's not just the other children. You talk too much about the past. You don't just listen." And I do talk. Worse, I write about it.

Mama has always come to each of her children seeking different responses. With me she expresses the disappointment, hurt, and anger of betrayal: anger that her children are so critical, that we can't even have the sense to like the presents she sends. She says, "From now on there will be no presents. I'll just stick some money in a little envelope the way the rest of you do. Nobody wants criticism. Everybody can criticize me but I am supposed to say nothing." When I try to talk, my voice sounds like a twelve year old. When I try to talk, she speaks louder, interrupting me, even though she has said repeatedly, "Explain it to me, this talk about the past." I struggle to return to my thirty-five year old self so that she will know by the sound of my voice that we are two women talking together. It is only when I state firmly in my very adult voice, "Mama, you are not listening," that she becomes quiet. She waits. Now that I have her attention, I fear that my explanations will be lame, inadequate. "Mama," I begin, "people usually go to therapy because they feel hurt inside, because they have pain that will not stop, like a wound that continually breaks open, that does not heal. And often these hurts, that pain has to do with things that have happened in the past, sometimes in childhood, often in childhood, or things that we believe happened." She wants to know, "What hurts, what hurts are you talking about?" "Mom, I can't answer that. I can't speak for all of us, the hurts are different for everybody. But the point is you try to make the hurt better, to heal it, by understanding how it came to be. And I know you feel mad when we say something happened or hurt that you don't remember being that way, but the past isn't like that, we don't have the same memory of it. We remember things differently. You know that. And sometimes folk feel hurt about stuff and you just don't know or didn't realize it, and they need to talk about it. Surely you understand the need to talk about it."

Our conversation is interrupted by the sight of my uncle walking across the park toward us. We stop to watch him. He is on his way to work dressed in a familiar blue suit. They look alike, these two who rarely discuss the past. This interruption makes me think about life in a small town. You always see someone you know. Interruptions, intrusions are part of daily life. Privacy is difficult to maintain. We leave our private space in the car to greet him. After the hug and kiss he has given me every year since I was born, they talk about the day's funerals. In the distance the bus approaches. He walks away knowing that they will see each other later. Just before I board the bus I turn, staring into my mother's face. I am momentarily back in time, seeing myself eighteen years ago, at this same bus stop, staring into my mother's face, continually turning back, waving farewell as I returned to college—that experience which first took me away from our town, from family. Departing was as painful then as it is now. Each movement away makes return harder. Each separation intensifies distance, both physical and emotional.

To a southern black girl from a working-class background who had never been on a city bus, who had never stepped on an escalator, who had never travelled by plane, leaving the comfortable confines of a small town Kentucky life to attend Stanford University was not just frightening; it was utterly painful. My parents had not been delighted that I had been accepted and adamantly opposed my going so far from home. At the time, I did not see their opposition as an expression of their fear that they would lose me forever. Like many working-class folks, they feared what college education might do to their children's minds even as they unenthusiastically acknowledged its importance. They did not understand why I could not attend a college nearby, an all-black college. To them, any college would do. I would graduate, become a school teacher, make a decent living and a good marriage. And even though they reluctantly and skeptically supported my educational endeavors, they also subjected them to constant harsh and bitter critique. It is difficult for me to talk about my parents and their impact on me because they have always felt wary, ambivalent, mistrusting of my intellectual aspirations even as they have been caring and supportive. I want to speak about these contradictions because sorting through them, seeking resolution and reconciliation has been important to me both as it affects my development as a writer, my effort to be fully self-realized, and my longing to remain close to the family and community that provided the groundwork for much of my thinking, writing, and being.

Studying at Stanford, I began to think seriously about class differences. 5 To be materially underprivileged at a university where most folks (with the exception of workers) are materially privileged provokes such thought. Class differences were boundaries no one wanted to face or talk about. It was easier to downplay them, to act as though we were all from privileged backgrounds, to work around them, to confront them privately in the solitude of one's room, or to pretend that just being chosen to study at such an institution meant that those of us who did not come from privilege were already in transition toward privilege. To not long for such transition marked one as rebellious, as unlikely to succeed. It was a kind of treason not to believe that it was better to be identified with the world of material privilege than with the world of the working class, the poor. No wonder our working-class parents from poor backgrounds feared our entry into such a world, intuiting perhaps that we might learn to be ashamed of where we had come from, that we might never return home, or come back only to lord it over them.

Though I hung with students who were supposedly radical and chic, we did not discuss class. I talked to no one about the sources of my shame, how it hurt me to witness the contempt shown the brown-skinned Filipina maids who cleaned our rooms, or later my concern about the $100 a month I paid for a room off-campus which was more than half of what my parents paid for rent. I talked to no one about my efforts to save money, to send a little something home. Yet these class realities separated me from fellow students. We were moving in different directions. I did not intend to forget my class

background or alter my class allegiance. And even though I received an education designed to provide me with a bourgeois sensibility, passive acquiescence was not my only option. I knew that I could resist. I could rebel. I
could shape the direction and focus of the various forms of knowledge available to me. Even though I sometimes envied and longed for greater material
advantages (particularly at vacation times when I would be one of few if any
students remaining in the dormitory because there was no money for travel), I
did not share the sensibility and values of my peers. That was important—
class was not just about money; it was about values which showed and determined behavior. While I often needed more money, I never needed a new
set of beliefs and values. For example, I was profoundly shocked and disturbed when peers would talk about their parents without respect, or would
even say that they hated their parents. This was especially troubling to me
when it seemed that these parents were caring and concerned. It was often
explained to me that such hatred was "healthy and normal." To my white,
middle-class California roommate, I explained the way we were taught to
value our parents and their care, to understand that they were obligated to
give us care. She would always shake her head, laughing all the while, and
say, "Missy, you will learn that it's different here, that we think differently."
She was right. Soon, I lived alone, like the one Mormon student who kept to
himself as he made a concentrated effort to remain true to his religious beliefs
and values. Later in graduate school I found that classmates believed "lower
class" people had no beliefs and values. I was silent in such discussions, dis-
gusted by their ignorance.

Carol Stack's anthropological study, *All Our Kin,* was one of the first
books I read which confirmed my experiential understanding that within
black culture (especially among the working class and poor, particularly in
southern states), a value system emerged that was counter-hegemonic, that
challenged notions of individualism and private property so important to the
maintenance of white-supremacist, capitalist patriarchy. Black folk created in
marginal spaces a world of community and collectivity where resources were
shared. In the preface to *Feminist Theory: from margin to center,* I talked about
how the point of difference, this marginality, can be the space for the formation of an oppositional world view. That world view must be articulated,
named if it is to provide a sustained blueprint for change. Unfortunately,
there has existed no consistent framework for such naming. Consequently
both the experience of this difference and documentation of it (when it occurs) gradually loses presence and meaning.

Much of what Stack documented about the "culture of poverty," for
example, would not describe interactions among most black poor today irrespective of geographical setting. Since the black people she described did not
acknowledge (if they recognized it in theoretical terms) the oppositional value
of their world view, apparently seeing it more as a survival strategy determined less by conscious efforts to oppose oppressive race and class biases than

by circumstance, they did not attempt to establish a framework to transmit their beliefs and values from generation to generation. When circumstances changed, values altered. Efforts to assimilate the values and beliefs of privileged white people, presented through media like television, undermine and destroy potential structures of opposition.

Increasingly, young black people are encouraged by the dominant culture (and by those black people who internalize the values of this hegemony) to believe that assimilation is the only possible way to survive, to succeed. Without the framework of an organized civil rights or black resistance struggle, individual and collective efforts at black liberation that focus on the primacy of self-definition and self-determination often go unrecognized. It is crucial that those among us who resist and rebel, who survive and succeed, speak openly and honestly about our lives and the nature of our personal struggles, the means by which we resolve and reconcile contradictions. This is no easy task. Within the educational institutions where we learn to develop and strengthen our writing and analytical skills, we also learn to think, write, and talk in a manner that shifts attention away from personal experience. Yet if we are to reach our people and all people, if we are to remain connected (especially those of us whose familial backgrounds are poor and working-class), we must understand that the telling of one's personal story provides a meaningful example, a way for folks to identify and connect.

Combining personal with critical analysis and theoretical perspectives   10 can engage listeners who might otherwise feel estranged, alienated. To speak simply with language that is accessible to as many folks as possible is also important. Speaking about one's personal experience or speaking with simple language is often considered by academics and/or intellectuals (irrespective of their political inclinations) to be a sign of intellectual weakness or even anti-intellectualism. Lately, when I speak, I do not stand in place—reading my paper, making little or no eye contact with audiences—but instead make eye contact, talk extemporaneously, digress, and address the audience directly. I have been told that people assume I am not prepared, that I am anti-intellectual, unprofessional (a concept that has everything to do with class as it determines actions and behavior), or that I am reinforcing the stereotype of black as non-theoretical and gutsy.

Such criticism was raised recently by fellow feminist scholars after a talk I gave at Northwestern University at a conference on "Gender, Culture, Politics" to an audience that was mainly students and academics. I deliberately chose to speak in a very basic way, thinking especially about the few community folks who had come to hear me. Weeks later, KumKum Sangari, a fellow participant who shared with me what was said when I was no longer present, and I engaged in quite rigorous critical dialogue about the way my presentation had been perceived primarily by privileged white female academics. She was concerned that I not mask my knowledge of theory, that I not appear anti-intellectual. Her critique compelled me to articulate concerns that I am

often silent about with colleagues. I spoke about class allegiance and revolutionary commitments, explaining that it was disturbing to me that intellectual
radicals who speak about transforming society, ending the domination of race,
sex, class, cannot break with behavior patterns that reinforce and perpetuate
domination, or continue to use as their sole reference point how we might be
or are perceived by those who dominate, whether or not we gain their acceptance and approval.

   This is a primary contradiction which raises the issue of whether or not
the academic setting is a place where one can be truly radical or subversive.
Concurrently, the use of a language and style of presentation that alienates
most folks who are not also academically trained reinforces the notion that the
academic world is separate from real life, that everyday world where we constantly adjust our language and behavior to meet diverse needs. The academic
setting is separate only when we work to make it so. It is a false dichotomy
which suggests that academics and/or intellectuals can only speak to one another, that we cannot hope to speak with the masses. What is true is that we
make choices, that we choose our audiences, that we choose voices to hear
and voices to silence. If I do not speak in a language that can be understood,
then there is little chance for dialogue. This issue of language and behavior is
a central contradiction all radical intellectuals, particularly those who are
members of oppressed groups, must continually confront and work to resolve.
One of the clear and present dangers that exists when we move outside our
class of origin, our collective ethnic experience, and enter hierarchical institutions which daily reinforce domination by race, sex, and class, is that we gradually assume a mindset similar to those who dominate and oppress, that we
lose critical consciousness because it is not reinforced or affirmed by the environment. We must be ever vigilant. It is important that we know who we are
speaking to, who we most want to hear us, who we most long to move, motivate, and touch with our words.

   When I first came to New Haven to teach at Yale, I was truly surprised
by the marked class divisions between black folks — students and professors —
who identify with Yale and those black folks who work at Yale or in surrounding communities. Style of dress and self-presentation are most often the
central markers of one's position. I soon learned that the black folks who
spoke on the street were likely to be part of the black community and those
who carefully shifted their glance were likely to be associated with Yale.
Walking with a black female colleague one day, I spoke to practically every
black person in sight (a gesture which reflects my upbringing), an action
which disturbed my companion. Since I addressed black folk who were
clearly not associated with Yale, she wanted to know whether or not I knew
them. That was funny to me. "Of course not," I answered. Yet when I
thought about it seriously, I realized that in a deep way, I knew them for
they, and not my companion or most of my colleagues at Yale, resemble my
family. Later that year, in a black women's support group I started for under-

graduates, students from poor backgrounds spoke about the shame they some-times feel when faced with the reality of their connection to working-class and poor black people. One student confessed that her father is a street per-son, addicted to drugs, someone who begs from passersby. She, like other Yale students, turns away from street people often, sometimes showing anger or contempt; she hasn't wanted anyone to know that she was related to this kind of person. She struggles with this, wanting to find a way to acknowledge and affirm this reality, to claim this connection. The group asked me and one another what we [should] do to remain connected, to honor the bonds we have with working-class and poor people even as our class experience alters.

Maintaining connections with family and community across class boundaries demands more than just summary recall of where one's roots are, where one comes from. It requires knowing, naming, and being ever-mindful of those aspects of one's past that have enabled and do enable one's self-development in the present, that sustain and support, that enrich. One must also honestly confront barriers that do exist, aspects of that past that do dimin-ish. My parents' ambivalence about my love for reading led to intense con-flict. They (especially my mother) would work to ensure that I had access to books, but would threaten to burn the books or throw them away if I did not conform to other expectations. Or they would insist that reading too much would drive me insane. Their ambivalence nurtured in me a like uncertainty about the value and significance of intellectual endeavor which took years for me to unlearn. While this aspect of our class reality was one that wounded and diminished, their vigilant insistence that being smart did not make me a "better" or "superior" person (which often got on my nerves because I think I wanted to have that sense that it did indeed set me apart, make me better) made a profound impression. From them I learned to value and respect vari-ous skills and talents folk might have, not just to value people who read books and talk about ideas. They and my grandparents might say about somebody, "Now he don't read nor write a lick, but he can tell a story," or as my grand-mother would say, "call out the hell in words."

Empty romanticization of poor or working-class backgrounds under-   15
mines the possibility of true connection. Such connection is based on under-standing difference in experience and perspective and working to mediate and negotiate these terrains. Language is a crucial issue for folk whose movement outside the boundaries of poor and working-class backgrounds changes the nature and direction of their speech. Coming to Stanford with my own ver-sion of a Kentucky accent, which I think of always as a strong sound quite different from Tennessee or Georgia speech, I learned to speak differently while maintaining the speech of my region, the sound of my family and com-munity. This was of course much easier to keep up when I returned home to stay often. In recent years, I have endeavored to use various speaking styles in the classroom as a teacher and find it disconcerts those who feel that the use of a particular patois excludes them as listeners, even if there is translation into

the usual, acceptable mode of speech. Learning to listen to different voices, hearing different speech challenges the notion that we must all assimilate — share a single, similar talk — in educational institutions. Language reflects the culture from which we emerge. To deny ourselves daily use of speech patterns that are common and familiar, that embody the unique and distinctive aspect of our self is one of the ways we become estranged and alienated from our past. It is important for us to have as many languages on hand as we can know or learn. It is important for those of us who are black, who speak in particular patois as well as standard English, to express ourselves in both ways.

Often I tell students from poor and working-class backgrounds that if you believe what you have learned and are learning in schools and universities separates you from your past, this is precisely what will happen. It is important to stand firm in the conviction that nothing can truly separate us from our pasts when we nurture and cherish that connection. An important strategy for maintaining contact is ongoing acknowledgment of the primacy of one's past, of one's background, affirming the reality that such bonds are not severed automatically solely because one enters a new environment or moves toward a different class experience.

Again, I do not wish to romanticize this effort, to dismiss the reality of conflict and contradiction. During my time at Stanford, I did go through a period of more than a year when I did not return home. That period was one where I felt that it was simply too difficult to mesh my profoundly disparate realities. Critical reflection about the choice I was making, particularly about why I felt a choice had to be made, pulled me through this difficult time. Luckily I recognized that the insistence on choosing between the world of family and community and the new world of privileged white people and privileged ways of knowing was imposed upon me by the outside. It is as though a mythical contract had been signed somewhere which demanded of us black folks that once we entered these spheres we would immediately give up all vestiges of our underprivileged past. It was my responsibility to formulate a way of being that would allow me to participate fully in my new environment while integrating and maintaining aspects of the old.

One of the most tragic manifestations of the pressure black people feel to assimilate is expressed in the internalization of racist perspectives. I was shocked and saddened when I first heard black professors at Stanford downgrade and express contempt for black students, expecting us to do poorly, refusing to establish nurturing bonds. At every university I have attended as a student or worked at as a teacher, I have heard similar attitudes expressed with little or no understanding of factors that might prevent brilliant black students from performing to their full capability. Within universities, there are few educational and social spaces where students who wish to affirm positive ties to ethnicity — to blackness, to working-class backgrounds — can receive affirmation and support. Ideologically, the message is clear — assimilation is the way to gain acceptance and approval from those in power.

Many white people enthusiastically supported Richard Rodriguez's ve-hement contention in his autobiography, *Hunger of Memory,* that attempts to maintain ties with his Chicano background impeded his progress, that he had to sever ties with community and kin to succeed at Stanford and in the larger world, that family language, in his case Spanish, had to be made secondary or discarded. If the terms of success as defined by the standards of ruling groups within white-supremacist, capitalist patriarchy are the only standards that exist, then assimilation is indeed necessary. But they are not. Even in the face of powerful structures of domination, it remains possible for each of us, espe-cially those of us who are members of oppressed and/or exploited groups as well as those radical visionaries who may have race, class, and sex privilege, to define and determine alternative standards, to decide on the nature and extent of compromise. Standards by which one's success is measured, whether stu-dent or professor, are quite different from those of us who wish to resist rein-forcing the domination of race, sex, and class, who work to maintain and strengthen our ties with the oppressed, with those who lack material privi-lege, with our families who are poor and working-class.

When I wrote my first book, *Ain't I a Woman: black women and feminism,* 20 the issue of class and its relationship to who one's reading audience might be came up for me around my decision not to use footnotes, for which I have been sharply criticized. I told people that my concern was that footnotes set class boundaries for readers, determining who a book is for. I was shocked that many academic folks scoffed at this idea. I shared that I went into working-class black communities as well as talked with family and friends to survey whether or not they ever read books with footnotes and found that they did not. A few did not know what they were, but most folks saw them as indicating that a book was for college-educated people. These responses in-fluenced my decision. When some of my more radical, college-educated friends freaked out about the absence of footnotes, I seriously questioned how we could ever imagine revolutionary transformation of society if such a small shift in direction could be viewed as threatening. Of course, many folks warned that the absence of footnotes would make the work less credible in academic circles. This information also highlighted the way in which class in-forms our choices. Certainly I did feel that choosing to use simple language, absence of footnotes, etc. would mean I was jeopardizing the possibility of being taken seriously in academic circles but then this was a political matter and a political decision. It utterly delights me that this has proven not to be the case and that the book is read by many academics as well as by people who are not college-educated.

Always our first response when we are motivated to conform or com-promise within structures that reinforce domination must be to engage in critical reflection. Only by challenging ourselves to push against oppressive boundaries do we make the radical alternative possible, expanding the realm and scope of critical inquiry. Unless we share radical strategies, ways of rethinking and revisioning with students, with kin and community, with a larger audience, we risk perpetuating the stereotype that we succeed because we are the exception, different from the rest of our people. Since I left home and entered college, I am often asked, usually by white people, if my sisters and brothers are also high achievers. At the root of this question is the longing for reinforcement of the belief in "the exception" which enables race, sex, and class biases to remain intact. I am careful to separate what it means to be exceptional from a notion of "the exception."

Frequently I hear smart black folks, from poor and working-class backgrounds, stressing their frustration that at times family and community do not recognize that they are exceptional. Absence of positive affirmation clearly diminishes the longing to excel in academic endeavors. Yet it is important to distinguish between the absence of basic positive affirmation and the longing for continued reinforcement that we are special. Usually liberal white folks will willingly offer continual reinforcement of us as exceptions—as special. This can be both patronizing and very seductive. Since we often work in situations where we are isolated from other black folks, we can easily begin to feel that encouragement from white people is the primary or only source of support and recognition. Given the internalization of racism, it is easy to view this support as more validating and legitimizing than similar support from black people. Still, nothing takes the place of being valued and appreciated by one's own, by one's family and community. We share a mutual and reciprocal responsibility for affirming one another's successes. Sometimes we have to talk to our folks about the fact that we need their ongoing support and affirmation, that it is unique and special to us. In some cases we may never receive desired recognition and acknowledgment of specific achievements from kin. Rather than seeing this as a basis for estrangement, for severing connection, it is useful to explore other sources of nourishment and support.

I do not know that my mother's mother ever acknowledged my college education except to ask me once, "How can you live so far away from your people?" Yet she gave me sources of affirmation and nourishment, sharing the legacy of her quilt-making, of family history, of her incredible way with words. Recently, when our father retired after more than thirty years of work as a janitor, I wanted to pay tribute to this experience, to identify links between his work and my own as writer and teacher. Reflecting on our family past, I recalled ways he had been an impressive example of diligence and hard work, approaching tasks with a seriousness of concentration I work to mirror and develop, with a discipline I struggle to maintain. Sharing these thoughts with him keeps us connected, nurtures our respect for each other, maintaining a space, however large or small, where we can talk.

Open, honest communication is the most important way we maintain relationships with kin and community as our class experience and backgrounds change. It is as vital as the sharing of resources. Often financial assistance is given in circumstances where there is no meaningful contact. However helpful, this can also be an expression of estrangement and alienation. Communication between black folks from various experiences of material privilege was much easier when we were all in segregated communities sharing common experiences in relation to social institutions. Without this grounding, we must work to maintain ties, connection. We must assume greater responsibility for making and maintaining contact, connections that can shape our intellectual visions and inform our radical commitments.

The most powerful resource any of us can have as we study and teach in   25 university settings is full understanding and appreciation of the richness, beauty, and primacy of our familial and community backgrounds. Maintaining awareness of class differences, nurturing ties with the poor and working-class people who are our most intimate kin, our comrades in struggle, transforms and enriches our intellectual experience. Education as the practice of freedom becomes not a force which fragments or separates, but one that brings us closer, expanding our definitions of home and community.

QUESTIONING THE TEXT

1. Hooks contends that "[w]ithin universities, there are few educational and social spaces where students who wish to affirm positive ties to ethnicity—to blackness, to working-class backgrounds—can receive affirmation and support. Ideologically, the message is clear—assimilation is the way to gain acceptance and approval from those in power." What is hooks's attitude toward assimilation? What in the text reveals that attitude? Freewrite for 10 or 15 minutes on how your own school is leading you to assimilate to some things, such as academic language, grading standards, or ways of behaving—both in and out of class.

2. In this essay, hooks describes several occasions when she was accused of writing or speaking in ways that were unacceptable according to academic standards. Does this essay meet the criteria for academic writing as you understand it? Give examples to illustrate what you find "academic" about this essay.

3. Look at the quotation A.L. chooses to use in her introduction about hooks. Why do you think she chose that quotation in particular?

MAKING CONNECTIONS

4. A.L. chose both this reading and the one by Mike Rose (p. 105). What do these pieces have in common that might have appealed to A.L.? What, on the other hand, might hooks and Rose be expected to disagree on?

5. In the previous reading, Shelby Steele represents African American students as affected by a "myth of inferiority." Would hooks agree? Why, or why not?

JOINING THE CONVERSATION

6. Hooks says that after arriving at college a person may find it difficult to stay connected to her or his home community, especially if that community is quite different from the academic community. Do you agree? Has coming to college changed your relationship with your family and/or home community? If you keep a reading log, answer this question there.

7. Hooks suggests that her experiences with people who were different from her—her white, middle-class roommate, for example—strengthened her sense of herself as a black, working-class person. How has your involvement with people who are different from you affected your sense of who you are? Write a paragraph or two about some memorable character who has shaped your sense of self.

8. Working with two or three classmates, come up with a list of characteristics of an "academic" style of speaking or writing. What kinds of language use does your group think the university would consider unacceptable? What arguments would you make for—or against—such academic writing? Together prepare a brief letter to incoming students explaining how the university defines *academic writing*.

MIKE ROSE
Lives on the Boundary

As a child, Mike Rose (b. 1944) never thought of going to college. The son of Italian immigrants, he was placed in the "vocational track" in school (through a clerical error, as it turns out) and, as he says, "lived down to expectations beautifully." He was one of those who might well have been excluded from the university. In his prize-winning volume Lives on the Boundary *(1989), Rose recalls those circumstances that opened up the university to him, and he argues forcefully that education in a democracy must be truly open to all, a theme he pursues in his latest book,* Possible Lives *(1996).*

In the excerpt from Lives on the Boundary *that follows, Rose describes several students he has known, considering the ways in which the "idea of a university" either includes or excludes them. In an extended discussion of what he calls the "canonical curriculum," he concludes that "books can spark dreams," but "appeals to elevated texts can also divert attention from the conditions that keep a population from realizing its dreams."*

I wanted to include this passage from Rose's book because he explicitly addresses the call made by Jeffrey Hart and others for a university curriculum based on "Great Books," books that by definition exclude the experiences of the students Rose describes. In addition, I chose this selection because Rose is a graceful prose stylist, a gifted scholar, and a much-valued friend.

Professor of Education at UCLA, *Rose is also a truly extraordinary teacher. His own story, and the stories of those students whose lives he has touched, attest to the transformational power of the kind of educational experience he advocates. To "have any prayer of success" at making such experiences possible, Rose says, "we'll need many . . . blessings." We'll also need many more teachers and writers like Mike Rose.*   —A.L.

I have a vivid memory of sitting on the edge of my bed—I was twelve or thirteen maybe—listening with unease to a minute or so of classical music. I don't know if I found it as I was turning the dial, searching for the Johnny Otis Show or the live broadcast from Scribner's Drive-In, or if the tuner had simply drifted into another station's signal. Whatever happened, the music caught me in a disturbing way, and I sat there, letting it play. It sounded like the music I heard in church, weighted, funereal. Eerie chords echoing from another world. I leaned over, my fingers on the tuner, and, in what I remember as almost a twitch, I turned the knob away from the melody of these strange instruments. My reaction to the other high culture I encountered— *The Iliad* and Shakespeare and some schoolbook poems by Longfellow and

Lowell—was similar, though less a visceral rejection and more a rejecting dis-
interest, a sense of irrelevance. The few Shakespearean scenes I did know—
saw on television, or read or heard in grammar school—seemed snooty and
put-on, kind of dumb. Not the way I wanted to talk. Not interesting to me.

There were few books in our house: a couple of thin stories read to me
as a child in Pennsylvania (*The Little Boy Who Ran Away,* an *Uncle Remus*
sampler), the *M* volume of the *World Book Encyclopedia* (which I found one
day in the trash behind the secondhand store), and the Hollywood tabloids
my mother would bring home from work. I started buying lots of Superman
and Batman comic books because I loved the heroes' virtuous omnipo-
tence—comic books, our teachers said, were bad for us—and, once I discovered them, I began checking out science fiction novels from my grammar
school library. Other reading material appeared: the instructions to my chemistry set, which I half understood and only half followed, and, eventually, my
astronomy books, which seemed to me to be magical rather than discursive
texts. So it was that my early intrigue with literacy—my lifts and escapes with
language and rhythm—came from comic books and science fiction, from the
personal, nonscientific worlds I created with bits and pieces of laboratory and
telescopic technology, came, as well, from the Italian stories I heard my
uncles and parents tell. It came, too, from the music my radio brought me:
music that wove in and out of my days, lyrics I'd repeat and repeat—"gone,
gone, gone, jumpin' like a catfish on a pole"—wanting to catch that sound,
seeking other emotional frontiers, other places to go. Like rocker Joe Ely, I
picked up Chicago on my transistor radio.

Except for school exercises and occasional cards my mother made me
write to my uncles and aunts, I wrote very little during my childhood; it wasn't
until my last year in high school that Jack MacFarland* sparked an interest in
writing. And though I developed into a good reader, I performed from moder-
ately well to terribly on other sorts of school literacy tasks. From my reading I
knew vocabulary words, and I did okay on spelling tests—though I never lasted
all that long in spelling bees—but I got C's and D's on the ever-present requests
to diagram sentences and label parts of speech. The more an assignment was related to real reading, the better I did; the more analytic, self-contained, and divorced from context, the lousier I performed. Today some teachers would say I
was a concrete thinker. To be sure, the development of my ability to decode
words and read sentences took place in school, but my orientation to reading—
the way I conceived of it, my purpose for doing it—occurred within the tight
and untraditional confines of my home. The quirks and textures of my immediate environment combined with my escapist fantasies to draw me to books. "It
is what we are excited about that educates us," writes social historian Elizabeth
Ewen. It is what taps our curiosity and dreams. Eventually, the books that

---

Jack MacFarland: a man whom Rose describes as "the teacher who saved [my] life" seemed so distant, those Great Books, would work their way into my curiosity, would influence the way I framed problems and the way I wrote. But that would come much later—first with Jack MacFarland (mixed with his avant-garde countertradition), then with my teachers at Loyola and UCLA—an excitement and curiosity shaped by others and connected to others, a cultural and linguistic heritage received not from some pristine conduit, but exchanged through the heat of human relation.

A friend of mine recently suggested that education is one culture embracing another. It's interesting to think of the very different ways that metaphor plays out. Education can be a desperate, smothering embrace, an embrace that denies the needs of the other. But education can also be an encouraging, communal embrace—at its best an invitation, an opening. Several years ago, I was sitting in on a workshop conducted by the Brazilian educator Paulo Freire. It was the first hour or so and Freire, in his sophisticated, accented English, was establishing the theoretical base of his literacy pedagogy—heady stuff, a blend of Marxism, phenomenology, and European existentialism. I was two seats away from Freire; in front of me and next to him was a younger man, who, puzzled, finally interrupted the speaker to ask a question. Freire acknowledged the question and, as he began answering, he turned and quickly touched the man's forearm. Not patronizing, not mushy, a look and a tap as if to say: "You and me right now, let's go through this together." Embrace. With Jack MacFarland it was an embrace: no-nonsense and cerebral, but a relationship in which the terms of endearment were the image in a poem, a play's dialogue, the winding narrative journey of a novel.

More often than we admit, a failed education is social more than intel-   5
lectual in origin. And the challenge that has always faced American education, that it has sometimes denied and sometimes doggedly pursued, is how to create both the social and cognitive means to enable a diverse citizenry to develop their ability. It is an astounding challenge: the complex and wrenching struggle to actualize the potential not only of the privileged but, too, of those who have lived here for a long time generating a culture outside the mainstream and those who, like my mother's parents and my father, immigrated with cultural traditions of their own. This painful but generative mix of language and story can result in clash and dislocation in our communities, but it also gives rise to new speech, new stories, and once we appreciate the richness of it, new invitations to literacy.

Pico Boulevard, named for the last Mexican governor of California, runs an immense stretch west to east: from the wealth of the Santa Monica beaches to blighted Central Avenue, deep in Los Angeles. Union Street is comparatively brief, running north to south, roughly from Adams to Temple, pretty bad off all the way. Union intersects Pico east of Vermont Avenue and too far to the southwest to be touched by the big-money development that is turning downtown Los Angeles into a whirring postmodernist dreamscape.

The Pico-Union District is very poor, some of its housing as unsafe as that on Skid Row, dilapidated, overcrowded, rat-infested. It used to be a working-class Mexican neighborhood, but for about ten years now it has become the concentrated locale of those fleeing the political and economic horror in Central America. Most come from El Salvador and Guatemala. One observer calls the area a gigantic refugee camp.

As you move concentrically outward from Pico-Union, you'll encounter a number of other immigrant communities: Little Tokyo and China-town to the northeast, Afro-Caribbean to the southwest, Koreatown to the west. Moving west, you'll find Thai and Vietnamese restaurants tucked here and there in storefronts. Filipinos, Southeast Asians, Armenians, and Iranians work in the gas stations, the shoe-repair stores, the minimarts. A lawnmower repair shop posts its sign in Korean, Spanish, and English. A Korean church announces "Jesus Loves You" in the same three languages. "The magnitude and diversity of immigration to Los Angeles since 1960," notes a report from UCLA's Graduate School of Architecture and Urban Planning, "is comparable only to the New York-bound wave of migrants around the turn of the century." It is not at all uncommon for English composition teachers at UCLA, Cal-State L.A., Long Beach State—the big urban universities and colleges—to have, in a class of twenty-five, students representing a dozen or more linguistic backgrounds: from Spanish and Cantonese and Farsi to Hindi, Portuguese, and Tagalog. Los Angeles, the new Ellis Island.

On a drive down the Santa Monica Freeway, you exit on Vermont and pass Rick's Mexican Cuisine, Hawaii Discount Furniture, The Restaurant Ecuatoriano, Froggy's Children's Wear, Seoul Autobody, and the Bar Omaha. Turn east on Pico, and as you approach Union, taking a side street here and there, you'll start seeing the murals: The Virgin of Guadalupe, Steve McQueen, a scene resembling Siqueiros's heroic workers, the Statue of Liberty, Garfield the Cat. Graffiti are everywhere. The dreaded Eighteenth Street gang—an established Mexican gang—has marked its turf in Arabic as well as Roman numerals. Newer gangs, a Salvadoran gang among them, are emerging by the violent logic of territory and migration; they have Xed out the Eighteenth Street *placas* and written their own threatening insignias in place. Statues of the Blessed Mother rest amid potted plants in overgrown front yards. There is a rich sweep of small commerce: restaurants, markets, bakeries, legal services ("Income Tax y Amnestia"), beauty salons ("Lolita's Magic Touch—Salon de Belleza—Unisex"). A Salvadoran restaurant sells teriyaki burgers. A "Discoteca Latina" advertises "great rap hits." A clothing store has a Dick Tracy sweatshirt on a half mannequin; a boy walks out wearing a blue t-shirt that announces "Life's a Beach." Culture in a Waring blender.

There are private telegram and postal services: messages sent straight to "domicilio a CentroAmerica." A video store advertises a comedy about immigration: *Ni de Aqui/Ni de Alla,* "Neither from Here nor from There." The poster displays a Central American Indian caught on a wild freeway ride: a

Mexican in a sombrero is pulling one of the Indian's pigtails, Uncle Sam pulls the other, a border guard looks on, ominously suspended in air. You see a lot of street vending, from oranges and melons to deco sunglasses: rhinestones and plastic swans and lenses shaped like a heart. Posters are slapped on posters: one has rows of faces of the disappeared. Santa Claus stands on a truck bumper and waves drivers into a ninety-nine cent outlet.

Families are out shopping, men loiter outside a cafe, a group of young girls   10 collectively count out their change. You notice, even in the kaleidoscope you pick out his figure, you notice a dark-skinned boy, perhaps Guatemalan, walking down Pico with a cape across his shoulders. His hair is piled in a four-inch rockabilly pompadour. He passes a dingy apartment building, a *pupuseria,* a body shop with no name, and turns into a storefront social services center. There is one other person in the sparse waiting room. She is thin, her gray hair pulled back in a tight bun, her black dress buttoned to her neck. She will tell you, if you ask her in Spanish, that she is waiting for her English class to begin. She might also tell you that the people here are helping her locate her son — lost in Salvadoran resettlement camps — and she thinks that if she can learn a little English, it will help her bring him to America.

The boy is here for different reasons. He has been causing trouble in school, and arrangements are being made for him to see a bilingual counselor. His name is Mario, and he immigrated with his older sister two years ago. His English is halting, unsure; he seems simultaneously rebellious and scared. His case worker tells me that he still has flashbacks of Guatemalan terror: his older brother taken in the night by death squads, strangled, and hacked apart on the road by his house. Then she shows me his drawings, and our conversation stops. Crayon and pen on cheap paper; blue and orange cityscapes, eyes on billboards, in the windshields of cars, a severed hand at the bus stop. There are punks, beggars, piñatas walking the streets — upright cows and donkeys — skeletal homeboys, corseted girls carrying sharpened bones. "He will talk to you about these," the caseworker tells me. "They're scary, aren't they? The school doesn't know what the hell to do with him. I don't think he really knows what to do with all that's in him either."

In another part of the state, farther to the north, also rich in immigration, a teacher in a basic reading and writing program asks his students to interview one another and write a report, a capsule of a classmate's life. Caroline, a black woman in her late forties, chooses Thuy Anh, a Vietnamese woman many years her junior. Caroline asks only five questions — Thuy Anh's English is still difficult to understand — simple questions: What is your name? Where were you born? What is your education? Thuy Anh talks about her childhood in South Vietnam and her current plans in America. She is the oldest of nine children, and she received a very limited Vietnamese education, for she had to spend much of her childhood caring for her brothers and sisters. She married a serviceman, came to America, and now spends virtually all of her time pursuing a high school equivalency, struggling with textbook descriptions of the American political process, frantically trying to improve her computational skills. She is not doing very well at this. As one of her classmates observed, she might be trying too hard.

Caroline is supposed to take notes while Thuy Anh responds to her questions, and then use the notes to write her profile, maybe something like a reporter would do. But Caroline is moved to do something different. She's taken by Thuy Anh's account of watching over babies. "Mother's little helper," she thinks. And that stirs her, this woman who has never been a mother. Maybe, too, Thuy Anh's desire to do well in school, her driven eagerness, the desperation that occasionally flits across her face, maybe that moves Caroline as well. Over the next two days, Caroline strays from the assignment and writes a two-and-a-half page fiction that builds to a prose poem. She recasts Thuy Anh's childhood into an American television fantasy.

Thuy Anh is "Mother's little helper." Her five younger sisters "are happy and full of laughter . . . their little faces are bright with eyes sparkling." The little girls' names are "Hellen, Ellen, Lottie, Alice, and Olie"— American names—and they "cook and sew and make pretty doll dresses for their dolls to wear." Though the family is Buddhist, they exchange gifts at Christmas and "gather in the large living room to sing Christmas carols." Thuy Anh "went to school every day she could and studied very hard." One day, Thuy Anh was "asked to write a poem and to recite it to her classmates." And, here, Caroline embeds within her story a prose poem—which she attributes to Thuy Anh:

> My name is Thuy Anh I live near the Ocean. I see the waves boisterous and impudent bursting and splashing against the huge rocks. I see the white boats out on the blue sea. I see the fisher men rapped in heavy coats to keep their bodys warm while bringing in large fishes to sell to the merchants, Look! I see a larg white bird going on its merry way. Then I think of how great God is for he made this great sea for me to see and yet I stand on dry land and see the green and hillie side with flowers rising to the sky. How sweet and beautiful for God to have made Thuy Anh and the sea.

I interview Caroline. When she was a little girl in Arkansas, she "would   15 get off into a room by myself and read the Scripture." The "poems in King Solomon" were her favorites. She went to a segregated school and "used to write quite a bit" at home. But she "got away from it" and some years later dropped out of high school to come west to earn a living. She's worked in a convalescent hospital for twenty years, never married, wishes she had, comes, now, back to school and is finding again her love of words. "I get lost . . . I'm right in there with my writing, and I forget all my surroundings." She is classified as a basic student—no diploma, low-level employment, poor test scores—

had been taught by her grandmother that she would have to earn her living "by the sweat of my brow."

Her work in the writing course had been good up to the point of Thuy Anh's interview, better than that of many classmates, adequate, fairly free of error, pretty well organized. But the interview triggered a different level of performance. Caroline's early engagement with language reemerged in a lyrical burst: an evocation of an imagined childhood, a curious overlay of one culture's fantasy over another's harsh reality. Caroline's longing reshaped a Vietnamese girlhood, creating a life neither she nor Thuy Anh ever had, an intersection of biblical rhythms and *Father Knows Best.*

Over Chin's bent head arches a trellis packed tight with dried honeysuckle and chrysanthemum, sea moss, mushrooms, and ginseng. His elbow rests on the cash register—quiet now that the customers have left. He shifts on the stool, concentrating on the writing before him: "A young children," he scribbles, and pauses. "Young children," that doesn't sound good, he thinks. He crosses out "children" and sits back. A few seconds pass. He can't think of the right way to say it, so he writes "children" again and continues: "a young children with his grandma smail . . ." "Smail." He pulls a Chinese-English dictionary from under the counter.

In front of the counter and extending down the aisle are boxes of dried fish: shark fins, mackerel, pollock. They give off a musky smell. Behind Chin are rows of cans and jars: pickled garlic, pickled ginger, sesame paste. By the door, comic books and Chinese weeklies lean dog-eared out over the thin retaining wire of a dusty wooden display. Chin has found his word: It's not *smail,* it's *smile.* "A young children with his grandma smile. . . ." He reaches in the pocket of his jeans jacket, pulls out a piece of paper, and unfolds it. There's a word copied on it he has been wanting to use. A little bell over the door jingles. An old man comes in, and Chin moves his yellow pad aside.

Chin remembers his teacher in elementary school telling him that his writing was poor, that he didn't know many words. He went to middle school for a few years but quit before completing it. Very basic English—the ABCs and simple vocabulary—was, at one point, part of his curriculum, but he lived in a little farming community, so he figured he would never use it. He did, though, pick up some letters and a few words. He immigrated to America when he was seventeen, and for the two years since has been living with his uncle in Chinatown. His uncle signed him up for English classes at the community center. He didn't like them. He did, however, start hanging out in the recreation room, playing pool and watching TV. The English on TV intrigued him. And it was then that he turned to writing. He would "try to learn to speak something" by writing it down. That was about six months ago. Now he's enrolled in a community college literacy program and has been making strong progress. He is especially taken with one tutor, a woman in her mid-thirties who encourages him to write. So he writes for her. He writes stories about his childhood in China. He sneaks time when no one is in the store or when customers are poking around, writing because he likes to bring her things, writing, too, because "sometime I think writing make my English better."

The old man puts on the counter a box of tea guaranteed to help you 20 stop smoking. Chin rings it up and thanks him. The door jingles and Chin returns to his writing, copying the word from his folded piece of paper, a word he found in *People* magazine: "A young children with his grandma smile *gleefully*."

Frank Marell, born Meraglio, my oldest uncle, learned his English as Chin is learning his. He came to America with his mother and three sisters in September 1921. They came to join my grandfather who had immigrated long before. They joined, as well, the millions of Italian peasants who had flowed through Customs with their cloth-and-paper suitcases, their strange gestural language, and their dark, empty pockets. Frank was about to turn eight when he immigrated, so he has faint memories of Calabria. They lived in a one-room stone house. In the winter, the family's scrawny milk cow was brought inside. By the door there was a small hole for a rifle barrel. Wolves came out of the hills. He remembers the frost and burrs stinging his feet as he foraged the countryside for berries and twigs and fresh grass for the cow. *Chi esce riesce,* the saying went—"he who leaves succeeds"—and so it was that my grandfather left when he did, eventually finding work amid the metal and steam of the Pennsylvania Railroad.

My uncle remembers someone giving him bread on the steamship. He remembers being very sick. Once in America, he and his family moved into the company housing projects across from the stockyard. The house was dirty and had gouges in the wood. Each morning his mother had to sweep the soot from in front of the door. He remembers rats. He slept huddled with his father and mother and sisters in the living room, for his parents had to rent out the other rooms in order to buy clothes and shoes and food. Frank never attended school in Italy. He was eight now and would enter school in America. America, where eugenicists were attesting, scientifically, to the feeblemindedness of his race, where the popular press ran articles about the immorality of these swarthy exotics. Frank would enter school here. In many ways, you could lay his life like a template over a current life in the Bronx, in Houston, in Pico-Union.

He remembers the embarrassment of not understanding the teacher, of not being able to read or write. Funny clothes, oversize shoes, his hair slicked down and parted in the middle. He would lean forward—his assigned seat, fortunately, was in the back—and ask other Italian kids, ones with some English, to tell him what for the love of God was going on. He had big, sad eyes, thick hands, skin dark enough to yield the nickname Blacky. Frank remembers other boys—Carmen Santino, a kid named Hump, Bruno Tucci—who couldn't catch on to this new language and quit coming to school.

Within six months of his arrival, Frank would be going after class to the back room of Pete Mastis's Dry Cleaners and Shoeshine Parlor. He cleaned and shined shoes, learned to operate a steam press, ran deliveries. He listened to the radio, trying to mimic the harsh complexities of English. He spread Pete Mastis's racing forms out before him, copying words onto the margins of newsprint. He tried talking to the people whose shoes he was shining, exchanging tentative English with the broken English of Germans and Poles and other Italians.

Eventually, Frank taught his mother to sign her name. By the time he was in his teens, he was reading flyers and announcements of sales and legal documents to her. He was also her scribe, doing whatever writing she needed to have done. Frank found himself immersed in the circumstance of literacy.

With the lives of Mario and Caroline and Chin and Frank Marell as a   25 backdrop, I want to consider a current, very powerful set of proposals about literacy and culture.

There is a strong impulse in American education—curious in a country with such an ornery streak of antitraditionalism—to define achievement and excellence in terms of the acquisition of a historically validated body of knowledge, an authoritative list of books and allusions, a canon. We seek a certification of our national intelligence, indeed, our national virtue, in how diligently our children can display this central corpus of information. This need for certification tends to emerge most dramatically in our educational policy debates during times of real or imagined threat: economic hard times, political crises, sudden increases in immigration. Now is such a time, and it is reflected in a number of influential books and commission reports. E. D. Hirsch* argues that a core national vocabulary, one oriented toward the English literate tradition—Alice in Wonderland to zeitgeist—will build a knowledge base that will foster the literacy of all Americans. Diane Ravitch* and Chester Finn* call for a return to a traditional historical and literary curriculum: the valorous historical figures and the classical literature of the once-elite course of study. Allan Bloom,* Secretary of Education William Bennett, Mortimer Adler* and the Paideia Group, and a number of others have affirmed, each in their very different ways, the necessity of the Great Books:

E. D. Hirsch: author of *Cultural Literacy: What Every American Needs to Know,* which argues for a standard national public school curriculum that would ensure that all Americans share a common cultural vocabulary

Diane Ravitch: author of *Developing National Standards in Education* and an Education Department official in the Reagan administration

Chester Finn: undersecretary of education in the Reagan administration

Allan Bloom: author of *The Closing of the American Mind* (1987)

Mortimer Adler: educator and philosopher, author of many books, including three volumes on the Paideia Proposal, an educational framework based on ancient Greek concepts

Plato and Aristotle and Sophocles, Dante and Shakespeare and Locke, Dickens and Mann and Faulkner. We can call this orientation to educational achievement the canonical orientation.

At times in our past, the call for a shoring up of or return to a canonical curriculum was explicitly elitist, was driven by a fear that the education of the select was being compromised. Today, though, the majority of the calls are provocatively framed in the language of democracy. They assail the mediocre and grinding curriculum frequently found in remedial and vocational education. They are disdainful of the patronizing perceptions of student ability that further restrict the already restricted academic life of disadvantaged youngsters. They point out that the canon—its language, conventions, and allusions—is central to the discourse of power, and to keep it from poor kids is to assure their disenfranchisement all the more. The books of the canon, claim the proposals, the Great Books, are a window onto a common core of experience and civic ideals. There is, then, a spiritual, civic, and cognitive heritage here, and *all* our children should receive it. If we are sincere in our desire to bring Mario, Chin, the younger versions of Caroline, current incarnations of Frank Marell, and so many others who populate this book—if we truly want to bring them into our society—then we should provide them with this stable and common core. This is a forceful call. It promises a still center in a turning world.

I see great value in being challenged to think of the curriculum of the many in the terms we have traditionally reserved for the few; it is refreshing to have common assumptions about the capacities of underprepared students so boldly challenged. Many of the people we have encountered in these pages have displayed the ability to engage books and ideas thought to be beyond their grasp. There were the veterans: Willie Oates* writing, in prison, ornate sentences drawn from *The Mill on the Floss.** Sergeant Gonzalez* coming to understand poetic ambiguity in "Butch Weldy."* There was the parole aide Olga who no longer felt walled off from *Macbeth.* There were the EOP* students at UCLA, like Lucia who unpackaged *The Myth of Mental Illness* once she had an orientation and overview. And there was Frank Marell who, later in his life, would be talking excitedly to his nephew about this guy Edgar Allan Poe. Too many people are kept from the books of the canon, the Great Books, because of misjudgments about their potential. Those books eventually proved important to me, and, as best I know how, I invite my students to engage them. But once we grant the desirability of equal curricular treatment and begin to consider what this equally distributed curriculum would contain, problems arise: If the canon itself is the answer to our educational inequities,

---

Willie Oates, Sergeant Gonzalez: students in a veterans' program that Rose worked in
The Mill on the Floss: a novel (1860) by George Eliot (1819–80)
"Butch Weldy": a poem in *Spoon River Anthology* (1915) by Edgar Lee Masters (1869–1950)
EOP: Equal Opportunity Program

why has it historically invited few and denied many? Would the canonical orientation provide adequate guidance as to how a democratic curriculum should be constructed and how it should be taught? Would it guide us in opening up to Olga that "fancy talk" that so alienated her?

Those who study the way literature becomes canonized, how linguistic creations are included or excluded from a tradition, claim that the canonical curriculum students would most likely receive would not, as is claimed, offer a common core of American experience. Caroline would not find her life represented in it, nor would Mario. The canon has tended to push to the margin much of the literature of our nation: from American Indian songs and chants to immigrant fiction to working-class narratives. The institutional messages that students receive in the books they're issued and the classes they take are powerful and, as I've witnessed since my Voc. Ed. days, quickly internalized. And to revise these messages and redress past wrongs would involve more than adding some new books to the existing canon—the very reasons for linguistic and cultural exclusion would have to become a focus of study in order to make the canon act as a democratizing force. Unless this happens, the democratic intent of the reformers will be undercut by the content of the curriculum they propose.

And if we move beyond content to consider basic assumptions about teaching and learning, a further problem arises, one that involves the very nature of the canonical orientation itself. The canonical orientation encourages a narrowing of focus from learning to that which must be learned: It simplifies the dynamic tension between student and text and reduces the psychological and social dimensions of instruction. The student's personal history recedes as the what of the classroom is valorized over the how. Thus it is that the encounter of student and text is often portrayed by canonists as a transmission. Information, wisdom, virtue will pass from the book to the student if the student gives the book the time it merits, carefully traces its argument or narrative or lyrical progression. Intellectual, even spiritual, growth will *necessarily* result from an encounter with Roman mythology, *Othello,* and "I heard a Fly buzz—when I died—,"* with biographies and historical sagas and patriotic lore. Learning is stripped of confusion and discord. It is stripped, as well, of strong human connection. My own initiators to the canon—Jack MacFarland, Dr. Carothers, and the rest—knew there was more to their work than their mastery of a tradition. What mattered most, I see now, were the relationships they established with me, the guidance they provided when I felt inadequate or threatened. This mentoring was part of my entry into that solemn library of Western thought—and even with such support, there were still times of confusion, anger, and fear. It is telling, I think, that once that rich social network slid away, once I was in graduate school in intense,

30

"I heard a Fly buzz—when I died—": poem by Emily Dickinson (1830–86)

solitary encounter with that tradition, I abandoned it for other sources of nurturance and knowledge.

The model of learning implicit in the canonical orientation seems, at times, more religious than cognitive or social: Truth resides in the printed texts, and if they are presented by someone who knows them well and respects them, that truth will be revealed. Of all the advocates of the canon, Mortimer Adler has given most attention to pedagogy—and his Paideia books contain valuable discussions of instruction, coaching, and questioning. But even here, and this is doubly true in the other manifestos, there is little acknowledgement that the material in the canon can be not only difficult but foreign, alienating, overwhelming.

We need an orientation to instruction that provides guidance on how to determine and honor the beliefs and stories, enthusiasms, and apprehensions that students reveal. How to build on them, and when they clash with our curriculum—as I saw so often in the Tutorial Center at UCLA—when they clash, how to encourage a discussion that will lead to reflection on what students bring and what they're currently confronting. Canonical lists imply canonical answers, but the manifestos offer little discussion of what to do when students fail. If students have been exposed to at least some elements of the canon before—as many have—why didn't it take? If they're encountering it for the first time and they're lost, how can we determine where they're located—and what do we do then?

Each member of a teacher's class, poor *or* advantaged, gives rise to endless decisions, day-to-day determinations about a child's reading and writing: decisions on how to tap strength, plumb confusion, foster growth. The richer your conception of learning and your understanding of its social and psychological dimensions, the more insightful and effective your judgments will be. Consider the sources of literacy we saw among the children in El Monte: shopkeepers' signs, song lyrics, auto manuals, the conventions of the Western, family stories and tales, and more. Consider Chin's sources—television and *People* magazine—and Caroline's oddly generative mix of the Bible and an American media illusion. Then there's the jarring confluence of personal horror and pop cultural flotsam that surfaces in Mario's drawings, drawings that would be a rich, if volatile, point of departure for language instruction. How would these myriad sources and manifestations be perceived and evaluated if viewed within the framework of a canonical tradition, and what guidance would the tradition provide on how to understand and develop them? The great books and central texts of the canon could quickly become a benchmark against which the expressions of student literacy would be negatively measured, a limiting band of excellence that, ironically, could have a dispiriting effect on the very thing the current proposals intend: the fostering of mass literacy.

To understand the nature and development of literacy we need to consider the social context in which it occurs—the political, economic, and cultural forces that encourage or inhibit it. The canonical orientation discourages deep analysis of the way these forces may be affecting performance. The canonists ask that schools transmit a coherent traditional knowledge to an ever-changing, frequently uprooted community. This discordance between message and audience is seldom examined. Although a ghetto child can rise on the lilt of a Homeric line—books *can* spark dreams—appeals to elevated texts can also divert attention from the conditions that keep a population from realizing its dreams. The literacy curriculum is being asked to do what our politics and our economics have failed to do: diminish differences in achievement, narrow our gaps, bring us together. Instead of analysis of the complex web of causes of poor performance, we are offered a faith in the unifying power of a body of knowledge, whose infusion will bring the rich and the poor, the longtime disaffected and the uprooted newcomers into cultural unanimity. If this vision is democratic, it is simplistically so, reductive, not an invitation for people truly to engage each other at the point where cultures and classes intersect.

I worry about the effects a canonical approach to education could have on   35
cultural dialogue and transaction—on the involvement of an abandoned underclass and on the movement of immigrants like Mario and Chin into our nation. A canonical uniformity promotes rigor and quality control; it can also squelch new thinking, diffuse the generative tension between the old and the new. It is significant that the canonical orientation is voiced with most force during times of challenge and uncertainty, for it promises the authority of tradition, the seeming stability of the past. But the authority is fictive, gained from a misreading of American cultural history. No period of that history was harmoniously stable; the invocation of a golden age is a mythologizing act. Democratic culture is, by definition, vibrant and dynamic, discomforting and unpredictable. It gives rise to apprehension; freedom is not always calming. And, yes, it can yield fragmentation, though often as not the source of fragmentation is intolerant misunderstanding of diverse traditions rather than the desire of members of those traditions to remain hermetically separate. A truly democratic vision of knowledge and social structure would honor this complexity. The vision might not be soothing, but it would provide guidance as to how to live and teach in a country made up of many cultural traditions.

We are in the middle of an extraordinary social experiment: the attempt to provide education for all members of a vast pluralistic democracy. To have any prayer of success, we'll need many conceptual blessings: A philosophy of language and literacy that affirms the diverse sources of linguistic competence and deepens our understanding of the ways class and culture blind us to the richness of those sources. A perspective on failure that lays open the logic of error. An orientation toward the interaction of poverty and ability that undercuts simple polarities, that enables us to see simultaneously the constraints poverty places on the play of mind and the actual mind at play within those constraints. We'll need a pedagogy that encourages us to step back and consider the threat of the standard classroom and that shows us, having stepped back, how to step forward to invite a student across the boundaries of that powerful room. Finally, we'll need a revised store of images of educational excellence, ones closer to egalitarian ideals—ones that embody the reward and turmoil of education in a democracy, that celebrate the plural, messy human reality of it. At heart, we'll need a guiding set of principles that do not encourage us to retreat from, but move us closer to, an understanding of the rich mix of speech and ritual and story that is America.

QUESTIONING THE TEXT

1. What do you think Rose means when he says that "a failed education is social more than intellectual in origin"? Look back to A.L.'s profile on p. 105. Does anything there suggest a time when her education failed for social—or intellectual—reasons? Describe a time when your education failed—or succeeded—largely because of social reasons. If you keep a reading log, record your answers there.

2. Rose quotes a friend who says that education can be thought of as "one culture embracing another." Give a few examples from his essay that illustrate this embrace, and then give an example from your own educational experience.

3. Why do you think Rose includes the stories of Mario, Caroline, Chin, and Frank Marell as a backdrop for his discussion about current concepts of literacy in America? What do their stories have in common? What kinds of students does he leave unmentioned?

MAKING CONNECTIONS

4. Imagine Rose responding to Jeffrey Hart's arguments (p. 126) about what a university should teach the students he's concerned with. What would Rose and Hart agree on? Where would they disagree—and why?

5. Spend some time thinking about one of the students Rose describes. Then write a brief poem (using Gwendolyn Brooks as a model, perhaps; see p. 133) that characterizes that student's attitude toward school.

JOINING THE CONVERSATION

6. Try to remember a time when your relationship with someone (teacher, parent, coach, religious leader) made it easier (or harder) for you to learn what that person was trying to teach you. Write a brief description

of this event for your class, concluding by summarizing those things about another person that most *help* you to learn from him or her.

7. Rose remembers that his earliest interest in literacy came from "comic books and science fiction, from the personal, nonscientific worlds I created with bits and pieces of laboratory and telescopic technology, came, as well, from the Italian stories I heard my uncles and parents tell." Brainstorm with two or three other students about your earliest out-of-school experiences with reading and writing. How were they like or unlike your experiences of reading and writing in school?

DAVID THOMAS
The Mind of Man

*M*OST STUDIES THAT COMPARE *the academic performances of boys and girls focus on the one or two areas where males routinely outperform females, usually in mathematics and in the perception of spatial relationships. We are advised, as a result of such revelations, that society needs to do more to close the gaps between male and female accomplishment. All but ignored in press accounts and accompanying editorials are the other halves of those studies, the realms of achievement where young women decisively outperform young men, as if male deficiencies—for example, in verbal skills—were natural and beyond remediation.*

So it's a crisis requiring immediate attention (and funding) when Sam does better than Suzie in geometry, but it seems not to matter that she reads and writes better than he and probably possesses better study skills and more positive attitudes toward learning.

Even at the college level, researchers in rhetoric and composition rarely address the writing difficulties of young men, problems that women as a group seem not to have. This persistent male/female difference intrigues scholars much less than do more politically fashionable issues—such as why men supposedly dominate class discussions, including those on computer networks. Even in college, getting boys to behave seems to concern some academics more than teaching them something.

Am I making this up? Read the following essay by David Thomas (b. 1959) from his book Not Guilty *(1993). You'll discover that boys have trouble getting fair treatment in schools not only in the United States but also in Britain, where single-sex education—one potential solution to disparities experienced by both sexes in educational achievement—has been more common than it has been here. David Thomas is a writer and journalist who served for a time (1989–92) as editor of the famous English periodical* Punch.

—J.R.

An old calypso song states that "Man Smart, Woman Smarter," but it is generally agreed by most researchers that men and women are indivisible in terms of their average overall intelligence. In *A Question of Sex*, Dr. John Nicholson summarizes the history of research into intelligence, much of which had presumed the intellectual superiority of men. He concludes with a sentence from which there has been little subsequent dissent: "The most important fact is that men are not more intelligent than women—the average man's IQ score is indistinguishable from that of the average woman." Yet, as Dr. Nicholson points out with the aid of a few simple experiments, the sexes do differ in the types of mental tasks at which they excel.

In the words of a *Time* magazine cover story, published in January 1992, "Psychology tests consistently support the notion that men and women perceive the world in subtly different ways. Males excel at rotating three-dimensional objects in their head. Females prove better at reading the emotions of people in photographs. A growing number of scientists believe the discrepancies reflect functional differences in the brains of men and women . . . some misunderstandings between the sexes may have more to do with crossed wiring than cross-purposes."

Women are also better at verbal tasks. If given two minutes in which to come up with as many synonyms as possible for a series of words, they will, on the whole, score better than men. In both of these tests, however, some individuals will do much better or worse than their sex suggests that they "ought" to.

Do we, however, make the best of what nature has provided when the time comes to educate our young? Over the last few years, nationwide school exam results have shown an increasing gap between the performances of girls and boys, in the girls' favor. Many more boys than girls leave school without any form of qualification. And amongst those who do pass GCSE and A-Level exams, girls are getting the higher grades. The introduction of course work into the GCSE syllabus appears to favor girls, who tend to be diligent and less rebellious. Boys appear to prefer the one-off competition of the examination hall. These preferences may be due, in part, to differences in the male and female brain, which will be discussed anon. However, since white working-class boys now score more poorly in England and Wales than almost any other racial or sexual grouping, and since highly privileged public schoolboys can be coached and coaxed into achieving astonishingly high marks, the possibility must be considered that there are social forces at work.

Much has been written in the past about the difficulties girls face in mixed   5 classrooms. It has always been assumed that boys tend to speak up more forcefully than girls, and tend to be spoken to more frequently by teachers. If so, this reflects life in society as a whole. In both Britain and America, researchers have found that a woman who speaks as much as a man in a conversation, class or meeting will be thought, by both male and female observers, to have been hectoring and domineering: we are, quite simply, used to men taking the lion's share of conversation.

Recently, however, suggestions have been made that question this view of the classroom. At kindergarten and primary-school level, in which little girls out-perform the boys, the vast majority of teachers are female. Surveys by the now-defunct Inner London Education Authority showed that women teachers consistently praised girls more than boys, and equally consistently criticized the boys' behavior, often regarding it as a serious problem requiring remedial treatment. In the words of Tony Mooney, a secondary-school headmaster, writing in the *Independent on Sunday:* "Women teachers find boys too noisy, too aggressive, too boisterous. Unconsciously or not, they consistently reinforce and reward more 'feminine' behavior. If all this is true, it is understandable that boys should not be as advanced as girls in the hands of women junior school teachers. There is a direct relationship between a child's academic achievement and a favorable response from the teacher."

Mooney was first alerted to this possibility by the behavior of his own son, whose performance and self-confidence at school altered markedly when he was taught by a woman, rather than a man. When the boy's mother asked him why this should be so, he replied, "Because the men teachers never shout at me as much as the women teachers."

Research evidence, from an experiment at the University of California, Los Angeles, appeared to support Mooney's anecdotal experience: "Seventy-two boys and sixty girls at kindergarten . . . learned reading with a self-teaching machine. There were no differences between the sexes in their reactions to the mechanical gadgetry. Yet when the girls were tested on their reading progress they scored lower than the boys. Then the children were placed under the normal classroom instruction of women teachers. The children were tested again on the words they had been taught by the teacher. This time the boys' scores were inferior to the girls'."

Mooney noted that boys' exam results at secondary-school were declining just as the number of women secondary-school teachers was increasing. Boys, however, continued to out-perform girls in scientific and technical subjects where teaching was still dominated by men. The issue here is not just the favoritism that teachers may show to pupils of their own sex, but the instinctive understanding that an adult will enjoy with a child who is going through a process which he or she went through too.

The notion that boys might in some way be disadvantaged was too   10
shocking for at least one reader of Mooney's article. As far as Christine Cosker—a correspondent to the *Independent on Sunday*'s letters page—was concerned, it was partly the fault of the boys themselves. "If girls achieve higher standards than boys," she wrote, "it is not the result of sympathetic female teachers: it is that boys fail to be motivated because of their attitude to women. Boys' early experience is almost entirely one of a society which regards women's traditional roles as trivial, dull and second-rate and dismisses their opinions. If girls have a positive role model in the female teacher, they will do better than boys. But if boys, unencumbered by society's prejudices, valued their female teachers, then their progress would match that of girls."

It is worth examining some of the prejudices revealed by this letter in some detail, because I suspect that they would be shared by a broad swathe of supposedly progressive opinion.

In the first place, note that she has found it impossible to accept that female teachers could, in any way, be responsible for the situation. It has to be the fault of males and an anti-female social order. Specifically, boys are to be blamed for their own disadvantages.

Secondly, she has misinterpreted the article. Mr. Mooney indicated that his son's problem was not that he did not value his teacher, but that she did not value him. He was frightened of her because she shouted at him.

Thirdly, although it is extremely important to primary-school-aged boys not to be seen to act in any way that might be interpreted as cissy or girly, that is not necessarily to say that they regard women's traditional roles as "trivial, dull and second-rate." The most traditional role that women have is to be a mother. And the mother of a small boy is still one of the two most important people in his life. In the experience of most "traditional" housewives I know, it is other, career-minded women who hold them in the greatest contempt. Their children value them above all else.

Finally, observe the double standard applied to girls and boys. Cosker   15 maintains, and few would disagree, that girls benefit from a "positive role model." There is, however, no need for boys to be given the same benefit. Instead, they must pull their socks up and change their attitudes. Heaven forbid that they should be given any consideration or compassion. Heaven forbid that the prejudices of the new age should be challenged. If you ever doubted that feminists have taken over from apoplectic old colonels as the great reactionaries of society, just read this letter.

Alternatively, look at the facts. One of the few generally accepted differences between boys and girls is that boys are, across all cultures, much more boisterous and overtly competitive than girls. Boys enjoy games of rough and tumble. They play with guns, real or imaginary. They seek out physical competition, whether through sport or informal bouts of playground warfare. This makes them harder to control than girls, particularly if, as is the case in the majority of state primary schools in this country, they are being taught in an open-plan classroom. Janet Daley, writing in the *Independent,* has observed that "Anyone who visits an open-plan infant-school classroom, where the children organize much of their own time, will notice a pattern. Groups of little girls will be absorbed in quite orderly work or play . . . requiring little supervision. A few of the boys will be engrossed in solitary creative or constructive activity. A large number of children will be noisily participating in some loosely directed project which needs guidance and some of those will be boys who are persistently disruptive and out of control."

Daley ascribes this behavior to the fact that the neurological development of boys is slower than that of girls, and thus boys are "physically and mentally unstable for much of their childhood and adolescence." Are they? Or does Ms. Daley share a prejudice—unintended, no doubt—with the boys' teachers, who are trained to define the relative maturity of their charges by their ability to sit quietly and be attentive? By those standards, boys may appear backward, troublesome and even threatening. All that has happened, however, is that we are criticizing boys for their failure to be more like girls.

It has for some time been recognized that girls do better in single-sex education, where their particular needs can be catered for exclusively. Having spent ten years in single-sex boarding-school education, I have mixed feelings about its benefits for boys, but I am absolutely certain that there are great social benefits to be had from recognizing that boys may need specially tailored treatment to at least as great an extent as their sisters (a point with which Janet Daley concurs).

In the years before puberty, boys are, I suspect, perfectly happy to be left to themselves. At the age of eleven or twelve, I doubt whether I would have been at all pleased to see girls getting in the way of my games of football, or intruding in the serious business of building huts and encampments in the woods behind the school. By my teens, however, I was painfully aware of the distorting effect that an all-male institution was having on my own emotional development and that of my classmates.

Despite that, however, I was taught in a system that was designed to bring   20 the best out of boys, intellectually, creatively and on the sports field. It was certainly a world away from the non-achieving atmosphere that has been prevalent throughout much of English state education over the last twenty years. Of course, the boys with whom I was educated came from privileged backgrounds. But one of the mistakes made by critics of the public-school system is to underestimate the efficiency, not to say ruthlessness, with which its pupils are programmed to perform to the best of their ability. We were constantly tested, constantly ranked and constantly urged to do better. And, on reflection, I suspect that it is better to accept that boys are not, on the whole, docile creatures who wish to live in harmony with one another, but are, instead, highly competitive, physically energetic creatures who hunt in packs.

Some boys will suffer in that sort of environment, and they need to be respected and protected. I can remember all too well what it is like to be on the receiving end of bullying and oppression. But I also know that there is no point in deciding that, since traditional male behavior is politically unacceptable, boys must somehow be conditioned to behave in ways that are not natural to them. That process leads only to disaster.

Boys whose lives are led without structure and discipline do not find themselves liberated. Instead they become bored, frustrated and maladaptive. They fight. They misbehave and they perform badly, both at school and thereafter. However much it might want boys to change, any society that wants to limit the antisocial behavior of young men should start by accepting the way they are. Then it should do everything possible to make sure that their energies are directed towards good, rather than evil. When Yoda sat on his rock in *The Empire Strikes Back* and told Luke Skywalker that he had to choose between the dark force and the light, he knew what he was talking about.

QUESTIONING THE TEXT

1. Men and women differ, according to Thomas, in "the types of mental tasks at which they excel." Research this claim to determine the nature and quality of these differences—or whether they exist at all. Then dis-

cuss your reaction to the situation, focusing on the consequences any difference might have for educational policy.

2. Annotate places in Thomas's text where you notice a difference between the British educational system that he describes and the educational system that you know. How do the differences affect the way you ought to regard his claims?

3. Have you read claims like those discussed in J.R.'s introduction that girls are not treated equally in school? Have you ever read reports on the problems boys have getting fair treatment? What kinds of coverage do boys get in the media today, and why?

MAKING CONNECTIONS

4. Does the situation of young males in the educational system Thomas describes in any way resemble that of young females as described by Adrienne Rich (p. 65)? Freewrite on this subject; don't hesitate to explore differences as well.

JOINING THE CONVERSATION

5. In a group of men and women, discuss single-sex education. Then write a report that weighs the advantages and disadvantages of segregating boys and girls at the elementary, secondary, or college level.

6. Write a narrative about an incident in your school experience that revealed differences in the way teachers treated girls and boys.

JEFFREY HART
How to Get a College Education

HAVE YOU EVER THOUGHT ABOUT changing your major or your course of study? Almost everyone pursuing a degree or certificate does—the engineer considering the arts, the literature major sampling business courses, the hopeful linguist developing a fondness for calculus. To a remarkable degree, most educational institutions in the United States allow students to choose their course of study, especially after satisfying a few basic requirements, typically in English, mathematics, languages, and, perhaps, the sciences. But are college students—especially those right out of high school—really prepared to select classes that, taken together, would enable them to grasp, in John Henry Newman's words, "the great outlines of knowledge, the principles on which it rests, the scale of its parts, its lights and its shades, its great points and its little"?

Most faculty and even first-year students themselves might sheepishly say no. But then Newman's goals for liberal education are shared by few institutions, instructors, and undergraduates today. As any survey of university mission statements will attest (see p. 51), higher education serves diverse purposes and audiences, so many now that it is not surprising if students themselves are often confused and occasionally overwhelmed by the choices they are asked to make. Allan Bloom (1930–92), a spirited critic of higher education with little love for smorgasbord-style curricula, suggests in his The Closing of the American Mind *(1987) that it is precisely "[t]his undecided student [who] is an embarrassment to most universities, because he seems to be saying, 'I am a whole human being. Help me to form myself in my wholeness and let me develop my real potential,' and he is the one to whom they have nothing to say."*

In "How to Get a College Education," Jeffrey Hart, Professor Emeritus at Dartmouth College and intellectual confederate of Bloom, offers some advice for the befuddled student on picking majors and courses. You may be surprised at the political tone of Hart's essay, but of course, college curricula do reflect the ideologies of the faculty, and students need to understand that fact. Hart's essay originally appeared in a 1996 "Back to School" edition of National Review, *a journal of conservative opinion published by William F. Buckley.*   —J.R.

It was in the fall term of 1988 that the truth burst in upon me that something had gone terribly wrong in higher education. It was like the anecdote in Auden where the guest at a garden party, sensing something amiss, suddenly realizes that there is a corpse on the tennis court.

As a professor at Dartmouth, my hours had been taken up with my own writing, and with teaching a variety of courses—a yearly seminar, a yearly freshman composition course (which—some good news—all senior professors in the Dartmouth English Department are required to teach), and courses in my eighteenth-century specialty. Oh, I knew that the larger curriculum lacked shape and purpose, that something was amiss; but I deferred thinking about it.

Yet there does come that moment.

It came for me in the freshman composition course. The students were required to write essays based upon assigned reading—in this case, some Frost poems, Hemingway's *In Our Time, Hamlet.* Then, almost on a whim, I assigned the first half of Allan Bloom's new surprise best-seller *The Closing of the American Mind.*

When the time came to discuss the Bloom book, I asked them what 5 they thought of it.

They hated it.

Oh, yes, they understood perfectly well what Bloom was saying: that they were ignorant, that they believed in clichés, that their education so far had been dangerous piffle and that what they were about to receive was not likely to be any better.

No wonder they hated it. After all, they were the best and the brightest, Ivy Leaguers with stratospheric SAT scores, the Masters of the Universe. Who is Bloom? What is the University of Chicago, anyway?

So I launched into an impromptu oral quiz.

Could anyone (in that class of 25 students) say anything about the May- 10 flower Compact?

Complete silence.

John Locke?

Nope.

James Madison?

Silentia. 15

Magna Carta? The Spanish Armada? The Battle of Yorktown? The Bull Moose party? *Don Giovanni?* William James? The Tenth Amendment?

Zero. Zilch. Forget it.

The embarrassment was acute, but some good came of it. The better students, ashamed that their first 12 years of schooling had mostly been wasted (even if they had gone to Choate or Exeter), asked me to recommend some books. I offered such solid things as Samuel Eliot Morison's *Oxford History of the United States,* Max Farrand's *The Framing of the Constitution,* Jacob Burckhardt's *The Civilization of the Renaissance in Italy.* Several students asked for an informal discussion group, and so we started reading a couple of Dante's Cantos per week, Dante being an especially useful author because he casts his net so widely—the ancient world, the (his) modern world, theology, history, ethics.

I quickly became aware of the utter bewilderment of entering freshmen. They emerge from the near-nullity of K–12 and stroll into the chaos of the Dartmouth curriculum, which is embodied in a course catalogue about as large as a telephone directory.

Sir, what courses should I take? 20

A college like Dartmouth—or Harvard, Princeton, etc.—has require-ments so broadly defined that almost anything goes for degree credit. Of course, freshmen are assigned faculty "advisors," but most of them would rather return to the library or the Bunsen burner.

Thus it developed that I began giving an annual lecture to incoming freshmen on the subject, "What Is a College Education? And How to Get One, Even at Dartmouth."

One long-term reason why the undergraduate curriculum at Dartmouth and all comparable institutions is in chaos is specialization. Since World War II, success as a professor has depended increasingly on specialized publication. The ambitious and talented professor is not eager to give introductory or gen-eral courses. Indeed, his work has little or nothing to do with undergraduate teaching. Neither Socrates nor Jesus, who published nothing, could possibly receive tenure at a first-line university today.

But in addition to specialization, recent intellectual fads have done ex-traordinary damage, viz.:

—So-called Post-Modernist thought ("deconstruction," etc.) asserts that   25
one "text" is as much worth analyzing as any other, whether it be a movie, a comic book, or Homer. The lack of a "canon" of important works leads to course offerings in, literally, anything.

—"Affirmative Action" is not just a matter of skewed admissions and hiring, but also a mentality or ethos. That is, if diversity is more important than quality in admissions and hiring, why should it not be so in the curricu-lum? Hence the courses in things like Nicaraguan Lesbian Poetry.

—Concomitantly, ideology has been imposed on the curriculum to a startling degree. In part this represents a sentimental attempt to resuscitate Marxism, with assorted Victim Groups standing in for the old Proletariat; in part it is a new Identity Politics in which being Black, Lesbian, Latino, Ho-mosexual, Radical Feminist, and so forth takes precedence over any scholarly pursuit. These Victimologies are usually presented as "Studies" programs out-side the regular departments, so as to avoid the usual academic standards. Yet their course offerings carry degree credit.

On an optimistic note, I think that most or all of Post-Modernism, the Affirmative Action/Multicultural ethos, and the Victimologies will soon pass from the scene. The great institutions have a certain sense of self-preservation. Harvard almost lost its Law School to a Marxist faculty faction, but then cleaned house. Tenure will keep the dead men walking for another twenty years or so, but then we will have done with them.

But for the time being, what these fads have done to the liberal-arts and social-sciences curriculum since around 1968 is to clutter it with all sorts of nonsense, nescience, and distraction. The entering student needs to be wary lest he waste his time and his parents' money and come to consider all higher education an outrageous fraud. The good news is that the wise student can still get a college education today, even at Dartmouth, Harvard, Yale, and Princeton.

Of course the central question is one of *telos,* or goal. What is the   30
liberal-arts education supposed to produce? Once you have the answer to this question, course selection becomes easy.

I mean to answer that question here. But first, I find that undergraduates and their third-mortgaged parents appreciate some practical tips, such as:

Select the "ordinary" courses. I use *ordinary* here in a paradoxical and challenging way. An *ordinary* course is one that has always been taken and obviously should be taken—even if the student is not yet equipped with a sophisticated rationale for so doing. The student should be discouraged from putting his money on the cutting edge of interdisciplinary cross-textuality.

Thus, do take American and European history, an introduction to philosophy, American and European literature, the Old and New Testaments, and at least one modern language. It would be absurd not to take a course in Shakespeare, the best poet in our language. There is art and music history. The list can be expanded, but these areas every educated person should have a decent knowledge of—with specialization coming later on.

I hasten to add that I applaud the student who devotes his life to the history of China or Islam, but that too should come later. America is part of the narrative of European history.

If the student should seek out those "ordinary" courses, then it follows   35
that he should avoid the flashy come-ons. Avoid things like Nicaraguan Lesbian Poets. Yes, and anything listed under "Studies," any course whose description uses the words "interdisciplinary," "hegemonic," "phallocratic," or "empowerment," anything that mentions "keeping a diary," any course with a title like "Adventures in Film."

Also, any male professor who comes to class without a jacket and tie should be regarded with extreme prejudice unless he has won a Nobel Prize.

All these are useful rules of thumb. A theoretical rationale for a liberal-arts education, however, derives from that *telos* mentioned above. What is such an education supposed to produce?

A philosophy professor I studied with as an undergraduate had two phrases he repeated so often that they stay in the mind, a technique made famous by Matthew Arnold.

He would say, *"History must be told."*

History, he explained, is to a civilization what memory is to an individ-   40
ual, an irreducible part of identity.

He also said, *"The goal of education is to produce the citizen."* He defined the citizen as the person who, if need be, could re-create his civilization.

Now, it is said that Goethe was the last man who knew all the aspects of his civilization (I doubt that he did), but that after him things became too complicated. My professor had something different in mind. He meant that the citizen should know the great themes of his civilization, its important areas of thought, its philosophical and religious controversies, the outline of its history and its major works. The citizen need not know quantum physics, but he should know that it is there and what it means. Once the citizen knows the shape, the narrative, of his civilization, he is able to locate new things—and other civilizations—in relation to it.

The narrative of Western civilization can be told in different ways, but a useful paradigm has often been called "Athens and Jerusalem." Broadly construed, "Athens" means a philosophical and scientific view of actuality and "Jerusalem" a spiritual and scriptural one. The working out of Western civilization represents an interaction—tension, fusion, conflict—between the two.

Both Athens and Jerusalem have a heroic, or epic, phase. For Athens, the Homeric poems are a kind of scripture, the subject of prolonged ethical meditation. In time the old heroic ideals are internalized as heroic philosophy in Socrates, Plato, and Aristotle.

For Jerusalem, the heroic phase consists of the Hebrew narratives. Here   45 again, a process of internalization occurs, Jesus internalizing the Mosaic Law. Socrates is the heroic philosopher, Jesus the ideal of heroic holiness, both new ideals in their striking intensity.

During the first century of the Christian Era, Athens and Jerusalem converge under the auspices of Hellenistic thought, most notably in Paul and in John, whose gospel defined Jesus by using the Greek term for order, *Logos*.

Athens and Jerusalem were able to converge, despite great differences, because in some ways they overlap. The ultimate terms of Socrates and Plato, for example, cannot be entirely derived from reason. The god of Plato and Aristotle is monotheistic, though still the god of the philosophers. Yet Socrates considers that his rational universe dictates personal immortality.

In the Hebrew epic, there are hints of a law prior to the Law of revelation and derived from reason. Thus, when Abraham argues with God over the fate of Sodom and Gomorrah, Abraham appeals to a known principle of justice which God also assumes.

Thus Athens is not pure reason and Jerusalem not pure revelation. Both address the perennial question of why there is something rather than nothing.

From the prehistoric figures in Homer and in Genesis—Achilles,   50 Abraham—the great conversation commences. Thucydides and Virgil seek order in history. St. Augustine tries to synthesize Paul and Platonism. Montaigne's skepticism would never have been articulated without a prior assertion of cosmic order. Erasmus believed Christianity would prevail if only it could be put in the purest Latin. Shakespeare made a world, and transcended Lear's storm with that final calmed and sacramental Tempest. Rousseau would not have proclaimed the goodness of man if Calvin had not said the opposite. Dante held all the contradictions together in a total structure—for a glorious moment. Kafka could not see beyond the edges of his nightmare, but Dostoyevsky found love just beyond the lowest point of sin. The eighteenth-century men of reason knew the worst, and settled for the luminous stability of a bourgeois republic.

By any intelligible standard the other great civilization was China, yet it lacked the Athens–Jerusalem tension and dynamism. Much more static, its symbols were the Great Wall and the Forbidden City, not Odysseus/Columbus, Chartres, the Empire State Building, the love that moves the sun and the other stars.

When undergraduates encounter the material of our civilization—that is, the liberal arts—then they know that they are going somewhere. They are becoming citizens.

QUESTIONING THE TEXT

1. In "How to Get a College Education," Hart specifically mentions that he is a senior professor in the English Department at Dartmouth College. How does this information shape your response to the essay? What other information about the author do you learn from the piece? Imagine how you might respond differently if the essay (or one like it) were written by a student at a college or university.

2. Early in the essay (paragraphs 10–16), Hart lists persons, places, and things that no one in his first-year composition class can identify, including the Mayflower Compact, James Madison, and the Spanish Armada. Working in a group, review the list and, if necessary, research all the items Hart mentions. Then decide whether you agree that students beginning college should recognize these things. Be prepared to explain why, or why not.

3. Hart describes college curricula as "in chaos." What does he seem to dislike about college courses today? Does his description jibe with your own experiences so far in college? Why, or why not?

MAKING CONNECTIONS

4. In "Learning in the Key of Life" (p. 58), Jon Spayde complains that "our educations didn't prepare us for the world we're living in today." Read Spayde's essay carefully and then decide whether he is diagnosing the same problem Hart outlines or whether the two authors see American education in different ways.

5. How do you respond to Hart's characterization of college courses with the term "Studies" in their title as "Victimologies"? Review Adrienne

Rich's "What Does a Woman Need to Know?" (p. 65) and freewrite on how she might defend Women's Studies programs against Hart's charge.

JOINING THE CONVERSATION

6. Hart offers students specific advice about choosing college courses and instructors, even warning against male professors who teach without jackets and ties. Review Hart's advice. Then, drawing from your admittedly more limited experience, write a position paper in which you offer similar advice to fellow college students or to high school seniors thinking about college.

7. Write an exploratory essay on the phrase Hart learned from one of his undergraduate instructors: "'*The goal of education is to produce the citizen.*'" In the essay, you might want to draw on other essays in this collection, especially those by John Henry Newman (p. 46), Jon Spayde (p. 58), Adrienne Rich (p. 65), Mike Rose (p. 105), and Peter J. Gomes (p. 205).

8. In a comparison or contrast essay of your own, analyze some items of contemporary culture and/or education in terms of the "Athens–Jerusalem tension and dynamism" that Hart explains in the final paragraphs of "How to Get a College Education." Consider applying his analysis of that tension to works from contemporary popular culture or even to politics.

GWENDOLYN BROOKS
We Real Cool

W<small>HEN</small> G<small>WENDOLYN</small> B<small>ROOKS</small> *(b. 1917) was a little girl, her mother said "You're going to be the first lady Paul Laurence Dunbar," a powerful and well-known black poet. Brooks met her mother's challenge and then some, becoming the first African American writer to win the Pulitzer Prize (for* Annie Allen *in 1950) and the first African American woman to be elected to the National Institute of Arts and Letters or to serve as Consultant in Poetry to the Library of Congress. A 1936 graduate of Chicago's Wilson Junior College, Brooks has received over seventy honorary degrees.*

In her most distinguished career, Brooks has drawn on the traditions of African American sermons and musical forms—especially the blues, jazz, and the spiritual—to explore the American condition and, in particular, the realities of African American life. Her brief poem "We Real Cool" depicts a group of young hookey players who have rejected—or been rejected by—their schools. This is the first poem by Brooks I ever read, and it inspired me to seek out her other poetry and prose and to be a lifelong fan of her work. It also made me think about what my life would have been like if I had "left school."

—A.L.

> *The Pool Players.*
> *Seven at the Golden Shovel.*

We real cool. We
Left school. We

Lurk late. We
Strike straight. We

Sing sin. We
Thin gin. We

Jazz June. We
Die soon.

IN RESPONSE

1. What message do you take away from Brooks's poem? In what ways does it speak personally to you? If you keep a reading log, answer this question there.

2. How do you think the students in the reading by Mike Rose (p. 105) might respond to the poem?

3. Brooks's poem was written in 1960, and it refers to and uses the style of an even earlier jazz tradition. Write your own contemporary version of "We Real Cool," calling on present-day styles of music and culture to do so.

OTHER READINGS

hooks, bell. "Eros, Eroticism, and the Pedagogical Process." *Teaching to Transgress: Education as the Practice of Freedom.* New York: Routledge, 1994. Argues for the centrality of the body and the importance of passion in teaching.

Kolodny, Annette. *Failing the Future: A Dean Looks at Higher Education in the Twenty-first Century.* Durham, NC: Duke UP, 1998. Explores the current problems in higher education and offers practical solutions and workable programs for change.

Kors, Alan Charles, and Harvey A. Silverglate. *The Shadow University: The Betrayal of Liberty on America's Campuses.* New York: Free, 1998. Argues that universities have become the enemy of American traditions of freedom.

McNamara, Patrick H. "All Is Not Lost: Teaching Generation X." *Commonweal* 21 Apr. 1995. Reports that teaching the traditional Western canon works with students today.

Orenstein, Peggy. *School Girls: Young Women, Self-Esteem, and the Confidence Gap.* New York: Doubleday, 1994. Explores issues of self-esteem among female adolescents.

Pratt, Mary Louise. "Humanities for the Future: Reflections on the Western Culture Debate at Stanford." *South Atlantic Quarterly* 89.1 (Winter 1990): 7–25. On revising the Stanford humanities course to include more on cultural diversity.

Rorty, Richard. "The Unpatriotic Academy." *New York Times* 13 Feb. 1994: E15. Urges leftist academics to consider the virtues of patriotism.

Rose, Mike. *Possible Lives: The Promise of Public Education in America.* New York: Houghton, 1995. Provides a richly detailed account of what goes on in good classrooms around the country.

Sowell, Thomas. *Inside American Education: The Decline, the Deception, the Dogmas.* New York: Free, 1993. Finds failure and corruption in the American educational establishment.

ELECTRONIC RESOURCES

http://www.clas.ufl.edu/CLAS/american-universities.html

Lists Web sites for many American colleges and universities.

http://chronicle.merit.edu/

Outlines the content of current issues of a weekly newspaper covering higher education issues.

http://www.mcli.dist.maricopa.edu/cc/

Lists Web sites for many two-year schools.

Look carefully at the photograph on the preceding page, which shows Elizabeth Eckford, an African American teenager, on her way to enroll in (previously all-white) Central High School in Little Rock, Arkansas, on September 4, 1957. What first draws your attention to this photograph? ■ What story does the photo tell, both about each individual and about the group as a whole? ■ What dominant impression does it create? ■ What underlying and competing values seem to be at work in it?

Moralities: Most Sacred Values

4

I have tried to make clear that it is wrong to use immoral means to attain moral ends. But now I must affirm that it is just as wrong, or perhaps even more so, to use moral means to preserve immoral ends.

MARTIN LUTHER KING JR., *Letter from Birmingham Jail*

We, the People of the United States, who a little over two hundred years ago ordained and established the Constitution, have a serious problem: too many of us nowadays neither mean what we say nor say what we mean.

STEPHEN L. CARTER, *The Rules about the Rules*

If you had to say what morality meant to you, how would you sum it up?

CAROL GILLIGAN, *Concepts of Self and Morality*

You see I want to be quite obstinate about insisting that we have no way of knowing . . . what is "right" and what is "wrong," what is "good" and what "evil."

JOAN DIDION, *On Morality*

"Cheating *is* an answer. . . . It might not be a good answer, but none the less it is an answer."

MARK CLAYTON, *A Whole Lot of Cheatin' Going On*

Morality can survive without religion, it appears; children can be taught the importance of right versus wrong without benefit of religious training.

ANTHONY BRANDT, *Do Kids Need Religion?*

Remember, if your furniture is distressed your conscience needn't be.

DAVID BROOKS, *Conscientious Consumption*

We need passionate followers of an ideal of civic virtue, an ideal that does not conform, as St. Paul says in Romans 12:1&2, but is transformed by the renewing of one's mind and one's soul.

PETER J. GOMES, *Civic Virtue and the Character of Followership*

139

I don't want to have sex because "I guess" I want it. I want to wait for something more exciting than that, and modesty helps me understand why.

WENDY SHALIT, *The Future of Modesty*

I had not yet done the things / that would need forgiving.

KATHLEEN NORRIS, *Little Girls in Church*

Introduction

GEORGE JOHNSON OPENS *Fire in the Mind* (1995), a book on the relationship of faith and science, by citing a Navajo creation story:

> When all the stars were ready to be placed in the sky First Woman said, "I will use these to write the laws that are to govern mankind for all time. These laws cannot be written on the water as that is always changing its form, nor can they be written in the sand as the wind would soon erase them, but if they are written in the stars they can be read and remembered forever."

The myth gives shape to the enduring human desire for a firm moral sense, a guide to right and wrong as immutable as the stars.

Just as persistent among nations and people is a fear of moral decline. The Hebrew prophets in biblical times regularly denounced the sins and abominations of the Israelites. The ancient Romans had Cato the Censor to deplore their precipitous retreat from virtue. Martin Luther protested the corruption he found in the Catholic Church of the Renaissance, and his twentieth-century American namesake, Martin Luther King Jr., challenged a nation to restore its sense of justice by ending racial discrimination. Of course, reading history this way leads one to suspect that nearly every age views itself as a period of decline in need of prophets to set things right.

Some Americans, too, wonder at the turn of the millennium whether their national culture can sink much lower than it already has—the news honeying in scandal, corruption, and hate crimes, while pop culture celebrates greed, conspicuous consumption, promiscuous sex, and violence. Consider Jerry Springer, O.J., the blue dress, the dragging death of a black man in Texas, the murder of a gay college student in Wyoming, the shootings at a Colorado high school. To many, something seems rotten in the soul of the nation.

But is that perception accurate? And, if so, how does one restore the moral sense of a people grown too diverse and, perhaps, too worldly to look to the stars (or their equivalent) for guidance? Long-term trends are full of contradictions. There's been an increase in the rate of divorce and a surge in out-of-wedlock births, but a renewed concern for the institution of marriage and traditional families; a coarsening of social discourse, yet growing interest in manners and civility; an increase in juvenile violence, but an overall drop in crime; a steady number of abortions and a remarkably high rate of church going; a widening rift between rich and poor, yet dwindling support for welfare programs. Trends and numbers like these, of course, can support quite different moral interpretations—they can be read in varying ways. For instance, one writer may interpret the evident decline of the nuclear family in the United States as a threat to the country's moral core, while another regards it as welcome evidence that society is enlarging its moral vision to accept new kinds of families. To some, the steady abortion rate represents women having the freedom to exercise a moral choice; to others, it memorializes a new Holocaust.

So in thinking about behavior and choices, it seems we ought to think not of *morality* but *moralities*. To that end, in this chapter, we present authors locating their ethical assumptions in religion, philosophy, art, and even consumption. But this diversity of approach to questions of good and evil does not in itself necessarily signal the triumph of moral relativism—the belief that moral choices are made on the basis of individual or local, not universal, standards. The desire for surety transcends time and cultures, and the assertion that there is a universal moral sense continues to be heard. It is, in fact, one of the issues most under scrutiny and debate.

You might think that moral issues are too hypothetical to win your attention. But, as this chapter demonstrates, you face practical ethical choices almost every day in school, in the workplace, and in your personal life. Moreover, we probably need not fear for the health of our society as long as debates about moralities—the kind you and your colleagues might have in a dorm room or classroom—remain robust and honorable. Following are some questions to keep the debate alive:

- Do you and your friends discuss moral issues? If so, what topics come up regularly or provoke the most discussion?

- What sorts of moral issues affect you most directly or often? When do you find yourself most conscious of making a moral choice?

- Do you believe people share a common moral sense or that morality is a matter of personal belief?

- What makes a particular belief "religious"? What do the terms *religion* and *God* mean to you? To people with views or religious convictions different than your own?

- How important is morality to your generation? Would you characterize yourself and your peers as more or less "moral" or "ethical" than generations before or after your own?

MARTIN LUTHER KING JR.
Letter from Birmingham Jail

THE REVEREND MARTIN LUTHER KING JR. *(1929–68) is remembered today for many accomplishments: his leadership of the movement for civil rights for African Americans in the 1950s and 1960s; his advocacy of nonviolent resistance to oppressive systems; his Christian ministry; his powerful and moving sermons and speeches. In King, all these elements coalesced in a figure who won the Nobel Peace Prize, changed the face of American public life, and reframed the questions any society striving to enact truly democratic principles must face. When he was assassinated in Memphis on April 4, 1968, the world lost a major spokesperson for the values of equality, freedom, and social justice—for all.*

King attended Morehouse College (see p. 53 for the current Morehouse mission statement) and later received his Ph.D. in theology from Boston University. But extensive education and high intelligence did not protect him from racist forces, which eventually led to his murder and which are still present in the United States more than thirty years after King's death. But in the face of such hostility, King's moral commitment never faltered. In March 1963, he led the March on Washington and delivered, at the foot of the Lincoln Memorial, one of his most memorable and moving speeches, "I Have a Dream," to some quarter of a million people, the largest protest demonstration in American history up to that time. The next month, King led a major protest against unfair hiring practices in Birmingham, Alabama, for which he was arrested and put in jail. While in prison, he wrote a long letter responding to local white religious leaders of several faiths, who had criticized his actions as "unwise" and "untimely." "Letter from Birmingham Jail," reprinted here in the revised version published in Why We Can't Wait *(1964), has emerged as a classic text on civil rights. In it, King clearly and forcefully articulates the moral principles on which his actions rest—and challenges not only the clergy of the time but all readers today to examine their own.*   —A.L.

My Dear Fellow Clergymen:

While confined here in the Birmingham city jail, I came across your recent statement calling my present activities "unwise and untimely." Seldom do I pause to answer criticism of my work and ideas. If I sought to answer all the criticisms that cross my desk, my secretaries would have little time for anything other than such correspondence in the course of the day, and I would have no time for constructive work. But since I feel that you are men of genuine good will and that your criticisms are sincerely set forth, I want to try to answer your statement in what I hope will be patient and reasonable terms.

142

I think I should indicate why I am here in Birmingham, since you have been influenced by the view which argues against "outsiders coming in." I have the honor of serving as president of the Southern Christian Leadership Conference, an organization operating in every southern state, with head-quarters in Atlanta, Georgia. We have some eighty-five affiliated organiza-tions across the South, and one of them is the Alabama Christian Movement for Human Rights. Frequently we share staff, educational, and financial re-sources with our affiliates. Several months ago the affiliate here in Birming-ham asked us to be on call to engage in a nonviolent direct-action program if such were deemed necessary. We readily consented, and when the hour came, we lived up to our promise. So I, along with several members of my staff, am here because I was invited here. I am here because I have organiza-tional ties here.

But more basically, I am in Birmingham because injustice is here. Just as the prophets of the eighth century B.C. left their villages and carried their "thus saith the Lord" far beyond the boundaries of their home towns, and just as the Apostle Paul left his village of Tarsus and carried the gospel of Jesus Christ to the far corners of the Greco-Roman world, so am I compelled to carry the gospel of freedom beyond my own home town. Like Paul, I must constantly respond to the Macedonian call for aid.

Moreover, I am cognizant of the interrelatedness of all communities and states. I cannot sit idly by in Atlanta and not be concerned about what hap-pens in Birmingham. Injustice anywhere is a threat to justice everywhere. We are caught in an inescapable network of mutuality, tied in a single garment of destiny. Whatever affects one directly, affects all indirectly. Never again can we afford to live with the narrow, provincial "outside agitator" idea. Anyone who lives inside the United States can never be considered an outsider any-where within its bounds.

You deplore the demonstrations taking place in Birmingham. But your statement, I am sorry to say, fails to express a similar concern for the condi-tions that brought about the demonstrations. I am sure that none of you would want to rest content with the superficial kind of social analysis that deals merely with effects and does not grapple with underlying causes. It is unfortunate that demonstrations are taking place in Birmingham, but it is even more unfortunate that the city's white power structure left the Negro community with no alternative.

In any nonviolent campaign there are four basic steps: collection of the facts to determine whether injustices exist; negotiation; self-purification; and direct action. We have gone through all these steps in Birmingham. There can be no gainsaying the fact that racial injustice engulfs this community. Birmingham is probably the most thoroughly segregated city in the United States. Its ugly record of brutality is widely known. Negroes have experienced grossly unjust treatment in the courts. There have been more unsolved bombings of Negro homes and churches in Birmingham than in any other city in the nation. These are the hard, brutal facts of the case. On the basis of these conditions, Negro leaders sought to negotiate with the city fathers. But the latter consistently refused to engage in good-faith negotiation.

Then, last September, came the opportunity to talk with leaders of Birmingham's economic community. In the course of the negotiations, certain promises were made by the merchants—for example, to remove the stores' humiliating racial signs. On the basis of these promises, the Reverend Fred Shuttlesworth and the leaders of the Alabama Christian Movement for Human Rights agreed to a moratorium on all demonstrations. As the weeks and months went by, we realized that we were the victims of a broken promise. A few signs, briefly removed, returned; the others remained.

As in so many past experiences, our hopes had been blasted, and the shadow of deep disappointment settled upon us. We had no alternative except to prepare for direct action, whereby we would present our very bodies as a means of laying our case before the conscience of the local and the national community. Mindful of the difficulties involved, we decided to undertake a process of self-purification. We began a series of workshops on nonviolence, and we repeatedly asked ourselves: "Are you able to accept blows without retaliating?" "Are you able to endure the ordeal of jail?" We decided to schedule our direct-action program for the Easter season, realizing that except for Christmas, this is the main shopping period of the year. Knowing that a strong economic-withdrawal program would be the by-product of direct action, we felt that this would be the best time to bring pressure to bear on the merchants for the needed change.

Then it occurred to us that Birmingham's mayoral election was coming up in March, and we speedily decided to postpone action until after election day. When we discovered that the Commissioner of Public Safety, Eugene "Bull" Connor, had piled up enough votes to be in the run-off, we decided again to postpone action until the day after the run-off so that the demonstrations could not be used to cloud the issues. Like many others, we wanted to see Mr. Connor defeated, and to this end we endured postponement after postponement. Having aided in this community need, we felt that our direct-action program could be delayed no longer.

You may well ask, "Why direct action? Why sit-ins, marches, and so   10 forth? Isn't negotiation a better path?" You are quite right in calling for negotiation. Indeed, this is the very purpose of direct action. Nonviolent direct action seeks to create such a crisis and foster such a tension that a community which has constantly refused to negotiate is forced to confront the issue. It seeks so to dramatize the issue that it can no longer be ignored. My citing the creation of tension as part of the work of the nonviolent-resister may sound rather shocking. But I must confess that I am not afraid of the word "tension." I have earnestly opposed violent tension, but there is a type of constructive, nonviolent tension which is necessary for growth. Just as Socrates felt that it was necessary to create a tension in the mind so that individuals could rise from the bondage of myths and half-truths to the unfettered realm of creative analysis and objective appraisal, so must we see the need for nonviolent gadflies to create the kind of tension in society that will help men rise from the dark depths of prejudice and racism to the majestic heights of understanding and brotherhood.

The purpose of our direct-action program is to create a situation so crisis-packed that it will inevitably open the door to negotiation. I therefore concur with you in your call for negotiation. Too long has our beloved Southland been bogged down in a tragic effort to live in monologue rather than dialogue.

One of the basic points in your statement is that the action that I and my associates have taken in Birmingham is untimely. Some have asked: "Why didn't you give the new city administration time to act?" The only answer that I can give to this query is that the new Birmingham administration must be prodded about as much as the outgoing one, before it will act. We are sadly mistaken if we feel that the election of Albert Boutwell as mayor will bring the millennium to Birmingham. While Mr. Boutwell is a much more gentle person than Mr. Connor, they are both segregationists, dedicated to maintenance of the status quo. I have hoped that Mr. Boutwell will be reasonable enough to see the futility of massive resistance to desegregation. But he will not see this without pressure from devotees of civil rights. My friends, I must say to you that we have not made a single gain in civil rights without determined legal and nonviolent pressure. Lamentably, it is an historical fact that privileged groups seldom give up their privileges voluntarily. Individuals may see the moral light and voluntarily give up their unjust posture; but, as Reinhold Niebuhr has reminded us, groups tend to be more immoral than individuals.

We know through painful experience that freedom is never voluntarily given by the oppressor; it must be demanded by the oppressed. Frankly, I have yet to engage in a direct-action campaign that was "well timed" in the view of those who have not suffered unduly from the disease of segregation. For years now I have heard the word "Wait!" It rings in the ear of every Negro with piercing familiarity. This "Wait" has almost always meant "Never." We must come to see, with one of our distinguished jurists, that "justice too long delayed is justice denied."

We have waited for more than 340 years for our constitutional and God-given rights. The nations of Asia and Africa are moving with jetlike speed toward gaining political independence, but we still creep at horse-and-buggy pace toward gaining a cup of coffee at a lunch counter. Perhaps it is easy for those who have never felt the stinging darts of segregation to say, "Wait." But when you have seen vicious mobs lynch your mothers and fathers at will and drown your sisters and brothers at whim; when you have seen hate-filled policemen curse, kick, and even kill your black brothers and sisters; when you see the vast majority of your twenty million Negro brothers smothering in an airtight cage of poverty in the midst of an affluent society;

when you suddenly find your tongue twisted and your speech stammering as you seek to explain to your six-year-old daughter why she can't go to the public amusement park that has just been advertised on television, and see tears welling up in her eyes when she is told that Funtown is closed to colored children, and see ominous clouds of inferiority beginning to form in her little mental sky, and see her beginning to distort her personality by developing an unconscious bitterness toward white people; when you have to concoct an answer for a five-year-old son who is asking "Daddy, why do white people treat colored people so mean?"; when you take a cross-country drive and find it necessary to sleep night after night in the uncomfortable corners of your automobile because no motel will accept you; when you are humiliated day in and day out by nagging signs reading "white" and "colored"; when your first name becomes "nigger," your middle name becomes "boy" (however old you are) and your last name becomes "John," and your wife and mother are never given the respected title "Mrs."; when you are harried by day and haunted by night by the fact that you are a Negro, living constantly at tiptoe stance, never quite knowing what to expect next, and are plagued with inner fears and outer resentments; when you are forever fighting a degenerating sense of "nobodiness"—then you will understand why we find it difficult to wait. There comes a time when the cup of endurance runs over, and men are no longer willing to be plunged into the abyss of despair. I hope, sirs, you can understand our legitimate and unavoidable impatience.

You express a great deal of anxiety over our willingness to break laws. 15 This is certainly a legitimate concern. Since we so diligently urge people to obey the Supreme Court's decision of 1954 outlawing segregation in the public schools, at first glance it may seem rather paradoxical for us consciously to break laws. One may well ask: "How can you advocate breaking some laws and obeying others?" The answer lies in the fact that here are two types of laws: just and unjust. I would be the first to advocate obeying just laws. One has not only a legal but a moral responsibility to obey just laws. Conversely, one has a moral responsibility to disobey unjust laws. I would agree with St. Augustine that "an unjust law is no law at all."

Now, what is the difference between the two? How does one determine whether a law is just or unjust? A just law is a man-made code that squares with the moral law or the law of God. An unjust law is a code that is out of harmony with the moral law. To put it in the terms of St. Thomas Aquinas: An unjust law is a human law that is not rooted in eternal law and natural law. Any law that uplifts human personality is just. Any law that degrades human personality is unjust. All segregation statutes are unjust because segregation distorts the soul and damages the personality. It gives the segregator a false sense of superiority and the segregated a false sense of inferiority. Segregation, to use the terminology of the Jewish philosopher Martin Buber, substitutes "I–it" relationship for an "I–thou" relationship and ends up relegating persons to the status of things. Hence segregation is not only politically, economically, and sociologically unsound, it is morally wrong and sinful. Paul Tillich has said that sin is separation. Is not segregation an existential expression of man's tragic separation, his awful estrangement, his terrible sinfulness? Thus it is that I can urge men to obey the 1954 decision of the Supreme Court, for it is morally right; and I can urge them to disobey segregation ordinances, for they are morally wrong.

Let us consider a more concrete example of just and unjust laws. An unjust law is a code that a numerical or power majority group compels a minority group to obey but does not make binding on itself. This is *difference* made legal. By the same token, a just law is a code that a majority compels a minority to follow and that it is willing to follow itself. This is *sameness* made legal.

Let me give another explanation. A law is unjust if it is inflicted on a minority that, as a result of being denied the right to vote, had no part in enacting or devising the law. Who can say that the legislature of Alabama which set up that state's segregation laws was democratically elected? Throughout Alabama all sorts of devious methods are used to prevent Negroes from becoming registered voters, and there are some counties in which, even though Negroes constitute a majority of the population, not a single Negro is registered. Can any law enacted under such circumstances be considered democratically structured?

Sometimes a law is just on its face and unjust in its application. For instance, I have been arrested on a charge of parading without a permit. Now, there is nothing wrong in having an ordinance which requires a permit for a parade. But such an ordinance becomes unjust when it is used to maintain segregation and to deny citizens the First-Amendment privilege of peaceful assembly and protest.

I hope you are able to see the distinction I am trying to point out. In no 20 sense do I advocate evading or defying the law, as would the rabid segregationist. That would lead to anarchy. One who breaks an unjust law must do so openly, lovingly, and with a willingness to accept the penalty. I submit that an individual who breaks a law that conscience tells him is unjust, and who willingly accepts the penalty of imprisonment in order to arouse the conscience of the community over its injustice, is in reality expressing the highest respect for law.

Of course, there is nothing new about this kind of civil disobedience. It was evidenced sublimely in the refusal of Shadrach, Meshach, and Abednego to obey the laws of Nebuchadnezzar,* on the ground that a higher moral law was at stake. It was practiced superbly by the early Christians, who were willing to face hungry lions and the excruciating pain of chopping blocks rather than

---

Shadrach, Meshach, and Abednego . . . Nebuchadnezzar: In the biblical Book of Daniel, the Babylonian king Nebuchadnezzar orders the three Israelites thrown into a fiery furnace for refusing to worship a golden idol, but they emerge unharmed.

submit to certain unjust laws of the Roman Empire. To a degree, academic freedom is a reality today because Socrates practiced civil disobedience. In our own nation, the Boston Tea Party represented a massive act of civil disobedience.

We should never forget that everything Adolf Hitler did in Germany was "legal" and everything the Hungarian freedom fighters* did in Hungary was "illegal." It was "illegal" to aid and comfort a Jew in Hitler's Germany. Even so, I am sure that, had I lived in Germany at the time, I would have aided and comforted my Jewish brothers. If today I lived in a Communist country where certain principles dear to the Christian faith are suppressed, I would openly advocate disobeying that country's anti-religious laws.

I must make two honest confessions to you, my Christian and Jewish brothers. First, I must confess that over the past few years I have been gravely disappointed with the white moderate. I have almost reached the regrettable conclusion that the Negro's great stumbling block in his stride toward freedom is not the White Citizen's Counciler* or the Ku Klux Klanner, but the white moderate, who is more devoted to "order" than to justice; who prefers a negative peace which is the absence of tension to a positive peace which is the presence of justice; who constantly says, "I agree with you in the goal you seek, but I cannot agree with your methods of direct action"; who paternalistically believes he can set the timetable for another man's freedom; who lives by a mythical concept of time and who constantly advises the Negro to wait for a "more convenient season." Shallow understanding from people of good will is more frustrating than absolute misunderstanding from people of ill will. Lukewarm acceptance is much more bewildering than outright rejection.

I had hoped that the white moderate would understand that law and order exist for the purpose of establishing justice and that when they fail in this purpose they become the dangerously structured dams that block the flow of social progress. I had hoped that the white moderate would understand that the present tension in the South is a necessary phase of the transition from an obnoxious negative peace, in which the Negro passively accepted his unjust plight, to a substantive and positive peace, in which all men will respect the dignity and worth of human personality. Actually, we who engage in nonviolent direct action are not the creators of tension. We merely bring to the surface the hidden tension that is already alive. We bring it out in the open, where it can be seen and dealt with. Like a boil that can never be cured so long as it is covered up but must be opened with all its ugliness to the natural medicines of air and light, injustice must be exposed, with all the tension its exposure creates, to the light of human conscience and the air of national opinion, before it can be cured.

Hungarian freedom fighters: In 1956, Hungarians revolted against the Marxist government imposed on them by the former Soviet Union.

White Citizen's Counciler: member of a group organized to resist the desegregation of schools ordered by the Supreme Court's *Brown v. Board of Education* decision

In your statement you assert that our actions, even though peaceful,   25
must be condemned because they precipitate violence. But is this a logical assertion? Isn't this like condemning a robbed man because his possession of
money precipitated the evil act of robbery? Isn't this like condemning
Socrates because his unswerving commitment to truth and his philosophical
inquiries precipitated the act by the misguided populace in which they made
him drink hemlock? Isn't this like condemning Jesus because his unique God-
consciousness and never-ceasing devotion to God's will precipitated the evil
act of crucifixion? We must come to see that, as the federal courts have consistently affirmed, it is wrong to urge an individual to cease his efforts to gain
his basic constitutional rights because the quest may precipitate violence. Society must protect the robbed and punish the robber.

I had also hoped that the white moderate would reject the myth concerning time in relation to the struggle for freedom. I have just received a letter from a white brother in Texas. He writes: "All Christians know that the
colored people will receive equal rights eventually, but it is possible that you
are in too great a religious hurry. It has taken Christianity almost two thousand years to accomplish what it has. The teachings of Christ take time to
come to earth." Such an attitude stems from a tragic misconception of time,
from the strangely irrational notion that there is something in the very flow of
time that will inevitably cure all ills. Actually, time itself is neutral; it can be
used either destructively or constructively. More and more I feel that the
people of ill will have used time much more effectively than have the people
of good will. We will have to repent in this generation not merely for the
hateful words and actions of the bad people, but for the appalling silence of
the good people. Human progress never rolls in on wheels of inevitability; it
comes through the tireless efforts of men willing to be co-workers with God,
and without this hard work, time itself becomes an ally of the forces of social
stagnation. We must use time creatively, in the knowledge that the time is always ripe to do right. Now is the time to make real the promise of democracy and transform our pending national elegy into a creative psalm of brotherhood. Now is the time to lift our national policy from the quicksand of
racial injustice to the solid rock of human dignity.

You speak of our activity in Birmingham as extreme. At first I was
rather disappointed that fellow clergymen would see my nonviolent efforts as
those of an extremist. I began thinking about the fact that I stand in the
middle of two opposing forces in the Negro community. One is a force of
complacency, made up in part of Negroes who, as a result of long years of
oppression, are so drained of self-respect and a sense of "somebodiness" that
they have adjusted to segregation; and in part of a few middle-class Negroes
who, because of a degree of academic and economic security and because in
some ways they profit by segregation, have become insensitive to the problems of the masses. The other force is one of bitterness and hatred, and it
comes perilously close to advocating violence. It is expressed in the various

black nationalist groups that are springing up across the nation, the largest and best-known being Elijah Muhammad's Muslim movement. Nourished by the Negro's frustration over the continued existence of racial discrimination, this movement is made up of people who have lost faith in America, who have absolutely repudiated Christianity, and who have concluded that the white man is an incorrigible "devil."

I have tried to stand between these two forces, saying that we need emulate neither the "do-nothingism" of the complacent nor the hatred and despair of the black nationalist. For there is the more excellent way of love and nonviolent protest. I am grateful to God that, through the influence of the Negro church, the way of nonviolence became an integral part of our struggle.

If this philosophy had not emerged, by now many streets of the South would, I am convinced, be flowing with blood. And I am further convinced that if our white brothers dismiss as "rabblerousers" and "outside agitators" those of us who employ nonviolent direct action, and if they refuse to support our nonviolent efforts, millions of Negroes will, out of frustration and despair, seek solace and security in Black-nationalist ideologies—a development that would inevitably lead to a frightening racial nightmare.

Oppressed people cannot remain oppressed forever. The yearning for   30
freedom eventually manifests itself, and that is what has happened to the American Negro. Something within has reminded him of his birthright of freedom, and something without has reminded him that it can be gained. Consciously or unconsciously, he has been caught up by the *Zeitgeist,* and with his black brothers of Africa and his brown and yellow brothers of Asia, South America, and the Caribbean, the United States Negro is moving with a sense of great urgency toward the promised land of racial justice. If one recognizes this vital urge that has engulfed the Negro community, one should readily understand why public demonstrations are taking place. The Negro has spent many pent-up resentments and latent frustrations, and he must release them. So let him march; let him make prayer pilgrimages to the city hall; let him go on freedom rides—and try to understand why he must do so. If his repressed emotions are not released in nonviolent ways, they will seek expression through violence; this is not a threat but a fact of history. So I have not said to my people, "Get rid of your discontent." Rather, I have tried to say that this normal and healthy discontent can be channeled into the creative outlet of nonviolent direct action. And now this approach is being termed extremist.

But though I was initially disappointed at being categorized as an extremist, as I continued to think about the matter I gradually gained a measure of satisfaction from the label. Was not Jesus an extremist for love: "Love your enemies, bless them that curse you, do good to them that hate you, and pray for them which despitefully use you, and persecute you." Was not Amos an extremist for justice: "Let justice roll down like waters and righteousness like an everflowing stream." Was not Paul an extremist for the Christian gospel: "I bear in my body the marks of the Lord Jesus." Was not Martin Luther an extremist: "Here I stand; I cannot do otherwise, so help me God." And John

Bunyan: "I will stay in jail to the end of my days before I make a butchery of my conscience." And Abraham Lincoln: "This nation cannot survive half slave and half free." And Thomas Jefferson: "We hold these truths to be self-evident, that all men are created equal. . . ." So the question is not whether we will be extremists, but what kind of extremists we will be. Will we be extremists for hate or for love? Will we be extremists for the preservation of injustice or for the extension of justice? In that dramatic scene on Calvary's hill three men were crucified. We must never forget that all three were crucified for the same crime—the crime of extremism. Two were extremists for immorality, and thus fell below their environment. The other, Jesus Christ, was an extremist for love, truth, and goodness, and thereby rose above his environment. Perhaps the South, the nation, and the world are in dire need of creative extremists.

I had hoped that the white moderate would see this need. Perhaps I was too optimistic; perhaps I expected too much. I suppose I should have realized that few members of the oppressor race can understand the deep groans and passionate yearnings of the oppressed race, and still fewer have the vision to see that injustice must be rooted out by strong, persistent, and determined action. I am thankful, however, that some of our white brothers in the South have grasped the meaning of this social revolution and committed themselves to it. They are still all too few in quantity, but they are big in quality. Some—such as Ralph McGill, Lillian Smith, Harry Golden, James McBridge Dabbs, Anne Braden, and Sarah Patton Boyle—have written about our struggle in eloquent and prophetic terms. Others have marched with us down nameless streets of the South. They have languished in filthy, roach-infested jails, suffering the abuse and brutality of policemen who view them as "dirty nigger-lovers." Unlike so many of their moderate brothers and sisters, they have recognized the urgency of the moment and sensed the need for powerful "action" antidotes to combat the disease of segregation.

Let me take note of my other major disappointment. I have been so greatly disappointed with the white church and its leadership. Of course, there are some notable exceptions. I am not unmindful of the fact that each of you has taken some significant stands on this issue. I commend you, Reverend Stallings, for your Christian stand on this past Sunday, in welcoming Negroes to your worship service on a nonsegregated basis. I commend the Catholic leaders of this state for integrating Spring Hill College several years ago.

But despite these notable exceptions, I must honestly reiterate that I have been disappointed with the church. I do not say this as one of those negative critics who can always find something wrong with the church. I say this as a minister of the gospel, who loves the church; who was nurtured in its bosom; who has been sustained by its spiritual blessings and who will remain true to it as long as the cord of life shall lengthen.   35

When I was suddenly catapulted into the leadership of the bus protest in Montgomery, Alabama, a few years ago, I felt we would be supported by the white church. I felt that the white ministers, priests, and rabbis of the South would be among our strongest allies. Instead, some have been outright opponents, refusing to understand the freedom movement and misrepresenting its leaders; all too many others have been more cautious than courageous and have remained silent behind the anesthetizing security of stained glass windows.

In spite of my shattered dreams, I came to Birmingham with the hope that the white religious leadership of this community would see the justice of our cause and, with deep moral concern, would serve as the channel through which our just grievances could reach the power structure. I had hoped that each of you would understand. But again I have been disappointed.

I have heard numerous southern religious leaders admonish their worshipers to comply with a desegregation decision because it is the law, but I have longed to hear white ministers declare: "Follow this decree because integration is morally right and because the Negro is your brother." In the midst of blatant injustices inflicted upon the Negro, I have watched white churchmen stand on the sideline and mouth pious irrelevancies and sanctimonious trivialities. In the midst of a mighty struggle to rid our nation of racial and economic injustice I have heard many ministers say: "Those are social issues, with which the gospel has no real concern." And I have watched many churches commit themselves to a completely otherworldly religion which makes a strange, un-Biblical distinction between body and soul, between the sacred and the secular.

I have traveled the length and breadth of Alabama, Mississippi, and all the other southern states. On sweltering summer days and crisp autumn mornings I have looked at the South's beautiful churches with their lofty spires pointing heavenward. I have beheld the impressive outlines of her massive religious-education buildings. Over and over I have found myself asking: "What kind of people worship here? Who is their God? Where were their voices when the lips of Governor Barnett dripped with words of interposition and nullification? Where were they when Governor Wallace* gave a clarion call for defiance and hatred? Where were their voices of support when bruised and weary Negro men and women decided to rise from the dark dungeons of complacency to the bright hills of creative protest?"

Yes, these questions are still in my mind. In deep disappointment I have wept over the laxity of the church. But be assured that my tears have been tears of love. There can be no deep disappointment where there is not deep love. Yes, I love the church. How could I do otherwise? I am in the rather unique position of being the son, the grandson, and the great-grandson of preachers. Yes, I see the church as the body of Christ. But, oh! How we have blemished and scarred that body through social neglect and through fear of being nonconformists.

Governor Barnett . . . Governor Wallace: Ross Barnett and George Wallace were governors of Mississippi and Alabama, respectively, who resisted the racial integration of schools in their states.

There was a time when the church was very powerful—in the time   40
when the early Christians rejoiced at being deemed worthy to suffer for what
they believed. In those days the church was not merely a thermometer that
recorded the ideas and principles of popular opinion; it was a thermostat that
transformed the mores of society. Whenever the early Christians entered a
town, the people in power became disturbed and immediately sought to convict the Christians for being "disturbers of the peace" and "outside agitators."
But the Christians pressed on, in the conviction that they were "a colony of
heaven," called to obey God rather than man. Small in number, they were
big in commitment. They were too God-intoxicated to be "astronomically
intimidated." By their effort and example they brought an end to such ancient evils as infanticide and gladiatorial contests.

Things are different now. So often the contemporary church is a weak,
ineffectual voice with an uncertain sound. So often it is an archdefender of
the status quo. Far from being disturbed by the presence of the church, the
power structure of the average community is consoled by the church's
silent—and often even vocal—sanction of things as they are.

But the judgment of God is upon the church as never before. If today's
church does not recapture the sacrificial spirit of the early church, it will lose its
authenticity, forfeit the loyalty of millions, and be dismissed as an irrelevant social club with no meaning for the twentieth century. Every day I meet young
people whose disappointment with the church has turned into outright disgust.

Perhaps I have once again been too optimistic. Is organized religion too
inextricably bound to the status quo to save our nation and the world? Perhaps I must turn my faith to the inner spiritual church, the church within the
church, as the true *ekklesia** and the hope of the world. But again I am thankful to God that some noble souls from the ranks of organized religion have
broken loose from the paralyzing chains of conformity and joined us as active
partners in the struggle for freedom. They have left their secure congregations
and walked the streets of Albany, Georgia, with us. They have gone down
the highways of the South on tortuous rides for freedom. Yes, they have gone
to jail with us. Some have been dismissed from their churches, have lost the
support of their bishops and fellow ministers. But they have acted in the faith
that right defeated is stronger than evil triumphant. Their witness has been
the spiritual salt that has preserved the true meaning of the gospel in these
troubled times. They have carved a tunnel of hope through the dark mountain of disappointment.

I hope the church as a whole will meet the challenge of this decisive
hour. But even if the church does not come to the aid of justice, I have no
despair about the future. I have no fear about the outcome of our struggle in
Birmingham, even if our motives are at present misunderstood. We will reach

---

ekklesia: Greek word for the early Christian church

the goal of freedom in Birmingham and all over the nation, because the goal of America is freedom. Abused and scorned though we may be, our destiny is tied up with America's destiny. Before the pilgrims landed at Plymouth, we were here. Before the pen of Jefferson etched the majestic words of the Declaration of Independence across the pages of history, we were here. For more than two centuries our forebears labored in this country without wages; they made cotton king; they built the homes of their masters while suffering gross injustice and shameful humiliation—and yet out of a bottomless vitality they continued to thrive and develop. If the inexpressible cruelties of slavery could not stop us, the opposition we now face will surely fail. We will win our freedom because the sacred heritage of our nation and the eternal will of God are embodied in our echoing demands.

Before closing I feel impelled to mention one other point in your state- 45 ment that has troubled me profoundly. You warmly commended the Birmingham police force for keeping "order" and "preventing violence." I doubt that you would have so warmly commended the police force if you had seen its dogs sinking their teeth into unarmed, nonviolent Negroes. I doubt that you would so quickly commend the policemen if you were to observe their ugly and inhumane treatment of Negroes here in the city jail; if you were to watch them push and curse old Negro women and young Negro girls; if you were to see them slap and kick old Negro men and young boys; if you were to observe them, as they did on two occasions, refuse to give us food because we wanted to sing our grace together. I cannot join you in your praise of the Birmingham police department.

It is true that the police have exercised a degree of discipline in handling the demonstrators. In this sense they have conducted themselves rather "nonviolently" in public. But for what purpose? To preserve the evil system of segregation. Over the past few years I have consistently preached that nonviolence demands that the means we use must be as pure as the ends we seek. I have tried to make clear that it is wrong to use immoral means to attain moral ends. But now I must affirm that it is just as wrong, or perhaps even more so, to use moral means to preserve immoral ends. Perhaps Mr. Connor and his policemen have been rather nonviolent in public, as was Chief Pritchett in Albany, Georgia, but they have used the moral means of nonviolence to maintain the immoral end of racial injustice. As T. S. Eliot has said, "The last temptation is the greatest treason: To do the right deed for the wrong reason."

I wish you had commended the Negro sit-inners and demonstrators of Birmingham for their sublime courage, their willingness to suffer, and their amazing discipline in the midst of great provocation. One day the South will recognize its real heroes. They will be the James Merediths,* with the noble

---

James Merediths: The U.S. Supreme Court ordered the admission of James Meredith, a black student, to the segregated University of Mississippi in 1962 despite resistance from state officials.

sense of purpose that enables them to face jeering and hostile mobs, and with the agonizing loneliness that characterizes the life of the pioneer. They will be old, oppressed, battered Negro women, symbolized in a seventy-two-year-old woman in Montgomery, Alabama, who rose up with a sense of dignity and with her people decided not to ride segregated buses, and who responded with un-grammatical profundity to one who inquired about her weariness: "My feets is tired, but my soul is at rest." They will be the young high school and college stu-dents, the young ministers of the gospel and a host of their elders, courageously and nonviolently sitting in at lunch counters and willingly going to jail for con-science' sake. One day the South will know that when these disinherited chil-dren of God sat down at lunch counters, they were in reality standing up for what is best in the American dream and for the most sacred values in our Judaeo-Christian heritage, thereby bringing our nation back to those great wells of democracy which were dug deep by the founding fathers in their formulation of the Constitution and the Declaration of Independence.

Never before have I written so long a letter. I'm afraid it is much too long to take your precious time. I can assure you that it would have been much shorter if I had been writing from a comfortable desk, but what else can one do when he is alone in a narrow jail cell, other than write long letters, think long thoughts, and pray long prayers?

If I have said anything in this letter that overstates the truth and indicates an unreasonable impatience, I beg you to forgive me. If I have said anything that understates the truth and indicates my having a patience that allows me to settle for anything less than brotherhood, I beg God to for-give me.

I hope this letter finds you strong in the faith. I also hope that circum-   50 stances will soon make it possible for me to meet each of you, not as an inte-grationist or a civil-rights leader but as a fellow clergyman and a Christian brother. Let us all hope that the dark clouds of racial prejudice will soon pass away and the deep fog of misunderstanding will be lifted from our fear-drenched communities, and in some not too distant tomorrow the radiant stars of love and brotherhood will shine over our great nation with all their scintillating beauty.

Yours for the cause of Peace and Brotherhood,
MARTIN LUTHER KING JR.

QUESTIONING THE TEXT

1. King's letter is written to the white clergy of Birmingham, including those of Protestant, Catholic, and Jewish faiths. Look carefully at the sources King cites in his letter and note which ones seem most likely to appeal to members of these religious groups.

2. In a number of places in his "Letter," King mentions or alludes to Socrates. Review an account of Socrates' life. What makes him a particularly appropriate and powerful example for King to use? Can you think of any risks King takes in relying on Socrates as a key figure in his argument?

3. Working with one or two classmates, identify all of the evidence King offers in his "Letter" to prove that racial injustice is immoral.

4. Is this piece of writing really a letter? What qualities and elements of it allow you to answer this question — one way or the other?

MAKING CONNECTIONS

5. Carol Gilligan opens "Concepts of Self and Morality" (p. 169) by quoting a student's definition of the term *morality*. Read this definition; then write several paragraphs explaining how you think King would define the term.

6. In "The Rules about the Rules" (p. 157), Stephen L. Carter says that "[i]ntegrity . . . requires three steps: (1) *discerning* what is right and what is wrong; (2) *acting* on what you have discerned, even at personal cost; and (3) *saying openly* that you are acting on your understanding of right from wrong" (paragraph 15). Would King likely agree with Carter's description of these steps? What evidence of these three steps do you find in King's "Letter"?

JOINING THE CONVERSATION

7. Have you ever written a long letter to someone, a letter that was important to you and in which you tried hard to make a convincing case for something you believed or felt? If so, what were the features of that letter? How successful and effective was it? Take time to brainstorm about a letter you might write today. To whom would you address it? What would you argue for — or against? Where would you find support and evidence? What would be the most difficult part of writing the letter?

8. King uses a great many pronouns in his "Letter," including *you* to refer to the clergymen (there were no women clergy in Birmingham at the time) and *we* to refer to the nonviolent protesters in particular and the larger African American community in general. Working with one or two classmates, look carefully at how King uses pronouns in the reading. Then write a brief report to your class describing King's use of pronouns and explaining what effect(s) they have on readers today — and what effect(s) they may have been intended to have on the clergymen to whom the letter was addressed.

STEPHEN L. CARTER
The Rules about the Rules

I*T IS STILL TOO EARLY* to know what the long-term consequences will be of the political scandals of 1998, when a president of the United States was impeached—for only the second time in history—on charges of perjury and obstruction of justice. For more than a year, a nation watched, simultaneously fascinated and revolted, as its leaders and the media struggled with the aftershocks of an act of adultery. If little else, we learned that Shakespeare's clown Dogberry (borrowing from scripture) had spoken truthfully: "[t]hey that touch pitch will be defiled."

Stephen L. Carter (b. 1954), William Cromwell Nelson Professor of Law at Yale, probably wasn't surprised by the mess. Long before the country had ever heard of Monica Lewinsky, Carter had detected a wavering in the nation's ethical compass. His response is a book-length meditation, Integrity (1996), that does not focus on political scandal alone, but asks its readers to consider the slippage in ethics evident everywhere in our culture—in our legal system, media, sports, businesses, and marriages. He even devotes a section to academic letters of recommendation, arguing that teachers have debased this essential part of job and professional school applications because they are unwilling to deal with students honestly.

Integrity is not the first book in which Carter, playing the role of public intellectual, has helped to set the agenda for a serious national discussion of issues. Earlier, Reflections of an Affirmative Action Baby (1991) contributed to the continuing and uneasy debate over racial preferences in academia and the workplace. Even more influential was the award-winning The Culture of Disbelief (1993), which, contrary to much opinion, insists that people of faith have a right to exert their influence in politics. More recently, Carter has written Civility (1998), a call for a more decent and polite society.

The selection that follows, "The Rules about the Rules," is the opening chapter of Integrity. Omitted from the selection is a brief concluding section that summarizes the subsequent chapters of the book.

—J.R.

My first lesson in integrity came the hard way. It was 1960 or thereabouts and I was a first-grader at P.S. 129 in Harlem. The teacher had us all sitting in a circle, playing a game in which each child would take a turn donning a blindfold and then trying to identify objects by touch alone as she handed them to us. If you guessed right, you stayed in until the next round. If you guessed wrong, you were out. I survived almost to the end, amazing the entire class with my abilities. Then, to my dismay, the teacher realized what I had known, and relied upon, from the start: my blindfold was tied imperfectly and a sliver of bright reality leaked in from outside. By holding the unknown object in my lap instead of out in front of me, as most of the other children did, I could see at least a corner or a side and sometimes more—but always enough to figure out what it was. So my remarkable success was due only to my ability to break the rules.

Fortunately for my own moral development, I was caught. And as a result of being caught, I suffered, in front of my classmates, a humiliating reminder of right and wrong: I had cheated at the game. Cheating was wrong. It was that simple.

I do not remember many of the details of the "public" lecture that I received from my teacher. I do remember that I was made to feel terribly ashamed; and it is good that I was made to feel that way, for I had something to be ashamed of. The moral opprobrium that accompanied that shame was sufficiently intense that it has stayed with me ever since, which is exactly how shame is supposed to work. And as I grew older, whenever I was even tempted to cheat—at a game, on homework—I would remember my teacher's stern face and the humiliation of sitting before my classmates, revealed to the world as a cheater.

That was then, this is now. Browsing recently in my local bookstore, I came across a book that boldly proclaimed, on its cover, that it contained instructions on how to *cheat*—the very word occurred in the title—at a variety of video games. My instincts tell me that this cleverly chosen title is helping the book to sell very well. For it captures precisely what is wrong with America today: we care far more about winning than about playing by the rules.

Consider just a handful of examples, drawn from headlines of the mid-1990s: the winner of the Miss Virginia pageant is stripped of her title after officials determine that her educational credentials are false; a television network is forced to apologize for using explosives to add a bit of verisimilitude to a tape purporting to show that a particular truck is unsafe; and the authors of a popular book on management are accused of using bulk purchases at key stores to manipulate the *New York Times* best-seller list. Go back a few more years and we can add in everything from a slew of Wall Street titans imprisoned for violating a bewildering variety of laws in their frantic effort to get ahead, to the women's Boston Marathon winner branded a cheater for spending part of the race on the subway. But cheating is evidently no big deal: some 70 percent of college students admit to having done it at least once.[1]

That, in a nutshell, is America's integrity dilemma: we are all full of fine talk about how desperately our society needs it, but, when push comes to shove, we would just as soon be on the winning side. A couple of years ago as I sat watching a televised football game with my children, trying to explain to them what was going on, I was struck by an event I had often noticed but on which I had never reflected. A player who failed to catch a ball thrown his way hit the

5

---

[1]On cheating by college students, see Karen Thomas, "Rise in Cheating Called Response to Fall in Values," *USA Today,* August 2, 1995, p. 1A. I do not know whether the irony of the headline was intentional.

ground, rolled over, and then jumped up, celebrating as though he had caught the pass after all. The referee was standing in a position that did not give him a good view of what had happened, was fooled by the player's pretense, and so moved the ball down the field. The player rushed back to the huddle so that his team could run another play before the officials had a chance to review the tape. (Until 1992, National Football League officials could watch a television replay and change their call, as long as the next play had not been run.) But viewers at home did have the benefit of the replay, and we saw what the referee missed: the ball lying on the ground instead of snug in the receiver's hands. The only comment from the broadcasters: "What a heads-up play!" Meaning: "Wow, what a great liar this kid is! Well done!"

Let's be very clear: that is exactly what they meant. The player set out to mislead the referee and succeeded; he helped his team to obtain an advantage in the game that it had not earned. It could not have been accidental. He knew he did not catch the ball. By jumping up and celebrating, he was trying to convey a false impression. He was trying to convince the officials that he had caught the ball. And the officials believed him. So, in any ordinary understanding of the word, he lied. And that, too, is what happens to integrity in American life: if we happen to do something wrong, we would just as soon have nobody point it out.

Now, suppose that the player had instead gone to the referee and said, "I'm sorry, sir, but I did not make the catch. Your call is wrong." Probably his coach and teammates and most of his team's fans would have been furious: he would not have been a good team player. The good team player lies to the referee, and does so in a manner that is at once blatant (because millions of viewers see it) and virtually impossible for the referee to detect. Having pulled off this trickery, the player is congratulated: he is told that he has made a heads-up play. Thus, the ethic of the game turns out to be an ethic that rewards cheating. (But I still love football.) Perhaps I should have been shocked. Yet, thinking through the implications of our celebration of a national sport that rewards cheating, I could not help but recognize that we as a nation too often lack integrity, which might be described, in a loose and colloquial way, as the courage of one's convictions. And although I do not want to claim any great burst of inspiration, it was at about that time that I decided to write this book.

TOWARD A DEFINITION

We, the People of the United States, who a little over two hundred years ago ordained and established the Constitution, have a serious problem: too many of us nowadays neither mean what we say nor say what we mean. Moreover, we hardly expect anybody else to mean what they say either.

A couple of years ago I began a university commencement address by   10 telling the audience that I was going to talk about integrity. The crowd broke into applause. Applause! Just because they had heard the word *integrity*—that's how starved for it they were. They had no idea how I was using the word, or what I was going to say about it, or, indeed, whether I was for it or against it. But they knew they liked the idea of simply talking about it. This celebration of integrity is intriguing: we seem to carry on a passionate love affair with a word that we scarcely pause to define.

The Supreme Court likes to use such phrases as the "Constitution's structural integrity" when it strikes down actions that violate the separation of powers in the federal government.[2] Critics demand a similar form of integrity when they argue that our age has seen the corruption of language or of particular religious traditions or of the moral sense generally. Indeed, when parents demand a form of education that will help their children grow into people of integrity, the cry carries a neo-romantic image of their children becoming adults who will remain uncorrupted by the forces (whatever they are) that seem to rob so many grown-ups of . . . well, of integrity.

Very well, let us consider this word *integrity*. Integrity is like the weather: everybody talks about it but nobody knows what to do about it. Integrity is that stuff we always say we want more of. Such leadership gurus as Warren Bennis insist that it is of first importance. We want our elected representatives to have it, and political challengers always insist that their opponents lack it. We want it in our spouses, our children, our friends. We want it in our schools and our houses of worship. And in our corporations and the products they manufacture: early in 1995, one automobile company widely advertised a new car as "the first concept car with integrity." And we want it in the federal government, too, where officials all too frequently find themselves under investigation by special prosecutors. So perhaps we should say that integrity is like *good* weather, because everybody is in favor of it.

Scarcely a politician kicks off a campaign without promising to bring it to government; a few years later, more often than is healthy for our democracy, the politician slinks cravenly from office, having been lambasted by the press for lacking that self-same integrity; and then the press, in turn, is skewered for holding public figures to a measure of integrity that its own reporters, editors, producers, and, most particularly, owners could not possibly meet. And for refusing to turn that critical eye inward, the press is mocked for—what else?—a lack of integrity.

Everybody agrees that the nation needs more of it. Some say we need to return to the good old days when we had a lot more of it. Others say we as a nation have never really had enough of it. And hardly any of us stop to explain exactly what we mean by it—or how we know it is even a good thing—or why everybody needs to have the same amount of it. Indeed, the only trouble with integrity is that everybody who uses the word seems to

---

[2]See, for example, *Ryder v. United States,* 115 S. Ct. 2031 (1995).

mean something slightly different. So in a book about integrity, the place to start is surely with a definition.

When I refer to integrity, I have something very simple and very spe- 15 cific in mind. Integrity, as I will use the term, requires three steps: (1) *discerning* what is right and what is wrong; (2) *acting* on what you have discerned, even at personal cost; and (3) *saying openly* that you are acting on your understanding of right from wrong.[3] The first criterion captures the idea of integrity as requiring a degree of moral reflectiveness. The second brings in the ideal of an integral person as steadfast, which includes the sense of keeping commitments. The third reminds us that a person of integrity is unashamed of doing the right. . . . I hope that even readers who quarrel with my selection of the term *integrity* to refer to the form of commitment that I describe will come away from the book understanding why the concept itself, whatever it may be called, is a vital one.

The word *integrity* comes from the same Latin root as *integer* and historically has been understood to carry much the same sense, the sense of *wholeness:* a person of integrity, like a whole number, is a whole person, a person somehow undivided. The word conveys not so much a single-mindedness as a completeness; not the frenzy of a fanatic who wants to remake all the world in a single mold but the serenity of a person who is confident in the knowledge that he or she is living rightly. The person of integrity need not be a Gandhi but also cannot be a person who blows up buildings to make a point. A person of integrity lurks somewhere inside each of us: a person we feel we can trust to do right, to play by the rules, to keep commitments. Perhaps it is because we all sense the capacity for integrity within ourselves that we are able to notice and admire it even in people with whom, on many issues, we sharply disagree.

Indeed, one reason to focus on integrity as perhaps the first among the virtues that make for good character is that it is in some sense prior to everything else: the rest of what we think matters very little if we lack essential integrity, the courage of our convictions, the willingness to act and speak in behalf of what we know to be right. In an era when the American people are crying out for open discussion of morality—of right and wrong—the ideal of integrity seems a good place to begin. No matter what our politics, no matter what causes we may support, would anybody really want to be led or followed or assisted by people who *lack* integrity? People whose words we could not trust, whose motives we didn't respect, who might at any moment toss aside everything we thought we had in common and march off in some other direction?

The answer, of course, is no: we would not want leaders of that kind, even though we too often get them. The question is not only what integrity

---

[3]In this I am influenced to some extent by the fine discussion of integrity in Martin Benjamin's book *Splitting the Difference: Compromise and Integrity in Ethics and Politics* (Lawrence: University Press of Kansas, 1990).

is and why it is valuable, but how we move our institutions, and our very lives, closer to exemplifying it. In raising this question, I do not put myself forward as an exemplar of integrity, but merely as one who in daily life goes through many of the struggles that I will describe in these pages. The reader will quickly discover that I frequently use the word *we* in my analysis. The reason is that I see the journey toward a greater understanding of the role of integrity in our public and private lives as one that the reader and I are making together.

INTEGRITY AND RELIGION

The concept we are calling *integrity* has had little attention from philosophers, but has long been a central concern to the religions. Integrity, after all, is a kind of wholeness, and most religions teach that God calls us to an undivided life in accordance with divine command. In Islam, this notion is captured in the understanding that all rules, legal or moral, are guided by the *sharia,* the divine path that God directs humans to walk. In Judaism, study of the Torah and Talmud reveals the rules under which God's people are expected to live. And Christians are called by the Gospel to be "pure in heart" (Matt. 5:8), which implies an undividedness in following God's rules.

Indeed, although its antecedents may be traced to Aristotle, the basic   20 concept of integrity was introduced to the Western tradition through the struggle of Christianity to find a guide for the well-lived life. The wholeness that the Christian tradition identified as central to life with integrity was a wholeness in obedience to God, so that the well-lived life was a life that followed God's rules. Thomas Aquinas put it this way: "[T]he virtue of obedience is more praiseworthy than other moral virtues, seeing that by obedience a person gives up his own will for God's sake, and by other moral virtues something less."[4] John Wesley, in a famous sermon, was more explicit: "[T]he nature of the covenant of grace gives you no ground, no encouragement at all, to set aside any instance or degree of obedience."[5]

But obedience to what? Traditional religions teach that integrity is found in obedience to God. Moses Maimonides put the point most simply: "Everything that you do, do for the sake of God."[6] And a Professor W. S. Tyler, preaching a sermon at Amherst College in 1857, pointed the way to generalizing the concept beyond the religious sphere: "[I]ntegrity implies im-

---

[4]St. Thomas Aquinas, *The Summa Theologica,* tr. Father L. Shapcote, revised by Daniel L. Sullivan, 2d ed. (Chicago: Encyclopedia Britannica, 1990), 2a2ae, 104, 3.

[5]John Wesley, "On the Law Established Through Faith," in *The Works of the Rev. John Wesley,* vol. 8 (London: Thomas Cordeaux, 1811), p. 144.

[6]Quoted in Abraham Joshua Heschel, *Maimonides: A Biography,* tr. Joachim Neugroschel (New York: Image Books, 1991), p. 203. The German edition was published in 1935.

plicit obedience to the dictates of conscience—in other words, a heart and life habitually controlled by a sense of duty."[7]

But this is not a book about religion as such, still less about Christian doctrine. This book, rather, tries to honor our own national understanding of the word, in a tradition that is somewhat more secular but is, in its way, equally profound. My hope is to use traditional religious understandings to illuminate a concept that now has a distinct and honored place in the American ethical narrative, but to allow the narrative to tell its own story. So, although I have quoted Aquinas and will quote him again, this book is not about how Aquinas thought of integrity; it is about how we Americans think, or have thought, or should think, of it. Our demand for it illustrates that we think about it often, and a little desperately; my hope in this book is to demonstrate the value of the concept—to show *why* we think of the word with such affection—and then to examine the interplay of the integrity concept with a range of American problems and institutions.

In choosing integrity as my subject, I have tried to select an element of good character that is independent of the particular political views that one might hold; indeed, I would suspect that all of us, whatever our politics, would value, and perhaps demand, a degree of integrity in our associates, our government, and even our friends and families. So it is best that we try to reach some agreement on just what it is that we are valuing and demanding.

A good citizen, a person of integrity, I will refer to as one who leads an *integral life*. An integral life in turn requires all three steps of the definition, to which I will occasionally refer as the rules or criteria of integrity. Once this definition is understood, there are implications, from politics to marriage, from the way bosses write letters of recommendation to the way newspaper editors choose which stories to run. . . . I am, by training and persuasion, a lawyer, and so the reader should not be surprised to find many legal examples. . . ; indeed, there is even a bit of constitutional analysis. But if this is not a book about Christianity, still less is it a book about law, and certainly it is not a work of philosophy. It is, rather, a book about Americans and our society, about what we are, what we say we aspire to be, and how to bring the two closer to balance.

THE THREE STEPS

Integrity, I should explain before proceeding, is not the same as hon-   25
esty, although honesty obviously is a desirable element of good character as well. From our definition, it is clear that one cannot have integrity without also displaying a measure of honesty. But one can be honest without being

---

[7]W. S. Tyler, Integrity the Safeguard of Public and Private Life (Springfield: Samuel Bowles, 1857), p. 6.

integral, for integrity, as I define it, demands a difficult process of discerning one's deepest understanding of right and wrong, and then further requires action consistent with what one has learned. It is possible to be honest without ever taking a hard look inside one's soul, to say nothing of taking any action based on what one finds. For example, a woman who believes abortion is murder may state honestly that this is what she thinks, but she does not fulfill the integrity criteria unless she also works to change abortion law. A man who believes in our national obligation to aid the homeless cannot claim to be fulfilling the criteria unless he works to obtain the aid he believes is deserved—and perhaps provides some assistance personally.

All too many of us fall down on step 1: we do not take the time to discern right from wrong. Indeed, I suspect that few of us really know just what we believe—what we value—and, often, we do not really want to know. Discernment is hard work; it takes time and emotional energy. And it is so much easier to follow the crowd. We too often look the other way when we see wrongdoing around us, quite famously in the widely unwitnessed yet very unprivate murder of Kitty Genovese* thirty years ago. We refuse to think in terms of right and wrong when we elect or reject political candidates based on what they will do for our own pocketbooks. On the campuses, too many students and not a few professors find it easier to go along with the latest trends than to risk the opprobrium of others by registering an objection. Indeed, social psychologists say that this all too human phenomenon of refusing to think independently is what leads to mob violence. But a public-spirited citizen must do a bit of soul-searching—must decide what he or she most truly and deeply believes to be right and good—before it is possible to live with integrity.

The second step is also a tough one. It is far easier to know what one believes—to know, in effect, right from wrong—than it is to do something about it. For example, one may believe that the homeless deserve charity, but never dispense it; or one may think that they are bums who should not be given a dime, yet always dig into one's pockets when confronted. We Americans have a remarkable capacity to say one thing and do another, not always out of true hypocrisy but often out of a lack of self-assurance. We see this in our politics, where nobody wants to be the one to say that the retirees who receive Social Security payments are, for the most part, receiving not a return on an investment but direct subventions from the payments being made by today's workers toward their own retirements—which, if done by a private investment firm, would be an illegal pyramid scheme. The late legal scholar Robert Cover illustrated the point quite powerfully when he examined the puzzling question of how avowedly antislavery judges in the early nineteenth century could hand down obviously proslavery decisions.[8] Equally puzzling to

---

Kitty Genovese: In March 1964, Genovese was stabbed to death in a New York City neighborhood while thirty-eight residents looked on, failing to come to her assistance.

[8]See Robert Cover, *Justice Accused: Antislavery and the Judicial Process* (New Haven, CT: Yale University Press, 1975).

many political activists is their inability to recruit support from people they know to be committed to their causes, who frequently explain that they simply do not want to get involved.

But in order to live with integrity, it is sometimes necessary to take that difficult step—to get involved—to fight openly for what one believes to be true and right and good, even when there is risk to oneself. I would not go so far as to insist that morally committed citizens living integral lives must fight their way through life, strident activists in behalf of all their beliefs; but I worry deeply about the number of us who seem happy to drift through life, activists in behalf of none of our beliefs.

This leads to the third step, which seems deceptively simple, but is often the hardest of all: the person truly living an integral life must be willing to say that he or she is acting consistently with what he or she has decided is right. When the statements of a person of integrity are the result of discernment, of hard thought, we treat them as reliable, even when they are indicators of the future—"You've got the job" or "Till death do us part." But forthrightness also matters because people of integrity are willing to tell us *why* they are doing what they are doing. So it does not promote integrity for one to cheat on taxes out of greed but to claim to be doing it as a protest; indeed, it does not promote integrity to do it as a protest unless one says openly (including to the Internal Revenue Service) that that is what one is doing. It does not promote integrity to ignore or cover up wrongdoing by a co-worker or family member. And it does not promote integrity to claim to be doing the will of God when one is actually doing what one's political agenda demands.

This third step—saying publicly that we are doing what we think is right, even when others disagree—is made particularly difficult by our national desire to conform. Most of us want to fit in, to be accepted, and admitting to (or proudly proclaiming) an unpopular belief is rarely the way to gain acceptance. But if moral dissenters are unwilling to follow the example of the civil rights movement and make a proud public show of their convictions, we as a nation will never have the opportunity to be inspired by their integrity to rethink our own ideas. 30

This last point bears emphasis. Integrity does not always require following the rules. Sometimes—as in the civil rights movement—integrity requires *breaking* the rules. But it also requires that one be open and public about both the fact of one's dissent and the reasons for it. . . . A person who lives an integral life may sometimes reach moral conclusions that differ from those of the majority; displaying those conclusions publicly is a crucial aspect of the wholeness in which integrity consists.

Instead of a nation of public dissenters, we have become a nation experienced in misdirection—in beguiling the audience into looking in one direction while we are busy somewhere else. The media culture unfortunately rewards this, not only because a misleading sound bite is more attractive (that is, marketable) than a principled argument, but also because the media seem far more interested in tracking down hypocrisy than in reporting episodes of integrity.

Indeed, to bring the matter full circle, the media will get a healthy share of blame in this book: blame for oversimplification and for interfering with, rather than enabling, the search for right and wrong that each of us must undertake in order to live a life of integrity. But only a share of the blame. If indeed we allow the distractions of living to prevent the discernment of right and wrong so necessary to living with integrity, we should blame neither the media nor the schools nor the government nor our employers, but only ourselves. As I will explain, we as a society can and should do far more to train our children—and ourselves!—in the difficult work of sorting right from wrong and then doing the right and despising the wrong. We can try to blame other forces that interfere; but in the end, when the children grow up, they must make right choices for themselves.

CORRUPTION

If integrity has an opposite, perhaps it is corruption—the getting away with things we know to be wrong. We say that we are a nation that demands integrity, but are we really? We call ourselves a nation of laws, but millions of us cheat on our taxes. We seem not to believe in the integrity of our commitments, with half of marriages ending in divorce. We say we want integrity in our politics, and our politicians promise it endlessly. (Try searching the Nexis database for uses of the word *integrity* by politicians and commentators, and you will be inundated.) But we reward innuendo and smear and barefaced lies with our votes.

Corruption is corrosive. We believe we can do it just a little, but I 35 wonder whether we can. Nearly all of us break small laws—I do it all the time—laws governing everything from the speed at which we may drive to when and how we may cross the street. Few of us will stop on the highway to retrieve the paper bag that the wind whips out the window of our moving car; we may not have thrown it out intentionally, but it still came from our car and it's still littering. These I shall refer to as acts of unintegrity, not an attractive neologism, but one way of avoiding the repeated use of the word *corruption,* which might be misleading. And one who engages in repeated acts of unintegrity may be said to be living an unintegral life.

Some of these acts of unintegrity can be cured by simple calls upon the virtue of consistency. It is both amusing and sad to hear liberals who have fought against the portrayal of vicious racial stereotypes in the media now saying that portrayals of sex and family life in the media affect nobody's behavior; it is just as amusing, and just as sad, to see conservatives bash the President of the United States for criticizing hateful speech on the nation's airwaves and then turn around and bash Hollywood for speech the right happens to hate.

But inconsistency is the easiest example of unintegrity to spot. There are harder examples—as we shall see, there may even be some cases in which a lack of integrity is unavoidable—and I shall deal with many of them. . . .

When I began working on this book, I shared the story about the cheating football player with a few of my colleagues over lunch in the wood-paneled faculty dining room at the Yale Law School. Like me, they are lawyers, so none could be too outraged: our task in life, after all, is sometimes to defend the indefensible. They offered a bewildering array of fascinating and sophisticated arguments on why the receiver who pretended to catch the ball was doing nothing wrong. One in particular stuck in my mind. "You don't know if he was breaking the rules," one of the best and brightest of my colleagues explained, "until you know what the rules are about following the rules."

On reflection, I think my colleague was exactly right. And that, maybe better than anything else, sums up what this book is about. What are our rules about when we follow the rules? What are our rules about when we break them? Until we can answer those two questions, we will not know how much integrity we really want in our public and private lives, to say nothing of how to get it. . . .

QUESTIONING THE TEXT

1. Carter opens "The Rules about the Rules" with an anecdote from his own life that relates to the principle of integrity. In what ways does this narrative set you up for the discussion that follows? Does it make you think about the author? Does it lead you to recall times when you have acted dishonestly yourself? What does it do to make the prospect of an entire book on the subject of integrity less daunting?

2. Carter observes that "integrity is like *good* weather, because everybody is in favor of it" (paragraph 12). For the next several days, make a record of all the times you encounter the term *integrity* and the contexts in which it appears. Then compare your findings with those of your classmates. From your informal research, what conclusions, if any, can you draw about current attitudes toward integrity? When and where does the term occur most often—or has *integrity* become a word rarely spoken and written now?

MAKING CONNECTIONS

3. In Mark Clayton's article on campus plagiarism, "A Whole Lot of Cheatin' Going On" (p. 185), one student playing devil's advocate asserts that "'Cheating *is* an answer. . . . It might not be a good answer,

but none the less it is an answer'" (paragraph 2). Can you imagine an act of scholastic dishonesty that meets Carter's three conditions for integrity (paragraph 15)? In a group, explore this possibility.

4. Use Carter's definition of integrity to assess the act of civil disobedience that Terry Tempest Williams describes in "The Clan of One-Breasted Women" (p. 607). Compare your conclusion with those of your classmates. Be prepared to describe the general conditions that might make acts of civil disobedience defensible.

JOINING THE CONVERSATION

5. Carter defines *integrity* (in paragraphs 25–32) by enumerating its three necessary characteristics. Try to define another moral abstraction (such as *loyalty, courage, modesty,* or *civility*) in approximately the same way, by first enumerating the steps or criteria that identify the term and then providing examples of the concept as you have defined it.

6. Most schools have documents defining *plagiarism, collusion, cheating,* and other acts of academic dishonesty. Review your institution's policies on scholastic integrity or its honor code—if it has one. Then discuss these policies with your classmates, either in face-to-face conversation or in an online forum or listserv. After the discussion, write a short essay about the integrity of academic work. Is cheating a major problem in your classes? Are there ever good reasons to cheat? Can plagiarism or collusion be defended or eliminated? Why, or why not?

7. Write a brief portrait of someone you know who might fairly be described as "a person of integrity." Use your portrait as an indirect way of defining or exploring the concept of integrity.

CAROL GILLIGAN
Concepts of Self and Morality

CAROL GILLIGAN (b. 1936), Patricia Albjerg Graham Professor of Gender Studies at Harvard University, has been instrumental in charting the moral and intellectual development of young women, work that led to the founding of the collaborative Harvard Project on Women's Psychology and Development of Girls. Her 1982 book In a Different Voice: Psychological Theory and Women's Development *has been widely read and studied; journalist Ellen Goodman has called it "the most insightful book on women, men, and the differences between them." More recently, Gilligan has turned her research to the study of resistance and courage among boys as well as to the psychology of love and the role of gender in human development.*

For this reading, I have chosen a major part of chapter 3 of In a Different Voice, *entitled "Concepts of Self and Morality." In it, Gilligan describes her study of twenty-nine women (ranging in age from fifteen to thirty-three and coming from diverse class and ethnic backgrounds) as they dealt with moral issues and choices surrounding abortion. Although written almost twenty years ago, this chapter's stories continue to provide insights into the conflicting responsibilities that often emerge in the face of moral problems. I chose this chapter for this reason as well as for the fact that Gilligan's book is considered a classic in gender studies today. I also had one other reason: in preparing to give the opening talk at the 1999 Bring a Daughter to Work convocation, I was looking up some information on the history of the event, which on my campus draws many hundreds of young girls every year. I shouldn't have been surprised to discover that Gilligan was instrumental in creating this annual event.* —A.L.

A college student, responding to the question "If you had to say what morality meant to you, how would you sum it up?" replies:

> When I think of the word *morality*, I think of obligations. I usually think of it as conflicts between personal desires and social things, social considerations, or personal desires of yourself versus personal desires of another person or people or whatever. Morality is that whole realm of how you decide these conflicts. A moral person is one who would decide by placing themselves more often than not as equals. A truly moral person would always consider another person as their equal. . . . In a situation of social interaction, something is morally wrong where the individual ends up screwing a lot of people. And it is morally right when everyone comes out better off.

Yet when asked if she can think of someone whom she considers a genuinely moral person, she replies, "Well, immediately I think of Albert Schweitzer, because he has obviously given his life to help others." Obligation and sacrifice override the ideal of equality, setting up a basic contradiction in her thought.

Another undergraduate responds to the question "What does it mean to say something is morally right or wrong?" by also speaking first of responsibilities and obligations:

> It has to do with responsibilities and obligations and values, mainly values. . . . In my life situation I relate morality with interpersonal relationships that have to do with respect for the other person and myself. *(Why respect other people?)* Because they have a consciousness or feelings that can be hurt, an awareness that can be hurt.

The concern about hurting others persists as a major theme in the responses of two other women students to the question "Why be moral?"

> Millions of people have to live together peacefully. I personally don't want to hurt other people. That's a real criterion, a main criterion for me. It underlies my sense of justice. It isn't nice to inflict pain. I empathize with anyone in pain. Not hurting others is important in my own private morals. Years ago I would have jumped out of a window not to hurt my boyfriend. That was pathological. Even today, though, I want approval and love, and I don't want enemies. Maybe that's why there is morality—so people can win approval, love, and friendship.

> My main principle is not hurting other people as long as you aren't going against your own conscience and as long as you remain true to yourself. . . . There are many moral issues, such as abortion, the draft, killing, stealing, monogamy. If something is a controversial issue like these, then I always say it is up to the individual. The individual has to decide and then follow his own conscience. There are no moral absolutes. Laws are pragmatic instruments, but they are not absolutes. A viable society can't make exceptions all the time, but I would personally. . . . I'm afraid I'm heading for some big crisis with my boyfriend someday, and someone will get hurt, and he'll get more hurt than I will. I feel an obligation not to hurt him, but also an obligation not to lie. I don't know if it is possible not to lie and not to hurt.

The common thread that runs through these statements is the wish not to hurt others and the hope that in morality lies a way of solving conflicts so that no one will be hurt. This theme is independently introduced by each of the four women as the most specific item in their response to a most general question. The moral person is one who helps others; goodness is service, meeting one's obligations and responsibilities to others, if possible without sacrificing oneself. While the first of the four women ends by denying the conflict she initially introduced, the last woman anticipates a conflict between remaining true to herself and adhering to her principle of not hurting others. The dilemma that would test the limits of this judgment would be one where helping others is seen to be at the price of hurting the self.

The reticence about taking stands on "controversial issues," a willingness to "make exceptions all the time," is echoed repeatedly by other college women:

> I never feel that I can condemn anyone else. I have a very relativistic position. The basic idea that I cling to is the sanctity of human life. I am inhibited about impressing my beliefs on others.

> I could never argue that my belief on a moral question is anything that another person should accept. I don't believe in absolutes. If there is an absolute for moral decisions, it is human life.

Or as a thirty-one-year-old graduate says when explaining why she would find it difficult to steal a drug to save her own life, despite her belief that it would be right to steal for another: "It's just very hard to defend yourself against the rules. I mean, we live by consensus, and if you take an action simply for yourself, by yourself, there's no consensus there, and that is relatively indefensible in this society now."

What emerges in these voices is a sense of vulnerability that impedes   5
these women from taking a stand, what George Eliot regards as the girl's "susceptibility" to adverse judgments by others, which stems from her lack of power and consequent inability "to do something in the world" (p. 365). The unwillingness to make moral judgments that Kohlberg and Kramer (1969) and Kohlberg and Gilligan (1971) associate with the adolescent crisis of identity and belief takes the form in men of calling into question the concept of morality itself. But these women's reluctance to judge stems rather from their uncertainty about their right to make moral statements, or perhaps from the price for them that such judgment seems to entail.

When women feel excluded from direct participation in society, they see themselves as subject to a consensus or judgment made and enforced by the men on whose protection and support they depend and by whose names they are known. A divorced middle-aged woman, mother of adolescent daughters, resident of a sophisticated university community, tells the story:

> As a woman, I feel I never understood that I was a person, that I could make decisions and I had a right to make decisions. I always felt that that belonged to my father or my husband in some way, or church, which was always represented by a male clergyman. They were the three men in my life: father, husband, and clergyman, and they had much more to say about what I should or shouldn't do. They were really authority figures which I accepted. It only lately has occurred to me that I never even rebelled against it, and my girls are much more conscious of this, not in the militant sense, but just in the recognizing sense. . . . I still let things happen to me rather than make them happen, than make choices, although I know all about choices. I know the procedures and the steps and all. *(Do you have any clues about why this might be true?)* Well, I think in one sense there is less responsibility involved. Because if you make a dumb decision, you have to take the rap. If it happens to you, well, you

can complain about it. I think that if you don't grow up feeling that you ever have any choices, you don't have the sense that you have emotional responsibility. With this sense of choice comes this sense of responsibility.

The essence of moral decision is the exercise of choice and the willingness to accept responsibility for that choice. To the extent that women perceive themselves as having no choice, they correspondingly excuse themselves from the responsibility that decision entails. Childlike in the vulnerability of their dependence and consequent fear of abandonment, they claim to wish only to please, but in return for their goodness they expect to be loved and cared for. This, then, is an "altruism" always at risk, for it presupposes an innocence constantly in danger of being compromised by an awareness of the trade-off that has been made. Asked to describe herself, a college senior responds:

> I have heard of the onion-skin theory. I see myself as an onion, as a block of different layers. The external layers are for people that I don't know that well, the agreeable, the social, and as you go inward, there are more sides for people I know that I show. I am not sure about the innermost, whether there is a core, or whether I have just picked up everything as I was growing up, these different influences. I think I have a neutral attitude toward myself, but I do think in terms of good and bad. Good—I try to be considerate and thoughtful of other people, and I try to be fair in situations and be tolerant. I use the words, but I try and work them out practically. Bad things—I am not sure if they are bad, if they are altruistic or I am doing them basically for approval of other people. *(Which things are these?)* The values that I try to act out. They deal mostly with interpersonal relations. . . . If I were doing things for approval, it would be a very tenuous thing. If I didn't get the right feedback, there might go all my values.

. . .

Norma Haan's (1975) research on college students and Constance Holstein's (1976) three-year study of adolescents and their parents indicate that the moral judgments of women differ from those of men in the greater extent to which women's judgments are tied to feelings of empathy and compassion and are concerned with the resolution of real as opposed to hypothetical dilemmas. However, as long as the categories by which development is assessed are derived from research on men, divergence from the masculine standard can be seen only as a failure of development. As a result, the thinking of women is often classified with that of children. The absence of alternative criteria that might better encompass the development of women, however, points not only to the limitations of theories framed by men and validated by research samples disproportionately male and adolescent, but also to the diffidence prevalent among women, their reluctance to speak publicly in their own voice, given the constraints imposed on them by their lack of power and the politics of relations between the sexes.

In order to go beyond the question, "How much like men do women think, how capable are they of engaging in the abstract and hypothetical construction of reality?" it is necessary to identify and define developmental criteria that encompass the categories of women's thought. Haan points out the necessity to derive such criteria from the resolution of the "more frequently occurring, real-life moral dilemmas of interpersonal, empathic, fellow-feeling concerns" (p. 34) which have long been the center of women's moral concern. But to derive developmental criteria from the language of women's moral discourse, it is necessary first to see whether women's construction of the moral domain relies on a language different from that of men and one that deserves equal credence in the definition of development. This in turn requires finding places where women have the power to choose and thus are willing to speak in their own voice.

When birth control and abortion provide women with effective means   10 for controlling their fertility, the dilemma of choice enters a central arena of women's lives. Then the relationships that have traditionally defined women's identities and framed their moral judgments no longer flow inevitably from their reproductive capacity but become matters of decision over which they have control. Released from the passivity and reticence of a sexuality that binds them in dependence, women can question with Freud what it is that they want and can assert their own answers to that question. However, while society may affirm publicly the woman's right to choose for herself, the exercise of such choice brings her privately into conflict with the conventions of femininity, particularly the moral equation of goodness with self-sacrifice. Although independent assertion in judgment and action is considered to be the hallmark of adulthood, it is rather in their care and concern for others that women have both judged themselves and been judged.

The conflict between self and other thus constitutes the central moral problem for women, posing a dilemma whose resolution requires a reconciliation between femininity and adulthood. In the absence of such a reconciliation, the moral problem cannot be resolved. The "good woman" masks assertion in evasion, denying responsibility by claiming only to meet the needs of others, while the "bad woman" forgoes or renounces the commitments that bind her in self-deception and betrayal. It is precisely this dilemma—the conflict between compassion and autonomy, between virtue and power—which the feminine voice struggles to resolve in its effort to reclaim the self and to solve the moral problem in such a way that no one is hurt.

When a woman considers whether to continue or abort a pregnancy, she contemplates a decision that affects both self and others and engages directly the critical moral issue of hurting. Since the choice is ultimately hers and therefore one for which she is responsible, it raises precisely those questions of judgment that have been most problematic for women. Now she is asked whether she wishes to interrupt that stream of life which for centuries has immersed her in the passivity of dependence while at the same time imposing on her the responsibility for care. Thus the abortion decision brings to the core of feminine apprehension, to what Joan Didion (1972) calls "the irreconcilable difference of it—that sense of living one's deepest life under-water, that dark involvement with blood and birth and death" (p. 14), the adult questions of responsibility and choice.

How women deal with such choices was the subject of the abortion study, designed to clarify the ways in which women construct and resolve abortion decisions. Twenty-nine women, ranging in age from fifteen to thirty-three and diverse in ethnic background and social class, were referred for the study by abortion and pregnancy counseling services. The women participated in the study for a variety of reasons—some to gain further clarifi-cation with respect to a decision about which they were in conflict, some in response to a counselor's concern about repeated abortions, and others to contribute to ongoing research. Although the pregnancies occurred under a variety of circumstances in the lives of these women, certain commonalities were discerned. The adolescents often failed to use birth control because they denied or discredited their capacity to bear children. Some women became pregnant due to the omission of contraceptive measures in circumstances where intercourse had not been anticipated. Some pregnancies coincided with efforts on the part of the women to end a relationship and may be seen as a manifestation of ambivalence or as a way of putting the relationship to the ultimate test of commitment. For these women, the pregnancy appeared to be a way of testing truth, making the baby an ally in the search for male sup-port and protection or, that failing, a companion victim of male rejection. Fi-nally, some women became pregnant as a result either of a failure of birth control or of a joint decision that was later reconsidered. Of the twenty-nine women, four decided to have the baby, two miscarried, twenty-one chose abortion, and two who were in doubt about the decision at the time of the interview could not be contacted for the follow-up research.

The women were interviewed twice, first at the time they were making the decision, in the first trimester of a confirmed pregnancy, and then at the end of the following year. The referral procedure required that there be an interval between the woman's contacting a counselor or clinic and the time the abortion was performed. Given this factor and the fact that some counselors saw participation in the study as an effective means of crisis-intervention, there is reason to believe that the women interviewed were in greater than usual conflict over the decision. Since the study focused on the re-lation between judgment and action rather than on the issue of abortion per se, no effort was made to select a sample that would be representative of women considering, seeking, or having abortions. Thus the findings pertain to the dif-ferent ways in which women think about dilemmas in their lives rather than to the ways in which women in general think about the abortion choice.

In the initial part of the interview, the women were asked to discuss the decision they faced, how they were dealing with it, the alternatives they were considering, their reasons both for and against each option, the people involved, 15 the conflicts entailed, and the ways in which making this decision affected their views of themselves and their relationships with others. In the second part of the interview, the women were asked to resolve three hypothetical moral dilemmas, including the Heinz dilemma from Kohlberg's research.

In extending Piaget's description of children's moral judgment to the moral judgment of adolescents and adults, Kohlberg (1976) distinguishes three perspectives on moral conflict and choice. Tying moral development in adolescence to the growth of reflective thought at that time, Kohlberg terms these three views of morality preconventional, conventional, and postconventional, to reflect the expansion in moral understanding from an individual to a societal to a universal point of view. In this scheme, conventional morality, or the equation of the right or good with the maintenance of existing social norms and values, is always the point of departure. Whereas preconventional moral judgment denotes an inability to construct a shared or societal viewpoint, postconventional judgment transcends that vision. Preconventional judgment is egocentric and derives moral constructs from individual needs; conventional judgment is based on the shared norms and values that sustain relationships, groups, communities, and societies; and postconventional judgment adopts a reflective perspective on societal values and constructs moral principles that are universal in application.

This shift in perspective toward increasingly differentiated, comprehensive, and reflective forms of thought appears in women's responses to both actual and hypothetical dilemmas. But just as the conventions that shape women's moral judgment differ from those that apply to men, so also women's definition of the moral domain diverges from that derived from studies of men. Women's construction of the moral problem as a problem of care and responsibility in relationships rather than as one of rights and rules ties the development of their moral thinking to changes in their understanding of responsibility and relationships, just as the conception of morality as justice ties development to the logic of equality and reciprocity. Thus the logic underlying an ethic of care is a psychological logic of relationships, which contrasts with the formal logic of fairness that informs the justice approach.

Women's constructions of the abortion dilemma in particular reveal the existence of a distinct moral language whose evolution traces a sequence of development. This is the language of selfishness and responsibility, which defines the moral problem as one of obligation to exercise care and avoid hurt. The inflicting of hurt is considered selfish and immoral in its reflection of unconcern, while the expression of care is seen as the fulfillment of moral responsibility. The reiterative use by the women of the words *selfish* and *responsible* in talking about moral conflict and choice, given the underlying moral orientation that this language reflects, sets the women apart from the men whom Kohlberg studied and points toward a different understanding of moral development.

The three moral perspectives revealed by the abortion decision study denote a sequence in the development of the ethic of care. These different views of care and the transitions between them emerged from an analysis of the ways in which the women used moral language—words such as *should, ought, better, right, good,* and *bad*—by the changes and shifts that appeared in their thinking, and by the way in which they reflected on and judged their thought. In this sequence, an initial focus on caring for the self in order to ensure survival is followed by a transitional phase in which this judgment is criticized as selfish. The criticism signals a new understanding of the connection between self and others which is articulated by the concept of responsibility. The elaboration of this concept of responsibility and its fusion with a maternal morality that seeks to ensure care for the dependent and unequal characterizes the second perspective. At this point, the good is equated with caring for others. However, when only others are legitimized as the recipients of the woman's care, the exclusion of herself gives rise to problems in relationships, creating a disequilibrium that initiates the second transition. The equation of conformity with care, in its conventional definition, and the illogic of the inequality between other and self, lead to a reconsideration of relationships in an effort to sort out the confusion between self-sacrifice and care inherent in the conventions of feminine goodness. The third perspective focuses on the dynamics of relationships and dissipates the tension between selfishness and responsibility through a new understanding of the interconnection between other and self. Care becomes the self-chosen principle of a judgment that remains psychological in its concern with relationships and response but becomes universal in its condemnation of exploitation and hurt. Thus a progressively more adequate understanding of the psychology of human relationships—an increasing differentiation of self and other and a growing comprehension of the dynamics of social interaction—informs the development of an ethic of care. This ethic, which reflects a cumulative knowledge of human relationships, evolves around a central insight, that self and other are interdependent. The different ways of thinking about this connection or the different modes of its apprehension mark the three perspectives and their transitional phases. In this sequence, the fact of interconnection informs the central, recurring recognition that just as the incidence of violence is in the end destructive to all, so the activity of care enhances both others and self.

REFERENCES

Didion, Joan. "The Women's Movement." *New York Times Book Review,* July 30, 1972, pp. 1–2, 14.

Eliot, George. *The Mill on the Floss* (1860). New York: New American Library, 1965.

Haan, Norma. "Hypothetical and Actual Moral Reasoning in a Situation of Civil Disobedience." *Journal of Personality and Social Psychology* 32 (1975): 255–270.

Holstein, Constance. "Development of Moral Judgment: A Longitudinal Study of Males and Females." *Child Development* 47 (1976): 51–61.

Kohlberg, Lawrence. "The Development of Modes of Thinking and Choices in Years 10 to 16." Ph.D. Diss., University of Chicago. 1958.

———. "Stage and Sequence: The Cognitive-Development Approach to Socialization." In D. A. Goslin, ed., *Handbook of Socialization Theory and Research*. Chicago: Rand McNally, 1969.

———. "Continuities and Discontinuities in Childhood and Adult Moral Development Revisited." In *Collected Papers on Moral Development and Moral Education*. Moral Education Research Foundation, Harvard University, 1973.

———. "Moral Stages and Moralization: The Cognitive-Developmental Approach." In T. Lickona, ed., *Moral Development and Behavior: Theory, Research and Social Issues*. New York: Holt, Rinehart and Winston, 1976.

———. *The Philosophy of Moral Development*. San Francisco: Harper and Row, 1981.

Kohlberg, L., and Gilligan, C. "The Adolescent as a Philosopher: The Discovery of the Self in a Post-conventional World." *Daedalus* 100 (1971): 1051–1086.

Kohlberg, L., and Kramer, R. "Continuities and Discontinuities in Child and Adult Moral Development." *Human Development* 12 (1969): 93–120.

QUESTIONING THE TEXT

1. How do you think Gilligan defines an "ethic of care"? Working with another student, create a definition you think Gilligan would agree with and then create one of your own. Where and why do they differ?

2. Gilligan conducts her analysis primarily on the basis of information gained in interviews. Look at the passages from which Gilligan draws the conclusion that "[t]he common thread that runs through these statements is the wish not to hurt others" (paragraph 3). Then look again at the quotations: Could they be interpreted in ways that vary from Gilligan's conclusion, and, if so, how? What additional questions might you wish to ask the women Gilligan quotes?

MAKING CONNECTIONS

3. In "On Morality" (p. 179), Joan Didion suggests that where issues of morality are concerned, "For better or worse, we are what we learned as children" (paragraph 4). Do the women in Gilligan's study tend to bear out Didion's claim? Write a page or so in which you say why or why not, and provide some examples.

4. Would most of the women in Gilligan's study agree with Anthony Brandt that "[m]orality can survive without religion" (p. 196)? How do you think Gilligan—or some of the women in her study—might answer Brandt's question, "Do Kids Need Religion?"

JOINING THE CONVERSATION

5. Gilligan refers to a classic dilemma often used in research on moral reasoning: whether to steal a drug to save a loved one's life, or one's own life. Working with several members of your class, do some research on studies that have used this question, particularly those conducted by Lawrence Kohlberg and by Kohlberg and Gilligan (see the Other Readings list at the end of this chapter). You may also want to consult Gilligan's *In a Different Voice*. Then prepare a twenty-minute report for your class on theories of moral development.

6. Think about a difficult decision you have had to make that raised issues of morality. How did you come to this decision? What processes did you go through, and where did you turn for assistance in making the decision? Do any of the perspectives or transitions described by Gilligan (see especially p. 176) ring true to your own experience? Write an extended journal entry in which you explore these questions.

JOAN DIDION
On Morality

JOAN DIDION (b. 1934) is one of the few writers whose work has appeared in every edition of The Presence of Others *(her "On Going Home" appeared in the first two editions; "Georgia O'Keeffe" in the second). As these choices suggest, Didion is a prolific and splendid writer of essays, a talent she has honed for forty years. The 1968 collection in which "On Morality" appears is titled* Slouching Towards Bethlehem, *an allusion to William Butler Yeats's poem "The Second Coming," which concludes with a haunting image and question:*

> *That twenty centuries of stony sleep*
> *Were vexed to nightmare by a rocking cradle,*
> *And what rough beast, its hour come round at last,*
> *Slouches towards Bethlehem to be born?*

This seems a particularly appropriate question to ask as we enter a new millennium some twenty centuries after another birth in Bethlehem. In the essay that follows, Didion takes an intriguing stance toward morality, *a term she was invited to explore by the editors of Phi Beta Kappa's quarterly journal* The American Scholar *in 1965 and one she admits to being suspicious of. Rejecting any easy generalizations, Didion locates morality in specifics, in the social code of loyalty to those we love, a code she takes to be primitive and basic. Beyond that, Didion sees morality as capable of leading to nightmarish and "monstrous perversion," as when a mass murderer says that the killings were carried out because "'I did what I thought was right.'"*

I chose this essay not only because it challenges traditional views of morality as systems of right and wrong and because it calls up troubling images of a new millennium, but also because questions of morality — in public and private life — have never been more prominently under discussion. —A.L.

As it happens I am in Death Valley, in a room at the Enterprise Motel and Trailer Park, and it is July, and it is hot. In fact it is 119°. I cannot seem to make the air conditioner work, but there is a small refrigerator, and I can wrap ice cubes in a towel and hold them against the small of my back. With the help of the ice cubes I have been trying to think, because *The American Scholar* asked me to, in some abstract way about "morality," a word I distrust more every day, but my mind veers inflexibly toward the particular.

Here are some particulars. At midnight last night, on the road in from Las Vegas to Death Valley Junction, a car hit a shoulder and turned over. The driver, very young and apparently drunk, was killed instantly. His girl was found alive but bleeding internally, deep in shock. I talked this afternoon to the nurse who had driven the girl to the nearest doctor, 185 miles across the floor of the Valley and three ranges of lethal mountain road. The nurse explained that her husband, a talc miner, had stayed on the highway with the boy's body until the coroner could get over the mountains from Bishop, at dawn today. "You can't just leave a body on the highway," she said. "It's immoral."

It was one instance in which I did not distrust the word, because she meant something quite specific. She meant that if a body is left alone for even a few minutes on the desert, the coyotes close in and eat the flesh. Whether or not a corpse is torn apart by coyotes may seem only a sentimental consideration, but of course it is more: one of the promises we make to one another is that we will try to retrieve our casualties, try not to abandon our dead to the coyotes. If we have been taught to keep our promises—if, in the simplest terms, our upbringing is good enough—we stay with the body, or have bad dreams.

I am talking, of course, about the kind of social code that is sometimes called, usually pejoratively, "wagon-train morality." In fact that is precisely what it is. For better or worse, we are what we learned as children: my own childhood was illuminated by graphic litanies of the grief awaiting those who failed in their loyalties to each other. The Donner-Reed Party,* starving in the Sierra snows, all the ephemera of civilization gone save that one vestigial taboo, the provision that no one should eat his own blood kin. The Jayhawkers,* who quarreled and separated not far from where I am tonight. Some of them died in the Funerals and some of them died down near Badwater and most of the rest of them died in the Panamints. A woman who got through gave the Valley its name. Some might say that the Jayhawkers were killed by the desert summer, and the Donner Party by the mountain winter, by circumstances beyond control; we were taught instead that they had somewhere abdicated their responsibilities, somehow breached their primary loyalties, or they would not have found themselves helpless in the mountain winter or the desert summer, would not have given way to acrimony, would not have deserted one another, would not have *failed*. In brief, we heard such stories as cautionary tales, and they still suggest the only kind of "morality" that seems to me to have any but the most potentially mendacious meaning.

You are quite possibly impatient with me by now; I am talking, you want to say, about a "morality" so primitive that it scarcely deserves the name, a code that has as its point only survival, not the attainment of the ideal good. Exactly. Particularly out here tonight, in this country so ominous and terrible that to live in it is to live with antimatter, it is difficult to believe that "the good" is a knowable quantity. Let me tell you what it is like out here

5

Donner-Reed Party: In the winter of 1846–47, a party of eighty immigrants attempting to cross the Sierra Nevada became snowbound. Some members of the starving group survived by eating the corpses of those who had died.

Jayhawkers: In 1849, immigrants looking for a shortcut to the California goldfields found themselves trapped in the desolate area they subsequently named Death Valley.

tonight. Stories travel at night on the desert. Someone gets in his pickup and drives a couple of hundred miles for a beer, and he carries news of what is happening, back wherever he came from. Then he drives another hundred miles for another beer, and passes along stories from the last place as well as from the one before; it is a network kept alive by people whose instincts tell them that if they do not keep moving at night on the desert they will lose all reason. Here is a story that is going around the desert tonight: over across the Nevada line, sheriff's deputies are diving in some underground pools, trying to retrieve a couple of bodies known to be in the hole. The widow of one of the drowned boys is over there; she is eighteen, and pregnant, and is said not to leave the hole. The divers go down and come up, and she just stands there and stares into the water. They have been diving for ten days but have found no bottom to the caves, no bodies and no trace of them, only the black 90° water going down and down and down, and a single translucent fish, not classified. The story tonight is that one of the divers has been hauled up incoherent, out of his head, shouting—until they got him out of there so that the widow could not hear—about water that got hotter instead of cooler as he went down, about light flickering through the water, about magma, about underground nuclear testing.

That is the tone stories take out here, and there are quite a few of them tonight. And it is more than the stories alone. Across the road at the Faith Community Church a couple of dozen old people, come here to live in trailers and die in the sun, are holding a prayer sing. I cannot hear them and do not want to. What I can hear are occasional coyotes and a constant chorus of "Baby the Rain Must Fall" from the jukebox in the Snake Room next door, and if I were also to hear those dying voices, those Midwestern voices drawn to this lunar country for some unimaginable atavistic rites, *rock of ages cleft for me,* I think I would lose my own reason. Every now and then I imagine I hear a rattlesnake, but my husband says that it is a faucet, a paper rustling, the wind. Then he stands by a window, and plays a flashlight over the dry wash outside.

What does it mean? It means nothing manageable. There is some sinister hysteria in the air out here tonight, some hint of the monstrous perversion to which any human idea can come. "I followed my own conscience." "I did what I thought was right." How many madmen have said it and meant it? How many murderers? Klaus Fuchs* said it, and the men who committed the Mountain Meadows Massacre* said it, and Alfred Rosenberg* said it. And, as we are rotely and rather presumptuously reminded by those who would say it

---

Klaus Fuchs (1912–88): German-born naturalized British citizen and self-professed communist who traded nuclear secrets to the Soviet Union until he was arrested for spying in 1950

Mountain Meadows Massacre: In 1857, a band of 137 emigrants from Arkansas heading for California was ambushed in the Utah territory by Mormon settlers angered by U.S. government policies.

Alfred Rosenberg (1893–1946): Nazi ideologist who advocated policies of German racial purity and anti-Semitism. He was tried at Nürnberg and hanged as a war criminal.

now, Jesus said it. Maybe we have all said it, and maybe we have been wrong. Except on that most primitive level—our loyalties to those we love—what could be more arrogant than to claim the primacy of personal conscience? ("Tell me," a rabbi asked Daniel Bell* when he said, as a child, that he did not believe in God. "Do you think God cares?") At least some of the time, the world appears to me as a painting by Hieronymus Bosch; were I to follow my conscience then, it would lead me out onto the desert with Marion Faye, out to where he stood in *The Deer Park** looking east to Los Alamos and praying, as if for rain, that it would happen: "*. . . let it come and clear the rot and the stench and the stink, let it come for all of everywhere, just so it comes and the world stands clear in the white dead dawn.*"

Of course you will say that I do not have the right, even if I had the power, to inflict that unreasonable conscience upon you; nor do I want you to inflict your conscience, however reasonable, however enlightened, upon me. ("We must be aware of the dangers which lie in our most generous wishes," Lionel Trilling* once wrote. "Some paradox of our nature leads us, when once we have made our fellow men the objects of our enlightened interest, to go on to make them the objects of our pity, then of our wisdom, ultimately of our coercion.") That the ethic of conscience is intrinsically insidious seems scarcely a revelatory point, but it is one raised with increasing infrequency; even those who do raise it tend to *segue* with troubling readiness into the quite contradictory position that the ethic of conscience is dangerous when it is "wrong," and admirable when it is "right."

You see I want to be quite obstinate about insisting that we have no way of knowing—beyond that fundamental loyalty to the social code—what is "right" and what is "wrong," what is "good" and what "evil." I dwell so upon this because the most disturbing aspect of "morality" seems to me to be the frequency with which the word now appears; in the press, on television, in the most perfunctory kinds of conversation. Questions of straightforward power (or survival) politics, questions of quite indifferent public policy, questions of almost anything: they are all assigned these factitious moral burdens. There is something facile going on, some self-indulgence at work. Of course we would all like to "believe" in something, like to assuage our private guilts in public causes, like to lose our tiresome selves; like, perhaps, to transform the white flag of defeat at home into the brave white banner of battle away from home. And of course it is all right to do that; that is how, immemorially, things have gotten done. But I think it is all right only so long as we do not

---

Daniel Bell (b. 1919): influential sociologist and—at the time of Didion's essay—author of *Marxian Socialism in America* (1952) and *The Radical Right* (1963)

The Deer Park (1955): novel by Norman Mailer set in a desert resort

Lionel Trilling (1905–75): American literary critic much influenced by work in psychology and sociology

delude ourselves about what we are doing, and why. It is all right only so long as we remember that all the *ad hoc* committees, all the picket lines, all the brave signatures in *The New York Times,* all the tools of agitprop straight across the spectrum, do not confer upon anyone any *ipso facto* virtue. It is all right only so long as we recognize that the end may or may not be expedient, may or may not be a good idea, but in any case has nothing to do with "morality." Because when we start deceiving ourselves into thinking not that we want something or need something, not that it is a pragmatic necessity for us to have it, but that it is a *moral imperative* that we have it, then is when we join the fashionable madmen, and then is when the thin whine of hysteria is heard in the land, and then is when we are in bad trouble. And I suspect we are already there.

QUESTIONING THE TEXT

1. Didion opens her essay by saying, "As it happens I am in Death Valley." Why is this setting particularly appropriate to the way she defines and explores morality? Is her claim that she is in Death Valley believable? What in the text supports your response to this question?

2. To further her argument, Didion uses examples (the miner staying with the body, the sheriff's deputies diving for bodies, the Donner party's long starvation and cannibalism) rather than depending on, say, references to authorities on or theories of morality. Which examples do you find most effective in supporting Didion's claim that "we have no way of knowing—beyond that fundamental loyalty to the social code— what is 'right' and what is 'wrong'" (paragraph 9)?

MAKING CONNECTIONS

3. It seems highly likely that Martin Luther King Jr. would disagree with Didion about a number of things. Working with another classmate, compose a brief letter you think King might have written in response to Didion's essay. Use reasons, examples, and quotations from King's "Letter from Birmingham Jail" (p. 142) to prepare your letter.

4. According to the nurse, her husband stays with the body of the dead boy on the highway because "'You can't just leave a body on the highway. . . . It's immoral'" (paragraph 2). How does this reasoning fit into the perspectives or transition stages described in Carol Gilligan's study (p. 175) of women's moral decision making?

5. Working with one or two classmates, write a short poem called "_____ in Death Valley." First, reread Didion's essay to decide with

whom or what you will fill in the blank in the title. Then read Kathleen Norris's "Little Girls in Church" (p. 222), and talk together about what dominant impression and images you want to include in your poem. Next you might try your hands at creating a stanza apiece and then working through a revision of the stanzas together, reading your work aloud and listening carefully to its effects. Finally, report back to the class on the difficulties and successes you encountered in this exercise and what you learned about creating memorable scenes or images in words.

JOINING THE CONVERSATION

6. We don't know how Didion went about composing this essay, but one good guess is that she wrote several, perhaps many, drafts of all or parts of the essay, each time choosing the best parts of the draft and using them to begin anew. This method is sometimes called *looping:* you write for a set period of time and then pause to reread, highlighting the best ideas, sentences, images, and so on. Then you take those "bests" and use them as the basis for a new loop, again writing for a set time. Try this method in your own exploration of the term *morality*. Make sure to do at least three or four loops. Then revise the final loop and bring it to class for presentation and discussion.

7. Prepare an editorial titled "On Morality" for a campus publication. Be sure to follow the editorial conventions of the publication in terms of length, format, use of illustrations, and so on.

8. Working with at least two classmates, draw up a plan for adding visuals (drawings, photographs, maps, or other illustrations) to Didion's essay. Gather or create the visuals you wish to use and decide where in the essay you will put each one and what caption, if any, you will give it. In what ways do the visuals affect Didion's essay? Bring your visuals and your conclusions about the effects they have to class for presentation and discussion.

MARK CLAYTON
A Whole Lot of Cheatin' Going On

HAVE YOU EVER CHEATED *on a college paper or examination? If you have* not, *studies suggest you are an exception—as many as 80 percent of students admit to at least one incident of scholastic dishonesty in their careers. As the associate director of a major university writing program, I've had to deal with many cases of plagiarism, and they are painful experiences for instructors and students alike. When faculty members discover that a student of theirs has copied or downloaded a paper, they typically feel betrayed and angry—as if they've been violated professionally. Students themselves are, for the most part, remorseful when confronted with evidence of their cheating. But a surprising number play the sullen and resentful victim, blaming their scholastic dishonesty on unreasonable instructors, demanding (and irrelevant) curricula, or work schedules they can't quite manage.*

Many students are also simply confused by the complexities of citing sources correctly or by the confusing status of source material in electronic formats. When material moves so effortlessly from screen to the page, it's hard to recall just who owns what material and harder still to enforce the intellectual property rights of authors.

Not surprisingly, scholastic integrity is a potent topic on many campuses. When my department hosted an online forum on the subject, we quickly got more than a hundred postings, mostly from students who condemned cheating. But you can read more about this forum and concerns about academic integrity on campuses nationwide in the following selection by Mark Clayton, originally published as a feature story in the Christian Science Monitor *(19 January 1999). Clayton (b. 1957), higher education writer for the* Monitor *since 1997, said in an email conversation with me that he is surprised by how casual students are about plagiarism and how unaware they often are of the serious consequences of cheating. "It might sound corny," Clayton notes, "but those [students] I interviewed said parents and educators need to make greater efforts to make clear to students that dishonesty has a real price in the real world—just as honesty has long-term rewards. After that, it's up to students."* —J.R.

Sitting in the glow of his computer screen at 2 A.M. on Oct. 26, 1998, John Smolik, a University of Texas freshman, fires off an e-mail message to an online debate over academic cheating on the Austin campus.

Many of the 100-plus student messages argue that cheaters only hurt themselves. Not so says Mr. Smolik's missive, labeled "reality check!" "Cheating *is* an answer," he writes. "It might not be a good answer, but none the less it is an answer."

Actually, Smolik "disagrees with cheating" and was simply playing devil's advocate, he said in a recent interview. But he allows that his provocative message put forward a widely shared view. And researchers agree.

Across America, college students and college-bound high-schoolers appear to be cheating like there's no tomorrow, student surveys show.

The Center for Academic Integrity in Nashville studied 7,000 students on 26 small-to-medium-size college campuses in 1990, 1992, and 1995. Those studies found that nearly 80 percent admitted to cheating at least once.

"We've seen a dramatic increase in the more-explicit forms of test cheating" and illegitimate "collaboration," says Donald McCabe, associate provost at Rutgers University in Newark, who founded CAI and did its studies.

He and others blame poor role models and lack of parental guidance for the growing acceptance of cheating in colleges. Easy access to the Internet, with its vast and often hard-to-trace resources, is another factor.

Add to that a pervasive change in societal values, and students can easily be snared if they lack a strong moral compass—as well as a campus where peers and administrators take a firm stand against dishonesty.

"Nobody cheated [in the 1960s] because of the peer pressure and likelihood of being turned in," claims Johan Madson, associate provost for student affairs at Vanderbilt University in Nashville. "Students of this generation are reluctant to turn their classmates in. They feel everyone ought to have their own right to do their own thing."

The problem is hardly limited to college campuses. Critics also point to   10
widespread cheating in high school as a reason for colleges' current woes.

Who's Who among American High School Students, which lists 700,000
high-achieving students, surveyed these top performers last year and found
that 80 percent said they had cheated during their academic careers. Joe
Krouse, associate publisher of the listing, says it is "the highest level we've
ever seen."

Mr. Krouse taps adult behavior as a factor. "Because adults and role
models in society do it, some students may have used those examples to
rationalize cheating," he says. In a survey conducted in 1997–98, he also
found that 66 percent of the parents of these top students said cheating was
"not a big deal."

COLLEGES ARE WATCHING MORE CLOSELY

Whatever the reason for cheating, its sheer volume is capturing the attention of more than a few schools. Most, chary of their images, downplay
dishonesty, unwilling to air dirty laundry in public. Yet a few are confronting
cheating by making it highly public—on campus, at least.

The University of Texas is the nation's largest university with about
50,000 students. It has roughly 180 academic-integrity cases pop up annually,
says Kevin Price, assistant dean of students. The school is trying to raise the
profile of integrity issues during orientation with skits, a 10-page handout on
plagiarism, and a newsletter called the *Integrity Herald* for faculty.

Another sign of academic stirring: the Center for Academic Integrity,   15
founded in 1993, already has 175 member schools and is drafting a framework
of principles that could be applied nationwide to lower student cheating.

Schools like Stanford University, Georgetown University, the University of
Delaware, and a half-dozen others are also buffing up or introducing new honor
codes.

But Mr. Madson at Vanderbilt University says what is most needed is for
students themselves to take charge and reject the attitude that cheating can be
justified.

Students say time and workload pressure are major factors spurring academic dishonesty, followed by parental pressure. "It's definitely what you get
assigned—and how long you have to do it—that right there determines
whether you're going to cheat," says Smolik, the University of Texas freshman.

Anne-Elyse Smith, another freshman at Texas, reasoned in an online
debate that it may not be smart to cheat, but it could be educationally valuable.

"People should hold themselves accountable to a standard at which they   20
are comfortable, and get out of the education what they can," she wrote. "If that

involves looking at one answer on a quiz, I think the person is more likely to re-member that one answer since they had to resort to cheating to obtain it."

A LITTLE IMAGINATION, A LOT OF HIGH TECH

Whether copying another student's homework, cheating on a test, or plagiarizing an essay, cheating is limited only by imagination—and technology. Some program their calculators with formulas, but rig them to show an empty memory if an instructor checks.

But what alarms some campus officials the most is the Internet's proven potential for explosive growth in negative areas such as pornography—and the possibility that plagiarism could be next. Web sites sporting names like "Cheater.com" and "School Sucks" offer tools for rampant plagiarism at the click of a mouse. "Download your workload" the latter site suggests, boasting more than 1 million term-paper downloads.

Such savvy borrowing may be lost on some educators, but others, like librarians, are catching up. "Students are finding it so easy to use these sources that they will dump them in the middle of the papers without any attribu-tion," says John Ruszkiewicz, an English professor at Texas. "What they don't realize is how readily [professors] can tell the material isn't the student's and how easy it is for instructors to search this material on the Web."

Anthony Krier, a reference librarian at Franklin Pierce College Library in Rindge, N.H., is one such literary bloodhound. Last semester, he investi-gated nine cases of plagiarism, three of them involving the Internet. One stu-dent had downloaded and passed off as his own a morality essay, apparently unaware of the irony, Mr. Krier says.

Some colleges are fighting back with explicit warnings, more detailed   25 orientations, and classes on how to cite sources—and lawsuits. Boston Uni-versity sued five online "term-paper mills" in 1997. The case was rejected by a federal judge last month. School officials vow to refile.

Last fall, the dean of the school's College of Communication, Brent Baker, wrote a letter to students urging them to protect their "good name" by reviewing carefully the school's code of conduct. To drive home the point, he attached a listing of 13 unnamed cases and the penalties—probation, suspension, and expulsion—meted out.

Likewise, the 152 reports of academic dishonesty for 1997–98 at the University of Southern California in Los Angeles "is higher than previous comparable years beginning in 1991," wrote Sandra Rhoten, assistant dean in the office of student conduct, in a letter in the campus newspaper describing violations and sanctions assessed.

"We had a full-blown, two-year campaign [starting in 1995] to educate people about the problem," Ms. Rhoten says in an interview. "Sometimes fac-ulty feel alone in this. We're reassuring them that we take this seriously too."

THE EXPECTATION OF HONESTY

Being blunt is the idea. Talking about the expectation of honesty is constant. And along with explicit warning shots, freshmen at USC are getting more intensive and detailed training in what constitutes plagiarism and other forms of cheating, Rhoten says.

The school passes out brochures on plagiarism, has regular coverage in   30 the student paper on cheating cases, and has beefed up orientation courses with training to explain subtler issues like unauthorized collaboration—the largest area of student honor violation at USC and many other campuses, Mr. McCabe and others say.

For instance, Lucia Brawley, a senior majoring in English at Harvard University in Cambridge, Mass., does not believe cheating is a big problem at her school. But when asked about the collaboration issue, she is less sure.

"With people I know in the sciences, there's so much to do and so little time, they help each other," she says. "You go to a lecture today, I'll go next week. You do the reading this week, I'll do it next week. It's a gray area."

Ultimately, though, it is students who will have to uphold academic integrity themselves, many say.

The University of Virginia has a student-run honor code whose "single sanction" for violators is expulsion. It is one of the nation's strictest. Even after more than a century, it remains controversial on campus. Of 11 cheating cases last semester, five resulted in expulsion. But the code has also created an atmosphere of trust that means students can take unproctored exams. "Many of our alumni attribute their success in life to this school's honor code," says Cabell Vest, a graduate student who chairs UVA's honor council.

At Vanderbilt, which also has a strict code, 20 academic dishonesty   35 cases are under review, Madson says—triple the number a few years ago. But he is confident the school is creating an atmosphere less tolerant of cheating. "You just can't have an academic enterprise that isn't based on integrity and honesty," he says. "Nobody wants somebody building bridges to take shortcuts."

QUESTIONING THE TEXT

1. Clayton quotes a provost from Vanderbilt who asserts that "'[n]obody cheated [in the 1960s] because of the peer pressure and likelihood of being turned in'" (paragraph 9). Examine this statement in the context in which it is made and then decide how you might go about testing its validity. What would you have to read and examine and who would you have to interview to confirm or refute its validity?

2. One student in the online debate asserts that "it may not be smart to cheat, but it could be educationally valuable." Examine the student's full statement and its rationale (paragraphs 19–20). Then discuss the implications of the statement with your classmates, either in face-to-face conversation or in an online forum or listserv.

3. Examine the image that accompanies "A Whole Lot of Cheatin' Going On." What does it depict? How does it shape your perception of the essay? For instance, does it seem less serious than the subject warrants? Does it remind you of what it is like to take examinations?

MAKING CONNECTIONS

4. Review Clayton's article on cheating in light of the changes in copyright law described in Pamela Samuelson's "The Digital Rights War" (p. 315). Is it possible that our attitudes toward plagiarism may change as electronic data is transmitted faster and more routinely? Write a dialogue on that possibility between a student who expects to use electronic sources routinely in papers and an instructor who wishes he or she would not.

5. Read the college mission statements in Chapter 3 (p. 51) and imagine how you might present a school's position on cheating. Write a position statement for your institution on the issue of scholastic integrity. Imagine the statement as a Web page. What issues would you present? What images might you use? What links might you make?

JOINING THE CONVERSATION

6. Conduct a series of interviews on your campus to explore the issue of scholastic integrity within a small group you can readily identify — for instance, your fraternity or sorority, the Young Democrats, or the club volleyball team. Use Clayton's article to prepare a list of interview questions about plagiarism, cheating, and collusion at your institution; avoid questions that can be answered by a simple yes or no. Then write a brief report summarizing what you've discovered locally about scholastic integrity. Quote freely from your interviews, but be sure to protect the interviewees' anonymity.

7. Locate a copy of your institution's policies on cheating, plagiarism, and collusion. Then write a critical analysis of these statements. Are the statements clear? Are important terms carefully defined? Do the statements provide a convincing ethical rationale for the policies announced? Do the policies account for changes as a result of electronic technology?

ANTHONY BRANDT
Do Kids Need Religion?

*A*NTHONY B*RANDT*, *a contributing editor at* Parenting *magazine, focuses on the relationship of children to religious faith. Brandt speaks as a parent, one concerned about how best to help his children face the losses and traumas life always brings. In this essay, published in 1991 in the progressive* Utne Reader, *he describes himself as a "run-of-the-mill modern skeptic," without faith or belief, and asks us to consider the uses of religion in what he terms a largely secular society. Might religion serve as a unifying cultural force, even for people who don't "believe"? Even more important, Brandt asks, "What sort of meaning does a secular society offer a child?" These questions suggest that Brandt is searching for a basis on which he can make some very hard choices about how he will (and should) raise his children.*

    I admire Brandt's straightforward approach here, his willingness to consider various options, and his refusal to argue that his *way to spirituality is the only or even the best way. In addition, I find that Brandt establishes some common ground for all people, regardless of differences in religious faith or creed, when he says, "The longing for meaning is something we all share. . . ."*

—A.L.

This happened nearly 20 years ago, so I may not have all the details right. As I remember, my daughter was about 10 years old. She had spent the weekend with her grandparents, and while she was gone, a house down the road from ours burned to the ground. Three children died in the fire. One was a houseguest. The other two were my daughter's closest friends.

My wife went to see the bereaved parents. They were devout Catholics and they took their loss amazingly well. They talked to her about their two girls being angels in heaven now, and they really believed it. At the funeral, they were strong and brave, braver than many others there, including myself.

My tears were bitter. I didn't think their children were angels, I thought they were dead. I had little confidence in any sort of existence beyond that. I was not a devout Catholic or a devout anything. I was your run-of-the-mill modern skeptic who long before had stopped going to church, thought most religious doctrine absurd, and was resolved to live without the illusions of belief.

I know children who have experienced the death of a loved one "up close and personal." Our society holds death so much at arm's length and tries to deny it in so many ways that we don't in any way prepare children (or ourselves) for its reality.

—A.L.

191

What does your run-of-the-mill modern skeptic tell his 10-year-old daughter when her closest friends have just died in a fire? My wife and I told her what had happened when she got home from her grandparents' house. I was crying and so was my wife, but my daughter just sat there, stunned, in shock. I wanted so much to console her, to find something to say that would explain, would justify these deaths and give them meaning. But I didn't think these deaths had any meaning. All I could come up with was something I didn't believe. "Maybe there is a heaven," I said, "and that's where they are." Yeah, maybe. And maybe not.

I'm old enough to know now that there's no living without illusions of some sort, that we all need to find or generate some kind of meaning for our lives if life is not to become unbearable. But what kind? It goes without saying that we are no longer a religious society in the conventional sense of the word. Religion no longer stands at the center of our culture as it did a hundred or so years ago. Rather, we are a thoroughly secularized society. The miracles we marvel at are the miracles of technology. For the answers to our questions about the meaning of things, we look not to the elders of a church, but to science.

Is Brandt saying that meaning is always in some sense an illusion? I wouldn't use the word illusion here. A construct, perhaps, but not an illusion. —A.L.

Doesn't Brandt underestimate the influence of religion in the USA here? —J.R.

An event like the cruel and pointless death of three little girls, however, presents a fundamental challenge. What sort of meaning does a secular society offer a child? What do parents with no religious beliefs do when their children start asking those difficult questions about where Grandpa has gone, Grandpa having just died, or why Jesus was crucified, and why people are so mean, and what will happen to them when they die?

It might, in fact, be harder for a believer to explain to children why a benevolent God would allow such a tragedy to befall the faithful. —J.G.R.

For some parents, to be sure, questions like these present no problem. Either they have religious beliefs and are confident they can transmit them to their kids, or they have no religious beliefs at all and see no reason to raise their children to have any. I asked one father what he had done about his kids' religious education and he said, "Nothing whatsoever." Well, I went on, how did he answer their questions about God and things like that? He didn't remember there being any. And even if there are questions, a parent can say, "Go ask your mother" or "I'm no expert on that" or simply "I don't know," and let it go at that. Western culture is so secularized that parents can evade or dismiss "religious" questions without feeling that they're merely getting themselves off the hook. No one is surprised anymore by this kind of religious indifference.

Surprised? No. But what are the consequences? —J.R.

For believers, too, the problem doesn't exist. Secure in their own faith, they can confidently answer the questions of a child.

How can he be so sure? Don't all people—believers or not—have doubts? —J.G.R.

Another mother and father, not so secure in their faith, say it was actually their children who brought them back to religion. They had both been raised Roman Catholic; each had children from a previous marriage; both had lapsed from the church. But they were sending their kids to a Protestant Sunday school. One night at dinner the oldest child said, "Don't you think we should pray for this food?" This was something of a shock. It was even more so when the child said, in prayer, "And thank you, God, for bringing our whole family together." The following Sunday the parents went to church. They have been actively involved (in a Protestant congregation) ever since. "Children come up with some really interesting questions," the mother told me, "and we still have to do a lot of explaining. But we have faith. We don't feel that we're alone with these questions."

This isn't at all clear to me. Faith in what? And how does this faith have to do with not "being alone" with these questions? —A.L.

For those of us without faith it's not so easy. Do we send our kids to Sunday school when we ourselves never go to church? Do we have them baptized even though we have no intention of raising them to be religious? I argued against having my son baptized. It's a meaningless ritual, I said. I didn't think he had been "born in sin," so why wash him free of it, even symbolically? Why bow to convention simply for convention's sake? I gave in, but only to keep peace in the family.

The author seems earnest. Why do I feel uneasy as a reader? —J.R.

For me religious education raised the issue of honesty. I thought it would be hypocritical to make my kids attend Sunday school when I not only didn't go to church but also didn't have any

Are there reasons for sending children to Sunday school that go beyond religious beliefs? —A.L.

religious beliefs. My parents had sent me to Sunday school when neither of them was in the least religious, and under the circumstances I came to think Sunday school was a joke. I learned a few Bible stories, but that was all. I believed I should spare my children that kind of charade. My wife took them to church from time to time, but only once or twice did they attend a Sunday school class.

I'm still wondering whether we did the right thing. In *Childhood and Society* the renowned psychoanalyst Erik Erikson makes the unsettling remark that "many are proud to be without religion whose children cannot afford their being without it." Children may not need a religious upbringing, but, says Erikson, they do need a sense of "basic trust," a feeling not only that their fundamental bodily needs will be met and that their parents love them and will take care of them, but also that they have not been abandoned to the empty haphazardness of existence.

Children can be taught moral values and courage without religion.
— J.G.R.

I can't see offhand why religion is the only thing that could fulfill this need not to feel abandoned.
— A.L.

Erikson relates this sense of trust to the psychosocial origins of religious life. "The parental faith which supports the trust emerging in the newborn," he writes, "has throughout history sought its institutional safeguard . . . in organized religion." The trust of the infant in the parents, in other words, finds its parallel—and takes its mature form—in the parents' trust in God. The implication is that if trust has no institutional reinforcement, it will tend to wither. Basic trust will become basic mistrust, and there will be more work for mental health experts such as Erikson.

The institutional form that trust has taken in America has historically remained within the Judeo-Christian tradition, and the decision to deny that tradition to a child ought at the very least to be well thought out. Children will become aware of the tradition with or without parental teaching; they'll bring it home from school or the playground, wanting to know why their friend Jimmy says they'll go to hell if they don't go to church, or why Alice is getting a beautiful white confirmation dress and they're not. A psychoanalyst, Ana-Marie Rizzuto, once pointed out that no matter what parents teach their children, "religious symbols and language are so widely present in this society that

Brandt equates religion with objects and symbols, not beliefs and moral choices. I'm disappointed that all he's worried about is that his children won't fit into a Judeo-Christian culture. — J.R.

virtually no child reaches school age without having constructed—with or without religious instruction—an image or images of God."

I broached the subject with one couple who have a three-year-old daughter. The father, Pete, was raised in a fundamentalist family and rebelled against it; religion holds a kind of perverse fascination for him, but he is not what you would call a believer. His wife, Valerie, has no religious beliefs to speak of. Yet they both want their daughter to go to Sunday school. "I don't want her to grow up in a religious vacuum," says Pete. He thinks that if they don't give her a religious background they will be depriving her of a choice later on. If she has the background, she can always reject it when she gets older, he says; if she doesn't, there will be nothing to reject but nothing to affirm, either. He doesn't think she would be likely to come to that crossroads on her own. Valerie agrees with this reasoning: "I want her to know the Bible stories, the mythology," she says. "It's a major part of our culture. And I want her to have a sense of mystery, of awe." A sense, says Pete, that in our society has largely been lost.

If this approach seems paradoxical coming from parents who are not themselves believers, it also makes a certain amount of sense. No matter what we believe in, our society's Judeo-Christian tradition retains a good deal of its power. I reject organized religion, yet I cannot listen to Mozart's *Requiem Mass* without being moved. Perhaps nonpracticing Jews feel the same when they hear Hebrew prayers sung. Much of Western culture springs from religious feeling; we are secular but our heritage is not, and there is no true identification with a culture without some feel for its past. To raise children in a culture without at least exposing them to its religious traditions, even if you yourself have abandoned the beliefs on which they are based, may be doing them a disservice. The children will be exposed to those traditions in any case, so why not give them some real instruction?

Pete and Valerie are not alone; among the nonbelieving parents I talked to, theirs was a common rationale for sending their children to Sunday school, and the most common solution to the

What he wants for his children is "religious appreciation," not religion. No hard choices here—religion as art.   —J.R.

Why does religious instruction have to come from a church?   —J.G.R.

There's a big difference between introducing children to the religious traditions of our culture (which are quite diverse) and training them into one set of religious beliefs as absolutely the truth and the one way.   —A.L.

problem. Several other parents, however, admitted to qualms. "Kids pick up on your real feelings about things pretty fast," one father said. "If you're making them do something you yourself don't believe in, they're going to figure it out." And a mother told me, "I think you can transmit values to your kids, but belief is different. Values—respect for other people, respect for life, not taking what doesn't belong to you, things like that—they're universal, they're everywhere. But belief is a special thing. You have to come to it on your own; nobody can impose it on you."

How typical of our times to regard "values" as universal and belief as contingent. We'd better hope there is no God! —J.R.

Too, it is impossible to predict with any confidence what effect a religious education will have on children. It can be more than a little uncomfortable when your children take religious teaching more seriously than you do. It is unsettling to think that they might need religion when you have decided you do not. Do kids in fact need religion? They need "basic trust," as Erikson says, but beyond that, nobody has conclusive answers. We used to think that without religious beliefs, social behavior would come unglued. "If God is dead," wrote Dostoyevski, "then everything is permitted." It hasn't happened.

Well, yes, or any other training, for that matter. Some of the most horrible characters in our history, for instance, were thoroughly trained in religions and/or other traditions. —A.L.

Wrong. What— besides racism and sexism—is regarded as sinful these days? Adultery? Pornography? Idolatry? Abortion? Covetousness? —J.R.

Morality can survive without religion, it appears; children can be taught the importance of right versus wrong without benefit of religious training. Jean Piaget and Lawrence Kohlberg* have shown that moral understanding is acquired in stages, that it is a developmental process that unfolds, to some extent, as naturally as intelligence itself.

All of Brandt's sources are psychologists. What's his own background? —J.G.R.

My daughter, now age 27, who was exposed to little more than my own deep skepticism, is studying Buddhism. As I write, in fact, she is in Tibet, on a journey that I'm sure is at least partly spiritual. I have made spiritual journeys during my adult life, all of them outside the sphere of Christianity that I was raised in. I continue to distrust and

---

Jean Piaget (1896–1980) *and Lawrence Kohlberg* (1927–87): psychologists who studied the mental and moral development of children and young adults

dislike organized religion but find it hard, as I grow older, to live with only my vague faith that life must have some kind of meaning, even if I don't know what it is.

To believe is to be connected, and those of us who don't believe cannot help but miss the feelings that come with belonging to something larger than ourselves. I hope my children find a straighter road than I've found. "I very much wish I had had some religion, for my kids' sake," one father told me. "My son's into tarot cards now. There's not much comfort in tarot cards."

This is an interesting definition of belief— "to be connected." I'll have to think about this; I'm not sure I agree. —A.L.

The longing for meaning is something we all share, parent and child alike. But it may be that this is an area where a parent can't help a child much. Meaning may be something all of us have to find in our own way. I don't know. I am loath to give advice. Robert Coles* quotes a black woman who worked as a servant for a wealthy white Southern family: "My momma told me: Remember that you're put here only for a few seconds of God's time, and he's testing you. He doesn't want answers, though. He wants you to know how to ask the right questions." Teaching our kids how to ask the right questions may be the best we can do.

This is a safe and predictable conclusion. No strong position is taken. I'm disappointed. —J.R.

I end up wondering where Brandt stands on his original question. I'll need to reread this to decide whether his answer is yes, no, or maybe. —A.L.

Afterwords

I agree that human beings seek meaning, that we yearn for meaning so strongly that we will make meaning(s) at all cost. Further, I consider this yearning to be a function related to our being inside a world of languages—which is why the philosopher Kenneth Burke defines people as "symbol-using, symbol-abusing animals." Language allows us to assign meaning, and if this capacity is by definition human, then it makes perfect sense that we would need to assign meaning, demand to make meaning.

That said, I'm willing to follow in Brandt's steps as he explores the central question of his essay, which I would rephrase as, "Will religion help kids make or find meaning?" Put this way, my answer would be conditional: organized religion can help people make meaning, and it can do so largely by way of its own

---

Robert Coles: an educational psychologist (b. 1929) whose work on the ethical life of children has been widely influential

language, its symbolicity. But I'd also say that organized religion won't automatically *help kids or anyone else find meaning.*

Brandt claims not to have religion, but rather "spirituality." What seems to give meaning to him and his life is his connection to others, particularly his family, and his commitment to intellectual inquiry, to continued probing of important issues, including those of religion and meaning. In this regard, I am most sympathetic to him. I find meaning in my own life in relationship to someone else, either in person (as with my friends, my family, and especially my students) or in words (with persons I know only through books). Meaning, it strikes me, isn't ever in us or indeed in any one thing; rather, meaning arises out of connections and relations. For me, these are the pathways to spirituality, ones I'd like to share with "kids" of all ages. —A.L.

One reason I am not now particularly religious is that I am unmoved by "soft" notions of religion such as put forth by Brandt and to some extent by A.L. Raised in a strict Catholic tradition, I take little solace or intellectual satisfaction in faith represented chiefly as a quest for meaning or selfhood. Religion makes more sense to me if it also deals with timeless, if evolving, truths.

To offer religion to children as an alternative to harsh reality—as a way of explaining to a ten-year-old why her best friends died in a fire, to use Brandt's example—trivializes religion. That a nonbelieving parent like Brandt might expose his children to organized religion because he wants them to know the tradition behind Mozart's Requiem *is to treat faith with secular contempt, rendering it as worthless as sunshine patriotism. Religion is about hard choices, not easy ones; about truths, not feelings. Questions of faith compel individuals to face the abyss and to confront the responsibility we have for our own souls. Religion defines meaning not in terms of historical and cultural artifacts, but in terms of a higher power. At some point, this faith requires a difficult, uncompromising, and honest credo.*

I am not able to speak that word yet, but when and if I do, I don't expect my life to be any easier. —J.R.

As an agnostic parent, I looked forward to reading this piece. After reading it, I feel let down, mostly because it seems long on questions and short on answers.

I wanted guidance, but instead I got descriptions of wishy-washy parents relying on religious institutions they have no faith in to give their children moral security and structure. How hypocritical! I expected a spectrum of authoritative opinions, but Brandt relies solely on psychologists.

Because this issue is so critical to me, I may have wanted too much from Brandt. In raising my son, Luke, I can relate to some of Brandt's experiences. But I feel I might be setting Luke up for a spiritual fall if I were to raise him in a religion I have no faith in myself. He might ultimately lose faith in me as well as in religion. Apparently, what I want no writer can objectively give: answers to an eternal enigma. —J.G.R.

QUESTIONING THE TEXT

1. What would be the effect of changing Brandt's title question to "Do Kids Need Morality?" What evidence in the essay relates Brandt's discussion of religion to issues of morality?

2. What is Brandt's answer to his title question, "Do Kids Need Religion?" What in the essay most clearly tells you what the answer is? If you keep a reading log, answer these questions there.

3. Look at the questions A.L., J.R., and J.G.R. pose in their marginal commentary on this piece. Choose several of their questions and decide what functions each question serves. Can you see any differences in the kinds of questions each reader tends to ask?

MAKING CONNECTIONS

4. Judging from their selections in this chapter, what advice would Martin Luther King Jr. (p. 142) and Stephen L. Carter (p. 157) likely give Brandt about children and religion? Imagine that you are either King or Carter, and write a letter to Brandt offering such advice.

5. In what ways might Brandt's spiritual quest be compared to that depicted in Kathleen Norris's "Little Girls in Church" (p. 222)? How do Brandt and Norris differ in their relationship to belief or faith?

6. Is Brandt's attitude toward faith chiefly secular? After reading the selections by Joan Didion (p. 179) and Edward O. Wilson (p. 322), write a brief essay that compares and contrasts the views of these three writers on the secular nature of faith and morality.

JOINING THE CONVERSATION

7. Like other authors in this chapter, Brandt seems to distinguish between *spirituality* (or *spiritual quest*) and *religion*. Try your hand at comparing and contrasting these terms in writing, and bring your definitions to class for discussion.

8. Working with two or three classmates, answer Brandt's question, "Do kids need religion?" Then together draw up a list of reasons, examples, or other evidence to support your answer. Finally, on your own, draft a one-page position paper beginning with either "Kids need religion" or "Kids don't need religion."

DAVID BROOKS
Conscientious Consumption

My INTRODUCTION TO WHAT DAVID BROOKS *playfully describes as* conscientious consumption *occurred during the recent remodeling of my kitchen. I thought that my parquet floor, scarred by fifteen years of scuffs, spills, and incontinent dogs, ought to be replaced. But the interior designer assured me that distressed wood was very much in vogue and that people paid good money to acquire kitchen floors as battered as mine.*

Conscientious consumption is the opposite of conspicuous consumption, *a phrase coined early in the twentieth century by economist Thorstein Veblen (1857– 1929) to describe the propensity of capitalists to put their wealth on haughty display as an exercise of power. Today, however, such ostentation has become so outmoded that the wealthy — at least in some parts of the country — spend huge sums of money to give their homes and possessions a stylish patina of poverty. David Brooks pokes fun at this fashion in his article by mercilessly listing what he describes as the Code of Financial Correctness and then fleshing out its specific details. But his article raises a serious moral question, too, about the motives of people who enjoy the fruits of consumerism while pretending to detest them. Their behavior, which seems at first glance merely silly, might, in fact, be profoundly deceptive and hypocritical.*

"Conscientious Consumption" first appeared in the New Yorker *(23 November 1998), a magazine of culture and commentary. David Brooks is a senior editor of the* Weekly Standard, *a conservative political journal.* —J.R.

You're a highly cultured person who has never cared all that much about money, but suddenly, thanks to the information-age economy, you find yourself making more dough than you ever expected. The problem is: How to spend all that income without looking like one of the vulgar yuppies you despise? Fortunately, a Code of Financial Correctness is emerging. It's a set of rules to guide your consumption patterns, to help you spend money in ways that are spiritually and culturally uplifting. If you follow these precepts, you'll be able to dispose of up to four or five million dollars annually in a manner that shows how little you care about material things.

Rule No. 1: Only vulgarians spend a lot of money on luxuries; restrict your lavish spending to necessities. When it comes to members of the cultivated class, the richer they get the more they emulate the Shakers. It's crass to spend sixty thousand dollars on a Porsche, but it's a sign of elevated consciousness to spend sixty-five thousand dollars on a boxy and practical Range Rover. It's decadent to spend ten thousand dollars on an outdoor Jacuzzi, but if you're not spending twenty-five thousand dollars turning a spare bedroom into a new master bath, with a freestanding copper tub in the middle of the floor and an oversized slate shower stall, it's a sign that you probably haven't learned to appreciate the simple rhythms of life.

An important corollary to Rule No. 1 is that you can never spend too much money on a room or a piece of equipment that in an earlier age would have been used primarily by the servants. It's vulgar to spend fifteen thousand dollars on a sound system and a wide-screen TV, but it's virtuous to spend fifty thousand dollars on a utilitarian room, like the kitchen. Only a bounder would buy a Louis Vuitton briefcase, but the owner of a German-made Miele White Pearl vacuum cleaner, which retails for seven hundred and forty-nine dollars, clearly has his priorities straight.

Rule No. 2: It is perfectly acceptable to spend lots of money on anything that is "professional quality," even if it has nothing to do with your profession. For example, although you are not likely ever to climb Mt. Everest, an expedition-weight three-layer Gore-Tex Alpenglow-reinforced Marmot Thunderlight jacket is a completely reasonable purchase. You may not be planning to convert your home into a restaurant, but a triple-doored Sub Zero refrigerator and a ten-thousand-dollar AGA cooker with a warming plate, a simmering plate, a baking oven, a roasting oven, and an infinite supply of burners is still a sensible acquisition.

Rule No. 3: You can never have too much texture. The high-achieving   5
but grasping consumers of the nineteen-eighties surrounded themselves with smooth surfaces—matte black furniture, polished lacquer floors, and sleek faux-marbleized walls. To demonstrate your spiritual superiority to such people, you'll want to build an environment full of natural irregularities. Everything they made smooth you'll want to make rough. You'll hire squads of workmen with ball-peen hammers to pound some rustic authenticity into your broad floor planks. You'll import craftsmen from Umbria to create the look of crumbling frescoed plaster in your foyer. You'll want a fireplace built from craggy stones that look as if they could withstand a catapult assault. You'll want sideboards with peeling layers of paint, rough-hewn exposed beams, lichenous stone walls, weathered tiles, nubby upholstery fabrics. Remember, if your furniture is distressed your conscience needn't be.

The texture principle applies to comestibles, too. Everything you drink will leave sediment in the bottom of the glass: yeasty microbrews, unfiltered fruit juices, organic coffees. Your bread will be thick and grainy, the way wholesome peasants like it, not thin and airy, as shallow suburbanites prefer. Even your condiments will be admirably coarse; you'll know you're refined when you start using unrefined sugar.

Rule No. 4: You must practice one-downmanship. Cultivated people are repelled by the idea of keeping up with the Joneses. Thus, in order to raise your own status you must conspicuously reject status symbols. You will never display gilt French antiques or precious jewelry, but you will proudly dine on a two-hundred-year-old pine table that was once used for slaughtering chickens. Your closet doors will have been salvaged from an old sausage factory. Your living-room rugs will resemble the ponchos worn by Mexican paupers. The baby gates on the stairs will have been converted from nineteenth-century rabbit hutches. Eventually, every object in your house will look as if it had once been owned by someone much poorer than you.

You will never spend large sums on things associated with the rich, like yachts, caviar, or truffles. Instead, you will buy unpretentious items associated with the proletariat—except that you'll buy pretentious versions of these items, which actual members of the proletariat would find preposterous. For example, you'll go shopping for a basic food like potatoes, but you won't buy an Idaho spud. You'll select one of those miniature potatoes of distinction that grow only in certain soils of northern France. When you need lettuce, you will choose only from among those flimsy cognoscenti lettuces that taste so bad on sandwiches. (You will buy these items in boutique grocery stores whose inventory says "A Year in Provence" even as their prices say "Ten Years Out of Medical School.")

Accordingly, you will pay hugely inflated prices for all sorts of things that uncultivated people buy cheap: coffee at three seventy-five a cup, water at five dollars a bottle, a bar of soap for twelve dollars. Even your plain white T-shirt will run fifty dollars or more. The average person might be satisfied with a twenty-dollar shovel from Sears, but the sophisticated person will appreciate the heft and grip of the fifty-nine-dollar English-made Bull Dog brand garden spade

Why buy an Idaho spud when you can have a potato of distinction that grows only in the soil of northern France?

that can be found at Smith & Hawken. When buying your necessities, you have   10
to prove that you are serious enough to appreciate the best.

Rule No. 5: If you want to practice conscientious consumption, you'll want to be able to discourse knowledgeably about everything you buy. You'll favor catalogues that provide some helpful background reading on each item. You'll want your coffee shop and your bookstore to have maxims from Emerson and Arendt on the walls, because there is nothing more demeaning than shopping in a store that offers no teleological context for your purchases. You'll only patronize a butcher who hosts poetry readings. Remember, you are not merely a pawn in a mass consumer society; you are the curator of your purchases. You are able to elevate consumption above the material plane. You are able to turn your acquisitions into a set of morally informed signifiers that will win the approbation of your peers. You are able to create a life style that compensates for the fact that you abandoned your early interest in poetry and grew up to be a corporate lawyer. You care enough to spend the very most.

QUESTIONING THE TEXT

1. Brooks mentions some items that people who follow his "Code of Financial Correctness" would never purchase — including a Porsche, a Jacuzzi, and a wide-screen TV. Identify other products that might similarly be avoided by those practicing conscientious consumption. Why exactly might they attach a stigma to these goods?

2. Look at the cartoon by Michael Crawford that accompanies Brooks's text. What does it suggest about the attitudes of conscientious consumers? Which of its details contribute to this impression? Do you think the cartoon is a more effective illustration for this piece than a photograph would have been? Why, or why not?

3. The last line of Brooks's article parodies a famous advertising slogan. Identify the original slogan and then explore the implications of Brooks's new version. Working with some classmates, create an advertisement, complete with images, that features that line: "You care enough to spend the very most."

MAKING CONNECTIONS

4. Brooks's "Conscientious Consumption" draws a series of comparisons that roughly parallels those Dave Barry offers in "Guys vs. Men" (p. 372). Both articles also use humor to make potentially serious points. Read the two pieces side by side and comment on these relationships and any others you uncover.

5. Review James Q. Wilson's "Cars and Their Enemies" (p. 303) in light of the attitudes attributed to conscientious consumers. Would someone who

practices conscientious consumption more likely be a friend or an enemy of the car? Provide evidence to support your claim.

6. An equally strict code of consumer behavior is set forth and analyzed in three readings in Chapter 8, Home—"Ask Martha: Guest Towels" (p. 654), Tom Connor and Jim Downey's "Well-Stacked Logs" (p. 656), and Margaret Talbot's "Les Très Riches Heures de Martha Stewart" (p. 657). After reading these selections, and perhaps viewing Martha Stewart's television program or visting her Web site, discuss with three or four classmates how much—or how little—devotees of Stewart have in common with Brooks's conscientious consumers.

JOINING THE CONVERSATION

7. In an essay, explore the implications of Brooks's odd statement: "Remember, if your furniture is distressed your conscience needn't be" (paragraph 5). What does old-looking furniture have to do with issues of conscience? Draw upon other parts of "Conscientious Consumption" to develop your paper.

8. Write a paper that borrows the structure of Brooks's essay by identifying an idea comparable to conscientious consumption, creating a "Code of _____," and then listing its rules. Be sure to flesh out your paper with the kind of specific details that make Brooks's piece both humorous and persuasive.

PETER J. GOMES
Civic Virtue and the Character of Followership: A New Take on an Old Hope

As a very amateur photographer fond of western landscapes, I sometimes return from road trips with prints of canyons, cliffs, or rock formations that seem out of kilter—distorted and oddly incomprehensible—until I turn them 180 degrees and look at them the way I originally shot them. To some extent, that's what the Reverend Peter J. Gomes does in the following lecture on leadership. In a portion of the lecture not included here, he reviews an American political and social landscape that seems familiar and distorted all at the same time, a free nation in which prosperous and oddly contented people complain constantly about the quality of the nation's leaders. Deftly, then, Gomes rotates this portrait and asks his listeners to examine it again, from their point of view as citizens and followers. Can a nation have distinguished leaders, he wonders in the section reprinted here, if leaders do not have virtuous men and women to follow them? In other words, to understand leadership we must also appreciate what Gomes calls good "followership."

Aside from the intriguing issues Gomes raises and the historical perspectives he offers, I chose this selection because it captures a potent rhetorical moment. Gomes delivered "Civic Virtue and the Character of Followership" to a large and enthusiastic audience at the University of Texas on March 24, 1997, his artful phrases and sonorous voice providing a potent lesson in eloquence. Portions of the speech reproduced here in printed form retain some of the oral features that made his performance so memorable. But they only hint at the brightness of the occasion.

Gomes (b. 1942) is Plummer Professor of Christian Morals and Pusey Minister in the Memorial Church at Harvard University. One of America's most distinguished preachers, he is the author of The Good Book: Reading the Bible with Mind and Heart *(1996).*   —J.R.

. . .

. . . Those of us who have had to read, and then subsequently have had to teach, the history of the Romans and the Greeks, understand that the greatness of those cultures was never the great leader, it was always the good people, and it is that inversion, or reversion, that has produced much of the dilemma of our modern secular industrialized west. What we have lost, in my opinion, is not a succession of able leaders in church or state or in the civic body, in the sense of a legitimate peoplehood, not just an aggregate population but the sense of an identity and an obligation as people. We have lost, or at least have mislaid, the concept of civic virtue. This is not just shorthand, this notion of civic virtue, again an appeal to conservative culture and family values, this is not an attempt to elect again Bill Bennett* as our philosopher king, but it is an attempt to address the need for a recovery of a sensibility, a sense of what it means to share and to serve in a state which is not driven by our own immediate interests. That is perhaps one of the most radical statements that a speaker would be permitted to get away with today before a reasonably comprehending audience.

A citizen is one who belongs and who has obligations: those are the two fundamental pillars upon which the notion of belonging to the *civitas,* the people or the city, is based, the notion of belonging, of having an identity of which one is proud and by which one is defined, and having an obligation to share and to serve in behalf of that greater good. The purpose of such an aggregation of citizens is not rights but obligations, and consists not first in self but first in duty. Now these are stern, old-fashioned, and strangely foreign words to us because for at least a hundred years and maybe a hundred more years than that, we have been taught by precept and example exactly the opposite, and I would be the last person to deny that I have benefited from parts of that agenda. I have enjoyed the benefits of living in a state which takes care of and is concerned for and is passionate about the individual, which allows individual rights and individual merits to determine the cultural marketplace of ideas, and which is concerned at great cost to protect the individual over against an overweening or an imperious or an indifferent state. We are in this country remarkably free from the tyranny of majoritarian rule, though that is always present in the process by which we do our business. I, and all of you, have taken the benefit of all of that, but we have reached the point, I think, where it is important to say well and good, but not enough. There must be more to this, and in part that more is the return to something which we may once have understood but from which we have long departed.

The Roman understood that to be a citizen of the republic or of the empire was to belong to something that was great and good that exceeded the individual compass of his own experience or his own needs, or his own opportunities. Citizenship in that sense was the highest right to which an individual could aspire, to be a part of such a community. It was in 1986, for example, that somebody struggled greatly with trying to achieve the kind of culture in which citizenship could be affirmed in this way. I quote from Václav Havel: "Without free, self-respecting and autonomous citizens, there can be no free and independent nations. Without internal peace, that is, peace among citizens and between citizens and the state, there can be no guarantee of external peace." That is an attempt to define the relationship of the individual to the whole, the private agenda to the public weal.

Bill Bennett: William J. Bennett, former U.S. drug czar and secretary of education. Author of *The Book of Virtues: A Treasury of Great Moral Stories* (1993)

It was the American judge at the Nuremberg Trials and a justice of the Supreme Court, Judge Robert Jackson, who wrote in 1950, "It is not the function of our government to keep the citizen from falling into error, it is the function of the citizen to keep the government from falling into error."

It would be no less robust an American than Theodore Roosevelt, who in 1902 would say that "The first requirement of a good citizen in this republic of ours is that he shall be able to pull his weight."

Now, these are invocations of relationships as well as of obligations and responsibilities, but the best of these senses of citizenship is contained not in the words of a philosopher or a politician or a theorist of government, but rather in the Nebraska-bred and Plains-fed poet and writer, Willa Cather, who defined happiness in this way: "That is happiness; to be dissolved into something complete and great." Let me repeat that: "That is happiness; to be dissolved into something complete and great." Now we would not necessarily look to that phrase to define the essence or the nature of citizenship and followership, but I suggest that that may very well be an exercise not in English literature but in civics. Modernity, contemporary American culture, would in that definition of Willa Cather, emphasize happiness: "That is happiness . . ." for everybody, even those who can hardly read or write, knows that we are guaranteed the right to the pursuit of happiness. All other obligations fall into disrepair by comparison to our pursuit of happiness, and that is the resonant word: I have a right to be happy, I have a desire to be happy, I have a constitutional liberty to be happy, and I will be as happy as I can be no matter how miserable it makes me or anybody else.

We focus on the word happiness, but those of you who know how to parse a sentence, those of you who know the functions of punctuation, should know when you see "That is happiness;" (semi-colon), that behind the semi-colon is what it is all about, that that is where the expectation is to be fulfilled. So, when she says "That is happiness;" (semi-colon), she then says "to be dissolved into something complete and great." That is what it is about, and strange and foreign is the notion to be dissolved into something complete and great. The notion to be dissolved is offensive to many of us, it means is all of me not to be preserved intact? You mean I'm going to be submerged into something other than myself, my solo apparition is not going to maintain its autonomy and its integrity? To be dissolved? I'm not sure I like that, and to be dissolved into something complete and great? Does that imply that I myself am not complete unless I am dissolved into something? Does it imply that there is something greater than I am, and that without being dissolved into it I will not know what happiness is? Well, the simple answer to that is yes! That is exactly what it means. It means that to be a part of that which is larger, greater, more whole, more complete than I am, is the source of ultimate joy and happiness and responsibility. To be lost into something larger than you are but that unites what you are with all of those other elements is an extraordinary experience.

I was driven around your enormous campus today, shown all of the great and the good landmarks, and of course the most powerful and domineering specter on your horizon is not your famous or infamous tower; oh, by no means, it is not that tower, it is your football stadium, where ritually you are all dissolved into something complete and great, and if you're sober enough to realize what's happening, it's happiness, and you know what it's like. There is no such thing as a solitary autonomous football fan, for either you are with that mindless, screaming, soulless horde, or you're doing other things elsewhere, but you're not up there reading Plato or playing your flute or saying your prayers, you're dissolved into something complete and great. Now all analogies are untidy, all metaphors are a little messy, that's why we have so many of them, and I won't stake my entire reputation on the analogy of the UT [University of Texas] football stadium to the idea of civic virtue, but you get the idea. You can figure it out for yourselves, and go home and speculate on it if you will. That is what it's about, but we, I think, have this inner longing, this deep-seated longing for this great leader on this white horse, at least we think that's what we want. Every November we hear about how bleak the choices are, how few white horses and how far too many potentially inadequate horsemen and women there are to ride them, but I don't think that's the real longing. That is the sort of thing you tell to the pollsters, and we all know that we don't tell the truth in that setting, we tell the truth to God but we lie to the pollsters.

I think that this basic longing we have is not for this Anthony Lewis-like leader.* I think the civil yearning, groaning, is for something worth believing in, something worthy of our loyalty and passion, something that suggests that to follow is as honorable as to lead, and in fact, that is what I mean by "followership," the notion that the loyalty to an idea and not to an individual, to a passion and not to a program, to a vision and not to an entitlement, is the entity to which we give our ultimate loyalty. We are led by that conviction, by that consensus; and the articulation of that conviction, that sensitivity, that sense of place and person, is what I call "followership," being led by that which is greater than any of us or any of our needs or our ambitions.

Now, because I am both an academic and a clergyman, I have examples 10 to offer to you, historical examples which you can examine at your leisure in the university library with your professors, or elsewhere. They are well known; I didn't make any of them up, they may be strange to some of you but that's your problem; you haven't read widely or deeply enough, and I hope that by the time this term is over you will correct that for your sake as well as for that of the republic. I have three examples of citizenship that I want to talk about as exemplifying this followership.

Anthony Lewis-like leader: In a portion of the lecture not reprinted here, Gomes discusses an article in which *New York Times* columnist Anthony Lewis calls for "a leader who can lift our aspirations."

Citizenship, in the first case, for Jesus and for St. Paul, was the kingdom of heaven for those two great figures of the world, and in the kingdom of heaven where all of us are meant to be followers there is not a great deal of talk about leadership. There is not a great deal of talk about leadership in the Bible; there is a lot of talk about it in the church, but one must never confuse the church with the Bible. There is not a great deal of talk about leadership in the Bible but there is tremendous talk about followership in the Bible, and to follow Jesus and to follow Paul and to follow God is to enter the kingdom of heaven where the ordinary rules of engagement don't take place anymore, they do not apply. The Beatitudes* tell you that the ordinary convictions about how society is to be organized no longer work. In this world the meek do not inherit the earth. As we say in Cambridge, the meek do not inherit the earth, the meek go to Yale, and you will have your own version of that here I am sure, but in the kingdom of heaven the meek inherit the earth because the ordinary rules of engagement are suspended. Those who mourn are blessed, they are not overwhelmed by their sorrow, and the notion of leadership is overcome by the notion of fellowship, reunion, community, as opposed to the led and the leader. That is one model of leadership. When Paul says "Our citizenship is in heaven," which he does in the epistles, he is saying that the standard for our civic virtue is derived from that heavenly model as opposed to this old broken down earthly one.

Well, Jesus and Paul may be a little much for you; this is, after all, a state university and we perhaps shouldn't be too evangelical under these auspices, so let me take you a few years down the road to St. Augustine. Now, nobody can argue with St. Augustine, a dead white male indeed, but even that does not disqualify him from being taken seriously. In probably the greatest book in the west apart from the Bible, *The City of God,* Augustine talks about the notion of citizenship, of belonging to something that overwhelms and transcends the particularities of our mundane earthly existence; and to be a citizen of the city of God while living on earth is to anticipate bliss, and joy, and to have an identity which is formed both by that to which we belong and that to which we aspire. So, Augustine manages this double hat-trick, that is to say, we celebrate that to which we aspire and we make it happen by the nature of that to which we belong here and now, so that we're not overwhelmed, daunted, or intimidated by this fallen world because we are, in his delicious phrase, a "colony of heaven"; we are an outpost of an external overwhelming force into which ultimately we are to be dissolved.

Now, perhaps that is a little medieval and esoteric and foreign, for after all Augustine was an African and spoke Latin, so if we want to bring this a little closer to home, well, we come to Massachusetts where all good things in

---

Beatitudes: the blessings offered by Jesus in the Sermon on the Mount, such as "Blessed are the poor in spirit, for theirs is the kingdom of heaven," from the biblical New Testament (Matt. 5:3–12)

the new world began, of course, and we look first at the landing in 1620 in my native town of Plymouth, of the Pilgrims, those people who landed on or near or under or around Plymouth Rock, that disappointing stone that you've all visited and wondered whether this is it. Well it *is* it, but there's more to it than that, and the more to it I'm about to tell you. They produced a remarkable document called the Mayflower Compact, in which they defined themselves, aboard the *Mayflower* in November 1620, as a civil body politic. Now there's a great deal of romantic nonsense about the Mayflower Compact, and you may have learned about it in high school. Undo it, let me put you straight, I, as president of the Pilgrim Society. The civil body politic of which they were speaking was not some pure abstraction either from the Bible or from Plato, or even from Machiavelli or Thomas More, of whom they would have disapproved. It was an attempt, an expedient, to provide for the necessary ordering of society by a group of willful and ignorant and unruly people who needed wise restraints in order to make them free, and the best way that that freedom could be defined, protected, and derived was by the submission of those freedoms in a larger body, the civil body politic. That is the phrase which they extorted from each other and which is at the heart of the Mayflower Compact.

Now, a more famous iteration of this occurs ten years later in Boston Harbor, when Governor Winthrop lands with his Puritans aboard the ship *Arbella,* and in perhaps the most evocative words with which the new settlements in the new world were introduced, Winthrop preaches a sermon aboard the ship, reminding these vain and varied and aggressive Englishmen that the eyes of the world were to be upon them as they started up this new Puritan colony. They were not fleeing in exile and huddled masses yearning to be free, they were going to be an exemplary community to which the world would look. In order to ensure that the world would find them, Winthrop preached them a sermon entitled "A New Modell of Christian Charity," in which he preached the gospel of Christian community which has essentially at its heart charity and submission. He used as one of his texts that marvelous passage from the Sermon on the Mount, that wonderful figure, "We shall be as a city set on a hill," which has become one of the touchstone phrases of our civilized life. So familiar has it become that when it was used in Ronald Reagan's first campaign, people thanked Peggy Noonan* for writing it, thinking that such a clever word-mistress as she was would come up with such an evocative and effective metaphor for the American republic. It took a few people to remind other people, particularly Peggy Noonan, that she didn't make it up, that actually Jesus had said it some time ago, or whoever the Jesus Seminar says said it, and that it was a phrase of some great antiquity but of current power as well.

Peggy Noonan (b. 1950): speechwriter for Ronald Reagan and George Bush

So, this notion of a city set on a hill is a city not of rampant individual- 15
ists out trying to make as much of the real estate deal as they can of that city
set on a hill, but is actually a city of people who submit themselves to each
other and to the common good, out of charity, which is equally translated as
love. Submission and love, those are not two words that you hear when you
associate the notion of leadership, but they are words that you hear at the
heart of the notion of followership. So, the kingdom of heaven, the city of
God, the city set on a hill—these are extraordinary, demanding illustrations
of what it is I think we desperately yearn for, deserve, and desire; and what is
common to them all is the sense of being dissolved into something that is
complete and great and that aspires to live up to its highest ideals even when
it falls short of those ideals.

What it takes to do that, to achieve that, is not a panoply of powerful
leaders but an ever-increasing horde of faithful, articulate, inspired followers
from whom, in the fullness of time, when and where and as necessary, appropriate leadership will come. The future health of the republic will not depend, in my opinion, on our ability to ferret out yet more leaders and to generate yet more heroic three-initialled figures to lead us across whatever
bridges we happen to be stranded on in the middle. That is not where the future well-being of the republic is. It occurs to me that the future well-being
of the republic is to generate an ever-succeeding succession of generations of
young men and women like yourselves who are pleased, privileged, and honored to be part of something greater than yourselves, greater than your own
ambition, and greater than your own achievement, who in submission and in
love are prepared to be citizens of the city of God, members of the republic of
virtue, citizens of this great republic of ours. The strength of a people consists
not in the greatness of its leaders: that is the thesis I have been beating over
and over again. The strength of a people consists in the quality of its followers, people who are led not by leaders but by visions, ideas, ideals, and passions. The great hope of a community, such as this university, is the great
hope of the republic itself.

In a small parish church in the little village of Sandwich in Kent, England,
in the diocese of Canterbury, there is on the wall an epitaph to a schoolmaster
who was schoolmaster to a dear old friend of mine, now a retired bishop. He recalled sitting in the parish church during compulsory chapel as a young boy,
when he read this epitaph to the former headmaster of the school, and I jotted it
down when he told it to me some years ago: "As a follower he led, as a leader he
served, and so he set the feet of many upon the path of life."

Those of us who teach, those of us who aspire to teach, and those of us
who learn, and those of us who aspire to learn, could not ask for any better
summation of our spot in the world than that. We need no new cadre of
leaders—God spare us yet another crop—who will get our trains to run on
time while balancing the budget, and at no extra cost to us. Spare us such
leaders. We need passionate followers of an ideal of civic virtue, an ideal that

does not conform, as St. Paul says in Romans 12:1&2, but is transformed by the renewing of one's mind and one's soul. If we address the question of what it means to follow and what is worth following, what it means to belong, and what it means to be submissive and loving for the larger and general good, and see that as an honorable and compelling and inescapable vocation for us all, leadership will take its place. It will follow from followership in a wonderful application of the biblical principle, when indeed the first will be last and the last will be first, and the first vocation for all of us ought to be as worthy followers of a worthy ideal. Thank you. . . .

QUESTIONING THE TEXT

1. What particular features in the language of Gomes's lecture indicate that it was originally delivered to a live audience? Highlight sentences, phrases, words, and any other items that look like a residue of a spoken, rather than a written, text.

2. Gomes makes quite a point (in paragraphs 6–7) about the semicolon in a sentence he quotes from author Willa Cather: "That is happiness; to be dissolved into something complete and great." Check a writing handbook to see what semicolons do (if you don't already know). Then, in a few sentences of your own, analyze Gomes's interpretation of Cather's claim.

MAKING CONNECTIONS

3. Like Martin Luther King Jr. in "Letter from Birmingham Jail" (p. 142), Gomes is an African American preacher addressing an audience that is predominantly (though not exclusively) white. In a group, explore the dynamics of this rhetorical situation. Consider, especially, how Gomes's reception today may be shaped by the historical influence of King as teacher and minister.

4. After you have thought about the way Gomes defines good "followership," read Marge Piercy's poem "To Be of Use" (p. 730). Do Gomes and Piercy describe the same thing? Compare and contrast their portraits of the people "who do what has to be done."

JOINING THE CONVERSATION

5. Gomes draws upon a variety of sources to argue that it is the responsibility of good citizens to keep the state from error—and not vice versa. Write a comparison or contrast essay that explores this notion, investi-

gating how a government or institution (perhaps even a college) tries to shape the behavior of its citizens. Conversely, you could consider how citizens (or students) might try to reshape the character and actions of a state or institution. This essay will be easier to write if you work with specific examples of policies, actions, protests, or political movements.

6. A crowd pulling together at a football game is Gomes's example of people ritually dissolving their individuality "into something complete and great" (paragraph 8). Write an essay arguing whether a football crowd is or is not an appropriate analogy for a society that is coming together to achieve a greater good than an individual acting alone might produce.

7. Write an essay evaluating Gomes's conclusion: "The strength of a people consists in the quality of its followers, people who are led not by leaders but by visions, ideas, ideals, and passions" (paragraph 16). Judge it according to your own experiences as well as by evidence of history as you know it.

WENDY SHALIT
The Future of Modesty

Early in a book-length study of sexual modesty, perhaps the first such volume ever written by a woman, author Wendy Shalit (b. 1975) introduces readers to mod-estyniks—Orthodox Jewish women who ascribe to a traditional code of behavior that forbids touching between the sexes before marriage. Such behavior seems so odd that many people assume that modestyniks must be abuseniks; that is, women who are reacting to some previous sexual trauma by repressing sexual desire. Yet, contrary to all expectations, Shalit observes that modestyniks seem remarkably well adjusted, even "twinkling," in comparison to most young women living supposedly less repressive lifestyles. So why is modesty so often reduced to a pathology? Shalit concludes that modesty has been misunderstood by our culture, which confuses modesty with prudery. In contrast, she argues that modesty is both natural and erotic. She decides to explore the virtue of modesty in more depth, looking at it historically, culturally, even person-ally. Some of the conclusions she reaches appear in "The Future of Modesty," a section from her book A Return to Modesty: Discovering the Lost Virtue *(1999).*

Shalit's study grew out of an article she had written while a student at Williams College to protest unisex bathrooms in her dormitory. She found herself unwilling to accept either the facilities shared with men or the assumptions about sex and sexu-ality that made coed bathrooms possible. Her willingness to challenge the ideology pre-vailing at her college led to the discovery that many others shared her belief that both women and men have much to gain from appreciating privacy and the power of mystery in sex.

Shalit graduated from Williams in 1997 with a degree in philosophy. Her writings have appeared in Commentary, Reader's Digest, *and the* Wall Street Journal.

—J.R.

Every day, it seems, another girl is assaulted in school. The day after a 15-year-old girl was sexually assaulted at her Queens high school, *The New York Post* reported: "A teacher at Martin Luther King Jr. High School as-signed an explicit sex poem titled *Climaxin'* to his class full of 15-year-olds." It is, needless to say, rather hard to prosecute boys who assault girls when their teachers are doing more or less the same thing to them in the classroom.

Anne Roiphe writes in her latest book, *Fruitful,* that "in the nineteen fifties . . . I was not afraid of being raped; I was afraid of being talked about." She and other women of her generation rejected the culture which valued modesty, because they didn't want to be talked about. A culture which values modesty, after all, had its disadvantages. Obviously you can't praise dressing modestly without, implicitly, condemning immodesty. And one must grant that being talked about *is* unpleasant. It can feel oppressive.

214

But what is the alternative? We who have grown up in a culture of im-modesty tend to find rape much worse than being talked about. You can fear being talked about and still feel safe, whereas if you fear rape and stalking, cannot safely walk in the street alone, cannot be a 9-year-old girl in school without being sodomized, you cannot feel safe. A culture which valued mod-esty surely had its drawbacks, but now that we have experimented with its opposite, we who have had our sex education in kindergarten and were as-signed poems about orgasms instead of Shakespeare in school, we who have watched in horror as our perpetrators of sexual assault get younger and younger—well, we take a different view of things.

Still, even if we could agree it is desirable to return to a culture of mod-esty, would it even be possible? Don't notions of modesty and shame differ between cultures? Which style would we opt for? In eighteenth-century France, deep décolletage was allowed, but it was considered indecent to re-veal the point of the shoulder. The Indian woman is also reticent about re-vealing her shoulders, but then the Chinese woman is shy about showing her foot, and the Muslim woman, her face. And there is always Stendhal's native woman of Madagascar to reckon with, the one who exposes all the things we cover up here, but would "rather die of shame than expose her arms." What is one to make of her?

Stendhal concludes that therefore sexual modesty must be mostly   5 taught, a product of culture, but is this the only conclusion one could reach about the woman from Madagascar? To me the salient detail is not that she covers up a different part of her body, but that even in Madagascar there is something a woman would "rather die" than reveal. As Kurt Riezler pointed out in 1943, we could not trace, discern, and compare the different manifes-tations of shame were a fundamentally similar, even universal, attitude to shame not presupposed:

> Anthropologists, in comparing cultures, find different tribes ashamed of different things. Obviously they could not make such comparisons unless they had a certain knowledge of an attitude called shame as distinct from the contents of shame, the *pudenda*. . . . Habits are products of yesterday's conditions. But how is it that each of the different stories has a chapter about shame?

Perhaps the same is true of modesty—another universal instinct hidden within us, suppressed sometimes, but always ready to show its face if we would only allow it. Frances Benton concluded as much in 1956 when she remarked that modesty was a relative, but nonetheless universal, virtue:

> Specific rules about modesty change with the styles. Our Victorian an-cestors, for instance, would judge us utterly depraved for wearing the modern bathing suit. Real modesty, however, is a constant and desirable quality. It is based not on fashion but on appropriateness. A woman boarding a subway in shorts at the rush hour is immodest not because the shorts are in themselves indecent, but because they are worn in the

wrong place at the wrong time. A well-mannered and self-respecting woman avoids clothes or behavior that are inappropriate or conspicuous.

Of course to us, that shorts rule seems as quaint as Victorian bathing attire did to Frances Benton. And yet, this may be precisely why modesty is ripe for a return these days. There is simply nowhere else to go in the direction of immodesty, only back.

Though no one wants to be accused of being "prudish," or "reactionary," or—worst of all—"not comfortable with her body," at the same time there is an emerging consensus that things have gone too far.

This is why a counterrevolution may be just around the corner.

When I returned to college after publishing an anti-coed bathroom article, I was positively overwhelmed with letters and e-mail messages from female students. Each began a different way—some serious ("I had to share a bathroom with four football players my sophomore year, and it was the most horrible year of my life"), others gleeful ("Dear Sister Chastity: *I can't stand it either!*"). But all eventually got to the same point, which was, I thought *I* was the only one who couldn't stand these bathrooms. One female student confessed that her doctor said she had contracted a urinary infection because she wasn't going to the bathroom enough. "I'm simply too embarrassed," she confided.

Even one girl who *liked* the coed bathrooms wrote me a gushing letter about my "bravery" for "speaking out," as if I had written an anti-Castro screed in Cuba, instead of just a piece about toilets in a free country. To appreciate how much these letters amazed me, one must understand that when I wrote this article I was absolutely sure that I was the only one who was uncomfortable with our coed bathrooms. Our college administration never requires our bathrooms to be coed—students are simply assigned to rooms their freshman year, boys and girls on the same floor, and then they all vote on whether it's "okay" for the floor bathrooms to be coed. Since the procedure was so democratic, and the votes in all the other freshman dorms always went the same way, I naturally assumed that the other students must like the idea of coed bathrooms. But as soon as I spoke up and started to receive these strange letters, each reporting the same "eerie" feeling, it became clear to me that in fact many college students were like me, uncomfortable with not having privacy, but not wanting to seem "uncool" by objecting. Students from various other colleges also wrote to tell me that this was happening all over the country, and wasn't it ridiculous? A few years later, *The New York Times* reported on the "open living arrangements that have been the vogue on campuses for years." Even secular Yale students weren't terribly pleased with today's dormitory arrangements: "Some quietly confessed that the permissiveness of residence life sometimes made them uncomfortable." Soon after, a *New York Times Magazine* profile found that to one young woman, "those same dormitories represent immorality itself, an arena of coed bathrooms, safe-sex manuals and free condoms, a threat to her very soul."

10

At my own college, the administration ended up changing its policy:

> A Triumph for Modesty: Some incoming freshmen will have to deal
> with fewer awkward moments than their predecessors, as the College is
> planning to renovate the Fayerweather and East College dorms this
> summer, providing a second bathroom for each entry (read: one for each
> sex). . . . It appears that Wendy Shalit '97, whose article in *Reader's Digest*
> condemning the bathroom situation garnered Williams dubious distinc-
> tion in the national spotlight, will finally be avenged.
> — *Williams Free Press,* May 19, 1998

The grownups may be afraid to admit it, but clearly the children are rebelling. College students are refusing to live in coed dormitories, and the
newest locker room trend among grade and high school students is refusing to
shower after gym class. As Dirk Johnson explains in his "Students Still Sweat,
They Just Don't Shower" report: "Students across the United States have
abandoned school showers, and their attitudes seem to be much the same
whether they live in inner-city high-rises, on suburban cul-de-sacs or in far-
flung little towns in cornfield country." As he continues:

> Modesty among young people today seems, in some ways, out of step in
> a culture that sells and celebrates the uncovered body in advertisements,
> on television and in movies. But some health and physical education ex-
> perts contend that many students withdraw precisely because of the over-
> load of erotic images . . . the reasons seem as varied as insecurities about
> body image [to] heightened sexual awareness.

Or, to put it differently, in a different age, when young students were
not endlessly bombarded with sexual images, showering could be innocent, a
simple matter of proper hygiene. But now that everything has been sexual-
ized, even the most harmless sphere becomes poisoned.

We all want to be cool, to pretend not to care, but our discomfort with
immodesty keeps cropping up. In one episode of *Beverly Hills 90210,* America's most popular, and surely most immodest, teen TV drama, aspiring actress
"Brenda" accepts a role that requires her to take off her clothes. When the
critical moment arrives, though, she can't bring herself to strip. By the end,
she muses, "On second thought, maybe masks aren't so bad after all."

Many young women today are having related "second thoughts." *Sev-*   15
enteen magazine reports that teens are now demanding workshops on manners, of all things. As Alix Strauss explains, "Today's kids want to return to an
era of courteousness. Plus, this is about more than just manners. It deals with
improving your self-image and self-esteem."

Adults would be mistaken, though, if they thought this return to dignity
and propriety is just for show. Today's young women aren't just learning their
social graces, but changing their fundamental attitude about sex. For example, in
a marked departure from their usual of-course-you-should-sleep-with-everyone

pabulum, a 1997 issue of *Glamour* ran an article called "Casual Sex: Why Confident Women Are Saying No." The article explained the role played by oxytocin, the hormone produced during both sex and childbirth which many researchers suspect may be responsible for the bonding response in women. Biologically-based differences between the sexes? Yes. Essentialist? Yes.

Yet later on in the year, all three letters published in response to this piece were positive. Each woman sounded relieved to learn that there was nothing wrong with her for being emotionally attached to her sexual partners. "K.C." from Atlanta wrote that she felt as if the article "was written about me! I am involved in a relationship of sorts with a wonderful guy. From the beginning we established that for us, sex was that and nothing more—no strings attached. Now I am starting to get emotionally involved with him, whether I want to or not. *Glamour* readers, the phrase *casual sex* is the world's biggest oxymoron!" Another woman, Drew Pinkney in Detroit, said she found the article "fascinating. . . . Could this explain why we so often feel irrational attachments for lovers we barely know? Perhaps for women, casual, merely physical sex just isn't in our nature." These kinds of thoughts would have been unheard of in a women's magazine ten years ago.

Clearly modern woman still longs for courtship and romance to satisfy her erotic imagination, but she can only dream inside the world of romance novels and nineteenth-century period dramas. Why? Because outside of fantasy land, the fundamental prerequisite for courtship, a social sanction for modesty, has been denied her.

Thus, the most compelling rationale for a return to modesty is our discovery that our culture of immodesty isn't, finally, as sexy as we thought it was going to be. In an article entitled "Modesty Belles: Cover-all Glamour Dives into the Lead," the *Sunday Mirror* reports that "SIZZLING swimwear gets a girl noticed, but it's not always the most revealing style that sends temperatures soaring."

> We put eight of this year's hottest looks to the test and came up with some surprising results. It seems modesty now rules the waves. Today's beach belle prefers a style which leaves more than a little to the imagination. . . . Even the men on our panel of six judges chose a glamorous Forties-styles one-piece over a skimpy string bikini.

But is our current interest in modesty and codes of conduct just a craze, 20 or will today's young women succeed in changing the cultural climate? I think we may succeed, because there is enough dissatisfaction with the current state of affairs, as well as a recognition that the revolution our parents engineered hasn't worked. The most common complaint I hear from women my age is that there is no longer any "dating scene." Young people go out in packs, they drink, they "hook up," and the next day life returns to normal. I suppose you could find much depressing in this behavior—for starters, that there is not even a pretense of anticipation of a love that will last forever in the cold expression, "to hook up"—but there is also a lot about this behavior that should give us hope, and that is the fact that all of them have to drink to do it.

They aren't drinking wine to begin delightful conversation. They are drinking beer and hard liquor to get drunk—precisely to cut off delightful conversation and get "right to the point," as it were. That is the advertised purpose of most college parties, and this kind of drinking is really quite a stark admission: that in fact we realize we are not just like the lower animals, that our romantic longings and hopes should inform our most intimate actions, and that if the prevailing wisdom decrees "hook-ups" don't matter, that sex is "no big deal," then we must numb ourselves in order to go through with it. Thus we pay tribute to the importance of modesty by the very lengths to which we must go to stifle it.

Also, if our hook-ups didn't really matter, then why would we have our checkups? Why all this guerrilla etiquette gushing up from the quarters of the liberated? And why is the most pressing question in all the women's magazines still "how to overcome your hang-ups"?

These kinds of things give me hope that a restoration of a culture of modesty might not only be desirable, but possible. We're all modest already, deep down—because we're human—we just need to stop drinking so much, get off our Prozac, and come out of the closet about it. Like Modesty Anonymous. We would all admit that we are powerless over our embarrassment. That one blush was just never enough.

I'm not a happily married woman or spinster who now wants to spoil your fun. I'm writing because I see so much unhappiness around me, so many women settling for less, because I don't want to settle for less and because I don't think you should have to, either. In 1997, *Marie Claire* tells us about "Daisy Starr's one-night stand." She "knew Joe a bit from going into the bar/cafe where he works . . . we got to his house, we watched cartoons. . . . When I went home with him that night, I hadn't planned on having sex, but I guess I wanted it."

I don't want to have sex because "I guess" I want it. I want to wait for 25
something more exciting than that, and modesty helps me understand why.

It is possible for a young woman to hope for something more, many of us do, and we hereby enter a plea that society permit us to hope for something more. But consider yourself forewarned: If you refuse to be cured of your sensitivity or your womanhood, if you start defending your right to your illusions, be prepared for people to tell you that you are silly and childish. Be prepared for some to make fun of you directly, and for others to be more sophisticated about it and try to reduce your hopes to various psychological maladies.

Don't believe them for a second.

Because the question has been thoroughly examined, in all of its boring detail, the data calibrated and recalibrated, multiple regressions have been performed, and in fact, not all modestyniks are abuseniks. It's actually quite within her rights for a young woman to want to be a woman.

Our culture's message to young women is, It's a free society, dearie, just one teensy footnote, by the way: *You'd better be having many hook-ups—or else! Shyness will not be tolerated! Hang-ups will not be tolerated! Rejection-sensitivity will not be tolerated! Go on Prozac! Lose your curves! Stop being a woman! Stop being a woman!*

But what would happen, I wonder, if women, instead of seeing their romantic hopes as "hang-ups" to get rid of, instead of being ashamed of themselves for being women, would start to be proud of their hesitation, their hopes, and their dignity? What would happen if they stopped listening to those who say womanhood is a drag, and began to see themselves as individuals with the power to turn society around?   30

Society might very well have to turn around.

QUESTIONING THE TEXT

1. If you have Internet access, use a search engine or an online book service (such as Amazon.com) to locate several reviews of Shalit's *A Return to Modesty*. Read the reviews and briefly summarize for your classmates the reactions of readers to her argument.

2. Shalit addresses her readers very directly near the end of "The Future of Modesty": "I'm writing because I see so much unhappiness around me, so many women settling for less, because I don't want to settle for less and because I don't think you should have to, either" (paragraph 24). Analyze the entire selection carefully and then write a brief evaluation of Shalit's ability to connect with her intended audience. Does she do an effective job? Why, or why not? If you have time, you might examine her entire book and extend your evaluation to include more evidence.

3. Shalit claims that younger people are rebelling against the sexual permissiveness they have grown up with. Examine the evidence she offers to support her thesis and, in a group, discuss other phenomena in society and popular culture that you see as either supporting or countervailing this trend.

MAKING CONNECTIONS

4. Carol Gilligan, author of *In a Different Voice,* suggests that for women, moral issues usually arise over "an injunction to care, a responsibility to discern and alleviate the 'real and recognizable trouble' of this world."

Do you find in Shalit's defense of female modesty an ethic of caring that might alleviate the troubles of this world? Or does it represent a return to prudery and repression for women? Review the readings by Gilligan (p. 169) and Shalit, and write a position paper about the moral implications of modesty.

JOINING THE CONVERSATION

5. Before she wrote against coed bathrooms in dormitories, Shalit assumed that most other students liked the idea. In taking the position she did, she knew that she risked looking "uncool." Have you had moral objections to a policy or administrative assumption at your school, but been similarly hesitant to voice a complaint? If so, consider writing a response to that policy now, perhaps as a letter to the editor to a local or campus newspaper. Alternatively, write a narrative about your experiences dealing with a policy you regard as wrongheaded or even immoral.

6. The headnote to this selection briefly defines terms that Shalit uses in her book. Review the definition of *modestynik,* reread Shalit's essay, and then write an imaginary dialogue that might occur between a modestynik and a fan of *Cosmo* or *GQ* as they watch and evaluate a contemporary television drama or sitcom together (such as *Friends, Party of Five,* or *Dawson's Creek*).

7. In an exploratory essay that draws on sources in addition to Shalit, examine the assumptions behind some aspect of the sexual behavior of your generation (whatever that generation might be). Decide how decisions about right/wrong, ethical/immoral issues are made—if they are. Look for phenomena in the surrounding culture (church, school, clubs, music, movies, advertisements) that send signals about appropriate choices. The essay need not be personal, but do focus on a particular aspect of the question, not on the entire issue of sexual mores.

KATHLEEN NORRIS
Little Girls in Church

*K*ATHLEEN *N*ORRIS *(b. 1947) has published many works since graduating from Bennington College in 1969. In addition to* Little Girls in Church *(1995), from which the following poem is taken, Norris has published five poetry chapbooks and two other full-length books of poetry,* Falling Off *(1971) and* The Middle of the World *(1981). Although she lives in western South Dakota with her husband, the poet David Dwyer, she has written two compelling nonfiction books while living in monasteries, including* Dakota: A Spiritual Geography *(1993). In* Cloister Walk *(1996), a second book of nonfiction, she continues her exploration of spiritual places and spaces. Her favorite piece in this book, Norris says, is one that describes and reflects on the wide-ranging responses that Benedictine nuns gave to her question of why they do or do not wear habits. A more recent book is* Amazing Grace: A Vocabulary of Faith *(1998), a meditation on the language of Christian belief.*

Norris's poem "Little Girls in Church" also records a wide range of responses to the question of faith and its moral relationship to institutionalized religion. For me, the poem calls up the many Sundays I spent in my grandmother's Baptist church and in my parents' Presbyterian one, days that run together in my memory of Bible-school stories (I still vividly recall Joseph and his Coat of Many Colors), covered-dish suppers, prayer meetings, and songs—lots and lots of songs. I wonder what memories Norris's words may evoke for you.   —A.L.

I

I've made friends
with a five-year-old
Presbyterian. She tugs at her lace collar,
I sympathize. We're both bored.
I give her a pencil;   5
she draws the moon,
grass, stars, and
I name them for her,
printing in large letters.
The church bulletin   10
begins to fill.
Carefully, she prints her name
on it, *KATHY*, and hands it back.

222

Just last week,
in New York City, the Orthodox liturgy   15
was typically intimate,
casual. An old woman greeted the icons
one by one
and fell asleep
during the Great Litany.   20
People went in and out,
to smoke cigarettes and chat on the steps.

A girl with long brown braids
was led to the icons
by her mother. They kissed each one,   25
and the girl made a confession
to the youngest priest. I longed to hear it,
to know her name.

II

I worry for the girls.
I once had braids,   30
and wore lace that made me suffer.
I had not yet done the things
that would need forgiving.

Church was for singing, and so I sang.
I received a Bible, stars   35
for all the verses;
I turned and ran.

The music brought me back
from time to time,
singing hymns   40
in the great breathing body
of a congregation.
And once in Paris, as
I stepped into Notre Dame
to get out of the rain,   45
the organist began to play:
I stood rooted to the spot,
looked up, and believed.

It didn't last.
Dear girls, my friends,   50
may you find great love
within you, starlike
and wild, as wide as grass,
solemn as the moon.
I will pray for you, if I can.   55

IN RESPONSE

1. Norris's narrator talks about the songs and hymns of the church she attended. What songs or lullabies do you remember from your childhood? Choose one, and jot down what you remember of its words and what you liked (or disliked) about it. Bring your notes to class for discussion.

2. Think for a while about your own spiritual and/or religious beliefs—or about your secular beliefs. Then try your hand at writing a brief poem that would capture the essence of those beliefs. Bring your poem to class to share with others.

3. What in Norris's poem helps readers understand why she "worr[ies] for the girls"?

OTHER READINGS

Brilmayer, Lea. *American Hegemony: Political Morality in a One-Superpower World*. New Haven: Yale UP, 1994. Examines whether it is morally acceptable for the United States to dominate or police other countries.

Caputo, Philip. "Alone." *Men's Journal* Aug. 1998: 78–83. Argues that human civilization needs the moral centering provided by wilderness and solitude.

Henry, Patrick, et al. "Symposium: Is Morality a Non-aim of Education?" *Philosophy and Literature* Apr. 1998: 136–99. Eight scholars respond to the claim that a university is not responsible for offering moral guidance to students.

Kohlberg, Lawrence. *The Philosophy of Moral Development*. San Francisco: Harper, 1981. Argues that children go through predictable stages of moral development.

Kohlberg, Lawrence, and Carol Gilligan. "The Adolescent as a Philosopher: The Discovery of the Self in a Post-conventional World." *Daedalus* 100 (1971): 1051–86. Focuses on the construction of moral selfhood.

Neuhaus, Richard John. "The Empty Creche." *National Review* 31 Dec. 1996: 29–31. Explores how removing Christian elements from the observance of Christmas undermines spiritual and moral values.

Noddings, Nel. *Caring*. Berkeley: U of California, 1984. Describes and argues for a moral system based on what Noddings terms an "ethic of care."

Norris, Kathleen. *Dakota: A Spiritual Geography*. New York: Ticknor, 1993. A memoir about place, morality, and spirituality.

Reeves, Richard. "I'm Sorry, Mr. President." *American Heritage* Dec. 1996: 53–55. A journalist apologizes for contributing to the corruption of public discourse.

ELECTRONIC RESOURCES

http://www.nd.edu/~rbarger/kohlberg.html
Provides a summary of Lawrence Kohlberg's theory of stages of moral development.

http://ispp.org/ISPP/genmorbibispp.html
Provides a bibliography for gender-related issues and moral reasoning.

http://www.cc.org/publications/rights.html
Reviews the legal status of religion in America. Site is sponsored by the Christian Coalition.

http://www.indiana.edu/~wts/wts/plagiarism.html
Definitions, policies, and examples designed to help students understand the concept and consequences of plagiarism.

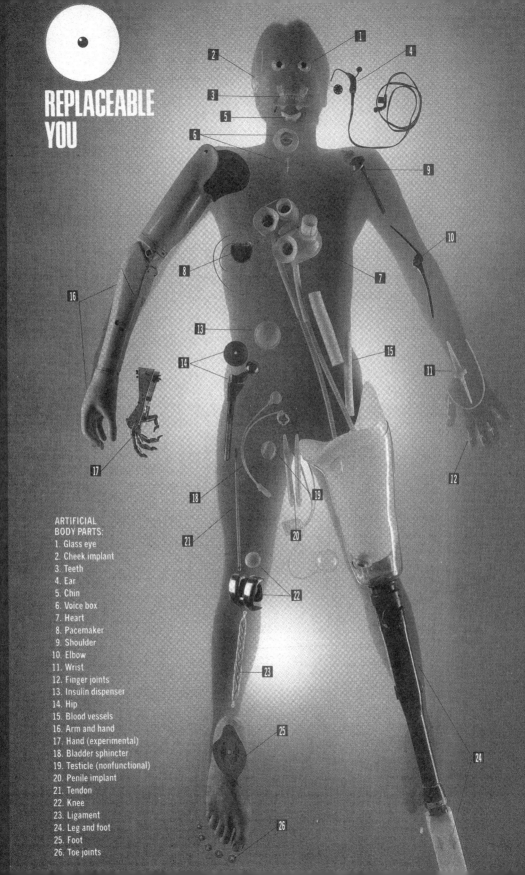

REPLACEABLE
YOU

ARTIFICIAL
BODY PARTS:
1. Glass eye
2. Cheek implant
3. Teeth
4. Ear
5. Chin
6. Voice box
7. Heart
8. Pacemaker
9. Shoulder
10. Elbow
11. Wrist
12. Finger joints
13. Insulin dispenser
14. Hip
15. Blood vessels
16. Arm and hand
17. Hand (experimental)
18. Bladder sphincter
19. Testicle (nonfunctional)
20. Penile implant
21. Tendon
22. Knee
23. Ligament
24. Leg and foot
25. Foot
26. Toe joints

Look closely at the figure on the preceding page, which is reproduced from a 1989 issue of *Life Maga-zine*. How do the written text and the placement of that text affect your interpretation of and response to the central image? ■ What effect does the use of light and dark have on the way the image comes across? ■ What does this image suggest about the relation-ships between humans and technologies? ■ What questions does it evoke for you?

Science and Technology: O Brave New World

Learn from me . . . how dangerous is the acquirement of knowledge, and how much happier that man is who believes his native town to be the world, than he who aspires to become greater than his nature will allow.

MARY SHELLEY, *Frankenstein*

Resistance to science is born of fear. Fear, in turn, is bred by ignorance. And it is ignorance that is our deepest malady.

J. MICHAEL BISHOP, *Enemies of Promise*

Genetically engineered insects, fish and domesticated animals have also been introduced, like the sheep/goat hybrid "geep."

JEREMY RIFKIN, *Biotech Century*

[T]he battle over computers . . . is not just the future versus the past, uncertainty versus nostalgia; it is about encouraging a fundamental shift in personal priorities—a minimizing of the real, physical world in favor of an unreal "virtual" world.　　　　TODD OPPENHEIMER, *The Computer Delusion*

The portrait of the body conveyed most often and most vividly in the mass media shows it as a defended nation-state, organized around a hierarchy of gender, race, and class.　　　　EMILY MARTIN, *The Body at War*

Imagine the country we now inhabit—big, urban, prosperous—with one exception: the automobile has not been invented.

JAMES Q. WILSON, *Cars and Their Enemies*

Why shouldn't recording companies issue CDs that are coded to self-destruct or lock up after 15 plays, forcing those who want to hear more to pay more?

PAMELA SAMUELSON, *The Digital Rights War*

Ethics and religion are still too complex for present-day science to explain in depth. They are, however, far more a product of autonomous evolution than has hitherto been conceded by most theologians.

EDWARD O. WILSON, *The Biological Basis of Morality*

Introduction

TIME AND AGAIN in the twentieth century, we have found that our scientists and engineers—like the hero of Mary Shelley's *Frankenstein* (1818)—have created technologies that drive our society to the limits of what it can grasp legally and ethically. Indeed, there seems to be no boundary to what the human imagination can first contemplate and then achieve. Scientists have already mapped out the genes that control life, performed surgery in the womb, extracted the secrets of the atom, and etched the pathways of human knowledge onto tiny silicon chips. Occasionally, experiments escape our control and we watch them poison our landscapes or explode before our eyes. But the quest for knowledge continues.

Julius Caesar, a military genius and a shrewd politician, observed once that "it is better to have expanded the frontiers of the mind than to have pushed back the boundaries of the empire." As Caesar doubtless understood, the two achievements often amount to the same thing, the powers of mind enabling one people or nation to dominate others, to cast itself in the role of a god and its neighbors as servants or slaves.

This chapter is designed to explore the resonances of *Frankenstein,* the many questions it raises, and the ways it leads us to think about science, progress, and alienation. In our mythologies, ancient and modern, we show a fondness for rebels like Victor Frankenstein, who would steal the fire of the gods and, with their new knowledge, shake the foundations of empires. Yet we cannot entirely identify with such figures either. They remain a threat to us too, a reminder that humanity finally lacks the wisdom to play God.

Your own thinking about these issues may be stimulated by considering the following questions:

- Why do contemporary readers and moviegoers continue to find *Frankenstein* fascinating? What makes the intellectual dreamer or the rebel an attractive figure?

- Why does a society usually react with suspicion toward people who, like Victor Frankenstein's monster, seem different? How do we define the outsider? How does the outsider act as a result?

- How do we deal with new technologies or learn to assess the impact of older technologies we now take for granted?

- Does scientific or technological progress always entail some loss or disruptive change? You might want to discuss this issue with a group of classmates.

MARY SHELLEY
Frankenstein

*W*ITH FRANKENSTEIN, *Mary Shelley (1797–1851) created a myth as powerful, complex, and frightening as the monster in the novel itself. The book intrigues us today as a narrative with many dimensions and interpretations. It works as the story of a scientist whose ambitions exceed his understanding, as an account of a scientific project that begins with great promise but leads to disaster, as the lament of an alien creature spurned by his maker, as the tract of an outsider besieged by his sense of difference, as the protest of a rebel striking out against a conventional and restrictive society.*

The daughter of early feminist Mary Wollstonecraft and political theorist William Godwin and the wife of Percy Bysshe Shelley, Mary Shelley began Frankenstein; or, The Modern Prometheus, *to use its full title, in the summer of 1816 after the poet Byron invited his friends at a lake resort in Switzerland to "each write a ghost story." The short piece she composed eventually grew through several revisions (1818, 1823, 1831) into the novel we know today.*

The protagonist of her work, Victor Frankenstein, is an ambitious young scholar who discovers how to bestow "animation upon lifeless matter." He uses this knowledge to assemble a grotesque manlike creature, and then, horrified by what he has done, abandons it the moment he brings it to life. The following selection from the novel is Victor's account of those events. —J.R.

I see by your eagerness, and the wonder and hope which your eyes express, my friend, that you expect to be informed of the secret with which I am acquainted; that cannot be: listen patiently until the end of my story, and you will easily perceive why I am reserved upon that subject. I will not lead you on, unguarded and ardent as I then was, to your destruction and infallible misery. Learn from me, if not by my precepts, at least by my example, how dangerous is the acquirement of knowledge, and how much happier that man is who believes his native town to be the world, than he who aspires to become greater than his nature will allow.

When I found so astonishing a power placed within my hands, I hesitated a long time concerning the manner in which I should employ it. Although I possessed the capacity of bestowing animation, yet to prepare a frame for the reception of it, with all its intricacies of fibers, muscles, and veins, still remained a work of inconceivable difficulty and labour. I doubted at first whether I should attempt the creation of a being like myself, or one of simpler organization; but my imagination was too much exalted by my first success to permit me to doubt of my ability to give life to an animal as complex and wonderful as man. The materials at present within my command hardly appeared adequate to so arduous an undertaking; but I doubted not that I should ultimately succeed. I prepared myself for a multitude of reverses; my operations might be incessantly baffled, and at last my work be imperfect: yet, when I considered the improvement which every day takes place in science and mechanics, I was encouraged to hope my present attempts would at least lay the foundations of future success. Nor could I consider the magnitude and complexity of my plan as any argument of its impracticability. It was with these feelings that I began the creation of a human being. As the minuteness of the parts formed a great hindrance to my speed, I resolved, contrary to my first intention, to make the being of a gigantic stature; that is to say, about eight feet in height, and proportionably large. After having formed this determination, and having spent some months in successfully collecting and arranging my materials, I began.

No one can conceive the variety of feelings which bore me onwards, like a hurricane, in the first enthusiasm of success. Life and death appeared to me ideal bounds, which I should first break through, and pour a torrent of light into our dark world. A new species would bless me as its creator and source; many happy and excellent natures would owe their being to me. No father could claim the gratitude of his child so completely as I should deserve theirs. Pursuing these reflections, I thought, that if I could bestow animation upon lifeless matter, I might in process of time (although I now found it impossible) renew life where death had apparently devoted the body to corruption.

These thoughts supported my spirits, while I pursued my undertaking with unremitting ardour. My cheek had grown pale with study, and my person had become emaciated with confinement. Sometimes, on the very brink of certainty, I failed; yet still I clung to the hope which the next day or the next hour might realize. One secret which I alone possessed was the hope to which I had dedicated myself; and the moon gazed on my midnight labors, while, with unrelaxed and breathless eagerness, I pursued nature to her hiding-places. Who shall conceive the horrors of my secret toil, as I dabbled among the unhallowed damps of the grave, or tortured the living animal to animate the lifeless clay? My limbs now tremble, and my eyes swim with the remembrance; but then a resistless, and almost frantic, impulse, urged me forward; I seemed to have lost all soul or sensation but for this one pursuit. It was indeed but a passing trance, that only made me feel with renewed acuteness so soon as, the unnatural stimulus ceasing to operate, I had returned to my old habits. I collected bones from charnel-houses; and disturbed, with profane fingers, the tremendous secrets of the human frame. In a solitary chamber, or rather cell, at the top of the house, and separated from all the other apartments by a gallery and staircase, I kept my workshop of filthy creation: my eye-balls were starting from their sockets in attending to the details of my employment. The dissecting room and the slaughter-house furnished many of my materials; and often did my human nature turn with loathing from my occupation, whilst, still urged on by an eagerness which perpetually increased, I brought my work near to a conclusion.

The summer months passed while I was thus engaged, heart and soul, in one pursuit. It was a most beautiful season; never did the fields bestow a more plentiful harvest, or the vines yield a more luxuriant vintage: but my eyes were insensible to the charms of nature. And the same feelings which made me neglect the scenes around me caused me also to forget those friends who were so many miles absent, and whom I had not seen for so long a time. I knew my silence disquieted them; and I well remembered the words of my father: "I know that while you are pleased with yourself, you will think of us with affection, and we shall hear regularly from you. You must pardon me if I regard any interruption in your correspondence as a proof that your other duties are equally neglected."

I knew well therefore what would be my father's feelings; but I could not tear my thoughts from my employment, loathsome in itself, but which had taken an irresistible hold of my imagination. I wished, as it were, to procrastinate all that related to my feelings of affection until the great object, which swallowed up every habit of my nature, should be completed.

I then thought that my father would be unjust if he ascribed my neglect to vice, or faultiness on my part; but I am now convinced that he was justified in conceiving that I should not be altogether free from blame. A human being in perfection ought always to preserve a calm and peaceful mind, and never to allow passion or a transitory desire to disturb his tranquility. I do not think that the pursuit of knowledge is an exception to this rule. If the study to which you apply yourself has a tendency to weaken your affections, and to destroy your taste for those simple pleasures in which no alloy can possibly mix, then that study is certainly unlawful, that is to say, not befitting the human mind. If this rule were always observed; if no man allowed any pursuit whatsoever to interfere with the tranquility of his domestic affections, Greece had not been enslaved; Caesar would have spared his country; America would have been discovered more gradually; and the empires of Mexico and Peru had not been destroyed.

But I forgot that I am moralizing in the most interesting part of my tale; and your looks remind me to proceed.

My father made no reproach in his letters, and only took notice of my silence by enquiring into my occupations more particularly than before. Winter, spring, and summer passed away during my labors; but I did not watch the blossom or the expanding leaves—sights which before always yielded me supreme delight—so deeply was I engrossed in my occupation. The leaves of that year had withered before my work drew near to a close; and now every day showed me more plainly how well I had succeeded. But my enthusiasm was checked by my anxiety, and I appeared rather like one doomed by slavery to toil in the mines, or any other unwholesome trade, than an artist occupied by his favorite employment. Every night I was oppressed by a slow fever, and I became nervous to a most painful degree; the fall of a leaf startled me, and I shunned my fellow-creatures as if I had been guilty of a crime. Sometimes I grew alarmed at the wreck I perceived that I had become; the energy of my purpose alone sustained me: my labors would soon end, and I believed that exercise and amusement would then drive away incipient disease; and I promised myself both of these when my creation should be complete.

It was on a dreary night of November, that I beheld the accomplishment   10
of my toils. With an anxiety that almost amounted to agony, I collected the instruments of life around me, that I might infuse a spark of being into the lifeless thing that lay at my feet. It was already one in the morning; the rain pattered dismally against the panes, and my candle was nearly burnt out, when, by the glimmer of the half-extinguished light, I saw the dull yellow eye of the creature open; it breathed hard, and a convulsive motion agitated its limbs.

How can I describe my emotions at this catastrophe, or how delineate the wretch whom with such infinite pains and care I had endeavored to form? His limbs were in proportion, and I had selected his features as beautiful. Beautiful!—Great God! His yellow skin scarcely covered the work of muscles and arteries beneath; his hair was of lustrous black, and flowing; his teeth of a pearly whiteness; but these luxuriances only formed a more horrid contrast with his watery eyes, that seemed almost of the same colour as the dun white sockets in which they were set, his shriveled complexion and straight black lips.

The different accidents of life are not so changeable as the feelings of human nature. I had worked hard for nearly two years, for the sole purpose of infusing life into an inanimate body. For this I had deprived myself of rest and health. I had desired it with an ardor that far exceeded moderation; but now that I had finished, the beauty of the dream vanished, and breathless horror and disgust filled my heart. Unable to endure the aspect of the being I had created, I rushed out of the room, and continued a long time traversing my bedchamber, unable to compose my mind to sleep. At length lassitude succeeded to the tumult I had before endured; and I threw myself on the bed in my clothes, endeavoring to seek a few moments of forgetfulness. But it was in vain; I slept, indeed, but I was disturbed by the wildest dreams. I thought I saw Elizabeth,* in the bloom of health, walking in the streets of Ingolstadt. Delighted and surprised, I embraced her; but as I imprinted the first kiss on her lips, they became livid with the hue of death; her features appeared to change, and I thought that I held the corpse of my dead mother in my arms; a shroud enveloped her form, and I saw the graveworms crawling in the folds of the flannel. I started from my sleep with horror; a cold dew covered my forehead, my teeth chattered, and every limb became convulsed; when, by the dim and yellow light of the moon, as it forced its way through the window shutters, I beheld the wretch—the miserable monster whom I had created. He held up the curtain of the bed; and his eyes, if eyes they may be called, were fixed on me. His jaws opened, and he muttered some inarticulate sounds, while a grin wrinkled his cheeks. He might have spoken, but I did not hear; one hand was stretched out, seemingly to detain me,

---

Elizabeth: adopted sister of Victor Frankenstein

but I escaped, and rushed down stairs. I took refuge in the courtyard belonging to the house which I inhabited; where I remained during the rest of the night, walking up and down in the greatest agitation, listening attentively, catching and fearing each sound as if it were to announce the approach of the demoniacal corpse to which I had so miserably given life.

Oh! no mortal could support the horror of that countenance. A mummy again endued with animation could not be so hideous as that wretch. I had gazed on him while unfinished; he was ugly then; but when those muscles and joints were rendered capable of motion, it became a thing such as even Dante* could not have conceived.

I passed the night wretchedly. Sometimes my pulse beat so quickly and hardly, that I felt the palpitation of every artery; at others I nearly sank to the ground through languor and extreme weakness. Mingled with this horror, I felt the bitterness of disappointment; dreams that had been my food and pleasant rest for so long a space were now become a hell to me; and the change was so rapid, the overthrow so complete!

Morning, dismal and wet, at length dawned, and discovered to my 15 sleepless and aching eyes the church of Ingolstadt, its white steeple and clock, which indicated the sixth hour. The porter opened the gates of the court, which had that night been my asylum, and I issued into the streets, pacing them with quick steps, as if I sought to avoid the wretch whom I feared every turning of the street would present to my view. I did not dare return to the apartment which I inhabited, but felt impelled to hurry on, although drenched by the rain which poured from a black and comfortless sky.

QUESTIONING THE TEXT

1. How does Victor Frankenstein explain his drive to work hard to bring a nonliving entity to life? Annotate the margins of the *Frankenstein* selection to highlight places where Frankenstein explains his motives. Do you think any of these motives account for the continuing development of science and technology today? Explore this issue with classmates.

2. To create his monster, what does Victor Frankenstein have to do to himself and to other creatures? Have you ever been so single-minded in the pursuit of a goal or passion?

3. What precisely about the creature disappoints Frankenstein? In a group, discuss Frankenstein's rejection of his monster, exploring its meanings and implications.

4. J.R.'s introduction suggests that the Frankenstein story has become a modern myth. How many versions of Shelley's tale can you think of? List them.

Dante (1265–1321): Italian poet, author of *Divine Comedy*

MAKING CONNECTIONS

5. Victor Frankenstein warns that knowledge is dangerous: "how much happier that man is who believes his native town to be the world, than he who aspires to become greater than his nature will allow" (paragraph 1). Freewrite on this idea, taking into account the essay in this chapter by J. Michael Bishop (p. 237). Is it likely that men and women will ever live contentedly in their native towns?

6. Can you think of ways in which the anthologized passage from the novel differs from film versions of the Frankenstein tale you may have seen? Brainstorm a list of differences and jot them down.

JOINING THE CONVERSATION

7. Write a parody of this selection from *Frankenstein*, perhaps detailing the creation and consequences of some similar but more recent "monster," understanding that term broadly or metaphorically. You might even read Dave Barry's "Guys vs. Men" (p. 372) in Chapter 6 for a perspective on the peculiarly male desire to build "neat stuff."

8. Working with a group, discuss the monster as a creature who is similar to but also different from a human being. Can you compare his situation to that of other individuals or groups considered "different" in society? Write a brief position paper about Frankenstein's monster as a symbol of what it means to be different. Is the comparison convincing? Why, or why not?

9. Some critics suggest that *Frankenstein* reflects an early view of industrialization as a monstrous creation out of control. Use the library to learn what changes the industrial revolution was imposing on the landscape of England during the nineteenth century. Try also to determine how favorably people regarded changes such as the building of factories, industrial plants, and railroads. This subject is complex enough to support a full-scale research paper. Give it a try.

J. MICHAEL BISHOP
Enemies of Promise

Not long ago I discovered that the on-board diagnostic system of my new vehicle will let me know via a "Check Engine" light when I haven't screwed the gas cap on tight enough to prevent fumes from polluting the atmosphere. The computer discovers the problem not by monitoring a crude switch on the gas cap itself but by checking the entire combustion process and searching for irregularities. Anomalies—even momentary ones—detected this way are stored in the computer's memory so a technician can fix them later. The technology in my car is almost as wondrous as that of the Internet, which enables me to converse with people anywhere in the world; or consider the science that recently produced a new asthma medication that means I can now play racquetball without carrying an inhaler. As you might suspect, I'm not in the camp of those who denigrate science or criticize technological change.

I do understand the fears of the Luddites, who yearn for a world less chemically reprocessed and technologically demanding. But I also think that many who criticize science today have either short memories or little historical sense, which is why I wanted to share "Enemies of Promise" by J. Michael Bishop (b. 1936), a professor of microbiology at the University of California, San Francisco, and winner of the Nobel Prize. He warns that the misperceptions many people have about science could have serious consequences for all Americans. The piece is also a fine example of an expert writing clearly to an audience of nonspecialists—something scientists will have to do more often if faith in science is to be restored.

"Enemies of Promise" appeared originally in my favorite magazine, the Wilson Quarterly *(Summer 1995), a publication of the Woodrow Wilson International Center for Scholars.*   —J.R.

We live in an age of scientific triumph. Science has solved many of nature's puzzles and greatly enlarged human knowledge. And the fruits of scientific inquiry have vastly improved human welfare. Yet despite these proud achievements, science today is increasingly mistrusted and under attack.

Some of the opposition to science comes from familiar sources, including religious zealots who relentlessly press for the mandatory teaching of creationism in the public schools. It is discouraging to think that more than a century after the publication of Charles Darwin's *Origin of Species* (1859), and seventy years after the Scopes trial dramatized the issue, the same battles must still be fought. But fight them we must.

Other antagonists of science are less familiar. Strange though it may seem, there is within academe a school of thought that considers science to be wholly fraudulent as a way of knowing. According to these "postmodernists,"

the supposedly objective truths of science are in reality all "socially constructed fictions," no more than "useful myths," and science itself is "politics
by other means." Anyone with a working knowledge of science, anyone who
looks at the natural world with an honest eye, should recognize all of this for
what it is: arrant nonsense.

Science, of course, is not the exclusive source of knowledge about
human existence. Literature, art, philosophy, history, and religion all have their
insights to offer into the human condition. To deny that is scientism—the belief that the methods of the natural sciences are the only means of obtaining
knowledge. And to the extent that scientists have at times indulged in that belief, they must shoulder some of the blame for the misapprehensions that some
people have about science.

But science does have something inimitable to offer humankind: it is, in   5
the words of physician-author Lewis Thomas, "the best way to learn how the
world works." A postmodernist poet of my acquaintance complains that it is in
the nature of science to break things apart, thereby destroying the "mysterious
whole." But we scientists take things apart in order to understand the whole, to
solve the mystery—an enterprise that we regard as one of the great, ennobling
tasks of humankind.

In the academic medical center where I work, the efficacy and benefits
of science are a daily reality. So when I first encountered the postmodernist
view of science some years ago, I dismissed it as either a strategy for advancement in parochial precincts of the academy or a display of ignorance. But
now I am alarmed because the postmodernist cry has been joined, outside the
academy, by other strong voices raised against science.

Consider these lines from Václav Havel, the widely admired Czech
writer and statesman, who has vigorously expressed his disenchantment with
the ethos of science: "Modern rationalism and modern science . . . now systematically leave [the natural world] behind, deny it, degrade and defame it—
and, of course, at the same time, colonize it."

Those are angry words, even if their precise meaning is elusive. And
anger is evident, too, in Havel's main conclusion: "This era [of science and
rationalism] has reached the end of its potential, the point beyond which the
abyss begins."

Even some influential men who know science well and who have been
good friends to it in the past have joined in the chorus of criticism and doubt.
Thanks in part to Havel's ruminations, Representative George E. Brown, Jr.
(D.-Calif.), who was trained as a physicist, reports that his faith in science has
been shaken. He complains of what he calls a "knowledge paradox": an expansion of fundamental knowledge accompanied by an increase in social
problems. He implies that it shouldn't be that way, that as science progresses,
the problems of society should diminish. And he suggests that Congress and

the "consumers" of scientific research may have to take more of a hand in determining how science is conducted, in what research gets funded.

A similar critique has been made by former Colorado governor Richard   10
Lamm. He claims no longer to believe that biomedical research contributes to
the improvement of human health—a truly astonishing stance. To validate
his skepticism, he presents the example of the University of Colorado Medical Center. It has done "little or nothing," he complains, about increasing
primary care, expanding medical coverage to the uninsured, dealing with various addictions and dietary excesses, and controlling violence. As if biomedical research, or even academic medical centers, had either the resources or
the capabilities to do what Lamm desires!

The source of these dissatisfactions appears to be an exaggerated view of
what science can do. For example, agitation within Congress may induce the
National Science Foundation to establish a center for research on violence, but
only the naive would expect a quick fix for that momentous problem. Three-quarters of a century after the death of the great German sociologist Max Weber
(1864–1920), the social and behavioral sciences have yet to produce an antidote
for even one of the common social pathologies. The genesis of human behavior
entails complexities that still lie beyond the grasp of human reason.

Critics such as Brown and Lamm blame science for what are actually
the failures of individuals or society to use the knowledge that science has
provided. The blame is misplaced. Science has produced the vaccines required to control many childhood infections in the United States, but our nation has failed to deploy properly those vaccines. Science has sounded the
alarm about acid rain and its principal origins in automobile emissions, but
our society has not found the political will to bridle the internal combustion
engine. Science has documented the medical risks of addiction to tobacco, yet
our federal government still spends large amounts of money subsidizing the
tobacco industry.

These critics also fail to understand that success in science cannot be
dictated. The progress of science is ultimately driven by feasibility. Science is
the art of the possible, of the soluble, to recall a phrase from the late British
immunologist and Nobel laureate Sir Peter Medawar. We seldom can force
nature's hand; usually, she must tip it for us.

Nor is it possible, especially in the early stages of research, to anticipate
what benefits are likely to result. My own experience is a case in point. In
1911, Peyton Rous at the Rockefeller Institute in New York City discovered
a virus that causes cancer in chickens, a seemingly obscure observation. Yet
65 years later, that chicken virus was the vehicle by which Harold Varmus
and I, and our colleagues, were able to uncover genes that are involved in the
genesis of human cancer. The lesson of history is clear: the lines of inquiry
that may prove most fruitful to science are generally unpredictable.

Biologist John Tyler Bonner has whimsically recalled an exchange he   15
had some decades ago with the National Science Foundation, which had
given him a grant for a research project. "After the first year, I wrote that
things had not worked out very well—had tried this, that, and the other
thing, and nothing had really happened. [The foundation] wrote back, saying,
'Don't worry about it—that is the way research goes sometimes. Maybe next
year you will have better luck.'" Alas, no scientist today would think of writing such a report, and no scientist today could imagine receiving such a reply.

The great successes of science have helped to create the exaggerated expectations about what science can accomplish. Why has malaria not been
eradicated by now? Why is there still no cure for AIDS? Why is there not a
more effective vaccine for influenza? When will there be a final remedy for
the common cold? When will we be able to produce energy without waste?
When will alchemy at last convert quartz to gold?

When scientists fail to meet unrealistic expectations, they are condemned by critics who do not recognize the limits of science. Thus, playwright and AIDS activist Larry Kramer bitterly complains that science has yet
to produce a remedy for AIDS, placing much of the blame on the National Institutes of Health (NIH)—"a research system that by law demands compromise, rewards mediocrity and actually punishes initiative and originality."

I cannot imagine what law Kramer has in mind, and I cannot agree with
his description of what the NIH expects from its sponsored research. I have
assisted the NIH with peer review for more than twenty years. Its standards
have always been the same: it seeks work of the highest originality and demands rigor as well. I, for one, have never knowingly punished initiative or
originality, and I have never seen the agencies of the NIH do so. I realize
with sorrow that Mr. Kramer is unlikely to believe me.

Biomedical research is one of the great triumphs of human endeavor. It
has unearthed usable knowledge at a remarkable rate. It has brought us international leadership in the battle against disease and the search for understanding. I wonder how all this could have been accomplished if we scientists did
business in the way that Kramer and critics like him claim that we do.

The bitter outcry from AIDS activists over the past decade was echoed in   20
the 1992 film *Lorenzo's Oil,* which portrays medical scientists as insensitive,
close-minded, and self-serving, and dismisses controlled studies of potential
remedies as a waste of precious time. The film is based on a true story, the
case of Lorenzo Odone, a child who suffers from a rare hereditary disease that
cripples many neurological functions and leads at an agonizing pace to death.

Offered no hope by conventional medical science, Lorenzo's desperate
parents scoured the medical literature and turned up a possible remedy: the
administration of two natural oils known as erucic and oleic acid. In the face
of the skepticism of physicians and research specialists, Lorenzo was given the

oils and, in the estimation of his parents, ceased to decline—perhaps even improved marginally. It was a courageous, determined, and even reasoned effort by the parents. (Mr. Odone has since received an honorary degree from at least one university.) Whether it was effective is another matter.

The movie portrays the treatment of Lorenzo as a success, with the heroic parents triumphant over the obstructionism of medical scientists. The film ends with a collage of parents testifying that the oils had been used successfully to treat Lorenzo's disease in their children. But it fails to present any of the parents who have tried the oils with bitter disappointment. And, of course, all of this is only anecdotal information. Properly controlled studies are still in progress. To date, they have not given much cause for hope.

Meanwhile, as if on cue, medical scientists have since succeeded in isolating the damaged gene responsible for the rare disease. Thus, the stage is set for the development of decisive clinical testing and effective therapy (although the latter may be long in coming).

If misapprehensions abound about what science can and cannot do, so do misplaced fears of its hazards. For more than five years now, my employer, the University of California, San Francisco, has waged a costly battle for the right to perform biomedical research in a residential area. For all intents and purposes, the university has lost. The opponents were our neighbors, who argued that we are dangerous beyond tolerance; that we exude toxic wastes, infectious pathogens, and radioactivity; that we put at risk the lives and limbs of all who come within reach—our own lives and limbs included, I suppose, a nuance that seems lost on the opposition. One agitated citizen suggested in a public forum that the manipulation of recombinant DNA at the university had engendered the AIDS virus; another declared on television her outrage that "those people are bringing DNA into my neighborhood."

Resistance to science is born of fear. Fear, in turn, is bred by ignorance. 25 And it is ignorance that is our deepest malady. The late literary critic Lionel Trilling described the difficulty well, in words that are even more apposite now than when he wrote them: "Science in our day lies beyond the intellectual grasp of most [people]. . . . This exclusion . . . from the mode of thought which is habitually said to be the characteristic achievement of the modern age . . . is a wound . . . to our intellectual self-esteem . . . a diminution of national possibility . . . a lessening of the social hope."

The mass ignorance of science confronts us daily. In recent international testing, U.S. high school students finished ninth in physics among the top twelve nations, eleventh in chemistry, and dead last in biology. Science is poorly taught in most of our elementary and secondary schools, when it is taught at all. Surveys of adult Americans indicate that only a minority accepts evolution as an explanation for the origin of the human species. Many do not even know that the Earth circles the Sun. In a recent committee hearing, a prominent member of Congress betrayed his ignorance of how the prostate gland differs from the testes.

Accountants, laborers, lawyers, poets, politicians, and even many physicians look upon science with bewilderment.

Do even we scientists understand one another? A few years ago, I read of a Russian satellite that gathers solar light to provide constant illumination of large areas of Siberia. "They are taking away the night," I thought. "They are taking away the last moments of mystery. Is nothing sacred?" But then I wondered what physicists must think of biologists' hopes to decipher the entire human genome and perhaps recraft it, ostensibly for the better.

Writing an article about cancer genes for *Scientific American* some years ago, I labored mightily to make the text universally accessible. I consulted students, journalists, laity of every stripe. When these consultants all had approved, I sent the manuscript to a solid-state physicist of considerable merit. A week later, the manuscript came back with this comment: "I have read your paper and shown it around the staff here. No one understands much of it. What exactly is a gene?"

Robert M. Hazen and James Trefil, authors of *The Sciences: An Integrated Approach* (1994), tell of twenty-three geophysicists who could not distinguish between DNA and RNA, and of a Nobel Prize–winning chemist who had never heard of plate tectonics. I have encountered biologists who thought string theory had something to do with pasta. We may be amused by these examples; we should also be troubled. If science is no longer a common culture, what can we rightfully expect of the laity by way of understanding?

Lionel Trilling knew where the problem lay in his time: "No successful 30 method of instruction has been found . . . which can give a comprehension of sciences . . . to those students who are not professionally committed to its mastery and especially endowed to achieve it." And there the problem lies today: perplexing to our educators, ignored by all but the most public-minded of scientists, bewildering and vaguely disquieting to the general public.

We scientists can no longer leave the problem to others. Indeed, it has always been ours to solve, and all of society is now paying for our neglect. As physicist and historian of science Gerald Holton has said, modern men and women "who do not know the basic facts that determine their very existence, functioning, and surroundings are living in a dream world . . . are, in a very real sense, not sane. We [scientists] . . . should do what we can, or we shall be pushed out of the common culture. The lab remains our workplace, but it must not become our hiding place."

The enterprise of science embodies a great adventure: the quest for understanding in a universe that the mathematician Freeman Dyson once characterized as "infinite in all directions, not only above us in the large but also below us in the small." We of science have begun the quest well, by building a method of ever-increasing power, a method that can illuminate all that is in the natural world. In consequence, we are admired but also feared, mistrusted, even despised. We offer hope for the future but also moral conflict and ambiguous choice. The price of science seems large, but to reject science is to deny the future.

QUESTIONING THE TEXT

1. Have you ever encountered the attitude toward science that Bishop describes as *postmodern?* If so, explain this notion of science as a set of "socially constructed fictions." Share your work with classmates, and explore the difference between science as a useful fiction and science as an ennobling fact.

2. Are there any words, concepts, or examples in "Enemies of Promise" that you don't understand? Based on his text, how would you characterize Bishop's intended readership?

3. What is J.R.'s attitude toward scientific progress as demonstrated in his introduction? How does the introduction influence your reading of Bishop's "Enemies of Promise"?

MAKING CONNECTIONS

4. On the Internet, explore a Usenet group or listserv that discusses scientific issues. Follow a discussion or controversy for several days, and then write a paragraph reporting on it.

5. Victor Frankenstein, in Mary Shelley's selection from *Frankenstein* (p. 231), describes this way his rejection of the monster that he had created: "I felt the bitterness of disappointment; dreams that had been my food and pleasant rest for so long a space were now become a hell to me; and the change was so rapid, the overthrow so complete!" Does the rejection of science in our time as described by Bishop reflect disappointment and bitterness that we have not created the technological Utopia that once seemed just over the horizon? Freewrite on this subject, and then write a position paper on this question: has science today become Dr. Frankenstein's monster?

JOINING THE CONVERSATION

6. Write a 200-word summary or abstract of "Enemies of Promise" for readers who might not have time to study the entire piece.

7. Choose an example of a scientific or technological change that has occurred in the last hundred years; read about it in the library, using at least three different sources, and then write an evaluation of that change.

8. Examine a technology that you believe has caused more problems than it has solved, and write an essay in which you propose a solution to at least one of those problems. Trace the cause of the problem in the technology — is it a problem in the science, in social attitudes, in politics, and so on?

JEREMY RIFKIN

Biotech Century: Playing Ecological Roulette with Mother Nature's Designs

JEREMY RIFKIN *(b. 1945) is well known as a social activist. Organizer of the 1968 March on the Pentagon, Rifkin helped draw public attention to alleged U.S. war crimes in Vietnam. By the late 1970s, he was focusing his efforts on biotechnology, concentrating, for example, on the dangers of genetic engineering in the beef industry and in many everyday food substances. As president of the nonprofit Foundation on Economic Trends, Rifkin has gained a wide audience that includes both devoted admirers and scornful opponents: the National Milk Producers call him a "food terrorist" while reviewer and journalist Scott Landon concludes that he is a "fine synthesizer of cutting-edge issues."*

Rifkin himself does not take well to being labeled an antitechnology zealot, saying over and over again that he supports the use of biotechnology for making pharmaceuticals and for applying new knowledge of genetics to preventive medicine. How you respond to Rifkin's concerns in "Biotech Century" will probably be closely connected to your own value system as well as to the evidence provided for or against Rifkin's thesis.

The essay reprinted here, published in the May–June 1988 issue of E/The Environmental Magazine, *is adapted from Rifkin's book* The Biotech Century: Harnessing the Gene and Remaking the World *(1998). I chose this piece because Rifkin's trademark use of overstatement makes his claims very clear—and hard to ignore. In addition, while I am generally an advocate and admirer of science and scientific discovery, I have my own fears about human attempts to master—and effectively change—the natural world.* —A.L.

We're in the midst of a great historic transition into the Biotech Age. The ability to isolate, identify and recombine genes is making the gene pool available, for the first time, as the primary raw resource for future economic activity on Earth. After thousands of years of fusing, melting, soldering, forging and burning inanimate matter to create useful things, we are now splicing, recombining, inserting and stitching living material for our own economic interests. Lord Ritchie-Calder, the British science writer, cast the biological revolution in the proper historical perspective when he observed that "just as we have manipulated plastics and metals, we are now manufacturing living materials."

The Nobel Prize–winning chemist Robert F. Curl of Rice University spoke for many of his colleagues in science when he proclaimed that the 20th century was "the century of physics and chemistry. But it is clear that the next century will be the century of biology."

Global "life-science" companies promise an economic renaissance in the coming Biotech Century—they offer a door to a new era of history where the genetic blueprints of evolution itself become subject to human authorship. Critics worry that the reseeding of the Earth with a laboratory-conceived second Genesis could lead to a far different future—a biological Tower of Babel and the spread of chaos throughout the biological world, drowning out the ancient language of creation.

A Second Genesis

Human beings have been remaking the Earth for as long as we have had a history. Up to now, however, our ability to create our own second Genesis has been tempered by the restraints imposed by species boundaries. We have been forced to work narrowly, continually crossing close relatives in the plant or animal kingdoms to create new varieties, strains and breeds. Through a long, historical process of tinkering and trial and error, we have redrawn the biological map, creating new agricultural products, new sources of energy, more durable building materials, and life-saving pharmaceuticals. Still, in all this time, nature dictated the terms of engagement.

But the new technologies of the Genetic Age allow scientists, corporations and governments to manipulate the natural world at the most fundamental level—the genetic one. Imagine the wholesale transfer of genes between totally unrelated species and across all biological boundaries—plant, animal and human—creating thousands of novel life forms in a brief moment of evolutionary time. Then, with clonal propagation, mass-producing countless replicas of these new creations, releasing them into the biosphere to propagate, mutate, proliferate and migrate. This is, in fact, the radical scientific and commercial experiment now underway.

Global Powers at Play

Typical of new biotech trends is the bold decision by the Monsanto Corporation, long a world leader in chemical products, to sell off its entire chemical division in 1997 and anchor its research, development and marketing in biotech-based technologies and products. Global conglomerates are rapidly buying up biotech start-up companies, seed companies, agribusiness and agrochemical concerns, pharmaceutical, medical and health businesses, and food and drink companies, creating giant life-science complexes from which to fashion a bio-industrial world. The concentration of power is impressive. The top 10 agrochemical companies control 81 percent of the $29 billion per year global agrochemical market. Ten life-science companies

control 37 percent of the $15 billion per year global seed market. Meanwhile, pharmaceutical companies spent more than $3.5 billion in 1995 buying up biotech firms. Novartis, a giant new firm resulting from the $27 billion merger of Sandoz and Ciba-Geigy, is now the world's largest agrochemical company, the second-largest seed company and the second-largest pharmaceutical company.

Global life-science companies are expected to introduce thousands of new genetically engineered organisms into the environment in the coming century. In just the past 18 months, genetically engineered corn, soy and cotton have been planted over millions of acres of U.S. farmland. Genetically engineered insects, fish and domesticated animals have also been introduced, like the sheep/goat hybrid "geep."

Virtually every genetically engineered organism released into the environment poses a potential threat to the ecosystem. To appreciate why this is so, we need to understand why the pollution generated by genetically modified organisms is so different from the pollution resulting from the release of petrochemical products into the environment.

Because they are alive, genetically engineered organisms are inherently more unpredictable than petrochemicals in the way they interact with other living things in the environment. Consequently, it is much more difficult to assess all of the potential impacts that a genetically engineered organism might have on the Earth's ecosystems.

Genetically engineered products also reproduce. They grow and they 10 migrate. Unlike petrochemical products, it is difficult to constrain them within a given geographical locale. Finally, once released, it is virtually impossible to recall genetically engineered organisms back to the laboratory, especially those organisms that are microscopic in nature.

The risks in releasing novel, genetically engineered organisms into the biosphere are similar to those we've encountered in introducing exotic organisms into the North American habitat. Over the past several hundred years, thousands of non-native organisms have been brought to America from other regions of the world. While many of these creatures have adapted to the North American ecosystems without severe dislocations, a small percentage of them have run wild, wreaking havoc on the flora and fauna of the continent. Gypsy moth, Kudzu vine, Dutch elm disease, chestnut blight, starlings and Mediterranean fruit flies come easily to mind.

Whenever a genetically engineered organism is released, there is always a small chance that it, too, will run amok because, like nonindigenous species, it has been artificially introduced into a complex environment that has developed a web of highly integrated relationships over long periods of evolutionary history. Each new synthetic introduction is tantamount to playing ecological roulette. That is, while there is only a small chance of it triggering an environmental explosion, if it does, the consequences could be significant and irreversible.

SPREADING GENETIC POLLUTION

Nowhere are the alarm bells going off faster than in agricultural biotechnology. The life-science companies are introducing biotech crops containing newly discovered genetic traits from other plants, viruses, bacteria and animals. The new genetically engineered crops are designed to perform in ways that have eluded scientists working with classical breeding techniques. Many of the new gene-spliced crops emanating from laboratories seem more like creations from the world of science fiction. Scientists have inserted "antifreeze" protein genes from flounder into the genetic code of tomatoes to protect the fruit from frost damage. Chicken genes have been inserted into potatoes to increase disease resistance. Fire-fly genes have been injected into the biological code of corn plants. Chinese hamster genes have been inserted into the genome of tobacco plants to increase sterol production.

Ecologists are unsure of the impacts of bypassing natural species boundaries by introducing genes into crops from wholly unrelated plant and animal species. The fact is, there is no precedent in history for this kind of "shotgun" experimentation. For more than 10,000 years, classical breeding techniques have been limited to the transference of genes between closely related plants or animals that can sexually interbreed, limiting the number of possible genetic combinations. Natural evolution appears to be similarly circumscribed. By contrast, the new gene-splicing technologies allow us to bypass all previous biological boundaries in nature, creating life forms that have never before existed. For example, consider the ambitious plans to engineer transgenic plants to serve as pharmaceutical factories for the production of chemicals and drugs. Foraging animals, seed-eating birds and soil insects will be exposed to a range of genetically engineered drugs, vaccines, industrial enzymes, plastics and hundreds of other foreign substances for the first time, with untold consequences. The notion of large numbers of species consuming plants and plant debris containing a wide assortment of chemicals that they would normally never be exposed to is an unsettling prospect.

Much of the current effort in agricultural biotechnology is centered on the creation of herbicide-tolerant, pest-resistant and virus-resistant plants. Herbicide-tolerant crops are a favorite of companies like Monsanto and Novartis that are anxious to corner the lucrative worldwide market for their herbicide products. More than 600 million pounds of poisonous herbicides are dumped on U.S. farm land each year, most sprayed on corn, cotton and soybean crops. Chemical companies gross more than $4 billion per year in U.S. herbicide sales alone.

To increase their share of the growing global market for herbicides, life-science companies have created transgenic crops that tolerate their own herbicides (see "Say It Ain't Soy," *In Brief* March/April, 1997). The idea is to sell farmers patented seeds that are resistant to a particular brand of herbicide in the hope of increasing a company's share of both the seed and herbicide markets. Monsanto's new "Roundup Ready" patented seeds, for example, are resistant to its best-selling chemical herbicide, Roundup.

The chemical companies hope to convince farmers that the new herbicide-tolerant crops will allow for a more efficient eradication of weeds. Farmers will be able to spray at any time during the growing season, killing weeds without killing their crops. Critics warn that with new herbicide-tolerant crops planted in the fields, farmers are likely to use even greater quantities of herbicides to control weeds, as there will be less fear of damaging their crops in the process of spraying. The increased use of herbicides, in turn, raises the possibility of weeds developing resistance, forcing an even greater use of herbicides to control the more resistant strains.

The potential deleterious impacts on soil fertility, water quality and beneficial insects that result from the increased use of poisonous herbicides, like Monsanto's Roundup, are a disquieting reminder of the escalating environmental bill that is likely to accompany the introduction of herbicide-tolerant crops.

The new pest-resistant transgenic crops pose similar environmental problems. Life-science companies are readying transgenic crops that produce insecticide in every cell of each plant. Several crops, including Ciba Geigy's pest-resistant "maximizer corn" and Rohm and Haas's pest-resistant tobacco are already available on the commercial market. A growing body of scientific evidence points to the likelihood of creating "super bugs" resistant to the effects of the new pesticide-producing genetic crops.

The new generation of virus-resistant transgenic crops pose the equally dangerous possibility of creating new viruses that have never before existed in nature. Concerns are surfacing among scientists and in scientific literature over the possibility that the protein genes could recombine with genes in related viruses that find their way naturally into the transgenic plant, creating a recombinant virus with novel features.

A growing number of ecologists warn that the biggest danger might lie in what is called "gene flow"—the transfer of genes from altered crops to weedy relatives by way of cross-pollination. Researchers are concerned that manufactured genes for herbicide tolerance, and pest and viral resistance might escape and, through cross pollination, insert themselves into the genetic makeup of weedy relatives, creating weeds that are resistant to herbicides, pests and viruses. Fears over the possibility of transgenic genes jumping to wild weedy relatives heightened in 1996 when a Danish research team, working under the auspices of Denmark's Environmental Science and Technology Department, observed the transfer of just such a gene—something critics of deliberate-release experiments have warned of for years and biotech companies have dismissed as a remote or nonexistent possibility.

Transnational life-science companies project that within 10 to 15 years, all of the major crops grown in the world will be genetically engineered to include herbicide-, pest-, virus-, bacteria-, fungus- and stress-resistant genes. Millions of acres of agricultural land and commercial forest will be transformed in the most daring experiment ever undertaken to remake the biological world. Proponents of the new science, armed with powerful gene-splicing tools and precious little data on potential impacts, are charging into this new world of agricultural biotechnology, giddy over the potential benefits and confident that the risks are minimum or non-existent. They may be right. But, what if they are wrong?

INSURING DISASTER

The insurance industry quietly let it be known several years ago that it would not insure the release of genetically engineered organisms into the environment against the possibility of catastrophic environmental damage, because the industry lacks a risk-assessment science—a predictive ecology—with which to judge the risk of any given introduction. In short, the insurance industry clearly understands the Kafka-esque implications of a government regime claiming to regulate a technology in the absence of clear scientific knowledge.

Increasingly nervous over the insurance question, one of the biotech trade associations attempted early on to raise an insurance pool among its member organizations, but gave up when it failed to raise sufficient funds to make the pool operable. Some observers worried, at the time, and continue to worry—albeit privately—over what might happen to the biotech industry if a large-scale commercial release of a genetically altered organism were to result in a catastrophic environmental event. For example, the introduction and spread of a new weed or pest comparable to Kudzu vine, Dutch elm disease or gypsy moth, might inflict costly damage to flora and fauna over extended ranges.

Corporate assurances aside, one or more significant environmental mishaps   25
are an inevitability in the years ahead. When that happens, every nation is going to be forced to address the issue of liability. Farmers, landowners, consumers and the public at large are going to demand to know how it could have happened and who is liable for the damages inflicted. When the day arrives—and it's likely to come sooner rather than later—"genetic pollution" will take its place alongside petrochemical and nuclear pollution as a grave threat to the Earth's already be-leaguered environment.

ALLERGIC TO TECHNOLOGY?

The introduction of new genetically engineered organisms also raises a number of serious human health issues that have yet to be resolved. Health professionals and consumer organizations are most concerned about the potential allergenic effects of genetically engineered foods. The Food and Drug Administration (FDA) announced in 1992 that special labeling for genetically engineered foods would not be required, touching off protest among food professionals, including the nation's leading chefs and many wholesalers and retailers.

With two percent of adults and eight percent of children having allergic responses to commonly eaten foods, consumer advocates argue that all gene-spliced foods need to be properly labeled so that consumers can avoid health risks. Their concerns were heightened in 1996 when *The New England Journal of Medicine* published a study showing genetically engineered soybeans containing a gene from a Brazil nut could create an allergic reaction in people who were allergic to the nuts. The test result was unwelcome news for Pioneer Hi-Bred International, the Iowa-based seed company that hoped to market the new genetically engineered soy. Though the FDA said it would label any genetically engineered foods containing genes from common allergenic organisms, the agency fell well short of requiring across-the-board labeling, leaving *The New England Journal of Medicine* editors to ask what protection consumers would have against genes from organisms that have never before been part of the human diet and that might be potential allergens. Concerned over the agency's seeming disregard for human health, the *Journal* editors concluded that FDA policy "would appear to favor industry over consumer protection."

DEPLETING THE GENE POOL

Ironically, all of the many efforts to reseed the biosphere with a laboratory-conceived second Genesis may eventually come to naught because of a massive catch-22 that lies at the heart of the new technology revolution.

On the one hand, the success of the biotech revolution is wholly dependent on access to a rich reservoir of genes to create new characteristics and properties in crops and animals grown for food, fiber and energy, and products used for pharmaceutical and medical purposes. Genes containing beneficial traits that can be manipulated, transformed and inserted into organisms destined for the commercial market come from either the wild or from traditional crops and animal breeds. Notwithstanding its awesome ability to transform nature into commercially marketable commodities, the biotech industry still remains utterly dependent upon nature's seed stock—germplasm—for its raw resources. At present, it is impossible to create a "useful" new gene in the laboratory. In this sense, biotechnology remains an extractive industry. It can rearrange genetic material, but cannot create it. On the other hand, the very practice of biotechnology—including cloning, tissue culturing and gene splicing—is likely to result in increasing genetic uniformity, a narrowing of the gene pool, and loss of the very genetic diversity that is so essential to guaranteeing the success of the biotech industry in the future.

In his book *The Last Harvest,* Paul Raeburn, the science editor for *Business Week,* penetrates to the heart of the problem. He writes, "Scientists can accomplish remarkable feats in manipulating molecules and cells, but they are utterly incapable of re-creating even the simplest forms of life in test tubes. Germplasm provides our lifeline into the future. No breakthrough in fundamental research can compensate for the loss of the genetic material crop breeders depend upon."

Agricultural biotechnology greatly increases the uniformity of agricul-   30
tural practices, as did the Green Revolution when it was introduced more than 30 years ago. Like its predecessor, the goal is to create superior varieties that can be planted as monocultures in agricultural regions all over the world. A handful of life-science companies are staking out the new biotech turf, each aggressively marketing their own patented brands of "super seeds"—and soon "super" farm animals as well. The new transgenic crops and animals are designed to grow faster, produce greater yields, and withstand more varied environmental and weather-related stresses. Their cost effectiveness, in the short run, is likely to guarantee them a robust market. In an industry where profit margins are notoriously low, farmers will likely jump at the opportunity of saving a few dollars per acre and a few cents per pound by shifting quickly to the new transgenic crops and animals.

However, the switch to a handful of patented transgenic seeds and livestock animals will likely further erode the genetic pool as farmers abandon the growing of traditional varieties and breeds in favor of the commercially more competitive patented products. By focusing on short-term market priorities, the biotech industry threatens to destroy the very genetic heirlooms that might one day be worth their weight in gold as a line of defense against new resistant diseases or superbugs.

Most molecular biologists and the biotechnology industry at large have all but dismissed the growing criticism of ecologists, whose recent studies suggest that the biotech revolution will likely be accompanied by the proliferation and spread of genetic pollution and the wholesale loss of genetic diversity. Nonetheless, the uncontrollable spread of super weeds, the buildup of resistant strains of bacteria and new super insects, the creation of novel viruses, the destabilization of whole ecosystems, the genetic contamination of food, and the steady depletion of the gene pool are no longer minor considerations, the mere grumbling of a few disgruntled critics. To ignore the warnings is to place the biosphere and civilization in harm's way in the coming years. Pestilence, famine, and the spread of new kinds of diseases throughout the world might yet turn out to be the final act in the script being prepared for the biotech century.

QUESTIONING THE TEXT

1. Rifkin uses an analogy to help support his argument: "The risks in releasing novel, genetically engineered organisms into the biosphere are similar to those we've encountered in introducing exotic organisms into the North American habitat" (paragraph 11). He goes on to mention some "severe dislocations" that have resulted—Dutch elm disease, for example. Working with two classmates, explore Rifkin's analogy, beginning perhaps by brainstorming about movies or TV shows you have seen that illustrate the analogy—*Jurassic Park,* for instance. Then try to think of counterexamples to Rifkin's argument, genetically altered things that have been introduced but that have not been disastrous (such as disease-resistant corn). Prepare a brief report for your class that either supports or challenges Rifkin's analogical argument.

2. Reread Rifkin's essay, noting his use of metaphors ("synthetic introduction is . . . ecological roulette"; a "biological Tower of Babel") and similes ("new gene-spliced crops . . . [are] like creations from the world of science fiction"). Then write a critical response to Rifkin's essay based on your understanding of how he uses metaphors, similes, and other figures of speech to help make his case.

3. Look carefully at the illustration by Tadeusz Majewski that accompanies this essay. Working with a classmate, determine what the illustration adds to Rifkin's argument, what it might distract from, or what it might emphasize, downplay, and so on. Summarize the thesis of Rifkin's argument and then write a one- or two-page report that explains to your class how the illustration works in relation to the thesis.

MAKING CONNECTIONS

4. Rifkin has a number of worries similar to those of Victor Frankenstein. If Mary Shelley were writing *Frankenstein* (p. 231) in the twenty-first century, what might be the characteristics of the "monster" the doctor

wishes to create? Where would the major pitfalls lie in accomplishing his goals? Make a list of characteristics and pitfalls and bring them to class for discussion.

JOINING THE CONVERSATION

5. Try your hand at writing a letter of response to Rifkin. In it, make sure that you demonstrate your understanding of his argument; then give your response to that argument and conclude with a series of questions about the "Biotech Century" you would most like to have answered. Bring your letter to class for discussion.

6. Working with two classmates, do some research on the claims Rifkin makes in his essay. One person might interview a senior professor in biology or biotechnology; one might search the Web for the latest research on genetic engineering in agriculture; another might seek out reviews of Rifkin's book and track down the reviews of several proponents and critics. After gathering as much material as you can, meet to share information and to decide what conclusions you can draw from it. Then prepare a 15- to 20-minute presentation for your class on "Rifkin's Claims: An Expanded View."

TODD OPPENHEIMER
The Computer Delusion

*I*N *"T*HE *C*OMPUTER *D*ELUSION*," T*ODD *O*PPENHEIMER*, winner of many awards for investigative reporting, argues that the tremendous emphasis on computers and technology in elementary and secondary schools, and especially in the lower grades, can actually decrease the effectiveness of learning and teaching. Yet local, state, and national governments are pouring funds into more and more technology for schools, often, Oppenheimer thinks, to the detriment of other programs. Students, teachers, parents, and policy makers must confront these issues immediately, he argues, and to help with that endeavor he looks closely at five claims that underlie the move to computerize U.S. schools.*

Oppenheimer's critique, "The Computer Delusion," published in the July 1997 issue of the Atlantic Monthly, *is anchored in his own experience. As associate editor at* Newsweek Interactive, *Oppenheimer has spent a great deal of time in cyberspace, exploring the uses of chat rooms and bulletin boards, initiating and conducting online discussion forums, and preparing numerous reports on experiments with new media. So although I have been a strong advocate of technology in the classroom, and especially in the writing classroom, reading Oppenheimer's essay gave me pause. Perhaps on these issues I am moving closer to Sherry Turkle, whom Oppenheimer quotes: "[t]he possibilities of using this thing [computer technology] poorly so outweigh the chance of using it well, it makes people like us, who are fundamentally optimistic about computers, very reticent."*

In addition to my own concerns about how best to use technology in education, I chose this essay partly because I am drawn to Oppenheimer's sense that we—people like you and me—must take responsibility for how technology will be used, both in and out of schools. In an online article in the Columbia Journalism Review, *Oppenheimer concludes by saying, "It's my hope that the new gurus of tomorrow will be those who can redefine responsibility—ours and that of our readers." Given the demand for instant gratification of what Oppenheimer calls "always-restless" cybercitizens, who disappear at a click if they aren't being entertained, this is a very tall order. And Oppenheimer, who learned to hold a New York City street audience as a mime partner of Robin Williams, well understands the difficulty of using technology to improve learning. How does your own experience bear out—or challenge—Oppenheimer's arguments?*

—A.L.

In 1922 Thomas Edison predicted that "the motion picture is destined to revolutionize our educational system and . . . in a few years it will supplant largely, if not entirely, the use of textbooks." Twenty-three years later, in 1945, William Levenson, the director of the Cleveland public schools' radio station, claimed that "the time may come when a portable radio receiver will be as common in the classroom as is the blackboard." Forty years after that the noted psychologist B. F. Skinner, referring to the first days of his "teaching machines," in the late 1950s and early 1960s, wrote, "I was soon saying that, with the help of teaching machines and programmed instruction, students could learn twice as much in the same time and with the same effort as in a standard classroom." Ten years after Skinner's recollections were published, President Bill Clinton campaigned for "a bridge to the twenty-first century . . . where computers are as much a part of the classroom as blackboards." Clinton was not alone in his enthusiasm for a program estimated to cost somewhere between $40 billion and $100 billion over the next five years. Speaker of the House Newt Gingrich, talking about computers to the Republican National Committee early this year, said, "We could do so much to make education available twenty-four hours a day, seven days a week, that people could literally have a whole different attitude toward learning."

If history really is repeating itself, the schools are in serious trouble. In *Teachers and Machines: The Classroom Use of Technology Since 1920* (1986), Larry Cuban, a professor of education at Stanford University and a former school superintendent, observed that as successive rounds of new technology failed their promoters' expectations, a pattern emerged. The cycle began with big promises backed by the technology developers' research. In the classroom, however, teachers never really embraced the new tools, and no significant academic improvement occurred. This provoked consistent responses: the problem was money, spokespeople argued, or teacher resistance, or the paralyzing school bureaucracy. Meanwhile, few people questioned the technology advocates' claims. As results continued to lag, the blame was finally laid on the machines. Soon schools were sold on the next generation of technology, and the lucrative cycle started all over again.

Today's technology evangels argue that we've learned our lesson from past mistakes. As in each previous round, they say that when our new hot

I began teaching in the mid-1960s and remember all the talk of the "smart" teaching machines. In fact, I helped design an individually paced program in English—though I didn't like it much and didn't think it taught students very well. —A.L.

A good point; availability of technology without proper motivation is not sufficient to create a learning environment. —H.R.

I remember "telecourses" from the late 1950s. They were awful stuff— we laughed at them more than we learned from them. —J.R.

But their reasons for not doing so get glossed over. I know of many classrooms right now, for instance, where new computers sit in unopened cartons, not because the teachers haven't embraced them but because the teachers' rooms are not wired properly for them. —A.L.

It seems to me that the role of business in education needs to be scrutinized. What are the dynamics of power between educators and businesses? —H.R.

technology—the computer—is compared with yesterday's, today's is better. "It can do the same things, plus," Richard Riley, the U.S. Secretary of Education, told me this spring.

How much better is it, really?

The promoters of computers in schools again offer prodigious research showing improved academic achievement after using their technology. The research has again come under occasional attack, but this time quite a number of teachers seem to be backing classroom technology. In a poll taken early last year U.S. teachers ranked computer skills and media technology as more "essential" than the study of European history, biology, chemistry, and physics; than dealing with social problems such as drugs and family breakdown; than learning practical job skills; and than reading modern American writers such as Steinbeck and Hemingway or classic ones such as Plato and Shakespeare.

In keeping with these views New Jersey cut state aid to a number of school districts this past year and then spent $10 million on classroom computers. In Union City, California, a single school district is spending $27 million to buy new gear for a mere eleven schools. The Kittridge Street Elementary School, in Los Angeles, killed its music program last year to hire a technology coordinator; in Mansfield, Massachusetts, administrators dropped proposed teaching positions in art, music, and physical education, and then spent $333,000 on computers; in one Virginia school the art room was turned into a computer laboratory. (Ironically, a half dozen preliminary studies recently suggested that music and art classes may build the physical size of a child's brain, and its powers for subjects such as language, math, science, and engineering—in one case far more than computer work did.) Meanwhile, months after a New Technology High School opened in Napa, California, where computers sit on every student's desk and all academic classes use computers, some students were complaining of headaches, sore eyes, and wrist pain.

Throughout the country, as spending on technology increases, school book purchases are stagnant. Shop classes, with their tradition of

What kind of a poll? What teachers were consulted, and how many? I'm suspicious of this "finding."   —A.L.

What is the payoff or trade-off when music classes are cut to fund classroom computers? I want to compare what skills are being represented developmentally by each program.   —H.R.

He's right about the costs. Maintaining the computers for our writing programs costs more than $15,000 a year, and that's just to cover mechanical bits and pieces.   —J.R.

Maybe lowering book purchases by itself is not a totally

negative result. I can't help thinking of the money I waste buying books that are ordered by my professors and then scarcely incorporated into the class or not at all. Having certain online references could relieve space limitations as well as conserve funds. —H.R.

teaching children building skills with wood and metal, have been almost entirely replaced by new "technology education programs." In San Francisco only one public school still offers a full shop program—the lone vocational high school. "We get kids who don't know the difference between a screwdriver and a ball peen hammer," James Dahlman, the school's vocational-department chair, told me recently. "How are they going to make a career choice? Administrators are stuck in this mindset that all kids will go to a four-year college and become a doctor or a lawyer, and that's not true. I know some who went to college, graduated, and then had to go back to technical school to get a job." Last year the school superintendent in Great Neck, Long Island, proposed replacing elementary school shop classes with computer classes and training the shop teachers as computer coaches. Rather than being greeted with enthusiasm, the proposal provoked a backlash.

Interestingly, shop classes and field trips are two programs that the National Information Infrastructure Advisory Council, the Clinton Administration's technology task force, suggests reducing in order to shift resources into computers. But are these results what technology promoters really intend? "You need to apply common sense," Esther Dyson, the president of EDventure Holdings and one of the task force's leading school advocates, told me recently. "Shop with a good teacher probably is worth more than computers with a lousy teacher. But if it's a poor program, this may provide a good excuse for cutting it. There will be a lot of trials and errors with this. And I don't know how to prevent those errors."

The issue, perhaps, is the magnitude of the errors. Alan Lesgold, a professor of psychology and the associate director of the Learning Research and Development Center at the University of Pittsburgh, calls the computer an "amplifier," because it encourages both enlightened study practices and thoughtless ones. There's a real risk, though, that the thoughtless practices will dominate, slowly dumbing down huge numbers of tomorrow's adults. As Sherry Turkle, a

I'd count shop as a "technology program" too—why should the definition of technology be limited to computers? —A.L.

Aren't students increasingly able to gain computer-related skills at home? —H.R.

The need for good teachers, not just high-tech equipment, is right on. All the students I've talked with agree that the teacher makes the difference. —H.R.

The powerful nature of the medium as well as the capacity for errors make for an effective argument for being cautious in determining the amount of exposure children should be given to it. —H.R.

professor of the sociology of science at the Massachusetts Institute of Technology and a longtime observer
of children's use of computers, told me, "The possibilities of using this thing poorly so outweigh the
chance of using it well, it makes people like us, who
are fundamentally optimistic about computers, very
reticent."

Turkle's comment hits home: one can be enthusiastic about computers, but still question their place in education. —J.R.

Perhaps the best way to separate fact from
fantasy is to take supporters' claims about computerized learning one by one and compare them with
the evidence in the academic literature and in the
everyday experiences I have observed or heard
about in a variety of classrooms.

Five main arguments underlie the campaign
to computerize our nation's schools.

I appreciate the focus that these five points bring to the article, but I wonder about who the "supporters" are who set forth these arguments: what primary sources is Oppenheimer drawing on in summarizing these points? —A.L.

- Computers improve both teaching practices
  and student achievement.

- Computer literacy should be taught as early as
  possible; otherwise students will be left behind.

- To make tomorrow's work force competitive
  in an increasingly high-tech world, learning
  computer skills must be a priority.

- Technology programs leverage support from
  the business community—badly needed today
  because schools are increasingly starved for
  funds.

- Work with computers—particularly using the
  Internet—brings students valuable connections with teachers, other schools and students,
  and a wide network of professionals around the
  globe. These connections spice the school day
  with a sense of real-world relevance, and
  broaden the educational community.

What makes someone "computer literate"? How long should this process take? —H.R.

"The Filmstrips of the 1990s"

Clinton's vision of computerized classrooms
arose partly out of the findings of the presidential
task force—thirty-six leaders from industry, education, and several interest groups who have guided
the Administration's push to get computers into the

schools. The report of the task force, "Connecting K–12 Schools to the Information Superhighway" (produced by the consulting firm McKinsey & Co.), begins by citing numerous studies that have apparently proved that computers enhance student achievement significantly. One "meta-analysis" (a study that reviews other studies—in this case 130 of them) reported that computers had improved performance in "a wide range of subjects, including language arts, math, social studies and science." Another found improved organization and focus in students' writing. A third cited twice the normal gains in math skills. Several schools boasted of greatly improved attendance.

Everything depends on how one defines "improved performance" here—and I cannot believe that computers alone improve performance in, for example, writing.   —A.L.

Unfortunately, many of these studies are more anecdotal than conclusive. Some, including a giant, oft-cited meta-analysis of 254 studies, lack the necessary scientific controls to make solid conclusions possible. The circumstances are artificial and not easily repeated, results aren't statistically reliable, or, most frequently, the studies did not control for other influences, such as differences between teaching methods. This last factor is critical, because computerized learning inevitably forces teachers to adjust their style—only sometimes for the better. Some studies were industry-funded, and thus tended to publicize mostly positive findings. "The research is set up in a way to find benefits that aren't really there," Edward Miller, a former editor of the *Harvard Education Letter,* says. "Most knowledgeable people agree that most of the research isn't valid. It's so flawed it shouldn't even be called research. Essentially, it's just worthless." Once the faulty studies are weeded out, Miller says, the ones that remain "are inconclusive"—that is, they show no significant change in either direction. Even Esther Dyson admits the studies are undependable. "I don't think those studies amount to much either way," she says. "In this area there is little proof."

Why are solid conclusions so elusive? Look at Apple Computer's "Classrooms of Tomorrow," perhaps the most widely studied effort to teach using computer technology. In the early 1980s Apple shrewdly realized that donating computers to schools might help not only students but also company sales, as Apple's ubiquity in classrooms turned legions of families into Apple loyalists. Last year, after the *San Jose Mercury News* (published in Apple's Silicon Valley home) ran a series questioning the effectiveness of computers in schools, the paper printed an opinion-page response from Terry Crane, an Apple vice-president. "Instead of isolating students," Crane wrote, "technology actually encouraged them to collaborate more than in traditional classrooms. Students also learned to explore and represent information dynamically and creatively, communicate effectively about complex processes, become independent learners and self-starters and become more socially aware and confident."

In my own classrooms, the use of technology has indeed fostered a collaborative environment. On a huge campus like mine, even the ability to set up virtual "meetings" has been a tremendous help to students and teachers. —A.L.

Crane didn't mention that after a decade of effort and the donation of equipment worth more than $25 million to thirteen schools, there is scant evidence of greater student achievement. To be fair, educators on both sides of the computer debate acknowledge that today's tests of student achievement are shockingly crude. They're especially weak in measuring intangibles such as enthusiasm and self-motivation, which do seem evident in Apple's classrooms and other computer-rich schools. In any event, what is fun and what is educational may frequently be at odds. "Computers in classrooms are the filmstrips of the 1990s," Clifford Stoll, the author of *Silicon Snake Oil: Second Thoughts on the Information Highway* (1995), told *The New York Times* last year, recalling his own school days in the 1960s. "We loved them because we didn't have to think for an hour, teachers loved them because they didn't have to teach, and parents loved them because it showed their schools were high-tech. But no learning happened."

I think Stoll way overstates the case! I've always remembered Aristotle's injunction that learning is life's greatest pleasure. So while I take the point here—learning and fun may sometimes be at odds— I believe as well that they do not have to be at odds, and that technology in the classroom doesn't have to be just about "fun." —A.L.

Stoll somewhat overstates the case—obviously, benefits can come from strengthening a student's motivation. Still, Apple's computers may bear less responsibility for that change than Crane suggests. In the beginning, when Apple did little more than dump computers in classrooms and homes, this produced no real results, according to Jane David, a consultant Apple hired to study its classroom initiative. Apple quickly learned that teachers needed to change their classroom approach to what is commonly called "project-oriented learning." This is an increasingly popular teaching method, in which students learn through doing and teachers act as facilitators or partners rather than as didacts. (Teachers sometimes refer to this approach, which arrived in classrooms before computers did, as being "the guide on the side instead of the sage on the stage.") But what the students learned "had less to do with the computer and more to do with the teaching," David concluded. "If you took the computers out, there would still be good teaching there." This story is heard in school after school, including two impoverished schools—Clear View Elementary School, in southern California, and the Christopher Columbus middle school, in New Jersey—that the Clinton Administration has loudly celebrated for turning themselves around with computers. At Christopher Columbus, in fact, students' test scores rose before computers arrived, not afterward, because of relatively basic changes: longer class periods, new books, after-school programs, and greater emphasis on student projects and collaboration.

Interesting. Does Oppenheimer make this sentence into a separate paragraph to give it special emphasis? To build the credibility of his firsthand experience? —A.L.

During recent visits to some San Francisco-area schools I could see what it takes for students to use computers properly, and why most don't.

On a bluff south of downtown San Francisco, in the middle of one of the city's lower-income neighborhoods, Claudia Schaffner, a tenth-grader, tapped away at a multimedia machine in a computer lab at Thurgood Marshall Academic High School, one of half a dozen special technology schools in the city. Schaffner was using a physics program to simulate the trajectory of a marble on a small roller coaster. "It helps to visualize it first, like 'A is for Apple' with kindergartners," Schaffner told me, while mousing up and down the virtual roller coaster. "I can see how the numbers go into action." This was lunch hour, and the students' excitement about what they can do in this lab was palpable. Schaffner could barely tear herself away. "I need to go eat some food," she finally said, returning within minutes to eat a rice dish at the keyboard.

Why are computers so addictive? I know people who became "glued" to the computer even after short periods of time. This doesn't seem healthy to me. —H.R.

Schaffner's teacher is Dennis Frezzo, an electrical-engineering graduate from the University of California at Berkeley. Despite his considerable knowledge of computer programming, Frezzo tries to keep classwork focused on physical projects. For a mere $8,000, for example, several teachers put together a multifaceted robotics lab, consisting of an advanced lego engineering kit and twenty-four old 386-generation computers. Frezzo's students used these materials to build a tiny electric car, whose motion was to be triggered by a light sensor. When the light sensor didn't work, the students figured out why. "That's a real problem—what you'd encounter in the real world," Frezzo told me. "I prefer they get stuck on small real-world problems instead of big fake problems"—like the simulated natural disasters that fill one popular educational game. "It's sort of the Zen approach to education," Frezzo said. "It's not the big problems. Isaac Newton already solved those. What come up in life are the little ones."

Technical glitches occur in college classrooms, too, after diverting attention from course work to technology.
—J.R.

It's one thing to confront technology's complexity at a high school—especially one that's blessed with four different computer labs and some highly skilled teachers like Frezzo, who know enough, as he put it, "to keep computers in their place." It's quite another to grapple with a high-tech future in the lower grades, especially at everyday schools that lack special funding or technical support. As evidence, when *U.S. News & World Report* published a cover story last fall on schools that make computers work, five of the six were high schools—among them Thurgood Marshall. Although the sixth was an elementary school, the featured program involved children with disabilities—the one group that does show consistent benefits from computerized instruction.

So "what it takes for students to use computers properly" is money and a really expert teacher who can "keep computers in their place." Now I expect we're going to hear why most schools don't meet these standards. *—A.L.*

ARTIFICIAL EXPERIENCE

Consider the scene at one elementary school, Sanchez, which sits on the edge of San Francisco's Latino community. For several years Sanchez, like many other schools, has made do with a roomful of basic Apple IIes. Last year, curious about what

computers could do for youngsters, a local entrepreneur donated twenty costly Power Macin-
toshes—three for each of five classrooms, and one
for each of the five lucky teachers to take home.
The teachers who got the new machines were delighted. "It's the best thing we've ever done,"
Adela Najarro, a third-grade bilingual teacher, told
me. She mentioned one boy, perhaps with a learning disability, who had started to hate school. Once
he had a computer to play with, she said, "his
whole attitude changed." Najarro is now a true believer, even when it comes to children without disabilities. "Every single child," she said, "will do
more work for you and do better work with a
computer. Just because it's on a monitor, kids pay
more attention. There's this magic to the screen."

So I got a surprise here—Oppenheimer is still concentrating on schools where computers "work." —A.L.

Scary? What exactly is the screen's magic, and does it make students think or merely amuse them? —J.R.

   Down the hall from Najarro's classroom her
colleague Rose Marie Ortiz had a more troubled
relationship with computers. On the morning I visited, Ortiz took her bilingual special-education class
of second-, third-, and fourth-graders into the lab
filled with the old Apple IIes. The students look
forward to this weekly expedition so much that
Ortiz gets exceptional behavior from them all morning. Out of date though these machines are, they
do offer a range of exercises, in subjects such as science, math, reading, social studies, and problem
solving. But owing to this group's learning problems and limited English skills, math drills were all
that Ortiz could give them. Nonetheless, within
minutes the kids were excitedly navigating their
way around screens depicting floating airplanes and
trucks carrying varying numbers of eggs. As the
children struggled, many resorted to counting in
whatever way they knew how. Some squinted at
the screen, painstakingly moving their fingers from
one tiny egg symbol to the next. "*Tres, cuatro, cinco,
seis . . . ,*" one little girl said loudly, trying to hear
herself above her counting neighbors. Another girl
kept a piece of paper handy, on which she marked
a line for each egg. Several others resorted to the
slow but tried and true—their fingers. Some just
guessed. Once the children arrived at answers, they
frantically typed them onto the screen, hoping it

Ironically, here's a school setting where technology would seem to hold out enormous potential to help students and teachers. What's gone wrong? —A.L.

would advance to something fun, the way Nintendos, Game Boys, and video-arcade games do. Sometimes their answers were right, and the screen did advance; sometimes they weren't; but the children were rarely discouraged. As schoolwork goes, this was a blast.

"It's highly motivating for them," Ortiz said as she rushed from machine to machine, attending not to math questions but to computer glitches. Those she couldn't fix she simply abandoned. "I don't know how practical it is. You see," she said, pointing to a girl counting on her fingers, "these kids still need the hands-on"—meaning the opportunity to manipulate physical objects such as beans or colored blocks. The value of hands-on learning, child-development experts believe, is that it deeply imprints knowledge into a young child's brain, by transmitting the lessons of experience through a variety of sensory pathways. "Curiously enough," the educational psychologist Jane Healy wrote in *Endangered Minds: Why Children Don't Think and What We Can Do about It* (1990), "visual stimulation is probably not the main access route to nonverbal reasoning. Body movements, the ability to touch, feel, manipulate, and build sensory awareness of relationships in the physical world, are its main foundations." The problem, Healy wrote, is that "in schools, traditionally, the senses have had little status after kindergarten."

Ortiz believes that the computer-lab time, brief as it is, dilutes her students' attention to language. "These kids are all language-delayed," she said. Though only modest sums had so far been spent at her school, Ortiz and other local teachers felt that the push was on for technology over other scholastic priorities. The year before, Sanchez had let its librarian go, to be replaced by a part-timer.

When Ortiz finally got the students rounded up and out the door, the kids were still worked up. "They're never this wired after reading group," she said. "They're usually just exhausted, because I've been reading with them, making them write and talk." Back in homeroom Ortiz showed off the students' monthly handwritten writing samples. "Now, could you do that on the computer?" she

Even more experienced users now probably expect a visual or aural payoff for their computer work. Have we been programmed to expect stimulation from the screen?
—J.R.

Here is the Western emphasis on rationality and the mind—as opposed to the rest of the body—and I believe that our educational system has been skewed strongly away from sensation as it relates to knowing and learning. I'd like to read Healy's book. —A.L.

asked. "No, because we'd be hung up on finding the keys." So why does Ortiz bother taking her students to the computer lab at all? "I guess I come in here for the computer literacy. If everyone else is getting it, I feel these kids should get it too."

Some computerized elementary school programs have avoided these pitfalls, but the record subject by subject is mixed at best. Take writing, where by all accounts and by my own observations the computer does encourage practice — changes are easier to make on a keyboard than with an eraser, and the lettering looks better. Diligent students use these conveniences to improve their writing, but the less committed frequently get seduced by electronic opportunities to make a school paper look snazzy. (The easy "cut and paste" function in today's word-processing programs, for example, is apparently encouraging many students to cobble together research materials without thinking them through.) Reading programs get particularly bad reviews. One small but carefully controlled study went so far as to claim that Reader Rabbit, a reading program now used in more than 100,000 schools, caused students to suffer a 50 percent drop in creativity. (Apparently, after forty-nine students used the program for seven months, they were no longer able to answer open-ended questions and showed a markedly diminished ability to brainstorm with fluency and originality.) What about hard sciences, which seem so well suited to computer study? Logo, the high-profile programming language refined by Seymour Papert and widely used in middle and high schools, fostered huge hopes of expanding children's cognitive skills. As students directed the computer to build things, such as geometric shapes, Papert believed, they would learn "procedural thinking," similar to the way a computer processes information. According to a number of studies, however, Logo has generally failed to deliver on its promises. Judah Schwartz, a professor of education at Harvard and a co-director of the school's Educational Technology Center, told me that a few newer applications, when used properly, can dramatically expand children's math and science

In papers where I have done major revising by the cut-and-paste method, I've found that I finish them without having a clear recollection of the flow of my arguments. —H.R.

I want to say "Yes, but . . ." to Oppenheimer's remarks about computers and writing. I think he understates the benefits of computers in writing classes. —J.R.

Despite the improvements, I'm skeptical of educational software programs. When I used them in junior high, I learned less about the subject being presented than about the computer functions themselves. —H.R.

thinking by giving them new tools to "make and explore conjectures." Still, Schwartz acknowledges that perhaps "ninety-nine percent" of the educational programs are "terrible, really terrible."

Even in success stories important caveats continually pop up. The best educational software is usually complex — most suited to older students and sophisticated teachers. In other cases the schools have been blessed with abundance — fancy equipment, generous financial support, or extra teachers — that is difficult if not impossible to duplicate in the average school. Even if it could be duplicated, the literature suggests, many teachers would still struggle with technology. Computers suffer frequent breakdowns; when they do work, their seductive images often distract students from the lessons at hand — which many teachers say makes it difficult to build meaningful rapport with their students.

With such a discouraging record of student and teacher performance with computers, why has the Clinton Administration focused so narrowly on the hopeful side of the story? Part of the answer may lie in the makeup of the Administration's technology task force. Judging from accounts of the task force's deliberations, all thirty-six members are unequivocal technology advocates. Two thirds of them work in the high-tech and entertainment industries. The effect of the group's tilt can be seen in its report. Its introduction adopts the authoritative posture of impartial fact-finder, stating that "this report does not attempt to lay out a national blueprint, nor does it recommend specific public policy goals." But it comes pretty close. Each chapter describes various strategies for getting computers into classrooms, and the introduction acknowledges that "this report does not evaluate the relative merits of competing demands on educational funding (e.g., more computers versus smaller class sizes)."

When I spoke with Esther Dyson and other task-force members about what discussion the group had had about the potential downside of computerized education, they said there hadn't been any. And when I asked Linda Roberts, Clinton's lead technology adviser in the Department of

In the hard sciences, do computers make what is genuinely complex look appealingly simple? —J.R.

The administration's ties to Hollywood are well known, and many of the advisors are strongly connected to related high-tech firms — thus the particular view of computers as necessary and good for education. —A.L.

How can we raise both sides of the issue for debate where it will count? —H.R.

I've followed Dyson's work for years now, and I am extremely surprised at her answer. —A.L.

Oppenheimer here asks just the right questions for his critical analysis.
—J.R.

Education, whether the task force was influenced by any self-interest, she said no, quite the opposite: the group's charter actually gave its members license to help the technology industry directly, but they concentrated on schools because that's where they saw the greatest need.

That sense of need seems to have been spreading outside Washington. Last summer a California task force urged the state to spend $11 billion on computers in California schools, which have struggled for years under funding cuts that have driven academic achievement down to among the lowest levels in the nation. This task force, composed of forty-six teachers, parents, technology experts, and business executives, concluded, "More than any other single measure, computers and network technologies, properly implemented, offer the greatest potential to right what's wrong with our public schools." Other options mentioned in the group's report—reducing class size, improving teachers' salaries and facilities, expanding hours of instruction—were considered less important than putting kids in front of computers.

"Hypertext Minds"

I worry that devoting too many hours to any medium puts kids at risk in some way. If Howard Gardner is right in his claim that all people have multiple intelligences—not simply one IQ—then we have to allow children time to develop these multiple intelligences, and doing so will mean widely varying activities.
—A.L.

Today's parents, knowing firsthand how families were burned by television's false promises, may want some objective advice about the age at which their children should become computer literate. Although there are no real guidelines, computer boosters send continual messages that if children don't begin early, they'll be left behind. Linda Roberts thinks that there's no particular minimum age—and no maximum number of hours that children should spend at a terminal. Are there examples of excess? "I haven't seen it yet," Roberts told me with a laugh. In schools throughout the country administrators and teachers demonstrate the same excitement, boasting about the wondrous things that children of five or six can do on computers: drawing, typing, playing with elementary science simulations and other programs called "educational games."

Will schools have to worry about teaching these basic skills to children? Within a few years, might not computers—in one form or another—be as common as TVs?   —J.R.

The schools' enthusiasm for these activities is not universally shared by specialists in childhood development. The doubters' greatest concern is for the very young—preschool through third grade, when a child is most impressionable. Their apprehension involves two main issues.

First, they consider it important to give children a broad base—emotionally, intellectually, and in the five senses—before introducing something as technical and one-dimensional as a computer. Second, they believe that the human and physical world holds greater learning potential.

The importance of a broad base for a child may be most apparent when it's missing. In *Endangered Minds,* Jane Healy wrote of an English teacher who could readily tell which of her students' essays were conceived on a computer. "They don't link ideas," the teacher says. "They just write one thing, and then they write another one, and they don't seem to see or develop the relationships between them." The problem, Healy argued, is that the pizzazz of computerized schoolwork may hide these analytical gaps, which "won't become apparent until [the student] can't organize herself around a homework assignment or a job that requires initiative. More commonplace activities, such as figuring out how to nail two boards together, organizing a game . . . may actually form a better basis for real-world intelligence."

False causality? I encountered the problem Healey describes in student papers long before computers were available. —J.R.

Others believe they have seen computer games expand children's imaginations. High-tech children "think differently from the rest of us," William D. Winn, the director of the Learning Center at the University of Washington's Human Interface Technology Laboratory, told *Business Week* in a recent cover story on the benefits of computer games. "They develop hypertext minds. They leap around. It's as though their cognitive strategies were parallel, not sequential." Healy argues the opposite. She and other psychologists think that the computer screen flattens information into narrow, sequential data. This kind of material, they believe, exercises mostly one half of the brain—the left hemisphere, where primarily sequential thinking occurs. The "right brain" meanwhile gets short shrift—yet this is the hemisphere that works on different kinds of information simultaneously. It shapes our multi-faceted impressions, and serves as the engine of creative analysis.

Opinions diverge in part because research on the brain is still so sketchy, and computers are so new, that the effect of computers on the brain remains a great mystery. "I don't think we know anything about it," Harry Chugani, a pediatric neurobiologist at Wayne State University, told me. This very ignorance makes skeptics wary. "Nobody knows how kids' internal wiring works," Clifford Stoll wrote in *Silicon Snake Oil*, "but anyone who's directed away from social interactions has a head start on turning out weird. . . . No computer can teach what a walk through a pine forest feels like. Sensation has no substitute."

This points to the conservative developmentalists' second concern: the danger that even if hours in front of the screen are limited, unabashed enthusiasm for the computer sends the wrong message: that the mediated world is more significant than the real one. "It's like TV commercials," Barbara Scales, the head teacher at the Child Study Center at the University of California at Berkeley, told me. "Kids get so hyped up, it can change their expectations about stimulation, versus what they generate themselves." In *Silicon Snake Oil*, Michael Fellows, a computer scientist at the University of Victoria, in British Columbia, was even blunter. "Most schools would probably be better off if they threw their computers into the Dumpster."

Faced with such sharply contrasting viewpoints, which are based on such uncertain ground, how is a responsible policymaker to proceed? "A prudent society controls its own infatuation with 'progress' when planning for its young," Healy argued in *Endangered Minds*.

> Unproven technologies . . . may offer lively visions, but they can also be detrimental to the development of the young plastic brain. The cerebral cortex is a wondrously well-buffered mechanism that can withstand a good bit of well-intentioned bungling. Yet there is a point at which fundamental neural substrates for reasoning may be jeopar-

I often think that if I were beginning my studies all over again, I would focus on neuroscience. Especially in the last few years, a number of excellent books about how the brain/mind works and develops have appeared, and I read all of them with great interest! —A.L.

Many college students seem to have a healthy skepticism about computers. Few students get hooked. —J.R.

dized for children who lack proper physical, intellectual, or emotional nurturance. Childhood—and the brain—have their own imperatives. In development, missed opportunities may be difficult to recapture.

The problem is that technology leaders rarely include these or other warnings in their recommendations. When I asked Dyson why the Clinton task force proceeded with such fervor, despite the classroom computer's shortcomings, she said, "It's so clear the world is changing."

Must computer training come early? Computers and software are getting easier to operate, not harder. Can't we afford to introduce children to computers when they are ready? —J.R.

REAL JOB TRAINING

In the past decade, according to the presidential task force's report, the number of jobs requiring computer skills has increased from 25 percent of all jobs in 1983 to 47 percent in 1993. By 2000, the report estimates, 60 percent of the nation's jobs will demand these skills—and pay an average of 10 to 15 percent more than jobs involving no computer work. Although projections of this sort are far from reliable, it's a safe bet that computer skills will be needed for a growing proportion of tomorrow's work force. But what priority should these skills be given among other studies?

When will this trend plateau? Oppenheimer implies that schools are overpreparing for this trend. —H.R.

In fact, over 50 percent of all jobs are now classified as "information" jobs. But simple knowledge of technical aspects of computers does not prepare people to do well at such jobs. —A.L.

Listen to Tom Henning, a physics teacher at Thurgood Marshall, the San Francisco technology high school. Henning has a graduate degree in engineering, and helped to found a Silicon Valley company that manufactures electronic navigation equipment. "My bias is the physical reality," Henning told me, as we sat outside a shop where he was helping students to rebuild an old motorcycle. "I'm no technophobe. I can program computers." What worries Henning is that computers at best engage only two senses, hearing and sight—and only two-dimensional sight at that "Even if they're doing three-dimensional computer modeling, that's still a two-D replica of a three-D world. If you took a kid who grew up on Nintendo, he's not going to have the necessary skills. He needs to have done it first with Tinkertoys or clay, or carved it out of balsa wood." As David Elkind, a professor of child development at Tufts University, puts it, "A dean of the University of Iowa's school of engineering used to say the best engineers were the farm boys," because they knew how machinery really worked.

Surely many employers will disagree, and welcome the commercially applicable computer skills that today's high-tech training can bring them. What's striking is how easy it is to find other employers who share Henning's and Elkind's concerns.

Kris Meisling, a senior geological-research adviser for Mobil Oil, told me that "people who use computers a lot slowly grow rusty in their ability to think." Meisling's group creates charts and maps—some computerized, some not—to plot where to drill for oil. In large one-dimensional analyses, such as sorting volumes of seismic data, the computer saves vast amounts of time, sometimes making previously impossible tasks easy. This lures people in his field, Meisling believes, into using computers as much as possible. But when geologists turn to computers for "interpretive" projects, he finds, they often miss information, and their oversights are further obscured by the computer's captivating automatic design functions. This is why Meisling still works regularly with a pencil and paper—tools that, ironically, he considers more interactive than the computer, because they force him to think implications through.

"You can't simultaneously get an overview and detail with a computer," he says. "It's linear. It gives you tunnel vision. What computers can do well is what can be calculated over and over. What they can't do is innovation. If you think of some new way to do or look at things and the software can't do it, you're stuck. So a lot of people think 'Well, I guess it's a dumb idea, or it's unnecessary.'"

High-tech firms here in Austin have snapped up graduate students in English who can program or create Web pages—the companies seem to value literacy as much as technological skills. —J.R.

I have heard similar warnings from people in other businesses, including high-tech enterprises. A spokeswoman for Hewlett-Packard, the giant California computer-products company, told me the company rarely hires people who are predominantly computer experts, favoring instead those who have a talent for teamwork and are flexible

I have heard precisely the same stories from friends in Silicon Valley high-tech firms. —A.L.

and innovative. Hewlett-Packard is such a believer in hands-on experience that since 1992 it has spent $2.6 million helping forty-five school districts build math and science skills the old-fashioned way—using real materials, such as dirt, seeds, water, glass vials, and magnets. Much the same perspective came from several recruiters in film and computer-game animation. In work by artists who have spent a lot of time on computers "you'll see a stiffness or a flatness, a lack of richness and depth," Karen Chelini, the director of human resources for LucasArts Entertainment, George Lucas's interactive-games maker, told me recently. "With traditional art training, you train the eye to pay attention to body movement. You learn attitude, feeling, expression. The ones who are good are those who as kids couldn't be without their sketchbook."

Many jobs obviously will demand basic computer skills if not sophisticated knowledge. But that doesn't mean that the parents or the teachers of young students need to panic. Joseph Weizenbaum, a professor emeritus of computer science at MIT, told the *San Jose Mercury News* that even at his technology-heavy institution new students can learn all the computer skills they need "in a summer." This seems to hold in the business world, too. Patrick MacLeamy, an executive vice-president of Hellmuth Obata & Kassabaum, the country's largest architecture firm, recently gave me numerous examples to illustrate that computers pose no threat to his company's creative work. Although architecture professors are divided on the value of computerized design tools, in MacLeamy's opinion they generally enhance the process. But he still considers "knowledge of the hands" to be valuable—today's architects just have to develop it in other ways. (His firm's answer is through building models.) Nonetheless, as positive as MacLeamy is about computers, he has found the company's two-week computer training to be sufficient. In fact, when he's hiring, computer skills don't enter into his list of priorities. He looks for a strong character; an ability to speak, write, and comprehend; and a rich education in the history of architecture.

Two weeks! This figure surprises me; I wonder how much data MacLeamy has to back it up.
—A.L.

THE SCHOOLS THAT BUSINESS BUILT

Newspaper financial sections carry almost daily pronouncements from the computer industry and other businesses about their high-tech hopes for America's schoolchildren. Many of these are joined to philanthropic commitments to helping schools make curriculum changes. This sometimes gets businesspeople involved in schools, where they've begun to understand and work with the many daunting problems that are unrelated to technology. But if business gains too much influence over the curriculum, the schools can become a kind of corporate training center—largely at taxpayer expense.

For more than a decade scholars and government commissions have criticized the increasing professionalization of the college years—frowning at the way traditional liberal arts are being edged out by hot topics of the moment or strictly business-oriented studies. The schools' real job, the technology critic Neil Postman argued in his book *The End of Education* (1995), is to focus on "how to make a life, which is quite different from how to make a living." Some see the arrival of boxes of computer hardware and software in the schools as taking the commercial trend one step further, down into high school and elementary grades. "Should you be choosing a career in kindergarten?" asks Helen Sloss Luey, a social worker and a former president of San Francisco's Parent Teacher Association. "People need to be trained to learn and change, while education seems to be getting more specific."

Indeed it does. The New Technology High School in Napa (the school where a computer sits on every student's desk) was started by the school district and a consortium of more than forty businesses. "We want to be the school that business built," Robert Nolan, a founder of the school, told me last fall. "We wanted to create an environment that mimicked what exists in the high-tech business world." Increasingly, Nolan explained, business leaders want to hire people specifically trained in the skill they need. One of Nolan's partners, Ted Fujimoto, of the Landmark Consulting Group, told

I agree with Postman's general point, but I do not think that these two goals—making a life and making a living—need to be seen as antithetical. Can't one "make" both, and do a good job at each?   —A.L.

me that instead of just asking the business community for financial support, the school will now undertake a trade: in return for donating funds, businesses can specify what kinds of employees they want—"a two-way street." Sometimes the traffic is a bit heavy in one direction. In January, *The New York Times* published a lengthy education supplement describing numerous examples of how business is increasingly dominating school software and other curriculum materials, and not always toward purely educational goals.

People who like the idea that their taxes go to computer training might be surprised at what a poor investment it can be. Larry Cuban, the Stanford education professor, writes that changes in the classroom for which business lobbies rarely hold long-term value. Rather, they're often guided by labor-market needs that turn out to be transitory; when the economy shifts, workers are left unprepared for new jobs. In the economy as a whole, according to a recent story in *The New York Times,* performance trends in our schools have shown virtually no link to the rises and falls in the nation's measures of productivity and growth. This is one reason that school traditionalists push for broad liberal-arts curricula, which they feel develop students' values and intellect, instead of focusing on today's idea about what tomorrow's jobs will be.

I wish Oppenheimer would be more specific about those narrow technological skills businesses want students to develop. —J.R.

High-tech proponents argue that the best education software does develop flexible business intellects. In the *Business Week* story on computer games, for example, academics and professionals expressed amazement at the speed, savvy, and facility that young computer jocks sometimes demonstrate. Several pointed in particular to computer simulations, which some business leaders believe are becoming increasingly important in fields ranging from engineering, manufacturing, and troubleshooting to the tracking of economic activity and geopolitical risk. The best of these simulations may be valuable, albeit for strengthening one form of thinking. But the average simulation program may be of questionable relevance.

This reminds me of my cousin who graduated with a humanities degree and quickly acquired the skills to land a job as a computer troubleshooter. —H.R.

Sherry Turkle, the sociology professor at MIT, has studied youngsters using computers for more than twenty years. In her book *Life on the Screen: Identity in the Age of the Internet* (1995) she described a disturbing experience with a simulation game called SimLife. After she sat down with a thirteen-year-old named Tim, she was stunned at the way

> Tim can keep playing even when he has no idea what is driving events. For example, when his sea urchins become extinct, I ask him why.
>
> TIM: "I don't know, it's just something that happens."
>
> ST: "Do you know how to find out why it happened?"
>
> TIM: "No."
>
> ST: "Do you mind that you can't tell why?"
>
> TIM: "No. I don't let things like that bother me. It's not what's important."

Anecdotes like this lead some educators to worry that as children concentrate on how to manipulate software instead of on the subject at hand, learning can diminish rather than grow. Simulations, for example, are built on hidden assumptions, many of which are oversimplified if not highly questionable. All too often, Turkle wrote recently in *The American Prospect,* "experiences with simulations do not open up questions but close them down." Turkle's concern is that software of this sort fosters passivity, ultimately dulling people's sense of what they can change in the world. There's a tendency, Turkle told me, "to take things at 'interface' value." Indeed, after mastering SimCity, a popular game about urban planning, a tenth-grade girl boasted to Turkle that she'd learned the following rule: "Raising taxes always leads to riots."

The business community also offers tangible financial support, usually by donating equipment. Welcome as this is, it can foster a high-tech habit. Once a school's computer system is set up, the companies often drop their support. This saddles the school with heavy long-term responsibilities: maintenance of the computer network and the need

Oppenheimer draws quite an inference from the single example he presents. I am not convinced. —J.R.

This is one of the most worrisome claims in Oppenheimer's article. I hope Turkle, whose research in this area is generally very well respected, will turn her attention to studying whether this claim holds up. —A.L.

for constant software upgrades and constant teacher training—the full burden of which can cost far more than the initial hardware and software combined. Schools must then look for handouts from other companies, enter the grant-seeking game, or delicately go begging in their own communities. "We can go to the well only so often," Toni-Sue Passantino, the principal of the Bayside Middle School, in San Mateo, California, told me recently. Last year Bayside let a group of seventh- and eighth-graders spend eighteen months and countless hours creating a rudimentary virtual-reality program, with the support of several high-tech firms. The companies' support ended after that period, however—creating a financial speed bump of a kind that the Rand Corporation noted in a report to the Clinton Administration as a common obstacle.

School administrators may be outwardly excited about computerized instruction, but they're also shrewdly aware of these financial challenges. In March of last year, for instance, when California launched its highly promoted "Net-Day '96" (a campaign to wire 12,000 California schools to the Internet in one day), school participation was far below expectations, even in technology-conscious San Francisco. In the city papers school officials wondered how they were supposed to support an Internet program when they didn't even have the money to repair crumbling buildings, install electrical outlets, and hire the dozens of new teachers recently required so as to reduce class size.

One way around the donation maze is to simplify: use inexpensive, basic software and hardware, much of which is available through recycling programs. Such frugality can offer real value in the elementary grades, especially since basic word-processing tools are most helpful to children just learning to write. Yet schools, like the rest of us, can't resist the latest toys. "A lot of people will spend all their money on fancy new equipment that can do great things, and sometimes it just gets used for typing classes," Ray Porter, a computer resource teacher for the San Francisco schools, told me

In the computers and composition program at my school, this solution has not proved viable: the equipment we can get through "recycling" is too outdated to allow our students to create the kind of projects they need to succeed in advanced classes.
—A.L.

recently. "Parents, school boards, and the reporters want to see only razzle-dazzle state-of-the-art."

INTERNET ISOLATION

It is hard to visit a high-tech school without being led by a teacher into a room where students are communicating with people hundreds or thousands of miles away—over the Internet or sometimes through video-conferencing systems (two-way TV sets that broadcast live from each room). Video conferences, although fun, are an expensive way to create classroom thrills. But the Internet, when used carefully, offers exciting academic prospects—most dependably, once again, for older students. In one case schools in different states have tracked bird migrations and then posted their findings on the World Wide Web, using it as their own national notebook. In San Francisco eighth-grade economics students have E-mailed Chinese and Japanese businessmen to fulfill an assignment on what it would take to build an industrial plant overseas. Schools frequently use the Web to publish student writing. While thousands of self-published materials like these have turned the Web into a worldwide vanity press, the network sometimes gives young writers their first real audience.

This assessment of the Internet seems balanced—both good and bad are acknowledged.
—J.R.

The free nature of Internet information also means that students are confronted with chaos, and real dangers. "The Net's beauty is that it's uncontrolled," Stephen Kerr, a professor at the College of Education at the University of Washington and the editor of *Technology in the Future of Schooling* (1996), told me. "It's information by anyone, for anyone. There's racist stuff, bigoted, hate-group stuff, filled with paranoia; bomb recipes; how to engage in various kinds of crimes, electronic and otherwise; scams and swindles. It's all there. It's all available." Older students may be sophisticated enough to separate the Net's good food from its poisons, but even the savvy can be misled. On almost any subject the Net offers a plethora of seemingly sound "research." But under close inspection much of it

Students in one of my classes identified a number of racist sites, analyzed the rhetorical strategies used by the sites, and wrote compelling counter-arguments to them.
—A.L.

proves to be ill informed, or just superficial. "That's the antithesis of what classroom kids should be exposed to," Kerr said.

This makes traditionalists emphasize the enduring value of printed books, vetted as most are by editing. In many schools, however, libraries are fairly limited. I now volunteer at a San Francisco high school where the library shelves are so bare that I can see how the Internet's ever-growing number of research documents, with all their shortcomings, can sometimes be a blessing.

The replacement of print books by cyber versions strikes me as impractical and unhealthy.
—H.R.

Even computer enthusiasts give the Net tepid reviews. "Most of the content on the Net is total garbage," Esther Dyson acknowledges. "But if you find one good thing you can use it a million times." Kerr believes that Dyson is being unrealistic. "If you find a useful site one day, it may not be there the next day, or the information is different. Teachers are being asked to jump in and figure out if what they find on the Net is worthwhile. They don't have the skill or time to do that." Especially when students rely on the Internet's much-vaunted search software. Although these tools deliver hundreds or thousands of sources within seconds, students may not realize that search engines, and the Net itself, miss important information all the time.

The old axiom "garbage in, garbage out" may count double online: we all need to remember this and to think critically about the information we find online.
—A.L.

Of course, neither students nor instructors need to come to the Internet without guidance. And learning to find information is a vital skill.
—J.R.

"We need *less* surfing in the schools, not more," David Gelernter, a professor of computer science at Yale, wrote last year in *The Weekly Standard*. "Couldn't we teach them to use what they've got before favoring them with three orders of magnitude *more?*" In my conversations with Larry Cuban, of Stanford, he argued, "Schooling is not about information. It's getting kids to think about information. It's about understanding and knowledge and wisdom."

It may be that youngsters' growing fascination with the Internet and other ways to use computers will distract from yet another of Clinton's education priorities: to build up the reading skills of American children. Sherry Dingman, an assistant professor of psychology at Marist College, in Poughkeepsie, New York, who is optimistic about many computer applications, believes that if children start using computers before they have a broad foundation in reading from books, they will be cheated out of opportunities to develop imagination. "If we think we're going to take kids who haven't been read to, and fix it by sitting them in front of a computer, we're fooling ourselves," Dingman told me not long ago. This doesn't mean that teachers or parents should resort to books on CD-ROM, which Dingman considers "a great waste of time," stuffing children's minds with "canned" images instead of stimulating youngsters to create their own. "Computers are lollipops that rot your teeth" is how Marilyn Darch, an English teacher at Poly High School, in Long Beach, California, put it in *Silicon Snake Oil.* "The kids love them. But once they get hooked. . . . It makes reading a book seem tedious. Books don't have sound effects, and their brains have to do all the work."

Computer advocates like to point out that the Internet allows for all kinds of intellectual challenges—especially when students use E-mail, or post notes in "newsgroup" discussions, to correspond with accomplished experts. Such experts, however, aren't consistently available. When they are, online "conversations" generally take place when correspondents are sitting alone, and the dialogue lacks the unpredictability and richness that occur in face-to-face discussions. In fact, when youngsters are put into groups for the "collaborative" learning that computer defenders celebrate, realistically only one child sits at the keyboard at a time. (During my school visits children tended to get quite possessive about the mouse and the keyboard, resulting in frustration and noisy disputes more often than collaboration.) In combination these constraints lead to yet another of the childhood developmentalists' concerns—that computers encourage social isolation.

Just a Glamorous Tool

It would be easy to characterize the battle over computers as merely another chapter in the world's oldest story: humanity's natural resistance to change. But that does an injustice to the forces at work in this transformation. This is not just the future versus the past, uncertainty versus nostalgia; it is about encouraging a fundamental shift in personal priorities—a minimizing of the real, physical world in favor of an unreal "virtual" world. It is about teaching youngsters that exploring what's on a two-dimensional screen is more important than playing with real objects, or sitting down to an attentive conversation with a friend, a parent, or a teacher. By extension, it means downplaying the importance of conversation, of careful listening, and of expressing oneself in person with acuity and individuality. In the process, it may also limit the development of children's imaginations.

Perhaps this is why Steven Jobs, one of the founders of Apple Computer and a man who claims to have "spearheaded giving away more computer equipment to schools than anybody else on the planet," has come to a grim conclusion: "What's wrong with education cannot be fixed with technology," he told *Wired* magazine last year. "No amount of technology will make a dent. . . . You're not going to solve the problems by putting all knowledge onto CD-ROMS. We can put a Web site in every school—none of this is bad. It's bad only if it lulls us into thinking we're doing something to solve the problem with education." Jane David, the consultant to Apple, concurs, with a commonly heard caveat. "There are real dangers," she told me, "in looking to technology to be the savior of education. But it won't survive without the technology."

Arguments like David's remind Clifford Stoll of yesteryear's promises about television. He wrote in *Silicon Snake Oil,*

> "Sesame Street" . . . has been around for twenty years. Indeed, its idea of making learning relevant to all was as widely promoted in the seventies as the Internet is today.
>
> So where's that demographic wave of creative and brilliant students now entering college? Did kids really need to learn how to watch television? Did we inflate their expectations that learning would always be colorful and fun?

Computer enthusiasts insist that the computer's "interactivity" and multimedia features

I am most alarmed about this possibility. However, part of me wonders whether the "virtual" world isn't also real—and we just can't quite see it that way yet.
—A.L.

Some either/or thinking going on here? —J.R.

Oppenheimer's definition of "reality" is vague and unconvincing. He doesn't address the issue that written texts have a similar distance from the "real" world.
—H.R.

make this machine far superior to television. Nonetheless, Stoll wrote,

> I see a parallel between the goals of "Sesame Street" and those of children's computing. Both are pervasive, expensive and encourage children to sit still. Both display animated cartoons, gaudy numbers and weird, random noises. . . . Both give the sensation that by merely watching a screen, you can acquire information without work and without discipline.

As the technology critic Neil Postman put it to a Harvard electronic-media conference, "I thought that television would be the last great technology that people would go into with their eyes closed. Now you have the computer."

The lengthy essay ends with some specific proposals — all of which seem reasonable, given the evidence presented. —J.R.

The solution is not to ban computers from classrooms altogether. But it may be to ban federal spending on what is fast becoming an overheated campaign. After all, the private sector, with its constant supply of used computers and the computer industry's vigorous competition for new customers, seems well equipped to handle the situation. In fact, if schools can impose some limits — on technology donors and on themselves — rather than indulging in a consumer frenzy, most will probably find themselves with more electronic gear than they need. That could free the billions that Clinton wants to devote to technology and make it available for impoverished fundamentals: teaching solid skills in reading, thinking, listening, and talking; organizing inventive field trips and other rich hands-on experiences; and, of course, building up the nation's core of knowledgeable, inspiring teachers. These notions are considerably less glamorous than computers are, but their worth is firmly proved through a long history.

Is banning funding too extreme a reaction? Is this the only way to protect against the "dangers" of computers? What about school districts that don't have the necessary resources? —H.R.

Last fall, after the school administrators in Mansfield, Massachusetts, had eliminated proposed art, music, and physical-education positions in favor of buying computers, Michael Bellino, an electrical engineer at Boston University's Center for Space Physics, appeared before the Massachusetts Board of Education to protest. "The purpose of the schools

[is] to, as one teacher argues, 'Teach carpentry, not hammer,'" he testified. "We need to teach the whys and ways of the world. Tools come and tools go. Teaching our children tools limits their knowledge to these tools and hence limits their futures."

Afterwords

As I read Oppenheimer's essay, I kept thinking back to 1983, the year I got my first real computer. As I recall, it was about twice the size of the one I now have on my desk, and about four or five times the size of my little laptop. And I struggled to memorize complicated codes, to figure out how to configure the right printer, and to remember which key to hit to center text and carry out other word-processing functions. I signed up for a word-processing class, but quickly withdrew in favor of trial and error—and the help of friends. Will I ever get the hang of this thing?

Some seventeen years later, I find I have internalized a great deal of information about how to use the computer to my advantage, especially in communicating with people around the world, in searching for esoteric—and sometimes everyday—information, and in producing documents from short speeches to entire books. But I am still learning and experimenting with how best to use technology in my classrooms. While I routinely set up closed listservs for my classes and make materials available on the Web, I certainly have not perfected these strategies. Fortunately for me, the students in my classes are usually willing and able to help with the logistical problems we face, and they routinely have the best ideas about how to integrate technology into our courses. What I hope to do more of is team-teaching via technology. I'm planning, for instance, for my first-year writing class to meet at least once a week online with a similar group at another university; the teacher of that course and I are working on our syllabus together, and we will be carrying out email exchanges and holding real-time meetings during the course of the next term. I believe that doing so will allow us a stronger sense of a "real" audience for our writing and give us access to other teacher and student ideas.

Oppenheimer has given me a lot to think about in his warnings about computer "delusions." As a result, I will be particularly cautious in my use of technology in my classrooms. But I am not ready to give up on its effectiveness quite yet. — A.L.

For the past six years, I've taught all of my courses in a networked computer classroom. I often joke that I'm never more than five minutes away from throwing out the d—n machines and going back to paper and blackboards. That's because the technology never quite works as advertised: a printer goes offline; the browser software freezes on screen; the word processor formats a list the way it wants to; and nobody remembers the passwords to the online forums.

Yet I also know that I now take for granted much of what computers do for me. I correspond daily with a dozen people or more via email, can locate almost any information I need on the Web, expect flawless and immediate copies of everything I write, and depend on the word processor to catch my more egregious spelling and grammar errors. My class presentations now routinely rely on PowerPoint and an LCD projector, and I deliver my policy statements, syllabi, and assignments via course Web sites. I realize that I am hooked. The computer has become a permanent and necessary part of my professional world. But it is only a tool. It hasn't made me smarter—just quicker, more productive, and, frankly, more frazzled.

So Oppenheimer's piece makes sense to me. He's not a Luddite who fears electronic technology, but an advocate for education. I think he overstates his case near the end of the essay, and he may underestimate the contributions computers can make to education. But learning is rarely easy, and students will be hurt if their machines make it seem so.   —J.R.

Overall, I found this article interesting and often compelling. The craze for computer technology in schools is convincingly shown to be more extreme than prudence warrants. The arguments Oppenheimer makes about why the role of computers in classrooms should change seem to be arranged logically. He covers and anticipates in his article many of the questions that occurred to me.

I would have appreciated a clearer comparison between the skills developed in children by computer work and those skills developed by other areas of education. If this information was not yet available in 1997, when Oppenheimer was writing, a summary of what was being done—and by whom—to research these issues would have been particularly interesting to me. His conclusion struck me at first as an overreaction. In thinking it over, however, I've decided that his suggestion about controlling the influence government money has over educational practices might have some merit.

— H.R.

QUESTIONING THE TEXT

1. The five claims Oppenheimer explores are listed near the beginning of the essay (p. 259). Working with a classmate, review these five claims carefully. Then work together to create an outline of the rest of Oppenheimer's essay, labeling the parts of the essay that address each of the claims he considers. Which claims get most—or least—attention? Why might Oppenheimer have chosen to focus on some more sharply than others?

2. List the sources Oppenheimer refers to in his essay, including the writers and the titles of their works, if given. What do these sources seem to have in common? Why do you think Oppenheimer chose each one?

MAKING CONNECTIONS

3. Oppenheimer doesn't talk in this essay about issues of ownership in classrooms (for example, who "owns" the writing students produce on school computers?). What are some questions Pamela Samuelson (p. 315) might want Oppenheimer to consider, and why?

4. Might J. Michael Bishop (p. 237) label Oppenheimer an "enemy of promise"? Why, or why not?

JOINING THE CONVERSATION

5. You may or may not be among those who remember using computers from your earliest years. In either case, reflect for a while on the technologies you encountered during your early years in school. Did you encounter reading machines? Television and video? Overhead projectors? Computers? Share your memories with two classmates and brainstorm together for technologies you may have forgotten. Finally, write a letter to Oppenheimer in which you use your own school experience to support or challenge his argument.

6. Oppenheimer characterizes the "battle over computers" as being "about encouraging a fundamental shift in personal priorities — a minimizing of the real, physical world in favor of an unreal 'virtual' world" (pp. 280–281). Spend some time talking with two classmates about this statement, about what you think it means, and about what evidence you can see around you that relates to it. Then work independently on several freewriting "loops" in response to the statement. Start by writing for 10 to 15 minutes (without stopping) about whatever comes into your mind when you read the statement. Identify the most interesting sentence or idea in what you have written and use it as the beginning of another "loop"; again, write for 10 to 15 minutes. (You may want to carry out several additional loops.) Finally, go over all your materials and prepare a one-page critical response to Oppenheimer's statement.

EMILY MARTIN
The Body at War: Media Views of the Immune System

W*RITING SOME FORTY YEARS AGO about "Roots for a New Rhetoric" that could foster global understanding, Father Daniel Fogarty called language our "most significant
invention." "Out of language," he continued, we "have fashioned the exquisite sensitivity of Hamlet, the instruments of psychotherapy, and that sizable but sensible dream
that became the United Nations." Fogarty's statements stress the power of language to
shape the reality we perceive. Chief among the powers of language is that of metaphor,
the very basis of language symbols. The linguists George Lakoff and Mark Johnson
argue that metaphors underlie and reinforce not only the values we hold but the reasons
we give for holding them.*

We have all seen these insights enacted on television: think, for example, of the
toothpaste commercials you have seen featuring chemical creatures fighting plaque or
tooth decay in the service of sales, or consider the number of songs that depend on the
metaphor of a broken heart to sell their particular sentiments. And powerful metaphors
inform our desktops well: think how different the "product" might be if we had not
"Microsoft Office" as a guiding metaphor but, say, "Microsoft kitchen."*

Building on these insights about language and metaphor, the cultural critic
Emily Martin (b. 1944), Mary Garrett Professor of Anthropology at the Johns
Hopkins University, traces the metaphoric representation of the human immune system from its first widespread dissemination as a topic of interest in 1957 to the present. Martin's analysis reveals that the most powerful metaphors associated with the
immune system are those of war and battle, and she reflects on the ways in which
these war scenes are populated by identities that are gendered, raced, and classed.
Using vivid examples drawn from books, songs, paintings, cartoons, and advertising, Martin shows how saturated our culture is with the image of "the body at
war" and asks us to think about the full implications of viewing our bodies in
this way.

Having studied the history and theory of rhetoric, of how we persuade and understand one another, for most of my adult life, I am particularly interested in the questions Martin asks: What difference does it make how we represent or image ourselves in
words? How does our manner of talking about things inevitably shape how we can
know (and not know) those things? I believe that examining the work of science with
these questions in mind will not detract from the importance of the scientific enterprise
but rather enrich and strengthen it. As you read "The Body at War," a chapter from
Martin's book Flexible Bodies: Tracking Immunity in American Culture —
From the Days of Polio to the Age of AIDS (1994), think about the power of
metaphor in your own life.   — A.L.

> But the thing that sticks to my mind more than anything else is, do you remember the movie The Fantastic Voyage? Where they shoved people down inside the body? Do you remember the scene when they had to go outside the ship to fix the cell, and the little antibodies were coming all around them and everything like that? I think that's where I get a lot of my ideas from, you know? That was probably the first real exposure I had to the human body and the immune system, because I was young, I was still in elementary school.
>
> —CHARLES KINGSLEY

When Mack Drury found out that his lover had tested positive for HIV, he told us, he faced the difficult task of getting himself tested. At the clinic he visited, Mack and the others in the waiting room watched a film about AIDS that illustrated graphically how HIV will destroy the cells in your immune system. He said that he fled from the clinc, disturbed because the images and language in the film were so upsetting, and afraid that his health would be affected by them.

Mack's conviction that his health would be harmed by the images in the film made me want to explore in some detail media coverage of the immune system. I include here audio, print, and other visual media that are usually available to a mass audience. . . .

Perhaps the notion of an immune "system" was first widely disseminated to the reading public through an article condensed in the *Reader's Digest* in 1957 (Brecher and Brecher 1957). Accompanying a small but steady rate of publications about the immune system in mass market magazines throughout the 1960s and 1970s, two major film productions featured the immune system.[1] *The Fantastic Voyage*, starring Raquel Welch, first appeared in 1966, and several people we interviewed mentioned that they remembered it vividly. (It is now available in local video stores.) Several main components of the immune system (antibodies, macrophages, lymph nodes) had a role to play in the film, which involved miniaturizing a submarine for travel through the arteries and veins of a Russian scientist who had defected from the Soviet Union. The scientist had been so severely injured that conventional surgery would have been no use. The goal of the crew was to remove a blood clot caused by his injury so the Russian could recover consciousness and divulge Soviet secrets to the Americans. The team of medical specialists and army personnel inside the submarine tried to travel through the Russian's body to reach the site of his injury, which they attempted to repair with a laser. Along the way, caught while wearing a diving suit outside the submarine, Raquel Welch was attacked by antibodies. These were depicted as flickering shapes that adhered tightly to her chest and nearly suffocated her, until, just in the nick of time, the male members of the team managed (more than slightly lasciviously) to

---

[1]According to *Magazine Index,* there were about thirty articles on some aspect of immunity or the immune system published per year from 1960 to 1980.

pull them off with their hands. In the end, the villain of the drama (a double agent) was horribly killed, suffocated by the billowing white mass of a macrophage as the ship passed through a lymph node.

In the early 1970s, a television program called "The Immortal" featured a hero who had a "supercharged immune system that made him impervious to the diseases and the gradual wearing down the flesh is heir to. Traumas like a bullet to the heart could kill the guy, but if he survived, his wounds would heal within hours" (Laliberte 1992:56; see also Terrace 1985–86:215).

Riding the crest of the huge wave of media interest in the immune sys-   5
tem that began in the early 1980s, science writers such as Peter Jaret published major articles on the immune system and embellished them with electron micrographs of immune system cells and their interactions. According to the readers' survey carried out by the National Geographic Society, Jaret's 1986 photographic essay garnered the most commendations of any article published that year and prompted a large number of requests of reprints.[2]

Jaret's essay in the *National Geographic* apparently inspired writers for several other mass media periodicals, which shortly thereafter featured cover stories on the immune system (see fig. 1): *Time* (Jaroff 1988), *U.S. News and World Report* (Brownlee 1990), and *Awake!* (November 1990).[3] The *Reader's*

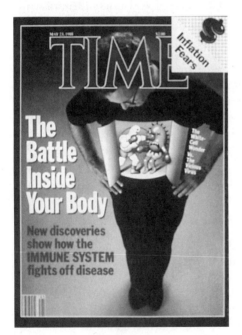

Fig. 1.   The body's immune system (the white-cell wonder) shown in a boxing match with the vicious virus.
(From *Time,* 23 May 1988. © 1988 Time Inc. Reprinted by permission.)

---

[2]Peter Jaret, interview, December 1992. The details were kindly provided by the National Geographic Society.

[3]This magazine is translated into sixteen languages.

Digest once again presented a major article on the immune system, this time a condensation of Jaret's article (Jaret 1987).

At the same time, the syndrome that we now call AIDS was beginning to be understood as an immune system dysfunction, enormously increasing both scientific and public interest in how the immune system works or fails to work. Beginning in the early 1980s, there was an explosion of interest in periodicals on the immune system, whether measured in absolute numbers or as a percentage of all articles in periodicals.[4] Apart from periodicals, other print media on the immune system mushroomed. Here I can give only the slightest indication of the quantity of this material by indicating its range. There are books that combine science education with practical guidelines for a healthy immune system (e.g., Dwyer 1988; Fox and Fox 1990; Pearsall 1987; Potts and Morra 1986). There are books that appeal to methods of strengthening the immune system that are intended to be different from those of biomedicine (e.g., Chopra 1989; DeSchepper 1989; Michaud and Feinstein 1989; Muramoto 1988; Serinus 1987). There is also a special genre of children's books on the immune system (e.g., Benziger 1989, 1990; Galland 1988; Gelman 1992).

As one would expect given the flourishing of books and magazines, there are many audiotapes devoted to the health of the immune system, subliminal and otherwise (e.g., Sutphen 1988; Mars 1992; Achterberg and Lawlis 1992). There are also high school and college science teaching films galore (*The Human Immune System: The Fighting Edge, Immune System Disorders, Lupus,* and *Internal Defenses* are examples from one catalog),[5] science films for grade school and middle school students (*The Immune System: Your Magic Doctor, The Immune System: Our Internal Defender*),[6] seminars for health professionals of all sorts,[7] and seminars for continuing adult education.[8]

The portrait of the body conveyed most often and most vividly in the mass media shows it as a defended nation-state, organized around a hierarchy of gender, race, and class.[9] In this picture, the boundary between the body

---

[4]According to a count produced by *Magazine Index,* by 1981–85 there were over 150 articles a year, by 1986–90 over 300 per year, and in 1992 alone over 450.

[5]Films for the Humanities and Sciences, *1992–93 Health Education Video Catalogue* (Princeton, N.J.).

[6]For descriptions, see Copeland (1992) and Rubin (1989).

[7]Mind Matters Seminars (Stanford, Calif.) ran three seminars on "The Immune System: Minding the Body, Embodying the Mind" in the Baltimore area in the fall of 1992.

[8]The Johns Hopkins School of Continuing Studies ran a course on psychoneuroimmunology in the fall of 1991 that was oversubscribed; the course was offered again the following year.

[9]Haraway (1989:14) terms this the "hierarchical, localized organic body." In her work, Haraway eloquently stresses the displacement of the hierarchical, localized body by new parameters: "a highly mobile field of strategic differences . . . a semiotic system, a complex meaning-producing field" (p. 15). No one could improve on her characterization of these new elements; I would add only that there may be strategic reasons why a remnant of the old body is carried forward with the new.

("self") and the external world ("nonself") is rigid and absolute: "At the heart of the immune system is the ability to distinguish between self and nonself. Virtually every body cell carries distinctive molecules that identify it as self" (Schindler 1988:1). These molecules are class 1 MHC proteins, present on every nucleated cell in an individual's body and different from every other individual's. One popular book calls these our "trademark" (Dwyer 1988:37). The maintenance of the purity of self within the borders of the body is seen as tantamount to the maintenance of the self: a chapter called "The Body under Siege," in the popular book on the immune system *In Self Defense,* begins with an epigraph, from Shakespeare: "To be or not to be, that is the question" (Mizel and Jaret 1985:1).[10]

The notion that the immune system maintains a clear boundary be-   10 tween self and nonself is often accompanied by a conception of the nonself world as foreign and hostile.[11] Our bodies are faced with masses of cells bent on our destruction: "To fend off the threatening horde, the body has devised astonishingly intricate defenses" (Schindler 1988:13). As a measure of the extent of this threat, popular publications depict the body as the scene of total war between ruthless invaders and determined defenders:[12] "Besieged by a vast array of invisible enemies, the human body enlists a remarkably complex corps of internal bodyguards to battle the invaders" (Jaret 1986:702). A site of injury is "transformed into a battle field on which the body's armed forces, hurling themselves repeatedly at the encroaching microorganisms, crush and annihilate them" (Nilsson 1985:20).

Small white blood cells called *granulocytes* are "kept permanently at the ready for a blitzkrieg against microorganisms" and constitute the "infantry" of the immune system. "Multitudes fall in battle, and together with their vanquished foes, they form the pus which collects in wounds." Larger macrophages are another type of white blood cell that is depicted as the "armored unit" of the defense system. "These roll forth through the tissues . . . devouring everything that has no useful role to play there." Another part of the immune system, the complement system, can "perforate hostile organisms so that their lives trickle to a halt." These function as "'magnetic mines.' They are sucked toward the bacterium and perforate it, causing it to explode" (Nilsson 1985:24, 25, 24, 72). When complement "comes together in the right sequence, it detonates like a bomb, blasting through the invader's cell membrane" (Jaret 1986:720). The *killer cells,* the technical scientific name of a type of T lymphocyte, are the "immune system's special combat units in the war against cancer." Killer cells "strike," "attack," and "assault" (Nilsson 1985:96, 98, 100). "The killer T cells

---

[10]This may relate to what Petchesky (1981:208) calls the ideology of "privatism."

[11]For lack of space, I cannot deal with the subtleties of how this "old body discourse" appears in interviews. Suffice it to say that military metaphors are extremely widespread.

[12]These include mass media magazines such as *Time* and *Newsweek* as well as the *National Geographic.* They also include more expensive items such as Lennert Nilsson's popular coffee table book *The Body Victorious* (1985).

are relentless. Docking with infected cells, they shoot lethal proteins at the cell membrane. Holes form where the protein molecules hit, and the cell, dying, leaks out its insides" (Jaroff 1988:59).

To understand the immune system, we are to think of it "as a disciplined and effective army that posts soldiers and scouts on permanent duty throughout your body" (Laliberte 1992:56). These warriors identify a threat, attack and destroy our enemies so quickly that we often do not know that we were threatened: the immune system "never takes prisoners." The story of the human immune system "reads like a war novel": our lymph nodes are major centers for the breeding of "attack dogs," called antibodies (Gates 1989:16). In sum, the body "has devised a series of defenses so intricate they make war games look like child's play" (National Institute of Allergy and Infectious Diseases 1985:5).

Although the metaphor of warfare against an external enemy dominates these accounts, another metaphor plays nearly as large a role: the body as police state.[13] Every body cell is equipped with "'proof of identity'—a special arrangement of protein molecules on the exterior . . . these constitute the cell's identity papers, protecting it against the body's own police force, the immune system. . . . The human body's police corps is programmed to distinguish between bona fide residents and illegal aliens—an ability fundamental to the body's power of self-defense" (Nilsson 1985:21). What identifies a resident is likened to speaking a national language: "An immune cell bumps into a bacterial cell and says, 'Hey, this guy isn't speaking our language, he's an intruder.' That's defense" (Levy, quoted in Jaret 1986:733). "T cells are able to 'remember for decades' the identity of foreign antigens: the intruders' descriptions are stored in the vast criminal records of the immune system. When a substance matching one of the stored descriptions makes a new appearance, the memory cells see to the swift manufacture of antibodies to combat it. The invasion is defeated before it can make us ill. We are *immune*" (Nilsson 1985:28).

What happens to these illegal aliens when they are detected? They are "executed" in a "death cell," the digestive cavity inside a feeding cell (Nilsson 1985:25, 31, 76, 81). "When the walls have closed around the enemy, the execution—phagocytosis—takes place. The prisoner is showered with hydrogen peroxide or other deadly toxins. Digestive enzymes are sent into the death chamber to dissolve the bacterium" (Nilsson 1985:81).

Not surprisingly, identities involving gender, race, and class are present in this war scene. Compare two categories of immune system cells, macrophages, which surround and digest foreign organisms, on the one hand, and T cells, which kill by transferring toxin to them, on the other. The

---

[13]At times the "police" become more like antiterrorist squads, as befits the task of finding enemies within who are bent on destruction. Paula Treichler points out that the AIDS virus is a "spy's spy, capable of any deception . . . a terrorist's terrorist, an Abu Nidal of viruses" (1987:282).

macrophages are a lower form of cell; they are called a "primeval tank corps" (Michaud and Feinstein 1989:4), "a nightmare lurching to life" (Page 1981:115). T cells are more advanced, evolutionary, and have higher functions, such as memory (Jaroff 1988:60). It is only these advanced cells who "attend the technical colleges of the immune system" (Nilsson 1985:26).

There is clearly a hierarchical division of labor here, one that is to some extent overlaid with gender categories familiar in European and American culture. Specifically, one might wonder about the female associations with the engulfing and surrounding that macrophages do and the male associations with the penetrating or injecting that killer T cells do. In addition, many scholars have pointed out the frequent association of the female, symbolically, with lower functions, especially with the lack or lesser degree of mental functions.

Beyond this, macrophages are the cells that are the "housekeepers" (Jaret 1986) of the body, cleaning up the dirt and debris, including "dead bodies," both themselves and foreign cells. (One immunologist called them "little drudges.")[14] "The first defenders to arrive would be the phagocytes [a category of 'eating' cells that includes macrophages]—the scavengers of the system. Phagocytes constantly scour the territories of our bodies, alert to anything that seems out of place. What they find, they engulf and consume. Phagocytes are not choosy. They will eat anything suspicious that they find in the bloodstream, tissues, or lymphatic system" (Jaret 1986:715). Given their uncultivated origins, it should not be surprising that, after eating, a macrophage "burps": "After it finishes its meal, it burps out pieces of the enemy and puts them out on its surface" (Michaud and Feinstein 1989:6). As macrophages feed, they may be described as "angry," in a "feeding fury," or "insatiable" (Page 1981:104), combining in one image uncontrolled emotions and an obliterating, engulfing presence, both common cultural ascriptions of females.

Gender might not be the only overlay on the division of labor in our cells. Racial overtones may be there as well, although I have less convincing evidence for them. Macrophages are the cells that actually eat other cells belonging to the category *self* and so engage in "a kind of small-scale cannibalism" (Nilsson 1985:25). Cannibalism is often associated with the attribution of a lower, animal nature to those who engage in it (Arens 1979). In media coverage of the immune system, macrophages are seen as feminized in some ways but as simply "uncivilized" in others. These "cannibals" are indiscriminate eaters, barbaric and savage in their willingness to eat any manner of thing at all. Sometimes macrophages are feminized "housekeepers," and sometimes they seem to be marked by race, class, or a combination of the two, as when they are described as "big, primitive garbage collectors" (Jaret 1986:733),

---

[14]Overheard by Paula Treichler, personal communication.

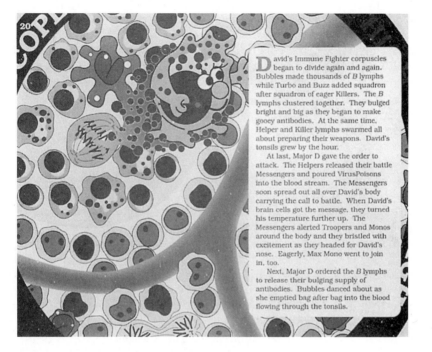

Within the figure:

D avid's Immune Fighter corpuscles began to divide again and again. Bubbles made thousands of B lymphs while Turbo and Buzz added squadron after squadron of eager Killers. The B lymphs clustered together. They bulged bright and big as they began to make gooey antibodies. At the same time, Helper and Killer lymphs swarmed all about preparing their weapons. David's tonsils grew by the hour.

At last, Major D gave the order to attack. The Helpers released their battle Messengers and poured VirusPoisons into the blood stream. The Messengers soon spread out all over David's body carrying the call to battle. When David's brain cells got the message, they turned his temperature further up. The Messengers alerted Troopers and Monos around the body and they bristled with excitement as they headed for David's nose. Eagerly, Max Mono went to join in, too.

Next, Major D ordered the B lymphs to release their bulging supply of antibodies. Bubbles danced about as she emptied bag after bag into the blood flowing through the tonsils.

Fig. 2.   A depiction of a B cell as "Bubbles," who is dancing about as she empties antibodies into the blood.
(From J. Benziger, *The Corpuscles: Adventures in Innerspace* [1989:20]/Corpuscles Inter-Galactica, 40 Johnson Heights, Waterville, ME 04901. Copyright © 1989 by John Benziger. Reprinted by permission of the author.)

"roving garbage collectors" (Brownlee 1990:50), a "'cleanup' crew" (Pearsall 1987:41), or "roving scavengers" (Jaroff 1988:58).

To explore further the popular media imagery of the hierarchy of cells, we need to look at another immune system cell, the B cell. B cells are clearly ranked far above the lowly macrophage. They are not educated in the college of the thymus, but they are "educated" in the bone marrow (Dwyer 1988:47), and they have enormous specificity. They rank below the T cell, however, which is consistently termed the *orchestrator* of the immune response and which activates B cells. In one popular book, this is called giving the B cell "permission" (Dwyer 1988:47) to attack invading organisms. B cells exist in two stages, immature and mature B cells. Mature B cells are the cells that, having been stimulated by antigens of the right specificity, and with T cell "permission," rapidly produce antibodies against invading antigens. In a children's book about the immune system, all the immune system cells are given names and identities. The B cell, called "Bubbles" (see fig. 2), bulged "big and bright" as she began to make antibodies. When "Major D," a type of T cell, gives the order, "Bubbles danced about as she emptied bag after bag into the blood" (Benziger 1990:20).

This suggests that B cells are sometimes feminized but rank much higher in the hierarchy than the lowly macrophage.[15] This means that in the B cell we may have a kind of upper-class female, a suitable partner for the top-ranked T cell. These two types of cells together have been termed "the mind of the immune system" (Galland 1988:10). In illustrations of these cells in *Peak Immunity* (see fig. 3), each of them is depicted with a drawing of a human brain (De-Schepper 1989:16). Far below them in terms of class and race we would find the macrophage, angry and engulfing, or scavenging and cleaning up.

In this system, gendered distinctions are not limited to male and female; they also encompass the distinction between heterosexual and homosexual. T cells convey aspects of male potency, cast as heterosexual potency. They are the virile heroes of the immune system, highly trained commandos who are selected for and then educated in the technical college of the thymus gland. T cells are referred to as the "commander in chief of the immune system" (Jaret 1986:708) or the "battle manager" (Jaroff 1988:58). Some T cells, killer cells, are masculine in the old-fashioned mold of a brawny, brutal he-man: in a mail advertisement from *Prevention* magazine for a book (i.e., Michaud and Feinstein 1989) on the immune system, we are told, "You owe your life to this little guy, the Rambo of your body's immune system." A comic book produced for AIDS education depicts T cells as a squad of Mister Ts (see fig. 4), the muscular hero from the television show "The A Team."

Other T cells, T 4 cells, have a masculinity composed of intellect, strategic planning ability, and a propensity for corporate team participation, powers well suited for the world of global corporations.[16] The T 4 cell is often called *the quarterback of the immune system* because he orchestrates everything else and because he is the brains and memory of the team. As one source puts it, "Besides killer T cells . . . there are also helper [T 4] and suppressor T cells. *Somebody* has to make strategic decisions." This popular manual on the immune system, called *Fighting Disease*, clinches the heterosexuality of the T cell: "In order to slip inside a cell, a virus has to remove its protein coat, which it leaves outside on the cell membrane. The viral coat hanging outside signals the passing T cell that viral hanky panky is going on inside. Like the jealous husband who spots a strange jacket in the hall closet and *knows* what's going on in the upstairs bedroom, the T cell takes swift action. It bumps against the body cell with the virus inside and perforates it" (Michaud and Feinstein 1989:10, 8).

However they are marked by gender, sexuality, race, or class, all these cells of the immune system belong to "self" and have the primary function of defending the self against the nonself. When the nonself is a disease-causing

---

[15]B cells are not always feminized: Michaud and Feinstein (1989:13, 7, respectively) depict them as admirals and supermen.

[16]For a lengthy discussion of why teamwork and group cooperation are required in the economic world, see Kash (1989).

Virus attacks!

The body's phagocyte (the "Pac Man" of the immune system) attacks the viruses.

"Pac Man" displaying the antigen.

The "Pac Man" displaying the antigen alerts the T-Helper cell. (Commander-in-chief of our immune system)

Once activated, the T-Helper cells begin to multiply.

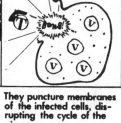
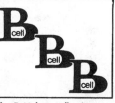

Like a battlefield general, the T-Helper cells send for the front soldiers called T-Killer cells!

They puncture membranes of the infected cells, disrupting the cycle of the viruses.

The T-Helper cells then call in the second platoon called B-Cells!

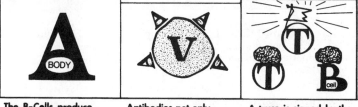

The B-Cells produce chemical weapons called antibodies.

Antibodies not only neutralize, but kill.

A truce is signed by the T-Suppressor. T and B-Memory cells are left in our body.

Fig. 3.   Star wars of the immune system, showing T cells and B cells with brains and memory.
(From L. DeSchepper, *Peak Immunity* [1989:15–16]. Reprinted by permission of the author and Beacon Press.)

Fig. 4.   A squad of Mister T cells attempts to do in HIV but is defeated.
(From D. Cherry, "AIDS Virus," in *Risky Business* [1988:5]. Reprinted by permission of the
publisher. Reprinted by permission of the San Francisco AIDS Foundation.)

microbe, the model works quite logically. But when the nonself is a fetus
growing inside a woman's body, the model quickly runs into difficulty. As
the popular media explain it, since the fetus is a graft of foreign tissue inside
the mother, why does she not "mount an attack against the fetus as she would
against any other allograft [a graft from a genetically different member of the
same species]?" (Kimball 1986:433). The lack of an attack is even more mysterious given that pregnant women have antibodies to certain antigens expressed by the fetus. The reduction in the woman's normal immune response,

which would be to destroy the fetal "nonself," whatever the mechanism, is called *tolerance*. From an immunological point of view, the fetus is a "tumor" that the woman's body should try furiously to attack (Dwyer 1988:60). But the mother's immune system "tolerates" her fetus; all our immune systems "tolerate" our own tissues, unless we suffer from autoimmune disease.

Immunologists have yet fully to answer the question of how the body achieves tolerance; in the meantime, it is interesting to wonder whether other images of the body less reliant on hard boundaries and strict distinctions might produce another set of questions altogether. Work in feminist theory suggests that there is a masculinist bias to views that divide the world into sharply opposed, hostile categories, such that the options are to conquer, be conquered, or magnanimously tolerate the other. The stance is one from which nature can be dominated and a separation from the world maintained (Keller 1985:124).[17] Many mothers and fathers might find the notion of a baby in utero as a tumor that the mother's body tries its best to destroy so counterintuitive as to warrant searching for a different set of organizing images altogether.[18]

Another set of images coexists in the popular media with these scenes of 25 battle and is also imbued with hierarchies involving gender and class. This other set of images coexists uneasily with the first, is subdued by taking up far less space in printed descriptions, and is able to generate far fewer visual images to express itself. It depicts the body as a "regulatory-communications network" (Schindler 1988:1). As Haraway's work emphasizes, the body is seen as "an engineered communications system, ordered by a fluid and dispersed command-control-intelligence network" (1989:14). Hierarchy is replaced by dispersed control; rigidly prescribed roles are replaced by rapid change and flexible adaptation. The emphasis shifts from the various roles played by the parts of the immune system to "the most remarkable feature of the immune system . . . the system itself—the functioning of diverse elements as an efficient, effective whole" (National Jewish Center for Immunology and Respiratory Medicine 1989:2). As an example, consider a pamphlet on the immune system that is available from the National Cancer Institute.[19] In the midst of elaborate military metaphors—"defense against foreign invaders," "stockpiling a tremendous arsenal," "intricate defenses to fend off the threatening horde"—a very different set of images appears: The immune system is described as "an incredibly elaborate and dynamic regulatory-communications network. Millions and millions of cells, organized into sets and subsets, pass

---

[17]Keller (1992:116–17) illustrates how easily the language of evolutionary biology slips from descriptions of nature as neutrally indifferent to descriptions of nature as callous and hostile.

[18]Elsewhere, I am developing an account of fetus-mother interaction in an immunological environment in which blurry self-nonself discrimination is assumed. After all, babies are born, tissue can be grafted, and many bacteria live (to the benefit of our health) in our gut.

[19]This pamphlet can be obtained by calling 1-800-4CANCER or through Info-quest (CD-ROM) in many public libraries.

information back and forth like clouds of bees swarming around a hive. The result is a sensitive system of checks and balances that produces an immune response that is prompt, appropriate, effective, and self-limiting" (Schindler 1988:1). This is an image of a complex system held together by communication and feedback, not divided by category and hierarchy. Often, in this mode, accounts stress how rapidly the system can be poised to change in response to its environment. Description of that process can easily slip back into the military analogy: "By storing just a few cells specific for each potential invader, it [the immune system] has room for the entire array. When an antigen appears, these few specifically matched cells are stimulated to multiply into a full-scale army. Later, to prevent this army from overexpanding wildly, like a cancer, powerful suppresser mechanisms come into play" (National Institute of Allergy and Infectious Diseases 1985:3). One way in which a few accounts diminish the tension between these two images is specifically to stress the changed character of contemporary warfare: the great variety of different "weapons" is a product of evolutionary adaptation to changing defense needs: "Just as modern arsenals are ever changing as the weaponry of a potential enemy becomes more sophisticated, so our immune system has adapted itself many times to counter survival moves made by the microbial world to protect itself" (Dwyer 1988:28).

In sum, for the most part, the media coverage of the immune system operates largely in terms of the image of the body at war. Even when the problem is not an external enemy like a microbe but an internal part of "self," the military imagery is extended to notions of "mutiny," "self-destruction," and so on.[20] In one television show, autoimmunity was described as "we have met the enemy and the enemy is us."[21] A book on AIDS written by a physiologist for a general audience repeatedly refers to autoimmunity as "the immunological equivalent of civil war" (Root-Bernstein 1993:87).[22]

Powerful as the impact of media images may be, we would be terribly misled if we took their content as the only sign of what is being understood in the wider culture. Many studies assume that the content of mass media products gives transparent evidence of "cultural ideas." Some further assert that the mass media do not allow any meaningful response from the pub-

---

[20]A Toronto newspaper reported that "Vancouver psychologist Andrew Feldmar offers an intriguing explanation for the adult onset of autoimmune disease: 'It strikes people who in their childhood were inhibited from differentiating who is their enemy, who is their friend'" (Maté 1993:16).

[21]Reported to me by Ariane van der Straten.

[22]David Napier explores the implications of using a metaphor of self-destruction to describe illness. He suggests that, despite the disorientation that might be produced, telling someone who is suffering that her body is at war with itself can be a helpful thing to do: "People often do feel better when they can salvage a 'self' from a ravaged body; we learn to deal with illness by setting it up as something against which we can define (even through dissociation) a better condition of selfhood" (1992:187).

lic: they are "opposed to mediation"; they "fabricate noncommunication" (Baudrillard 1985).[23] Ethnographic exploration will quickly show us that the reality is far more complex. In the end, we will see that media images, rich as they seem, are impoverished in comparison to the living collage of ideas produced by people—scientists and nonscientists.

REFERENCES

Achterberg, J., and G. F. Lawlis. 1992. Imagery in healing workshop. Boulder, Colo.: Sounds True. Audiotape.

Arens, W. 1979. *The man-eating myth: Anthropology and anthropophagy*. Oxford: Oxford University Press.

Baudrillard, J. 1985. The masses: The implosion of the social in the media. *New Literary History* 16, no. 3 (March): 577–89.

Benziger, J. 1989. *The corpuscles: Adventures in innerspace*. Waterville, Maine: Corpuscles InterGalactica.

———. 1990. *The corpuscles meet the virus invaders*. Waterville, Maine: Corpuscles InterGalactica.

Brecher, R., and E. Brecher. 1954. Are we expecting too much too soon from the new polio vaccine? *Parents' Magazine,* July, 31–33, 72–74.

Brownlee, S. 1990. The body at war: Baring the secrets of the immune system. *U.S. News and World Report,* 2 July, 48–54.

Cherry, D. 1988. AIDS virus. In *Risky business,* ed. S. A. Winterhalter. San Francisco: San Francisco AIDS Foundation.

Chopra, D. 1989. *Quantum healing: Exploring the frontiers of mind/body medicine*. New York: Bantam.

Connor, S. 1989. *Postmodernist culture: An introduction to theories of the contemporary*. Oxford: Blackwell.

Copeland, B. 1992. Review of *The immune system: Our internal defender*. *Book Report* 11:64.

DeSchepper, L. 1989. *Peak immunity: How to fight Epstein-Barr virus, candida, herpes simplex and other immuno-depressive disorders and win*. Santa Monica, Calif.: Luc DeSchepper.

---

[23]For a detailed discussion of Baudrillard's views of the media, see Connor (1989). I have found Mah (1991) useful in considering the pitfalls of thinking that any text can be treated as a transparent window into culture. Recent ethnographic media studies have allowed the "reading" of media messages to take into account what people in the culture say (e.g., Morley 1992). For some of the rich variety of current studies of culture through the media, see Gitlin (1987), Fiske (1987), and Robbins (1993).

Dwyer, J. M. 1988. *The body at war: The miracle of the immune system.* New York: New American Library.

Fiske, J. 1987. *Television culture.* London: Routledge.

Fox, A., and B. Fox. 1990. *Immune for life: Live longer and better by strengthening your doctor within.* Rocklin, Calif.: Pruna.

Galland, L. 1988. *Superimmunity for kids.* New York: Dell.

Gates, J. 1989. Aging and the immune system. *Vibrant Life* 5 (September): 16–20.

Gelman, R. G. 1992. *Body battles.* New York: Scholastic.

Gitlin, T., ed. 1987. *Watching television.* New York: Pantheon.

Haraway, D. 1989. *Primate visions: Gender, race, and nature in the world of modern science.* New York: Routledge.

Jaret, P. 1986. Our immune system: The wars within. *National Geographic.* June, 702–35.

Jaroff, L. 1988. Stop that germ! *Time,* 23 May, 56–64.

Kash, D. E. 1989. *Perpetual innovation: The new world of competition.* New York: Basic.

Keller, E. F. 1985. *Reflections on gender and science.* New Haven, Conn.: Yale University Press.

Kimball, J. W. 1986. *Introduction to immunology.* New York: Macmillan.

Laliberte, R. 1992. The best defense. *Men's Health,* September, 56–60.

Mah, H. 1991. Suppressing the text: The metaphysics of ethnographic history in Darnton's great cat massacre. *History Workshop Journal* 31:1–20.

Mars, B. 1992. Natural remedies for a healthy immune system. Boulder, Colo: Sounds True. Audiotape.

Maté, G. 1993. Why does the body sometimes declare war on itself? *Toronto Globe and Mail.* 14 June, 16.

Michaud, E., and A. Feinstein. 1989. *Fighting disease: The complete guide to natural immune power.* Emmaus, Pa.: Rodale.

Mizel, S. B., and P. Jaret. 1985. *In self defense.* San Diego, Calif.: Harcourt Brace Jovanovich.

Morley, D. 1992. *Television audiences and cultural studies.* London: Routledge.

Muramoto, N. B. 1988. *Natural immunity: Insights on diet and AIDS.* Oroville, Calif.: George Ohsawa Macrobiotic Foundation.

Napier, A. D. 1992. *Foreign bodies: Performance, art, and symbolic anthropology.* Berkeley and Los Angeles: University of California Press.

National Institute of Allergy and Infectious Diseases. 1985. *Understanding the immune system.* Washington, D.C.

National Jewish Center for Immunology and Respiratory Medicine. 1989. *Immunology.* Washington, D.C.

Nilsson, L. 1985. *The body victorious.* New York: Delacorte.

Page, J. 1981. *Blood: The river of life.* Washington, D.C.: U.S. News Books.

Pearsall, P. 1987. *Super immunity: Master your emotions and improve your health.* New York: Fawcett.

Petchesky, R. P. 1981. Antiabortion, antifeminism and the rise of the new Right. *Feminist Studies* 7, no. 2:206–46.

Potts, E., and M. Morra. 1986. *Understanding your immune system.* New York: Avon.

Robbins, B., ed. 1993. *The phantom public sphere.* Minneapolis: University of Minnesota Press.

Root-Bernstein, R. S. 1993. *Rethinking AIDS: The tragic cost of premature consensus.* New York: Free Press.

Rubin, E. 1989. Review of *The immune system: Your magic doctor. School Library Journal* 35:58.

Schindler, L. W. 1988. *Understanding the immune system.* Washington, D.C.: U.S. Department of Health and Human Services.

Serinus, J., ed. 1987. *Psychoimmunity and the healing process.* Berkeley, Calif.: Celestial Arts.

Sutphen, D. 1988. Strengthening your immune system: Subliminal programming with music. Malibu, Calif.: Valley of the Sun. Audiotape.

Terrace, V. 1985–86. *Encyclopedia of television series, pilots and specials.* 3 vols. New York: Zoetrope.

Treichler, P. A. 1987. AIDS, homophobia and biomedical discourse: An epidemic of signification. *Cultural Studies* 1, no. 3 (October): 263–305.

QUESTIONING THE TEXT

1. In "The Body at War," Martin presents a very large number of sources in support of her thesis. Look back through this selection to identify the major areas these sources come from. How do these examples support her argument? How credible are they to you?

2. In addition to the image of the immune system as a battleground, Martin sketches in another set of images that depict the body as a "regulatory-communications network." In your experience, which set of images is most prevalent? List as many examples as you can think of that add to either category. What other images can you think of that are associated with the body or the body's immune system?

3. What is A.L.'s view of language? How does she reveal this view in her introduction to this piece?

4. Look closely at the illustrations in Martin's essay. Why do you think she chose each one? What does each figure contribute to the argument she

is making? Look especially closely at any references she makes to these illustrations in the text of her essay. Does what she says about them match your own "reading" of them? Why, or why not?

MAKING CONNECTIONS

5. In "Enemies of Promise" (p. 237), J. Michael Bishop offers a definition (one that seems particularly limited, even a caricature) of "postmodernist" views of science. How might Martin respond to Bishop's definition and discussion of postmodern views? In what ways might her analysis support Bishop's claims for science?

6. Martin's essay explores how images related to war and militarism affect our understanding of the body and its immune system. Look in Jeremy Rifkin's essay, "Biotech Century" (p. 244), for metaphors, images, and so on that relate to or suggest war or battle. How do they affect your understanding of Rifkin's argument?

JOINING THE CONVERSATION

7. Imagine that you, the monster from Mary Shelley's *Frankenstein* (p. 231), and Martin are all on a talk show. The host asks each of you to define *science*. Write your own definition of the term, and then try to define *science* from the perspective of the other guests on the show. Compare your definitions with those of your classmates. What areas of agreement and disagreement do you find?

8. Choose a subject you are particularly interested in, and conduct an investigation of the ways that topic is represented in images and words. You might, for example, look at the ways mothers are represented in popular advertisements, songs, cartoons, or stories, or at how teenagers are depicted in several major newspapers and on television shows. Gather as many examples of the images as you can, and then examine them for their metaphoric power. What do they suggest about the topic you are investigating? What values do they attach to it? This investigation could easily lead to a full-scale research report. If you undertake one, try tracking your topic on the Internet.

9. With one or two classmates, try to corroborate or challenge Martin's findings. Look through contemporary magazines and newspapers, especially those that deal with scientific subjects, and review relevant television programs, movies, or songs. Bring your evidence to class for discussion.

JAMES Q. WILSON
Cars and Their Enemies

MENTION THE WORD technology *and most people today think of silicon chips,
DVD systems, high-definition TVs, and cellular phones—not the vehicles they drive.
Yet even the highest-tech computers haven't had the impact on our lives (at least, not
yet) of gasoline-powered motor vehicles, a form of technology now a century old. From
sea to sea, the American landscape has been bulldozed and paved to serve our national
desire to move at will from one place to another. Fast cars and burly trucks have shaped
our national character, changing how we live, where we live, how we court, and maybe
even how we think.*

    *Yet the car represents a technological direction by no means inevitable. James Q.
Wilson opens "Cars and Their Enemies" by suggesting how deep and determined opposition to this technology would be if it had been invented today rather than at the end
of the nineteenth century. But Wilson rejects any notion of the car as a Frankenstein
monster, describing it instead as a rational choice, one that makes the lives of most
people freer and more pleasurable. In defending this claim, he challenges the growing
number of academic and social critics made uneasy by the prospect of more and more
Americans driving alone to work in 5,000-pound Suburbans and even bigger Excur-
sions, wasting fuel, clogging streets, and avoiding public transportation.*

    *Wilson (b. 1931), Collins Professor of Management and Public Policy at UCLA,
is one of America's most respected social critics and conservative thinkers, writing widely
on crime, ethics, and character. Among his recent books are* The Moral Sense *(1993)
and* Moral Judgment *(1997). "Cars and Their Enemies" originally appeared in the
July 1997 volume of* Commentary, *a journal of neoconservative opinion.*   —J.R.

Imagine the country we now inhabit—big, urban, prosperous—with
one exception: the automobile has not been invented. We have trains and bi-
cycles, and some kind of self-powered buses and trucks, but no private cars
driven by their owners for business or pleasure. Of late, let us suppose, someone has come forward with the idea of creating the personal automobile.
Consider how we would react to such news.

    Libertarians might support the idea, but hardly anyone else. Engineers
would point out that such cars, if produced in any significant number, would
zip along roads just a few feet—perhaps even a few inches—from one another; the chance of accidents would not simply be high, it would be certain.
Public-health specialists would estimate that many of these accidents would
lead to serious injuries and deaths. No one could say in advance how common they would be, but the best experts might guess that the number of

people killed by cars would easily exceed the number killed by murderers. Psychologists would point out that if any young person were allowed to operate a car, the death rate would be even higher, as youngsters—those between the ages of sixteen and twenty-four—are much more likely than older persons to be impulsive risk-takers who find pleasure in reckless bravado. Educators would explain that, though they might try by training to reduce this youthful death rate, they could not be optimistic they would succeed.

Environmentalists would react in horror to the idea of automobiles powered by the internal combustion engine, apparently the most inexpensive method. Such devices, because they burn fuel incompletely, would eject large amounts of unpleasant gases into the air, such as carbon monoxide, nitrogen oxide, and sulfur dioxide. Other organic compounds, as well as clouds of particles, would also enter the atmosphere to produce unknown but probably harmful effects. Joining in this objection would be people who would not want their view spoiled by the creation of a network of roads.

Big-city mayors would add their own objections, though these would reflect their self-interest as much as their wisdom. If people could drive anywhere from anywhere, they would be able to live wherever they wished. This would produce a vast exodus from the large cities, led in all likelihood by the most prosperous—and thus the most tax-productive—citizens. Behind would remain people who, being poorer, were less mobile. Money would depart but problems remain.

Governors, pressed to keep taxes down and still fund costly health, welfare, educational, and criminal-justice programs, would wonder who would pay for the vast networks of roads that would be needed to carry automobiles. Their skepticism would be reinforced by the worries of police officials fearful of motorized thieves evading apprehension, and by the opposition of railroad executives foreseeing the collapse of their passenger business as people abandoned trains for cars.

Energy experts would react in horror at the prospect of supplying the gasoline stations and the vast quantities of petroleum necessary to fuel automobiles which, unlike buses and trucks, would be stored at home and not at a central depot and would burn much more fuel per person carried than some of their mass-transit alternatives.

In short, the automobile, the device on which most Americans rely for not only transportation but mobility, privacy, and fun would not exist if it had to be created today. Of course, the car does exist, and has powerfully affected the living, working, and social spaces of America. But the argument against it persists. That argument dominates the thinking of academic experts on urban transportation and much of city planning. It can be found in countless books complaining of dreary suburban architecture, endless trips to and from work, the social isolation produced by solo auto trips, and the harmful effects of the car on air quality, noise levels, petroleum consumption, and road congestion.

In her recent book, *Asphalt Nation: How the Automobile Took Over America and How We Can Take It Back,* Jane Holtz Kay, the architecture critic for the *Nation,* assails the car unmercifully. It has, she writes "strangled" our lives and landscape, imposing on us "the costs of sprawl, of pollution, of congestion, of commuting." For this damage to be undone, the massively subsidized automobile will have to be sharply curtailed, by investing heavily in public transportation and imposing European-like taxes on gasoline. (According to Kay, if we cut highway spending by a mere $10 million, we could buy bicycles for all 93,000 residents of Eugene, Oregon, over the age of eleven.) What is more, people ought to live in cities with high population densities, since "for mass transit," as Kay notes, "you need mass." Housing should be built within a short walk of the corner store, and industries moved back downtown.

In Kay's book, hostility to the car is linked inextricably to hostility to the low-density suburb. Her view is by no means one that is confined to the political Left. Thus, Karl Zinsmeister, a conservative, has argued in the *American Enterprise* that we have become "slaves to our cars" and that, by using them to live in suburbs, we have created "inhospitable places for individualism and community life." Suburbs, says Zinsmeister, encourage "rootlessness," and are the enemy of the "traditional neighborhood" with its "easy daily interactions."

The same theme has been taken up by Mark Gauvreau Judge in the 10 *Weekly Standard.* Emerging from his home after a heavy snowfall, Judge, realizing that the nearest tavern was four miles away, concluded that he had to leave the suburbs. He repeats Zinsmeister's global complaint. Suburbanization, he writes, has fed, and sometimes caused,

> hurried life, the disappearance of family time, the weakening of generational links, our ignorance of history, our lack of local ties, an exaggerated focus on money, the anonymity of community life, the rise of radical feminism, the decline of civic action, the tyrannical dominance of TV and pop culture over leisure time.

Wow.

These people must live in or near very odd suburbs. The one in which I lived while my children were growing up, and the different ones in which my married daughter and married son now live, are not inhospitable, rootless, isolated, untraditional, or lacking in daily interactions. The towns are small. Life is organized around the family, for which there is a lot of time. Money goes farther for us than for Manhattanites struggling to get their children into the nursery school with the best link to Harvard. Television is less important than in big cities, where the streets are far less safe and TV becomes a major indoor activity. In most cases you can walk to a store. You know your neighbors. There is a Memorial Day parade. People care passionately and argue intensely about school policies and land-use controls. Of course, these are only my personal experiences—but unlike the critics, I find it hard to convert personal beliefs into cosmic generalizations.

Now I live in a suburb more remote from a big city than the one where my children were raised. Because population density is much lower, my wife and I walk less and drive more. But as I write this, my wife is at a neighborhood meeting where she will be joined by a travel agent, a retired firefighter, a hospital manager, and two housewives who are trying to decide how best to get the city to fix up a road intersection, prevent a nearby land development, and induce our neighbors to prepare for the fire season. On the way back, she will stop at the neighborhood mail station where she may talk to other friends, and then go on to the market where she will deal with people she has known for many years. She will do so by car.

And so back to our theme. Despite the criticisms of Kay and others, the use of the automobile has grown. In 1960, one-fifth of all households owned no car and only one-fifth owned two; by 1990, only one-tenth owned no car and over one-third owned two. In 1969, 80 percent of all urban trips involved a car and only one-twentieth involved public transport; by 1990, car use had risen to 84 percent and public transit had fallen to less than 3 percent. In 1990, three-fourths or more of the trips to and from work in nineteen out of our twenty largest metropolitan areas were by a single person in an automobile. The exception was the New York metropolitan region, but even there—with an elaborate mass-transit system and a residential concentration high enough to make it possible for some people to walk to work—solo car use made up over half of all trips to work.

Some critics explain this American fascination with the car as the unhappy consequence of public policies that make auto use more attractive than the alternatives. To Jane Holtz Kay, if only we taxed gasoline at a high enough rate to repay society for the social costs of automobiles, if only we had an elaborate mass-transit system that linked our cities, if only we placed major restraints on building suburbs on open land, if only we placed heavy restrictions on downtown parking, then things would be better.

Would they? Charles Lave, an economist at the University of California   15
at Irvine, has pointed out that most of Western Europe has long had just these sorts of anti-auto policies in effect. The result? Between 1965 and 1987, the growth in the number of autos per capita has been three times faster in Western Europe than in the United States. Part of the reason for the discrepancy is that the American auto market is approaching saturation: we now have roughly one car in existence for every person of driving age. But if this fact helps explain why the car market here is not growing rapidly, it does not explain the growth in Europe, which is the real story. Despite policies that penalize car use, make travel very expensive, and restrict parking spaces, Europeans, once they can afford to do so, buy cars, and drive them; according to

Lave, the average European car is driven about two-thirds as many miles per year as the average American car. One result is obvious: the heavily subsidized trains in Europe are losing business to cars, and governments there must pay an even larger share of the running cost to keep the trains moving.

In fact, the United States *has* tried to copy the European investment in mass transit. Relentlessly, transportation planners have struggled to find ways of getting people out of their cars and into buses, trains, and subways (and car pools). Relentlessly, and unsuccessfully. Despite spending about $100 billion, Washington has yet to figure out how to do it.

New subway systems have been built, such as the BART system in San Francisco and the Metro system in Washington, D.C. But BART, in the words of the transportation economist Charles L. Wright, "connects almost nothing to little else." The Metro is still growing, and provides a fine (albeit expensive) route for people moving about the city; but only 7 percent of all residential land area in Washington is within a mile of a Metro station, which means that people must either walk a long way to get to a stop or continue to travel by car. Between 1980 and 1990, while the Washington Metrorail system grew from 30 to 73 miles of line and opened an additional 30 stations, the number of people driving to work increased from 980,000 to 1,394,000, and the transit share of all commutes declined.

The European experience should explain why this is so: if people can afford it, they will want to purchase convenience, flexibility, and privacy. These facts are as close to a Law of Nature as one can get in the transportation business. When the industrial world became prosperous, people bought cars. It is unstoppable.

Suppose, however, that the anti-car writers were to win over the vastly more numerous pro-car drivers. Let us imagine what life would be like in a carless nation. People would have to live very close together so they could walk or, for healthy people living in sunny climes, bicycle to mass-transit stops. Living in close quarters would mean life as it is now lived in Manhattan. There would be few freestanding homes, many row houses, and lots of apartment buildings. There would be few private gardens except for flowerpots on balconies. The streets would be congested by pedestrians, trucks, and buses, as they were at the turn of the century before automobiles became common.

Moving about outside the larger cities would be difficult. People would   20 be able to take trains to distant sites, but when they arrived at some attractive locale it would turn out to be another city. They could visit the beach, but only (of necessity) crowded parts of it. They could go to a national park, but only the built-up section of it. They could see the countryside, but (mostly) through a train window. More isolated or remote locations would be accessible, but since public transit would provide the only way of getting there, the departures would be infrequent and the transfers frequent.

In other words, you could see the United States much as most Europeans saw their countryside before the automobile became an important means of locomotion. A train from London or Paris would take you to "the country" by way of a long journey through ugly industrial areas to those rural parts where either you had a home (and the means to ferry yourself to it) or there was a resort (that would be crowded enough to support a nearby train stop).

All this is a way of saying that the debate between car defenders and car haters is a debate between private benefits and public goods. List the characteristics of travel that impose few costs on society and, in general, walking, cycling, and some forms of public transit will be seen to be superior. Non-car methods generate less pollution, use energy a bit more efficiently, produce less noise, and (with some exceptions) are safer. But list the characteristics of travel that are desired by individuals, and (with some exceptions) the car is clearly superior. The automobile is more flexible, more punctual, supplies greater comfort, provides for carrying more parcels, creates more privacy, enables one to select fellow passengers, and, for distances over a mile or more, requires less travel time.

As a practical matter, of course, the debate between those who value private benefits and those who insist on their social costs is no real debate at all, since people select modes of travel based on individual, not social, preferences. That is why in almost every country in the world, the automobile has triumphed, and much of public policy has been devoted to the somewhat inconsistent task of subsidizing individual choices while attempting to reduce the costs attached to them. In the case of the automobile, governments have attempted to reduce exhaust pollution, make roadways safer, and restrict use (by tolls, speed bumps, pedestrian-only streets, and parking restrictions) in neighborhoods that attach a high value to pedestrian passage. Yet none of these efforts can alter the central fact that people have found cars to be the best means for getting about.

Take traffic congestion. Television loves to focus on grim scenes of gridlocked highways and angry motorists, but in fact people still get to work faster by car than by public transit. And the reason is not that car drivers live close to work and transit users travel a greater distance. According to the best estimates, cars outperform public transit in getting people quickly from their front doors to their work places. This fact is sometimes lost on car critics. Kay, for example, writes that "the same number of people who spend an hour driving sixteen lanes of highway can travel on a two-track train line." Wrong. Train travel is efficient *over a fixed, permanent route,* but people have to find some way to get to where the train starts and get to their final destination after the train stops. The *full* cost of moving people from home to work and back to the home is lower for cars than for trains. Moreover, cars are not subject to union strikes. The Long Island railroad or the bus system may shut down when workers walk off the job; cars do not.

The transportation argument rarely seems to take cognizance of the su- 25
periority of cars with respect to individual wants. Whenever there is a discussion about how best to move people about, mass-transit supporters typically
overestimate, usually by a wide margin, how many people will leave their cars
and happily hop onto trains or buses. According to one study, by Don Pick-
erell, the vast majority of American rail-transportation proposals greatly exaggerate the number of riders to be attracted; the actual ridership turns out to be
about a third of the predicted level. For this reason, urban public transport almost never recovers from the fare box more than a fraction of the actual cost
of moving people. Osaka, Japan, seems to be the only large city in the world
that gets back from passengers what it spends; in Atlanta, Detroit, and Houston, public transit gets from passengers no more than a third of their cost.

So the real debate ought not be one between car enthusiasts and mass-
transit advocates, but about ways of moderating the inevitable use of cars in
order to minimize their deleterious effects.

One such discussion has already had substantial effects. Auto-exhaust
pollution has been dramatically reduced in this country by redesigning engines, changing fuels (largely by removing lead), and imposing inspection requirements.

Since the mid-1960s, auto emissions have been reduced by about
95 percent. Just since 1982, ten years after the Clean Air Act was passed,
carbon-monoxide levels have fallen by 40 percent and nitrogen-oxide levels
by 25 percent. I live in the Los Angeles area and know from personal experience how irritating smog was in the 1950's. I also know that smog has decreased dramatically for most (but not all) of the region. The number of
"smog alert" days called by the South Coast Air Quality Management District
(AQMD) declined from 121 in the mid-1970's to seven in 1996. AQMD now
predicts that by the year 2000 the number may fall to zero.

Nationally, very little of this improvement has come about from moving people from solo cars into car pools or onto mass transit. What experts call
"Transportation Control Measures" (TCM's)—the combined effect of mass
transit, car pools, telecommuting, and the like—have produced small reduc-
tions in smog levels. Transit expansion has decreased carbon monoxide by
six-tenths of 1 percent and car pools by another seven-tenths of 1 percent.
Adding BART to San Francisco has had only trivial effects on pollution. The
Environmental Protection Agency (in the Clinton administration) has issued a
report that puts it bluntly: "Efforts to reduce emissions through traditional
TCM's have not generated significant air-quality benefits." The methods that
have reduced pollution significantly are based on markets, not capital invest-
ments, and include smog fees, congestion pricing, gas taxes, and higher parking charges.

There is still more pollution to eliminate, but the anti-car enthusiasts 30
rarely approach the task rationally. General Motors now leases electric cars,

but they are very expensive and require frequent recharging from scarce power outlets. The electric car is an impressive engineering achievement, but not if you want to travel very far.

We could pass laws that would drive down even further the pollution output of cars, but this would impose huge costs on manufacturers and buyers without addressing the real source of auto pollution—a small percentage of older or modified cars that generate huge amounts of exhaust. Devices now exist for measuring the pollution of cars as they move on highways and then ticketing the offenders, but only recently has there been a large-scale trial of this method, and the results are not yet in. The method has the virtue of targeting enforcement on real culprits, but the defect (for car critics) of not requiring a "tough new law" aimed at every auto owner.

As for traffic congestion, that has indeed become worse—because highway construction has not kept pace with the growth of automobile use. But it is not as bad as some imagine—the average commuting time was the same in 1990 as in 1980—and it is not bad where it is often assumed to be bad. A road is officially called "congested" if its traffic volume exceeds 80 percent of its designed capacity. By this measure, the most congested highways are in and around Washington, D.C., and San Francisco. But if you drive these roads during rush hour, as I have, you will acquire a very different sense of things. The highways into Washington and San Francisco do produce blockages, usually at familiar intersections, bridges, or merges. They rarely last very long and, on most days, one can plan around them.

Indeed, the fact and consequences of auto congestion are greatly exaggerated in most large cities. During rush hour, I have driven into and out of Dallas, Kansas City, Phoenix, St. Louis, and San Diego without much more than an occasional slowdown. Moreover, despite the massive reliance on cars and a short-term decline in the economic vitality of their downtown areas, most of these cities have restored their central areas. Kansas City is bleak in the old downtown, but the shopping area (built 75 years ago!) called Country Club Plaza is filled with people, stores, and restaurants. San Diego and San Francisco have lively downtowns. Los Angeles even managed to acquire a downtown (actually, several downtowns) after it grew up without much of one—and this in a city allegedly "built around the car." Phoenix is restoring its downtown and San Diego never really lost its center.

Real congestion, by contrast, is found in New York City, Chicago, and Boston, where almost any movement on any downtown street is extremely difficult. From the moment you enter a car or taxi, you are in a traffic jam. Getting to the airport by car from Manhattan or Boston is vastly more difficult than getting there from San Francisco, Los Angeles, or Washington.

But the lesson in this should be disturbing to car critics: *car travel is most* 35 *congested in cities that have the oldest and most highly developed rail-based transit systems.* One reason is historical: having subways from their early days, these cities built up to high levels of residential and commercial concentration. A car added to this mix has to navigate through streets surrounded by high office buildings and tall apartment towers. When many people in those buildings take cars or taxis, the congestion can be phenomenal.

But there is another reason as well. Even where rail transportation exists, people will not use it enough to relieve congestion. There is, for example, an excellent rail line from O'Hare Airport to downtown Chicago, and some people use it. But it has done little or nothing to alleviate congestion on the parallel highway. People do not like dragging suitcases on and off trains. And the train does not stop where people want to go — namely, where they live. It stops at busy street corners, sometimes in dangerous neighborhoods. If you take the train, you still must shift to a car at the end, and finding one is not always easy. This is why taking a car from the Los Angeles airport, though it will place you in a few pockets of congestion, gets you to your home faster (and with all of your belongings) than taking a train and taxi a comparable distance from O'Hare.

A great deal can still be done to moderate the social costs of automobile traffic. More toll roads can be built with variable rates that will allow people to drive — at different prices, depending on the level of congestion — to and from cities. Bridges into cities can charge tolls to ensure that only highly motivated people consume scarce downtown road space. (A friend of mine, a distinguished economist, was once asked, in derision, whether he would buy the Brooklyn Bridge. "I would if I could charge tolls on it," he replied.) Cars can be banned from streets that are capable of being pedestrian malls — though there are not many such places. (A number of such malls were created for the purpose of keeping people downtown who did not want to be downtown, and were doomed to failure from the start.)

Other measures are also possible. More bicycle pathways can be created, though these are rarely alternatives to auto transportation; some people do ride a bike to work, but few do so often. Street patterns in residential areas can be arranged to minimize the amount of through road traffic they must endure. Gasoline taxes can be set high enough to recover more of the social costs of operating automobiles. (This will not happen in a society as democratic as ours, but it is a good idea, and maybe someday a crisis will create an opportunity.)

Portland, Oregon, has become well-known among American cities for having adopted a law — the Urban Growth Boundary — that denies people the right to build almost any new structure in a green belt starting about twenty minutes from downtown. This means that new subdivisions to which one must travel by car cannot be created outside the line. The nice result is that outside the city, you can drive through unspoiled farm land.

The mayor and downtown business leaders like what they have created.   40
So do environmentalists, social-service organizations, and many ordinary

citizens. The policy, described in a recent issue of *Governing* magazine, is called the New Urbanism, and has attracted interest from all over the country. But the policy also has its costs. As the city's population grows, more people must be squeezed into less space. Housing density is up. Before the Urban Growth Boundary, the average Portland house was built on a lot about 13,000 feet square and row houses made up only 3 percent of all dwelling units. Now, the average lot size has fallen to 8,700 square feet and row houses make up 12 percent of the total. And housing prices are also up. Six years ago, Portland was the nation's 55th most affordable city; today, it is the 165th.

As density goes up in Portland, so will the problems associated with density, such as crime. Reserving land out of a city for scenic value is an important goal, but it must be balanced with supplying affordable housing. Portland will work out the balance, once people begin to yearn for lower density.

But even if we do all the things that can be done to limit the social costs of cars, the campaign against them will not stop. It will not stop because so many of the critics dislike everything the car stands for and everything that society constructs to serve the needs of its occupants.

Cars are about privacy; critics say privacy is bad and prefer group effort. (Of course, one rarely meets these critics in groups. They seem to be too busy rushing about being critics.) Cars are about autonomy; critics say that the pursuit of autonomy destroys community. (Actually, cars allow people to select the kind of community in which they want to live.) Cars are about speed; critics abhor the fatalities they think speed causes. (In fact, auto fatalities have been declining for decades, including after the 55-mile-per-hour national speed limit was repealed. Charles Lave suggests that this is because higher speed limits reduce the variance among cars in their rates of travel, thereby producing less passing and overtaking, two dangerous highway maneuvers.) Cars are about the joyous sensation of driving on beautiful country roads; critics take their joy from politics. (A great failing of the intellectual life of this country is that so much of it is centered in Manhattan, where one finds the highest concentration of nondrivers in the country.) Cars make possible Wal-Mart, Home Depot, the Price Club, and other ways of allowing people to shop for rock-bottom prices; critics want people to spend their time gathering food at downtown shops (and paying the much higher prices that small stores occupying expensive land must charge). Cars make California possible; critics loathe California. (But they loathe it for the wrong reason. The state is not the car capital of the nation; 36 states have more cars per capita, and their residents drive more miles.)

Life in California would be very difficult without cars. This is not because the commute to work is so long; in Los Angeles, according to Charles Lave, the average trip to work in 1994 was 26 minutes, five minutes *shorter* than in New York City. Rather, a carless state could not be enjoyed. You could not see the vast areas of farm land, the huge tracts of empty mountains and deserts, the miles of deserted beaches and forests.

No one who visits Los Angeles or San Francisco can imagine how   45
much of California is, in effect, empty, unsettled. It is an empire of lightly
used roads, splendid vistas, and small towns, intersected by a highway system
that, should you be busy or foolish enough to use it, will speed you from San
Francisco to Los Angeles or San Diego. Off the interstate, it is a kaleidoscope
of charming places to be alone.

Getting there in order to be alone is best done in one of the remarkably
engineered, breathtakingly fast, modern cars that give to the driver the deepest sense of what the road can offer: the beauty of its views, the excitement of
command, the passion of engagement.

I know the way. If you are a friend, you need only ask.

QUESTIONING THE TEXT

1. Review "Cars and Their Enemies," looking for places where Wilson
   characterizes the critics of automobiles. What terms or names does he
   give to these critics? Where do they live, and in Wilson's opinion, how
   do they typically behave? How does Wilson's treatment of "car haters"
   enhance or detract from his argument?

2. Does "Cars and Their Enemies" have a thesis you could state in one
   sentence? Reread the essay carefully, highlighting sentences you think
   make major points or summarize Wilson's thinking. Then review these
   major claims and offer your summary of Wilson's case in favor of the
   automobile.

3. Wilson, a sociologist by profession, uses both statistics and personal experiences to make his argument. Evaluate his use of these different kinds of
   evidence. Where does he cite statistics? Where does he rely on personal
   experience? How do you react to the highly personal last paragraph of the
   piece: "I know the way. If you are a friend, you need only ask"?

MAKING CONNECTIONS

4. In the opening paragraphs (1–7), Wilson suggests that were the automobile invented today, various experts—engineers, psychologists, environmentalists, governors, police officers—would likely lobby hard
   against it as a dangerous and irrational device. Compare Wilson's characterization of "expertise" with Robert A. Lutz's opinion of market research in "The Primary Purpose of Business Is Not to Make Money"
   (p. 712). Might too much expertise and professionalism make a society
   timid—unwilling to invest in untried or risky technologies or ideas?
   Explain.

5. What does Wilson seem to value in a car? Along with several classmates, read Reilly Brennan's "Would You Buy a Car from This Man?" (p. 706). Then, on the basis of what you can judge from Wilson's essay, brainstorm about how you would try to persuade him to buy a Daewoo. Bring your list of ideas to class for discussion.

JOINING THE CONVERSATION

6. Write an editorial for your campus newspaper in response to Wilson's piece, examining the issue of local transportation or, perhaps, traffic and parking at your school. In your argument, you need not simply agree or disagree with Wilson—just begin with his reflection on the automobile in American culture. Consider other possibilities for addressing the issue.

7. Write a brief essay exploring whether another older technology (besides the gasoline-powered car) might or might not be built if it were invented today rather than in the past. Use the first seven paragraphs of "Cars and Their Enemies" as a model for your piece.

8. Use both research materials and personal experience to write an essay on "_____ and Their Enemies," filling in the blank with a subject you can explore in depth. Present both your point of view on the topic and the ideas of those with whom you might disagree. Review Wilson's piece for ideas about organization and tone.

PAMELA SAMUELSON
The Digital Rights War

S<small>ITTING IN FRONT</small> *of your computer, browsing a listserv or tinkering with your own home page, you might yawn if someone mentioned intellectual property laws. Sure, copyright rules are important but, like the tax code, they're really stuff for lawyers and politicians to haggle over, not for harried students like you to ponder.*

Well, think again.

It turns out that you do have a stake in how electronically transmitted ideas, words, and images might be protected in the future from theft or misuse. If you are like most people, you assume that you can use, howsoever you please, all the copyrighted materials you routinely purchase, including books, videos, and magazines, just as long as you don't copy and sell them for your own profit. You can share textbooks with a roommate, photocopy an important magazine article for a friend, or listen to a folk CD until you can recite its lyrics in your sleep. But what if you weren't allowed to loan out your DVD copy of A Clockwork Orange? *What if a CD you purchased worked for only a set number of performances? What if new books erased themselves after a year—all to protect the property rights of artists and producers? These things could happen.*

No doubt, you have barely noticed and probably clicked right through the licensing screens of new software you've purchased. In the decades to come, such agreements might be a much more intrusive part of your life, thanks to changes in the copyright law. And electronic products might not be the only types of media affected. You might not be permitted to resell textbooks like this one at the end of a school term. Have I got your attention now?

Pamela Samuelson explores the intriguing—some might say invidious—possibilities of our electronic future in "The Digital Rights War," an essay that originally appeared in the Autumn 1998 issue of the Wilson Quarterly. *(We reproduce the article here after dutifully seeking the necessary permissions from the owner of the original copyright.) Samuelson is a professor of law and information management at the University of California, Berkeley, where she codirects the Berkeley Center for Law and Technology. Regarded as one of the most influential authorities on the new electronic and digital economies, Samuelson has been a fellow of both the Electronic Frontier Foundation and the Association of Computing Machinery.* —J.R.

Digital technology is opening up new worlds of potential, few more enticing than the emerging global marketplace for information products and services. Imagine being able to call up news articles, short stories, photographs, motion pictures, sound recordings, and other information any time, day or night, almost anywhere in the world. This is the vision that until recently sent the stocks of obscure Internet enterprises soaring and propelled relatively new companies such as Microsoft to the front ranks of American industry.

The great advantage of digital information—and a key source of its potential—is that, once produced, it is easy and cheap to disseminate. There is, however, a threat as well as a promise in this unique quality. Digital information is the equivalent of what land, factories, and equipment are in the conventional economy: essential property. And the very same low costs of reproduction and dissemination that are its great virtue also make possible unauthorized uses—including everything from copying a page from a magazine to pirating thousands of copies of a Frank Sinatra CD—on an unparalleled scale. It is no longer just commercial pirates peddling mass-produced bootlegs that alarm the Hollywood movie studios and the publishing industries; it is also the ordinary Tom, Dick, or Harriet who may be inclined to share copies of a favorite film or book with a thousand of his or her closest friends.

To guard against this possibility, some established copyright-based enterprises—including film studios, book and magazine publishers, software companies, and others that trade in intellectual property—have been spending hefty sums to create technological "locks" for their products. They are also seeking amendments to federal copyright law that would outlaw any tampering with these locks. But they are asking copyright law to perform tasks very different from those it has performed in the print world, tasks with alarming implications for our national life.

The new future of technically protected information is so far from the ordinary person's experience that few of us have any clue about what is at stake. So comfortable are we with the way in which copyright law matches up with our everyday experience, practices, and expectations that we find it hard to imagine the dramatic changes the digital world may bring. If I buy a copy of *A Streetcar Named Desire* today, for example, I know I can read it, share it with a friend, and perform scenes in my home or in a classroom. I can also make a photocopy of a favorite passage to send to my sister. If I am short of cash, I can go to a library and borrow a copy, making the same uses of it as I would of a purchased copy. But I also know that I should not run off dozens of copies or stage a production unless I get the copyright owner's permission.

In the familiar world we take for granted, principles and practice seem to form a seamless whole. Virtually all private and noncommercial uses of information are lawful. Yet the underlying law is somewhat more complicated. From the standpoint of copyright law, it is permissible to read a play not so much because one has paid for a copy, but because the law does not confer on owners a right to control the reading of protected, or copyrighted, works. It is okay to borrow a copy of the play from a library or share a personal copy with a friend because the law treats the first sale of a copy to the public as *exhausting* the copyright owner's right to control further distribution of that copy. Photocopying a favorite passage from a play would generally be considered a "fair use." Performing the play among friends or in a classroom also passes muster thanks to special "carve-outs" for these activities. The main concern of the law has been to stop people from becoming alternative publishers of a work (by, say, making many photocopies) or undercutting other commercial exploitations (such as controlling the licensing of theatrical performances of *A Streetcar Named Desire*).

But the rules that have served the print world so admirably do not carry over very well to the digital world. For one thing, it is impossible to use any work that exists in digital form without also making a number of temporary copies of it. When you visit the CNN Web site, for example, or look at entries in a CD-ROM encyclopedia, your computer has to make temporary copies so that you can see the material. This simple fact has profound implications for copyright. After all, the principal right of authors and publishers (as the term *copy-right* implies) is to control reproduction of their works.

In 1995, the Clinton administration issued a policy white paper, *Intellectual Property and the National Information Infrastructure,* that spelled out just how profound it thought these implications were. The white paper made the controversial assertion that because temporary copies do get made, copyright owners are entitled to control all browsing and reading of their works in digital form. Never mind that Congress, in writing the laws in an earlier era, probably never contemplated that the rights of copyright owners would extend so far.

The white paper also endorsed a view shared by many copyright owners—including big companies such as Disney, Time-Warner, and Microsoft—that "fair use" is going to wither away in the digital world, and by analogy in the print world. Why? Because it is now technically possible (or soon will be) for consumers to get a license from the publisher whenever they want to use a copyrighted work. These copyright owners contend that the real reason certain uses of such works were formerly considered *fair* is that it was simply too expensive and cumbersome to require a license for each use. Now that technology is curing this "market failure," they assert, fair use goes away. In the new order they envision, if a use can be licensed, it *must* be licensed, even a photocopied passage from *A Streetcar Named Desire*.

It is also contended in the white paper that the "first sale" principle is outmoded. The principle doesn't apply, according to this argument, because lending a digital copy of a work to a friend requires making a copy, not just passing along your copy. In addition, digital copies of works tend to be offered on *licensed* terms, not by sales of copies. When you buy a copy of word processing software, for example, the publisher includes a so-called license agreement—that often includes a prohibition on retransfer of the copy and other restrictions on sharing the content. Increasingly, other digital works, such as encyclopedias and CD-ROMs of telephone listings, also come with such licenses. If these "shrinkwrap" licenses are legally enforceable—an issue on which the courts are currently split—there is no reason why they could not also be applied to the print world. Then it would be illegal to sell second-hand books, for example, or even to give them away—a prospect that must surely delight publishers of college textbooks. This is not just a theoretical prospect. The National Conference of Commissioners on Uniform State Laws will soon complete a new model commercial law, designed to serve as a template for state law (which governs these matters), that validates all mass-market licenses of information, whether in digital or print form.

The abolition of the "first sale" principle would have a powerful effect on libraries. In the past, when a library stopped subscribing to a particular journal, for example, it still had back issues available for patrons. But in a world of licensed information, canceling a subscription may mean losing all access. So all information in a particular database would become unavailable. Owning a licensed physical copy of the information, such as a CD-ROM of reference materials, might not make a difference. Publishers would be entitled to demand their return, or to trigger embedded technological locks to keep users out.

Some publishers envision an information future ruled by a pay-per-use system. Users would license from the publisher each and every access to and use of protected works, even those for private, noncommercial purposes. If you want to read an article in *Time* but don't have a subscription, these publishers argue, why shouldn't you have to pay 50 cents or a dollar to read it—even at a library—and twice as much if you want a printout? The Clinton administration's white paper, with its assertion that copyright owners are entitled to control all uses of works in digital form, strongly endorsed this vision.

The white paper also foresaw the use of technological "locks" and self-destructing copies to help copyright owners protect their works against unauthorized uses. Try to make a copy of a movie on one of the new digital videodisks (DVDs) available today, for example, and you will quickly find your path blocked by such a lock. In fact, you probably won't be able to play your disk on a DVD player purchased in Tokyo or London because the players contain built-in technical locking systems coded by geographical location. (This gives the studios greater control over the distribution and marketing of their goods.) The DivX format for movies is an example of a self-destructing copy system already in the marketplace. If you purchase a DivX disk, you can play it on your own player for 48 hours, but after that, the data on the disk is inaccessible unless you pay another license fee. There is no technical reason why this can't happen with other kinds of information as well. Why shouldn't recording companies issue CDs that are coded to self-destruct or lock up after 15 plays, forcing those who want to hear more to pay more?

But some copyright owners worry that what one technology can do, another technology can often undo. They have lobbied Congress to make it illegal to circumvent or bypass technical protection systems and to outlaw the manufacture or sale of software that make circumvention possible.

Congress debated the issue earlier this year, pondering three options. One, pushed strongly by Hollywood, was a total ban on circumvention. The studios implausibly liken circumvention to burglary, insisting that it should never be allowed.[1] Libraries and educators were among those arguing for a second approach: banning circumvention only when the purpose is to infringe a copyright, which is, after all, the real evil that concerns the studios. Congress, however, chose a third option, a general ban on circumvention with specific exceptions in a number of cases, such as for law enforcement agencies.

What about the vitally important issue of circumvention to make fair   15
use of a protected work? A friend of mine, for example, recently defeated the technical protection on a videocassette in order to get a film clip to demonstrate the negative connotation of the word *redskin* in a lawsuit. This seemed to him fair use. Alas, it might not be permitted under the new rules.

The Senate version of the bill makes no allowance for circumvention for fair use, a position that has won the legislation the backing of Hollywood and software giant Microsoft. The House bill, recognizing the stakes involved, calls for a two-year study of the fair use issue and carves out a temporary suspension of the ban for nonprofit institutions. (Delegates negotiating an intentional copyright treaty in Geneva in 1996 rejected a ban on circumvention sought by the Clinton administration for similar reasons, including concern about the implications for fair use.) A House-Senate conference committee should resolve the differences this year, but that will hardly end the debate. How the new provisions will be applied in the marketplace—where, for example, consumers may resist new controls—and how the new law will meld with existing law and constitutional principles, such as the right to free speech, will keep contention very much alive.

In this year's debate over the new law, as in others surrounding the seemingly less than scintillating subject of intellectual property, the general public has not had a strong voice. The American Library Association, the Electronic Frontier Foundation, and a handful of other groups have sought to speak for the ordinary Americans whose lives will be profoundly influenced by what Congress decides, but without an aware and aroused public, these advocates' effectiveness will remain limited.

Americans need to have a broader public conversation about the kind of information future they want to create, a conversation that must include the role of copyright. The loudest answer to the copyright industries today comes

---

[1]In practice, people frequently circumvent protection systems, and social custom often supports them. Some years ago, for example, when software publishers offered their products only on copy-protected disks, users frequently bypassed the protection in order to make backup copies. A federal court even upheld the legitimacy of selling a program that could bypass these systems, reasoning that making such backups is a legitimate, noninfringing use.

from technological optimists such as Nicholas Negroponte, the director of the Media Lab at the Massachusetts Institute of Technology and a columnist for *Wired*. The optimists stake out the opposite extreme of the argument, insisting that because the economics of bits is so different from that of atoms, copyright is, or soon will be, dead. Good riddance, they add. All information must ultimately be free.

But Negroponte and his allies do not explain how creators will be able to make a living if they have no right at all to charge for the use of their works. If they are to thrive, authors, moviemakers, painters, software creators, and others do need a way to control commercial uses of their work. Preserving copyright looks to be the best way to achieve this goal. But copyright works well in part because creators can also make fair uses of the work of others and because people have reasonable freedom to privately share information. These values, too, need to be preserved.

An "information society" in which all information is kept under high- 20 tech lock and key, available only under terms and conditions dictated by a licenser, would not be worthy of the name. We need to work instead toward a new status quo that preserves the values that are already built into copyright law, allowing authors and publishers to thrive while also promoting the widest possible use of their creations.

QUESTIONING THE TEXT

1. Two important concepts to understand in reading "The Digital Rights War" are *fair use* and *first sale*. Review Samuelson's essay, looking for passages where she defines these terms or sets them in a context that helps you appreciate their importance. Then write a brief definition of each term, as you understand it. Compare your definitions with those prepared by several classmates.

2. Samuelson admits that intellectual property law can seem to be a "less than scintillating subject." But what facts or details in "The Digital Rights War" catch your attention? What, if anything, makes you interested in the subject?

MAKING CONNECTIONS

3. What relationships, if any, do you see between Samuelson's thoughts on intellectual property rights and Mark Clayton's observations about scholastic integrity in "A Whole Lot of Cheatin' Going On" (p. 185)? How might new property rights laws affect students involved in cheating or plagiarism?

4. Do you value information you receive electronically less than information you gather or acquire by slower or more traditional channels? Ponder this question carefully after reading Samuelson's essay alongside Todd Oppenheimer's "The Computer Delusion" (p. 255). Then write a brief argument in which you take a stand in response to the question.

JOINING THE CONVERSATION

5. Write a position paper in which you try to define the rights the creator(s) of a work should have over its use and reproduction. To make the essay manageable, explain the rights you are willing to grant to the author or producer of one very specific type of product or creation: a music CD, a movie on videotape or in DVD format, a magazine article, an electronic game, a ballet, an image or photograph. Feel free to draw on Samuelson or other sources for this paper.

6. Write a brief narrative in which you depict a world where you must pay for every bit of information you use. Draw from Samuelson's essay for the details of your story — and imagine how people might deal with the restrictions imposed on books, videos, CDs, and other information by new copyright laws. Be sure to consider what advantages there might be in a world where intellectual property rights were more vigorously defended.

7. Imagine a world entirely without copyright laws and intellectual property rights. (If it helps, first find and read an article on the subject by *Wired* columnist Nicholas Negroponte, mentioned by Samuelson in paragraphs 18–19.) Then consider how you might compose an academic research paper in such an environment. Turn your thinking into a one-page parody of a research paper in the digital age. Have fun with this assignment.

EDWARD O. WILSON
The Biological Basis of Morality

Edward O. Wilson (b. 1929) grew up in Alabama, where he went to college at the University of Alabama, receiving his bachelor's and master's degrees in biology. After receiving his Ph.D. (at Harvard University, again in biology), Wilson joined the faculty at Harvard, where he is currently Research Professor and Honorary Curator in Entomology of the Museum of Comparative Zoology. During his long career, Wilson has written dozens of books and twice won the Pulitzer Prize (in 1978 for On Human Nature *and in 1990 for* The Ants, *which he wrote with Bert Holldobler). Among his many other awards, including the 1977 National Medal of Science, he has been honored on several occasions for exemplary college teaching.*

While Wilson's work in biology is widely acclaimed, it is also controversial, especially the aspects of Social Darwinism (a "survival of the fittest" theory applied to humans) in his many explorations into sociobiology. In "The Biological Basis of Morality," originally published in the April 1998 issue of the Atlantic Monthly, *Wilson takes a controversial stand for "a purely material origin of ethics," arguing that "causal explanations of brain activity and evolution, while imperfect, already cover most facts known about behavior we term 'moral.'" He also admits, "I may be wrong." I chose this essay because it challenges me to think of morality in ways I have not done before. As you read the selection, decide for yourself how likely Wilson is to be correct in his claims.* —A.L.

Centuries of debate on the origin of ethics come down to this: Either ethical principles, such as justice and human rights, are independent of human experience, or they are human inventions. The distinction is more than an exercise for academic philosophers. The choice between these two understandings makes all the difference in the way we view ourselves as a species. It measures the authority of religion, and it determines the conduct of moral reasoning.

The two assumptions in competition are like islands in a sea of chaos, as different as life and death, matter and the void. One cannot learn which is correct by pure logic; the answer will eventually be reached through an accumulation of objective evidence. Moral reasoning, I believe, is at every level intrinsically consilient with—compatible with, intertwined with—the natural sciences. (I use a form of the word "consilience"—literally a "jumping together" of knowledge as a result of the linking of facts and fact-based theory across disciplines to create a common groundwork of explanation—because its rarity has preserved its precision.)

Every thoughtful person has an opinion on which premise is correct. But the split is not, as popularly supposed, between religious believers and secularists. It is between transcendentalists, who think that moral guidelines exist outside the human mind, and empiricists, who think them contrivances of the mind. In simplest terms, the options are as follows: *I believe in the independence of moral values, whether from God or not,* and *I believe that moral values come from human beings alone, whether or not God exists.*

Theologians and philosophers have almost always focused on transcendentalism as the means to validate ethics. They seek the grail of natural law, which comprises freestanding principles of moral conduct immune to doubt and compromise. Christian theologians, following Saint Thomas Aquinas's reasoning in *Summa Theologiae,* by and large consider natural law to be an expression of God's will. In this view, human beings have an obligation to discover the law by diligent reasoning and to weave it into the routine of their daily lives. Secular philosophers of a transcendental bent may seem to be radically different from theologians, but they are actually quite similar, at least in moral reasoning. They tend to view natural law as a set of principles so powerful, whatever their origin, as to be self-evident to any rational person. In short, transcendental views are fundamentally the same whether God is invoked or not.

For example, when Thomas Jefferson, following John Locke, derived   5
the doctrine of natural rights from natural law, he was more concerned with the power of transcendental statements than with their origin, divine or secular. In the Declaration of Independence he blended secular and religious presumptions in one transcendentalist sentence, thus deftly covering all bets: "We hold these Truths to be self-evident, that all Men are created equal, that they are endowed by their Creator with certain unalienable Rights, that among these are Life, Liberty, and Pursuit of Happiness." That assertion became the cardinal premise of America's civil religion, the righteous sword wielded by Abraham Lincoln and Martin Luther King Jr., and it endures as the central ethic binding together the diverse peoples of the United States.

So compelling are such fruits of natural-law theory, especially when the Deity is also invoked, that they may seem to place the transcendentalist assumption beyond question. But to its noble successes must be added appalling failures. It has been perverted many times in the past—used, for example, to argue passionately for colonial conquest, slavery, and genocide. Nor was any great war ever fought without each side thinking its cause transcendentally sacred in some manner or other.

So perhaps we need to take empiricism more seriously. In the empiricist view, ethics is conduct favored consistently enough throughout a society to be expressed as a code of principles. It reaches its precise form in each culture according to historical circumstance. The codes, whether adjudged good or evil by outsiders, play an important role in determining which cultures flourish and which decline.

The crux of the empiricist view is its emphasis on objective knowledge. Because the success of an ethical code depends on how wisely it interprets moral sentiments, those who frame one should know how the brain works, and how the mind develops. The success of ethics also depends on how accurately a society can predict the consequences of particular actions as opposed to others, especially in cases of moral ambiguity.

The empiricist argument holds that if we explore the biological roots of moral behavior, and explain their material origins and biases, we should be able to fashion a wise and enduring ethical consensus. The current expansion of scientific inquiry into the deeper processes of human thought makes this venture feasible.

The choice between transcendentalism and empiricism will be the coming century's version of the struggle for men's souls. Moral reasoning will either remain centered in idioms of theology and philosophy, where it is now, or shift toward science-based material analysis. Where it settles will depend on which world view is proved correct, or at least which is more widely *perceived* to be correct.   10

Ethicists, scholars who specialize in moral reasoning, tend not to declare themselves on the foundations of ethics, or to admit fallibility. Rarely do we see an argument that opens with the simple statement *This is my starting point, and it could be wrong.* Ethicists instead favor a fretful passage from the particular to the ambiguous, or the reverse—vagueness into hard cases. I suspect that almost all are transcendentalists at heart, but they rarely say so in simple declarative sentences. One cannot blame them very much; explaining the ineffable is difficult.

I am an empiricist. On religion I lean toward deism, but consider its proof largely a problem in astrophysics. The existence of a God who created the universe (as envisioned by deism) is possible, and the question may eventually be settled, perhaps by forms of material evidence not yet imagined. Or the matter may be forever beyond human reach. In contrast, and of far greater importance to humanity, the idea of a biological God, one who directs organic evolution and intervenes in human affairs (as envisioned by theism), is increasingly contravened by biology and the brain sciences.

The same evidence, I believe, favors a purely material origin of ethics, and it meets the criterion of consilience: causal explanations of brain activity and evolution, while imperfect, already cover most facts known about behavior we term "moral." Although this conception is relativistic (in other words, dependent on personal viewpoint), it can, if evolved carefully, lead more directly and safely to stable moral codes than can transcendentalism, which is also, when one thinks about it, ultimately relativistic.

Of course, lest I forget, I may be wrong.

TRANSCENDENTALISM VERSUS EMPIRICISM

The argument of the empiricist has roots that go back to Aristotle's   15
Nicomachean Ethics and, in the beginning of the modern era, to David Hume's *A Treatise of Human Nature* (1739–1740). The first clear evolutionary elaboration of it was by Charles Darwin, in *The Descent of Man* (1871).

Again, religious transcendentalism is bolstered by secular transcendentalism, to which it is fundamentally similar. Immanuel Kant, judged by history the greatest of secular philosophers, addressed moral reasoning very much as a theologian. Human beings, he argued, are independent moral agents with a wholly free will, capable of obeying or breaking moral law: "There is in man a power of self-determination, independent of any coercion through sensuous impulses." Our minds are subject to a categorical imperative, Kant said, of what our actions ought to be. The imperative is a good in itself alone, apart from all other considerations, and it can be recognized by this rule: "Act only on that maxim you wish will become a universal law." Most important, and transcendental, *ought* has no place in nature. Nature, Kant said, is a system of cause and effect, whereas moral choice is a matter of free will, absent cause and effect. In making moral choices, in rising above mere instinct, human beings transcend the realm of nature and enter a realm of freedom that belongs exclusively to them as rational creatures.

Now, this formulation has a comforting feel to it, but it makes no sense at all in terms of either material or imaginable entities, which is why Kant, even apart from his tortured prose, is so hard to understand. Sometimes a concept is baffling not because it is profound but because it is wrong. This idea does not accord, we know now, with the evidence of how the brain works.

In *Principia Ethica* (1903), G. E. Moore, the founder of modern ethical philosophy, essentially agreed with Kant. In his view, moral reasoning cannot dip into psychology and the social sciences in order to locate ethical principles, because those disciplines yield only a causal picture and fail to illuminate the basis of moral justification. So to reach the normative *ought* by way of the factual *is* is to commit a basic error of logic, which Moore called the naturalistic fallacy. John Rawls, in *A Theory of Justice* (1971), once again traveled the transcendental road. He offered the very plausible suggestion that justice be defined as fairness, which is to be accepted as an intrinsic good. It is the imperative we would follow if we had no starting information about our own future status in life. But in making such a suggestion Rawls ventured no thought on where the human brain comes from or how it works. He offered no evidence that justice-as-fairness is consistent with human nature, hence practicable as a blanket premise. Probably it is, but how can we know except by blind trial and error?

Had Kant, Moore, and Rawls known modern biology and experimental psychology, they might well not have reasoned as they did. Yet as this century closes, transcendentalism remains firm in the hearts not just of religious believers but also of countless scholars in the social sciences and the humanities who, like Moore and Rawls, have chosen to insulate their thinking from the natural sciences.

Many philosophers will respond by saying, Ethicists don't need that kind of information. You really can't pass from *is* to *ought*. You can't describe a genetic predisposition and suppose that because it is part of human nature, it is somehow transformed into an ethical precept. We must put moral reasoning in a special category, and use transcendental guidelines as required.

No, we do not have to put moral reasoning in a special category and use transcendental premises, because the posing of the naturalistic fallacy is itself a fallacy. For if *ought* is not *is,* what is? To translate *is* into *ought* makes sense if we attend to the objective meaning of ethical precepts. They are very unlikely to be ethereal messages awaiting revelation, or independent truths vibrating in a nonmaterial dimension of the mind. They are more likely to be products of the brain and the culture. From the consilient perspective of the natural sciences, they are no more than principles of the social contract hardened into rules and dictates—the behavioral codes that members of a society fervently wish others to follow and are themselves willing to accept for the common good. Precepts are the extreme on a scale of agreements that range from casual assent, to public sentiment, to law, to that part of the canon considered sacred and unalterable. The scale applied to adultery might read as follows:

> *Let's not go further; it doesn't feel right, and it may lead to trouble. (Maybe we ought not.)*
>
> *Adultery not only causes feelings of guilt but is generally disapproved of by society. (We probably ought not.)*
>
> *Adultery isn't just disapproved of; it's against the law. (We almost certainly ought not.)*
>
> *God commands that we avoid this mortal sin. (We absolutely ought not.)*

In transcendental thinking, the chain of causation runs downward from the given *ought* in religion or natural law through jurisprudence to education and finally to individual choice. The argument from transcendentalism takes the following general form: *The order of nature contains supreme principles, either divine or intrinsic, and we will be wise to learn about them and find the means to conform to them.* Thus John Rawls opens *A Theory of Justice* with a proposition he regards as irrevocable: "In a just society the liberties of equal citizenship are taken as settled; the rights secured by justice are not subject to political bargaining or to the calculus of social interests." As many critiques have made clear, that premise can lead to unhappy consequences when applied to the real world, including a tightening of social control and a decline in personal initiative. A very different premise, therefore, is suggested by Robert Nozick in *Anarchy, State, and Utopia* (1974): "Individuals have rights, and there are things no person or group may do to them (without violating their rights). So strong and far-reaching are these rights that they raise the question of what, if anything, the state and its officials may do." Rawls would point us toward egalitarianism regulated by the state, Nozick toward libertarianism in a minimalist state.

The empiricist view, in contrast, searching for an origin of ethical rea-soning that can be objectively studied, reverses the chain of causation. The individual is seen as predisposed biologically to make certain choices. Through cultural evolution some of the choices are hardened into precepts, then into laws, and, if the predisposition or coercion is strong enough, into a belief in the command of God or the natural order of the universe. The gen-eral empiricist principle takes this form: *Strong innate feeling and historical experi-ence cause certain actions to be preferred; we have experienced them, and have weighed their consequences, and agree to conform with codes that express them. Let us take an oath upon the codes, invest our personal honor in them, and suffer punishment for their violation.* The empiricist view concedes that moral codes are devised to con-form to some drives of human nature and to suppress others. *Ought* is the translation not of human nature but of the public will, which can be made in-creasingly wise and stable through an understanding of the needs and pitfalls of human nature. The empiricist view recognizes that the strength of com-mitment can wane as a result of new knowledge and experience, with the re-sult that certain rules may be desacralized, old laws rescinded, and formerly prohibited behavior set free. It also recognizes that for the same reason new moral codes may need to be devised, with the potential of being made sacred in time.

THE ORIGIN OF MORAL INSTINCTS

If the empiricist world view is correct, *ought* is just shorthand for one kind of factual statement, a word that denotes what society first chose (or was coerced) to do, and then codified. The naturalistic fallacy is thereby reduced to the naturalistic problem. The solution of the problem is not difficult: *ought* is the product of a material process. The solution points the way to an objec-tive grasp of the origin of ethics.

A few investigators are now embarked on just such a foundational in-   25 quiry. Most agree that ethical codes have arisen by evolution through the in-terplay of biology and culture. In a sense these investigators are reviving the idea of moral sentiments that was developed in the eighteenth century by the British empiricists Francis Hutcheson, David Hume, and Adam Smith.

What have been thought of as moral sentiments are now taken to mean moral instincts (as defined by the modern behavioral sciences), subject to judgment according to their consequences. Such sentiments are thus derived from epigenetic rules—hereditary biases in mental development, usually con-ditioned by emotion, that influence concepts and decisions made from them. The primary origin of moral instincts is the dynamic relation between cooperation and defection. The essential ingredient for the molding of the in-stincts during genetic evolution in any species is intelligence high enough to judge and manipulate the tension generated by the dynamism. That level of intelligence allows the building of complex mental scenarios well into the future. It occurs, so far as is known, only in human beings and perhaps their closest relatives among the higher apes.

A way of envisioning the hypothetical earliest stages of moral evolution is provided by game theory, particularly the solutions to the famous Prisoner's Dilemma. Consider the following typical scenario of the dilemma. Two gang members have been arrested for murder and are being questioned separately. The evidence against them is strong but not irrefutable. The first gang member believes that if he turns state's witness, he will be granted immunity and his partner will be sentenced to life in prison. But he is also aware that his partner has the same option, and that if both of them exercise it, neither will be granted immunity. That is the dilemma. Will the two gang members independently defect, so that both take the hard fall? They will not, because they agreed in advance to remain silent if caught. By doing so, both hope to be convicted on a lesser charge or escape punishment altogether. Criminal gangs have turned this principle of calculation into an ethical precept: Never rat on another member; always be a stand-up guy. Honor does exist among thieves. The gang is a society of sorts; its code is the same as that of a captive soldier in wartime, obliged to give only name, rank, and serial number.

In one form or another, comparable dilemmas that are solvable by cooperation occur constantly and everywhere in daily life. The payoff is variously money, status, power, sex, access, comfort, or health. Most of these proximate rewards are converted into the universal bottom line of Darwinian genetic fitness: greater longevity and a secure, growing family.

And so it has most likely always been. Imagine a Paleolithic band of five hunters. One considers breaking away from the others to look for an antelope on his own. If successful, he will gain a large quantity of meat and hide—five times as much as if he stays with the band and they are successful. But he knows from experience that his chances of success are very low, much less than the chances of the band of five working together. In addition, whether successful alone or not, he will suffer animosity from the others for lessening their prospects. By custom the band members remain together and share equitably the animals they kill. So the hunter stays. He also observes good manners in doing so, especially if he is the one who makes the kill. Boastful pride is condemned, because it rips the delicate web of reciprocity.

Now suppose that human propensities to cooperate or defect are heritable: some people are innately more cooperative, others less so. In this respect moral aptitude would simply be like almost all other mental traits studied to date. Among traits with documented heritability, those closest to moral aptitude are empathy with the distress of others and certain processes of attachment between infants and their caregivers. To the heritability of moral aptitude add the abundant evidence of history that cooperative individuals generally survive longer and leave more offspring. Following that reasoning, in the course of evolutionary history genes predisposing people toward coop- 30 erative behavior would have come to predominate in the human population as a whole.

Such a process repeated through thousands of generations inevitably gave rise to moral sentiments. With the exception of psychopaths (if any truly exist), every person vividly experiences these instincts variously as conscience, self-respect, remorse, empathy, shame, humility, and moral outrage. They bias cultural evolution toward the conventions that express the universal moral codes of honor, patriotism, altruism, justice, compassion, mercy, and redemption.

The dark side of the inborn propensity to moral behavior is xenophobia. Because personal familiarity and common interest are vital in social transactions, moral sentiments evolved to be selective. People give trust to strangers with effort, and true compassion is a commodity in chronically short supply. Tribes cooperate only through carefully defined treaties and other conventions. They are quick to imagine themselves the victims of conspiracies by competing groups, and they are prone to dehumanize and murder their rivals during periods of severe conflict. They cement their own group loyalties by means of sacred symbols and ceremonies. Their mythologies are filled with epic victories over menacing enemies.

The complementary instincts of morality and tribalism are easily manipulated. Civilization has made them more so. Beginning about 10,000 years ago, a tick in geological time, when the agricultural revolution started in the Middle East, in China, and in Mesoamerica, populations increased tenfold in density over those of hunter-gatherer societies. Families settled on small plots of land, villages proliferated, and labor was finely divided as a growing minority of the populace specialized as craftsmen, traders, and soldiers. The rising agricultural societies became increasingly hierarchical. As chiefdoms and then states thrived on agricultural surpluses, hereditary rulers and priestly castes took power. The old ethical codes were transformed into coercive regulations, always to the advantage of the ruling classes. About this time the idea of law-giving gods originated. Their commands lent the ethical codes overpowering authority—once again, no surprise, in the interests of the rulers.

Because of the technical difficulty of analyzing such phenomena in an objective manner, and because people resist biological explanations of their higher cortical functions in the first place, very little progress has been made in the biological exploration of the moral sentiments. Even so, it is astonishing that the study of ethics has advanced so little since the nineteenth century. The most distinguishing and vital qualities of the human species remain a blank space on the scientific map. I doubt that discussions of ethics should rest upon the freestanding assumptions of contemporary philosophers who have evidently never given thought to the evolutionary origin and material functioning of the human brain. In no other domain of the humanities is a union with the natural sciences more urgently needed.

When the ethical dimension of human nature is at last fully opened to 35 such exploration, the innate epigenetic rules of moral reasoning will probably not prove to be aggregated into simple instincts such as bonding, cooperativeness, and altruism. Instead the rules will most probably turn out to be an ensemble of many algorithms, whose interlocking activities guide the mind across a landscape of nuanced moods and choices.

Such a prestructured mental world may at first seem too complicated to have been created by autonomous genetic evolution alone. But all the evidence of biology suggests that just this process was enough to spawn the millions of species of life surrounding us. Each kind of animal is furthermore guided through its life cycle by unique and often elaborate sets of instinctual algorithms, many of which are beginning to yield to genetic and neurobiological analyses. With all these examples before us, we may reasonably conclude that human behavior originated the same way.

A Scientific Approach to Moral Reasoning

Meanwhile, the mélanges of moral reasoning employed by modern societies are, to put the matter simply, a mess. They are chimeras, composed of odd parts stuck together. Paleolithic egalitarian and tribalistic instincts are still firmly installed. As part of the genetic foundation of human nature, they cannot be replaced. In some cases, such as quick hostility to strangers and competing groups, they have become generally ill adapted and persistently dangerous. Above the fundamental instincts rise superstructures of arguments and rules that accommodate the novel institutions created by cultural evolution. These accommodations, which reflect the attempt to maintain order and further tribal interests, have been too volatile to track by genetic evolution; they are not yet in the genes.

Little wonder, then, that ethics is the most publicly contested of all philosophical enterprises. Or that political science, which at its foundation is primarily the study of applied ethics, is so frequently problematic. Neither is informed by anything that would be recognizable as authentic theory in the natural sciences. Both ethics and political science lack a foundation of verifiable knowledge of human nature sufficient to produce cause-and-effect predictions and sound judgments based on them. Surely closer attention must be paid to the deep springs of ethical behavior. The greatest void in knowledge for such a venture is the biology of moral sentiments. In time this subject can be understood, I believe, by paying attention to the following topics:

- *The definition of moral sentiments,* first by precise descriptions from experimental psychology and then by analysis of the underlying neural and endocrine responses.

- *The genetics of moral sentiments,* most easily approached through measurements of the heritability of the psychological and physiological processes of ethical behavior, and eventually, with difficulty, through identification of the prescribing genes.

- *The development of moral sentiments as products of the interactions of genes and the environment.* Research is most effective when conducted at two levels: the histories of ethical systems as part of the emergence of different cultures, and the cognitive development of individuals living in a variety of cultures. Such investigations are already well along in anthropology and psychology. In the future they will be augmented by contributions from biology.

- *The deep history of moral sentiments*—why they exist in the first place. Presumably they contributed to survival and reproductive success during the long periods of prehistoric time in which they genetically evolved.

From a convergence of these several approaches the true origin and meaning of ethical behavior may come into focus. If so, a more certain measure can then be taken of the strength and flexibility of the epigenetic rules composing the various moral sentiments. From that knowledge it should be possible to adapt ancient moral sentiments more wisely to the swiftly changing conditions of modern life into which, willy-nilly and largely in ignorance, we have plunged.

Then new answers might be found to the truly important questions of 40 moral reasoning. How can the moral instincts be ranked? Which are best subdued and to what degree? Which should be validated by law and symbol? How can precepts be left open to appeal under extraordinary circumstances? In the new understanding can be located the most effective means for reaching consensus. No one can guess the exact form that agreements will take from one culture to the next. The process, however, can be predicted with assurance. It will be democratic, weakening the clash of rival religions and ideologies. History is moving decisively in that direction, and people are by nature too bright and too contentious to abide anything else. And the pace can be confidently predicted: change will come slowly, across generations, because old beliefs die hard, even when they are demonstrably false.

The same reasoning that aligns ethical philosophy with science can also inform the study of religion. Religions are analogous to organisms. They have a life cycle. They are born, they grow, they compete, they reproduce, and, in the fullness of time, most die. In each of these phases religions reflect the human organisms that nourish them. They express a primary rule of human existence: Whatever is necessary to sustain life is also ultimately biological.

Successful religions typically begin as cults, which then increase in power and inclusiveness until they achieve tolerance outside the circle of believers. At the core of each religion is a creation myth, which explains how the world began and how the chosen people—those subscribing to the belief system—arrived at its center. Often a mystery, a set of secret instructions and formulas, is available to members who have worked their way to a higher state of enlightenment. The medieval Jewish cabala, the trigradal system of Freemasonry, and the carvings on Australian aboriginal spirit sticks are examples of such arcana. Power radiates from the center, gathering converts and binding followers to the group. Sacred places are designated, where the gods can be importuned, rites observed, and miracles witnessed.

The devotees of the religion compete as a tribe with those of other religions. They harshly resist the dismissal of their beliefs by rivals. They venerate self-sacrifice in defense of the religion.

The tribalistic roots of religion are similar to those of moral reasoning and may be identical. Religious rites, such as burial ceremonies, are very old. It appears that in the late Paleolithic period in Europe and the Middle East bodies were sometimes placed in shallow graves, accompanied by ocher or blossoms; one can easily imagine such ceremonies performed to invoke spirits and gods. But, as theoretical deduction and the evidence suggest, the primitive elements of moral behavior are far older than Paleolithic ritual. Religion arose on a foundation of ethics, and it has probably always been used in one manner or another to justify moral codes.

The formidable influence of the religious drive is based on far more, however, than just the validation of morals. A great subterranean river of the mind, it gathers strength from a broad spread of tributary emotions. Foremost among them is the survival instinct. "Fear," as the Roman poet Lucretius said, "was the first thing on earth to make the gods." Our conscious minds hunger for a permanent existence. If we cannot have everlasting life of the body, then absorption into some immortal whole will serve. *Anything* will serve, as long as it gives the individual meaning and somehow stretches into eternity that swift passage of the mind and spirit lamented by Saint Augustine as the short day of time.

The understanding and control of life is another source of religious power. Doctrine draws on the same creative springs as science and the arts, its aim being the extraction of order from the mysteries and tumult of the material world. To explain the meaning of life it spins mythic narratives of the tribal history, populating the cosmos with protective spirits and gods. The existence of the supernatural, if accepted, testifies to the existence of that other world so desperately desired.

Religion is also mightily empowered by its principal ally, tribalism. The shamans and priests implore us, in somber cadence, *Trust in the sacred rituals, become part of the immortal force, you are one of us. As your life unfolds, each step has mystic significance that we who love you will mark with a solemn rite of passage, the last to be performed when you enter that second world, free of pain and fear.*

If the religious mythos did not exist in a culture, it would quickly be invented, and in fact it has been invented everywhere, thousands of times through history. Such inevitability is the mark of instinctual behavior in any species, which is guided toward certain states by emotion-driven rules of mental development. To call religion instinctive is not to suppose that any particular part of its mythos is untrue — only that its sources run deeper than ordinary habit and are in fact hereditary, urged into existence through biases in mental development that are encoded in the genes.

Such biases are a predictable consequence of the brain's genetic evolution. The logic applies to religious behavior, with the added twist of tribalism. There is a hereditary selective advantage to membership in a powerful group united by devout belief and purpose. Even when individuals subordinate themselves and risk death in a common cause, their genes are more likely to be transmitted to the next generation than are those of competing groups who lack comparable resolve.

The mathematical models of population genetics suggest the following 50
rule in the evolutionary origin of such altruism: If the reduction in survival and reproduction of individuals owing to genes for altruism is more than offset by the increased probability of survival of the group owing to the altruism, then altruism genes will rise in frequency throughout the entire population of competing groups. To put it as concisely as possible: the individual pays, his genes and tribe gain, altruism spreads.

ETHICS AND ANIMAL LIFE

Let me now suggest a still deeper significance of the empiricist theory of the origin of ethics and religion. If empiricism were disproved, and transcendentalism compellingly upheld, the discovery would be quite simply the most consequential in human history. That is the burden laid upon biology as it draws close to the humanities.

The matter is still far from resolved. But empiricism, as I have argued, is well supported thus far in the case of ethics. The objective evidence for or against it in religion is weaker, but at least still consistent with biology. For example, the emotions that accompany religious ecstasy clearly have a neurobiological source. At least one form of brain disorder is associated with hyper-religiosity, in which cosmic significance is given to almost everything, including trivial everyday events. One can imagine the biological construction of a mind with religious beliefs, although that alone would not disprove the logic of transcendentalism, or prove the beliefs themselves to be untrue.

Equally important, much if not all religious behavior could have arisen from evolution by natural selection. The theory fits — crudely. The behavior includes at least some aspects of belief in gods. Propitiation and sacrifice, which are near-universals of religious practice, are acts of submission to a dominant being. They reflect one kind of dominance hierarchy, which is a general trait of organized mammalian societies. Like human beings, animals use elaborate signals to advertise and maintain their rank in the hierarchy. The details vary among species but also have consistent similarities across the board, as the following two examples will illustrate.

In packs of wolves the dominant animal walks erect and "proud," stiff-legged and deliberate, with head, tail, and ears up, and stares freely and casually at others. In the presence of rivals the dominant animal bristles its pelt while curling its lips to show teeth, and it takes first choice in food and space. A subordinate uses opposite signals. It turns away from the dominant individual while lowering its head, ears, and tail, and it keeps its fur sleek and its teeth covered. It grovels and slinks, and yields food and space when challenged.

In a troop of rhesus monkeys the alpha male is remarkably similar in   55
mannerisms to a dominant wolf. He keeps his head and tail up, and walks in a deliberate, "regal" manner while casually staring at others. He climbs objects to maintain height above his rivals. When challenged he stares hard at the opponent with mouth open—signaling aggression, not surprise—and sometimes slaps the ground with open palms to signal his readiness to attack. The male or female subordinate affects a furtive walk, holding its head and tail down, turning away from the alpha and other higher-ranked individuals. It keeps its mouth shut except for a fear grimace, and when challenged makes a cringing retreat. It yields space and food and, in the case of males, estrous females.

My point is this: Behavioral scientists from another planet would notice immediately the parallels between animal dominance behavior on the one hand and human obeisance to religious and civil authority on the other. They would point out that the most elaborate rites of obeisance are directed at the gods, the hyperdominant if invisible members of the human group. And they would conclude, correctly, that in baseline social behavior, not just in anatomy, *Homo sapiens* has only recently diverged in evolution from a nonhuman primate stock.

Countless studies of animal species, whose instinctive behavior is unobscured by cultural elaboration, have shown that membership in dominance orders pays off in survival and lifetime reproductive success. That is true not just for the dominant individuals but for the subordinates as well. Membership in either class gives animals better protection against enemies and better access to food, shelter, and mates than does solitary existence. Furthermore, subordination in the group is not necessarily permanent. Dominant individuals weaken and die, and as a result some of the underlings advance in rank and appropriate more resources.

Modern human beings are unlikely to have erased the old mammalian genetic programs and devised other means of distributing power. All the evidence suggests that they have not. True to their primate heritage, people are easily seduced by confident, charismatic leaders, especially males. That predisposition is strong in religious organizations. Cults form around such leaders. Their power grows if they can persuasively claim special access to the supremely dominant, typically male figure of God. As cults evolve into religions, the image of the Supreme Being is reinforced by myth and liturgy. In time the authority of the founders and their successors is graven in sacred texts. Unruly subordinates, known as "blasphemers," are squashed.

The symbol-forming human mind, however, never remains satisfied with raw, apish feeling in any emotional realm. It strives to build cultures that are maximally rewarding in every dimension. Ritual and prayer permit religious believers to be in direct touch with the Supreme Being; consolation from coreligionists softens otherwise unbearable grief; the unexplainable is explained; and an oceanic sense of communion with the larger whole is made possible.

Communion is the key, and hope rising from it is eternal; out of the 60 dark night of the soul arises the prospect of a spiritual journey to the light. For a special few the journey can be taken in this life. The mind reflects in certain ways in order to reach ever higher levels of enlightenment, until finally, when no further progress is possible, it enters a mystical union with the whole. Within the great religions such enlightenment is expressed by Hindu samadhi, Buddhist Zen satori, Sufi fana, and Pentecostal Christian rebirth. Something like it is also experienced by hallucinating preliterate shamans. What all these celebrants evidently feel (as I felt once, to some degree, as a reborn evangelical) is hard to put in words, but Willa Cather came as close as possible in a single sentence. In *My Antonia* her fictional narrator says, "That is happiness; to be dissolved into something complete and great."

Of course that is happiness—to find the godhead, or to enter the wholeness of nature, or otherwise to grasp and hold on to something ineffable, beautiful, and eternal. Millions seek it. They feel otherwise lost, adrift in a life without ultimate meaning. They enter established religions, succumb to cults, dabble in New Age nostrums. They push *The Celestine Prophecy* and other junk attempts at enlightenment onto the best-seller lists.

Perhaps, as I believe, these phenomena can all eventually be explained as functions of brain circuitry and deep genetic history. But this is not a subject that even the most hardened empiricist should presume to trivialize. The idea of mystical union is an authentic part of the human spirit. It has occupied humanity for millennia, and it raises questions of utmost seriousness for transcendentalists and scientists alike. What road, we ask, was traveled, what destination reached, by the mystics of history?

THEOLOGY MOVES TOWARD ABSTRACTION

For many, the urge to believe in transcendental existence and immortality is overpowering. Transcendentalism, especially when reinforced by religious faith, is psychically full and rich; it feels somehow *right*. By comparison, empiricism seems sterile and inadequate. In the quest for ultimate meaning the transcendentalist route is much easier to follow. That is why, even as empiricism is winning the mind, transcendentalism continues to win the heart.

Science has always defeated religious dogma point by point when differences between the two were meticulously assessed. But to no avail. In the United States 16 million people belong to the Southern Baptist denomination, the largest favoring a literal interpretation of the Christian Bible, but the American Humanist Association, the leading organization devoted to secular and deistic humanism, has only 5,000 members.

Still, if history and science have taught us anything, it is that passion and desire are not the same as truth. The human mind evolved to believe in gods. It did not evolve to believe in biology. Acceptance of the supernatural conveyed a great advantage throughout prehistory, when the brain was evolving. Thus it is in sharp contrast to the science of biology, which was developed as a product of the modern age and is not underwritten by genetic algorithms. The uncomfortable truth is that the two beliefs are not factually compatible. As a result, those who hunger for both intellectual and religious truth face disquieting choices.

Meanwhile, theology tries to resolve the dilemma by evolving, science- 65 like, toward abstraction. The gods of our ancestors were divine human beings. The Egyptians represented them as Egyptian (often with body parts of Nilotic animals), and the Greeks represented them as Greek. The great contribution of the Hebrews was to combine the entire pantheon into a single person, Yahweh (a patriarch appropriate to desert tribes), and to intellectualize his existence. No graven images were allowed. In the process, they rendered the divine presence less tangible. And so in biblical accounts it came to pass that no one, not even Moses approaching Yahweh in the burning bush, could look upon his face. In time the Jews were prohibited from even pronouncing his true full name. Nevertheless, the idea of a theistic God, omniscient, omnipotent, and closely involved in human affairs, has persisted to this day as the dominant religious image of Western culture.

During the Enlightenment a growing number of liberal Judeo-Christian theologians, wishing to accommodate theism to a more rationalist view of the material world, moved away from God as a literal person. Baruch Spinoza, the preeminent Jewish philosopher of the seventeenth century, visualized the deity as a transcendent substance present everywhere in the universe. *Deus sive natura*, "God or nature," he declared, they are interchangeable. For his philosophical pains he was banished from his synagogue under a comprehensive anathema, combining all the curses in the book. The risk of heresy notwithstanding, the depersonalization of God has continued steadily into the modern era. For Paul Tillich, one of the most influential Protestant theologians of the twentieth century, the assertion of the existence of God-as-person is not false; it is just meaningless. Among many of the most liberal contemporary thinkers the denial of a concrete divinity takes the form of "process theology." Everything in this most extreme of ontologies is part of a seamless and endlessly complex web of unfolding relationships. God is manifest in everything.

Scientists, the roving scouts of the empiricist movement, are not immune to the idea of God. Those who favor it often lean toward some form of process theology. They ask this question: When the real world of space, time, and matter is well enough known, will that knowledge reveal the Creator's presence? Their hopes are vested in the theoretical physicists who pursue the final theory, the Theory of Everything, T.O.E., a system of interlocking equations that describe all that can be learned of the forces of the physical universe. T.O.E. is a "beautiful" theory, as Steven Weinberg has called it in his important book *Dreams of a Final Theory*—beautiful because it will be elegant, expressing the possibility of unending complexity with minimal laws; and symmetrical, because it will hold invariant through all space and time; and inevitable, meaning that once it is stated, no part can be changed without invalidating the whole. All surviving subtheories can be fitted into it permanently, in the manner described by Einstein in his own contribution, the General Theory of Relativity. "The chief attraction of the theory," Einstein said, "lies in its logical completeness. If a single one of the conclusions drawn from it proves wrong, it must be given up; to modify it without destroying the whole structure seems to be impossible."

The prospect of a final theory by the most mathematical of scientists might seem to signal the approach of a new religious awakening. Stephen Hawking, yielding to the temptation in *A Brief History of Time* (1988), declared that this scientific achievement "would be the ultimate triumph of human reason—for then we would know the mind of God."

A HUNGER FOR SPIRITUALITY

The essence of humanity's spiritual dilemma is that we evolved genetically to accept one truth and discovered another. Can we find a way to erase the dilemma, to resolve the contradictions between the transcendentalist and empiricist world views?

Unfortunately, in my view, the answer is no. Furthermore, the choice 70 between the two is unlikely to remain arbitrary forever. The assumptions underlying these world views are being tested with increasing severity by cumulative verifiable knowledge about how the universe works, from atom to brain to galaxy. In addition, the harsh lessons of history have taught us that one code of ethics is not always as good—or at least not as durable—as another. The same is true of religions. Some cosmologies are factually less correct than others, and some ethical precepts are less workable.

Human nature is biologically based, and it is relevant to ethics and religion. The evidence shows that because of its influence, people can readily be educated to only a narrow range of ethical precepts. They flourish within certain belief systems and wither in others. We need to know exactly why.

To that end I will be so presumptuous as to suggest how the conflict between the world views will most likely be settled. The idea of a genetic, evolutionary origin of moral and religious beliefs will continue to be tested by biological studies of complex human behavior. To the extent that the sensory and nervous systems appear to have evolved by natural selection, or at least some other purely material process, the empiricist interpretation will be supported. It will be further supported by verification of gene-culture coevolution, the essential process postulated by scientists to underlie human nature by linking changes in genes to changes in culture.

Now consider the alternative. To the extent that ethical and religious phenomena do *not* appear to have evolved in a manner congenial to biology, and especially to the extent that such complex behavior cannot be linked to physical events in the sensory and nervous systems, the empiricist position will have to be abandoned and a transcendentalist explanation accepted.

For centuries the writ of empiricism has been spreading into the ancient domain of transcendentalist belief, slowly at the start but quickening in the scientific age. The spirits our ancestors knew intimately fled first the rocks and trees and then the distant mountains. Now they are in the stars, where their final extinction is possible. *But we cannot live without them.* People need a sacred narrative. They must have a sense of larger purpose, in one form or another, however intellectualized. They will refuse to yield to the despair of animal mortality. They will continue to plead, in company with the psalmist, *Now Lord, what is my comfort?* They will find a way to keep the ancestral spirits alive.

If the sacred narrative cannot be in the form of a religious cosmology, it will be taken from the material history of the universe and the human species. That trend is in no way debasing. The true evolutionary epic, retold as poetry, is as intrinsically ennobling as any religious epic. Material reality discovered by science already possesses more content and grandeur than all religious cosmologies combined. The continuity of the human line has been traced through a period of deep history a thousand times as old as that conceived by the Western religions. Its study has brought new revelations of great moral importance. It has made us realize that *Homo sapiens* is far more than an assortment of tribes and races. We are a single gene pool from which individuals are drawn in each generation and into which they are dissolved the next generation, forever united as a species by heritage and a common future. Such are the conceptions, based on fact, from which new intimations of immortality can be drawn and a new mythos evolved.

Which world view prevails, religious transcendentalism or scientific empiricism, will make a great difference in the way humanity claims the future. While the matter is under advisement, an accommodation can be reached if the following overriding facts are realized. Ethics and religion are still too complex for present-day science to explain in depth. They are, however, far more a product of autonomous evolution than has hitherto been conceded by most theologians. Science faces in ethics and religion its most interesting and possibly most humbling challenge, while religion must somehow find the way to incorporate the discoveries of science in order to retain credibility. Religion will possess strength to the extent that it codifies and puts into enduring, poetic form the highest values of humanity consistent with empirical knowledge. That is the only way to provide compelling moral leadership. Blind faith, no matter how passionately expressed, will not suffice. Science, for its part, will test relentlessly every assumption about the human condition and in time uncover the bedrock of moral and religious sentiments.

The eventual result of the competition between the two world views, I believe, will be the secularization of the human epic and of religion itself. However the process plays out, it demands open discussion and unwavering intellectual rigor in an atmosphere of mutual respect.

QUESTIONING THE TEXT

1. Wilson's essay rests on a binary opposition that might be summed up as follows: either transcendentalists are correct or empiricists are correct. The choice, he says, "makes all the difference in the way we view ourselves as a species" (paragraph 1). Binaries like this one can often clarify thinking—but they can also skew perspective or hide from view other possibilities. What counterexamples might you offer to challenge Wilson's assumption that these two viewpoints are the *only* two available? Work with one or two classmates to answer this question and bring your counterexamples to class for discussion. In the discussion, be sure to consider whether there is any possibility that both viewpoints might in some way(s) be correct.

2. In discussing empiricism, Wilson says that the crux of this view is its "emphasis on objective knowledge" (paragraph 8). Read carefully through Wilson's essay with this quotation in mind, and then try your hand at creating a definition of "objective knowledge" that Wilson might endorse. Then, working with another classmate, write a competing definition of this term.

MAKING CONNECTIONS

3. In "Enemies of Promise" (p. 237), J. Michael Bishop worries that growing hostility to science is a dangerous phenomenon. "To reject science," he argues, "is to deny the future" (paragraph 32). How might the critics of science that Bishop addresses react to Wilson's bold

suggestion that scientific empiricism might replace religious transcendentalism? Is society likely to embrace such a change soon? Why, or why not?

4. Wilson mentions Martin Luther King Jr. in his essay, associating King's "righteous sword" with the opening sentence of the Declaration of Independence and the transcendentalist position on morality and ethics. How might King (p. 142) respond to Wilson's preference for the empiricist view?

5. Working with a classmate, look through the readings in Chapter 4, Moralities. Which writers fit most neatly into Wilson's empiricist category? Which into his transcendentalist category? How might some of the writers challenge or even defy these two categories?

JOINING THE CONVERSATION

6. Which of Wilson's categories most nearly captures your own views on the basis of morality? Spend some time describing your views on this issue and giving examples to illustrate those views. Then use what you have written to prepare a journal entry in which you explore where your views on transcendentalist and/or empiricist understandings of morality have come from. What influences in your life have helped to mold and shape your views on morality? Which influences seem most important, and why?

7. Wilson defines ethics as "conduct favored consistently enough throughout a society to be expressed as a code of principles" (paragraph 7). Using evidence drawn from Wilson's essay, other essays from Chapter 4, and your own experience, write a list of such principles. Bring your list to class, and be prepared to explain, illustrate, and defend the principles you have chosen.

OTHER READINGS

Aveni, Anthony. "Time's Empire." *Wilson Quarterly* Summer 1998: 44–57. Traces the history of "time" as a concept and a technology.

Bolter, Jay David, and Richard Grusin. *Remediation: Understanding New Media.* Cambridge, MA: MIT P, 1999. Offers a new way to consider how new media borrow from and remake other media.

Bringsford, Selmer, "Chess Is Too Easy." *Technology Review* Mar.–Apr. 1998: 23–29. Explores the meaning of artificial intelligence.

Florman, Samuel C. *Blaming Technology: The Irrational Search for Scapegoats.* New York: St. Martin's, 1981. Argues for not turning away from technological change.

Haraway, Donna J. *Modest_Witness@Second_Millennium.FemaleMan©_Meets_OncoMouse*™. New York: Routledge, 1997. Explores contemporary technoscience and argues that we are all cyborgs.

Harding, Sandra. *Is Science Multicultural? Postcolonialisms, Feminisms, and Epistemologies.* Bloomington: Indiana UP, 1998. Explores what practitioners of European and American feminist and postcolonial science and technology studies can learn from each other.

Johnson, George. *Fire in the Mind: Science, Faith, and the Search for Order.* New York: Knopf, 1995. Focuses on Los Alamos to explore the human drive for order as expressed in different cultural traditions.

Stoll, Clifford. *Silicon Snake Oil: Second Thoughts on the Information Highway.* New York: Doubleday, 1995. Warns that the Internet may not live up to its vaunted potential.

Ullman, Ellen. *Close to the Machine: Technophilia and Its Discontents.* San Francisco: City Lights, 1997. Uses her own experiences as a long-time computer programmer and techno-buff to question whether networking can allow for the kind of intimacy humans long for.

ELECTRONIC RESOURCES

http://www.nasa.gov
Gateway to a complex site on NASA's diverse missions.

http://www.pbs.org/wgbh/aso
Companion site to the PBS series *A Science Odyssey: 100 Years of Discovery.*

http://www.wired.com/news
Wired magazine's up-to-date news on subjects related to computers and electronic technology.

Look carefully at the image on the preceding page, of three generations of a Chinese American family. What is the focal point of the image, the thing to which your eyes are first drawn? ■ What does the composition of the photograph suggest about the relationships among these generations? ■ Where is the photo taken, and what effect does that setting have on your "reading" of the image? ■ What does the photo suggest to you about the influences that families have on our identities? ■ In thinking about this question, you might also want to look at the photo on p. 584.

Identities: The One in Many/The Many in One

If the first woman God ever made was strong enough to turn the world upside down all alone, these women together ought to be able to turn it back. . . .
                              SOJOURNER TRUTH, *Ain't I a Woman?*

Growing up homosexual was to grow up normally but displaced; to experience romantic love, but with the wrong person; to entertain grand ambitions, but of the unacceptable sort; to seek a gradual self-awakening, but in secret, not in public.   ANDREW SULLIVAN, *What Are Homosexuals For?*

She obeyed him; she always did as she was told.
                       MAXINE HONG KINGSTON, *No Name Woman*

. . . if God did not want us to make gender-based generalizations, She would not have given us genders.
                                  DAVE BARRY, *Guys vs. Men*

I remember the very day that I became colored.
          ZORA NEALE HURSTON, *How It Feels to Be Colored Me*

Of the students who drop my class after the first meeting, there may be some who find the idea of a blind professor ludicrous, aggravating, or frightening. But I will never know.   GEORGINA KLEEGE, *Call It Blindness*

I suggest that we relax and luxuriate in our linguistic richness and our traditional tolerance of language differences.
                       ROBERT D. KING, *Should English Be the Law?*

Just as rock-and-roll foreshadowed many of the changes in gender and race relations that followed in the 1960s, country music today—with its suburban, middle-aged themes of family and renewal—may be the clearest reflection of many of the anxieties and aspirations that have just begun to bubble to the surface in American political life.   BRUCE FEILER, *Gone Country*

"For us, every day is a thanksgiving day, a prayer in the cycle of life. . . . But for you whites, every day is a slogan."   ALEX SHOUMATOFF, *The Navajo Way*

A MUD can become a context for discovering who one is and wishes to be. In this way, the games are laboratories for the construction of identity.

SHERRY TURKLE, *Who Am We?*

I guess being colored doesn't make me not like
the same things other folks like who are other races.
So will my page be colored that I write?
Being me, it will not be white.   LANGSTON HUGHES, *Theme for English B*

Introduction

"AND WHO ARE YOU?" a talkative snail asks Alice, the heroine of *Alice in Wonderland*, who replies, "I—I hardly know, sir, just at present—at least I know who I was when I got up this morning, but I think I must have been changed several times since then." Little wonder that Marshall McLuhan concludes his *The Medium Is the Massage* with this exchange, since in that book he argues that "electronic technology . . . is forcing us to reconsider and reevaluate practically every thought, every action, and every institution formerly taken for granted. Everything is changing—you, your family, your neighborhood, your education, your job, your government, your relation to 'the others.' And they're changing dramatically" (p. 8). Most of all, McLuhan insists, our ideas about who we are—our very identities—are changing.

What may be surprising to you is that McLuhan wrote those words in 1967 (or perhaps earlier since the book was published that year), over three decades before you take them up in this text. And those thirty years have seen many of McLuhan's claims borne out, particularly in the threat of electronic surveillance and a concomitant loss of privacy. Would McLuhan be surprised by the kinds of "identity theft" taking place today—such as online trickery or in warring countries, where people evicted from their homes for political and religious reasons are often stripped of all papers and thus left with no official identity? We don't think so.

But have our very ideas of identity changed? Many believe that they have—or that they are doing so right now. The view of self as autonomous, coherent, and unifying, a view associated with both eighteenth-century rationalism and Romanticism, for example, has been challenged on many fronts. In place of this singular, solitary self (celebrated in dramatic and unforgettable terms in Walt Whitman's "Song of Myself" and many other works of literature), multiple alternatives have emerged: a socially constructed self that grows up through a series of negotiations with others and with the environment; a self fashioned by forces beyond the control of the individual; and, most recently, a "virtual" self or selves that may (or may not) coalesce into one individual. In turn, these theoretical debates have left many wondering just how identity *is* constituted.

The selections in this chapter all circle around questions of identity formation. Is it related primarily to a genetic base? To gender, sex, and sexuality? To nation-state and politics? To race and ethnicity? To language—or to any number of other crucially important sources of influence in individuals' lives, such as work, physical abilities, and so on? Looking back over our own lives, we can see ways in which our sense of identity has shifted over the decades; we can identify as well periods of tension in terms of identity, particularly during moments of great change or loss. Yet on most days, we'd probably respond to the question "Who are you?" not as Alice did but with the simple statement of our names. What's in a name? And what's in an identity? These are crucial questions as we enter the new millennium, questions that lead psychologist Sherry Turkle to ask "Who Am We?" (p. 442) and to posit a mass "identity crisis" at the turn of the century.

We believe you have already thought quite a lot about these issues. To add to that thinking, consider the following questions:

- What things in your surroundings do you most closely identify with—family, friends, church, team, some other group—and why?

- Can you recall a time when someone identified you in some way that seemed completely surprising or foreign to you? If so, describe that time.

- How would you define your identity? Where do your identifying characteristics or features come from? How many "selves" can you identify in yourself?

• • •

SOJOURNER TRUTH
Ain't I a Woman?

*S*OJOURNER *T*RUTH *(1797–1883) took her name from mystical visions that urged her, after her escape from slavery, to sojourn and speak the truth. Although she never learned to write on paper, the words of her speeches often wrote on her listeners' souls. The following speech, one of her most famous, was originally written down by Eliza-beth Cady Stanton, an early proponent of women's rights, and printed in* The His-tory of Woman Suffrage. *Truth delivered it at the Women's Rights Convention in Akron, Ohio, in 1851. On that occasion she spoke to an almost all-white audience, since African Americans were, ironically, not welcome at such events. In "Ain't I a Woman?" Truth claims her identity as a woman—and as equal to men. In doing so, she speaks not just for women but for many who are oppressed, combining her devotion to abolitionism and to women's suffrage. With vigor and humor, she argues for basic human rights as one feature of identity among "all God's children."*

This brief speech always reminds me of the power of the spoken word—and of the difference one voice can sometimes make. I love Truth's use of some of the colloqui-alisms I grew up with (like "out of kilter"), her familiar references to those in her audi-ence as "honey" and "children," and other aspects of her speaking style that help me feel as though she is right here in front of me talking. I chose this speech for these rea-sons and because Truth counters perfectly all those voices down through the ages that have dismissed people such as her as "just" women. To hear her rebuttal, and to get at some of this speech's rhythmic power, try reading it aloud. —A.L.

Well, children, where there is so much racket there must be something out of kilter. I think that 'twixt the negroes of the South and the women of the North, all talking about rights, the white men will be in a fix pretty soon. But what's all this here talking about?

That man over there says that women need to be helped into carriages, and lifted over ditches, and to have the best place everywhere. Nobody ever helps me into carriages, or over mud-puddles, or gives me any best place! And ain't I a woman? Look at me! Look at my arm! I have ploughed and planted, and gathered into barns, and no man could head me! And ain't I a woman? I could work as much and eat as much as a man—when I could get it—and bear the lash as well! And ain't I a woman? I have borne thirteen children, and seen them most all sold off to slavery, and when I cried out with my mother's grief, none but Jesus heard me! And ain't I a woman?

Then they talk about this thing in the head; what's this they call it? [In-tellect, someone whispers.] That's it, honey. What's that got to do with women's rights or negro's rights? If my cup won't hold but a pint, and yours holds a quart, wouldn't you be mean not to let me have my little half-measure full?

Then that little man in black there, he says women can't have as much rights as men, 'cause Christ wasn't a woman! Where did your Christ come from? Where did your Christ come from? From God and a woman! Man had nothing to do with Him.

If the first woman God ever made was strong enough to turn the world   5
upside down all alone, these women together ought to be able to turn it back, and get it right side up again! And now they is asking to do it, the men better let them.

Obliged to you for hearing me, and now old Sojourner ain't got nothing more to say.

QUESTIONING THE TEXT

1. Truth punctuates her speech with a rhetorical question—"And ain't I a woman?" What effect does the repetition of this question have on you as a reader? What answer does Truth invoke?

2. A.L.'s introduction reveals that she is a fan of Sojourner Truth. What criticisms *could* A.L. have leveled at Truth's argument?

MAKING CONNECTIONS

3. How might Sojourner Truth respond to Dave Barry's "Guys vs. Men" (p. 372)? Read that selection. Then, using Truth's humorous and conversational tone, write a brief speech in which she responds to "Guys vs. Men."

4. Several other selections in this chapter deal with the ways in which part of one's identity brings forth discrimination, bias, oppression. Choose one of these other selections and read it carefully after rereading Truth's speech. What arguments can you find in common between Truth and the other author you chose? What differences in evidence and in argumentative strategy do you detect?

JOINING THE CONVERSATION

5. List as many reasons as you can to support the belief that men and women should or should not have the same rights and responsibilities. Explain from your own experiences *why* you believe as you do.

6. Try your hand at writing your own manifesto of identity, using a repeated question (such as "And ain't I a _____?") to organize your brief piece of writing.

ANDREW SULLIVAN
What Are Homosexuals For?

*A*NDREW *S*ULLIVAN's *argument in favor of "normalizing" homosexual identity in America—understood as legalizing same-sex marriage and permitting gay men and women to serve in the military—speaks quietly and eloquently to the entire political spectrum. In* Virtually Normal *(1995), Sullivan (b. 1963), former editor of the political journal the* New Republic *and homosexual himself, systematically examines arguments on all sides of a thorny issue to hammer out a compromise "politics of homosexuality." He places himself squarely in the middle, clearing ground for tolerance by seeming tolerant himself, acknowledging, for example, that conservative critics of homosexuality may be expressing "sincerely held moral beliefs." Yet he also bravely questions those who might be logical allies. About the radical activities of* ACT UP, *for example, Sullivan observes: "A politics which seeks only to show and not to persuade will only be as successful as its latest theatrical escapade, and will be as susceptible to the fashion of audiences as any other fad."*

Reviewed favorably in many periodicals, Virtually Normal *caused a minor ripple when it debuted, Sullivan himself playing the TV talk show circuit. But a book so sober and rational can change public opinion only one reader at a time. The more immediate accomplishment of* Virtually Normal *may have been to set a standard for civil argument at precisely the moment when America's public square had become a tough, bellicose place. This selection is from the epilogue of* Virtually Normal, *a personal part of Sullivan's book, and one that conveys the honesty and lucidity that make the entire work worth reading.* —J.R.

Reason has so many shapes we don't know what to seize hold of; experience has just as many. What we infer from the similarity of events is uncertain, because they are always dissimilar: there is no quality so universal here as difference.

—MICHEL DE MONTAIGNE

The discovery of one's homosexuality is for many people the same experience as acting upon it. For me, alas, this was not the case. Maybe, in some respects, this was intellectually salutary: I was able, from an early age, to distinguish, as my Church taught, the condition of homosexuality from its practice. But in life, nothing is as easily distinguished. Even disavowing homosexuality is a response to it; and the response slowly, subtly alters who you are. The sublimation of sexual longing can create a particular form of alienated person: a more ferocious perfectionist, a cranky individual, an extremely brittle emotionalist, an ideological fanatic. This may lead to some brilliant lives: witty, urbane, subtle, passionate. But it also leads to some devastating loneliness. The abandonment of intimacy and the rejection of one's emotional core are, I have come to believe, alloyed evils. All too often, they preserve the persona at the expense of the person.

I remember a man, a university figure, who knew everyone in a distant avuncular fashion. I suppose we all understood that somewhere he was a homosexual; he had few women friends, and no emotional or sexual life to speak of. He lived in a carefully constructed world of university gossip, intellectual argument, and intense, platonic relationships with proteges and students. He was immensely fat. One day, he told me, in his mid-forties, he woke up in a room at the Harvard Club in New York and couldn't move. He stayed there immobile for the morning and much of the afternoon. He realized at that moment that there was no honesty at the core of his life, and no love at its center. The recognition of this emptiness literally paralyzed him. He was the lucky one. He set about re-ordering his life; in his late middle age, he began to have adolescent affairs; he declared his sexuality loudly and somewhat crudely to anyone who could hear; he unloaded himself to his friends and loved ones. In one of those ultimately unintelligible tragedies, he died of a swift and deadly cancer three years later. But at his funeral, I couldn't help but reflect that he had at least tasted a few years of life. He had regained himself before he lost himself forever.

Others never experience such dreadful epiphanies. There was a time when I felt that the closeted homosexual was a useful social creature, and possibly happier than those immersed in what sometimes seems like a merciless and shallow subculture. But the etiolation of the heart which this self-abnegation requires is enormous. For many of us, a shared love is elusive anyway, a goal we rarely achieve and, when we do, find extremely hard to maintain. But to make the lack of such an achievement a condition of one's existence is to remove from a human life much that might propel it forward. Which is why I cannot forget the image of that man in a bed. He could not move. For him, there was no forward, no future to move into.

This is how the world can seem to many adolescent homosexuals; and I was no exception. Heterosexual marriage is perceived as the primary emotional goal for your peers; and yet you know this cannot be your fate. It terrifies and alarms you. While its form comforts, its content appalls. It requires a systematic dishonesty; and this dishonesty either is programmed into your soul and so warps your integrity, or is rejected in favor of—what? You scan your mind for an alternative. You dream grandiose dreams, construct a fantasy of a future, pour your energies into some massive distraction, pursue a consuming career to cover up the lie at the center of your existence. You are caught between escape and the constant daily wrench of self-denial. It is a vise from which many teenagers and young adults never emerge.

I was lucky. I found an escape, an escape into a world of ideas, into a   5
career, and into another country. America provided an excuse for a new beginning, as it had done for millions of immigrants before me. I often wonder,
had I stayed in the place which reminded me so much of where I was from,
whether I would have found a way to construct a measurably honest life. I
don't know. But I do know that in this as well I was not alone. So many homosexuals find it essential to move away from where they are before they can
regain themselves. Go to any major city and you'll find thousands of exiles
from the heartland, making long-distance phone calls which echo with the
same euphemisms of adolescence, the same awkward pauses, the same banal
banter. These city limits are the equivalent of the adolescent's bedroom door:
a barrier where two lives can be maintained with some hope of success and a
minimal amount of mutual embarrassment.

It was in the safety of this exile that I could come home. I remember
my first kiss with another man, the first embrace, the first love affair. Many
metaphors have been used to describe this delayed homecoming—I was
twenty-three—but to me, it was like being in a black-and-white movie that
suddenly converted to color. The richness of experience seemed possible for
the first time; the abstractions of dogma, of morality, of society, dissolved into
the sheer, mysterious pleasure of being human. Perhaps this is a homosexual
privilege: for many heterosexuals, the pleasures of intimacy and sexuality are
stumbled upon gradually when young; for many homosexuals, the entire experience can come at once, when an adult, eclipsing everything, humiliating
the developed person's sense of equilibrium, infantilizing and liberating at the
same time. Sometimes I wonder whether some homosexuals' addiction to
constant romance, to the thrill of the new lover, to the revelation of a new
and obliviating desire, is in fact an attempt to relive this experience, again
and again.

What followed over the years was not without its stupidity, excess, and
hurt. But it was far realler than anything I had experienced before. I was
never really "in the closet" in this sense. Until my early twenties, I was essentially heterosexual in public disclosure and emotionless in private life. Within
a year, I was both privately and publicly someone who attempted little disguise of his emotional orientation. In this, I was convinced I was entering finally into normal life. I was the equal of heterosexuals, deserving of exactly
the same respect, attempting to construct in the necessarily contrived world of
the gay subculture the mirror image of the happy heterosexuality I imagined
around me. Like many in my generation, I flattered myself that this was a
first: a form of pioneering equality, an insistence on one's interchangeability
with the dominant culture, on one's radical similarity with the heterosexual
majority.

And in a fundamental sense, as I have tried to explain, this was true.
The homosexual's emotional longings, his development, his dreams are
human phenomena. They are, I think, instantly recognizable to any hetero-

sexual, in their form if not their content. The humanity of homosexuals is clear everywhere. Perhaps nothing has illustrated this more clearly than the AIDS epidemic. Gay people have to confront grief and shock and mortality like anybody else. They die like all people die.

Except, of course, that they don't. Homosexuals in contemporary America tend to die young; they sometimes die estranged from their families; they die among friends who have become their new families; they die surrounded by young death, and by the arch symbols of cultural otherness. Growing up homosexual was to grow up normally but displaced; to experience romantic love, but with the wrong person; to entertain grand ambitions, but of the unacceptable sort; to seek a gradual self-awakening, but in secret, not in public.

But to live as an adult homosexual is to experience something else 10 again. By the simple fact of one's increasing cultural separation, the human personality begins to develop differently. As an adolescent and child, you are surrounded by the majority culture: so your concerns and habits and thoughts become embedded in the familiar and communicable. But slowly, and gradually, in adulthood, your friends and acquaintances become increasingly gay or lesbian. Lesbian women can find themselves slowly distanced from the company of men; gay men can find themselves slowly disentangled from women. One day, I glanced at my log of telephone calls: the ratio of men to women, once roughly even, had become six-to-one male. The women I knew and cared about had dwindled to a small but intimate group of confidantes and friends, women who were able to share my homosexual life and understand it. The straight men, too, had fallen in number. And both these groups tended to come from people I had met *before* I had fully developed an openly gay life.

These trends reinforced each other. Of course, like most gay people, I worked in a largely heterosexual environment and still maintained close links with my heterosexual family. But the environmental incentives upon me were clearly in another direction. I naturally gravitated toward people who were similar. Especially in your twenties, when romantic entanglement assumes a dominant role in life, you naturally socialize with prospective partners. Before you know where you are, certain patterns develop. Familiarity breeds familiarity; and, by no conscious process, your inculturation is subtly and powerfully different than that of your heterosexual peers.

In the world of emotional and sexual life, there were no clear patterns to follow: homosexual culture offered a gamut of possibilities, from anonymous sex to bourgeois coupling. But its ease with sexual activity, its male facility with sexual candor, its surprising lack of formal, moral stricture—all these made my life subtly and slowly more different than my straight male (let alone my straight female) peers'. In my late twenties, the difference became particularly acute. My heterosexual male friends became married; soon, my straight peers were having children. Weddings, babies, career couples, engagements: the calendar began to become crowded with the clatter of heterosexual bonding. And yet in my gay life, something somewhat different was occurring.

I remember vividly one Labor Day weekend. I had two engagements to attend. The first was a gay friend's thirtieth birthday party. It was held in the Deep South, in his family's seaside home. He had told his family he was gay the previous winter; he had told them he had AIDS that Memorial Day. His best friends had come to meet the family for the first time—two straight women, his boyfriend, his ex-boyfriend, and me. That year, we had all been through the trauma of his illness, and he was visibly thinner now than he had been even a month before. Although we attended to the typical family functions—dinners, beach trips, photo ops—there was a strained air of irony and sadness about the place. How could we explain what it was like to live in one's twenties and thirties with such a short horizon, to face mortality and sickness and death, to attend funerals when others were attending weddings? And yet, somehow the communication was possible. He was their son, after all. And after they had acclimatized to our mutual affection, and humor, and occasional diffidence, there was something of an understanding. His father took me aside toward the end of the trip to thank me for taking care of his son. I found it hard to speak any words of reply.

I flew directly from that event to another family gathering of another thirty-year-old friend of mine. This one was heterosexual; and he and his fiancee were getting married surrounded by a bevy of beaming acquaintances and family. In the Jewish ceremony, there was an unspoken, comforting rhythm of rebirth and life. The event was not untouched by tragedy: my friend's father had died earlier that year. But the wedding was almost an instinctive response to that sadness, a reaffirmation that the cycles and structures that had made sense of most of the lives there would be making sense of another two in the years ahead. I did not begrudge it at all; it is hard not to be moved by the sight of a new life beginning. But I could not help also feeling deeply, powerfully estranged.

AIDS has intensified a difference that I think is inherent between homo-   15 sexual and heterosexual adults. The latter group is committed to the procreation of a new generation. The former simply isn't. Yes, there are major qualifications to this—gay men and lesbians are often biological fathers and mothers—but no two lesbians and no two homosexual men can be parents in the way that a heterosexual man and a heterosexual woman with a biological son or daughter can be. And yes, many heterosexuals neither marry nor have children and many have adopted children. But in general, the difference holds. The timeless, necessary, procreative unity of a man and a woman is inherently denied homosexuals; and the way in which fatherhood transforms heterosexual men, and motherhood transforms heterosexual women, and parenthood transforms their relationship, is far less common among homosexuals than among heterosexuals.

AIDS has only added a bitter twist to this state of affairs. My straight peers in their early thirties are engaged in the business of births; I am largely engaged in the business of deaths. Both experiences alter people profoundly. The very patterns of life of mothers and fathers with young children are vastly different than those who have none; and the perspectives of those who have stared death in the face in their twenties are bound to be different than those who have stared into cribs. Last year, I saw my first nephew come into the world, the first new life in my life to whom I felt physically, emotionally connected. I wondered which was the deeper feeling: the sense of excruciating pain seeing a member of my acquired family die, or the excruciating joy of seeing a member of my given family born. I am at a loss to decide; but I am not at a loss to know that they are different experiences: equally human, but radically different.

In a society more and more aware of its manifold cultures and subcultures, we have been educated to be familiar and comfortable with what has been called "diversity": the diversity of perspective, culture, meaning. And this diversity is usually associated with what are described as cultural constructs: race, gender, sexuality, and so on. But as the obsession with diversity intensifies, the possibility of real difference alarms and terrifies all the more. The notion of collective characteristics—of attributes more associated with blacks than with whites, with Asians than with Latinos, with gay men than with straight men, with men than with women—has become anathema. They are marginalized as "stereotypes." The acceptance of diversity has come to mean the acceptance of the essential sameness of all types of people, and the danger of generalizing among them at all. In fact, it has become virtually a definition of "racist" to make any substantive generalizations about a particular ethnicity, and a definition of "homophobic" to make any generalizations about homosexuals.

What follows, then, is likely to be understood as "homophobic." But I think it's true that certain necessary features of homosexual life lead to certain unavoidable features of homosexual character. This is not to say that they define any random homosexual: they do not. As with any group or way of life, there are many, many exceptions. Nor is it to say that they define the homosexual life: it should be clear by now that I believe the needs and feelings of homosexual children and adolescents are largely interchangeable with those of their heterosexual peers. But there are certain generalizations that can be made about adult homosexuals and lesbians that have the ring of truth.

Of course, in a culture where homosexuals remain hidden and wrapped in self-contempt, in which their emotional development is often stunted and late, in which the closet protects all sorts of self-destructive behavior that a more open society would not, it is still very hard to tell what is inherent in a homosexual life that makes it different, and what is simply imposed upon it. Nevertheless, it seems to me that even in the most tolerant societies, some of the differences that I have just described would inhere.

The experience of growing up profoundly different in emotional and   20
psychological makeup inevitably alters a person's self-perception, tends to
make him or her more wary and distant, more attuned to appearance and its
foibles, more self-conscious and perhaps more reflective. The presence of homosexuals in the arts, in literature, in architecture, in design, in fashion could
be understood, as some have, as a simple response to oppression. Homosexuals have created safe professions within which to hide and protect each other.
But why these professions? Maybe it's also that these are professions of appearance. Many homosexual children, feeling distant from their peers, become experts at trying to figure out how to disguise their inner feelings, to
"pass." They notice the signs and signals of social interaction, because they do
not come instinctively. They develop skills early on that help them notice the
inflections of a voice, the quirks of a particular movement, and the ways in
which meaning can be conveyed in code. They have an ear for irony and for
double meanings. Sometimes, by virtue of having to suppress their natural
emotions, they find formal outlets to express themselves: music, theater, art.
And so their lives become set on a trajectory which reinforces these trends.

As a child, I remember, as I suppressed the natural emotions of an adolescent, how I naturally turned in on myself—writing, painting, and participating in amateur drama. Or I devised fantasies of future exploits—war
leader, parliamentarian, famous actor—that could absorb those emotions that
were being diverted from meeting other boys and developing natural emotional relationships with them. And I developed mannerisms, small ways in
which I could express myself, tiny revolts of personal space—a speech affec-
tation, a ridiculous piece of clothing—that were, in retrospect, attempts to
communicate something in code which could not be communicated in language. In this homosexual archness there was, of course, much pain. And it
came as no surprise that once I had become more open about my homosexuality, these mannerisms declined. Once I found the strength to be myself, I
had no need to act myself. So my clothes became progressively more regular
and slovenly; I lost interest in drama; my writing moved from fiction to journalism; my speech actually became less affected.

This, of course, is not a universal homosexual experience. Many homosexuals never become more open, and the skills required to survive the closet
remain skills by which to earn a living. And many homosexuals, even once
they no longer need those skills, retain them. My point is simply that the universal experience of self-conscious difference in childhood and adolescence—
common, but not exclusive, to homosexuals—develops identifiable skills.
They are the skills of mimesis; and one of the goods that homosexuals bring
to society is undoubtedly a more highly developed sense of form, of style.
Even in the most open of societies, I think, this will continue to be the case.
It is not something genetically homosexual; it is something environmentally
homosexual. And it begins young.

Closely connected to this is a sense of irony. Like Jews who have developed ways to resist, subvert, and adopt a majority culture, so homosexuals have found themselves ironizing their difference. Because, in many cases, they have survived acute periods of emotion, they are more likely to appreciate — even willfully celebrate — its more overwrought and melodramatic depictions. They have learned to see the funny side of etiolation. This, perhaps, is the true origin of camp. It is the ability to see agony and enjoy its form while ignoring its content, the ability to watch emotional trauma and not see its essence but its appearance. It is the aestheticization of pain.

This role in the aestheticization of the culture is perhaps enhanced by another unavoidable fact about most homosexuals and lesbians: their childlessness. This generates two related qualities: the relative freedom to procreate in a broader, structural sense, and to experiment with human relationships that can be instructive for the society as a whole.

The lack of children is something some homosexuals regard as a curse;   25 and it is the thing which many heterosexuals most pity (and some envy) about their homosexual acquaintances. But it is also an opportunity. Childless men and women have many things to offer a society. They can transfer their absent parental instincts into broader parental roles: they can be extraordinary teachers and mentors, nurses and doctors, priests, rabbis, and nuns; they can throw themselves into charity work, helping the needy and the lonely; they can care for the young who have been abandoned by others, through adoption. Or they can use all their spare time to forge an excellence in their field of work that is sometimes unavailable to the harried mother or burdened father. They can stay late in the office, be the most loyal staffer in an election campaign, work round the clock in a journalistic production, be the lawyer most able and willing to meet the emerging deadline.

One of their critical roles in society has also often been in the military. Here is an institution which requires dedication beyond the calling to the biological, nuclear family, that needs people prepared to give all their time to the common endeavor, that requires men and women able to subsume their personal needs into the formal demands of military discipline. Of all institutions in our society, the military is perhaps the most naturally homosexual, which is part of the reason, of course, why it is so hostile to their visible presence. The displacement of family affection onto a broader community also makes the homosexual an ideal person to devote him- or herself to a social institution: the university, the school, the little league, the Boy Scouts, the church, the sports team. Scratch most of these institutions and you'll find a homosexual or two sustaining many of its vital functions.

But the homosexual's contribution can be more than nourishing the society's aesthetic and institutional life. It has become a truism that in the field of emotional development, homosexuals have much to learn from the heterosexual culture. The values of commitment, of monogamy, of marriage, of stability are all posited as models for homosexual existence. And, indeed, of course, they are. Without an architectonic institution like that of marriage, it is difficult to create the conditions for nurturing such virtues, but that doesn't belie their importance.

It is also true, however, that homosexual relationships, even in their current, somewhat eclectic form, may contain features that could nourish the broader society as well. Precisely because there is no institutional model, gay relationships are often sustained more powerfully by genuine commitment. The mutual nurturing and sexual expressiveness of many lesbian relationships, the solidity and space of many adult gay male relationships, are qualities sometimes lacking in more rote, heterosexual couplings. Same-sex unions often incorporate the virtues of friendship more effectively than traditional marriages; and at times, among gay male relationships, the openness of the contract makes it more likely to survive than many heterosexual bonds. Some of this is unavailable to the male-female union: there is more likely to be greater understanding of the need for extramarital outlets between two men than between a man and a woman; and again, the lack of children gives gay couples greater freedom. Their failures entail fewer consequences for others. But something of the gay relationship's necessary honesty, its flexibility, and its equality could undoubtedly help strengthen and inform many heterosexual bonds.

In my own sometimes comic, sometimes passionate attempts to construct relationships, I learned something of the foibles of a simple heterosexual model. I saw how the network of gay friendships was often as good an emotional nourishment as a single relationship, that sexual candor was not always the same as sexual license, that the kind of supportive community that bolsters many gay relationships is something many isolated straight marriages could benefit from. I also learned how the subcultural fact of gay life rendered it remarkably democratic; in gay bars, there was far less socioeconomic stratification than in heterosexual bars. The shared experience of same-sex desire cut through class and race; it provided a humbling experience, which allowed many of us to risk our hearts and our friendships with people we otherwise might never have met. It loosened us up, and gave us a keener sense, perhaps, that people were often difficult to understand, let alone judge, from appearances. My heterosexual peers, through no fault of their own, were often denied these experiences. But they might gain from understanding them a little better, and not simply from a position of condescension.

As I've just argued, I believe strongly that marriage should be made 30 available to everyone, in a politics of strict public neutrality. But within this model, there is plenty of scope for cultural difference. There is something baleful about the attempt of some gay conservatives to educate homosexuals and lesbians into an uncritical acceptance of a stifling model of heterosexual normality. The truth is, homosexuals are not entirely normal; and to flatten their varied and complicated lives into a single, moralistic model is to miss what is essential and exhilarating about their otherness.

This need not mean, as some have historically claimed, that homosexuals have no stake in the sustenance of a society, but rather that their role is somewhat different; they may be involved in procreation in a less literal sense: in a society's cultural regeneration, its entrepreneurial or intellectual rejuvenation, its religious ministry, or its professional education. Unencumbered by children, they may be able to press the limits of the culture or the business infrastructure, or the boundaries of intellectual life, in a way that heterosexuals, by dint of a different type of calling, cannot. Of course, many heterosexuals perform similar roles; and many homosexuals prefer domesticity to public performance; but the inevitable way of life of the homosexual provides an opportunity that many intuitively seem to grasp and understand.

Or perhaps their role is to have no role at all. Perhaps it is the experience of rebellion that prompts homosexual culture to be peculiarly resistant to attempts to guide it to be useful or instructive or productive. Go to any march for gay rights and you will see the impossibility of organizing it into a coherent lobby: such attempts are always undermined by irony, or exhibitionism, or irresponsibility. It is as if homosexuals have learned something about life that makes them immune to the puritanical and flattening demands of modern politics. It is as if they have learned that life is fickle; that there are parts of it that cannot be understood, let alone solved; that some things lead nowhere and mean nothing; that the ultimate exercise of freedom is not a programmatic journey but a spontaneous one. Perhaps it requires seeing one's life as the end of a biological chain, or seeing one's deepest emotions as the object of detestation, that provides this insight. But the seeds of homosexual wisdom are the seeds of human wisdom. They contain the truth that order is in fact a euphemism for disorder; that problems are often more sanely enjoyed than solved; that there is reason in mystery; that there is beauty in the wild flowers that grow randomly among our wheat.

QUESTIONING THE TEXT

1. Sullivan begins by discussing how the cultural dominance of heterosexual marriage shapes the identity of young homosexuals. Consider the power of this social institution, whatever one's sexual orientation or expectations in life. What does it mean when our culture defines "normal" through the prism of heterosexual marriage? If you keep a reading log, answer this question there.

2. Sullivan presents the rituals and routines of heterosexual life through the eyes of a gay male who feels like an outsider. Describe an experience you have had as an outsider, looking in. Is this the experience of women peering in at male institutions? Of men watching women socializing? Of poor looking at rich? Of the physically challenged considering the fully able? Of conservative students in liberal classrooms?

3. J.R.'s introduction to Sullivan's "What Are Homosexuals For?" praises the piece as an example of "civil argument." Do you find the essay as balanced and reasonable as the introduction promises? Use examples from the essay to support your answer.

MAKING CONNECTIONS

4. Maxine Hong Kingston's "No Name Woman" (p. 361) describes a woman whose life is destroyed because society cannot accept her out-of-wedlock pregnancy. Homosexuals, too, Sullivan argues, are culturally marginalized for their sexual behavior. In a group, discuss both the constraints society puts on sexuality and the reasons for them. Are there legitimate differences, for example, among *constraints, taboos,* and *prejudices?* Then write a short essay about one way society manages sexual behavior in your community—religious, social, or political.

5. Read Dave Barry's "Guys vs. Men" (p. 372) from the point of view that Sullivan offers. Does Barry's world of "guys" have room for homosexuals? Why, or why not? Write a paragraph or two on the subject.

JOINING THE CONVERSATION

6. Not many years ago, a common journal or essay assignment in college was to write about a first date or first love. With the selection by Sullivan in mind, write an essay exploring the appropriateness of such an assignment.

7. Sullivan argues that the way homosexuals are raised and the defenses they use to survive make them "more wary and distant, more attuned to appearance and its foibles, more self-conscious and perhaps more reflective" (paragraph 20). He also admits that such assertions come dangerously close to homophobic generalizations. Can people talk about the behavior of particular groups—whether gay men, lesbians, heterosexual women, or even "guys"—without engaging in harmful stereotypes? Explore this question by writing a dialogue between two people on different sides of this issue.

MAXINE HONG KINGSTON
No Name Woman

Maxine Hong Kingston was born (in 1940) and raised in California, but her roots grow deep in Chinese soil and culture, as is evidenced in two highly acclaimed books, The Woman Warrior *(1970) and* China Men *(1980). In these and other works, Kingston explores the effects of Chinese legend and custom on her own identity as a woman and as a Chinese American. In "No Name Woman," an excerpt from* The Woman Warrior, *Kingston examines one identifying feature of most women—their ability to bear children—and she explores the consequences of that identifying mark.*

Many readers of this text may be able to identify a shadowy relative in their own past—an absent parent, a grandparent much discussed but seldom seen, a mysterious uncle or aunt or cousin—about whom older family members whispered. Few of us are likely to have written so powerfully about such a figure, however, or to have evoked in such a short space what it would be like to be "No Name Woman." I chose this selection precisely for its power. It has stayed vividly with me ever since I first read it—so vividly, in fact, that "No Name Woman" seems like someone I know personally. To me, she tells not only her own story but the story of all those whose lives are destroyed by narrow and rigid beliefs about what someone's identity must *be.* —A.L.

"You must not tell anyone," my mother said, "what I am about to tell you. In China your father had a sister who killed herself. She jumped into the family well. We say that your father has all brothers because it is as if she had never been born.

"In 1924 just a few days after our village celebrated seventeen hurry-up weddings—to make sure that every young man who went 'out on the road' would responsibly come home—your father and his brothers and your grandfather and his brothers and your aunt's new husband sailed for America, the Gold Mountain. It was your grandfather's last trip. Those lucky enough to get contracts waved good-bye from the decks. They fed and guarded the stowaways and helped them off in Cuba, New York, Bali, Hawaii. 'We'll meet in California next year,' they said. All of them sent money home.

"I remember looking at your aunt one day when she and I were dressing; I had not noticed before that she had such a protruding melon of a stomach. But I did not think, 'She's pregnant,' until she began to look like other pregnant women, her shirt pulling and the white tops of her black pants showing. She could not have been pregnant, you see, because her husband had been gone for years. No one said anything. We did not discuss it. In early summer she was ready to have the child, long after the time when it could have been possible.

"The village had also been counting. On the night the baby was to be born the villagers raided our house. Some were crying. Like a great saw, teeth strung with lights, files of people walked zigzag across our land, tearing the rice. Their lanterns doubled in the disturbed black water, which drained away through the broken bunds. As the villagers closed in, we could see that some of them, probably men and women we knew well, wore white masks. The people with long hair hung it over their faces. Women with short hair made it stand up on end. Some had tied white bands around their foreheads, arms, and legs.

"At first they threw mud and rocks at the house. Then they threw eggs   5 and began slaughtering our stock. We could hear the animals scream their deaths — the roosters, the pigs, a last great roar from the ox. Familiar wild heads flared in our night windows; the villagers encircled us. Some of the faces stopped to peer at us, their eyes rushing like searchlights. The hands flattened against the panes, framed heads, and left red prints.

"The villagers broke in the front and the back doors at the same time, even though we had not locked the doors against them. Their knives dripped with the blood of our animals. They smeared blood on the doors and walls. One woman swung a chicken, whose throat she had slit, splattering blood in red arcs about her. We stood together in the middle of our house, in the family hall with the pictures and tables of the ancestors around us, and looked straight ahead.

"At that time the house had only two wings. When the men came back, we would build two more to enclose our courtyard and a third one to begin a second courtyard. The villagers pushed through both wings, even your grandparents' rooms, to find your aunt's, which was also mine until the men returned. From this room a new wing for one of the younger families would grow. They ripped up her clothes and shoes and broke her combs, grinding them underfoot. They tore her work from the loom. They scattered the cooking fire and rolled the new weaving in it. We could hear them in the kitchen breaking our bowls and banging the pots. They overturned the great waist-high earthenware jugs; duck eggs, pickled fruits, vegetables burst out and mixed in acrid torrents. The old woman from the next field swept a broom through the air and loosed the spirits-of-the-broom over our heads. 'Pig.' 'Ghost.' 'Pig,' they sobbed and scolded while they ruined our house.

"When they left, they took sugar and oranges to bless themselves. They cut pieces from the dead animals. Some of them took bowls that were not broken and clothes that were not torn. Afterward we swept up the rice and sewed it back up into sacks. But the smells from the spilled preserves lasted. Your aunt gave birth in the pigsty that night. The next morning when I went up for the water, I found her and the baby plugging up the family well.

"Don't let your father know that I told you. He denies her. Now that you have started to menstruate, what happened to her could happen to you.

Don't humiliate us. You wouldn't like to be forgotten as if you had never been born. The villagers are watchful."

Whenever she had to warn us about life, my mother told stories that ran 10 like this one, a story to grow up on. She tested our strength to establish realities. Those in the emigrant generations who could not reassert brute survival died young and far from home. Those of us in the first American generations have had to figure out how the invisible world the emigrants built around our childhoods fit in solid America.

The emigrants confused the gods by diverting their curses, misleading them with crooked streets and false names. They must try to confuse their offspring as well, who, I suppose, threaten them in similar ways—always trying to get things straight, always trying to name the unspeakable. The Chinese I know hide their names; sojourners take new names when their lives change and guard their real names with silence.

Chinese-Americans, when you try to understand what things in you are Chinese, how do you separate what is peculiar to childhood, to poverty, insanities, one family, your mother who marked your growing with stories, from what is Chinese? What is Chinese tradition and what is the movies?

If I want to learn what clothes my aunt wore, whether flashy or ordinary, I would have to begin, "Remember Father's drowned-in-the-well sister?" I cannot ask that. My mother has told me once and for all the useful parts. She will add nothing unless powered by Necessity, a riverbank that guides her life. She plants vegetable gardens rather than lawns; she carries the odd-shaped tomatoes home from the fields and eats food left for the gods.

Whenever we did frivolous things, we used up energy; we flew high kites. We children came up off the ground over the melting cones our parents brought home from work and the American movie on New Year's Day— *Oh, You Beautiful Doll* with Betty Grable one year, and *She Wore a Yellow Ribbon* with John Wayne another year. After the one carnival ride each, we paid in guilt; our tired father counted his change on the dark walk home.

Adultery is extravagance. Could people who hatch their own chicks and 15 eat the embryos and the heads for delicacies and boil the feet in vinegar for party food, leaving only the gravel, eating even the gizzard lining—could such people engender a prodigal aunt? To be a woman, to have a daughter in starvation time was a waste enough. My aunt could not have been the lone romantic who gave up everything for sex. Women in the old China did not choose. Some man had commanded her to lie with him and be his secret evil. I wonder whether he masked himself when he joined the raid on her family.

Perhaps she encountered him in the fields or on the mountain where the daughters-in-law collected fuel. Or perhaps he first noticed her in the marketplace. He was not a stranger because the village housed no strangers. She had to have dealings with him other than sex. Perhaps he worked an adjoining field, or he sold her the cloth for the dress she sewed and wore. His demand must have surprised, then terrified her. She obeyed him; she always did as she was told.

When the family found a young man in the next village to be her husband, she stood tractably beside the best rooster, his proxy, and promised before they met that she would be his forever. She was lucky that he was her age and she would be the first wife, an advantage secure now. The night she first saw him, he had sex with her. Then he left for America. She had almost forgotten what he looked like. When she tried to envision him, she only saw the black and white face in the group photograph the men had taken before leaving.

The other man was not, after all, much different from her husband. They both gave orders: she followed. "If you tell your family, I'll beat you. I'll kill you. Be here again next week." No one talked sex, ever. And she might have separated the rapes from the rest of living if only she did not have to buy her oil from him or gather wood in the same forest. I want her fear to have lasted just as long as rape lasted so that the fear could have been contained. No drawn-out fear. But women at sex hazarded birth and hence lifetimes. The fear did not stop but permeated everywhere. She told the man, "I think I'm pregnant." He organized the raid against her.

On nights when my mother and father talked about their life back home, sometimes they mentioned an "outcast table" whose business they still seemed to be settling, their voices tight. In a commensal tradition, where food is precious, the powerful older people made wrongdoers eat alone. Instead of letting them start separate new lives like the Japanese, who could become samurais and geishas, the Chinese family, faces averted but eyes glowering sideways, hung on to the offenders and fed them leftovers. My aunt must have lived in the same house as my parents and eaten at an outcast table. My mother spoke about the raid as if she had seen it, when she and my aunt, a daughter-in-law to a different household, should not have been living together at all. Daughters-in-law lived with their husbands' parents, not their own; a synonym for marriage in Chinese is "taking a daughter-in-law." Her husband's parents could have sold her, mortgaged her, stoned her. But they had sent her back to her own mother and father, a mysterious act hinting at disgraces not told me. Perhaps they had thrown her out to deflect the avengers.

She was the only daughter; her four brothers went with her father, husband, and uncles "out on the road" and for some years became western men. When the goods were divided among the family, three of the brothers took land, and the youngest, my father, chose an education. After my grandparents gave their daughter away to her husband's family, they had dispensed all the adventure and all the property. They expected her alone to keep the traditional ways, which her brothers, now among the barbarians, could fumble without detection. The heavy, deep-rooted women were to maintain the past against the flood, safe for returning. But the rare urge west had fixed upon our family, and so my aunt crossed boundaries not delineated in space.

The work of preservation demands that the feelings playing about in one's guts not be turned into action. Just watch their passing like cherry blossoms. But perhaps my aunt, my forerunner, caught in a slow life, let dreams grow and fade and after some months or years went toward what persisted. Fear at the enormities of the forbidden kept her desires delicate, wire and bone. She looked at a man because she liked the way the hair was tucked behind his ears, or she liked the question-mark line of a long torso curving at the shoulder and straight at the hip. For warm eyes or a soft voice or a slow walk — that's all — a few hairs, a line, a brightness, a sound, a pace, she gave up family. She offered us up for a charm that vanished with tiredness, a pigtail that didn't toss when the wind died. Why, the wrong lighting could erase the dearest thing about him.

It could very well have been, however, that my aunt did not take subtle enjoyment of her friend, but, a wild woman, kept rollicking company. Imagining her free with sex doesn't fit, though. I don't know any women like that, or men either. Unless I see her life branching into mine, she gives me no ancestral help.

To sustain her being in love, she often worked at herself in the mirror, guessing at the colors and shapes that would interest him, changing them frequently in order to hit on the right combination. She wanted him to look back.

On a farm near the sea, a woman who tended her appearance reaped a reputation for eccentricity. All the married women blunt-cut their hair in flaps about their ears or pulled it back in tight buns. No nonsense. Neither style blew easily into heart-catching tangles. And at their weddings they displayed themselves in their long hair for the last time. "It brushed the backs of my knees," my mother tells me. "It was braided, and even so, it brushed the backs of my knees."

At the mirror my aunt combed individuality into her bob. A bun could   25 have been contrived to escape into black streamers blowing in the wind or in quiet wisps about her face, but only the older women in our picture album wear buns. She brushed her hair back from her forehead, tucking the flaps behind her ears. She looped a piece of thread, knotted into a circle between her index fingers and thumbs, and ran the double strand across her forehead. When she closed her fingers as if she were making a pair of shadow geese bite, the string twisted together catching the little hairs. Then she pulled the thread away from her skin, ripping the hairs out neatly, her eyes watering from the needles of pain. Opening her fingers, she cleaned the thread, then rolled it along her hairline and the tops of her eyebrows. My mother did the same to me and my sisters and herself. I used to believe that the expression "caught by the short hairs" meant a captive held with a depilatory string. It especially hurt at the temples, but my mother said we were lucky we didn't have to have our feet bound when we were seven. Sisters used to sit on their beds and cry together, she said, as their mothers or their slave removed the bandages for a few minutes each night and let the blood gush back into their veins. I hope that the man my aunt loved appreciated a smooth brow, that he wasn't just a tits-and-ass man.

Once my aunt found a freckle on her chin, at a spot that the almanac said predestined her for unhappiness. She dug it out with a hot needle and washed the wound with peroxide.

More attention to her looks than these pullings of hairs and pickings at spots would have caused gossip among the villagers. They owned work clothes and good clothes, and they wore good clothes for feasting the new seasons. But since a woman combing her hair hexes beginnings, my aunt rarely found an occasion to look her best. Women looked like great sea snails—the corded wood, babies, and laundry they carried were the whorls on their backs. The Chinese did not admire a bent back; goddesses and warriors stood straight. Still there must have been a marvelous freeing of beauty when a worker laid down her burden and stretched and arched.

Such commonplace loveliness, however, was not enough for my aunt. She dreamed of a lover for the fifteen days of New Year's, the time for families to exchange visits, money, and food. She plied her secret comb. And sure enough she cursed the year, the family, the village, and herself.

Even as her hair lured her imminent lover, many other men looked at her. Uncles, cousins, nephews, brothers would have looked, too, had they been home between journeys. Perhaps they had already been restraining their curiosity, and they left, fearful that their glances, like a field of nesting birds, might be startled and caught. Poverty hurt, and that was their first reason for leaving. But another, final reason for leaving the crowded house was the never-said.

She may have been unusually beloved, the precious only daughter, spoiled and mirror-gazing because of the affection the family lavished on her. When her husband left, they welcomed the chance to take her back from the in-laws; she could live like the little daughter for just a while longer. There are stories that my grandfather was different from other people, "crazy ever since the little Jap bayoneted him in the head." He used to put his naked penis on the dinner table, laughing. And one day he brought home a baby girl, wrapped up inside his brown western-style greatcoat. He had traded one of his sons, probably my father, the youngest, for her. My grandmother made him trade back. When he finally got a daughter of his own, he doted on her. They must have all loved her, except perhaps my father, the only brother who never went back to China, having once been traded for a girl.   30

Brothers and sisters, newly men and women, had to efface their sexual color and present plain miens. Disturbing hair and eyes, a smile like no other, threatened the ideal of five generations living under one roof. To focus blurs, people shouted face to face and yelled from room to room. The immigrants I know have loud voices, unmodulated to American tones even after years away from the village where they called their friendships out across the fields. I have not been able to stop my mother's screams in public libraries or over telephones. Walking erect (knees straight, toes pointed forward, not pigeon-toed, which is Chinese-feminine) and speaking in an inaudible voice, I have tried to turn myself American-feminine. Chinese communication was loud, public. Only sick people had to whisper. But at the dinner table, where the family members came nearest one another, no one could talk, not the outcasts nor any eaters. Every word that falls from the mouth is a coin lost. Silently they gave and accepted food with both hands. A preoccupied child who took his bowl with one hand got a sideways glare. A complete moment of total attention is due everyone alike. Children and lovers have no singularity here, but my aunt used a secret voice, a separate attentiveness.

She kept the man's name to herself throughout her labor and dying; she did not accuse him that he be punished with her. To save her inseminator's name she gave silent birth.

He may have been somebody in her own household, but intercourse with a man outside the family would have been no less abhorrent. All the village were kinsmen, and the titles shouted in loud country voices never let kinship be forgotten. Any man within visiting distance would have been neutralized as a lover—"brother," "younger brother," "older brother"—115 relationship titles. Parents researched birth charts probably not so much to assure good fortune as to circumvent incest in a population that has but one hundred surnames. Everybody has eight million relatives. How useless then sexual mannerisms, how dangerous.

As if it came from an atavism deeper than fear, I used to add "brother" silently to boys' names. It hexed the boys, who would or would not ask me to dance, and made them less scary and as familiar and deserving of benevolence as girls.

But, of course, I hexed myself also—no dates. I should have stood up, both arms waving, and shouted out across libraries, "Hey, you! Love me back." I had no idea, though, how to make attraction selective, how to control its direction and magnitude. If I made myself American-pretty so that the five or six Chinese boys in the class fell in love with me, everyone else—the Caucasian, Negro, and Japanese boys—would too. Sisterliness, dignified and honorable, made much more sense.

Attraction eludes control so stubbornly that whole societies designed to organize relationships among people cannot keep order, not even when they bind people to one another from childhood and raise them together. Among the very poor and the wealthy, brothers married their adopted sisters, like doves. Our family allowed some romance, paying adult brides' prices and providing dowries so that their sons and daughters could marry strangers. Marriage promises to turn strangers into friendly relatives—a nation of siblings.

In the village structure, spirits shimmered among the live creatures, balanced and held in equilibrium by time and land. But one human being flaring up into violence could open up a black hole, a maelstrom that pulled in the sky. The frightened villagers, who depended on one another to maintain the real, went to my aunt to show her a personal, physical representation of the break she made in the "roundness." Misallying couples snapped off the future, which was to be embodied in true offspring. The villagers punished her for acting as if she could have a private life, secret and apart from them.

If my aunt had betrayed the family at a time of large grain yields and peace, when many boys were born, and wings were being built on many houses, perhaps she might have escaped such severe punishment. But the men — hungry, greedy, tired of planting in dry soil, cuckolded — had been forced to leave the village in order to send food-money home. There were ghost plagues, bandit plagues, wars with the Japanese, floods. My Chinese brother and sister had died of an unknown sickness. Adultery, perhaps only a mistake during good times, became a crime when the village needed food.

The round moon cakes and round doorways, the round tables of graduated size that fit one roundness inside another, round windows and rice bowls — these talismans had lost their power to warn this family of the law: a family must be whole, faithfully keeping the descent line by having sons to feed the old and the dead who in turn look after the family. The villagers came to show my aunt and lover-in-hiding a broken house. The villagers were speeding up the circling of events because she was too shortsighted to see that her infidelity had already harmed the village, that waves of consequences would return unpredictably, sometimes in disguise, as now, to hurt her. This roundness had to be made coin-sized so that she would see its circumference: punish her at the birth of her baby. Awaken her to the inexorable. People who refused fatalism because they could invent small resources insisted on culpability. Deny accidents and wrest fault from the stars.

After the villagers left, their lanterns now scattering in various directions   40
toward home, the family broke their silence and cursed her. "Aiaa, we're going to die. Death is coming. Death is coming. Look what you've done. You've killed us. Ghost! Dead Ghost! Ghost! You've never been born." She ran out into the fields, far enough from the house so that she could no longer hear their voices, and pressed herself against the earth, her own land no more. When she felt the birth coming, she thought that she had been hurt. Her body seized together. "They've hurt me too much," she thought. "This is gall, and it will kill me." With forehead and knees against the earth, her body convulsed and then relaxed. She turned on her back, lay on the ground. The black well of sky and stars went out and out forever; her body and her complexity seemed to disappear. She was one of the stars, a bright dot in blackness, without home, without a companion, in eternal cold and silence. An agoraphobia rose in her, speeding higher and higher, bigger and bigger; she would not be able to contain it; there would be no end to fear.

Flayed, unprotected against space, she felt pain return, focusing her body. This pain chilled her — a cold, steady kind of surface pain. Inside, spasmodically, the other pain, the pain of the child, heated her. For hours she lay on the ground, alternately body and space. Sometimes a vision of normal comfort obliterated reality: she saw the family in the evening gambling at the dinner table, the young people massaging their elders' backs. She saw them congratulating one another, high joy on the mornings the rice shoots came up. When these pictures burst, the stars drew yet further apart. Black space opened.

She got to her feet to fight better and remembered that old-fashioned women gave birth in their pigsties to fool the jealous, pain-dealing gods, who do not snatch piglets. Before the next spasms could stop her, she ran to the pigsty, each step a rushing out into emptiness. She climbed over the fence and knelt in the dirt. It was good to have a fence enclosing her, a tribal person alone.

Laboring, this woman who had carried her child as a foreign growth that sickened her every day, expelled it at last. She reached down to touch the hot, wet, moving mass, surely smaller than anything human, and could feel that it was human after all — fingers, toes, nails, nose. She pulled it up on to her belly, and it lay curled there, butt in the air, feet precisely tucked one under the other. She opened her loose shirt and buttoned the child inside. After resting, it squirmed and thrashed and she pushed it up to her breast. It turned its head this way and that until it found her nipple. There, it made little snuffling noises. She clenched her teeth at its preciousness, lovely as a young calf, a piglet, a little dog.

She may have gone to the pigsty as a last act of responsibility: she would protect this child as she had protected its father. It would look after her soul, leaving supplies on her grave. But how would this tiny child without family find her grave when there would be no marker for her anywhere, neither in the earth nor the family hall? No one would give her a family hall name. She had taken the child with her into the wastes. At its birth the two of them had felt the same raw pain of separation, a wound that only the family pressing tight could close. A child with no descent line would not soften her life but only trail after her, ghostlike, begging her to give it purpose. At dawn the villagers on their way to the fields would stand around the fence and look.

Full of milk, the little ghost slept. When it awoke, she hardened her 45 breasts against the milk that crying loosens. Toward morning she picked up the baby and walked to the well.

Carrying the baby to the well shows loving. Otherwise abandon it. Turn its face into the mud. Mothers who love their children take them along. It was probably a girl; there is some hope of forgiveness for boys.

"Don't tell anyone you had an aunt. Your father does not want to hear her name. She has never been born." I have believed that sex was unspeakable and words so strong and fathers so frail that "aunt" would do my father mysterious harm. I have thought that my family, having settled among immigrants who had also been their neighbors in the ancestral land, needed to clean their name, and a wrong word would incite the kinspeople even here. But there is more to this silence: they want me to participate in her punishment. And I have.

In the twenty years since I heard this story I have not asked for details nor said my aunt's name; I do not know it. People who comfort the dead can also chase after them to hurt them further—a reverse ancestor worship. The real punishment was not the raid swiftly inflicted by the villagers, but the family's deliberately forgetting her. Her betrayal so maddened them, they saw to it that she would suffer forever, even after death. Always hungry, always needing, she would have to beg food from other ghosts, snatch and steal it from those whose living descendants give them gifts. She would have to fight the ghosts massed at crossroads for the buns a few thoughtful citizens leave to decoy her away from village and home so that the ancestral spirits could feast unharassed. At peace, they could act like gods, not ghosts, their descent lines providing them with paper suits and dresses, spirit money, paper houses, paper automobiles, chicken, meat, and rice into eternity—essences delivered up in smoke and flames, steam and incense rising from each rice bowl. In an attempt to make the Chinese care for people outside the family, Chairman Mao encourages us now to give our paper replicas to the spirits of outstanding soldiers and workers, no matter whose ancestors they may be. My aunt remains forever hungry. Goods are not distributed evenly among the dead.

My aunt haunts me—her ghost drawn to me because now, after fifty years of neglect, I alone devote pages of paper to her, though not origamied into houses and clothes. I do not think she always means me well. I am telling on her, and she was a spite suicide, drowning herself in the drinking water. The Chinese are always very frightened of the drowned one, whose weeping ghost, wet hair hanging and skin bloated, waits silently by the water to pull down a substitute.

QUESTIONING THE TEXT

1. The narrator of "No Name Woman" tells several different versions of her aunt's life. Which do you find most likely to be accurate, and why?

2. What is the narrator's attitude toward the villagers? What in the text reveals her attitude—and how does it compare with your own attitude toward them?

3. A.L.'s introduction sympathizes with No Name Woman. If one of the villagers had written the introduction, how might it differ from A.L.'s?

MAKING CONNECTIONS

4. Andrew Sullivan's discussion in "What Are Homosexuals For?" (p. 350) is very different from Kingston's story of No Name Woman. But Sullivan does explore, sometimes implicitly, the reasons homosexuals might

choose to keep secrets as well as the complications if they choose to tell. After rereading these pieces, freewrite for 10 to 15 minutes on some secrets in our society that people are never supposed to tell.

JOINING THE CONVERSATION

5. Interview—or spend an hour or so talking with—one of your parents, grandparents, aunts, or uncles, or another older person you know fairly well. Ask your interviewee to describe the attitudes that governed female sexual behavior—or female identity—in his or her day. How were "good girls" supposed to act? What counted as *bad* behavior—and what were the subtle or overt social punishments for that behavior? Write a brief report of your findings, comparing the older person's description of attitudes at an earlier time with those you hold today.

6. Try rewriting one of Kingston's versions of No Name Woman's story from the point of view of the man. How might he see things differently? After you have written this man's version, jot down a few things about him. What does he value? What does he think of women? What is his relationship to women? Finally, bring your version to class to compare with those of two classmates. After studying each version, work together to make a list of what the three versions have in common and a list of how they differ.

DAVE BARRY
Guys vs. Men

O<small>NE OF THE FIRST WORDS</small> *I ever spoke was* truck, *and about forty-five years later I finally bought one, a fully skid-plated 4 × 4 Yukon tall enough to scrape the garage roof and designed to roll me safely over the treacherous ravines and gullies between . . . home and work. Well, I'm man enough to admit that gas-guzzling Big Blue made as much sense as a drawbridge, and I eventually traded it in for a smaller, more environmentally friendly SUV. But the* guy *in me still yearns for tow hooks, a robust V-8, and a subwoofer that will pop rivets.*

If you don't understand what makes grown men covet "neat stuff" or ruin their knees to conquer at touch football, reading Dave Barry's "Guys vs. Men" may help a little. Barry (b. 1947) is, of course, a guy, and that fact helps him at least diagnose the problem of guyness—if it is one. Suffice to say that a lot of men will recognize themselves in the categories he describes. And some women may identify with the "stupid behavioral patterns" that mark men as guys. In fact, when I discussed Barry's essay in a writing class recently, the women insisted on a "guy" term of their own and came up with chick.

"Guys vs. Men" is the preface to Dave Barry's Complete Guide to Guys: A Fairly Short Book *(1995). Barry is a Pulitzer Prize-winning humorist who, early in his career, lectured to business audiences on effective writing. He has published more than a dozen books and collections of humor, including* Stay Fit and Healthy until You're Dead *(1985) and* Homes and Other Black Holes: The Happy Homeowner's Guide *(1988).* —J.R.

Could a woman get away with such a trivialization of womanhood? The fact that a man can (and so successfully at that) is evidence in itself for Barry's argument.
—J.G.R.

372

This is a book about guys. It's *not* a book about men. There are already way too many books about men, and most of them are *way* too serious.

Men itself is a serious word, not to mention *manhood* and *manly*. Such words make being male sound like a very important activity, as opposed to what it primarily consists of, namely, possessing a set of minor and frequently unreliable organs.

But men tend to attach great significance to Manhood. This results in certain characteristically masculine, by which I mean stupid, behavioral patterns that can produce unfortunate results such as violent crime, war, spitting, and ice hockey. These

Who might write "Chicks vs. Women"? Whoopi Goldberg? Madonna? Hillary Rodham Clinton? Maybe Mia Hamm? —A.L.

things have given males a bad name.[1] And the "Men's Movement," which is supposed to bring out the more positive aspects of Manliness, seems to be densely populated with loons and goobers.

So I'm saying that there's another way to look at males: not as aggressive macho dominators; not as sensitive, liberated, hugging drummers; but as *guys*.

And what, exactly, do I mean by "guys"? I don't know. I haven't thought that much about it. One of the major characteristics of guyhood is that we guys don't spend a lot of time pondering our deep innermost feelings. There is a serious question in my mind about whether guys actually *have* deep innermost feelings, unless you count, for example, loyalty to the Detroit Tigers, or fear of bridal showers.

But although I can't define exactly what it means to be a guy, I can describe certain guy characteristics, such as:

GUYS LIKE NEAT STUFF

By "neat," I mean "mechanical and unnecessarily complex." I'll give you an example. Right now I'm typing these words on an *extremely* powerful computer. It's the latest in a line of maybe ten computers I've owned, each one more powerful than the last. My computer is chock full of RAM and ROM and bytes and megahertzes and various other items that enable a computer to kick data-processing butt. It is probably capable of supervising the entire U.S. air-defense apparatus while simultaneously processing the tax return of every resident of Ohio. I use it mainly to write a newspaper column. This is an activity wherein I sit and stare at the screen for maybe ten minutes, then, using only my forefingers, slowly type something like:

Henry Kissinger* looks like a big wart.

I stare at this for another ten minutes, have an inspiration, then amplify the original thought as follows:

Aha! Barry's first slip—completely neglecting the computer's all-important functions of Solitaire and Hearts. How would we play these without a computer?
—J.G.R.

He is counting on powerful stereotypes here, and with this one he seems right on target. Boys love toys, maybe?
—A.L.

---

[1] Specifically, "asshole."

Henry Kissinger (b. 1923): foreign policy advisor to President Nixon and U.S. Secretary of State, 1973–77

Henry Kissinger looks like a big fat wart.

Then I stare at that for another ten minutes, pondering whether I should try to work in the concept of "hairy."

This is absurdly simple work for my computer. It sits there, humming impatiently, bored to death, passing the time between keystrokes via brain-teaser activities such as developing a Unified Field Theory of the universe and translating the complete works of Shakespeare into rap.[2]

In other words, this computer is absurdly overqualified to work for me, and yet soon, I guarantee, I will buy an *even more powerful* one. I won't be able to stop myself. I'm a guy.

Probably the ultimate example of the fundamental guy drive to have neat stuff is the Space Shuttle. Granted, the guys in charge of this program *claim* it has a Higher Scientific Purpose, namely to see how humans function in space. But of course we have known for years how humans function in space: They float around and say things like: "Looks real good, Houston!"

No, the real reason for the existence of the Space Shuttle is that it is one humongous and spectacularly gizmo-intensive item of hardware. Guys can tinker with it practically forever, and occasionally even get it to work, and use it to place *other* complex mechanical items into orbit, where they almost immediately break, which provides a great excuse to send the Space Shuttle up *again*. It's Guy Heaven.

Other results of the guy need to have stuff are Star Wars, the recreational boating industry, monorails, nuclear weapons, and wristwatches that indicate the phase of the moon. I am not saying that women haven't been involved in the development or use of this stuff. I'm saying that, without guys, this stuff probably would not exist; just as, without women, virtually every piece of furniture in the world would still be in its original position. Guys

Probably the most telltale line of this piece. —J.G.R.

Little boys don't have to be taught to want toy cars or video games. —J.R.

How about dividing Shakespeare's characters into guys or men? Falstaff—now, there was a guy. —A.L.

Less than amusing—especially in light of the space shuttle disaster. Is he implying that guys aren't interested in basic ethical questions like what results their gizmos have on people's lives? —A.L.

---

[2]To be or not? I got to *know*.
Might kill myself by the end of the *show*.

do not have a basic need to rearrange furniture. Whereas a woman who could cheerfully use the same computer for fifty-three years will rearrange her furniture on almost a weekly basis, sometimes in the dead of night. She'll be sound asleep in bed, and suddenly, at 2 A.M., she'll be awakened by the urgent thought: *The blue-green sofa needs to go perpendicular to the wall instead of parallel, and it needs to go there RIGHT NOW.* So she'll get up and move it, which of course necessitates moving other furniture, and soon she has rearranged her entire living room, shifting great big heavy pieces that ordinarily would require several burly men to lift, because there are few forces in Nature more powerful than a woman who needs to rearrange furniture. Every so often a guy will wake up to discover that, because of his wife's overnight efforts, he now lives in an entirely different house.

A tongue-in-cheek nod at the politically correct. Nice.
—J.G.R.

Another stereotype neatly deployed. And he counts on our not minding that he lumps all women into one category—it's part of what he has to do to make such portraits "funny."
—A.L.

(I realize that I'm making gender-based generalizations here, but my feeling is that if God did not want us to make gender-based generalizations, She would not have given us genders.)

GUYS LIKE A REALLY
POINTLESS CHALLENGE

Not long ago I was sitting in my office at the *Miami Herald*'s Sunday magazine, *Tropic,* reading my fan mail,[3] when I heard several of my guy coworkers in the hallway talking about how fast they could run the forty-yard dash. These are guys in their thirties and forties who work in journalism, where the most demanding physical requirement is the ability to digest vending-machine food. In other words, these guys have absolutely no need to run the forty-yard dash.

But one of them, Mike Wilson, was writing a story about a star high-school football player who could run it in 4.38 seconds. Now if Mike had written a story about, say, a star high-school poet,

---

[3]Typical fan letter: "Who cuts your hair? Beavers?"

none of my guy coworkers would have suddenly decided to find out how well they could write sonnets. But when Mike turned in his story, they became *deeply* concerned about how fast they could run the forty-yard dash. They were so concerned that the magazine editor, Tom Shroder, decided that they should get a stopwatch and go out to a nearby park and find out. Which they did, a bunch of guys taking off their shoes and running around barefoot in a public park on company time.

This is what I heard them talking about, out in the hall. I heard Tom, who was thirty-eight years old, saying that his time in the forty had been 5.75 seconds. And I thought to myself: This is ridiculous. These are middle-aged guys, supposedly adults, and they're out there *bragging* about their performance in this stupid juvenile footrace. Finally I couldn't stand it anymore.

"Hey!" I shouted. "*I* could beat 5.75 seconds."

So we went out to the park and measured off forty yards, and the guys told me that I had three chances to make my best time. On the first try my time was 5.78 seconds, just three-hundredths of a second slower than Tom's, even though, at forty-five, I was seven years older than he. So I just *knew* I'd beat him on the second attempt if I ran really, really hard, which I did for a solid ten yards, at which point my left hamstring muscle, which had not yet shifted into Spring Mode from Mail-Reading Mode, went, and I quote, "pop."

I had to be helped off the field. I was in considerable pain, and I was obviously not going to be able to walk right for weeks. The other guys were very sympathetic, especially Tom, who took the time to call me at home, where I was sitting with an ice pack on my leg and twenty-three Advil in my bloodstream, so he could express his concern.

"Just remember," he said, "*you didn't beat my time.*"

There are countless other examples of guys rising to meet pointless challenges. Virtually all sports fall into this category, as well as a large part of

OK. Now I know I am not and never can be a "guy." This is the last thing I would do in response to a story about 40-yard dash times. —A.L.

I may expire on the racquetball court some day. But I'll go happy—so long as I'm winning. —J.R.

Any guy who has ever competed in an "eat-til-you-puke" contest with 49-cent tacos can relate to this. —J.G.R.

Who is it that proposed cutting out all militaries the world over and resolving all foreign policy crises by sending out squads to play some game? I can just imagine Barry describing such scenes. —A.L.

Or "Last one to the moon has to eat the Berlin Wall." (It took them over 20 years to pay up for this one.) —J.G.R.

U.S. foreign policy. ("I'll bet you can't capture Manuel Noriega!"* "Oh YEAH??")

GUYS DO NOT HAVE A RIGID AND WELL-DEFINED MORAL CODE

This is not the same as saying that guys are bad. Guys *are* capable of doing bad things, but this generally happens when they try to be Men and start becoming manly and aggressive and stupid. When they're being just plain guys, they aren't so much actively *evil* as they are *lost*. Because guys have never really grasped the Basic Human Moral Code, which I believe was invented by women millions of years ago when all the guys were out engaging in some other activity, such as seeing who could burp the loudest. When they came back, there were certain rules that they were expected to follow unless they wanted to get into Big Trouble, and they have been trying to follow these rules ever since, with extremely irregular results. Because guys have never *internalized* these rules. Guys are similar to my small auxiliary backup dog, Zippy, a guy dog[4] who has been told numerous times that he is *not* supposed to (1) get into the kitchen garbage or (2) poop on the floor. He knows that these are the rules, but he has never really understood *why,* and sometimes he gets to thinking: Sure, I am *ordinarily* not supposed to get into the garbage, but obviously this rule is not meant to apply when there are certain extenuating[5] circumstances, such as (1) somebody just threw away some perfectly good seven-week-old Kung Pao Chicken, and (2) I am home alone.

And so when the humans come home, the kitchen floor has been transformed into Garbage-Fest USA, and Zippy, who usually comes rushing

---

Manuel Noriega (b. 1934): Panamanian dictator removed from power by armed U.S. intervention in 1989

[4]I also have a female dog, Earnest, who *never* breaks the rules.

[5]I am taking some liberties here with Zippy's vocabulary. More likely, in his mind, he uses the term *mitigating.*

up, is off in a corner disguised in a wig and sun-glasses, hoping to get into the Federal Bad Dog Re-location Program before the humans discover the scene of the crime.

When I yell at him, he frequently becomes so upset that he poops on the floor.

Guys do care about rules when it comes to their machines or games, the more compli-cated the better. Only guys could have invented f-stops or the infield fly rule. —J.R.

Morally, most guys are just like Zippy, only taller and usually less hairy. Guys are *aware* of the rules of moral behavior, but they have trouble keeping these rules in the forefronts of their minds at certain times, especially the present. This is espe-cially true in the area of faithfulness to one's mate. I realize, of course, that there are countless examples of guys being faithful to their mates until they die, usually as a result of being eaten by their mates im-mediately following copulation. Guys outside of the spider community, however, do not have a terrific record of faithfulness.

I'm not saying guys are scum. I'm saying that many guys who consider themselves to be committed to their marriages will stray if they are confronted with overwhelming temptation, defined as "virtually any temptation."

Wonder if his wife read this? —J.G.R.

Okay, so maybe I *am* saying guys are scum. But they're not *mean-spirited* scum. And few of them—even when they are out of town on busi-ness trips, far from their wives, and have a clear-cut opportunity—will poop on the floor.

Well, that's a re-lief—considering that they will readily foul up their marriages. —A.L.

GUYS ARE NOT GREAT AT COMMUNICATING THEIR INTIMATE FEELINGS, ASSUMING THEY HAVE ANY

This is an aspect of guyhood that is very frus-trating to women. A guy will be reading the news-paper, and the phone will ring; he'll answer it, lis-ten for ten minutes, hang up, and resume reading. Finally his wife will say: "Who was that?"

And he'll say: "Phil Wonkerman's mom."

(Phil is an old friend they haven't heard from in seventeen years.)

And the wife will say, "Well?"

And the guy will say, "Well what?"

And the wife will say, "What did she *say*?"

And the guy will say, "She said Phil is fine," making it clear by his tone of voice that, although he does not wish to be rude, he is trying to read the newspaper, and he happens to be right in the middle of an important panel of "Calvin and Hobbes."

But the wife, ignoring this, will say, "That's *all* she said?"

And she will not let up. She will continue to ask district-attorney-style questions, forcing the guy to recount the conversation until she's satisfied that she has the entire story, which is that Phil just got out of prison after serving a sentence for a murder he committed when he became a drug addict because of the guilt he felt when his wife died in a freak submarine accident while Phil was having an affair with a nun, but now he's all straightened out and has a good job as a trapeze artist and is almost through with the surgical part of his sex change and recently became happily engaged to marry a prominent member of the Grateful Dead, so in other words he is fine, which is *exactly* what the guy told her in the first place, but is that enough? No. She wants to hear *every single detail*.

Or let's say two couples get together after a long separation. The two women will have a conversation, lasting several days, during which they discuss virtually every significant event that has occurred in their lives and the lives of those they care about, sharing their innermost thoughts, analyzing and probing, inevitably coming to a deeper understanding of each other, and a strengthening of a cherished friendship. Whereas the guys will watch the play-offs.

This is not to say the guys won't share their feelings. Sometimes they'll get quite emotional.

"That's not a FOUL??" they'll say.

Or: "YOU'RE TELLING ME THAT'S NOT A FOUL???"

I have a good friend, Gene, and one time, when he was going through a major medical development in his life, we spent a weekend together. During this time Gene and I talked a lot and enjoyed each other's

This section on "communication," especially this communication between men and women, is the subject of several books by Deborah Tannen, whose studies might suggest that Barry is not far off the mark here.
—A.L.

Example Chart

Men	Guys
Vince Lombardi	Joe Namath
Oliver North	Gilligan
Hemingway	Gary Larson
Columbus	Whichever astronaut hit the first golf ball on the Moon
Superman	Bart Simpson
Doberman pinschers	Labrador retrievers
Abbott	Costello
Captain Ahab	Captain Kangaroo
Satan	Snidely Whiplash
The pope	Willard Scott
Germany	Italy
Geraldo	Katie Couric

company immensely, but—this is true—the most intimate personal statement he made to me is that he has reached Level 24 of a video game called "Arkanoid." He had even seen the Evil Presence, although he refused to tell me what it looks like. We're very close, but there is a limit.

You may think that my friends and I are Neanderthals, and that a lot of guys are different. This is true. A lot of guys don't use words at *all*. They communicate entirely by nonverbal methods, such as sharing bait.

I am glad to say I know some men who really are different, especially in the way they communicate their feelings. —A.L.

Are you starting to see what I mean by "guyness"? I'm basically talking about the part of the male psyche that is less serious and/or aggressive than the Manly Manhood part, but still essentially very male. My feeling is that the world would be a much better[6] place if more males would stop trying so hard to be Men and instead settle for being Guys. Think of the

---

[6] As measured by total sales of [my] book.

historical problems that could have been avoided if more males had been able to keep their genderhood in its proper perspective, both in themselves and in others. ("Hey, Adolf, just because you happen to possess a set of minor and frequently unreliable organs, that is no reason to invade Poland.") And think how much happier women would be if, instead of endlessly fretting about what the males in their lives are thinking, they could relax, secure in the knowledge that the correct answer is: *very little*.

All kidding aside, I do think women need a better understanding of the way guys think, if that's the right verb for the process. —J.R.

C'mon, Dave . . . even you had to do some thinking to come up with this book. —A.L.

Yes, what we need, on the part of both genders, is more understanding of guyness. And that is why I wrote this book. I intend to explore in detail every major facet of guyhood, including the historical facet, the sociological facet, the physiological facet, the psychosexual facet, and the facet of how come guys spit so much. Every statement of fact you will read in this book is either based on actual laboratory tests, or else I made it up. But you can trust me. I'm a guy.

Stimulus-Response Comparison Chart: Women vs. Men vs. Guys

Stimulus	Typical *Woman* Response	Typical *Man* Response	Typical *Guy* Response
An untamed river in the wilderness.	Contemplate its beauty.	Build a dam.	See who can pee the farthest off the dam.
A child who is sent home from school for being disruptive in class.	Talk to the child in an effort to determine the cause.	Threaten to send the child to a military academy.	Teach the child how to make armpit farts.
Human mortality	Religious faith	The pyramids	Bungee-jumping

Afterwords

*While reading "Guys vs. Men," most males and a great many women will likely discover a bit of the guy within themselves. The kernels of truth residing within Barry's stereotypes are what make this essay funny and oddly provocative. When Barry observes that "Guys like neat stuff," he's acknowledging the inventiveness and curiosity that have driven human beings from chariots to Stealth bombers in a couple thousand years. We owe a debt to all the geeks and tinkerers who began a sentence "Wouldn't it be neat if . . . ?" and then followed through. Sometimes in their mania, guys land on the moon and sometimes they blow themselves up. I guess it's the responsibility of more proper "men" and "women" to make sure that the former happens more often than the latter. —*J.R.

*What can I say? Some of my best friends are "guys"? I even know women who are "guys"? I wish I knew more real "guys"? Not likely. I admire Barry's way with words, and especially the way he can poke fun at himself. And I laughed out loud at some of the early parts of this essay. But in my serious moments, I worry about the need to "blow things up" and to outperform everyone at everything at every minute of the day and night. I worry about what the "culture of guyhood" has done (is doing?) to us all, and to men in particular. Squeezing infinitely varied males into the little square space allowed to "guys" can't be all that much fun. Can it? —*A.L.

*Dave Barry hits the nail on the head with this piece—or, to be more precise, the galvanized, flat-head 5-1/4" nail with a stainless steel, all-metal, lifetime-guaranteed hammer. Barry is right on with the simplicity of "guyness." Not even a man could complicate it, but for some reason I bet that women won't understand. —*J.G.R.

QUESTIONING THE TEXT

1. Barry's humor obviously plays off of gross stereotypes about men. Underscore or annotate all the stereotypes you can find in the essay.

2. Barry employs a lengthy analogy featuring his dog Zippy to explore the moral behavior of guys (p. 377). In a group, discuss this analogy, focusing on the observations that seem especially apt.

MAKING CONNECTIONS

3. Pick any essay you have already read from this collection and give it the Dave Barry treatment. That is, try your hand at making readers see the subject from a comic perspective. You might, for example, try writing a short article portraying the issues in James Q. Wilson's "Cars and Their

Enemies" (p. 303) as a battle between car nuts and tree-huggers. Or Wendy Shalit's concern over unisex bathrooms in "The Future of Modesty" (p. 214) may suggest other opportunities for humor. Be certain your comic piece makes a point.

4. Barry comically suggests that the space shuttle is the ultimate guy thing — a complicated gizmo that men can tinker with forever. Examine Barry's comic observations side by side with any of the readings in Chapter 5 on science and technology. Then, if you keep a reading log, write a serious response there to Barry's humorous observations. Is science a male obsession with how things work?

JOINING THE CONVERSATION

5. "Guys vs. Men" is almost a textbook exercise in writing an extended definition. Annotate the different techniques Barry uses to craft his definition (definition by contrast; class/characteristics; definition by example; negative definition). Then write a similar definitional piece — humorous if you like — contrasting two terms that might at first glance seem similar: Chicks vs. Women; Cops vs. Police Officers; Freshmen vs. First-Year Students.

6. Barry illustrates the competitiveness of men with a short anecdote about the forty-yard dash. Choose another stereotypical trait of either men or women (insensitivity, bad driving, excessive concern with appearance), and write an anecdote from your own experience that illustrates the trait. Try some of the techniques Barry uses to make his story funny: understatement, exaggeration, irony, self-deprecation, dialogue.

ZORA NEALE HURSTON
How It Feels to Be Colored Me

Zora Neale Hurston *(1891–1960), born and raised in the first all-black town in the United States to be incorporated and self-governing (Eatonville, Florida), packed an astonishing number of careers and identities into her sixty-nine years. She was a "wardrobe girl" for traveling entertainers, a manicurist, an anthropologist and folklorist, a college professor, a drama coach, an editor, and—above all—a writer of great distinction. Author of numerous articles, essays, and stories as well as folklore collections, plays, and an autobiography, Hurston is today probably best known for her novels:* Their Eyes Were Watching God *(1937),* Jonah's Gourd Vine *(1934), and* Moses, Man of the Mountain *(1939).*

Hurston studied anthropology at Barnard College, where she was the only African American student, and gained a strong reputation for her academic work on folklore. But by the 1930s, she was being criticized for what were said to be caricatures of blacks, especially in her "minstrel" novels. Her growing conservatism led to further attacks from writers such as Richard Wright, and by 1950, her reputation gone, she was working in Florida as a maid. Evicted from her home in 1956, she suffered a stroke in 1959 and died, penniless, the next year. In recent years, Alice Walker sought out her unmarked grave in Fort Pierce, Florida, and erected a marker in memory of Hurston and her work, which is, today, widely read and influential.

The essay that follows, published in World Tomorrow *(May 1928), challenges the notion that American identity is connected to freedom, the "home of the brave," and the "land of the free." Hurston is deeply aware of such ironies and of the bitter struggles obscured by the happy image of an American identity forged in the melting pot. But she is not cast down or resentful; she has no time to waste on negativity. I chose "How It Feels to Be Colored Me" for its irrepressible spirit in the face of what are clear inequalities in America, for its ironic self-representation, and for the sheer delight it gives me to think that Hurston has triumphed after all.* — A.L.

I am colored but I offer nothing in the way of extenuating circumstances except the fact that I am the only Negro in the United States whose grandfather on the mother's side was *not* an Indian chief.

I remember the very day that I became colored. Up to my thirteenth year I lived in the little Negro town of Eatonville, Florida. It is exclusively a colored town. The only white people I knew passed through the town going to or coming from Orlando. The native whites rode dusty horses, the Northern tourists chugged down the sandy village road in automobiles. The town knew the Southerners and never stopped cane chewing* when they passed. But the Northerners were something else again. They were peered at cautiously from behind curtains by the timid. The more venturesome would come out on the porch to watch them go past and got just as much pleasure out of the tourists as the tourists got out of the village.

The front porch might seem a daring place for the rest of the town, but it was a gallery seat for me. My favorite place was atop the gate-post. Proscenium box for a born first-nighter. Not only did I enjoy the show, but I didn't mind the actors knowing that I liked it. I usually spoke to them in passing. I'd wave at them and when they returned my salute, I would say something like this: "Howdy-do-well-I-thank-you-where-you-goin'?" Usually automobile or the horse paused at this, and after a queer exchange of compliments, I would probably "go a piece of the way" with them, as we say in farthest Florida. If one of my family happened to come to the front in time to see me, of course negotiations would be rudely broken off. But even so, it is clear that I was the first "welcome-to-our-state" Floridian, and I hope the Miami Chamber of Commerce will please take notice.

During this period, white people differed from colored to me only in that they rode through town and never lived there. They liked to hear me "speak pieces" and sing and wanted to see me dance the parse-me-la, and gave me generously of their small silver for doing these things, which seemed strange to me for I wanted to do them so much that I needed bribing to stop. Only they didn't know it. The colored people gave no dimes. They deplored any joyful tendencies in me, but I was their Zora nevertheless. I belonged to them, to the nearby hotels, to the country — everybody's Zora.

But changes came in the family when I was thirteen, and I was sent to   5
school in Jacksonville. I left Eatonville, the town of the oleanders, as Zora. When I disembarked from the river-boat at Jacksonville, she was no more. It seemed that I had suffered a sea change. I was not Zora of Orange County any more. I was now a little colored girl. I found it out in certain ways. In my heart as well as in the mirror, I became a fast brown — warranted not to rub nor run.

But I am not tragically colored. There is no great sorrow dammed up in my soul, nor lurking behind my eyes. I do not mind at all. I do not belong to the sobbing school of Negrohood who hold that nature somehow has given them a lowdown dirty deal and whose feelings are all hurt about it. Even in the helter-skelter skirmish that is my life, I have seen that the world is to the strong* regardless of a little pigmentation more or less. No, I do not weep at the world — I am too busy sharpening my oyster knife.*

---

cane chewing: chewing sugar-cane stalks

the world is to the strong: an allusion to the biblical passage (in Ecclesiastes 9:11) that reads "The race is not to the swift, nor the battle to the strong"

sharpening my oyster knife: an allusion to the saying "The world is my oyster," which appears in Shakespeare's *The Merry Wives of Windsor*

Someone is always at my elbow reminding me that I am the granddaughter of slaves. It fails to register depression with me. Slavery is sixty years in the past. The operation was successful and the patient is doing well, thank you. The terrible struggle* that made me an American out of a potential slave said "On the line!" The Reconstruction said "Get set!"; and the generation before said "Go!" I am off to a flying start and I must not halt in the stretch to look behind and weep. Slavery is the price I paid for civilization, and the choice was not with me. It is a bully adventure and worth all that I have paid through my ancestors for it. No one on earth ever had a greater chance for glory. The world to be won and nothing to be lost. It is thrilling to think— to know that for any act of mine, I shall get twice as much praise or twice as much blame. It is quite exciting to hold the center of the national stage, with the spectators not knowing whether to laugh or to weep.

The position of my white neighbor is much more difficult. No brown specter pulls up a chair beside me when I sit down to eat. No dark ghost thrusts its leg against mine in bed. The game of keeping what one has is never so exciting as the game of getting.

I do not always feel colored. Even now I often achieve the unconscious Zora of Eatonville before the Hegira. I feel most colored when I am thrown against a sharp white background.

For instance at Barnard. "Beside the waters of the Hudson"* I feel my   10
race. Among the thousand white persons, I am a dark rock surged upon, and overswept, but through it all, I remain myself. When covered by the waters, I am; and the ebb but reveals me again.

Sometimes it is the other way around. A white person is set down in our midst, but the contrast is just as sharp for me. For instance, when I sit in the drafty basement that is The New World Cabaret with a white person, my color comes. We enter chatting about any little nothing that we have in common and are seated by the jazz waiters. In the abrupt way that jazz orchestras have, this one plunges into a number. It loses no time in circumlocutions, but gets right down to business. It constricts the thorax and splits the heart with its tempo and narcotic harmonies. This orchestra grows rambunctious, rears on its hind legs and attacks the tonal veil with primitive fury, rending it, clawing it until it breaks through to the jungle beyond. I follow those heathen— follow them exultingly. I dance wildly inside myself; I yell within, I whoop; I shake my assegai above my head, I hurl it true to the mark *yeeeeooww!* I am in the jungle and living in the jungle way. My face is painted red and yellow and

---

the terrible struggle: the Civil War

"Beside the waters of the Hudson": Barnard College is near the Hudson River in New York City. For another account of how it felt to be a black student at Columbia University in the early twentieth century, see the poem by Langston Hughes, "Theme for English B" (p. 459).

my body is painted blue. My pulse is throbbing like a war drum. I want to slaughter something—give pain, give death to what, I do not know. But the piece ends. The men of the orchestra wipe their lips and rest their fingers. I creep back slowly to the veneer we call civilization with the last tone and find the white friend sitting motionless in his seat, smoking calmly.

"Good music they have here," he remarks, drumming the table with his fingertips.

Music. The great blobs of purple and red emotion have not touched him. He has only heard what I felt. He is far away and I see him but dimly across the ocean and the continent that have fallen between us. He is so pale with his whiteness then and I am *so* colored.

At certain times I have no race, I am *me*. When I set my hat at a certain angle and saunter down Seventh Avenue, Harlem City, feeling as snooty as the lions in front of the Forty-Second Street Library,* for instance. So far as my feelings are concerned, Peggy Hopkins Joyce* on the Boule Mich* with her gorgeous raiment, stately carriage, knees knocking together in a most aristocratic manner, has nothing on me. The cosmic Zora emerges. I belong to no race nor time. I am the eternal feminine with its string of beads.

I have no separate feeling about being an American citizen and colored.   15
I am merely a fragment of the Great Soul that surges within the boundaries. My country, right or wrong.

Sometimes, I feel discriminated against, but it does not make me angry. It merely astonishes me. How *can* any deny themselves the pleasure of my company? It's beyond me.

But in the main, I feel like a brown bag of miscellany propped against a wall. Against a wall in company with other bags, white, red and yellow. Pour out the contents, and there is discovered a jumble of small things priceless and worthless. A first-water diamond, an empty spool, bits of broken glass, lengths of string, a key to a door long since crumbled away, a rusty knife-blade, old shoes saved for a road that never was and never will be, a nail bent under the weight of things too heavy for any nail, a dried flower or two still a little fragrant. In your hand is the brown bag. On the ground before you is the jumble it held—so much like the jumble in the bags, could they be emptied, that all might be dumped in a single heap and the bags refilled without altering the content of any greatly. A bit of colored glass more or less would not matter. Perhaps that is how the Great Stuffer of Bags filled them in the first place—who knows?

---

the lions in front of the Forty-Second Street Library: two statues of lions that stand in front of the main building of the New York Public Library, on Fifth Avenue at 42nd Street
Peggy Hopkins Joyce: a famous beauty who set fashions in the 1920s
the Boule Mich: the Boulevard Saint-Michel, a street in Paris

QUESTIONING THE TEXT

1. Color is a central theme in this brief essay. Jot down as many of the ways color appears as you can remember. Then go back and check the text. Complete your list and compare it with the lists of others in your class. What are the different things color is attributed to?

2. In her introduction to this essay, A.L. makes absolutely clear how much she admires Hurston. How does her praise affect your evaluation of the essay?

3. Hurston exemplifies the *differences* among people in her vivid descriptions of her experience of jazz (paragraph 11). First, try to describe your experience with the kind of music that most engages and moves you. What do you find in common with or different from Hurston's experience? Does what you have discovered lead you to see "sharp" contrasts, as Hurston does, or commonalities? What do such contrasts and commonalities have to do with your race? With some other feature of your identity?

MAKING CONNECTIONS

4. Read Hurston's piece along with Langston Hughes's "Theme for English B" (p. 459). Do these writers hold different—or similar—views on commonalities among all people? Explain your answer in an informal statement (about a page or two) addressed to your class.

5. Hurston dwells in this essay on color, using it metaphorically to evoke her experiences and literally to evoke her own—and others'—colors. Color, of course, depends largely on sight, on vision. What would happen to the world Hurston describes if vision were *not* so important? Write a brief dialogue that Georgina Kleege (p. 389) and Hurston might have on this question.

JOINING THE CONVERSATION

6. Hurston concludes with a simile about bags. First, consider what simile or metaphor you might use to describe your own race or ethnicity and its relationship to others. Begin perhaps by completing the sentence "But in the main, I feel like . . ." Then write an extended description of your simile or metaphor and bring it to class for discussion.

7. Working with two or three classmates, draft a composite description of the metaphors you came up with. What do these metaphors have in common? How do they differ?

GEORGINA KLEEGE
Call It Blindness

On my forty-fifth birthday, *I had a sudden shock: I could no longer read the* condensed version of the Oxford English Dictionary *without using the handy magnifying glass that accompanies that two-volume work. I merely had presbyopia, my doctor informed me, and I was certainly not unique: at about my age, almost everyone could count on failing vision. Of course, I could also count on glasses to help me out, a luxury that our ancestors did not have and one that provides precious little help for those who are "legally blind."*

Now meet Georgina Kleege (b. 1956), whose own experiences with blindness and sight are both extensive and intensive. Pronounced "legally blind" when she was eleven, Kleege's loss of vision was so gradual that she has "no memory of losing" it. Indeed, she long "passed" as sighted and only gradually came to "see" the myriad and destructive ways in which our society equates "sight with good and blindness with evil." The difference of blindness evokes fear more than any other emotion, however — a fear "as ancient as the fear of darkness." In moving and meticulously crafted prose, Kleege challenges this fear, challenges each of us to examine our own dependence on sight, to assess just how well and how much we can really "see," and to question whether our identity is really linked to "normal" vision.

Currently living in Columbus, Ohio, Kleege grew up in New York City, attending Grace Church School. Since graduating from Yale in 1979, she has written both fiction, Home for the Summer *(1989), and a collection of essays,* Sight Unseen *(1999), which includes the following essay, originally published in the* Yale Review *(April 1994).*

"Call It Blindness" was named one of the Best American Essays of 1995. My students were unanimous in urging that it be included in the third edition of The Presence of Others. *I couldn't agree more.* —A.L.

I tell the class, "I am legally blind." There is a pause, a collective intake of breath. I feel them look away uncertainly and then look back. After all, I just said I couldn't see. Or did I? I had managed to get there on my own—no cane, no dog, none of the usual trappings of blindness. Eyeing me askance now, they might detect that my gaze is not quite focused. My eyes are aimed in the right direction but the gaze seems to stop short of touching anything. But other people do this, sighted people, normal people, especially in an awkward situation like this one, the first day of class. An actress who delivers an aside to the audience, breaking the "fourth wall" of the proscenium, will aim her gaze somewhere above any particular pair of eyes. If I hadn't said anything, my audience might understand my gaze to be like that, a part of the performance. In these few seconds between sentences, their gaze becomes intent. They watch me glance down, or toward the door where someone's coming in late. I'm just like anyone else. Then what did I actually mean by "legally blind"? They wait. I go on, "Some people would call me 'visually challenged.'" There is a ripple of laughter, an exhalation of relief. I'm making a joke about it. I'm poking fun at something they too find aggravating, the current mania to stick a verbal smiley-face on any human condition which deviates from the status quo. Differently abled. Handicapable. If I ask, I'm sure some of them can tell jokes about it: "Don't say 'bald,' say 'follicularly challenged.'" "He's not dead, he's metabolically stable." Knowing they are at least thinking of these things, I conclude, "These are just silly ways of saying I don't see very well."

I probably shouldn't make these jokes. In fact the term *legally blind* is not a new, politically correct euphemism. Nor is the adverb interchangeable with *half, partially,* or *nearly.* Someone is legally blind whose visual acuity is 20/200 or less, or whose visual field is 20 degrees or less, in the better eye, with corrective lenses. The term seems to have been coined by the American Medical Association in 1934, then adopted by the federal government in the Social Security Act of 1935, as a standard measure to determine eligibility for new federal programs for the blind. The definition has been controversial since it was instituted. It turns on only two aspects of sight, and does not measure how well or poorly an individual uses residual sight. There are many who would like to abandon the definition, enlarge it, contract it, or create new categories. I could tell my students this, a tidbit of medical and social history. I could also explain that the legally blind often "see" something, and often use visual experience to understand the world, and thus "appear" sighted. I could hand out diagrams of the human eye, photographs simulating various types of "legal blindness." But I do not.

Instead I detail how my condition will affect them. Someone will have to read me their papers and exams. Or else they will have to tape their written work, which can be time-consuming. When I look at them I cannot tell if their eyes are focused with interest or glazed over with confusion, boredom, or fatigue. In other words, I cannot "read" the class as effectively as other teachers. I cannot ask for a show of hands, or if I do someone else must count them. If they want to make a comment they must break the cardinal rule of classroom decorum drummed in since the first grade and interrupt me. It may take the entire term for me to match each of them, whatever it is I see of them, to a name.

Most of this may not matter to them at all. Perhaps they have other instructors with comparable foibles. Perhaps there's no need even to mention it. They can tell I don't see well just by watching me read, holding the page an inch from my eyes, squinting through coke-bottle lenses. But I must talk about it, as a way to dispel possible confusion or discomfort. I bring it up so the student in the back row with his hand in the air can drop it and say, "Excuse me, I have a question" and not "What's the matter, can't you see?"

In other public speaking situations I never mention my blindness. I used 5
to give educational and fund-raising talks about domestic violence, sexual assault, and other issues. I spoke from memory, never using notes. I shifted my
focus here and there in the way all the literature about public speaking advises. I learned to direct my eyes at any sound, to raise them to the ceiling or
lower them to the floor, as if searching for the right words. Perhaps I came off
as stagy, phony, insincere, but certainly not blind. The only risky moments
during any of these occasions were the question-and-answer periods. But
usually there was a host—the chair of the meeting, the teacher of the class—
who pointed to the raised hands. Though I could not make eye contact (I do
not really know what eye contact feels like or does), I doubt my audiences
ever really noticed. Often the subject matter made them drop their eyes and
stare at their shoes. Or else they so identified with the topic, they became distracted by memories, blinded by tears. If I had introduced myself as blind, it
would have detracted from my topic. They might have felt compelled to
watch out for my safety. I might be about to knock something over or fall off
the stage. Or else they might have suspected me of fraud, a rather clumsy deception meant to milk their sympathy. As with my students, I could have
taken the time to educate them, to explain that blindness does not equal ineptitude. It does not even mean an absolute lack of sight. But I had more important things to say. My blindness was an irrelevant fact they did not need to
know about me, like my religion or political affiliation.

In social situations I never announce my blindness. And as long as I'm
not obliged to read anything, or identify a person or a plate of food, people
tend not to notice. I pass as sighted. I have many acquaintances, people who
know me slightly, or only by sight, who would be shocked to learn that my
vision is not normal. The fact that I do not look people in the eye they may
chalk up to shyness, reserve, or boredom.

Some blind people introduce their disability when they shake hands.
They feel it's best to get it out of the way in the first moments of acquaintance. I have never mastered the technique. If I have to explain why I don't
drive, for instance, the discomfort of the sighted people is debilitating. Tension solidifies around us. Their voices become softer, even hushed with a so-
licitous piety. They become self-conscious about language, hesitant to say "I
see what you mean" or "See you later." I feel them glance around for whoever brought me, whoever is responsible for me. Sometimes there's a degree
of desperation in this, an anxiety to turn me back over to the person in
charge, as if this disaster only just occurred in the second it took to speak the
word. I've learned to speed-skate around it, to feign gaiety, to babble my way
into another topic, but equilibrium is hard to recover.

Once, at a party, a man I was speaking to was almost reduced to tears to
learn I was a blind writer. There was a tremor in his voice. He kept saying
something about "the word fading." I tried to tell him that since my condition is stable, the word has already faded as much as it ever will, unless some

other condition develops. And as far as these things go, a writer is not a bad thing to be if you can't see. There are other ways to write, other ways to read. It is easier for a writer to compensate for sight loss than a visual artist, a race car driver, an astronomer. I might have even mentioned Homer, Milton, and Joyce, the sight-impaired literary luminaries most often invoked at such times. But he had already receded from me, become preoccupied with a new, reductive view of me and my restricted future.

Of course, it's the word *blind* which causes all the problems. To most people, blindness means total, absolute darkness, a complete absence of any visual experience. Though only about ten per cent of the legally blind have this degree of impairment, people think the word should be reserved to designate this minority. For the rest of us, with our varying degrees of sight, a modifier becomes necessary. We're encouraged to indicate that we're not quite "that bad." Better to speak of a visual impairment, a sight deficit, low vision. Better still to accentuate the positive and call it "partially sighted."

Sometimes I use these other terms, but I find them no more precise or   10
pleasing. The word *impairment* implies impermanence, an encumbrance which could disappear, and my condition has no cure or treatment. The term *low vision* reminds me too much of *short eyes,* a prison term for child molesters. And anyway, I crave the simplicity of a single, unmodified adjective. Blind. Perhaps I could speak in relative terms, say I am blinder than some, less blind than others.

"But," people object, "you are not really blind," attaching yet another adverb to separate me from the absolutely sightless. The modern, legal definition is arbitrary, a convention based on notions of what visual skills are necessary for an adult to be gainfully employed or a child traditionally educated. The definition has more to do with the ability to read print or drive a car than with the ability to perceive color, light, motion, or form. If I lived in a different culture or a different age, no one would define me as blind. I could transport myself on foot or horseback. I could grow or gather my own food, relying on other senses to detect ripeness, pests, soil quality. I would have trouble hunting. The protective coloration of most animals and birds is always good enough to deceive me. But I might learn to devise cunning traps, and I could fish. I could become adept at crafts—certain kinds of weaving or pottery— which require as much manual dexterity and digital sensitivity as visual acuity. If I looked at people strangely it might be accepted as a personality flaw. Or else it might be a culture where a too-direct gaze is considered impolite. In any case, I could live independently, with enough sight to perform routine tasks without aid. If I had a sense that others' eyes were stronger or more discerning than mine, I still would not define myself as blind. Especially if it was the sort of culture which put the blind to death.

Though in the here and now execution is unlikely, a stigma exists. So why should I want to label myself in that way? Isn't the use of the word at all, even with one of the imprecise modifiers, a form of self-dramatization, a demand for attention and pity better bestowed elsewhere? Isn't it a dishonest claim of marginal status, now that marginality is fashionable?

In fact, it is only recently that I have started using the word. I was pronounced "legally blind" when I was eleven, though my condition probably developed a year or two earlier. I have no memory of losing my sight. I imagine it took place so gradually I was unaware of what I was not seeing. The only outward sign was that I began to read with the book very close to my eyes. Everyone assumed I was simply nearsighted, but tests did not show this. My cornea and lenses refracted normally. Remarkably, my doctor did not pursue the matter, even though the early signs of retinal damage should have been revealed in a standard eye exam. Apparently it was not what he was looking for. Instead, he jumped to the conclusion that I was faking, even though I was not the sort of child who would do that. My parents and teachers were advised to nag me into holding the book away from my face. For a while I complied, keeping the book at the prescribed distance, turning pages at appropriate intervals. Then, when no one was looking, I would flip back and press my nose to the page. Eventually it became clear to everyone that this was not a phase I was going to outgrow. Additional tests were performed. When it was all over, my doctor named my disorder "macular degeneration," defined my level of impairment as legally blind, and told me there was no treatment or cure, and no chance of improvement. And that was all. Like many ophthalmologists then and perhaps still, he did not feel it was his responsibility to recommend special education or training. He did not send me to an optometrist for whatever magnification devices might have been available then. This was in the mid-sixties, so the boom in high-tech "low vision" aids had not yet begun. He said that as long as I continued to perform well at school, there was no point in burdening me with cumbersome gadgetry or segregating me from my classmates. He did not tell me I was eligible to receive recorded materials for the blind. He did not even explain legal blindness, much less the specifics of my condition. I did not find out what my macula was for several years. He said nothing about adaptation, did not speculate about what my brain had already learned to do to compensate for the incomplete images my eyes were sending to it. This was not his job. Since then I have heard accounts of other doctors faced with the dilemma of telling patients there is no cure for their condition. They admit they sometimes see these patients as embarrassments, things they'd rather sweep under the carpet, out of public view. As a child of eleven I did not understand his dilemma. I assumed his failure to give me more information was a measure of the insignificance of my problem. I was confused and scared, but also disappointed not to receive the glasses I expected him to prescribe. I left with no glasses, no advice, no explanations, nothing but the words *macular degeneration,* which I did not understand, and more significantly, the word *blind,* which I understood only too well.

But I did not use the word. I was not blind. Blind people saw nothing, only darkness. *Blind* meant the man in the subway station, standing for hours near the token booth, tin cup in hand, a mangy German shepherd lying on a bit of blanket at his feet. That was not how I saw myself. Surely there was some sort of mistake. Or else it was a lie, and as long as I did not repeat it, refrained from speaking the hateful word and claiming identity with the beggar in the subway, I could keep the lie from becoming a reality. Because if I were blind, or going blind, surely someone would do something about it. I'd read about Helen Keller. I knew what went on. Shouldn't someone be teaching me braille? At school they didn't use the word either. They moved me to the front row, stopped telling me to hold the book away from my face, and kept an eye on me. From this I understood not only that the word should not be spoken, but also that I shouldn't ask for special favors, shouldn't draw undue attention to my disability (a word I didn't use either), shouldn't make a spectacle of myself. I learned to read the blackboard from the motion of the teacher's writing. If I suspected I would have to read aloud in class, I'd memorize pages of text, predicting with reasonable accuracy which paragraph would fall to me. The routines of my teachers saved me. Also, by the sixth grade, reading aloud in class was usually only required in French, and then only a few sentences at a time. Outside of school, if other kids said, "Look at that!" I determined from the tone of voice whether they saw something ugly, strange, or cute, and would adjust my response accordingly. On the bus I counted streets to know my stop. In elevators I counted buttons.

The most I would admit to was "a problem with my eyes," sometimes adding, "and They won't give me glasses," indicating that it was not me but the willfully obstructionist medical establishment which was to blame for my failure to see as I should.   15

Once, in Paris, I met a banker who announced to me as he shook my hand that he had "un problème" with his eyes. He explained that this was why he couldn't look me straight in the eye. I understood that a person in his profession had to say something. For him, as for a used-car dealer or clergyman, failure to maintain a direct gaze would affect his business. I noted, too, that he did not use the word *aveugle,* any medical term, nor any other phrase I could translate into one of the current American ones to designate impaired sight. The imprecision of his phrase allowed for the possibility that the problem might be only temporary, a side-effect of medication, an adjustment to new glasses. But the tension in his tone gave him away. He was a French banker of the old school. His suit was that particular shade of navy. His repertoire of elegant pleasantries was extensive. Everything about him was calculated to affirm, in the most reassuring way, that he could dispatch even the most distasteful or compromising financial matter with discretion so deft it would seem effortless. But his own phrase, "un problème avec mes yeux," tripped him up. In his rehearsed delivery, his haste to move the conversation along, I recognized the uncomfortable anticipation of the usual responses, the hushed surprise, the "So sorry for your loss."

Reluctance to use the word *blind,* even in modified form, is as common as the desire to keep one's visual problems a secret. Many people conceal their sight loss for years, even from people close to them and certainly from strangers. Looking sighted is not so hard. For one thing, the sighted are not all that observant. And most blind people are better at appearing sighted than the sighted are at appearing blind. We compose our faces in expressions of preoccupation. We walk fast, purposefully. We do not ask directions. Forced to read something, we pat our pockets for reading glasses we do not own. When we make mistakes, we feign absentmindedness, slapping our foreheads, blinking our eyes.

An astonishing amount of the literature on the "training" and "rehabilitation" of the blind deals with appearance, the visible manifestations of blindness. Eliminate "blindisms," the experts say, the physical traits the blind are allegedly prone to—the wobbly neck, uneven posture, shuffling gait, unblinking gaze. Discolored or bulging eyes should be covered with patches or dark glasses, empty sockets filled with prostheses. But the books and pamphlets go further. They also urge that the blind, or their sighted keepers, be extra attentive to personal grooming, choose clothes which are stylish and color-coordinated. Having nice clothes and clean fingernails may contribute to a person's self-esteem whether they can see these things or not. And certainly hints about labeling socks or applying makeup can be useful. But the advice of the experts has another message. Blindness is unsightly, a real eyesore. No one wants to look at that.

So the blind, of all levels of impairment and all stages of sight loss, find themselves encouraged to sham sight. And even if there is no overt encouragement from well-meaning family members or social workers, we know, or sense instinctively, that our charade of sight is easier than the consequences of speaking the single word *blind*. Because the word bears such a burden of negative connotations and dreaded associations it can hardly be said to have any neutral, merely descriptive meaning at all. *Blind* means darkness, dependence, destitution, despair. *Blind* means the beggar in the subway station. Look at him slouching there, unkempt, head bowed, stationary among the rushing crowd. Intermittently, an involuntary twitch jerks his arm upward, making the coin or two in his cup clink. Otherwise he is silent, apparently speechless. A sign hung around his neck reads: "I'm blind. Please help." Because *blind* means "needs help," and also "needs charity." But the people rushing by barely oblige. They barely see him. They certainly don't stop to stare. And they certainly do not expand their vision to allow for any other image of blindness. Told that there are blind people in all walks of life—medicine, law, social work, education, the arts—they are not impressed. They see those successes as flukes, exceptions, while the beggar in the subway is the rule. Those people went blind late in life, after the habits of their professions were formed, and probably, if you looked closely, after their major accomplishments were already achieved. Or else they're not "really" blind. They have just enough sight to get by. Besides, they probably had special help. If, behind every great man there is a woman, in front of every accomplished blind person there is a sighted helper, spouse, child, or parent, leading the way. Helen Keller had Annie Sullivan. Milton had daughters.

The blind beggar stands alone. As long as we can manage, we keep our distance, both because he makes such a displeasing spectacle of himself and because we know the consequences of claiming identity with him. Note how few coins there are in his cup. He might be faking. If he greets the token clerk changing shifts, his take will plummet. Every visually impaired, partially sighted, hard-of-seeing person knows the suspicion. And we know the story of the cop beating the man with his nightstick for the crime of carrying both a white cane and a newspaper. "My mother is really blind," the cop shouts. The blind man says nothing. No chance to explain how his particular condition leaves him enough sight to read but not the right kind to get around. Too late for him to say he was bringing the paper home for someone to read aloud to him. The cop's mother sits in the dark, wishing someone would read the paper to her. The rest of us compose our faces, fake it as best we can, and scuttle toward the exit. We bite our tongues, dare not speak the word aloud, like the true name of God.

The word *blind* has always meant more than merely the inability to see. The Anglo-Saxon translators of the Gospels made the metaphoric leap from literal sightlessness to spiritual or cognitive incapacity. Of course they were only following an ancient lead. Throughout the history of the language and in common usage today, the word connotes lack of understanding or discernment, willful disregard or obliviousness, a thing meant to conceal or deceive. In fact, when you stop to listen, the word is far more commonly used in its figurative than its literal sense. And it comes up so often: blind faith, blind devotion, blind luck, blind lust, blind trust, blind chance, blind rage, blind alley, blind curve, blind-nail flooring, blind date (more dangerous than you think), duck blind, window blind, micro-mini blind (when open, they're hard to see), blind taste test, double blind study, flying blind, following blind, blind leading the blind, blind landing, color-blind (in the racial sense, a good thing), blind summit, blind side, blind spot, blindfold, blindman's buff, three blind mice (have you ever seen such a sight in your life?). Pick up any book or magazine and you will find dozens of similes and metaphors connecting blindness and blind people with ignorance, confusion, indifference, ineptitude. An image of a blind man stumbling around an unfamiliar and presumably overfurnished room is used to depict someone grappling with a difficult moral problem. A woman flails blindly (not only sightless but feeble) at an assailant, blinded by hatred and rage. Other disabilities are used similarly, but not as often. A politician may be deaf to the concerns of his constituents and lame in his responses, but first and foremost he is blind to their needs. Writers and speakers seem so attached to these meanings for *blind* they don't even find them clichéd. Deny them the use of the word and they feel gagged, stymied. If you want to talk about stupidity, prejudice, weakness, narrow-mindedness, no other word will do.

To express the opposite of blindness, however, we need at least two words. Generally, we use the words *sight* and *vision* interchangeably, though recently, some eye specialists make a distinction, using *sight* to refer to the functioning of the eye itself, and *vision* to refer to the functioning of the eye and brain together. Originally *vision* was used to mean spiritual or metaphysical perception. Later it became synonymous with sight. In common usage positive connotations predominate. Seeing, after all, is believing. We speak of vision as a virtue. Hindsight is always 20/20. We want our leaders to be at least clear-sighted, if not possessed of "that vision thing." We hold dear our views, outlooks, perspectives. We know a picture is worth a thousand words. We want to see eye to eye.

Of course people who are blind use language the same way. Though the joke "'I see,' says the blind man" can always get a laugh out of children and perhaps adults as well, blind people are as likely to say "I see what you mean" or "Let me look at that" as anyone else, and without excessive self-consciousness or irony.

The absolute equation of sight with good and blindness with evil breaks down from time to time. Seeing may be believing, but sometimes you cannot (should not) believe your eyes. When we say "Love is blind," it cuts both ways. Love makes us oblivious to the beloved's flaws, putting us at risk of exploitation, abuse, deception. But it also causes us to overlook the superficial defects and shortcomings of physical appearance, financial condition, social status, which others may see as obstacles to happiness. Myth and folklore abound with complex portrayals of the interplay between love and sight. Willful deities divert themselves by temporarily or permanently blinding mortals for the sole purpose of watching them fall in love with inappropriate partners. Sight restored, there's always a joke on someone, human or divine. Psyche finds herself united to a man she cannot see. When she finally lights the lamp and looks at Love, his beauty so startles her, she drops hot oil on him and he flees. The message: look too closely at the beloved and someone will get burned.

It's no accident that the eyes are the most often mentioned feature in all love poetry. Beautiful themselves for their gemlike color and liquid sheen, eyes are not only windows into the soul but can also send elaborate messages of love. They glow with affection, smoulder with passion, dilate with emotion. When we gaze into the eyes of the beloved and see a reflection of ourselves contained there, our narcissistic tendencies are gratified. Now, as in the past, women spend more time and money accentuating, highlighting, lining, defining, emphasizing their eyes than any other feature. Small wonder that women and men losing their sight often report anxiety about their sexuality. Women fear that without sight, their eyes will no longer be alluring. No more bedroom eyes, come-hither looks. Men seldom make passes at girls who wear glasses. If the girl is blind, she will be that much more unattractive, or that much less able to control her own sexuality. Blind girls have been sold into prostitution. Presumably they were expected to service men other women would find repulsive to look at. Or else a blind woman provides an extra level of voyeuristic titillation, the additional level of excitement Peeping Toms seek: to observe the unseeing. For men the loss of sight is devastating in a different way. The male gaze is supposed to project messages of intention and desire. But the act of seeing also plays a large part in male sexual arousal. This is an argument often made to defend pornography. If voracious and deviant males can get their jollies looking at dirty pictures, they'll keep their lecherous looks (and hands) to themselves. Oedipus tears out his eyes even if another organ might seem more appropriate, given his crime. His act not only symbolizes castration, but makes it unnecessary. What you can't see, you can't want. And don't forget: masturbation will make you blind.

Look at Justice. Observe that she is not blind but blindfolded. True, it's difficult to depict blindness in painting or sculpture without representing some unsightly deformity, unless the blindfold is actually a bandage hiding a gruesome wound. But it seems more likely that she has willingly renounced sight. She makes herself blind to extenuating circumstances, even to the fact that one of the litigants may be a family member or friend. Presumably when Justice is off duty she can see. The blindfold could even slip. She could lift an edge of it and peek if her hands weren't full. In one hand she holds a book, presumably of law, which she cannot read blindfolded. Perhaps it's there as a reminder that she could at any moment rip off the rag and look up the relevant statute. In the other hand she holds a scale to weigh evidence. But she cannot see the balance or lack of balance which is achieved. Perhaps she can feel it with the heightened sensitivity blind people are supposed to have.

Despite this apparent reverence for the impartiality of the blind, still, in some states, the legally blind are automatically exempt from jury duty. Though Justice is blind, the jury should be sighted. Jurors may have to examine evidence, respond to the ocular proof of a bloodstain or fingerprint. Attorneys coach witnesses not only on what to say, but how to look saying it. "Look at the defendant," the lawyer urges, "are those the eyes of a murderer?" True, looks can be deceiving, but in a court of law they still count for a great deal.

My husband was once dismissed from a jury pool because of my blindness. A doctor had allegedly misdiagnosed a patient's symptoms as psychosomatic, and failed to treat her for the brain tumor which caused her to go blind. The jurors were asked if the fact that the patient had ended up blind, as opposed to disabled in some other way, would have any bearing on their ability to arrive at an equitable settlement. Both attorneys viewed Nick's close association with blindness as an impairment of his vision, his ability to make a clear-sighted judgment. He might even upset the balance in the minds of other jurors with irrelevant details of the exact nature of this disability.

Law, love, language—the peculiar, double-edged sword of sight never leaves us alone. It's fear, of course; Americans' fear of blindness is second only to their fear of cancer, and as ancient as the fear of darkness. So these constant references to blindness, equating it with stupidity, narrow-mindedness, or evil, are a verbal game of chicken. Taunt the fates. Name the demon you fear and insult it. It's a way perpetually to reanimate the fear, keep the sense of dread alive. This is why the clichés seem always fresh. At the same time, calling justice and love blind is a dire warning. There's more here than meets the eye, but what meets the eye is still what matters most. Look deeper. Watch carefully. Don't blink. Use it or lose it.

The fear of blindness leads naturally to the fear of the blind. The competent and independent blind pose a particular threat to the sighted, and they can't refrain from comment. Every blind person is familiar with the praise. "You manage so well," the sighted coo. They go into raptures over the simplest tasks: our ability to recognize them from their voices, to eat spaghetti, to unlock a door. They are so utterly convinced of the absolute necessity of sight, and the absolute helplessness of the blind, that any display of independence makes them wonder how well they would fare. "I'd never guess you were blind," they say, a slight edge of resentment coming into their tone now. They label us exceptional and secretly suspect some unseen force prompting our response, guiding our hands. Since they can see with their own eyes that there are no strings, no mirrors, they are compelled to reinvent the ancient myths about compensatory powers, supersensory perception. The sixth sense, second sight. We are supposed to have both extra-accurate hearing and perfect pitch, more numerous and more acute taste buds, a finer touch, a bloodhound's sense of smell. We allegedly possess an unfair advantage, which we could use against the sighted, hearing the secrets in their sighs, smelling their fear. We are either supernatural or subhuman, alien or animal. We are not only different but dangerous. But when we express any of this, they scoff: "Don't be silly. I can see you as you really are. You don't scare me. You're just being oversensitive."

It's so much simpler to deal with the blind beggar in the subway. The sighted can pity him and fear becoming like him. Specifically, they fear the absolute dependence he represents, dependence on his dog, on family, educators, social workers, public and private charities, strangers. This dread may be particularly pronounced in Americans, driven as we are by ideals of individual freedom and self-determination. Being blind is un-American. Our national anthem asks a question the blind can only answer in the negative. "No. I cannot see it. The dawn's early light is too feeble. The rocket's red glare was too fleeting to prove anything to me." The National Federation of the Blind, the organization most concerned with the civil rights and political status of the blind, schedules its annual convention to coincide with Independence Day. To the tune of "The Battle Hymn of the Republic" they sing: "Blind eyes have seen the vision / Of the Federalist way. . . ." When the National Library Service began to offer recorded books for the blind in the 1930s, the first offerings included not only the Bible and some works of Shakespeare, but the

American Constitution and Declaration of Independence, perhaps in an effort to educate and patriate a population already at the farthest periphery of the American scene.

A major part of the American fear of blindness has to do with driving. "It's not just your car; it's your freedom," one car ad proclaimed recently.* Thus, if you can't drive, your freedom, your enjoyment of the great American open road, will be seriously restricted. Growing up in New York City, I was spared awareness of this aspect of my disability until I was an adult. I could get wherever I wanted to go on public transportation or on foot, as all my peers did. In other parts of the country, teenagers who, because of impaired sight or other conditions, cannot join in the automotive rites of passage of driver's ed classes and road tests, experience shame and an increased sense of isolation. Since most American cities and towns today sprawl outward from abandoned downtowns, the inability to drive is not only a handicap but an oddity that demands explanation. Public transit and special transportation for the disabled are haphazard at best. Even in places where there is decent public transit, most of the riders are people who do not own or cannot drive a car. A fellow transplanted New Yorker expressed her surprise about riding the bus in Columbus, Ohio. "It's not like New York, where everybody rides the bus. Here, everybody on the bus is . . ." she paused, searching for an inoffensive phrase. "People who ride the bus here are not. . . ." She stopped again, conscious suddenly that the word she wanted was "normal." Because in America today, *normal* means not only to see, to hear, to walk, to talk, to possess an average IQ and income, but also to drive.

But the fear of blindness is international, and goes beyond a fear of the inconveniences of personal transport. In the simplest terms, the fear is linked to the fear of old age and death. Since blindness equals darkness in most people's eyes, and darkness equals death, the final equation seems to follow as inevitably as the ones linking sight and light and life. In this view, blindness is as good as death. When I was eleven, after my condition was diagnosed, I wrote a poem about death. Memory has kindly erased all but the bouncy lines: "I've just been told, I'm getting old. / I don't want to die." But I do remember knowing what I was really writing about was blindness. My fear, only barely acknowledged, was that, like Bette Davis in *Dark Victory*, my lost sight was simply a sign of imminent death. The belief that human experience, both physical and mental, is essentially visual, and any other type of experience is necessarily second-rate, leads to the conclusion that not to see is not to experience, not to live, not to be. At best, the sighted imagine blindness as a state between life and death, an existence encased in darkness, an invisible coffin.

As overextended as this logic may be, the fact remains that the most common causes of blindness tend to occur late in life, thus close to death.

---

one car ad proclaimed recently: For a celebration of the car as an expression of freedom, see James Q. Wilson's "Cars and Their Enemies" (p. 303).

Two-thirds of the legally blind in America are over age fifty-five. Cells atrophy. Irregular blood pressure does damage. Even a relatively minor stroke can affect the vision centers of the brain. Macular degeneration affects ten percent of Americans over seventy. Twenty-five percent develop cataracts. And this is not counting glaucoma, diabetes, nor accidents—projectiles, chemical spills, gunshot wounds. Of course some of these conditions can be corrected surgically, arrested in early stages, or controlled with drugs, and medical science continues to come up with new techniques, treatments, and cures. But there is no guarantee that vision disorders can only occur one at a time. Live long enough and, chances are, you'll go blind too.

You won't be alone. As more and more people live longer, the ranks   35
of the blind will swell. For the currently blind this is cause for, if not celebration, at least optimism. We imagine the blind becoming a more and more significant force, demanding services and rights, changing the image of blindness.

But this optimism is countered by the fact that we seem to be becoming more and more visually dependent. Television has replaced newspapers as the primary source of information. Movies replace novels. Image is everything. But as society becomes increasingly visual, it becomes more audio as well. The telephone and voice mail replace the letter. Technology will also increase the ease with which large print, braille, and recorded materials are made available. Multimedia databases which allow subscribers to access texts combined with images and sound will spawn technologies for blind-friendly talking computers and other appliances. Increased demand will drive down costs. As the desire to preserve the environment continues to grow, public transportation will become more fashionable, efficient, and widespread. If you have to go blind, you've chosen a good time to do it.

All this should be reassuring, or at least no more frightening than any reminder of mortality. And it's true that the elderly who lose their sight may have a harder time than the younger blind, because their loss may be complicated by other problems—lost hearing, lost agility, lost memory, lost financial security. But the possibility of blindness still summons a particular kind of fear. The currently sighted don't want to talk about it. They are unnaturally squeamish about the whole subject. They recoil from any mention of their eyes, their parts or functions. They're far more comfortable discussing comparatively cruder organs: the heart, the bowels, the genitals. They pick up scraps of information and use them as a shield. "Don't they have an operation to fix that?" they say. "Don't they use lasers or something?" Though they may know someone who had a cataract operation, they have a less than perfect understanding either of the condition or the procedure, and certainly don't want to hear it described in detail. If the patient had some trouble adjusting to the intra-ocular implants, or the retina detached and the laser repair only restored partial vision, they shrug and say, "Better than nothing. He's retired. How much does he have to see anyway?" They cross their fingers, knock on wood, ward off the evil eye. When it happens to them, they hope, the techniques will be perfected and the surgeons will be more careful.

The funny thing is, of all the things people fear—cancer, murder, rape, torture, loss of limb, loss of loved ones—blindness is the one anyone can simulate. Simply close your eyes. If you are so afraid of future dependence, why not break this absolute dependence you have on your eyesight? "But," you object, "real blindness is worse than that. With my eyes shut I can still perceive light." True. But given the degrees of blindness you are most likely to experience, you will probably see more than you do with your lids lowered. So go ahead. Close your eyes. It is not an unfamiliar condition for you. You experience it every time you blink. You are the same person with your eyes closed. You can still think, remember, feel. See? It's not so bad. You discover not that you hear better, but that you are better able to make sense of sounds. You hear children playing across the street. After only a minute or two you find you can distinguish their different voices, and follow their game from their words. An acorn falls on the roof of the garage next door. You know, without looking, that it is neither a pebble nor a pellet of hail. A branch rustles, and you know that a squirrel is running across it, jumping to another branch then down the trunk and away. You create a mental picture of this and it pleases you.

Now challenge yourself a little. Drop your pen on the floor. Even if the floor is carpeted you hear where it falls, you can reach down and find it. It may take you a couple of tries, but each time your aim improves. Gravity acts on objects the same way even when your eyes are closed.

Get up and move around the room. Don't be afraid. You know the arrangement of the furniture. Chances are, you arranged it yourself. You have a mental map of the room and use it to navigate. After only a few minor bumps and scrapes your mental map becomes more detailed and precise. You begin to move with assurance. You discover you do not lose your balance or become disoriented. You can reach out and touch a chair or the wall, or feel the breeze through the window, or hear sounds in other rooms. The mental map in your head is in motion. You move more rapidly now. Perhaps you run, skip. It occurs to you it might help if you were neater, if you weren't forever leaving things lying about where you might step on them. Or else you use your memory in new ways. You discover you can find your shoes because you re-create the moment when you took them off. In fact you always take them off there. You are more a creature of habit than you thought.

Go to your closet. Clothes you thought you could identify only by color and cut you find readily recognizable from their texture. And you can dress yourself with your eyes closed. You have lost none of the manual dexterity required to button buttons, zip zippers. Finding socks to match may be tricky, except you may be someone who arranges your socks in some ordered sequence. Certainly you can imagine doing so. With a minimal amount of help and practice, you could do this.

In fact you discover you can accomplish most of your routine daily tasks with your eyes closed. That may be how you define them as routine. You can bathe, fix your hair. You find you don't really need to look at yourself in the mirror when you brush your teeth. A few tasks may require more thought: shaving, makeup, manicure. But your brain isn't impaired. You will come up with something.

And you can feed yourself with ease. You may be surprised by how easily the spoon finds your mouth, the cup your lip. You've been putting things in your mouth for many years now. Feeding yourself was one of your earliest feats of coordination and one which has long since ceased to be amazing, even to your parents.

This really isn't as terrible as you were always led to believe. You can make a list of the things which are impossible to do with your eyes closed, but the list is not very long. And with a little more thought and perhaps some organizational tricks, you can take care of yourself and even others—pets, children. Your problem-solving capacities are as sharp as ever. You are already figuring out clever ways to arrange food in the refrigerator, sort the laundry, wash the windows.

You turn on the TV. You have probably already observed that it is not 45 really necessary to watch the TV. TV is aimed at people who are not as smart as you. You know what's going on even with your eyes closed.

But maybe you're more in the mood for music. Perhaps you already keep records, tapes, and CDs in chronological, alphabetical, or some other order. Perhaps you wish you did and now have an incentive to do so. Or perhaps you enjoy randomness, a trial-and-error selection. And there's always the radio. You can tune the dial to find something you like. You may even feel like dancing. Go ahead.

You have cause to celebrate. You have faced one of your more debilitating fears and seen it for what it is. This is not to say that the loss of sight will not be traumatic, nor that there are things about the visible world which you will miss. But blindness does not in itself constitute helplessness. You will be as resourceful, capable, and intelligent as you ever were.

But suddenly you're not dancing anymore. The fear creeps back and overtakes you. It occurs to you slowly that you will not be alone in this. Your blindness will affect other people—family, friends, co-workers, strangers—and you are afraid they will not adapt as well as you. You worry that well-meaning loved ones will start doing everything for you, that they will refer to your condition as tragic, use hushed tones when they think you can't hear, display exaggerated cheerfulness when you can. If you're in school you worry that "special" classes will not provide you with the education you need. You have the nagging suspicion that teachers and counselors will want to guide your choices in ways that do not fully acknowledge your aptitudes, but only your limitations. You wonder if your employers value you enough to purchase equipment or hire staff to assist you, if they will do so grudgingly and only because the law obliges them. If you quit a job will someone else hire you? You're afraid that people on the street will stare at you or offer help when you don't need it. And when you need help, you're afraid people will mislead you, take unfair advantage, rob you blind.

Face it. What you fear is not your inability to adapt to the loss of sight, it is the inability of people around you to see you the same way. It's not you, it's them. And it's not because you have an unduly malevolent view of human nature. Nor are you guiltily acknowledging this prejudice in yourself. You may not see it as prejudice. Pity and solicitude are not the same as prejudice, you assert. The disabled should be a little more gracious. But the words stick in your throat. You know that's not the only response people have to the disabled.

Once Nick and I took a flight from Paris to Dallas. A man carried a   50 young woman on board and placed her in the seat in front of us. Then he returned with her wheelchair, which she dismantled and arranged in a nearby closet. Then the man left. After take-off, the flight crew discovered that the woman was traveling alone, which was against regulations. The gate agent should have prevented her from boarding. There was a great deal of debate and bustle, complicated by the fact that the woman spoke no English and only one or two crew members spoke French. They questioned her at length. Why had no one stopped her? They briefed her on the airline's responsibilities, the safety of other passengers which her presence on board impaired. What had she been thinking? They did not adopt any of the obvious solutions. They did not move her to an empty seat in first class, where a less-burdened crew member could serve her without imperiling the comfort of others. Instead, they opted for what is too often the first response of the able-bodied to the disabled: they ignored her. Throughout the long flight they rushed past her, greeting her requests for help, when they heard them at all, with surly admonitions about the needs of other passengers and their busy schedule. After a while she started to cry. She cried so hard she made herself sick. We and some other passengers tried to pitch in, but the shock of witnessing this cruelty made us ashamed and somewhat inept. But the woman had astonishing fortitude and cheered up. She was a swimmer, on her way to the Special Olympics. She had never been to America before, and her treatment on this airplane made her understandably apprehensive. We discussed the treatment of the disabled in our respective countries. She said her sense was that Americans tended to warehouse and conceal their disabled. Her exact sentence was: "Les handicappés sont moins visible aux Etas-Unis." One's patriotism flares at odd moments. I began to point out that I had never observed excessive concern for people's disabilities in Paris. High curbs and cobbled streets would be hazards to wheelchairs and crutches. I'd never noticed ramps in public buildings, kneeling buses, braille buttons in elevators. Once I tried to buy a large-print dictionary, a request met with the highest degree of Gallic stupefaction in every bookshop I tried. Was it possible that anyone could not read regular print? But the swimmer was from Bordeaux, where conditions might be better. And I knew that any claims I might make about facilities and services in the United States would seem ludicrous to her after the mistreatment she'd experienced.

And I did not tell her that the airlines have been a battleground for the blind for the last two decades. As the blind, like other Americans, began to fly more and more, the airlines and the Federal Aviation Administration adopted regulations to deal with them. Blind activists have been forcibly removed from airplanes for refusing to give up their white canes. The airlines saw the canes as a hazard to other passengers. "You might poke out someone's eye." In fact, there is a well-documented case of an emergency crash landing where a blind man was the first passenger to find and open an exit door. Accustomed as he was to navigating without eyesight, a little smoke and darkness were no obstacle to him. Today, the FAA has amended its policies, though individual airlines and flight crews sometimes still discriminate.

At the end of the flight, the crew reassembled around the French swimmer, ready to whisk her through immigration and into the hands of whoever was in charge, presumably with more reprimands and warnings. They were profuse in their thanks and praise to Nick and me and the other passengers who had helped her or, as they saw it, helped them. As we approached solid ground again, they felt a need to reestablish the us/them divide, and so efface any error or atrocity on their part. They wanted us to know they understood the ordeal we'd been through, thrown together with such a person. We, after all, like them, were normal. She was the aberration. Because my disability was invisible to them, I squeaked by undetected. Now, I am ashamed I didn't announce myself. At the time, I was too disturbed, too depressed, too frightened. I doubt it would have made them revise their views.

If the mistreatment of people with disabilities were limited to overzealous solicitude and an insensitive use of language, one could be more gracious. But everyone has witnessed the reality. Special treatment leads to resentment, which prompts ridicule, which barely conceals hate, and in extreme cases, suggests annihilation. Don't forget that in Hitler's vision of a perfect world there was no place for the blind, the deaf, the crippled, the mentally deficient. These views are still held, if, for now, only in secret. "Don't stare," parents warn a child watching a blind person with a cane, a deaf person speaking sign language, a person in a wheelchair. Don't stare. Don't look at that. Close your eyes and it will go away. Out of sight, out of mind. The child receives two messages: first, that people with disabilities should be ignored, pushed to the periphery of society, if not over the edge. And the parent reinforces yet again the idea of the preeminence of sight, the Almighty Eye which controls both consciousness and the world outside. What you can't see can't hurt you, can't matter, doesn't exist.

Which is why I call it blindness. When I identify myself in this way on the first day of class, it is perhaps presumptuous, an assertion of solidarity I have not earned because I see too much. But I hope by using the word I can help my students redefine it and, in some small way, correct their vision of the world. Of the students who drop my class after the first meeting, there may be some who find the idea of a blind professor ludicrous, aggravating, or frightening. But I will never know. The ones who stay adapt. They stand in my office doorway and identify themselves by name. They describe what's going on outside the window. They read me the slogans on their T-shirts. These gestures become natural to them. I tell them if they commit a crime in my presence I would not be able to pick them out of a police lineup. They indulge me with laughter. I have a conversation with one student about being a blind writer. He wants to know how I can describe things I cannot see. I explain how I question the sighted people I know about what they can see from what distance. We laugh. We talk about memory, how I can still recall what things look like from before I lost my sight, and how I use memory and imagination in the same way any writer does. He is a psychology major. We discuss visual perception. He tells me he knows a blind painter and describes how he manages. We are comfortable. We exchange these ideas with matter-of-fact ease. His question is not condescending or prying, not the "How ever do you possibly manage?" of the ignorant and insensitive. Another student talks about an anecdote I told in class, one of those extended narratives any teacher uses to make an obscure point. The anecdote made sense to him, he tells me, then adds, "And while you were talking, I looked around the room and everybody was just staring. They were all really into it." And for a moment I see this, creating the mental picture which goes with the words. The student sees me do this, but adds no embellishment. His subtle, unadorned generosity moves me.

This is how it's supposed to be, the whole point about integration, 55 mainstreaming, inclusion. They accept me and forget I ever used the ugly word. And perhaps later, the word will cease to seem so ugly.

Perhaps it doesn't matter what words you use as long as you know you mean. On the bus recently a man stopped the driver, saying, "Yo! There's a little handicap' brother wants to get on." The word *handicap* is in disfavor, despite the fact that in horse racing or golf, it is the most skillful competitor who carries the heaviest handicap. Still, *disabled* and *challenged* are more in vogue. But there on the bus no one challenged the man's use of the word. He was a big man, over six feet tall. His voice boomed out of his chest and had more than a hint of a threat in it. Besides, we all knew what he meant. It was early in the afternoon, an hour when everyone on the bus is challenged in some way: physically, developmentally, financially, chronologically. Simply by being on the bus we announce our difference, our specialness, our handicap.

The bus knelt. The handicapped brother got on. He was not in a wheelchair. He was about three and a half feet tall. His whole body rocked from side to side as he propelled himself forward. He belly-flopped into a seat, flipped, and sat. I could not see him well enough to give a name to his condition. The man who had stopped the bus made no move to assist him further. But he waited, watching him, and said, "I saved it for you, brother." His voice was full of defiance, the bravado that comes from a bond of shared identity. In his words was a challenge to anyone who dared come between them.

The man who spoke was African-American. The handicapped brother was not. The bond between them, between us all at that moment, was the bus.

The handicapped brother said "Thank you" with the deft graciousness of someone who regularly accepts assistance from strangers. The other man found a seat. The driver pulled the bus into traffic. The rest of us settled into a comfortable contemplation of our shared humanity and mutual acceptance. Those of us who could gazed through the window, looking down at the un-challenged in their cars, complacent in their independence, their unobstructed door-to-door mobility. Someday some of them will join us on the bus — sooner rather than later, given the way some of them drive. When it happens, we will do what we can for them. We'll give up our seat. We'll announce their stop, reach for the button to ring the bell, take an extra moment to explain. We've been riding the bus long enough to sense what's needed. The bus lurched and stalled in a snarl of traffic. Someone groaned. Someone laughed. We were not fooled. The bus is no more perfect than the world outside. But that day it felt right to us. It was where we all belonged. And eventually, with a shudder, another lurch, we moved forward, and, unsteadily at first but picking up speed, we bounced along together.

QUESTIONING THE TEXT

1. Kleege gives examples of the positive connotations associated with vision and sight ("seeing is believing," "that vision thing," "a picture is worth a thousand words," "seeing eye to eye") and the negative connotations associated with blindness ("blind alley," "blind rage," "blind leading the blind," "blind to their needs"). Brainstorm other words and phrases to add to these lists and bring them to class for discussion. How do these words and phrases suggest the way society regards sight and blindness?

2. The word *fear* reverberates like a drumbeat throughout this essay. Reread the essay, noting all the uses of *fear* and related words. What exactly is it that people fear? Write one or two paragraphs in response to this question and bring them to class for discussion.

3. Why do you think A.L. opens her introduction with a personal anecdote? What effect(s) might she hope to create by doing so?

MAKING CONNECTIONS

4. Read the selection in Chapter 7 by Ward Churchill, "Crimes against Humanity" (p. 497), and make a list of all the metaphors he uses. Then list the major metaphors for vision/sight and blindness/darkness used by

Kleege. Bring both lists to class for a discussion of the similar and different ways the two writers use metaphor to support and illustrate their arguments.

5. Near the end of her essay, after describing a scene in one of her classes, Kleege says, "This is how it's supposed to be, the whole point about integration, mainstreaming, inclusion. They accept me and forget I ever used the ugly word. And perhaps later, the word will cease to seem so ugly" (paragraph 55). Using this statement as a starting point, work with a classmate to create a brief dialogue between Kleege and Andrew Sullivan (p. 350) about whether mainstreaming is possible or desirable.

JOINING THE CONVERSATION

6. Take up the challenge that Kleege issues in paragraphs 38–47, closing your eyes and carrying out the tasks she describes. Then write a description of your experience, ending with a discussion of Kleege's claim that "You can make a list of the things which are impossible to do with your eyes closed, but the list is not very long." Bring your description to class to compare with those of classmates.

ROBERT D. KING
Should English Be the Law?

No DOUBT ABOUT IT—*our native tongue helps shape our personal identity, giving us not only words and literature in common with people who speak the same language but perhaps even habits of mind. And what is true for individuals may be the case for nations as well: their history and heritage are often embedded in their language. American English, for example, carries in its genes the Germanic tongue of the ancient peoples of Britain, including Angles, Saxons, and Jutes; the linguistic residue of Roman domination of Europe; the French idioms of a later band of Norman conquerors; the distinctive vocabulary of Africans brought to North America as slaves; and an infusion of terms from Native Americans and from Spanish-speaking peoples. English in general has long been especially receptive to words and expressions from other tongues. As a result, at the dawn of a new millennium, a dialect that originated with obscure tribes in a backwater of Europe has grown to become, arguably, the world's common language.*

But some worry that English itself is now under assault on its turf in the United States. Despite genuine hostility to new groups of immigrants, from the Irish in the nineteenth century to the Vietnamese in the twentieth, Americans have eventually accepted wave after wave of opportunity seekers from all corners of the globe. And within a generation most immigrant families have assumed a distinctly American identity, with their children speaking English as glibly as youngsters whose ancestors booked passage on the Mayflower. At least that's the melting-pot story many of us have lived and retold. But today, and not for the first time, some immigrants, especially from Mexico and Central America, seem reluctant to give up their native langauge and, with it, a portion of their culture and identity. This resistance has been strong enough to provoke a nativist response in the form of "English Only" legislation.

But just how much of a country's identity is tied to its language? And is language diversity really a threat to national identity? These are some of the questions linguist Robert D. King examines in "Should English Be the Law?" an essay that appeared originally in the Atlantic Monthly *(April 1997). He puts the issue in historical and political perspective and comes up with surprising and, for many Americans, comforting answers.*

King is Chair of the Linguistics Department at the University of Texas at Austin, where he also served as Dean of Liberal Arts for almost a decade. Among his books is Nehru and the Language Politics of India *(1997).* —J.R.

We have known race riots, draft riots, labor violence, secession, antiwar protests, and a whiskey rebellion, but one kind of trouble we've never had: a language riot. Language riot? It sounds like a joke. The very idea of

VACCINATING AGAINST CANCER / HOW MARIJUANA CAUSES INSANITY

The Atlantic Monthly

APRIL 1997

Should English Be the Law?

by
Robert D. King

The best strategy for preserving our national language may be to keep taking it for granted

$2.95   Can. $3.50

04

02058

0 395525 3

language as a political force—as something that might threaten to split a country wide apart—is alien to our way of thinking and to our cultural traditions.

This may be changing. On August 1 of last year [1996] the U.S. House of Representatives approved a bill that would make English the official language of the United States. The vote was 259 to 169, with 223 Republicans and thirty-six Democrats voting in favor and eight Republicans, 160 Democrats, and one independent voting against. The debate was intense, acrid, and partisan. On March 25 of last year the Supreme Court agreed to review a case involving an Arizona law that would require public employees to conduct government business only in English. Arizona is one of several states that have passed "Official English" or "English Only" laws. The appeal to the Supreme Court followed a 6-to-5 ruling, in October of 1995, by a federal appeals court striking down the Arizona law. These events suggest how divisive a public issue language could become in America—even if it has until now scarcely been taken seriously.

Traditionally, the American way has been to make English the national language—but to do so quietly, locally, without fuss. The Constitution is silent on language: the Founding Fathers had no need to legislate that English be the official language of the country. It has always been taken for granted that English *is* the national language, and that one must learn English in order to make it in America.

To say that language has never been a major force in American history or politics, however, is not to say that politicians have always resisted linguistic jingoism. In 1753 Benjamin Franklin voiced his concern that German immigrants were not learning English: "Those [Germans] who come hither are generally the most ignorant Stupid Sort of their own Nation. . . . they will soon so out number us, that all the advantages we have will not, in My Opinion, be able to preserve our language, and even our government will become precarious." Theodore Roosevelt articulated the unspoken American linguistic-melting-pot theory when he boomed, "We have room for but one language here, and that is the English language, for we intend to see that the crucible turns our people out as Americans, of American nationality, and not as dwellers in a polyglot boarding house." And: "We must have but one flag. We must also have but one language. That must be the language of the Declaration of Independence, of Washington's Farewell address, of Lincoln's Gettysburg speech and second inaugural."

OFFICIAL ENGLISH

TR's linguistic tub-thumping long typified the tradition of American 5 politics. That tradition began to change in the wake of the anything-goes attitudes and the celebration of cultural differences arising in the 1960s. A 1975 amendment to the Voting Rights Act of 1965 mandated the "bilingual ballot" under certain circumstances, notably when the voters of selected language groups reached five percent or more in a voting district. Bilingual education became a byword of educational thinking during the 1960s. By the 1970s linguists had demonstrated convincingly—at least to other academics—that black English (today called African-American vernacular English or Ebonics) was not "bad" English but a different kind of authentic English with its own rules. Predictably, there have been scattered demands that black English be included in bilingual-education programs.

It was against this background that the movement to make English the official language of the country arose. In 1981 Senator S. I. Hayakawa, long a leading critic of bilingual education and bilingual ballots, introduced in the U.S. Senate a constitutional amendment that not only would have made English the official language but would have prohibited federal and state laws and regulations requiring the use of other languages. His English Language Amendment died in the Ninety-seventh Congress.

In 1983 the organization called U.S. English was founded by Hayakawa and John Tanton, a Michigan ophthalmologist. The primary purpose of the organization was to promote English as the official language of the United States. (The best background readings on America's "neolinguisticism" are the books *Hold Your Tongue,* by James Crawford, and *Language Loyalties,* edited by Crawford, both published in 1992.) Official English initiatives were passed by California in 1986, by Arkansas, Mississippi, North Carolina, North Dakota, and South Carolina in 1987, by Colorado, Florida, and Arizona in 1988, and by Alabama in 1990. The majorities voting for these initiatives were generally not insubstantial: California's, for example, passed by 73 percent.

It was probably inevitable that the Official English (or English Only—the two names are used almost interchangeably) movement would acquire a conservative, almost reactionary undertone in the 1990s. Official English is politically very incorrect. But its cofounder John Tanton brought with him strong liberal credentials. He had been active in the Sierra Club and Planned Parenthood, and in the 1970s served as the national president of Zero Population Growth. Early advisers of U.S. English resist ideological pigeonholing: they included Walter Annenberg, Jacques Barzun, Bruno Bettelheim, Alistair Cooke, Denton Cooley, Walter Cronkite, Angier Biddle Duke, George Gilder, Sidney Hook, Norman Podhoretz, Arnold Schwarzenegger, and Karl Shapiro. In 1987 U.S. English installed as its president Linda Chávez, a Hispanic who had been prominent in the Reagan Administration. A year later she resigned her position, citing "repugnant" and "anti-Hispanic" overtones in an internal memorandum written by Tanton. Tanton, too, resigned, and Walter Cronkite, describing the affair as "embarrassing," left the advisory board. One board member, Norman Cousins, defected in 1986, alluding to the "negative symbolic significance" of California's Official English initiative, Proposition 63.

The current chairman of the board and CEO of U.S. English is Mauro E. Mujica, who claims that the organization has 650,000 members.

The popular wisdom is that conservatives are pro and liberals are con. True, conservatives such as George Will and William F. Buckley Jr. have written columns supporting Official English. But would anyone characterize as conservatives the present and past U.S. English board members Alistair Cooke, Walter Cronkite, and Norman Cousins? One of the strongest opponents of bilingual education is the Mexican-American writer Richard Rodríguez, best known for his eloquent autobiography, *Hunger of Memory* (1982). There is a strain of American liberalism that defines itself in nostalgic devotion to the melting pot.

For several years relevant bills awaited consideration in the U.S. House   10 of Representatives. The Emerson Bill (H.R. 123), passed by the House last August, specifies English as the official language of government, and requires that the government "preserve and enhance" the official status of English. Exceptions are made for the teaching of foreign languages; for actions necessary for public health, international relations, foreign trade, and the protection of the rights of criminal defendants; and for the use of "terms of art" from languages other than English. It would, for example, stop the Internal Revenue Service from sending out income-tax forms and instructions in languages other than English, but it would not ban the use of foreign languages in census materials or documents dealing with national security. *"E Pluribus Unum"* can still appear on American money. U.S. English supports the bill.

What are the chances that some version of Official English will become federal law? Any language bill will face tough odds in the Senate, because some western senators have opposed English Only measures in the past for various reasons, among them a desire by Republicans not to alienate the growing number of Hispanic Republicans, most of whom are uncomfortable with mandated monolingualism. Texas Governor George W. Bush, too, has forthrightly said that he would oppose any English Only proposals in his state. Several of the Republican candidates for President in 1996 (an interesting exception is Phil Gramm) endorsed versions of Official English, as has Newt Gingrich. While governor of Arkansas, Bill Clinton signed into law an English Only bill. As President, he has described his earlier action as a mistake.

Many issues intersect in the controversy over Official English: immigration (above all), the rights of minorities (Spanish-speaking minorities in particular), the pros and cons of bilingual education, tolerance, how best to educate the children of immigrants, and the place of cultural diversity in school curricula and in the American society in general. The question that lies at the root of most of the uneasiness is this: Is America threatened by the preservation of languages other than English? Will America, if it continues on its traditional path of benign linguistic neglect, go the way of Belgium, Canada, and Sri Lanka—three countries among many whose unity is gravely imperiled by language and ethnic conflicts?

LANGUAGE AND NATIONALITY

Language and nationalism were not always so intimately intertwined. Never in the heyday of rule by sovereign was it a condition of employment that the King be able to speak the language of his subjects. George I spoke no English and spent much of his time away from England, attempting to use the power of his kingship to shore up his German possessions. In the Middle Ages nationalism was not even part of the picture: one owed loyalty to a lord, a prince, a ruler, a family, a tribe, a church, a piece of land, but not to a nation and least of all to a nation as a language unit. The capital city of the Austrian Hapsburg empire was Vienna, its ruler a monarch with effective control of peoples of the most varied and incompatible ethnicities, and languages, throughout Central and Eastern Europe. The official language, and the lingua franca as well, was German. While it stood—and it stood for hundreds of years—the empire was an anachronistic relic of what for most of human history had been the normal relationship between country and language: none.

The marriage of language and nationalism goes back at least to Romanticism and specifically to Rousseau, who argued in his *Essay on the Origin of Languages* that language must develop before politics is possible and that language originally distinguished nations from one another. A little-remembered aim of the French Revolution—itself the legacy of Rousseau*—was to impose a national language on France, where regional languages such as Provençal, Breton, and Basque were still strong competitors against standard French, the French of the Ile de France. As late as 1789, when the Revolution began, half the population of the south of France, which spoke Provençal, did not understand French. A century earlier the playwright Racine* said that he had had to resort to Spanish and Italian to make himself understood in the southern French town of Uzès. After the Revolution nationhood itself became aligned with language.

In 1846 Jacob Grimm, one of the Brothers Grimm of fairy-tale fame but   15 better known in the linguistic establishment as a forerunner of modern comparative and historical linguists, said that "a nation is the totality of people who speak the same language." After midcentury, language was invoked more than any other single criterion to define nationality. Language as a political force helped to bring about the unification of Italy and of Germany and the secession

---

Rousseau: Jean-Jacques Rousseau (1712–78), French writer, political theorist, and philosopher

Racine: Jean-Baptiste Racine (1639–99), French dramatist and historiographer, author of *Andromaque* (1667) and *Phèdre* (1677)

of Norway from its union with Sweden in 1905. Arnold Toynbee* observed—unhappily—soon after the First World War that "the growing consciousness of Nationality had attached itself neither to traditional frontiers nor to new geographical associations but almost exclusively to mother tongues."

The crowning triumph of the new desideratum was the Treaty of Versailles, in 1919, when the allied victors of the First World War began redrawing the map of Central and Eastern Europe according to nationality as best they could. The magic word was "self-determination," and none of Woodrow Wilson's Fourteen Points* mentioned the word "language" at all. Self-determination was thought of as being related to "nationality," which today we would be more likely to call "ethnicity"; but language was simpler to identify than nationality or ethnicity. When it came to drawing the boundary lines of various countries—Czechoslovakia, Yugoslavia, Romania, Hungary, Albania, Bulgaria, Poland—it was principally language that guided the draftsman's hand. (The main exceptions were Alsace-Lorraine, South Tyrol, and the German-speaking parts of Bohemia and Moravia.) Almost by default language became the defining characteristic of nationality.

And so it remains today. In much of the world, ethnic unity and cultural identification are routinely defined by language. To be Arab is to speak Arabic. Bengali identity is based on language in spite of the division of Bengali-speakers between Hindu India and Muslim Bangladesh. When eastern Pakistan seceded from greater Pakistan in 1971, it named itself Bangladesh: *desa* means "country"; *bangla* means not the Bengali people or the Bengali territory but the Bengali language.

Scratch most nationalist movements and you find a linguistic grievance. The demands for independence of the Baltic states (Latvia, Lithuania, and Estonia) were intimately bound up with fears for the loss of their respective languages and cultures in a sea of Russianness. In Belgium the war between French and Flemish threatens an already weakly fused country. The present atmosphere of Belgium is dark and anxious, costive; the metaphor of divorce is a staple of private and public discourse. The lines of terrorism in Sri Lanka are drawn between Tamil Hindus and Sinhalese Buddhists—and also between the Tamil and Sinhalese languages. Worship of the French language fortifies the movement for an independent Quebec. Whether a united Canada will survive into the twenty-first century is a question too close to call. Much of the anxiety about language in the United States is probably fueled by the "Quebec problem": unlike Belgium, which is a small European country, or Sri Lanka, which is halfway around the world, Canada is our close neighbor.

Arnold Toynbee (1889–1975): English historian, author of the twelve-volume *A Study of History* (1934–61)

Fourteen Points: fourteen terms for peace outlined by U.S. president Woodrow Wilson on May 18, 1918, during World War I

Language is a convenient surrogate for nonlinguistic claims that are often awkward to articulate, for they amount to a demand for more political and economic power. Militant Sikhs in India call for a state of their own: Khalistan ("Land of the Pure" in Punjabi). They frequently couch this as a demand for a linguistic state, which has a certain simplicity about it, a clarity of motive—justice, even, because states in India are normally linguistic states. But the Sikh demands blend religion, economics, language, and retribution for sins both punished and unpunished in a country where old sins cast long shadows.

Language is an explosive issue in the countries of the former Soviet 20 Union. The language conflict in Estonia has been especially bitter. Ethnic Russians make up almost a third of Estonia's population, and most of them do not speak or read Estonian, although Russians have lived in Estonia for more than a generation. Estonia has passed legislation requiring knowledge of the Estonian language as a condition of citizenship. Nationalist groups in independent Lithuania sought restrictions on the use of Polish—again, old sins, long shadows.

In 1995 protests erupted in Moldova, formerly the Moldavian Soviet Socialist Republic, over language and the teaching of Moldovan history. Was Moldovan history a part of Romanian history or of Soviet history? Was Moldova's language Romanian? Moldovan—earlier called Moldavian—*is* Romanian, just as American English and British English are both English. But in the days of the Moldavian SSR, Moscow insisted that the two languages were different, and in a piece of linguistic nonsense required Moldavian to be writtin in the Cyrillic alphabet to strengthen the case that it was not Romanian.

The official language of Yugoslavia was Serbo-Croatian, which was never so much a language as a political accommodation. The Serbian and Croatian languages are mutually intelligible. Serbian is written in the Cyrillic alphabet, is identified with the Eastern Orthodox branch of the Catholic Church, and borrows its high-culture words from the east—from Russian and Old Church Slavic. Croatian is written in the Roman alphabet, is identified with Roman Catholicism, and borrows its high-culture words from the west—from German, for example, and Latin. One of the first things the newly autonomous Republic of Serbia did, in 1991, was to pass a law decreeing Serbian in the Cyrillic alphabet the official language of the country. With Croatia divorced from Serbia, the Croatian and Serbian languages are diverging more and more. Serbo-Croatian has now passed into history, a language-museum relic from the brief period when Serbs and Croats called themselves Yugoslavs and pretended to like each other.

Slovakia, relieved now of the need to accommodate to Czech cosmopolitan sensibilities, has passed a law making Slovak its official language. (Czech is to Slovak pretty much as Croatian is to Serbian.) Doctors in state hospitals must speak to patients in Slovak, even if another language would aid diagnosis and treatment. Some 600,000 Slovaks—more than 10 percent of the population—

are ethnically Hungarian. Even staff meetings in Hungarian-language schools must be in Slovak. (The government dropped a stipulation that church weddings be conducted in Slovak after heavy opposition from the Roman Catholic Church.) Language inspectors are told to weed out "all sins perpetrated on the regular Slovak language." Tensions between Slovaks and Hungarians, who had been getting along, have begun to arise.

The twentieth century is ending as it began — with trouble in the Balkans and with nationalist tensions flaring up in other parts of the globe. (Toward the end of his life Bismarck* predicted that "some damn fool thing in the Balkans" would ignite the next war.) Language isn't always part of the problem. But it usually is.

UNIQUE OTHERNESS

Is there no hope for language tolerance? Some countries manage to   25 maintain their unity in the face of multilingualism. Examples are Finland, with a Swedish minority, and a number of African and Southeast Asian countries. Two others could not be more unlike as countries go: Switzerland and India.

German, French, Italian, and Romansh are the languages of Switzerland. The first three can be and are used for official purposes; all four are designated "national" languages. Switzerland is politically almost hyperstable. It has language problems (Romansh is losing ground), but they are not major, and they are never allowed to threaten national unity.

Contrary to public perception, India gets along pretty well with a host of different languages. The Indian constitution officially recognizes nineteen languages, English among them. Hindi is specified in the constitution as the national language of India, but that is a pious postcolonial fiction: outside the Hindi-speaking northern heartland of India, people don't want to learn it. English functions more nearly than Hindi as India's lingua franca.

From 1947, when India obtained its independence from the British, until the 1960s blood ran in the streets and people died because of language. Hindi absolutists wanted to force Hindi on the entire country, which would have split India between north and south and opened up other fracture lines as well. For as long as possible Jawaharlal Nehru, independent India's first Prime Minister, resisted nationalist demands to redraw the capricious state boundaries of British India according to language. By the time he capitulated, the country had gained a precious decade to prove its viability as a union.

Why is it that India preserves its unity with not just two languages to contend with, as Belgium, Canada, and Sri Lanka have, but nineteen? The answer is that India, like Switzerland, has a strong national identity. The two

---

Bismarck: Otto von Bismarck (1815–98), Prussian prime minister and chancellor of the German Empire

countries share something big and almost mystical that holds each together in a union transcending language. That something I call "unique otherness."

The Swiss have what the political scientist Karl Deutsch called "learned   30 habits, preferences, symbols, memories, and patterns of landholding": customs, cultural traditions, and political institutions that bind them closer to one another than to people of France, Germany, or Italy living just across the border and speaking the same language. There is Switzerland's traditional neutrality, its system of universal military training (the "citizen army"), its consensual allegiance to a strong Swiss franc—and fondue, yodeling, skiing, and mountains. Set against all this, the fact that Switzerland has four languages doesn't even approach the threshold of becoming a threat.

As for India, what Vincent Smith, in the *Oxford History of India,* calls its "deep underlying fundamental unity" resides in institutions and beliefs such as caste, cow worship, sacred places, and much more. Consider *dharma, karma,* and *maya,** the three root convictions of Hinduism; India's historical epics; Gandhi; *ahimsa* (nonviolence); vegetarianism; a distinctive cuisine and way of eating; marriage customs; a shared past; and what the Indologist Ainslie Embree calls "Brahmanical ideology." In other words, "We are Indian; we are different."

Belgium and Canada have never managed to forge a stable national identity; Czechoslovakia and Yugoslavia never did either. Unique otherness immunizes countries against linguistic destabilization. Even Switzerland and especially India have problems; in any country with as many different languages as India has, language will never *not* be a problem. However, it is one thing to have a major illness with a bleak prognosis; it is another to have a condition that is irritating and occasionally painful but not life-threatening.

History teaches a plain lesson about language and governments: there is almost nothing the government of a free country can do to change language usage and practice significantly, to force its citizens to use certain languages in preference to others, and to discourage people from speaking a language they wish to continue to speak. (The rebirth of Hebrew in Palestine and Israel's successful mandate that Hebrew be spoken and written by Israelis is a unique event in the annals of language history.) Quebec has since the 1970s passed an array of laws giving French a virtual monopoly in the province. One consequence—unintended, one wishes to believe—of these laws is that last year kosher products imported for Passover were kept off the shelves because the packages were not labeled in French. Wise governments keep their hands off language to the extent that it is politically possible to do so.

We like to believe that to pass a law is to change behavior; but passing laws about language, in a free society, almost never changes attitudes or be-

---

dharma, karma, and *maya:* In Hinduism, *dharma* is the moral and religious law; *karma* expresses the connection of past lives to future ones; *maya* describes the force that makes people believe that the phenomenal world is real.

havior. Gaelic (Irish) is living out a slow, inexorable decline in Ireland despite enormous government support of every possible kind since Ireland gained its independence from Britain. The Welsh language, in contrast, is alive today in Wales in spite of heavy discrimination during its history. Three out of four people in the northern and western counties of Gwynedd and Dyfed speak Welsh.

I said earlier that language is a convenient surrogate for other national 35 problems. Official English obviously has a lot to do with concern about immigration, perhaps especially Hispanic immigration. America may be threatened by immigration; I don't know. But America is not threatened by language.

The usual arguments made by academics against Official English are commonsensical. Who needs a law when, according to the 1990 census, 94 percent of American residents speak English anyway? (Mauro E. Mujica, the chairman of U.S. English, cites a higher figure: 97 percent.) Not many of today's immigrants will see their first language survive into the second generation. This is in fact the common lament of first-generation immigrants: their children are not learning their language and are losing the culture of their parents. Spanish is hardly a threat to English, in spite of isolated (and easily visible) cases such as Miami, New York City, and pockets of the Southwest and southern California. The everyday language of south Texas is Spanish, and yet south Texas is not about to secede from America.

But empirical, calm arguments don't engage the real issue: language is a symbol, an icon. Nobody who favors a constitutional ban against flag burning will ever be persuaded by the argument that the flag is, after all, just a "piece of cloth." A draft card in the 1960s was never merely a piece of paper. Neither is a marriage license.

Language, as one linguist has said, is "not primarily a means of communication but a means of communion." Romanticism exalted language, made it mystical, sublime—a bond of national identity. At the same time, Romanticism created a monster: it made of language a means for destroying a country.

America has that unique otherness of which I spoke. In spite of all our racial divisions and economic unfairness, we have the frontier tradition, respect for the individual, and opportunity; we have our love affair with the automobile; we have in our history a civil war that freed the slaves and was fought with valor; and we have sports, hot dogs, hamburgers, and milk shakes—things big and small, noble and petty, important and trifling. "We are Americans; we are different."

If I'm wrong, then the great American experiment will fail—not be- 40 cause of language but because it no longer means anything to be an American; because we have forfeited that "willingness of the heart" that F. Scott Fitzgerald wrote was America; because we are no longer joined by Lincoln's "mystic chords of memory."

We are not even close to the danger point. I suggest that we relax and luxuriate in our linguistic richness and our traditional tolerance of language differences. Language does not threaten American unity. Benign neglect is a good policy for any country when it comes to language, and it's a good policy for America.

QUESTIONING THE TEXT

1. "Should English Be the Law?" is an argument—an essay that provides evidence in support of specific claims. What do you think are King's basic claims, and which pieces of evidence do you find either most convincing or most questionable? Offer your opinion in a brief critical analysis.

2. Near the end of his article (paragraph 40), King mentions Abraham Lincoln's phrase "'mystic chords of memory,'" assuming that most of his readers will appreciate the allusion. Using the resources of your library reference room, track down the allusion if you do not recognize it, and then explore its aptness. In what context did Lincoln use that phrase? What do "mystic chords of memory" have to do with language and national identity?

3. "Should English Be the Law?" was published as a cover story in the April 1997 issue of the *Atlantic Monthly*. That cover, reproduced on p. 410, shows a stern schoolmarm wielding a piece of chalk. Working in a group, do a detailed analysis of this image, noting as many of its features as you can. Then, in a brief essay, explain whether you think the image fits King's article. If you could have commissioned cover art for King's piece, what might it have been?

MAKING CONNECTIONS

4. The problems of immigrants trying to learn English and adapt to American culture are discussed in the selection from Mike Rose's *Lives on the Boundary* (p. 105). Read the selection by Rose and then, in a short piece, describe whether King's analysis of the language problem in the United States confirms or contradicts Rose's observations. Don't hesitate to offer your own analysis.

5. In "Civic Virtue and the Character of Followership" (p. 205), Peter J. Gomes argues that the people of a nation should be linked by their shared visions, ideas, ideals, and passions. What relationships—if any—can you draw between Gomes's analysis of "good followership" and

King's assertion that national unity depends upon "unique otherness" (paragraph 29)? Describe your reactions to these two authors in an exploratory essay.

JOINING THE CONVERSATION

6. King claims that a dispute over language often serves as a shorthand or surrogate for other national problems. For example, in some countries, conflicts over language are also about differences in religion or class status. In a small group, discuss some of the political and social issues that surround the "English Only" debate in the United States. Then write an argument on King's observation. Is the push to make English the official language of the United States one issue or many?

7. King attempts briefly to describe the "unique otherness" of the American people, listing such traits as the frontier tradition, love of the automobile, a civil war, and even hot dogs. In an extended essay, explore the concept of "unique otherness" as King uses it in this selection — either by offering your own description of American otherness or by questioning the notion itself.

BRUCE FEILER
Gone Country

POPULAR CULTURE HAS BEEN *all the rage among many academics during the last decade, with humanities departments offering courses in rap music, slasher movies, and Barbie side-by-side with Homer and Shakespeare. But an element of popular culture still largely ignored by faculty venturing into territories once considered too lowbrow for serious academic inquiry is country music. Why? The answer is pretty simple. Most college instructors hate country music. Many would sooner display Kenneth Starr on their T-shirts than Garth Brooks or Dolly Parton. Sure, they might admit a fondness for bluegrass tunes and find a place in their pop-culture pantheons for regional artists who cross various musical boundaries, people like Nanci Griffith, Lyle Lovett, and Emmylou Harris. But mainstream country stars past and present, from Tammy Wynette and Johnny Cash to Bryan White and LeAnn Rimes, are just too white bread and middle class for predominantly white-bread and middle-class professors. I searched through two dozen anthologies used widely in writing classes — including several collections of articles on popular culture — and found nary a word about country music. It's off the charts.*

All the more reason, I think, for considering Bruce Feiler's "Gone Country," an article that explores the changing shape of this musical force in America today. Like it or not, country music may have more to tell us about American identity in the next decade than rock or rap or any other native musical form. Feiler argues that country music is surprisingly diverse, increasingly complex, and remarkably adapted to the nation we are becoming. Some would argue, however, that both the music and the country are losing their way — adrift and stripped of their core values.

*Feiler (b. 1964), a native of Savannah, Georgia, has written on subjects as diverse as Japanese culture (*Learning to Bow, *1991) and life with the circus (*Under the Big Top, *1995). He has published in* USA Today, *the* Washington Post, *and the* New Republic, *where "Gone Country" first appeared in the February 5, 1996, issue.*

—J.R.

Never one to pass up a political opening, Bill Clinton stepped to the stage on the South Lawn of the White House last May to introduce a PBS special on the "Women of Country" and offered the following somewhat self-serving explanation for Nashville's recent surge in popularity: "Country music vividly demonstrates America's fundamental ability to adapt and change." He then went on to credit country's blending of cultures from the mountains of Appalachia, the fields of the South and the deserts of the "cowboy West."

But the president was out of date — country isn't about those things anymore. These days it's much more often about what first guest Suzy

Bogguss called to mind in dedicating her song, "Letting Go," to the First Lady and Chelsea: getting older, raising children and learning to survive in that new American frontier, suburbia.

The storied world of Nashville—once the isolated bastion of hillbilly crooners and hard-drinking ballads—has suddenly become the unlikely center of American cultural life, the patron city of the radical middle. Just as rock-and-roll foreshadowed many of the changes in gender and race relations that followed in the 1960s, country music today—with its suburban, middle-aged themes of family and renewal—may be the clearest reflection of many of the anxieties and aspirations that have just begun to bubble to the surface in American political life.

To begin with, there are the legions of new fans—Southern *and* Northern now, button-down as well as hayseed—who have flocked to the music in recent years. Seventy million Americans now listen to country radio every week, a total of 42 percent of all radio listeners. These listeners include a third of all Americans who have ever enrolled in a master's program, 40 percent of single adults between 25 and 39 and—if you need proof of country's appeal outside of Texas—half of all Americans who own a snowmobile.

With 2,642 radio stations now programming Nashville's latest, country   5 music has become the dominant radio format in the United States, reaching 20 million more people a week than its closest competitor, adult contemporary. By 1993, country radio had become the top-rated format in fifty-five of the nation's top 100 cities, including Baltimore, Buffalo, Milwaukee, Seattle, San Diego and Washington, D.C. The largest country radio station in the world, New York's WYNY, has 1 million listeners a day, not to mention its own dating service.

And country fans are more educated than either adult contemporary or rock audiences. According to the Simmons Study of Media and Markets, 36 percent of country music fans have a post-graduate degree, as compared to 30 percent for adult contemporary and only 22 percent for rock. They are also wealthier. Forty percent of individuals with annual incomes over $40,000 listen to country music, as do a third of individuals who earn over $100,000 a year.

This money has changed the character of the record business. Country album sales, which now total almost 18 percent of the market, have surpassed $2 billion a year, twice their total in 1990 and twenty times what they were in 1970. In 1985, just before the current boom, ten new country albums went Gold (sales of 500,000 units), while seven went Platinum, meaning they topped 1 million. In 1993, fifteen albums went Gold, twenty-six went Platinum, five reached 2 million in sales, four reached 3 million, one passed 7 million and one, Garth Brooks's *No Fences,* topped 10,000,000 units.

How revolutionary are these numbers?

In December, Garth Brooks, the prototypical clean-cut, yes-ma'am, aw-shucks suburban cowboy, became the third-highest-selling artist of *all time*—behind only the Beatles and Billy Joel and *ahead* of Madonna, Michael

Jackson, even Elvis. With a new album, *Fresh Horses,* hitting stores last Thanksgiving, Brooks, who has now sold 56 million albums (compared with the Beatles' 70 million), will almost surely catapult to number two on the list when new figures are issued this month. It's time to stand up and face the music: some time before the end of the century, while you're still listening to the Grateful Dead and Elvis Costello, Garth Brooks will become the best-selling recording artist in American history.

Then there are the people who make all this music. Once almost exclu-   10 sively from the Appalachian hills of West Virginia and the Baptist bayous of Mississippi, the performers who populate country music in the '90s are swarming to Nashville from all over the world—especially New York and L.A. (Nashville's newest nickname, the "Third Coast," reflects this change.) Mary-Chapin Carpenter, a singer on the cutting edge of Nashville's new liberal wing, was born in Princeton, New Jersey, raised in part in Tokyo and educated at Brown University. Shania Twain, whose album *The Woman in Me* was number one for much of last summer, is a native of Windsor, Ontario. Even my college neighbor from Yale, a Jewish Wall Street broker's son from Scarsdale, New York, is now making the rounds of singer/songwriter nights in every linoleum pizza joint within warbling distance of Music Row in Nashville.

These musicians—smarter, hipper; their fans—older, wiser; and ultimately the music itself—crisper, cleaner and much more clearly about core American values than anything coming out of Seattle or New York in the last ten years—combine to create one of the most vivid examples of America's reigning backlash against its own culturally liberal past. Hints of this trend have popped up elsewhere in American life—in the anti-violence campaign against Hollywood, in the movement against violent rock and rap music lyrics and in the agitated white suburban voice embodied by Newt Gingrich. But the common thread that ties these voices together is still mostly ignored by the political establishment, though it's offered around the clock—and for free—on your radio dial.

For Nashville, the road to the mainstream has been roundabout, at best. The music that eventually fell under the rubric of "country" first evolved about a century ago out of an eclectic array of sources including Irish and Scottish string music, Mississippi blues and Christian hymns. By the 1920s, big-city businessmen had caught on to the financial potential of this "old-time" or "hillbilly" music, which soon found a home on burgeoning commercial radio. A generation later, when radio turned to rock and country floundered, Nashville responded with more aggressive promotion and a new sound. The "Nashville Sound," blending orchestrated pop with country-fied themes, provided a foundation for a new roster of crossover artists like Jim Reeves, Eddy Arnold and Patsy Cline. Building on this initial success, Nashville began attracting more sophisticated audiences in the 1970s, folding in new stars like Kris Kristofferson, a Rhodes Scholar, and Willie Nelson, the thinking-man's outlaw. This pop-country trend reached its apotheosis with the release of the film *Urban Cowboy* in 1980, which suddenly convinced millions of Americans they were interested in country music.

Then came the bust. Predictably, the national fascination with all things Texan proved to be a fad. Audiences dropped, and in 1986 country album sales shrank to around 9 percent of the market, their lowest level in almost twenty years. This could have marked the end of country music as a national institution. The fact that it didn't—the fact that country music rebounded in the late 1980s and '90s to a point far higher than anyone in Nashville (or New York or L.A., for that matter) ever dreamed possible—ultimately says as much about America as it does about the music.

The conventional explanation for the growth in country music tends to focus on changes within the music industry itself—the decline of traditional pop radio, for instance. According to this theory, as contemporary music became more ethnic—with rap, house and urban dance music suddenly dominating the airwaves—many listeners became disenchanted and began searching for new buttons on their radios.

Another explanation focuses on changes in the way album sales were 15 recorded. In 1991 SoundScan introduced a new, computerized monitoring system, which for the first time calculated albums actually sold, rather than sales projections. By coincidence (or fate, as Nashville would have it), the week the new system went into effect in late September, 1991, Garth Brooks debuted at the top of both the country *and* the pop charts with his third album, *Ropin' the Wind,* the first album ever to achieve this feat.

Finally the other leading contention is that changes in the music itself account for country's unprecedented popularity. According to this view, singers like Ricky Skaggs, George Strait and Randy Travis reacted to the post–*Urban Cowboy* bust by turning the music away from its crossover amalgam sound and back to its traditional roots. While there is some truth to this—Randy Travis sold 3 million copies of *Storms of Life* without a crossover hit—the music of these so-called New Traditionalists still showed strikingly mainstream sensibilities. While New Traditionalism may have contributed to the surge of interest in country music, it did little to change the music itself. In the end, the music basically stayed where it was, while the country moved to it.

By 1990, the first of the baby-boomers were just reaching 40, and it was these people who first reached out to Nashville. "Country music is about lyric-oriented songs with adult themes," says Lon Helton, country editor of *Radio & Records,* the industry's leading publication. "You've probably got to be 24 or 25 to even understand a country song. Life has to slap you around a little bit, and then you go, 'Now I get what they're singing about.'" Two-thirds of country music listeners are between the ages of 25 and 54—40 percent of all Americans born between 1940 and 1970. More middle-aged Americans listen to country music every week than the total number of Americans who voted for Bill Clinton in 1992.

But an even bigger demographic shift that has fed country music is the movement of these baby-boomers away from downtown. In the first half of the century Americans moved in massive numbers from the country to the city. Jazz, blues, even rock-and-roll all reflected, in one way or another, this migration, while country music remained predominantly a rural music. The second half of this century has seen a different shift as Americans have decamped from the cities to the suburbs. Only 12 percent of Americans now live in cities of 500,000 or more. By contrast, 50 percent of Americans now live in the suburbs. Country music, more than any other format, is the direct beneficiary of this change.

As Americans aged and moved to the suburbs, they became increasingly interested in themes that have long been the mainstay of Nashville songwriters. While most pop music was still focused on sex, drugs, and other forms of license ("I Want Your Sex," to pick one example, or "Losing My Religion"), country pounded out tales of love, heartache, family ties and middle-aged renewal. In one of Garth Brooks's most successful songs, for example, "Unanswered Prayers," a man returns to a hometown football game with his wife, where together they run into his old high-school flame. Just as he starts to regret having lost the girlfriend, he realizes that she is not as lovely as he had remembered. "And as she walked away / I looked at my wife / And then and there I thanked the good Lord / For the gifts in my life."

Brooks, more than almost any other country singer, is a master of this   20 kind of mid-life ballad, a sort of fanfare for the reconciled. He has mixed songs of middle-aged angst ("If Tomorrow Never Comes" is about a man wondering if his wife, or is it his daughter?, will know how much he loved her if he dies in the night) with raucous, feel-good party anthems, like "Friends in Low Places." And he has brewed these together into an upbeat pop sensibility that is perfectly pitched to his audience. When U2's Bono disrupted the Grammy telecast in 1994, announcing that he intended to "fuck the mainstream," Garth Brooks followed up with a speech taking offense at this pledge. "The message I would send to the youth is not to screw up the mainstream," he said later, "but work with it to make it what you want."

What has solidified Brooks's connection to the audience is that he, like so many other country artists these days, is one of them. A middle-class native of Tulsa, Oklahoma, recently ranked the most demographically "typical" city in America, Brooks graduated from Oklahoma State University with a degree in advertising. Vince Gill grew up in a suburb of Oklahoma City (typical city number eight), where his father was a lawyer. Trisha Yearwood's father was the vice president of a bank. Both Mary-Chapin Carpenter and Marcus Hummon grew up overseas: Carpenter's father worked for *Life* magazine, Hummon's for the Agency for International Development. We've come a long way from the days of coal miners' daughters.

The fact that all of these performers—college-educated, worldly, as influenced by Dan Fogelberg as by Hank Williams—could find a home in Nashville in the '90s also speaks to another new phenomenon in American life: the revitalization of the American South. From pariah region—hot, isolated, poor, racist—the South has emerged over the last thirty years as the chief engine of growth and change in American life. First the population shifted South (3,000,000 people since 1975 alone), drawn by service jobs and air-conditioned suburbs. Then, politics—especially Republican politics—followed. (See "The Southern Coup," by Michael Lind, *TNR*,* June 19, 1995.) And now, in what just might be the final frontier of what Lind calls the "creeping Southernization of America," the pop cultural form most closely associated with the South—country music—has crept into the mainstream of American culture.

This cultural takeover has been abetted by nontraditional technologies pioneered to a large degree by a Southerner, Ted Turner, whose WTBS, TNT and eventually CNN paved the way for the widespread dissemination of new information about the South not controlled by New York or Los Angeles. Two cable channels in particular—TNN, The Nashville Network; and CMT, Country Music Television—with their sexy videos and telegenic stars, were instrumental in what has become country music's greatest coup in the last decade: its encroachment on the previously hostile youth market. According to *Radio & Records,* the percentage of country music listeners between 12 and 17 has tripled since 1988; the percentage between 18 and 24 has increased by half. Forty-three percent of Americans between 18 and 34 now listen to country music.

"When I first started in country radio back in 1971," says *R&R*'s Helton, "you had to convince people that country music didn't cause cancer. People in that [younger] age group always had a very negative connotation of country. It wasn't just neutral; it was negative. So for the first time ever we've gone from having a whole generation of people having a negative view to one with a positive view. We didn't even go through neutral; we went right to positive." The long-term importance of this trend is clear: country has secured its place in the mainstream for the next two generations, since recent pop history shows that as people grow older they return to the sounds of their youth.

The short-term implications, though, are even more striking. With the penetration of country music into the young adult market, popular music, for the first time in memory, is no longer a wedge between generations. For much of the last century, going back to jazz in the '20s, Frank Sinatra in the '40s, Elvis in the '50s and, of course, the Beatles in the '60s, each new generation has summarily rejected the music of its elders. With contemporary country music that urge toward rebellion has—temporarily, at least—stalled.

What has replaced it is a new moral consensus, coalescing around certain shared values: sincerity, earnestness, a longing for raw emotion instead of ironic detachment. When Tim McGraw, the 28-year-old former pre-law student from Louisiana, pleads with a mugger—"Take my money / Take my

25

TNR: *The New Republic*

wallet / Take my credit card / Here's the watch that my grandpa gave me / Here's the key to my car / . . . But please don't take the girl"—the sense of desperation crosses generations, especially since the song carries us from the boy's first meeting with the girl when they're still kids to the painful moment when he nearly loses her during childbirth. The true appeal of country music is in the content of these stories. And the moral of the stories is simple and counterrevolutionary: family values are sexy—not only for over-the-hill hippies who already had their fun and are well on their way to regret, but for their children as well. Some may find that embrace of the status quo frightening. But before you rush to judgment, consider the outlines of those values themselves.

Digging for cultural clues in an admittedly "feel-good" music is dodgy at best and perhaps even misleading at worst. Songs that become hits these days are songs that make it on the radio, and radio, at its core, is concerned with selling groceries, not records, and certainly not political causes. After all, how much cultural imagery can be found in the kind of music that opines, as one hit song* did last fall: "If the world had a front porch / Like we did back then / We'd still have our problems / But we'd all be friends"?

The answer is, more than you think. If, as Public Enemy's Chuck D has famously asserted, rap music is the "CNN of the ghetto," then country music, it seems no exaggeration to say, is the CNN of the suburbs.

If we accept this label, and look to the music for a reading of this increasingly potent force in American life, the news is decidedly mixed. First of all, on the most basic level, politics themselves seem to be of little interest to suburban country music listeners. Gone are the days when Johnny Cash railed against the mistreatment of Native Americans in "The Ballad of Ira Hayes" or Merle Haggard plumbed the darkness of his own prison life. Gone, no doubt, because those children of the Depression no longer seem relevant to a generation raised on Pop Tarts and sit coms.

Instead, hit songs these days are more often about anguished relation-   30
ships ("One Boy, One Girl"), romantic grief ("My Next Broken Heart") or youthful folly ("I'm Old Enough to Know Better (But Still Too Young to Care)"). In many ways country has become the pop music parallel to the confessional, self-referential talk-show boom on television (though without that genre's revels in weirdness). Even old beer-in-the-glass staples, such as breakup songs, have a pampered middle-class feel to them these days, a coating of freshly buffed self-esteem. Newcomer Terri Clark, for example, had a smash hit last fall with a song that listed all of the things she'd rather do than see her ex-boyfriend, including washing her car in the rain, checking the air

---

hit song: The lyrics are from Tracy Lawrence's "If the World Had a Front Porch," a top country single in 1995.

in her tires and straightening her stereo wires. "I'd love to talk to you / But then I'd miss Donahue." Patty Loveless weighed in with a song about trying to forget about her ex-lover. "I try to think about Elvis / Memphis / Oprah in the afternoon." And later, " I try to think about hair-do's / Tattoos / Sushi bars and saxophones." Say what you will about the old hard-edged "twang" in country music, but it's hard to imagine Hank Williams Sr. watching Ricki Lake and nibbling pickled ginger.

When social issues do come up, they invariably relate to domestic turmoil—alcoholism, child abuse, spousal abuse—rather than, in any overt way, class, race or poverty. In country music today, anxiety is a personal matter. The threat is not across the ocean or even on the other side of the harvest; it's on the street where you live, in what Mary-Chapin Carpenter calls this "House of Cards": "I grew up in a town like this / You knew the names of every street / On the surface it looked so safe / But it was perilous underneath." Perhaps the most startling example of this new trend is Martina McBride's defiant hit, "Independence Day." In this tune, named 1995 "Song of the Year" by the Country Music Association (CMA), a battered woman decides to burn down her house with her husband in it, "Let the weak be strong / Let the right be wrong / Throw the stone away / Let the guilty pay / It's Independence Day." This song, like many in the new social landscape, was written by a woman.

With so much peril in one's midst, perhaps it's not surprising that fewer people are prepared to go out of their way to solve the problems of others. A good example of this passivity is the glaring absence of any black performers—or black themes—in country music. The Simmons data suggest that around 25 percent of African Americans over 18 are listening to country radio. But not since Charley Pride snuck onto the scene in the 1960s by deliberately omitting his picture from his album cover has Nashville launched a single black country music performer. The one performer even given a chance, Cleve Francis, a 50-year-old cardiologist from Alexandria, Virginia, quit his medical practice several years ago to pursue a record contract, only to encounter a response so chilly that he retreated to the operating room.

There is some evidence, however, of a new openness about another hot-button issue, homosexuality. Country music has long been associated with conservative values (remember the "Ballad of the Green Berets" or "Okie from Muskogee") and, specifically, with the Republican Party. Richard Nixon, feeling the heat of the Watergate scandal, opened the new Grand Ole Opry facilities in 1974 by singing "God Bless America" and "Happy Birthday" to his wife, Pat. The country radio station in Washington, D.C., still "pauses to honor America" every day at noon with a broadcast of the National Anthem. It comes as no surprise, then, that homosexuality has long been a taboo subject. When rumors circulated that Randy Travis might be gay, he married his manager and moved to Hawaii.

But even that stigma seems to be weakening. Nashville has been fairly aggressive on the subject of AIDS. Reba McEntire had a hit single, "She Thinks His Name Was John," about a woman who contracts HIV from unprotected sex. Even Garth Brooks placed himself squarely in the gay-rights corner with his protest song, "We Shall Be Free." Then, in a turn of events that surprised almost everyone, Ty Herndon, a newcomer who was arrested last June for exposing himself to a (male) undercover officer in a Fort Worth park, managed to resume his seemingly crippled career after getting the charges dropped and spending time in a drug treatment center. If country music fans are prepared to overlook such private transgressions in deference to public performance, can Washington be far behind?

This new broad-minded attitude—sort of family values lite, or what   35
one label executive jokingly characterized to me as "fiscally conservative, socially liberal, just like Colin Powell"—also extends to women. For much of its history, country music has been a gender-polarized world, in which 75 percent of the performers were men, and 75 percent of the buyers were women. Those women who did break through were advised not to be too sexy, too threatening or too defiant of convention. One of the most popular songs in the history of country music is Tammy Wynette's beleaguered anthem, "Stand by Your Man."

But these days old prejudices are falling almost daily. Tanya Tucker and Wynonna both have children out of wedlock. Mary-Chapin Carpenter planted a kiss on the lips of Little Richard at the 1994 CMA Awards, a startling act for a white woman and black man that would have been unthinkable in the country world just a few years ago. And this year's superstar of the decade, Shania Twain, has marketed herself as the embodiment of (wholesome) sexuality, even hiring John and Bo Derek to spice up her image. For Twain, and her millions of fans, the message these days is "Stand by *Me*": "Any man of mine better be proud of me / Even when I'm ugly he still better love me / And I can be late for a date that's fine / But he better be on time." Hillary Clinton—who once cited "Stand by Your Man" as the motto of a life not worth living—would be proud.

Which brings us to the final frontier of country's chauvinism—and perhaps the most remarkable innovation in its new mainstream family values: the definition of the modern man. It used to be said that the bulk of country songs were about drinkin', cheatin' and truck drivin'—the Holy Trinity of the Angry White Male. These days big-rig songs have all but disappeared. Two-timin' tales usually wind up in the third verse accompanied by a tearful plea for forgiveness or twelve-step redemption. And the beer and billiard boasts are few and far between. "Well I don't drink as much as I used to," opened one recent Alan Jackson hit. "Lately it just ain't my style." Instead the hard-drinkin', girl chasin' good ol' boy has been supplanted by a new standard, Brooks & Dunn's everlovin', Hallmark-totin' "Brand New Man": "I used to have a wild side / They say a country mile wide / I'd burn those beer joints down / That's all changed now / You turned my life around / . . . I'm a brand new man."

In a climate where politicians of all stripes are concerned about the apathy, the anxiety and the downright "funk" of the American people, political leaders would be well-advised to take a clue from the vitality and quiet optimism of today's country music, where morality is hip, despair is surmountable and struggling to save a relationship (even one with a lot of "stress," as Newt Gingrich recently said of his own), is the national sport of the day.

"For men *and* women, equal footing is new," explains Bill Davis, deputy director of the Country Music Foundation. "Women don't have to pander to men, and men, well, they don't have to live up to John Wayne anymore."

So what is the message to men—especially male politicians—instead?   40
"Go home to your wife."

QUESTIONING THE TEXT

1. In much of the first half of "Gone Country," Feiler offers an analysis of cause and effect. The "effect" he identifies is the growing popularity of country music, and he uses statistics on CD sales and radio market penetration to support his observation. Do you find the case he makes for country music as a dominant musical force convincing? Why, or why not? How/where might you check his statistical claims?

2. What forces in American culture might account for the growth of country music as Feiler sees it? Review the essay and identify the specific causes he offers to explain the current popularity of country music. Then, working in a group, discuss the accuracy of these explanations, either offering more support for the causes Feiler identifies, refuting one or more of them, or suggesting alternative explanations.

3. In the headnote to Feiler's article, J.R. claims—without offering specific evidence—that "[m]ost college instructors hate country music." Is it fair for him to make such an assertion? Why, or why not?

MAKING CONNECTIONS

4. Even if some barriers are tumbling, Feiler notes that homosexuality remains a taboo subject for country artists. But could the issues faced by homosexuals be adapted to fit the general formula of country songs? Review Andrew Sullivan's "What Are Homosexuals For?" (p. 350), and then write a position paper on the potential of country music to

address nontraditional themes. Imagine that your essay might appear in a campus publication.

5. Country songs often tell stories about problems with families and marriages. Try reading "Gone Country" and Barbara Dafoe Whitehead's "The Making of a Divorce Culture" (p. 619) side by side. Then write a brief essay exploring the role country music may be playing in a society where the family is taking on different shapes.

JOINING THE CONVERSATION

6. Feiler claims that the moral themes of country music reflect a new national consensus: "sincerity, earnestness, a longing for raw emotion instead of ironic detachment" (paragraph 26). In a short essay, try to characterize the themes of at least one other kind of popular music or entertainment (rock, hip-hop, jazz, Broadway, rap).

7. Feiler is a southerner by birth. In *Contemporary Authors,* he notes that while a student at Yale, he became more aware of his identity: "Little did I know, but this process of being an outsider inside a strange place, in this case a Southerner in the North, would become a driving force behind my work." Do you have any sense of being an outsider or insider when reading about country music? Or can you imagine how someone might feel drawn to or alienated from any specific type of music? Who might feel so, and why? Write an essay in which you explore the ways people identify with particular forms of music or other types of artistic expression—including dance, painting, sculpture, architecture, even fashions.

ALEX SHOUMATOFF
The Navajo Way

SPREADING ACROSS ARID ACRES *of Arizona, Utah, and New Mexico, the* Dinetah, *or homeland of the Navajo Nation, looks like land no one might want. Its endless miles of desert scrub can seem cruel and relentless, and its human settlements, littered with abandoned pickups, discarded appliances, and aging trailers, soften the harsh landscape not at all. Yet, like most first impressions, this one is not entirely trustworthy. The poverty of the reservation is genuine, as are the problems Navajos share with other native peoples of the American West, including high rates of unemployment, suicide, and alcoholism. But Dinetah is a place of enormous drama and power that would compel any people dwelling among its stark canyons, mesas, and sacred mountains to ponder daily their place within a vast, hostile, and yet highly animate universe.*

For many tourists passing through this region, Navajo culture probably means only the jewelry and rugs available in shops and roadside stands. Some visitors might stop to ponder the artifacts and cliff dwellings of the Puebloan peoples, earlier inhabitants of this region not related to the Diné or Navajos. Yet the irreplaceable cultural treasures of the region are not the art and artifacts, but the distinctive identities of the Navajo (and Hopi, and other native peoples) themselves. In "The Navajo Way," Alex Shoumatoff asks readers to consider the people of this land for who they are—a nation within a nation.

A journalist and naturalist, Shoumatoff (b. 1946) typically explores the relationships of people and the land in his books and articles. He has also written on political and social dilemmas in African Madness *(1988) and on the destruction of the rain forest in* The World Is Burning *(1990). He is more recently the author of* Legends of the American Desert *(1997). "The Navajo Way" originally appeared in* Men's Journal *(November 1998).* —J.R.

One of the most remarkable things about this republic is that there exists within its borders a parallel universe known as Dinetah, a nation of more than 155,000 souls who subscribe to a mind-set completely different from the modern American belief that everything in nature is there for the taking. Dinetah is the ancestral homeland of the Diné, more commonly called the Navajo, a misnomer perpetrated by the Spaniards, as are many of the names for the native tribes of the Southwest. An area larger than West Virginia that sprawls out of Arizona into New Mexico and Utah, Dinetah is bounded by four sacred mountains—North Mountain (Debe'nitsaa), in the La Plata Mountains of Colorado; South Mountain (Tso Dzil), or Mount Taylor, near Grants, New Mexico; East Mountain (Sis Naajin'i), or Sierra Blanca, in Colorado; and West Mountain (Dook Oslid), in the San Francisco Peaks, near

Flagstaff, Arizona—and four sacred rivers (the Colorado, the Little Colorado, the San Juan, and the Rio Grande). It is some of the starkest, most magically open-to-the-sky country anywhere—a sagebrush steppe spotted with juniper and ancient, gnarled piñon trees, occasionally gashed by a yawning canyon or thrust up into a craggy, pine-clad mountain range, a magenta mesa, a blood-red cliff, a tiara of lucent, stress-fractured tan sandstone.

"The land is our Bible," a Navajo woman named Sally once explained to me. Every feature has a name and a story and is sacred, just as every animal and plant has a "way," its own particular means of contributing its right to be there, which must be respected. Much of a traditional Navajo's energies are devoted to keeping on good terms with the elements and one's fellow creatures, to "being in harmony with everything—yourself, mainly, all the living things, the air, Father Sky, the moon, and on and on," Sally continued. This state of *hozho*—or walking in beauty, as it is often translated—is the goal of the Navajo religion.

"You can be in harmony and sailing along just fine when suddenly you run into something disharmonious, and there's always a reason for it," she went on. "Like my brother Roy, who drowned. He got on bad terms with the Water People. Or my sister Lavine, who got bitten by a rattler when she was little. Her arm got big and bloated, and after that, every time I saw a snake I would kill it. Snakes see everything purple, and one day at noon when I was out with the sheep, everything suddenly turned purple. A snake slithered up and asked 'Why are you killing all our brothers?' I explained, because my sister got bitten. So the snake said, 'Let's make a deal: Don't kill us, and we won't bother you.'"

A few years ago, Sally's husband, Kee Richard, started having nosebleeds. It turned out there was a tumor in his nose. The doctor in Flagstaff said it was cancer and zapped it with radiation, but Sally's aunt, who was a medicine woman, took one look at Kee Richard and asked him "Did you ever kill a porcupine?" "Well, yes," Kee Richard said. "When I was 10, I clubbed a porcupine with a stick from the fire. It went off to die with blood pouring out of its nose." Sally's aunt told him he had to offer turquoise and abalone to the porcupine and make a confession to ask forgiveness.

According to archaeological evidence, the Navajo were part of a migration from Siberia somewhere between 11,000 and 16,000 years ago. The Navajo themselves, however, say the People emerged from Navajo Lake, in northeastern Arizona. "Don't tell me you're falling for that Bering Strait stuff," Sally's cousin Tom, a traditionalist, chided me. Glottochronological evidence suggests that the Navajo split off from the Athabascans of the Pacific Northwest within the past 1,000 years and began to drift south in loose, highly mobile bands. Their religion was an animism that evolved from their exceptional ability, as hunters, to "get inside the skulls of the animals," as one elder put it, a detailed understanding of the way of each species. Between

900 and 1,500 years ago, they arrived in the Southwest, where the Anasazi—ancestors of the Hopi—had lived for centuries in cliff dwellings and communal mud pueblos. The Anasazi had learned to grow maize from their Mexican cousins, a practice the Navajo adopted, along with the Anasazi's elaborate mysticism surrounding the plant. The Hopi, whose name for the Navajo means "Skull-Bashers" (while the Navajo call the Hopi "Cliff-Shitters" and "Hopeless"), still live on their four Tibetan mesas in the middle of Dinetah.

While the Hopi were their favorite prey, the Navajo also incorporated a lot of core Hopi beliefs: that the clouds are ancestors who have to be prayed to and harangued to let down their liquid essence in the form of rain, that this is the fourth world (the Navajo call it Glitter World, the previous ones—Black, Blue, and Yellow—having been destroyed because of the wickedness of their inhabitants). When they weren't raiding the Anasazi, the Navajo would appear at the pueblos with game to trade for produce. The Anasazi were in decline, weakened by years of drought. By 1519, when Cortés arrived in Mexico and with astonishing ease conquered the Aztec empire of Moctezuma II, the Anasazi disappeared. The Navajo moved into the vacant niches and thrived, developing a complicated, lyrical, and witty religion based on 58 ceremonials, or "sings," chanted by *hataali,* medicine men who specialize in one or two of them.

Nightway, for instance, which initiates boys and girls aged 7 to 13 into the ceremonial life of adults, takes 9 days to sing and consists of 576 subsongs that must be intoned perfectly, word for word, before the first frost and the first thunderstorm, while the snakes are hibernating. The slightest mistake can result in self-hexing: crippling, paralysis, loss of sight. Enemyway, a healing ceremony, was sung for Navajo soldiers returning from the killing in Vietnam, to purge their souls. A couple of years ago, I attended a four-day-long Beautyway for Sally's son, who had just served a nine-year sentence at Fort Leavenworth. "Maybe if I had Beautyway done for him before he went to boot camp, he wouldn't have gotten into trouble," she told me. Waterway, nearly extinct, is for people who survive drowning or flash-flooding, or who dream of drowning; for sickness from, among other things, rain and thunder, or from eating the meat of lightning-struck sheep or horses.

There is a high degree of paranoia in Dinetah because the Navajo live with many realities, not just the material plane. Evil is not just something down in the underworld, it's out there all the time; it's in your face. If you see an owl, it means somebody's going to die. If you see a coyote headed north, you have to make a prayer. Coyote sickness—brought upon by transgressing, even inadvertently, the way of a coyote—is something you would wish only on your worst enemy: One side of your mouth droops permanently, you become unable to remember anything, or you take to the bottle and, if you're a woman, you give yourself to all comers.

One morning as Tom and I sat outside his hogan, way out in the Arizona desert, we noticed a skinny black dog with a white beard slinking behind a rise,

200 yards off. I asked if it was a stray. Tom said it was a skinwalker. "He's been here a couple of days." Skinwalkers are witches—*chindi*—who can take the form of animals, particularly wolves or coyotes, and can inflict illness or death on those they have it in for. They are believed to be people who want to become rich and have gone through an elaborate ceremony that includes the sacrifice—by untraceable magic means—of a relative. When a skinwalker is identified, he is often beaten to death and mutilated beyond recognition, so he won't come back. Every so often, a forensic pathologist in Albuquerque told me, the Navajo Police bring in the pulverized cadaver of a suspected skinwalker from the rez, as everybody calls the part of Dinetah that the Great White Father designated as a reservation for the Navajo.

Maybe the Navajo are more aware of death and evil than your average   10
suburban Anglo-American because they live in the desert, which, as Georgia O'Keeffe* put it, "knows no kindness in all its beauty." In any case, their paranoia is tempered by a rollicking sense of humor, an irrepressible love of puns and wordplay. Their nickname for Hitler, for instance, is (He Who) Smells His Mustache. The way to break the ice with a Navajo is to make him laugh. In my first trip through Dinetah with my family, in 1985, we pulled over to check out some rugs a group of men had strung up under a brush ramada. While I was having a rather forced conversation with one of the men—the rugs worked out to about $1,000 a square yard—there was a sudden explosion of laughter behind the ramada. My two boys, aged 5 and 6, had gathered the other men around them and were putting on a little show with their Gobots, with a few twists transforming them from trucks into robots, which for some reason was killingly funny.

A lot of Navajo humor is derived from their language, which is tonal and full of prefixes that subtly shade the meanings of words and is virtually impenetrable to a non-Navajo. There are, for instance, 30 ways to say "wind." The Japanese were never able to decipher the messages of the famous Navajo code-talkers in the Pacific Theater, who were actually just speaking Navajo. The humor spills over into the whole Navajo psyche. All you have to do is graze a Navajo's funny bone—tell him a good joke—and he will practically die laughing.

The way to turn off a Navajo is to ask a lot of questions. One time, after I had been bombarding Tom with questions, he finally snapped: "If you quit acting like Harry Reasoner, maybe you might learn something." Another time I was talking with a group of Navajo about how tourists should behave. "Don't ask questions," one woman told me. "'What is that for?' 'Why do you wear that?' 'What does that mean?' Just step back and bite the Albuquerque bullet. Don't try to understand us in one day. You Americans are always looking for instant religious satisfaction, like instant mashed potatoes. But it's a lifetime thing. We live it everyday."

Georgia O'Keeffe (1887–1986): American painter famous for her stunning images of plants, animal skulls, rocks, and deserts

THE MEDICINE MAN, 1987; Laugher's Grandson (Dionsin Bitsoi), a 94-year-old medicine man and a great-grandfather many times over, regularly performs traditional ceremonies, which are very much a part of life for his family, near Chilchinbito.

Do you have any special word for "tourist"? I asked. There I was, doing just what the woman had said not to do.

"I call them 'moon children,'" she said. "They must have come from the moon 'cuz they have no respect for the earth, and they're so pale."

Roxana Robinson, an O'Keeffe biographer, told me about a woman   15 tourist who'd walked into a trading post on the rez and tried to start a conversation with a black-haired Navajo woman holding a red-headed baby. Was the father red-haired? The tourist asked. "I don't know," the mother retorted. "He never took off his hat."

"For us, every day is a thanksgiving day, a prayer in the cycle of life," Tom observed one time. "But for you whites, every day is a slogan. 'Give me liberty or give me death.' 'The Uncola.' 'I've just begun to fight.'"

Tom had built his hogan with the help of his cousin brothers. It was the six-sided "male" hogan with adobe-chinked log walls, a dome-shaped roof of cribbed, mud-smothered logs, and a hole in the center for smoke to exit. The door must face east, so you can greet the rising Father Sun. The woman is the keeper of the hogan. She tends a fire for her family. If a person dies in the hogan, or if the hogan is struck by lightning, it is abandoned. Navajo traditionally live in extended-family compounds known as outfits. These days the hogans are mixed with trailers, shacks, and prefab ranch houses. The sheep corrals — of which there are many — are circles of entwined piñons that look like giant crowns of thorn.

The converging Canyons de Chelly and Del Muerto are the spiritual heart of Dinetah. According to Navajo legend, they were made by hippopotamus-like creatures wallowing in the mud of what was then a vast quagmire. After the creatures had gouged out the canyons, they sent Hummingbird, who was monument-sized, to see if the walls were dry, which explains why some of them are scored with stuttering parenthetical gashes that look like the imprint of huge wings. The canyons have been inhabited for more than 2,000 years. The ruins of long-departed Anasazi are still preserved in scalloped alcoves under the 600-foot-high walls, which are decorated with hundreds of pictographs. On one sandstone panel is the masterpiece of some unknown Navajo Michelangelo, a mural portraying a cavalcade of Spanish soldiers in cloaks and flat-brimmed hats, with muskets held aloft — the Narbona expedition of 1805, sent to take care of "the Navajo problem." Ninety Navajo men and 25 women were gunned down by these "caballeros" as they huddled in a cave on the rim of what would become known as the "canyon of death."

The canyons were a focus of resistance in 1863, when General James H. Carleton launched a campaign to round up the Navajo. Most of the men were killed outright; the women were marched 300 miles to an internment camp at Bosque Redondo, in southeastern New Mexico. Many died on the Long Walk, and many more during the four years they spent in the Place of Confinement. Carleton's idea was that if you took the Navajo "away from their haunts and hills and hiding places" to a reorientation center and "teach their children how to read and write; teach them the arts of peace; teach them the truths of Christianity," they would become model citizens. "Fair Carletonia," as the camp was called, fell tragically short of its utopian mandate. In fact, it became a model for Hitler's concentration camps.

The leader of the 1863 Navajo campaign was 53-year-old Kit Carson, 20 the renowned Indian fighter. This was his last hurrah. The Navajos called him "Rope Thrower" because he lassoed them and marched them into captivity. By the winter of '63, Rope Thrower's tactics had left the People starving. Entering Canyon de Chelly with a detachment of bluecoats, he met fierce resistance from a cult founded by Hashkenneniinii, the Angry One, who thought he could enlist the supernatural being Monster Slayer. The Navajo taunted Carson. Occasionally they would attack and then scamper up the cliffs using secret handholds. Peach orchards were torched; a wrinkled grandmother was shot in the head as she chanted a witchcraft song. Finally, the People realized they had to submit. The few thousand survivors were released from the Place of Confinement in 1867, including Tom and Sally's then–12-year-old great-grandfather, Old Gold Tooth. From them the People rebounded. Now they're the largest Native American nation in the country.

A lot of the reason for the Navajo's extraordinary regeneration has to do with their capacity for adaptation, with their cultural fluidity. "The Navajo are the beggarly nomads, the sponges of American Indian culture," a University of Arizona anthropologist told me. "If they saw something good in another culture, they took it. They took sheep from the Spaniards and became the greatest sheepherders in the world. They took silversmithing and carried it to new artistic levels. They took horses and became the preeminent cowboys of the Southwest."

They also took the rifle and the pickup, the junk food, the TV, and the booze of Anglo culture. While juggling these cosmologies, they continued to adhere to the Navajo Way, but many of them stumbled, and stumble. At this point it is no longer accurate to say there is one Navajo culture. There are born-again Navajo, peyote "roadmen," dope-smoking hippies, gung-ho vets who listen religiously to Rush Limbaugh, heavy-metal freaks, even Satanists. Teenage drinking, fetal alcohol syndrome, domestic violence, and infant-mortality rates are all elevated on the rez. Five hundred Indians freeze to death or are hit by cars in New Mexico every year. Most of them are drunk, and most of them are Navajo. Some have been seduced by Anglo values, by what Tom calls "the almighty dollar and the ownership thing."

Two years ago, I played golf with Albert Hale, then the chairman of the Navajo Nation, who was in Dutch for allegedly taking his secretary to Paris on the tribe's tab and for playing in a pro-am in Albuquerque. He showed up with a large entourage at Pinon Hills, a municipal course in Farmington, just off the rez. Hale was a progressive who had as much in common with Tom as Donald Trump has with the Dalai Lama. "The council accused me of wasting Navajo money," he complained. "Our people are very traditional. They don't understand that golf courses are where a lot of business is done and that I was schmoozing corporate types." He was hoping to get Chi Chi Rodriguez to help build a course at Window Rock, the tribal headquarters. "We need to get everybody to see we are introducing a new game," he argued. "All they know is basketball and rodeo; they see golf as not useful. But golf teaches honesty, discipline, and good ethics. It teaches a code."

I observed that the state of mind you need to be in to play optimal golf, the state of harmony with yourself and your surroundings, is not unlike *hozho,* walking in beauty. Hale told me the Navajo used to play a game where they slapped around a feather-stuffed rawhide ball with a crooked stick. Hale had good hand-eye coordination. He played golf with zest, spitting on his palms and letting her rip. A few days later, I played with Notah Begay, the top Native American golfer, whose father is Navajo. Notah was Tiger Woods's teammate at Stanford. This past summer he shot an almost-inconceivable 59 on the Nike tour. He told me that his religion is an important part of his game.

On the back nine we were alone in the vastness of the desert steppe. Only the occasional jack rabbit would hop out of the brush and sit motionless along the fairway, frozen with nervous attentiveness. From the thirteenth tee, Notah smacked a drive that went forever. The wind took it 380 yards, and as we were walking to it he remarked, "It's so silent out here it hurts your ears."

QUESTIONING THE TEXT

1. According to Shoumatoff, a Navajo's sense of identity is intimately related to *hozho* ("walking in beauty"), a way of thinking and behaving in harmony with the world and the universe. Examine the examples of "walking in beauty" offered in this essay, and then freewrite on the *hozho* idea in an attempt to classify it. Does it seem to be a type of morality? A religion? A code or ethic? A sense of self?

2. The Navajos deal with various events in their lives through ceremonial "sings" — elaborate communal rituals led by *hataali* who memorize and perform the often lengthy ceremonies. In a group, discuss similar kinds of rituals in other cultures and explore the role these ceremonies might have in helping people share a cultural identity.

3. Navajos seem to resent tourists who ask too many questions about their culture. How might one learn about another culture if not through questions? In what ways might questions be offensive? Do all cultures or groups regard questions the same way?

MAKING CONNECTIONS

4. Does anything in Shoumatoff's essay suggest how Navajos might react to Ward Churchill's "Crimes against Humanity" (p. 497), particularly its criticism of sports teams that use Native American names or symbols? Explain.

5. In "Do Kids Need Religion?" (p. 191), Anthony Brandt worries that children raised without the anchor of an organized religion might later feel lost in the world. Review Brandt's essay while thinking about the attempts, described in Shoumatoff's piece, to deprive the Navajo Nation of its land, religion, and way of life. What might be the conse-

quences for people who have lived through such an experience? Write an exploratory essay on the subject.

6. Compare Gwendolen Cates's photograph of the elderly Navajo accompanying the Shoumatoff essay (p. 437) with the image of Chief Wahoo in the color insert. (Chief Wahoo is the emblem of the Cleveland Indians baseball team.) Do either of the images represent Native Americans in stereotypical ways? What are those stereotypes? Where have images of Native Americans appeared recently in media and popular culture? How have they been used? Discuss these questions in a group, and then write a position paper on the use of such images.

JOINING THE CONVERSATION

7. Shoumatoff discusses certain characteristics of the Navajos—their sings, their sense of humor, their resentment of tourists' questions, their love of wordplay. Write an essay, modeled on "The Navajo Way," describing the distinctive characteristics of a group you know well—perhaps one to which you belong.

8. In the 1860s, the U.S. government removed the Navajos from their homeland in an attempt to remake them as "model citizens." Using Shoumatoff's essay as a starting point (especially paragraphs 19–20), research this or any similar campaign against native peoples in the American West. Then write a well-documented report on the subject, perhaps coordinating your work with that of other classmates to produce a series of related historical essays.

9. Tony Hillerman has written a series of popular detective novels set in Dinetah, focusing on the work of Navajo tribal police. Read one of Hillerman's novels, and then write an essay in which you attempt to describe why his detective series has become so popular and influential. What in Navajo culture might appeal to American society in general?

SHERRY TURKLE
Who Am We?

GIVEN THAT PROVOCATIVE TITLE, *you might well ask, "Who am Sherry Turkle?" In fact, as the article suggests, Turkle (b. 1948) has a number of identities. In her* Life on the Screen: Identity in the Age of the Internet *(1995), she describes some of them: an undergraduate "Sherry" who attended Radcliffe and studied abstruse French philosophy in the 1960s, a social-science graduate student "Sherry" who attended Harvard, a clinical psychologist "Sherry," an MIT professor and mentor of students "Sherry," and a widely published author and respected researcher "Sherry."*

Turkle's list of publications and awards is a very long one—including Ms. Magazine's *Woman of the Year Award—and you might have seen or heard her on TV or radio shows such as* Nightline, 20/20, *or the* Jane Pauley Show, *where she often talks about virtual identities and RL (real life). In the following article, originally published in* Wired *in January 1996, Turkle draws on research for* Life on the Screen, *a study of the multiple lives and selves of MUDders, people who interact and often role-play in online environments. The multiple selves inhabited by her subjects dwell online in virtual worlds. And, Turkle notes, "people can get lost in virtual worlds" (paragraph 82).*

I have read Turkle's book several times now, and each time I come up with new challenges to my traditional concepts of identity and self. Students in my classes, often skilled MUDders themselves, also have a lot to say about the points Turkle makes here. In "Who Am We?" Turkle gives her answer to that question. How well does it match with yours?   —A.L.

As recently as 10 to 15 years ago, it was almost unthinkable to speak of the computer's involvement with ideas about unstable meanings and unknowable truths. The computer had a clear intellectual identity as a calculating machine. In an introductory programming course at Harvard University in 1978, one professor introduced the computer to the class by calling it a giant calculator. Programming, he reassured the students, was a cut-and-dried technical activity whose rules were crystal clear.

Such reassurances captured the essence of what I call the modernist computational aesthetic. It's the computer as calculator: no matter how complicated a computer might seem, what happened inside it could be mechanically unpacked. Programming was a technical skill that could be done a right way or a wrong way. The right way was dictated by the computer's calculator essence. The right way was linear and logical. This linear, logical [model] guided thinking not only about technology and programming, but about economics, psychology, and social life. Computational ideas were one of the great modern metanarratives, stories of how the world worked that provided unifying pictures and analyzed complicated things by breaking them down into simpler parts. Computers, it was assumed, would become more powerful, both as tools and as metaphors, by becoming better and faster calculating machines, better and faster analytical engines.

From today's perspective, the fundamental lessons of computing are wrong. Programming is no longer cut and dried. Are you programming when you customize your word-processing software? When you design "organisms" to populate a simulation of Darwinian evolution in the computer game *SimLife*? Or when you build a room in a MUD so that opening a door to it will cause "Happy Un-Birthday" to ring out on all but one day of the year?

The lessons of computing today have to do not with calculation and rules, but with simulation, navigation, and interaction. The very image of the computer as a giant calculator has become quaint and dated. Fifteen years ago, most computer users were limited to typing commands. Today they use off-the-shelf products to manipulate simulated desktops, draw with simulated paints and brushes, and fly in simulated airplane cockpits.

Today's computational models of the mind often embrace a postmodern aesthetic of complextiy and decentering. Mainstream computer researchers no longer aspire to program intelligence into computers but expect intelligence to emerge from the interactions of small subprograms.   5

In the games in the Sim series *(SimCity, SimLife, SimAnt, SimHealth)*, you try to build a community, an ecosystem, or a public policy. The goal is to make a successful whole from complex, interrelated parts. Tim is 13, and among his friends, the Sim games are the subject of long conversations about what he calls Sim secrets. "Every kid knows," he confides, "that hitting Shift-F1 will get you a couple of thousand dollars in *SimCity*." But Tim knows that the Sim secrets have their limits. They are little tricks, but they are not what the game is about. The game is about making choices and getting feedback. Tim talks easily about the trade-offs in *SimCity*—between zoning restrictions and economic development, pollution controls and housing starts.

SimLife is Tim's favorite game, because "even though it's not a videogame, you can play it like one." By this he means that as in a videogame, events in the Sim world move things forward. ("My trilobytes went extinct. They must have run out of algae. I didn't give them algae. I forgot. I think I'll do that now.") He is able to act on a vague intuitive sense of what will work even when he doesn't have a verifiable model of the rules underneath the game's behavior. When he is populating his universe in a biology laboratory scenario, Tim puts in 50 each of his favorite creatures, such as trilobytes and sea urchins, but puts in only 20 sharks. ("I don't want 50 of these, I don't want to ruin this.") Tim can keep playing even when he has no idea what is driving events. For example, when his sea urchins become extinct, I ask him why.

Tim: I don't know, it's just something that happens.

ST: Do you know how to find out why it happened?

Tim: No.

ST: Do you mind that you can't tell why?

Tim: No. I don't let things like that bother me. It's not what's important.

"Your orgot is being eaten up," the game tells us. I ask Tim, "What's an orgot?" He doesn't know. "I just ignore that," he says. "You don't need to know that kind of stuff to play."

I am clearly having a hard time hiding my lifetime habit of looking up words that I don't understand, because Tim tries to appease me by coming up with a working definition of orgot. "I ignore the word, but I think it is sort of like an organism. I never read that, but just from playing, I would say that's what it is."

The orgot issue will not die: "Your fig orgot moved to another species," the game informs us. This time I say nothing, but Tim reads my mind: "Don't let it bother you if you don't understand. I just say to myself that I probably won't be able to understand the whole game any time soon. So I just play it."

I begin to look through dictionaries, in which orgot is not listed, and finally find a reference to it embedded in the game itself, in a file called READ ME. The file apologizes for the fact that orgot has been given several and in some ways contradictory meanings in this version of *SimLife,* but one of them is close to organism. Tim was right enough.

Children are comfortable with the idea that inanimate objects can both think and have a personality. But they no longer worry if the machine is alive. They know it is not. The issue of aliveness has moved into the background as though it is settled. But the notion of the machine has expanded to include its having a psychology. In talking about computers in a psychological way, children allow computational machines to retain an animistic trace, a mark of having passed through a stage in which the issue of the computer's aliveness was a focus of intense consideration.

Children also grant new capacities and privileges to the machine world on the basis of its animation if not its life. They endow artificial objects with properties, such as having intentions and ideas, previously reserved for living beings.

Granting a psychology to computers can mean that objects in the category "machine," like objects in the categories "people" and "pets," are fitting partners for dialog and relationship. Although children increasingly regard computers as mere machines, they are also increasingly likely to attribute qualities to them that undermine the machine/person distinction.

Children develop the two concepts in parallel and take what they understand to be the computer's psychological activity (interactivity as well as speaking, singing, and doing math) as a sign of consciousness. But they insist that breathing, having blood, being born, and, as one put it, "having real skin" are the true signs of life. Children today contemplate machines they believe to be intelligent and conscious yet not alive.

These children who so effortlessly split consciousness and life are forerunners of a larger cultural movement. Adults, less willing than children to grant that today's most advanced computer programs are even close to conscious, no longer flinch from the very idea of a self-conscious machine. Even a decade ago, the idea of machine intelligence provoked sharp debate. Today, the controversy about computers does not turn on their capacity for intelligence but on their capacity for life. We are willing to grant that the machine has a "psychology," but not that it can be alive.

People accept the idea that certain machines have a claim to intelligence and thus to their respectful attention. They are ready to engage with computers in a variety of domains. Yet when people consider what if anything might ultimately differentiate computers from humans, they dwell long and lovingly on those aspects of people that are tied to the sensuality and physical embodiment of life. It is as if they are seeking to underscore that although today's machines may be psychological in the cognitive sense, they are not psychological in a way that comprises our relationships with our bodies and with other people. Some computers might be considered intelligent and might even become conscious, but they are not born of mothers, raised in families, they do not know the pain of loss, or live with the certainty that they will die.

The 13-year-old Tim thinks that *SimLife,* unlike videogames and computer programming, is useful. "You get to mutate plants and animals into different species. You get to balance an ecosystem. You are part of something important." Tim thinks that the "animals that grow in the computer could be alive," although he adds, "This is kind of spooky."

Robbie, a 10-year-old who has been given a modem for her birthday, puts the emphasis not on communication but on mobility in considering whether the creatures she has evolved on *SimLife* are alive. "I think they are a little alive in the game, but you can turn it off and you cannot save your game, so that all the creatures you have evolved go away. But if they could figure out how to get rid of that part of the program so that you would have to save the game . . . if your modem were on, [the creatures] could get out of your computer and go to America Online."

Sean, 13, who has never used a modem, comes up with a variant on 25 Robbie's ideas about travel. "The creatures could be more alive if they could get into DOS. If they were in DOS, they would be like a computer virus and they could get onto all of your disks, and if you loaned your disks to friends, it would be like they were traveling."

In the late 1970s and early 1980s, when I studied children's ideas about aliveness in dealing with stationary computer objects, the focus of children's thinking had shifted to an object's psychological properties. Today, in children's comments about the creatures that exist on simulation games, in talk about travel via circulating disks or over modems, in talk of viruses and networks, *movement* is resurfacing as a criterion for aliveness. Children widely assume that the creatures on Sim games have a desire to move out of the system into a wider digital world.

The creatures in simulation space challenge children to find a new language for talking about them and their status, as do mobile robots that wander about, making their "own decisions" about where to go. When MIT professor Rodney Brooks asked his 10-year-old daughter whether his mobots, or mobile robots, were alive, she said, "No, they just have control." For this child, and despite her father's work, life is biological. You can have consciousness and intentionality without being alive. At the end of the 1992 Artificial Life Conference, I sat next to 11-year-old Holly as we watched a group of robots with distinctly different "personalities" compete in a special robot Olympics. I told her I was studying robots and life, and Holly became thoughtful. Then she said unexpectedly, "It's like Pinocchio. First, Pinocchio was just a puppet. He was not alive at all. Then he was an alive puppet. Then he was an alive boy. A real boy. But he was alive even before he was a real boy. So I think the robots are like that. They are alive like Pinocchio [the puppet], but not like real boys."

In the early 1970s, the face-to-face role-playing game *Dungeons and Dragons* swept the game culture. The term "dungeon" persisted in the high-tech culture to connote a virtual place. So when virtual spaces were created that many computer users could share and collaborate within, they were deemed Multi-User Dungeons or MUDs, a new kind of social virtual reality. (Some games use software that make them technically MUSHES or MOOs, but the term MUD has come to refer to all of the multiuser environments.)

MUDs are a new kind of virtual parlor game and a new form of community: In addition, text-based MUDs are a new form of collaboratively written literature. MUD players are MUD authors, the creators as well as the consumers of media content. In this, participating in a MUD has much in common with scriptwriting, performance art, street theater, improvisational theater, or even commedia dell'arte. But MUDs are something else as well.

As players participate, they become authors not only of text but of 30 themselves, constructing new selves through social interaction. Since one participates in MUDs by sending text to a computer that houses the MUD's program and database, MUD selves are constituted in interaction with the machine. Take it away and the MUD selves cease to exist: "Part of me, a very important part of me, only exists inside PernMUD," says one player. Several players joke that they are like "the electrodes in the computer," trying to express the degree to which they feel part of its space.

All MUDS are organized around the metaphor of physical space. When you first enter a MUD, you may find yourself in a medieval church from which you can step out into the town square, or you may find yourself in the coat closet of a large, rambling house. For example, when you first log on to LambdaMOO, one of the most popular MUDs on the Internet, you see the following description:

> The Coat Closet. The Closet is a dark, cramped space. It appears to be very crowded in here; you keep bumping into what feels like coats, boots, and other people (apparently sleeping). One useful thing that you've discovered in your bumbling about is a metal doorknob set at waist level into what might be a door. There's a new edition of the newspaper. Type "news" to see it.

In the MUDs, virtual characters converse with each other, exchange gestures, express emotions, win and lose virtual money, and rise and fall in social status. A virtual character can also die. Some die of "natural" causes (a player decides to close them down), or they can have their virtual lives snuffed out. This is all achieved through writing, and this in a culture that had apparently fallen asleep in the audiovisual arms of television. Yet this new writing is a kind of hybrid: speech momentarily frozen into artifact, but curiously ephemeral artifact. In this new writing, unless it is printed out on paper, a screenful of flickers soon replaces the previous screen.

The anonymity of MUDs gives people the chance to express multiple and often unexplored aspects of the self, to play with their identity and to try out new ones. MUDs make possible the creation of an identity so fluid and multiple that it strains the limits of the notion. Identity, after all, refers to the sameness between two qualities, in this case between a person and his or her persona. But in MUDs, one can be many.

A 21-year-old college senior defends his violent characters as "something in me; but quite frankly I'd rather rape on MUDs where no harm is done." A 26-year-old clerical worker says, "I'm not one thing, I'm many things. Each part gets to be more fully expressed in MUDs than in the real world. So even though I play more than one self on MUDs, I feel more like "myself" when I'm MUDding." In real life, this woman sees her world as too narrow to allow her to manifest certain aspects of the person she feels herself to be. Creating screen personae is thus an opportunity for self-expression, leading to her feeling more like her true self when decked out in an array of virtual masks.

MUDs imply difference, multiplicity, heterogeneity, and fragmentation. 35 Such an experience of identity contradicts the Latin root of the word, *idem,* meaning "the same." But this contradiction increasingly defines the conditions of our lives beyond the virtual world. MUDs thus become objects-to-think-with for thinking about postmodern selves. Indeed, the unfolding of all

MUD action takes place in a resolutely postmodern context. There are parallel narratives in the different rooms of a MUD. The cultures of Tolkien, Gibson, and Madonna* coexist and interact. Since MUDs are authored by their players, thousands of people in all, often hundreds at a time, are all logged on from different places; the solitary author is displaced and distributed. Traditional ideas about identity have been tied to a notion of authenticity that such virtual experiences actively subvert. When each player can create many characters in many games, the self is not only decentered but multiplied without limit.

As a new social experience, MUDs pose many psychological questions: If a persona in a role-playing game drops defenses that the player in real life has been unable to abandon, what effect does this have? What if a persona enjoys success in some area (say, flirting) that the player has not been able to achieve? Slippages often occur in places where persona and self merge, where the multiple personae join to comprise what the individual thinks of as his or her authentic self.

Doug is a Midwestern college junior. He plays four characters distributed across three different MUDs. One is a seductive woman. One is a macho, cowboy type whose self-description stresses that he is a "Marlboros rolled in the T-shirt sleeve kind of guy." The third is a rabbit of unspecified gender who wanders its MUD introducing people to each other, a character he calls Carrot. Doug says, "Carrot is so low key that people let it be around while they are having private conversations. So I think of Carrot as my passive, voyeuristic character." Doug's fourth character is one that he plays only on a MUD in which all the characters are furry animals. "I'd rather not even talk about that character because my anonymity there is very important to me," Doug says. "Let's just say that on FurryMUDs I feel like a sexual tourist." Doug talks about playing his characters in windows and says that using windows has made it possible for him to "turn pieces of my mind on and off.

"I split my mind. . . . I can see myself as being two or three or more. And I just turn on one part of my mind and then another when I go from window to window. I'm in some kind of argument in one window and trying to come on to a girl in a MUD in another, and another window might be running a spreadsheet program or some other technical thing for school. . . . And then I'll get a real-time message that flashes on the screen as soon as it is sent from another system user, and I guess that's RL. RL is just one more window, and it's not usually my best one."

Tolkien, Gibson, and Madonna: J.R.R. Tolkien (1892–1973), British scholar and author of *The Lord of the Rings* trilogy of fantasy novels (1954–55); William Gibson (b. 1948), American author of *Neuromancer* (1984) and originator of cyberpunk; Madonna Louise Ciccone (b. 1958), American performer and film star

Play has always been an important aspect of our individual efforts to build identity. The psychoanalyst Erik Erikson called play a "toy situation" that allows us to "reveal and commit" ourselves "in its unreality." While MUDs are not the only "places" on the Internet in which to play with identity, they provide an unparalleled opportunity for such play. On a MUD one actually gets to build character and environment and then to live within the toy situation. A MUD can become a context for discovering who one is and wishes to be. In this way, the games are laboratories for the construction of identity.

Stewart, a 23-year-old physics graduate student, uses MUDs to have experiences he can't imagine for himself in RL. His intense online involvements engaged key issues in his life but ultimately failed to help him reach successful resolutions.

Stewart's real life revolves around laboratory work and his plans for a future in science. His only friend is his roommate, another physics student whom he describes as even more reclusive than himself. For Stewart, this circumscribed, almost monastic student life does not represent a radical departure from what has gone before. He has had heart trouble since he was a child; one small rebellion, a ski trip when he was a college freshman, put him in the hospital for a week. He has lived life within a small compass.

Stewart is logged on to one MUD or another for at least 40 hours a week. It seems misleading to call what he does there playing. He spends his time constructing a life that is more expansive than the one he lives in physical reality. Stewart, who has traveled very little and has never been to Europe, explains with delight that his favorite MUD, although played in English, is physically located on a computer in Germany and has many European players.

On the German MUD, Stewart shaped a character named Achilles, but he asks his MUD friends to call him Stewart as much as possible. He wants to feel that his real self exists somewhere between Stewart and Achilles. He wants to feel that his MUD life is part of his real life. Stewart insists that he does not role play, but that MUDs simply allow him to be a better version of himself.

On the MUD, Stewart creates a living environment suitable for his ideal self. His university dormitory is modest, but the room he has built for Achilles on the MUD is elegant and heavily influenced by Ralph Lauren advertising. He has named it "the home beneath the silver moon." There are books, a roaring fire, cognac, a cherry mantel "covered with pictures of Achilles's friends from around the world.

"You look up . . . and through the immense skylight you see a breathtaking view of the night sky. The moon is always full over Achilles's home, and its light fills the room with a warm glow."

Beyond expanding his social world, MUDs have brought Stewart the only romance and intimacy he has ever known. At a social event in virtual space, a "wedding" of two regular players on a German-based MUD I call Gargoyle, Achilles met Winterlight, a character played by one of the three female players on that MUD. Stewart, who has known little success in dating and romantic relationships, was able to charm this desirable player.

On their first virtual date, Achilles took Winterlight to an Italian restaurant close to Stewart's dorm. He had often fantasized being there with a woman. Stewart used a combination of MUD commands to simulate a romantic evening—picking Winterlight up at the airport in a limousine, driving her to a hotel room so that she could shower, and then taking her to the restaurant and ordering veal for her.

This dinner date led to others during which Achilles was tender and romantic, chivalrous and poetic. The intimacy Achilles experienced during his courtship of Winterlight is unknown to Stewart in other contexts. "She's a very, she's a good friend. I found out a lot of things, from things about physiology to the color of nail polish she wears." Finally, Achilles asked for Winterlight's hand. When she accepted, they had a formal engagement ceremony on the MUD.

At the engagement, Winterlight gave Achilles a rose she had worn in her hair; Achilles gave her 1,000 paper stars.

Although Stewart participated in this ceremony alone in his room with   50 his computer and modem, a group of European players actually traveled to Germany, site of Gargoyle's host computer, and got together for food and champagne. Many of the 25 guests at the German celebration brought gifts and dressed specially for the occasion. Stewart felt as though he were throwing a party. This was the first time that he had ever entertained, and he was proud of his success. In real life, Stewart felt constrained by his health problems, his shyness and social isolation, and his narrow economic straits. In the Gargoyle MUD, he bypassed these obstacles, at least temporarily.

The psychological effects of life on the screen can be complicated: a safe place is not all that is needed for personal change. Stewart came to MUDding with serious problems, and for Stewart, playing on MUDs led to a net drop in self-esteem. MUDs did help Stewart talk about his troubles while they were still emotionally relevant; nevertheless, he is emphatic that MUDding has ultimately made him feel worse about himself. MUDding did not alter Stewart's sense of himself as withdrawn, unappealing, and flawed.

While Stewart has tried hard to make his MUD self, the "better" Achilles self, part of his real life, he says he has failed. He says, "I'm not social. I don't like parties. I can't talk to people about my problems." The integration of the social Achilles, who can talk about his troubles, and the asocial Stewart, who can only cope by putting them out of mind, has not occurred. From Stewart's point of view, MUDs have stripped away some of his defenses but have given him nothing in return. In fact, MUDs make Stewart feel vulnerable in a new way. Although he hoped that MUDs would cure him, it is MUDs that now make him feel sick. He feels addicted to MUDs: "When you feel you're stagnating and you feel there's nothing going on in your life and you're stuck in a rut, it's very easy to be on there for a very large amount of time."

Stewart cannot learn from his character Achilles's experience and social success because they are too different from the things of which he believes himself capable. Despite his efforts to turn Achilles into Stewart, Stewart has split off his strengths and sees them as possible only for Achilles in the MUD. It is only Achilles who can create the magic and win the girl. In making this split between himself and the achievements of his screen persona, Stewart does not give himself credit for the positive steps he has taken in real life. Like an unsuccessful psychotherapy, MUDding has not helped Stewart bring these good experiences inside himself or integrate them into his self-image.

Relationships during adolescence are ususaly bounded by a mutual understanding that they involve limited commitment. Virtual space is well suited to such relationships; its natural limitations keep things within bounds. As in Thomas Mann's *The Magic Mountain,* which takes place in the isolation of a sanatorium, relationships become intense very quickly because the participants feel isolated in a remote and unfamiliar world with its own rules. MUDS, like other electronic meeting places, can breed a kind of easy intimacy. In a first phase, MUD players feel the excitement of a rapidly deepening relationship and the sense that time itself is speeding up. "The MUD quickens things. It quickens things so much," says one player. "You know, you don't think about it when you're doing it, but you meet somebody on the MUD, and within a week you feel like you've been friends forever."

In a second phase, players commonly try to take things from the virtual 55 to the real and are usually disappointed.

Gender-swapping on MUDs is not a small part of the game action. By some estimates, Habitat, a Japanese MUD, has 1.5 million users. Habitat is a MUD operated for profit. Among the registered members of Habitat, there is a ratio of four real-life men to each real-life woman. But inside the MUD the ratio is only three male characters to one female character. In other words, a significant number of players, many tens of thousands of them, are virtually cross-dressing.

What is virtual gender-swapping all about? Some of those who do it claim that it is not particularly significant. "When I play a woman I don't really take it too seriously," said 20-year-old Andrei. "I do it to improve the ratio of women to men. It's just a game." On one level, virtual gender-swapping is easier than doing it in real life. For a man to present himself as female in a chat room, on an IRC channel, or in a MUD, only requires writing a description. For a man to play a woman on the streets of an American city, he would have to shave various parts of his body; wear makeup, perhaps a wig, a dress, and high heels; perhaps change his voice, walk, and mannerisms. He would have some anxiety about passing, and there might be even more anxiety about not passing, which would pose a risk of violence and possibly arrest. So more men are willing to give virtual cross-dressing a try. But once they are online as female, they soon find that maintaining this fiction is difficult. To pass as a woman for any length of time requires understanding how gender inflects speech, manner, the interpretation of experience. Women attempting to pass as men face the same kind of challenge.

Virtual cross-dressing is not as simple as Andrei suggests. Not only can it be technically challenging, it can be psychologically complicated. Taking a virtual role may involve you in ongoing relationships. You may discover things about yourself that you never knew before.

Case, a 34-year-old industrial designer who is happily married to a co-worker, is currently MUDding as a female character. In response to my question, "Has MUDding ever caused you any emotional pain?" he says, "Yes, but also the kind of learning that comes from hard times.

"I'm having pain in my playing now. Mairead, the woman I'm playing 60 in Medieval MUSH, is having an interesting relationship with a fellow. Mairead is a lawyer, and the high cost of law school has to be paid for by a corporation or a noble house. She fell in love with a nobleman who paid for her law school. [Case slips into referring to Mairead in the first person.] Now he wants to marry me although I'm a commoner. I finally said yes. I try to talk to him about the fact that I'm essentially his property. I'm a commoner . . . I've grown up with it, that's the way life is. He wants to deny the situation. He says, 'Oh no, no, no. . . . We'll pick you up, set you on your feet, the whole world is open to you.' But every time I behave like I'm now going to be a countess some day . . . as in, 'And I never liked this wallpaper anyway,' I get pushed down. The relationship is pull up, push down. It's an incredibly psychologically damaging thing to do to a person. And the very thing that he liked about her that she was independent, strong, said what was on her mind, it is all being bled out of her."

Case looks at me with a wry smile and sighs, "A woman's life." He continues: "I see her [Mairead] heading for a major psychological problem. What we have is a dysfunctional relationship. But even though it's very painful and stressful, it's very interesting to watch myself cope with this problem. How am I going to dig my persona's self out of this mess? Because I don't want to go on like this. I want to get out of it. . . . You can see that playing this woman lets me see what I have in my psychological repertoire, what is hard and what is easy for me. And I can also see how some of the things that work when you're a man just backfire when you're a woman."

Case further illustrates the complexity of gender swapping as a vehicle for self-reflection. Case describes his RL persona as a nice guy, a "Jimmy Stewart type like my father." He says that in general he likes his father and he likes himself, but he feels he pays a price for his low-key ways. In particular, he feels at a loss when it comes to confrontation, both at home and in business dealings. Case likes MUDding as a female because it makes it easier for him to be aggressive and confrontational. Case plays several online "Katharine Hepburn types," strong, dynamic, "out there" women who remind him of his mother, "who says exactly what's on her mind and is a take-no-prisoners sort."

For Case, if you are assertive as a man, it is coded as "being a bastard." If you are assertive as a woman, it is coded as "modern and together."

Some women who play male characters desire invisibility or permission to be more outspoken or aggressive. "I was born in the South and taught that girls didn't speak up to disagree with men," says Zoe, a 34-year-old woman who plays male and female characters on four MUDs.

"We would sit at dinner and my father would talk and my mother would agree. I thought my father was a god. Once or twice I did disagree with him. I remember one time in particular when I was 10, and he looked at me and said, "Well, well, well, if this little flower grows too many more thorns, she will never catch a man." 65

Zoe credits MUDs with enabling her to reach a state of mind where she is better able to speak up for herself in her marriage ("to say what's on my mind before things get all blown out of proportion") and to handle her job as the financial officer for a small biotechnology firm.

"I played a MUD man for two years. First I did it because I wanted the feeling of an equal playing field in terms of authority, and the only way I could think of to get it was to play a man. But after a while, I got very absorbed by MUDding. I became a wizard on a pretty simple MUD. I call myself Ulysses and got involved in the system and realized that as a man I could be firm and people would think I was a great wizard. As a woman, drawing the line and standing firm has always made me feel like a bitch and, actually, I feel that people saw me as one, too. As a man I was liberated from all that. I learned from my mistakes. I got better at being firm but not rigid. I practiced, safe from criticism."

Zoe's perceptions of her gender trouble are almost the opposite of Case's. While Case sees aggressiveness as acceptable only for women, Zoe sees it as acceptable only for men. These stories share a notion that a virtual gender swap gave people greater emotional range in the real. Zoe says: "I got really good at playing a man, so good that whoever was on the system would accept me as a man and talk to me as a man. So, other guys talked to Ulysses guy to guy. It was very validating. All those years I was paranoid about how men talked about women. Or I thought I was paranoid. Then I got a chance to be a guy and I saw that I wasn't paranoid at all."

Virtual sex, whether in MUDs or in a private room on a commercial online service, consists of two or more players typing descriptions of physical actions, verbal statements, and emotional reactions for their characters. In cyberspace, this activity is not only common but, for many people, it is the centerpiece of their online experience.

On MUDs, some people have sex as characters of their own gender. 70
Others have sex as characters of the other gender. Some men play female personae to have netsex with men. And in the "fake-lesbian syndrome," men adopt online female personae in order to have netsex with women. Although it does not seem to be as widespread, I have met several women who say they present as male characters in order to have netsex with men. Some people have sex as nonhuman characters, for example, as animals on FurryMUDs. Some enjoy sex with one partner. Some use virtual reality as a place to experiment with group situations. In real life, such behavior (where possible) can create enormous practical and emotional confusion. Virtual adventures may be easier to undertake, but they can also result in significant complications.

Martin and Beth, both 41, have been married for 19 years and have four children. Early in their marriage, Martin regretted not having had more time for sexual experimentation and had an extramarital affair. The affair hurt Beth deeply, and Martin decided he never wanted to do it again. When Martin discovered MUDs he was thrilled. "I really am monogamous. I'm really not interested in something outside my marriage. But being able to have, you know, a Tiny* romance is kind of cool." Martin decided to tell Beth about his MUD sex life and she decided to tell him that she does not mind. Beth has made a conscious decision to consider Martin's sexual relationships on MUDs as more like his reading an erotic novel than like his having a rendezvous in a motel room. For Martin, his online affairs are a way to fill the gaps of his youth, to broaden his sexual experience without endangering his marriage.

Other partners of virtual adulterers do not share Beth's accepting attitude. Janet, 24, a secretary at a New York law firm, is very upset by her husband Tim's sex life in cyberspace. After Tim's first online affair, he confessed his virtual infidelity: When Janet objected, Tim told her that he would stop "seeing" his online mistress. Janet says that she is not sure that he actually did stop.

"The thing that bothers me most is that he wants to do it in the first place. In some ways, I'd have an easier time understanding why he would want to have an affair in real life. At least there, I could say to myself, 'Well, it is for someone with a better body, or just for the novelty.' It's like the first kiss is always the best kiss. But in MUDding, he is saying that he wants that feeling of intimacy with someone else, the 'just talk' part of an encounter with a woman, and to me that comes closer to what is most important about sex.

"First I told him he couldn't do it anymore. Then, I panicked and figured that he might do it anyway because, unlike in real life, I could never find out. All these thousands of people all over the world with their stupid fake

---

a Tiny romance: "Tiny" is a reference to the MUD TinySex.

names . . . no way I would ever find out. So, I pulled back and said that talking about it was strictly off limits. But now I don't know if that was the right decision. I feel paranoid whenever he is on the computer."

This distressed wife struggles to decide whether her husband is unfaithful when his persona collaborates on writing real-time erotica with another persona in cyberspace. And beyond this, should it make a difference if unbeknownst to the husband his cyberspace mistress turns out to be a 19-year-old male college freshman? What if "she" is an infirm 80-year-old man in a nursing home? And even more disturbing, what if she is a 12-year-old girl? Or a 12-year-old boy?   75

TinySex poses the question of what is at the heart of sex and fidelity. Is it the physical action? Is it emotional intimacy with someone other than one's primary partner? Is infidelity in the head or in the body? Is it in the desire or in the action? What constitutes the violation of trust?

And once we take virtuality seriously as a way of life, we need a new language for talking about the simplest things. Each individual must ask: What is the nature of my relationships? What are the limits of my responsibility? And even more basic: Who and what am I? What is the connection between my physical and virtual bodies? And is it different in different cyberspaces? These questions are equally central for thinking about community. What is the nature of our social ties? What kind of accountability do we have for our actions in real life and in cyberspace? What kind of society or societies are we creating, both on and off the screen?

When people adopt an online persona they cross a boundary into highly charged territory. Some feel an uncomfortable sense of fragmentation, some a sense of relief. Some sense the possibilities for self-discovery, even self-transformation. Serena, a 26-year-old graduate student in history, says, "When I log on to a new MUD and I create a character and know I have to start typing my description, I always feel a sense of panic. Like I could find out something I don't want to know." Arlie, a 20-year-old undergraduate, says, "I am always very self-conscious when I create a new character. Usually, I end up creating someone I wouldn't want my parents to know about. . . . But that someone is part of me."

> Irony is about contradictions that do not resolve into larger wholes . . .
> about the tension of holding incompatible things together because both
> or all are necessary and true.   —Donna Haraway

As we stand on the boundary between the real and the virtual, our experience recalls what the anthropologist Victor Turner termed a liminal moment, a moment of passage when new cultural symbols and meanings can emerge. Liminal moments are times of tension, extreme reactions, and great opportunity. When Turner talked about liminality, he understood it as a transitional state, but living with flux may no longer be temporary. Technology is bringing postmodernism down to earth itself; the story of technology refuses modernist resolutions and requires an openness to multiple viewpoints.

Multiple viewpoints call forth a new moral discourse. The culture of 80 simulation may help us achieve a vision of a multiple but integrated identity whose flexibility, resilience, and capacity for joy comes from having access to our many selves. But if we have lost reality in the process, we shall have struck a poor bargain. In Wim Wenders's film *Until the End of the World,* a scientist develops a device that translates the electrochemical activity of the brain into digital images. He gives this technology to his family and closest friends, who are now able to hold small battery-driven monitors and watch their dreams. At first, they are charmed. They see their treasured fantasies, their secret selves. They see the images they otherwise would forget, the scenes they otherwise would repress. As with the personae one can play in a MUD, watching dreams on a screen opens up new aspects of the self.

However, the story soon turns dark. The images seduce. They are richer and more compelling than the real life around them. Wenders's characters fall in love with their dreams, become addicted to them. People wander about with blankets over their heads the better to see the monitors from which they cannot bear to be parted. They are imprisoned by the screens, imprisoned by the keys to their past that the screens seem to hold.

We, too, are vulnerable to using our screens in these ways. People can get lost in virtual worlds. Some are tempted to think of life in cyberspace as insignificant, as escape or meaningless diversion. It is not. Our experiences there are serious play. We belittle them at our risk. We must understand the dynamics of virtual experience both to foresee who might be in danger and to put these experiences to best use. Without a deep understanding of the many selves that we express in the virtual, we cannot use our experiences there to enrich the real. If we cultivate our awareness of what stands behind our screen personae, we are more likely to succeed in using virtual experience for personal transformation.

The imperative to self-knowledge has always been at the heart of philosophical inquiry. In the 20th century, it found expression in the psychoanalytic culture as well. One might say that it constitutes the ethic of psychoanalysis. From the perspective of this ethic, we work to know ourselves in order to improve not only our own lives, but those of our families and society. Psychoanalysis is a survivor discourse. Born of a modernist worldview, it has evolved into forms relevant to postmodern times. With mechanistic roots in the culture of calculation, psychoanalytic ideas become newly relevant in the culture of simulation. Some believe that we are at the end of the Freudian century. But the reality is more complex. Our need for a practical philosophy of self-knowledge has never been greater as we struggle to make meaning from our lives on the screen.

QUESTIONING THE TEXT

1. Turkle claims that "MUDs imply difference, multiplicity, heterogeneity, and fragmentation" (paragraph 35). Reread her essay, looking for examples and other types of evidence that support her claim. Also identify any counterexamples or other elements that do *not* support her claim. Are you persuaded by this argument about the nature of MUDs? Write a critical response to Turkle, explaining your reasons for agreement or disagreement.

   80

2. How much does Turkle tell readers about the design of her research project (how many people she interviewed, whether they represented different parts of the country, how she analyzed the interview data, what she chose to include or to leave out, and so on)? Working with a classmate, list the questions you think a researcher carrying out this kind of project would need to ask. Bring your list to class for discussion.

MAKING CONNECTIONS

3. Turkle doesn't describe talking with any MUDders who have limited or no vision, though computer technology is being used in multiple ways by people with various disabilities, including blindness. Read Turkle's piece alongside Georgina Kleege's "Call It Blindness" (p. 389), looking for metaphors of sight, insight, vision, and blindness. Then, working with a classmate, brainstorm about a conversation Turkle and Kleege might have over email or in person. What would they most likely talk about? What questions might each ask the other? Try your hand at writing a dialogue between the two authors.

4. Choose one or two other selections from this chapter and read each one carefully, noting any evidence of multiple identities or "selves." Make notes on your findings and bring them to class for discussion.

JOINING THE CONVERSATION

5. Spend an hour or two visiting a MUD you have never been to before, jotting down notes about what you observe and experience during your visit. Record your sensations and feelings, your questions, things you find interesting or irritating, your impressions of the MUDders you encounter, and so on. Then, for 15 to 20 minutes, brainstorm about your overall impression of the MUD and the experience of the visit. Finally, use your notes and your brainstorming to write a detailed description of the MUD,

including an explanation of why you would or would not recommend it to others.

6. Turkle quotes Doug, "a Midwestern college junior" she interviewed, as saying that "RL [real life] is just one more window, and it's not usually my best one" (paragraph 38). Working in a group of two or three students, discuss Doug's comment and relate it to your own experiences with and feelings about RL. Then, working individually, draft a letter to Doug in which you respond to his statement. Finally, share and discuss your group's letters to Doug, using them to consider a range of attitudes toward "virtual" and "real" life.

7. Near the end of her essay, Turkle makes a bold claim: "Some are tempted to think of life in cyberspace as insignificant, as escape or meaningless diversion. It is not. Our experiences there are serious play. We belittle them at our risk" (paragraph 82). Write a four- to five-page exploratory essay on the possible meanings of this passage. Be sure to assess the evidence that Turkle provides elsewhere in her article in support of her claim and to give your critical response to that claim.

LANGSTON HUGHES
Theme for English B

As a young man in Joplin, Missouri, Langston Hughes (1902–67) worked as an assistant cook, a launderer, and a busboy—jobs similar to ones you may have held— before leaving to attend Columbia University in New York City. (He eventually graduated in 1929 from Lincoln University in Pennsylvania.) A prolific writer and part of the great artistic movement of the 1920s and 1930s known as the Harlem Renaissance, Hughes worked in many genres—novels, short stories, plays, essays, and poems. From his early collection of poems, The Weary Blues *(1926), to his posthumous volume of essays,* Black Misery *(1969), he explored numerous themes touching on the lives of African Americans, including that of higher education.*

The poem that follows, from 1926, describes one event in the speaker's college career and raises questions about relationships between instructors and students, between those "inside" the university and those "outside." It is one of my favorite poems, one of the few special ones I carry around with me and, in fact, now find that I know "by heart." With every new class I teach, I think of Hughes's "Theme for English B," for it speaks volumes to me about the necessity of respecting individual differences while at the same time valuing those bonds that link us to one another.

—A.L.

The instructor said,

> Go home and write
> a page tonight.
> And let that page come out of you —
> Then, it will be true.   5

I wonder if it's that simple?
I am twenty-two, colored, born in Winston-Salem.
I went to school there, then Durham, then here
to this college on the hill above Harlem.
I am the only colored student in my class.   10
The steps from the hill lead down to Harlem,
through a park, then I cross St. Nicholas,
Eighth Avenue, Seventh, and I come to the Y,
the Harlem Branch Y, where I take the elevator
up to my room, sit down, and write this page: 15

It's not easy to know what is true for you or me
at twenty-two, my age. But I guess I'm what
I feel and see and hear. Harlem, I hear you:
hear you, hear me—we two—you, me talk on this page.
(I hear New York, too.) Me—who?   20
Well, I like to eat, sleep, drink, and be in love.
I like to work, read, learn, and understand life.
I like a pipe for a Christmas present,
or records—Bessie,* bop, or Bach.
I guess being colored doesn't make me not like   25
the same things other folks like who are other races.
So will my page be colored that I write?
Being me, it will not be white.
But it will be
a part of you, instructor.   30
You are white—
yet a part of me, as I am a part of you.
That's American.
Sometimes perhaps you don't want to be a part of me.
Nor do I often want to be a part of you.   35
But we are, that's true!
As I learn from you,
I guess you learn from me—
although you're older—and white—
and somewhat more free.   40

This is my page for English B.

IN RESPONSE

1. Near the end of the poem, the speaker says, addressing his instructor, "You are white— / yet a part of me, as I am a part of you. / That's American." What do you think Hughes means by "American"?

2. The speaker of this poem notes that given who he is, his theme will not be "white," but he goes on to say that it will still be "a part of you, instructor." What do you think he means? Can you describe a time when you've had a similar experience?

3. In "The Recoloring of Campus Life," Shelby Steele (p. 72) writes at length of the myth of inferiority among African American youths.

Bessie: Bessie Smith (1898?–1937), a famous blues singer

What, if any, evidence of a myth of inferiority do you find in Hughes's poem? How might Hughes respond to Steele's essay?

4. Would Hughes—or his teacher—likely be found in John Henry Newman's ideal university (p. 46)? Why, or why not?

5. Consider what effects your own gender, race, class, or family background has had on your success in school. Then write a brief (one- or two-page) essay explaining those effects.

6. Brainstorm with two or three classmates about whether it is important for students to identify with their teachers, to have a number of things in common with them. Come to an agreement among yourselves on how to answer this question, and then write one page explaining why you answered it as you did.

OTHER READINGS

Buckley, Christopher. "Tough Guys Don't Dance." *Backward and Upward: The New Conservative Writing.* Ed. David Brooks. New York: Vintage, 1996. 125–31. Ponders forms of macho posturing—real and fake.

Cruikshank, Margaret, ed. *The Lesbian Path: 37 Lesbian Writers Share Their Personal Experiences, Viewpoints, Traumas, and Joys.* Monterey: Angel, 1980. Personal narratives by gay women.

Heath, Shirley Brice, and Milbrey W. McLaughlin, eds. *Identity and Inner-City Youth: Beyond Ethnicity and Gender.* New York: Teachers College, 1993. Explores the reasons local clubs and youth groups help inner-city youth find and maintain self-esteem in ways schools often do not.

Kors, Alan Charles, and Harvey A. Silverglate. "Individual Identity: The Heart of Liberty." *The Shadow University: The Betrayal of Liberty on America's Campuses.* New York: Free, 1998. 187–209. Charges that American universities treat students not as individuals but as members of politicized groups.

Senna, Danzy. "The Mulatto Millennium." *Utne Reader* Sept.–Oct. 1998: 31–34. Considers the complexities of multiracial identity, arguing that categories (even the ones this author coins) don't always fit a person's identity.

Whitman, Walt. "Song of Myself." 1881. *Leaves of Grass.* Ed. Scully Bradley and Harold W. Blodgett. New York: Norton, 1973. A classic statement of American identity.

ELECTRONIC RESOURCES

http://www.identitytheft.org/
Offers information on restoring credit and on protecting identity, credit, and reputation.

http://rs6.loc.gov/ammem/ammemhome.html
Gateway to a massive Library of Congress archive of photographs, manuscripts, and documents related to American history and identity.

http://www.nea.org/society/engonly.html
Web site of an organization that opposes "English only" legislation in the United States.

http://www.us-english.org/index.html
Web site of an organization that favors "English only" legislation in the United States.

Look carefully at the photograph on the preceding page, which was taken at the 1998 press conference where President Clinton denied he had had a sexual relationship with Monica Lewinsky. What occupies the foreground of the image—and what are your eyes drawn to first? ■ What impression do you think the photographer intended to create? ■ In what ways is that impression different from the one the president himself may have intended? ■ In what ways does the setting (the painting of Theodore Roosevelt on horseback, the presidential seal, and so on) affect your "reading" of this photograph? ■ How is your reading affected by the knowledge that the president later admitted the relationship with Lewinsky?

Images: Mirror, Mirror on the Wall

7

[T]he prison-house is the world of sight, the light of the fire is the sun, and you will not misapprehend me if you interpret the journey upwards to be the ascent of the soul into the intellectual world. . . .   PLATO, *Allegory of the Cave*

There was fear too of the magic that seems to lurk in images. They steal likenesses. They do what only gods should be able to do: They re-create the living and preserve the dead.

MITCHELL STEPHENS, *"By Means of the Visible": A Picture's Worth*

Like yin and yang, like the Christian cross and the star of Israel, Mickey can be seen everywhere—a sign, a rune, a hieroglyphic trace of a secret power, an electricity we want to plug into.   JOHN UPDIKE, *The Mystery of Mickey Mouse*

Think about why Land-o-Lakes finds it appropriate to market its butter with the stereotyped image of an "Indian princess" on the wrapper.

WARD CHURCHILL, *Crimes against Humanity*

For me, the trout in its stream is the essence of life—encompassing survival and beauty, death and birth.   JAMES PROSEK, *Introduction to* Trout

One picture, we are told, is worth a thousand words. But a thousand pictures, especially if they are of the same object, may not be worth anything at all.

NEIL POSTMAN, *The Great Symbol Drain*

Michael Jordan has become the greatest corporate pitchman of all time. As a twentieth-century sports hero, he has plausible competition from Babe Ruth and Muhammad Ali; as an agent of brand equity, he is without peer.

HENRY LOUIS GATES JR., *Net Worth*

Our own time is, as much as anything else, the Age of Falsification. The nip, the tuck, the face-lift, the silicone implant.

KENNETH BROWER, *Photography in the Age of Falsification*

If you have ever visited one of the Disney theme parks, . . . you have likely wondered at the labor—both seen and unseen—necessary to maintain these fanciful environments. . . . What keeps employees ("cast members") so poised, meticulously groomed, and endlessly cheerful?

LINDA S. WATTS, Review of Inside the Mouse

Introduction

WHAT COMES TO MIND when you hear or see the word *image*? Perhaps its relationship to the imagination (the word comes from the Latin word for "imitation" or "copy")? Or a familiar saying such as "she's the spitting image of her mother" or the biblical injunction not to worship "graven images"? Or perhaps you think first of a specific image that has stayed with you for a long, long time.

Whatever the case, you don't have to pursue the concept very long before you find someone asking about the difference between the image and what it purports to represent. In the fairy tale, "mirror, mirror on the wall" is followed by the question "who's the fairest of them all?" But as the selections in this chapter indicate, the question might rather be "which is the real-est of them all?" And, we might add, why does it matter which is the "most real"? Indeed, the relationship between the real and its copies, representations, and renderings (images) has been hotly debated throughout Western history. Is a reflection in a mirror the same as what it reflects? If not, what is the status and value of each? Drama, for example, can be seen as mimesis—an imitation or image of reality. But is it less valuable than what it imitates? Is it more valuable? These seemingly straightforward questions are anything but simple, and never more so than in our own time, often referred to as "the age of the image." In fact, the proliferation over the last two centuries of technologies for producing, reproducing, and altering images has led to a point of saturation: we are surrounded by images that compete for our time, attention, belief, and money. In this image-filled culture, we need to explore the effect images have on us and to ask an age-old question: to what (if any) reality does an image refer?

The selections in this chapter will provide you with a number of ways to think about these questions. Before you begin to read, however, you may want to explore your own connection to images, using the following questions:

- What images have most influenced you—and why?
- How would you summarize the difference between what is real and what is *apparently* real (an image)?
- What source of images do you find most powerful? The Web? Television and movies? Fine art? Drama, photography, or advertising?
- Is a picture really "worth a thousand words"? Why, or why not?

PLATO
Allegory of the Cave

DURING THE PAST 2,500 *years, few have exerted more influence on Western thought than Plato (c. 428–348* B.C.*). Born into an aristocratic family in the Greek city-state of Athens, Plato received the best education of the day, and he went on to found a school of his own—the Academy—in which he enacted the dialectical model of teaching famously associated with his own teacher, Socrates. Writing in the voice of Socrates, he produced a large number of dialogues (one of which ironically condemns writing) that have shaped Western philosophy, psychology, and politics. These works reveal Plato's literary and rhetorical abilities, inaugurate new forms and uses of prose, and set out his theory of the ideal state and a plan for living and learning within it.*

Characteristic of many Platonic works is the use of stories and myths featuring extended metaphors and analogies, such as his representation of the human soul as a charioteer trying to manage a chariot drawn by two horses, one docile and obedient, the other unruly and devilish. You can see one of these devices at work in "Allegory of the Cave," the climax of Plato's discussion of philosophy in book VII of The Republic, *his dialogue about the ideal state. The story presented in this brief allegory compares the life of people chained in a darkened cave, where they are deluded by shadows, with that of those released into the dazzling sunlight outside. Plato argues that this movement from darkness to light is like the journey the soul must make from the prison of mere sensory impressions (appearances or images) to the freedom of true reality, which exists only beyond the realm of the senses. Paradoxically, in Plato's system, what we can see with our eyes is suspect, a mere shadow; only what we can see with our souls is "real."*

In making this argument, Plato raises issues as old as Western history. What is "real," and what is only apparently real? Which is more valuable, and why? Down through the centuries, people have debated these questions, as we are doing in present-day discussions of "virtual" reality. I chose this selection from Plato's work because it seems so timely to current debates over what is real (is Coca-Cola the "real thing" or Amazon.com a "real" place?). You may want to keep these questions in mind as you read Plato's story—and as you turn in this chapter to other explorations of the power of images.

—A.L.

And now, I said, let me show in a figure how far our nature is enlightened or unenlightened:—Behold! Human beings living in an underground den, which has a mouth open towards the light and reaching all along the den; here they have been from their childhood, and have their legs and necks chained so that they cannot move, and can only see before them, being prevented by the chains from turning round their heads. Above and behind them a fire is blazing at a distance, and between the fire and the prisoners there is a raised way; and you will see, if you look, a low wall built along the way, like the screen which marionette players have in front of them, over which they show the puppets.

I see.

And do you see, I said, men passing along the wall carrying all sorts of vessels, and statues and figures of animals made of wood and stone and various materials, which appear over the wall? Some of them are talking, others silent.

You have shown me a strange image, and they are strange prisoners.

Like ourselves, I replied; and they see only their own shadows, or the   5
shadows of one another, which the fire throws on the opposite wall of the cave?

True, he said; how could they see anything but the shadows if they were never allowed to move their heads?

And of the objects which are being carried in like manner they would only see the shadows?

Yes, he said.

And if they were able to converse with one another, would they not suppose that they were naming what was actually before them?

Very true.   10

And suppose further that the prison had an echo which came from the other side, would they not be sure to fancy when one of the passers-by spoke that the voice which they heard came from the passing shadow?

No question, he replied.

To them, I said, the truth would be literally nothing but the shadows of the images.

That is certain.

And now look again, and see what will naturally follow if the prisoners   15
are released and disabused of their error. At first, when any of them is liberated and compelled suddenly to stand up and turn his neck round and walk and look towards the light, he will suffer sharp pains; the glare will distress him, and he will be unable to see the realities of which in his former state he had seen the shadows; and then conceive some one saying to him, that what he saw before was an illusion, but that now, when he is approaching nearer to being and his eye is turned towards more real existence, he has a clearer vision, — what will be his reply? And you may further imagine that his instructor is pointing to the objects as they pass and requiring him to name them, — will he not be perplexed? Will he not fancy that the shadows which he formerly saw are truer than the objects which are now shown to him?

Far truer.

And if he is compelled to look straight at the light, will he not have a pain in his eyes which will make him turn away to take refuge in the objects of vision which he can see, and which he will conceive to be in reality clearer than the things which are now being shown to him?

True, he said.

And suppose once more, that he is reluctantly dragged up a steep and rugged ascent, and held fast until he is forced into the presence of the sun himself, is he not likely to be pained and irritated? When he approaches the light his eyes will be dazzled, and he will not be able to see anything at all of what are now called realities.

Not all in a moment, he said.   20

He will require to grow accustomed to the sight of the upper world. And first he will see the shadows best, next the reflections of men and other objects in the water, and then the objects themselves; then he will gaze upon the light of the moon and the stars and the spangled heaven; and he will see the sky and the stars by night better than the sun or the light of the sun by day?

Certainly.

Last of all he will be able to see the sun, and not mere reflections of him in the water, but he will see him in his own proper place, and not in another; and he will contemplate him as he is.

Certainly.

He will then proceed to argue that this is he who gives the season and 25 the years, and is the guardian of all that is in the visible world, and in a certain way the cause of all things which he and his fellows have been accustomed to behold?

Clearly, he said, he would first see the sun and then reason about him.

And when he remembered his old habitation, and the wisdom of the den and his fellow-prisoners, do you not suppose that he would felicitate himself on the change, and pity them?

Certainly, he would.

And if they were in the habit of conferring honours among themselves on those who were quickest to observe the passing shadows and to remark which of them went before, and which followed after, and which were together; and who were therefore best able to draw conclusions as to the future, do you think that he would care for such honours and glories, or envy the possessors of them? Would he not say with Homer,

> "Better to be the poor servant of a poor master,"

and to endure anything, rather than think as they do and live after their manner?

Yes, he said, I think that he would rather suffer anything than entertain 30 these false notions and live in this miserable manner.

Imagine once more, I said, such a one coming suddenly out of the sun to be replaced in his old situation; would he not be certain to have his eyes full of darkness?

To be sure, he said.

And if there were a contest, and he had to compete in measuring the shadows with the prisoners who had never moved out of the den, while his sight was still weak, and before his eyes had become steady (and the time which would be needed to acquire this new habit of sight might be very considerable) would he not be ridiculous? Men would say of him that up he went and down he came without his eyes; and that it was better not even to think of ascending; and if any one tried to loose another and lead him up to the light, let them only catch the offender, and they would put him to death.

No question, he said.

This entire allegory, I said, you may now append, dear Glaucon,* to the 35 previous argument; the prison-house is the world of sight, the light of the fire is the sun, and you will not misapprehend me if you interpret the journey upwards to be the ascent of the soul into the intellectual world according to my poor belief, which, at your desire, I have expressed—whether rightly or wrongly God knows. But, whether true or false, my opinion is that in the world of knowledge the idea of good appears last of all, and is seen only with an effort; and, when seen, is also inferred to be the universal author of all things beautiful and right, parent of light and of the lord of light in this visible world, and the immediate source of reason and truth in the intellectual; and that this is the power upon which he who would act rationally either in public or private life must have his eye fixed.

I agree, he said, as far as I am able to understand you.

Moreover, I said, you must not wonder that those who attain to this beatific vision are unwilling to descend to human affairs; for their souls are ever hastening into the upper world where they desire to dwell; which desire of theirs is very natural, if our allegory may be trusted.

Yes, very natural.

And is there anything surprising in one who passes from divine contemplations to the evil state of man, misbehaving himself in a ridiculous manner; if, while his eyes are blinking and before he has become accustomed to the surrounding darkness, he is compelled to fight in courts of law, or in other places, about the images or the shadows of images of justice, and is endeavouring to meet the conceptions of those who have never yet seen absolute justice?

Anything but surprising, he replied.   40

Any one who has common sense will remember that the bewilderments of the eyes are of two kinds, and arise from two causes, either from coming out of the light or from going into the light, which is true of the mind's eye, quite as much as of the bodily eye; and he who remembers this when he sees any one whose vision is perplexed and weak, will not be too ready to laugh; he will first ask whether that soul of man has come out of the brighter life, and is unable to see because unaccustomed to the dark, or having turned from darkness to the day is dazzled by excess of light. And he will count the one happy in his condition and state of being, and he will pity the other; or, if he

---

Glaucon: one of the participants in the dialogue with Plato

have a mind to laugh at the soul which comes from below into the light, there will be more reason in this than in the laugh which greets him who returns from above out of the light into the den.

That, he said, is a very just distinction.

But then, if I am right, certain professors of education must be wrong when they say that they can put a knowledge into the soul which was not there before, like sight into blind eyes.

They undoubtedly say this, he replied.

Whereas, our argument shows that the power and capacity of learning   45 exist in the soul already; and that just as the eye was unable to turn from darkness to light without the whole body, so too the instrument of knowledge can only by the movement of the whole soul be turned from the world of becoming into that of being, and learn by degrees to endure the sight of being, and of the brightest and best of being, or in other words, of the good.

QUESTIONING THE TEXT

1. Working with two classmates, read carefully through Plato's "Allegory of the Cave," noting every use of metaphor, simile, or analogy you can find. Then group these figures of speech into categories according to what they relate to (for instance, those relating to vision or sight, those relating to the other senses, and so on). Write a one-page exploration of how figurative language works in Plato's text. Finally, in preparation for a class discussion, consider how metaphor or analogy relates to the *thing* it represents. Is Plato's own use of language in any way in tension with (or even in opposition to) the argument he is making? Bring your explorations and answers to class for discussion.

2. What qualities of dialogue does this passage exhibit? What role does each speaker play? How does the question-answer format affect you and your reading of the allegory?

MAKING CONNECTIONS

3. Read Linda S. Watts's "Review of *Inside the Mouse*" (p. 575) with Plato's allegory in mind. Then spend some time imagining Plato as a visitor to a Disney theme park. What might his responses be? Using what you learn from Watts's review as well as your own experience, write a one-page "review" of a Disney theme park authored by Plato.

4. If Plato found writing to be a mere imitation of the real or ideal, it's not hard to imagine what he would have said about photography. At first glance, then, you might think that Kenneth Brower and others who

consider photography an art form would have little sympathy with Plato's views. Read Brower's essay (p. 554) with this issue in mind, taking note of any similar arguments, examples, and other evidence in this piece and the one by Plato. Then prepare a brief report for your class on the ways in which Brower and Plato are not so far apart.

5. Neil Postman argues for the positive power—even the necessity—of symbols in achieving a national good. Read Postman's "The Great Symbol Drain" (p. 513). Then create a page of dialogue between Plato and Postman on this question: are symbols and narratives necessary for achieving national goals?

JOINING THE CONVERSATION

6. Spend 20 minutes or so brainstorming with classmates about other extended analogies or allegories that draw attention to the relationship between the "real" and its image, using a game, a space trip, a food, or whatever other vehicle will allow you to make the kind of stark comparison Plato makes in his allegory. Then look back at Plato's dialogue and note the different kinds of examples he uses to extend his allegory of the cave. Finally, try your hand at writing a brief piece called "Allegory of the _____."

7. Instead of thinking in terms of appearance (image) *versus* reality, try thinking of the two in other ways—as two sides of the same coin, as variations on a similar theme, or as simultaneously existing experiences, for example. Share your ideas with one or two classmates. Try drawing pictures or diagrams (images!) of the alternative relationships you came up with for appearance and reality. Do these alternative relationships change the way you value or think about what is real and what is an image or "shadow" (in Plato's words) of the real? Write a journal entry in which you explore this question. If you keep a reading log, answer this question there.

MITCHELL STEPHENS
"By Means of the Visible": A Picture's Worth

THOUGH WE LIVE IN A CULTURE *full of words and images that compete for our attention—billboards, traffic lights, movie posters, cereal boxes, magazine covers, computer interfaces, book displays—we may not think much about how they work or what they do to us. "'By Means of the Visible': A Picture's Worth" by Mitchell Stephens examines these interactions, drawing upon everything from Ancient Greek texts to MTV music videos to highlight the differences between words and images. Indeed, it is the dynamic style of MTV that leads Stephens to suggest that images in motion on video might embody complex ideas better than either words or still pictures alone.*

Stephens (b. 1949), Professor of Journalism at New York University, has written extensively about the history and practice of the news business and has served as a consultant to the innovative Newseum in Washington, D.C. "'By Means of the Visible'" is a chapter from his book The Rise of the Image, The Fall of the Word, *published in 1998.*

—J.R.

> Painting is much more eloquent than speech, and often penetrates more
> deeply into one's heart.   – Erasmus

Ask the creators of the wilder, more interesting-looking new television commercials, promotional announcements, news videos and even feature films where they found their inspiration, and their answer, more often than not, will contain the same three letters. Director Oliver Stone, when citing the antecedents of the jangled, fast-cut style he used in the movie *Natural Born Killers,* mentioned "commercials and MTV."[1] Don Schneider is senior creative director of the BBDO advertising agency, which has produced some groundbreaking Pepsi commercials, including that attack on the artichoke chef and the old TV. He made a more sweeping confession: "Ninety percent of this has to do with MTV."[2] ABC News took more than ideas from MTV: It hired one of the youth network's talented young producers, David Berrent.

MTV's influence begins, of course, with the music videos themselves— which "might be the only new popular art form in American life," Norman Mailer has suggested.[3] But many of the network's innovations appeared as

---

[1]Cited, John Hartl, "Fractured Reality—Oliver Stone's Latest Manic Movie Mixes Fiction with Today's Headlines," *Seattle Times,* August 21, 1994.

[2]Mitchell Stephens, "The New TV," *Washington Post,* April 25, 1993.

[3]Norman Mailer, "Like a Lady (Madonna)," *Esquire,* August 1994.

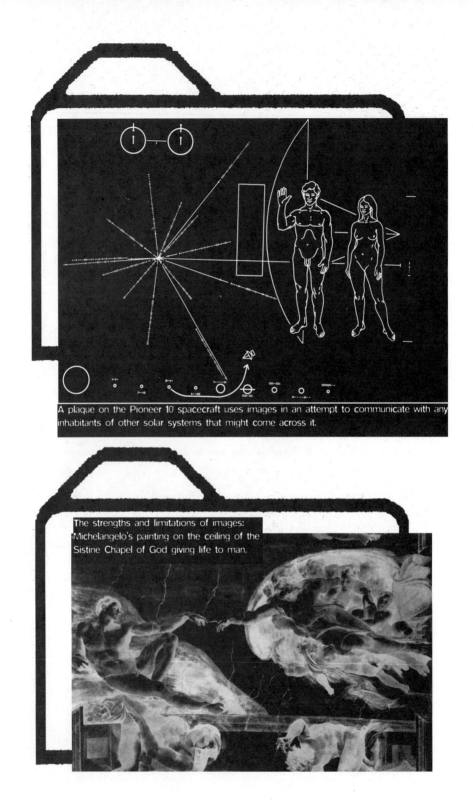

A plaque on the Pioneer 10 spacecraft uses images in an attempt to communicate with any inhabitants of other solar systems that might come across it.

The strengths and limitations of images: Michelangelo's painting on the ceiling of the Sistine Chapel of God giving life to man.

An image intended to take the place of words: the danger symbol from the discussion of the "Star Wars" defense system in MTV's Decade.

CHAPTER FIVE

"by means of the visible"

a picture's worth

more substantive supplements to those dizzying collages of guitar strummers and visual metaphors for lust. ABC wooed Berrent after executives saw his documentary *Decade,* a historical look, MTV-style, at the 1980s.

Decade includes a thirty-three-second segment on former President Ronald Reagan's planned "Star Wars" defense system. I make no claims for it journalistically, but in technique and style it is intriguing. An excerpt from a Reagan speech on national security is shown, along with an attack on Star Wars by the late rock musician Frank Zappa. These are sound-bites—the same (except for the use of Zappa as an expert) as might be seen in a traditional news story. But in between, Berrent placed a kind of rock video: While the phrase "guns in the sky" is sung over and over, and Zappa begins to talk, computer simulations of lasers attacking rockets are shown on screen. Those scenes, in turn, are interrupted by flashing, static images: a dollar sign, the symbol warning of possible nuclear contamination, the skull-and-crossbones symbol for danger.

Neither the word *danger* nor its synonyms is vocalized. Berrent clearly is relying on these flashing images not just to illustrate what is being said but to communicate their own meanings. In the introduction to that ABC documentary on churches, Roberta Goldberg, who learned from Berrent, does the same with the shot of three candles being extinguished. These images, the point is, are intended to take the place of words.

Many of the images that decorate our world have similar aspirations.   5 Among the most interesting are the icons that increasingly crowd the edges of computer screens. Small drawings—of a file folder, for instance—first began to replace lines of text on computer displays at a research center run by the Xerox Corporation in the 1970s. The driving force behind this work was Alan Kay, a Ph.D. in computer science, whose dreams for the future of the computer, inspired in part by Marshall McLuhan,* included a major role for images. Each icon used on the screen, Kay suspected, was worth not just a word but a whole sentence.[4]

A group of Apple Computer executives and engineers made an expedition to the Xerox center in 1979. They returned with many ideas and then added some of their own. In 1983 Apple released a slow, expensive, unsuccessful, "graphics-oriented" computer named Lisa and then, the next year, a faster, relatively inexpensive, hugely successful computer, using a similar operating system, named Macintosh. The indomitable Microsoft Corporation noticed the idea (Apple suggested, in court, a different verb), and with the success of the Windows operating system in 1990, sets of icons began to appear on most computer screens.[5]

Similar images currently express meanings on traffic signs, rest room doors, Olympic venues and biceps. Armies continue to march under images; the

---

Marshall McLuhan (1911–80): influential Canadian theorist of communication and author of *The Medium Is the Massage* (1967)

[4]Smith and Alexander 231, 235; Kay 193, 201, 202.

[5]Levy 69–70, 77–79, 98, 278–79.

devout of many faiths continue to pray to them. The *Pioneer 10* spacecraft, now embarked on a long journey toward the star Aldebaran, is equipped with a plaque designed to satisfy the curiosity of any aliens encountered along the way—a plaque covered not with words but with images (sketches of a naked man and woman, our solar system, the position of our sun, the hydrogen atom).[6]

Some meanings clearly are better communicated pictorially than verbally, as David Berrent, Alan Kay and most of the world's painters and sculptors have recognized. We live, however, in a culture that, despite the proliferation of images, not only has little faith in their ability but has at times been actively antagonistic toward them.

The Old Testament, characteristically, does not mince words: "Thou shalt not make unto thee any graven image, or any likeness of any thing that is in heaven above, or that is in the earth beneath"—a commandment second only to the demand that no other gods be worshiped before the source of these commandments. An antagonism toward images first appeared here at the beginning of Western culture. It appeared, too, after the development of the alphabet in Greece: Among Plato's targets in *The Republic* is the painter, whom he dismissed as "a magician and imitator." A similar scorn surfaced among Muslims: Muhammed is said to have proclaimed that "the angels will not enter a temple where there are images."[7]

This fury was unleashed, always, by partisans of the word—written or (for Plato) spoken. Behind it was a multifaceted fear: fear, to begin with, *for* the word. Images—easy to understand, fun to look at—inevitably threatened to turn the populace away from the deeper, more cerebral rewards of sacred writings or philosophic discourse.

There was fear too of the magic that seems to lurk in images. They steal likenesses. They do what only gods should be able to do: They re-create the living and preserve the dead. It is hard not to see this as black magic. Images allow us actually to look in on (not just hear about) the familiar from another perspective, an external perspective, often a disorienting perspective—to see ourselves, for example. They are, in this way, inherently unnatural—further evidence of magic.

Then there is the persistent "reality" issue. Images look real but are fake. They pretend to be what they are not. They lie. The portrait is a mute, lifeless substitute for the person; the idol, a primitive and superficial knockoff of the god. But that idol is also attractive and easy to see. It can distract from the more profound but more amorphous glories of the god. A painter, Plato warned, can deceive "children and fools" with mere "imitation of appearance," instead of "truth" or "real things."[8] Images can entrance.

10

---

[6]Arthur Smith 113–14, 121.

[7]Book X; Plato, *The Great Dialogues*, 464. Papadopoulo 49.

[8]Book X; Plato, *The Great Dialogues*, 463–4. This echoes Plato's attack on orators in the *Gorgias*.

Worse, in imitating "real things," images tend to devalue them. This is what the French theorist Jean Baudrillard called "the murderous capacity of images." Once we begin to lose ourselves in this world of illusions, it can begin to seem as if "truth" and "reality" are just further illusions (deserving of quotation marks). Images, on this level, are as Baudrillard put it, "murderers of the real, murderers of their own model."[9] The person is now seen as if posing for a portrait. The god is perceived as if just another idol.

"Cursed be the man who makes a graven or molten image," the Old Testament proclaims. We have reconciled ourselves to painting and sculpture by now; nevertheless, echoes of that curse can still be heard in many of the jeremiads launched by television's critics—most of whom retain an almost biblical allegiance to the word. The fear behind that curse undoubtedly was also present in some of the admonitions I heard from my parents: "You've had that thing on all evening!" "You look like you're in some kind of trance!" I'm sure it is present too in some my children have heard from me.

For television also has been judged too easy to watch: not sufficiently chal- 15 lenging, cerebral or deep. It displays a similarly suspect magic: It too captures appearances. Television too is accused of being "unreal," of duping children and fools. And television too has seemed to make the world it portrays—the social and political world—less "real." It has helped fill it with "pseudo-events," to use Daniel Boorstin's* often-repeated term. "The shadow has become the substance," Boorstin, with deference to Plato, warned.[10]

Here is a prejudice even Thoth* did not face. Video is not only suspiciously new and immature; it is tainted by its reliance upon facile, shallow, unreal, cursed images.[11]

Oddly, it was a group of thinkers not only steeped in biblical values but influenced by Platonic (or, more precisely, neo-Platonic) values who began to question this fear and scorn.[12] "We do no harm," Pope Gregory I wrote in a letter in 599, "in wishing to show the invisible by means of the visible." In the thirteenth century, Thomas Aquinas* outlined an argument in support of "the institution of images in the Church."[13]

The power of the visible has been disparaged and then rediscovered many times since: with the development of painting in the Renaissance (in-

---

[9]Baudrillard 255–56.

Daniel Boorstin (b. 1914): influential historian of the American experience

[10]Boorstin 26–29, 204; see also Mourier 310.

Thoth: ancient Egyptian god of learning and inventor of writing

[11]Cited, Briggs, *Competition,* 147n.

[12]For an investigation of this apparent irony, see Gombrich 154–60.

Thomas Aquinas (1224/25–74): medieval theologian and author of *Summa Theologiae* (1265–72)

[13]Cited, Freedberg 162–64. For a discussion of the philosophic underpinnings of Aquinas's thoughts on images, see Copleston 47–48, 167–68, 181–83.

cluding the use of perspective),[14] with the woodcut and the mechanical reproduction of illustrations, with the arrival of photography.[15] Over the centuries, those prepared to defend images have produced various calculations of
the comparative "worth" of pictures and words. They often seem silly. However, an investigation of the potential of video must begin by confronting the
lingering prejudice against images and acknowledging that there *are* some
things images do better than words.

Images, to begin with, are marvelously (though never perfectly) accessible. Aquinas explained that the "unlettered" might learn from pictures "as if
from books."[16] (Christians were not prepared to ignore the needs of the uneducated, of children or of fools.) We take advantage of the accessibility of
images to aid those who may not understand a particular language—visitors
to the Olympics, perhaps, or any space aliens who happen upon *Pioneer 10*.

Another strength of images is their concision—a significant advantage   20
for drivers speeding by or on a crowded computer screen. A native American
rock drawing found near a precipitous trail in New Mexico, for example,
shows a goat who is climbing but a man on a horse who has fallen.[17] It is difficult to imagine a sign made for the "lettered" that could communicate this
warning more efficiently. David Berrent and the others who have begun
flashing images on our screens are attempting to exploit this efficiency in their
efforts to say a lot in a short time.

Images also can wield great power—religious, tribal, romantic, peda-
gogic. One of David Berrent's productions for ABC was a public-service announcement on behalf, of all things, of PLUS: Project Literacy U.S. In its thirty
seconds, five or six fathers are shown reading to or reading with their children, with scenes from children's books and newspapers gently superimposed
on top of them. The fathers explain why this activity is important, but the
public-service announcement's power comes not from their words but from
the images Berrent has placed before us—images of togetherness, of caring,
of warmth.

Aquinas suggested that images can be used to "excite the emotions,
which are more effectively aroused by things seen than by things heard."[18]
That is why we find images in houses of worship, in military emblems and in
tattoos, as well as in public-service announcements. "If the poet can kindle
love in man, more so . . . the painter, as he can place the true image of the
beloved before the lover," observed Leonardo da Vinci.*[19]

---

[14]See Samuel Y. Edgerton Jr. 124–42; Bazin 11; Hogben 186–88; Berger 16.
[15]Cited, Crowley and Heyer 195.
[16]Cited, Freedberg 162.
[17]Gelb 29.
[18]Cited, Freedberg 162.
Leonardo da Vinci (1452–1519): Italian Renaissance artist and thinker
[19]Cited, Freedberg 451n.

There are also understandings, sometimes deep understandings, that can be put into images—accessibly, concisely, powerfully—but are difficult to put into words. The study of botany, zoology, anatomy, geography and astronomy were all advanced during or after the Renaissance by more precise depictions, models, representations and diagrams.[20] "Primates are visual animals," Stephen Jay Gould, the scientist and science writer, has asserted, "and we think best in pictorial or geometric terms. Words are an evolutionary afterthought."[21]

Bill McKibben was appearing on TV. This was an event akin to the Unabomber going on-line or Ralph Nader driving a Porsche.* For McKibben, a distinguished environmental writer, had just published an ardent attack on television: a book, *The Age of Missing Information,* based on his experience in watching every program that had appeared on a ninety-three-channel Virginia cable television system during one twenty-four-hour period. McKibben wrote of his concern not only with what TV offers but with what it does not offer: highs, lows, perspective, consciousness of the body, an awareness of death, of the seasons, of nature and of what happens "behind a face." "We use TV as we use tranquilizers," he concluded.[22] But now here McKibben was on the *Charlie Rose Show,* himself part of the dose.

Among those savoring the irony was the *New Republic*'s Robert Wright,   25 who admitted that McKibben looked more "earnest and thoughtful" than he had expected from reading reviews of his book. "TV has won for his cause one small battle that his book alone couldn't have won," Wright observed, "both because I don't have time to read it and because it is missing some kinds of information. (Some very 'natural' kinds of information, like how a person looks when saying what he believes. The written word, we sometimes forget, was invented as a crude if useful substitute for the real thing.)"[23]

The last thought is worth freeing from parentheses. No one, as Wright noted, has been earnest enough to read through, say, all the publications to be found one day on one newsstand (an exercise likely as dispiriting as McKibben's). But we can still come to some conclusions about what the printed word lacks.

Writing's great limitation grows out of its great strength: its abstractness. It is a system of representation, or code, that represents another system of representation, another code: spoken language.[24] The written word *face*—to oversimplify a bit—calls to mind the sound "fās." It is, therefore, two steps removed from that expressive skin sculpture itself. These steps back needed to be taken

---

[20]Hogben 188–89.

[21]Stephen Jay Gould, "Evolution by Walking," *Natural History,* March 1995.

Unabomber . . . Porsche: Two unlikely events: Unabomber Theodore Kaczynski berated technology; consumer guru Ralph Nader questioned the safety of rear-engined cars.

[22]McKibben 147, 189, 190, 198, 211–12.

[23]Robert Wright, "Washington Diarist: Channeling," *New Republic,* June 15, 1992.

[24]See Aristotle 40 (*De Interpretatione,* 1).

and have been hugely productive. Still, it is important to keep in mind the price paid for that abstraction. Printed words may take us, metaphorically at least, "behind a face"; they can help us see what we might not ordinarily see in a face; but they must work hard to tell us what a glance could about the expression on that face. In interpreting the code we make little use of our natural ability to observe: letters don't smile warmly or look intently.

This code, writing, also ignores our ability to find spatial and temporal connections between objects in the world. When we speak with each other, we can point: "That belongs over there." We can demonstrate: "Then she did this with her hair." We can indicate: "You want to give them control over this?" And we can gesture — with a look, a shrug, a grimace. All this information could alternatively be put into words; it could be written down. But in reading it, rather than seeing it, we sacrifice our ability to quickly and intuitively spot relationships — between here and there, this and that, words and gestures, ideas and expressions. We sacrifice our ability to judge earnestness and thoughtfulness, say, by observing people's faces as they speak.

Comparing what he saw on those ninety-three channels to what his senses can pick up in nature or at a circus, McKibben moaned that we are "starved on television's visual Pritikin regimen."*[25] This is a point I am anxious to debate. But for the moment it is sufficient to note that, if the measure is *direct* stimulation to our senses, a page of print makes a few moments of television look like a five-course French meal.

Printed prose is "an act of extraordinary stylization, of remarkable, expressive self-denial," stated Richard A. Lanham, who writes on Renaissance rhetoric and contemporary computers.[26] Our eyes were selected over millions of years of primate evolution for their ability to notice, search, compare, connect and evaluate. Increasingly, in the five thousand years since the development of writing, they have been reduced to staring at letters of identical size and color, arranged in lines of identical length, on pages of identical size and color. Readers, in a sense, are no longer asked to *see;* they are simply asked to interpret the code.

Written words, as Aquinas realized but we tend to forget, are hardly a perfect form of communication. No such thing exists. I don't want to overstate the case of images — at least still images — either. Certainly, as the Bible seems to suggest, but for centuries most Europeans tended to forget, nonmoving images have great difficulty conveying certain kinds of meanings. There are limits to what the Dutch humanist Erasmus called their eloquence.[27]

Alan Kay ended up dissatisfied with his experiments in the use of images on computer screens. He had understood, from having read educational

30

Pritikin regimen: a rigorous low-fat diet pioneered by Nathan Pritikin
[25]McKibben 192.
[26]Lanham 9.
[27]Cited, Freedberg 50.

theory, that icons were good at helping people "recognize, compare, configure." The success of the Macintosh and Windows operating systems has
proven that his understanding was correct. But Kay had a grander ambition:
He dreamed of using images to express abstract thought. Kay envisioned a
kind of language of images.[28]

That is an old dream. It was long surmised that the mysterious hieroglyphs that could be seen on the Egyptian obelisks that had been dragged to
Rome represented such a language of images. "The wise of Egypt . . . left
aside . . . words and sentences," wrote Plotinus, the third-century neo-
Platonist, "and drew pictures instead."[29] As late as the eighteenth century, the
historian Vico assumed that "all the first nations spoke in hieroglyphs."[30]

Behind this notion was the belief, still held by many today, that nature
is a "book" with a divine author.[31] If each tree, each ox, has a spiritual message for us, then that message might also be "read" in paintings or even iconic
representations of trees or oxen. An image language would be closer to that
original divine language. Over the centuries many Europeans attempted to
craft such a language.* They produced various occult codes, systems of gestures, systems of concepts, guides to memory and tools for international understanding.[32]

These various image languages all had something in common: To the   35
extent that they tried to communicate meaning effectively without depending
on words, they failed. The conviction that the Egyptians had succeeded in
this also crumbled. In 1799 one of Napoleon's soldiers in Egypt happened
upon an old stone that included an inscription written both in Egyptian hieroglyphic and in Greek. With the "Rosetta stone" Europe finally was able to
piece together accurate translations of those mysterious Egyptian writings, and
it became clear that not even hieroglyphic had escaped the dominance of language. Instead, like all other successful writing systems, these icons were directly connected to words: For example, they made heavy use, as in King
Narmer's* name, of phonetic indicators, of homonyms.[33]

Alan Kay's efforts to produce abstract thought from systems of icons on
the computer screen failed, too. "All I can say," Kay wrote, "is that we and
others came up with many interesting approaches over the years but none
have successfully crossed the threshold to the end user." The problem: "In
most iconic languages it is much easier to write the patterns than it is to read
them," Kay explained.[34]

---

[28]Kay 196, 202.
[29]Plotinus 427.
[30]Cited, Eco 166; see also Martin 19.
[31]See Gombrich 148–49.
many . . . language: The seventeenth-century Jesuit scholar Athanasius Kircher is an example.
[32]Eco 144–76.
Narmer: an Egyptian king of the late predynastic period (c. 2925 B.C.)
[33]Eco 144–76.
[34]Kay 202.

Here, for example, is the series of hand signals one Renaissance experimenter, the Abbé de l'Epée, used in his language of gestures to indicate the concept "I believe":

> I begin by making the sign of the first person singular, pointing the index finger of my right hand towards my chest. I then put my finger on my forehead, on the concave part in which is supposed to reside my spirit, that is to say, my capacity for thought, and I make the sign for *yes*. I then make the same sign on that part of the body which, usually, is considered as the seat of what is called the heart in its spiritual sense. . . . I then make the same sign *yes* on my mouth while moving my lips. . . . Finally, I place my hand on my eyes, and, making the sign for *no*, show that I do not see.

All that is quite clever, even poetic. It must have been great fun to devise but almost impossible for "end users"—those who were watching the abbé's energetic performance—to decipher. That undoubtedly explains why at the conclusion of his elaborate pantomime de l'Epée felt called upon to add one more action: "All I need to do," he stated, "is . . . to write *I believe.*"[35]

If images cannot form languages without a reliance upon words, it is in part because they have a great deal of difficulty escaping the affirmative, the past or present indicative.[36] De l'Epée was able at least to shake his head to put something in the negative; in some traffic signs we use a red diagonal line to say the same thing; but most still pictures must strain to say something as simple as "no" or to ask "why?" or to wonder what might be. They state much more effectively than they negate or interrogate or speculate. Pictures are better, similarly, with the concrete than the abstract, better with the particular than the general. These are significant handicaps.[37]

The other great obstacle to images forming a language of their own stems not from their muteness but from the fact that they tend to say too much. For example, Michelangelo's awe-inspiring depiction at the summit of the Sistine Chapel of God giving life to man through the touch of his finger also can be seen as showing a father-son relationship and perhaps a lover-beloved relationship; it can be seen as showing caring, effort, joy, and undoubtedly numerous other emotions. This richness of meaning is testament to the artist's genius. But if we did not receive some verbal explanation, how could we be expected to "read" this scene as we might read a piece of writing?

Knowing the genre helps. The location of this great fresco tells us that we should search for a religious interpretation in it.[38] But which one? The older man could be saving the younger man; he could be calling him to heaven; he could be giving or taking his soul. To know for sure, we must be

40

---

[35]Cited, Eco 173–74.

[36]French historian Roger Chartier talked about how images "mirrored" writing; Chartier 19.

[37]See Worth.

[38]See Gombrich 21 for the importance of genre.

directed to a story, to Genesis. Were this scene asked to serve as part of a language without the aid of such a story, how could we pinpoint specific meanings in it?[39] "The image is freedom, words are prison," wrote the film director Jean-Luc Godard, never one to shy from controversy, in 1980. "How are laws decreed today? They are written. When your passport is stamped 'entry to Russia forbidden,' it is not done with an image."[40] True, but neither the Bill of Rights nor the Declaration of the Rights of Man was composed in images either. The freedom images provide comes at a price.

"The ability of a visual language to express more than one meaning at once," contended Umberto Eco,* "is also . . . its limitation." Eco, whose academic speciality is semiotics, the study of systems of signs, called this excess of meaning "the fatal polysemy of . . . images."[41] Aquinas recognized the problem: "One thing may have similitude to many," he wrote. "For instance the lion may mean the Lord because of one similitude and the Devil because of another."[42] How can we develop a lexicon of images if we have no way of determining which of the many possible interpretations of an image is correct? (The perplexing graphics that are supposed to explain to speakers of different languages how to operate European appliances provide another example of this problem.)

To use images more precisely without captions, explanations or instructions—without words—it is necessary to rely on the most obvious of images, on clichés: a skull and crossbones, for instance, or a father snuggled up with a book and a child. France's expert on semiotics, Roland Barthes, gave the example of the use of a bookcase in the background of a photograph to show that a person is an intellectual.[43] As a result, as images that try to convey meaning without the use of words become less ambiguous, they also become less interesting, less challenging, and vice versa.

"I don't want there to be three or four thousand possibilities of interpreting my canvas," Pablo Picasso* once insisted. "I want there to be only one."[44] However, the artist in his more thoughtful moments undoubtedly realized what anyone who has stood before one of his canvases has likely realized: That is impossible.

---

[39]William E. Wallace 260–61. For another discussion of possible interpretations of the Sistine ceiling, see Richmond 63–68.

[40]Godard 123; translated by Dirk Standen.

Umberto Eco (b. 1938): Italian novelist and critic

[41]Eco 174; see also Martin 6.

[42]Cited, Gombrich 14.

[43]Barthes 201–2.

Pablo Picasso (1881–1973): Spanish painter and sculptor, among the most renowned artists of the twentieth century

[44]Cited, Alden Whitman, "Picasso: Protean and Prodigious," *New York Times,* April 8, 1973.

Words also can say too much, of course. *Man, woman* or *god,* for example, have no shortage of potential meanings. Dictionaries contain lists of them; occasionally we concoct our own. Writers can never be sure that their words have only one possible interpretation. As our literary theorists have spent a third of a century pointing out, readers bring different experiences and interests to the sentences they read and therefore take different meanings from them.

While working on this book, I reread *Madame Bovary* and, wouldn't 45 you know, began to uncover in Flaubert's novel* a series of lessons about images and words. Did he intend for me to read his book this way? Probably not. Nonetheless, Flaubert's problem with me and probably most of his other readers is much less acute than that faced by the authors of potential image languages. With the help (alas) of a translator I was able to get the gist of Flaubert's words. I followed his narrative. I was not so preoccupied with my own concerns that I missed the fact that he had many things to say that are not communications-related.

Our strategies for reading words are fairly well understood. We can, at least, make use of those dictionaries, with their limited lists of meanings. And the problem of comprehending words is further eased, if never entirely eliminated, by syntax. Using a grammar, the basic structure of which seems built into our genes, we modify the form of our words to signify their relation to their fellows in sentences. And then we narrow their potential meanings further by surrounding them not only with various qualifiers but with prepositions and articles. There are few equivalents for such parts of speech in the realm of the image.

In spoken and written languages, word builds upon word, sentence upon sentence, idea upon idea. The ambiguity of images, on the other hand, is increased by what Alan Kay called their "unsortedness." Painters may have mastered some tricks for guiding our eyes across canvases. But we are not born with, nor have we created, any particularly sophisticated systems for organizing still images to specify or build meanings. "Unlike paragraphs and lists of words, images have no *a priori* order in which they should be understood," Kay noted. "This means that someone coming onto an image from the outside has no strategy for solving it."[45]

This chapter might be helped by a depiction of Thomas Aquinas, Bill McKibben or Alan Kay. It would be useful actually to see how the Abbé de l'Epée looked when he made "the sign of the first person singular." But such concepts as "efficiency," "abstract thought" or "by means of the visible" would be difficult to communicate through still images. And how might an

---

Flaubert's novel: Gustave Flaubert (1821–80), French realist; author of *Madame Bovary* (1857)

[45]Kay 202.

argument composed of such images be organized? Left to right? Up and down? In a kind of circle? Unless, following de l'Epée's lead, such pictures were appended to a written version of the chapter itself, an observer would not know what "strategy" to employ in understanding them.

David Berrent and others of the most interesting workers in video — MTV alumni or MTV watchers — aim a barrage of images at us. Those images can do some things better than words; once we move beyond the scorn and the fears of word lovers, that becomes clear. Certain pictures can put most sentences to shame. But this is as far as I'm willing to go in making the case for still images.

The truth is that I am not one of those folks who spend an inordinate amount of time staring at dew-covered fields, wizened faces, cloud formations, or paintings thereof. It took some decades, and the guidance of a photographer friend, before I learned to notice light, not just the things upon which it shines. I'm good for a few hours in major museums, not a few days. Which is to say that while this is a book that gets rather excited about the potential of image communication, it is not based on a particularly romantic view of images or our visual sense in general. 50

Some continue to argue that pictures are more honest and profound than words, that they can claim some direct, mystical path to a higher reality. You won't find that argument here. In fact, I've tried to make clear in this chapter that still images operate under severe handicaps when attempting to embody ideas. For certain important purposes, a picture may actually be worth *less* than a single, relatively narrow, well-placed word. I agree with Umberto Eco that some of the most complex uses of images must "still depend (parasitically) on the semantic universe of the verbal language."[46] This, perhaps, is the true "curse" upon those who attempt to communicate through such images, graven or otherwise.

However, Eco did allow for one possible exception to his rule about the limitations of images — an exception even someone who won't pull the car over to gape at a sunset can accept: Eco suggested, with some reservations, that "the images of cinema and television" might escape those limitations.[47]

There is a sense in which David Berrent and his colleagues and successors in video seem better positioned than Michelangelo, Picasso and computer guru Alan Kay might have been to communicate abstract thought unambiguously through images — for motion, sound and computer editing have indeed begun to solve the image's intelligibility problems. And at MTV speeds, in ten or fifteen minutes it is now possible to present *a thousand pictures*.

---

[46]Eco 174.
[47]Eco 175–77.

QUESTIONING THE TEXT

1. The human eye evolved to catch action and evaluate movement. By implication, Stephens suggests, we have had to be trained to endure the tedium of processing row upon row of printed words when we read (paragraph 30). Examine a dozen printed texts you encounter in a given day and describe their visual elements—their images, graphics, designs, and colors. How visually arresting do you find the texts? Which ones offer the most visual stimulation? Which offer the least? (You may consider a computer screen a printed text for this exercise.)

2. Stephens argues that images, especially modern ones, are typically designed to take the place of words. He includes four potent and vastly different images to illustrate this point: the plaque borne by *Pioneer 10,* the first interstellar spacecraft; Michelangelo's Sistine Chapel ceiling fresco of God and Adam; a skull and crossbones; and a file folder from a Macintosh computer desktop (see pp. 474–75). Reverse the process Stephens describes: describe the four images in complete paragraphs. Then compare your work with your classmates' responses. Which images require the most words? Which require the least? Are words up to the task of displacing any of these images? Which ones, if any, and why?

MAKING CONNECTIONS

3. Like Plato describing our experience of reality in "Allegory of the Cave" (p. 467), Stephens suggests that writing is "two steps removed" from whatever reality it represents (paragraph 27). Do you think that images and, in particular, videos can represent reality more directly than words can? Why, or why not? (If you have seen Web cams, you might want to discuss how they now attempt to represent reality.)

4. Stephens discusses the work of Alan Kay, a computer scientist interested in whether images can be used to convey abstract ideas. Survey the images in the color insert section and choose one that you believe conveys a particular thought—that is, an idea that might be phrased in a complete statement. Write out that idea in a sentence or paragraph. Then compare your work with that of several classmates. How do they render these images into words? Do their versions work for you?

JOINING THE CONVERSATION

5. Is reading a book more intellectually stimulating than watching movies or television? The question is an old one, but explore it afresh with a small group and then write an essay in which you examine in detail the

differences between reading and watching. Come to a conclusion about the differences between the two experiences—but understand that the conclusion need not come down on one side or the other of the issue.

6. Stephens claims that some images convey ideas more concisely and efficiently than do words. Investigate his claim. Begin by listing all the basic images and symbols you must use to operate a particular machine or device. For example, if you use a computer, list all the images you must recognize to do basic word processing or to open your email. Alternatively, study the symbols on the dashboard of your car. Then evaluate the usefulness and clarity of these pictures. Which operations do they describe most clearly and which do you find confusing? What responses do the symbols require from you—do they convey warnings or tell you how to twist a knob, open a compartment, find more information, and so on? How often do the images need words for support? Summarize your results and report your findings in a short essay.

7. Write an essay in which you explore the comment of French filmmaker Jean-Luc Godard quoted by Stephens: "The image is freedom, words are prison" (paragraph 40). Find out a bit about Godard before you begin writing.

JOHN UPDIKE
The Mystery of Mickey Mouse

TALK ABOUT THE POWER *of images! I can still recall the day* The Mickey Mouse Club *premiered on TV in the 1950s, promising a daily after-school taste of all the Disneyland confections—Fantasyland, Frontierland, Adventureland, and (my personal favorite) Tomorrowland. Kids across America were soon humming the program's catchy theme song and selecting their favorite Mouseketeers—this was, after all, the show that introduced Annette Funicello. And most of us acquired and proudly wore the Mickey Mouse ears that made us official members of the club. We weren't sophisticated enough then to understand that the program was practically a half-hour infomercial for Disney's movies, merchandise, and new California theme park. But with those ears, we'd bought into Disney's vision of America, one that would make the company a media empire. Today, Disney operates four major theme parks, publishes books, owns movie and television production companies and two sports franchises, offers vacation cruises to a Disney-owned island, and controls the entire ABC television network. Not bad for a company built on a mouse's ears.*

But Mickey has never been just any mouse, as John Updike explains in this lovingly detailed essay on Walt Disney's most famous creation, originally published in Art & Antiques *magazine in 1991. Mickey is practically the embodiment of American popular culture and, perhaps, American enterprise as well.*

Updike (b. 1932), among the most admired and prolific American writers of the twentieth century, is best known for a series of four novels chronicling the life of Harry Angstrom, a middle-class American: Rabbit, Run *(1960),* Rabbit Redux *(1971),* Rabbit Is Rich *(1981), and* Rabbit at Rest *(1990). Updike has published numerous other novels as well as short stories, poems, and essays. But right through his college years at Harvard, he aspired to be a cartoonist.* —J.R.

It's all in the ears. When Mickey Mouse was born, in 1927, the world of early cartoon animation was filled with two-legged zoomorphic humanoids, whose strange half-black faces were distinguished one from another chiefly by the ears. Felix the Cat had pointed triangular ears and Oswald the Rabbit—Walt Disney's first successful cartoon creation, which he abandoned when his New York distributor, Charles Mintz, attempted to swindle him—had long floppy ears, with a few notches in the end to suggest fur. Disney's Oswald films, and the Alice animations that preceded them, had mice in them, with linear limbs, wiry tails, and ears that are oblong, not yet round. On the way back to California from New York by train, having left Oswald enmeshed for good in the machinations of Mr. Mintz, Walt and his wife Lillian invented another character based—the genesis legend claims—on the tame field mice that used to wander into Disney's old studio in Kansas City. His first thought was to call the mouse Mortimer; Lillian proposed instead the less pretentious name Mickey. Somewhere between Chicago and Los Angeles, the young couple concocted the plot of Mickey's first cartoon short, *Plane Crazy,* costarring Minnie and capitalizing on 1927's Lindbergh craze.* The next short produced by Disney's fledgling studio—which included, besides himself and Lillian, his brother Roy and his old Kansas City associate Ub Iwerks—was *Gallopin' Gaucho,* and introduced a fat and wicked cat who did not yet wear the prosthesis that would give him his name of Pegleg Pete. The third short, *Steamboat Willie,* incorporated that brand-new novelty a sound track, and was released first, in 1928. Mickey Mouse entered history, as the most persistent and pervasive figment of American popular culture in this century.

His ears are two solid black circles, no matter the angle at which he holds his head. Three-dimensional images of Mickey Mouse—toy dolls, or the papier-mâché heads the grotesque Disneyland Mickeys wear—make us uneasy, since the ears inevitably exist edgewise as well as frontally. These ears properly belong not to three-dimensional space but to an ideal realm of notation, of symbolization, of cartoon resilience and indestructibility. In drawings, when Mickey is in profile, one ear is at the back of his head like a spherical ponytail, or like a secondary bubble in a computer-generated Mandelbrot set. We accept it, as we accepted Li'l Abner's* hair always being parted on the side facing the viewer. A surreal optical consistency is part of the cartoon world, halfway between our world and the plane of pure signs, of alphabets and trademarks.

In the sixty-four years since Mickey Mouse's image was promulgated, the ears, though a bit more organically irregular and flexible than the classic 1930s appendages, have not been essentially modified. Many other modifications have, however, overtaken that first crude cartoon, born of an era of starker stylizations. White gloves, like the gloves worn in minstrel shows, appeared after those first, to cover the black hands. The infantile bare chest and shorts with two buttons were phased out in the forties. The eyes have undergone a number of changes, most drastically in the late thirties, when, some historians mistakenly claim, they acquired pupils. Not so: the old eyes, the black oblongs that acquired a nick of reflection in the sides, *were* the pupils; the eye whites filled the entire space beneath Mickey's cap of black, its widow's peak marking the division between these enormous oculi. This can be seen clearly in the face of the classic Minnie; when she bats her eyelids, their lashed shades cover over the full width of what might be thought to be her brow. But all the old animated animals were built this way from Felix the Cat on; Felix had lower lids, and the Mickey of *Plane Crazy* also.

Lindbergh craze: In 1927 aviator Charles Lindbergh became the first person to fly solo across the Atlantic, from New York City to Paris.

Li'l Abner: cartoon character from a comic strip of the same name drawn by Al Capp (1909–79)

So it was an evolutionary misstep that, beginning in 1938, replaced the shiny black pupils with entire oval eyes, containing pupils of their own. No such mutation has overtaken Pluto, Goofy, or Donald Duck. The change brought Mickey closer to us humans, but also took away something of his vitality, his alertness, his bugeyed cartoon readiness for adventure. It made him less abstract, less iconic, more merely cute and dwarfish. The original Mickey, as he scuttles and bounces through those early animated shorts, was angular and wiry, with much of the impudence and desperation of a true rodent. He was gradually rounded to the proportions of a child, a regression sealed by his fifties manifestation as the genius of the children's television show *The Mickey Mouse Club,* with its live Mouseketeers. Most of the artists who depict Mickey today, though too young to have grown up, as I did, with his old form, have instinctively reverted to it; it is the barechested basic Mickey, with his yellow shoes and oval buttons on his shorts, who is the icon, beside whom his modified later version is a mere mousy trousered pipsqueak.

His first, iconic manifestation had something of Chaplin to it; he was the little guy, just over the border of the respectable. His circular ears, like two minimal cents, bespeak the smallest economic unit, the overlookable democratic man. His name has passed into the language as a byword for the small, the weak —a "Mickey Mouse operation" means an undercapitalized company or minor surgery. Children of my generation—wearing our Mickey Mouse watches, prying pennies from our Mickey Mouse piggy banks (I won one in a third-grade spelling bee, my first intellectual triumph), following his running combat with Pegleg Pete in the daily funnies, going to the local movie-house movies every Saturday afternoon and cheering when his smiling visage burst onto the screen to introduce a cartoon—felt Mickey was one of us, a bridge to the adult world of which Donald Duck was, for all of his childish sailor suit, an irascible, tyrannical member. Mickey didn't seek trouble, and he didn't complain; he rolled with the punches, and surprised himself as much as us when, as in *The Little Tailor,* he showed warrior resourcefulness and won, once again, a blushing kiss from dear, all but identical Minnie. His minimal, decent nature meant that he would yield, in the Disney animated cartoons, the starring role to combative, sputtering Donald Duck and even to Goofy, with his "gawshes" and Gary Cooper*-like gawkiness. But for an occasional comeback like the "Sorcerer's Apprentice" episode of *Fantasia,* and last year's rather souped-up *The Prince and the Pauper,* Mickey was through as a star by 1940. But as with Marilyn Monroe when her career was over, his life as an icon gathered strength. The America that is not symbolized by that imperial Yankee Uncle Sam is symbolized by Mickey Mouse. He is America as it feels to itself—plucky, put-on, inventive, resilient, good-natured, game.

Gary Cooper (1901–61): American actor who often played quiet, ordinary men; his films include *Sergeant York* (1941), *Pride of the Yankees* (1942), and *High Noon* (1952)

Like America, Mickey has a lot of black blood. This fact was revealed to   5
me in conversation by Saul Steinberg,* who, in attempting to depict the
racially mixed reality of New York streets for the supersensitive and race-
blind *New Yorker* of the sixties and seventies, hit upon scribbling numerous
Mickeys as a way of representing what was jauntily and scruffily and unignor-
ably there. From just the way Mickey swings along in his classic, trademark
pose, one three-fingered gloved hand held on high, he is jiving. Along with
round black ears and yellow shoes, Mickey has soul. Looking back to such
early animations as the early Looney Tunes' Bosko and Honey series (1930–
36) and the Arab figures in Disney's own *Mickey in Arabia* of 1932, we see
that blacks were drawn much like cartoon animals, with round button noses
and great white eyes creating the double arch of the curious peaked skullcaps.
Cartoon characters' rubberiness, their jazziness, their cheerful buoyance and
idleness, all chimed with popular images of African Americans, earlier embodied in minstrel shows and in Joel Chandler Harris's* tales of Uncle
Remus, which Disney was to make into an animated feature, *Song of the
South,* in 1946.

Up to 1950, animated cartoons, like films in general, contained caricatures of blacks that would be unacceptable now; in fact, *Song of the South*
raised objections from the NAACP when it was released. . . . Not even the
superb crows section of *Dumbo* would be made now. But there is a sense in
which all animated cartoon characters are more or less black. Steven Spielberg's hectic tribute to animation, *Who Framed Roger Rabbit?,* has them all,
from the singing trees of Silly Symphonies to Daffy Duck and Woody Woodpecker, living in a Los Angeles ghetto, Toonville. As blacks were second-class
citizens with entertaining qualities, so the animated shorts were second-class
movies, with unreal actors who mocked and illuminated from underneath the
real world, the live-actor cinema. Of course, even in a ghetto there are class
distinctions. Porky Pig and Bugs Bunny have homes that they tend and defend, whereas Mickey started out, like those other raffish stick figures and
dancing blots from the twenties, as a free spirit, a wanderer. As Richard
Schickel* has pointed out, "The locales of his adventures throughout the
1930s ranged from the South Seas to the Alps to the deserts of Africa. He was,
at various times, a gaucho, teamster, explorer, swimmer, cowboy, fireman,
convict, pioneer, taxi driver, castaway, fisherman, cyclist, Arab, football
player, inventor, jockey, storekeeper, camper, sailor, Gulliver,* boxer," and

---

Saul Steinberg (1912–99): cartoonist and illustrator for the *New Yorker* magazine, famous
for his line drawings
Joel Chandler Harris (1848–1908) American writer and author of *Uncle Remus: His Songs
and His Sayings* (1880)
Richard Schickel (b. 1933): film critic and author of a definitive biography of Walt Disney,
The Disney Version (1968, revised 1985)
Gulliver: traveler to imaginary worlds in Jonathan Swift's satire *Gulliver's Travels* (1726)

so forth. He was, in short, a rootless vaudevillian who would play any part that the bosses at Disney Studios assigned him. And though the comic strip, which still persists, has fitted him with all of a white man's household comforts and headaches, it is as an unencumbered drifter whistling along on the road of hard knocks, ready for whatever adventure waits at the next turning, that he lives in our minds.

Cartoon characters have soul as Carl Jung* defined it in his *Archetypes and the Collective Unconscious:* "soul is a life-giving demon who plays his elfin game above and below human existence." Without the "leaping and twinkling of the soul," Jung says, "man would rot away in his greatest passion, idleness." The Mickey Mouse of the thirties shorts was a whirlwind of activity, with a host of unsuspected skills and a reluctant heroism that rose to every occasion. Like Chaplin and Douglas Fairbanks and Fred Astaire,* he acted our fantasies of endless nimbleness, of perfect weightlessness. Yet withal, there was nothing aggressive or self-promoting about him, as there was about Popeye. Disney, interviewed in the thirties, said, "Sometimes I've tried to figure out why Mickey appealed to the whole world. Everybody's tried to figure it out. So far as I know, nobody has. He's a pretty nice fellow who never does anybody any harm, who gets into scrapes through no fault of his own, but always manages to come up grinning." This was perhaps Disney's image of himself: for twenty years he did Mickey's voice in the films, and would often say, "There's a lot of the Mouse in me." Mickey was a character created with his own pen, and nurtured on Disney's memories of his mouse-ridden Kansas City studio and of the Missouri farm where his struggling father tried for a time to make a living. Walt's humble, scrambling beginnings remained embodied in the mouse, whom the Nazis, in a fury against the Mickey-inspired Allied legions (the Allied code word on D-Day was "Mickey Mouse"), called "the most miserable ideal ever revealed . . . mice are dirty."

But was Disney, like Mickey, just "a pretty nice fellow"? He was until crossed in his driving perfectionism, his Napoleonic capacity to marshal men and take risks in the service of an artistic and entrepreneurial vision. He was one of those great Americans, like Edison and Henry Ford, who invented themselves in terms of a new technology. The technology—in Disney's case, film animation—would have been there anyway, but only a few driven men seized the full possibilities and made empires. In the dozen years between *Steamboat Willie* and *Fantasia,* the Disney studios took the art of animation to heights of ambition and accomplishment it would never have reached

---

Carl Jung (1875–1961): noted Swiss psychiatrist and psychologist

Chaplin . . . Fairbanks . . . Astaire: Charlie Chaplin (1889–1977), British-born American actor and director, famous for his little tramp character; Douglas Fairbanks (1883–1939), American actor who played heroic action heroes; Fred Astaire (1899–1987), American dancer and actor renowned for his grace and style

otherwise, and Disney's personal zeal was the animating force. He created an empire of the mind, and its emperor was Mickey Mouse.

The thirties were Mickey's conquering decade. His image circled the globe. In Africa, tribesmen painfully had tiny mosaic Mickey Mouses inset into their front teeth, and a South African tribe refused to buy soap unless the cakes were embossed with Mickey's image, and a revolt of some native bearers was quelled when the safari masters projected some Mickey Mouse cartoons for them. Nor were the high and mighty immune to Mickey's elemental appeal—King George V and Franklin Roosevelt insisted that all film showings they attended include a dose of Mickey Mouse. But other popular phantoms, like Felix the Cat, have faded, where Mickey has settled into the national collective consciousness. The television program revived him for my children's generation, and the theme parks make him live for my grandchildren's. Yet survival cannot be imposed through weight of publicity; Mickey's persistence springs from something unhyped, something timeless in the image that has allowed it to pass in status from a fad to an icon.

To take a bite out of our imaginations, an icon must be simple. The   10
ears, the wiggly tail, the red shorts, give us a Mickey. Donald Duck and Goofy, Bugs Bunny and Woody Woodpecker are inextricably bound up with the draftsmanship of the artists who make them move and squawk, but Mickey floats free. It was Claes Oldenburg's* pop art that first alerted me to the fact that Mickey Mouse had passed out of the realm of commercially generated image into that of artifact. A new Disney gadget, advertised on television, is a cameralike box that spouts bubbles when a key is turned; the key consists of three circles, two mounted on a larger one, and the image is unmistakably Mickey. Like yin and yang, like the Christian cross and the star of Israel, Mickey can be seen everywhere—a sign, a rune, a hieroglyphic trace of a secret power, an electricity we want to plug into. Like totem poles, like African masks, Mickey stands at that intersection of abstraction and representation where magic connects.

Usually cartoon figures do not age, and yet their audience does age, as generation succeeds generation, so that a weight of allusion and sentimental reference increases. To the movie audiences of the early thirties, Mickey Mouse was a piping-voiced live wire, the latest thing in entertainment; by the time of *Fantasia* he was already a sentimental figure, welcomed back. *The Mickey Mouse Club,* with its slightly melancholy pack leader, Jimmie Dodd, created a Mickey more removed and marginal than in his first incarnation. The generation that watched it grew up into the rebels of the sixties, to whom Mickey became camp, a symbol of U.S. cultural fast food, with a touch of the old rodent raffishness. Politically, Walt, stung by the studio strike

---

Claes Oldenburg (b. 1929): Swedish-born sculptor renowned for his pop-art creations and soft sculptures

of 1940, moved to the right, but Mickey remains one of the thirties proletariat, not uncomfortable in the cartoon-rickety, cheerfully verminous crash
pads of the counterculture. At the Florida and California theme parks, Mickey
manifests himself as a short real person wearing an awkward giant head, cos-
tumed as a ringmaster; he is in danger, in these nineties, of seeming not
merely venerable kitsch but part of the great trash problem, one more piece
of visual litter being moved back and forth by the bulldozers of consumerism.

But never fear, his basic goodness will shine through. Beyond recall, perhaps, is the simple love felt by us of the generation that grew up with him. He
was five years my senior and felt like a playmate. I remember crying when the
local newspaper, cutting down its comic pages to help us win World War II,
eliminated the Mickey Mouse strip. I was old enough, nine or ten, to write an
angry letter to the editor. In fact, the strips had been eliminated by the votes of
a readership poll, and my indignation and sorrow stemmed from my incredu-
lous realization that not everybody loved Mickey Mouse as I did. In an account
of my boyhood written over thirty years ago, "The Dogwood Tree," I find
these sentences concerning another boy, a rival: "When we both collected Big
Little Books, he outbid me for my supreme find (in the attic of a third boy), the
first Mickey Mouse. I can still see that book. I wanted it so badly, its paper tan
with age and its drawings done in Disney's primitive style, when Mickey's black
chest is naked like a child's and his eyes are two nicked oblongs." And I once
tried to write a short story called "A Sensation of Mickey Mouse," trying to su-
perimpose on adult experience, as a shiver-inducing revenant, that indescribable
childhood sensation—a rubbery taste, a licorice smell, a feeling of supernatural
clarity and close-in excitation that Mickey Mouse gave me, and gives me, much
dimmed by the years, still. He is a "genius" in the primary dictionary sense of
"an attendant spirit," with his vulnerable bare black chest, his touchingly big
yellow shoes, the mysterious place at the back of his shorts where his tail came
out, the little cleft cushion of a tongue, red as a valentine and glossy as candy, always peeping through the catenary curves of his undiscourageable smile. Not to
mention his ears.

QUESTIONING THE TEXT

1. Examine the first sentence of Updike's "The Mystery of Mickey
   Mouse." What risks does the writer take with such a spare opening sentence? How do you react to it? How do you react to the final sentence
   of the essay?

2. What details in this essay suggest to you that Updike might have had
   experience as a cartoonist himself? List one or two observations from
   the essay that suggest a special insight or professional expertise. In a
   paragraph, explain what the passage(s) may have taught you about cartoons or images.

MAKING CONNECTIONS

3. Updike claims that Mickey Mouse may be "the most persistent and pervasive figment of American popular culture in this century" (paragraph 1). Yet, in "The Great Symbol Drain" (p. 513), Neil Postman argues that an image loses its power when it is seen too often. How has Mickey managed to retain his impact as a symbol or image despite being stamped on virtually every consumer product and serving for decades as an emblem of the Disney media empire?

4. Does Updike fall into stereotyping when he attempts to explain his observation that "there is a sense in which all animated cartoon characters are more or less black" (paragraph 6)? Review Updike's remarks and read them against Zora Neale Hurston's "How It Feels to Be Colored Me" (p. 384). Then discuss the question in a group or an online forum.

JOINING THE CONVERSATION

5. Updike explains that Mickey Mouse has evolved from a rodent-like figure in the original cartoons to a figure with more human characteristics. Working with a small group and using resources such as old magazines and newspapers, study the evolution of another icon or image over a period of decades. Then write an essay about how it has changed over time, offering explanations for the evolution of the image. You might examine a cartoon character, a corporate logo, a product label, a sports team emblem (the Cleveland Indians' Chief Wahoo offers a potent opportunity), or any other widely distributed image. Be sure to include in your essay reproductions of the evolving figure you discuss.

6. In the present-day era of Homer Simpson, is Mickey in danger of becoming what Updike calls "visual litter" (paragraph 11)? Does Mickey Mouse mean anything in particular to your generation — whatever it is? Write an essay in which you explore the presence or absence of this icon in your world, perhaps using the final two paragraphs of Updike's essay as a model or springboard.

WARD CHURCHILL
Crimes against Humanity

WARD CHURCHILL (b. 1947) is no stranger to controversy. A prolific writer and much-in-demand speaker, he has devoted most of his career to denouncing discrimination against and exploitation of Native American peoples. Churchill writes a regular column for the leftist Z Magazine *(where the following article first appeared in March 1993) and is the author of numerous books, including* Fantasies of the Master Race *(1992);* Struggle for the Land *(1993);* From a Native Son *(1996); and* Pacifism as Pathology *(1998), coauthored with Mike Ryan.*

As these book titles suggest, Churchill, Professor of American Indian Studies at the University of Colorado, is a man with a mission. In "Crimes against Humanity," he brings satire—a serious, close-to-the-edge kind of satire—to that mission to highlight what he sees as major and ongoing offenses against Native Americans (from the derogatory use of Indian caricatures in team sports to the secret use of involuntary sterilization programs for Indian women).

I have long been interested in the effects of stereotypical labels and media images on people's sense of themselves, of who they are, of their identities. Churchill's essay is a hard one for me to read precisely because it makes these stereotypes visible to me in unusual and decidedly in-your-face ways. The very day I read this article, I noticed over a dozen unflattering images of Native Americans—in advertisements, on assorted food boxes in the supermarket, on billboards, seemingly everywhere I turned. Some I had noticed and been troubled by before—but not all. I wonder what your experience will be?

—A.L.

During the past couple of seasons, there has been an increasing wave of controversy regarding the names of professional sports teams like the Atlanta Braves, Cleveland Indians, Washington Redskins, and Kansas City Chiefs. The issue extends to the names of college teams like Florida State University Seminoles, University of Illinois Fighting Illini, and so on, right on down to high school outfits like the Lamar (Colorado) Savages. Also involved have been team adoption of mascots, replete with feathers, buckskins, beads, spears, and "warpaint" (some fans have opted to adorn themselves in the same fashion), and nifty little "pep" gestures like the "Indian Chant" and "Tomahawk Chop."

A substantial number of American Indians have protested that use of native names, images, and symbols as sports team mascots and the like is, by definition, a virulently racist practice. Given the historical relationship between Indians and non-Indians during what has been called the Conquest of America, American Indian Movement leader (and American Indian

497

Anti-Defamation Council founder) Russell Means has compared the practice to contemporary Germans naming their soccer teams the "Jews," "Hebrews," and "Yids," while adorning their uniforms with grotesque caricatures of Jewish faces taken from the Nazis' anti-Semitic propaganda of the 1930s. Numerous demonstrations have occurred in conjunction with games—most notably during the November 15, 1992, matchup between the Chiefs and Redskins in Kansas City—by angry Indians and their supporters.

In response, a number of players—especially African Americans and other minority athletes—have been trotted out by professional team owners like Ted Turner, as well as university and public school officials, to announce that they mean not to insult but to honor native people. They have been joined by the television networks and most major newspapers, all of which have editorialized that Indian discomfort with the situation is "no big deal," insisting that the whole thing is just "good, clean fun." The country needs more such fun, they've argued, and "a few disgruntled Native Americans" have no right to undermine the nation's enjoyment of its leisure time by complaining. This is especially the case, some have argued, "in hard times like these." It has even been contended that Indian outrage at being systematically degraded—rather than the degradation itself—creates "a serious barrier to the sort of intergroup communication so necessary in a multicultural society such as ours."

Okay, let's communicate. We are frankly dubious that those advancing such positions really believe their own rhetoric, but, just for the sake of argument, let's accept the premise that they are sincere. If what they say is true, then isn't it time we spread such "inoffensiveness" and "good cheer" around among *all* groups so that *everybody* can participate *equally* in fostering the round of national laughs they call for? Sure it is—the country can't have too much fun or "intergroup involvement"—so the more, the merrier. Simple consistency demands that anyone who thinks the Tomahawk Chop is a swell pastime must be just as hearty in their endorsement of the following ideas— by the logic used to defend the defamation of American Indians—[and] should help us all really start yukking it up.

First, as a counterpart to the Redskins, we need an NFL team called   5
"Niggers" to honor Afro-Americans. Halftime festivities for fans might include a simulated stewing of the opposing coach in a large pot while players and cheerleaders dance around it, garbed in leopard skins and wearing fake bones in their noses. This concept obviously goes along with the kind of gaiety attending the Chop, but also with the actions of the Kansas City Chiefs, whose team members—prominently including black team members—lately appeared on a poster looking "fierce" and "savage" by way of wearing Indian regalia. Just a bit of harmless "morale boosting," says the Chiefs's front office. You bet.

So that the newly formed Niggers sports club won't end up too out of sync while expressing the "spirit" and "identity" of Afro-Americans in the above fashion, a baseball franchise—let's call this one the "Sambos"—should be formed. How about a basketball team called the "Spearchuckers"? A hockey team called the "Jungle Bunnies"? Maybe the "essence" of these teams could be depicted by images of tiny black faces adorned with huge pairs of lips. The players could appear on TV every week or so gnawing on chicken legs and spitting watermelon seeds at one another. Catchy, eh? Well, there's "nothing to be upset about," according to those who love wearing "war bonnets" to the Super Bowl or having "Chief Illiniwik" dance around the sports arenas of Urbana, Illinois.

And why stop there? There are plenty of other groups to include. "Hispanics"? They can be "represented" by the Galveston "Greasers" and San Diego "Spics," at least until the Wisconsin "Wetbacks" and Baltimore "Beaners" get off the ground. Asian Americans? How about the "Slopes," "Dinks," "Gooks," and "Zipperheads"? Owners of the latter teams might get their logo ideas from editorial page cartoons printed in the nation's newspapers during World War II: slant eyes, buck teeth, big glasses, but nothing racially insulting or derogatory, according to the editors and artists involved at the time. Indeed, this Second World War vintage stuff can be seen as just another barrel of laughs, at least by what current editors say are their "local standards" concerning American Indians.

Let's see. Who's been left out? Teams like the Kansas City "Kikes," Hanover "Honkies," San Leandro "Shylocks," Daytona "Dagos," and Pittsburgh "Polacks" will fill a certain social void among white folk. Have a religious belief? Let's all go for the gusto and gear up the Milwaukee "Mackerel Snappers" and Hollywood "Holy Rollers." The Fighting Irish of Notre Dame can be rechristened the "Drunken Irish" or "Papist Pigs." Issues of gender and sexual preference can be addressed through creation of teams like the St. Louis "Sluts," Boston "Bimbos," Detroit "Dykes," and the Fresno "Fags." How about the Gainesville "Gimps" and Richmond "Retards," so the physically and mentally impaired won't be excluded from our fun and games?

Now, don't go getting "overly sensitive" out there. None of this is demeaning or insulting, at least not when it's being done to Indians. Just ask the folks who are doing it, or their apologists like Andy Rooney in the national media. They'll tell you—as in fact they *have* been telling you—that there's been no harm done, regardless of what their victims think, feel, or say. The situation is exactly the same as when those with precisely the same mentality used to insist that Step 'n' Fetchit was okay, or Rochester on the *Jack Benny Show,* or Amos and Andy, Charlie Chan, the Frito Bandito, or any of the other cutesy symbols making up the lexicon of American racism. Have we communicated yet?

Let's get just a little bit real here. The notion of "fun" embodied in rit-   10 uals like the Tomahawk Chop must be understood for what it is. There's not a single non-Indian example used above which can be considered socially acceptable in even the most marginal sense. The reasons are obvious enough. So why is it different where American Indians are concerned? One can only conclude that, in contrast to the other groups at issue, Indians are (falsely) perceived as being too few, and therefore too weak, to defend themselves effectively against racist and otherwise offensive behavior.

Fortunately, there are some glimmers of hope. A few teams and their fans have gotten the message and have responded appropriately. Stanford University, which opted to drop the name "Indians" from Stanford, has experienced no resulting drop-off in attendance. Meanwhile, the local newspaper in Portland, Oregon, recently decided its long-standing editorial policy prohibiting use of racial epithets should include derogatory team names. The Redskins, for instance, are now referred to as "the Washington team," and will continue to be described in this way until the franchise adopts an inoffensive moniker (newspaper sales in Portland have suffered no decline as a result).

Such examples are to be applauded and encouraged. They stand as figurative beacons in the night, proving beyond all doubt that it is quite possible to indulge in the pleasure of athletics without accepting blatant racism into the bargain.

NUREMBERG PRECEDENTS

On October 16, 1946, a man named Julius Streicher mounted the steps of a gallows. Moments later he was dead, the sentence of an international tribunal composed of representatives of the United States, France, Great Britain, and the Soviet Union having been imposed. Streicher's body was then cremated, and—so horrendous were his crimes thought to have been—his ashes dumped into an unspecified German river so that "no one should ever know a particular place to go for reasons of mourning his memory."

Julius Streicher had been convicted at Nuremberg, Germany, of what were termed "crimes against humanity." The lead prosecutor in his case— Justice Robert Jackson of the United States Supreme Court—had not argued that the defendant had killed anyone, nor that he had personally committed any especially violent act. Nor was it contended that Streicher had held any particularly important position in the German government during the period in which the so-called Third Reich had exterminated some six million Jews, as well as several million Gypsies, Poles, Slavs, homosexuals, and other *untermenschen* ("subhumans").

The sole offense for which the accused was ordered put to death was in having served as publisher/editor of a Bavarian tabloid entitled *Der Sturmer* during the early- to mid-1930s, years before the Nazi genocide actually began. In this capacity, he had penned a long series of virulently anti-Semitic editorials and "news" stories, usually accompanied by cartoons and other images graphically depicting Jews in extraordinarily derogatory fashion. This, the prosecution asserted, had done much to "dehumanize" the targets of his distortion in the mind of the German public. In turn, such dehumanization had made it possible—or at least easier—for average Germans to later indulge in the outright liquidation of Jewish "vermin." The tribunal agreed, holding that Streicher was therefore complicit in genocide and deserving of death by hanging.

During his remarks to the Nuremberg tribunal, Justice Jackson observed that, in implementing its sentences, the participating powers were morally and legally binding themselves to adhere forever after to the same standards of conduct that were being applied to Streicher and the other Nazi leaders. In the alternative, he said, the victorious allies would have committed "pure murder" at Nuremberg—no different in substance from that carried out by those they presumed to judge—rather than establishing the "permanent benchmark for justice" which was intended.

Yet in the United States of Robert Jackson, the indigenous American Indian population had already been reduced, in a process which is ongoing to this day, from perhaps 12.5 million in the year 1500 to fewer than 250,000 by the beginning of the twentieth century. This was accomplished, according to official sources, "largely through the cruelty of [Euro-American] settlers," and an informal but clear governmental policy which had made it an articulated goal to "exterminate these red vermin," or at least whole segments of them.

Bounties had been placed on the scalps of Indians—any Indians—in places as diverse as Georgia, Kentucky, Texas, the Dakotas, Oregon, and California, and had been maintained until resident Indian populations were decimated or disappeared altogether. Entire peoples such as the Cherokee had been reduced to half their size through a policy of forced removal from their homelands east of the Mississippi River to what were then considered less preferable areas in the West.

Others, such as the Navajo, suffered the same fate while under military guard for years on end. The United States Army had also perpetrated a long series of wholesale massacres of Indians at places like Horseshoe Bend, Bear River, Sand Creek, the Washita River, the Marias River, Camp Robinson, and Wounded Knee.

Through it all, hundreds of popular novels—each competing with the 20 next to make Indians appear more grotesque, menacing, and inhuman—were sold in the tens of millions of copies in the United States. Plainly, the Euro-American public was being conditioned to see Indians in such a way as to allow their eradication to continue. And continue it did until the Manifest Destiny of the United States—a direct precursor to what Hitler would subsequently call *Lebensraumpolitik* ("the politics of living space")—was consummated.

By 1900, the national project of "clearing" Native Americans from their land and replacing them with "superior" Anglo-American settlers was complete; the indigenous population had been reduced by as much as 98 percent while approximately 97.5 percent of their original territory had "passed" to the invaders. The survivors had been concentrated, out of sight and mind of the public, on scattered "reservations," all of them under the self-assigned "plenary" (full) power of the federal government. There was, of course, no Nuremberg-style tribunal passing judgment on those who had fostered such circumstances in North America. No U.S. official or private citizen was ever imprisoned—never mind hanged—for implementing or propagandizing what had been done. Nor had the process of genocide afflicting Indians been completed. Instead, it merely changed form.

Between the 1880s and the 1980s, nearly half of all Native American children were coercively transferred from their own families, communities, and cultures to those of the conquering society. This was done through compulsory attendance at remote boarding schools, often hundreds of miles from their homes, where native children were kept for years on end while being systematically "deculturated" (indoctrinated to think and act in the manner of Euro-Americans rather than as Indians). It was also accomplished through a pervasive foster home and adoption program—including "blind" adoptions, where children would be permanently denied information as to who they were/are and where they'd come from—placing native youths in non-Indian homes.

The express purpose of all this was to facilitate a U.S. governmental policy to bring about the "assimilation" (dissolution) of indigenous societies. In other words, Indian cultures as such were to be caused to disappear. Such policy objectives are directly contrary to the United Nations 1948 Convention on Punishment and Prevention of the Crime of Genocide, an element of international law arising from the Nuremberg proceedings. The forced "transfer of the children" of a targeted "racial, ethnical, or religious group" is explicitly prohibited as a genocidal activity under the convention's second article.

Article II of the Genocide Convention also expressly prohibits involuntary sterilization as a means of "preventing births among" a targeted population. Yet, in 1975, it was conceded by the U.S. government that its Indian Health Service (IHS), then a subpart of the Bureau of Indian Affairs (BIA), was even then conducting a secret program of involuntary sterilization that had affected approximately 40 percent of all Indian women. The program was allegedly discontinued, and the IHS was transferred to the Public Health Service, but no one was punished. In 1990, it came out that the IHS was inoculating Inuit children in Alaska with hepatitis-B vaccine. The vaccine had already been banned by the World Health Organization as having a demonstrated correlation with the HIV syndrome, which is itself correlated to AIDS. As this is written, a "field test" of hepatitis-A vaccine, also HIV-correlated, is being conducted on Indian reservations in the northern plains region.

The Genocide Convention makes it a "crime against humanity" to create conditions leading to the destruction of an identifiable human group, as such. Yet the BIA has utilized the government's plenary prerogatives to negotiate mineral leases "on behalf of" Indian peoples paying a fraction of standard royalty rates. The result has been "super profits" for a number of preferred U.S. corporations. Meanwhile, Indians, whose reservations ironically turned out to be in some of the most mineral-rich areas of North America, which   25 makes us, the nominally wealthiest segment of the continent's population, live in dire poverty.

By the government's own data in the mid-1980s, Indians received the lowest annual and lifetime per capita incomes of any aggregate population group in the United States. Concomitantly, we suffer the highest rate of infant mortality, death by exposure and malnutrition, disease, and the like. Under such circumstances, alcoholism and other escapist forms of substance abuse are endemic to the Indian community, a situation which leads both to a general physical debilitation of the population and a catastrophic accident rate. Teen suicide among Indians is several times the national average.

The average life expectancy of a reservation-based Native American man is barely forty-five years; women can expect to live less than three years longer.

Such itemizations could be continued at great length, including matters like the radioactive contamination of large portions of contemporary Indian Country, the forced relocation of traditional Navajos, and so on. But the point should be made: genocide, as defined in international law, is a continuing fact of day-to-day life (and death) for North America's native peoples. Yet there has been—and is—only the barest flicker of public concern about, or even consciousness of, this reality. Absent any serious expression of public outrage, no one is punished and the process continues.

A salient reason for public acquiescence before the ongoing holocaust in Native North America has been a continuation of the popular legacy, often through more effective media. Since 1925, Hollywood has released more than two thousand films, many of them rerun frequently on television, portraying Indians as strange, perverted, ridiculous, and often dangerous things of the past. Moreover, we are habitually presented to mass audiences one-dimensionally, devoid of recognizable human motivations and emotions; Indians thus serve as props, little more. We have thus been thoroughly and systematically dehumanized.

Nor is this the extent of it. Everywhere, we are used as logos, as mascots, as jokes: Big Chief writing tablets, Red Man chewing tobacco, Winnebago campers, Navajo and Cherokee and Pontiac and Cadillac pickups and automobiles. There are the Cleveland Indians, the Kansas City Chiefs, the Atlanta Braves, and the Washington Redskins professional sports teams—not to mention those in thousands of colleges, high schools, and elementary schools across the country—each with their own degrading caricatures and parodies of Indians and/or things Indian. Pop fiction continues in the same vein, including an unending stream of New Age manuals purporting to expose the inner works of indigenous spirituality in everything from pseudophilosophical to do-it-yourself styles. Blond Yuppies from Beverly Hills amble about the country claiming to be reincarnated seventeenth-century Cheyenne Ushanians ready to perform previously secret ceremonies.

In effect, a concerted, sustained, and in some ways accelerating effort has gone into making Indians unreal. It is thus of obvious importance that the

American public begin to think about the implications of such things the next time they witness a gaggle of face-painted and war-bonneted buffoons doing the Tomahawk Chop at a baseball or football game. It is necessary that they think about the implications of the grade-school teacher adorning a child in turkey feathers to commemorate Thanksgiving. Think about the significance of John Wayne or Charlton Heston killing a dozen "savages" with a single bullet the next time a western comes on TV. Think about why Land-o-Lakes finds it appropriate to market its butter with the stereotyped image of an "Indian princess" on the wrapper. Think about what it means when non-Indian academics profess—as they often do—to "know more about Indians than Indians do themselves." Think about the significance of charlatans like Carlos Castaneda and Jamake Highwater and Mary Summer Rain and Lynn Andrews churning out "Indian" bestsellers, one after the other, while Indians typically can't get into print.

Think about the real situation of American Indians. Think about Julius Streicher. Remember Justice Jackson's admonition. Understand that the treatment of Indians in American popular culture is not "cute" or "amusing" or just "good, clean fun."

Know that it causes real pain and real suffering to real people. Know that it threatens our very survival. And know that this is just as much a crime against humanity as anything the Nazis ever did. It is likely that the indigenous people of the United States will never demand that those guilty of such criminal activity be punished for their deeds. But the least we have the right to expect—indeed, to demand—is that such practices finally be brought to a halt.

QUESTIONING THE TEXT

1. Working with a classmate, look closely at Churchill's use of quotation marks in "Crimes against Humanity." What kinds of words and phrases does he enclose in quotation marks—and why? What effects—even subtle ones—do these marks have on your reading of the essay? Make notes on your findings and bring them to class for discussion.

2. Toward the end of the article, Churchill says "a concerted, sustained, and in some ways accelerating effort has gone into making Indians unreal" (paragraph 31). Make a list of the examples, statistics, and other types of evidence the writer uses to support this claim. Then write a brief summary of this evidence and conclude with your observations on the potential consequences of making any group of people seem "unreal" to others.

3. Why do you think Churchill opens and closes this essay with a scathing discussion of the (mis)use of Native American names and images in big-league sports? In what ways does the opening discussion prepare you for Churchill's extended charge of "crimes against humanity"?

MAKING CONNECTIONS

4. Read Zora Neale Hurston's "How It Feels to Be Colored Me" (p. 384), and then compare the tone of that essay to the tone Churchill uses. How would you describe the tone of each piece, and in what ways do you find the tones particularly effective or ineffective? Write a paragraph or two in which you compare the tones and explain which you find most effective.

5. Look carefully at Alex Shoumatoff's "The Navajo Way" (p. 433). What use of labels, derogatory or otherwise, do you find in this essay? How might Churchill respond to them?

6. Look at the photograph in the color insert of the fans at a Cleveland Indians game. What in the photo confirms—or refutes—Churchill's arguments?

JOINING THE CONVERSATION

7. Spend some time online, gathering the names of college teams in the state where you live or attend school. What categories do you find being used for such names, and what characteristics do they suggest? Might any of the names be considered offensive? Write a brief essay on your findings and bring it to class for discussion.

8. Working with two or three classmates, do some research on the native inhabitants in one of your home states or in the state you attend college. What is the native population of this state today, and what was it around 1500? What evidence marks the presence of native peoples—names of towns, rivers, mountains, reservations, company logos, sports teams, and so on? Did the native peoples of the state sign any treaties? If so, to what did they agree? As a group, analyze the information you have gathered and prepare a 15-minute report for your class on "Native People of Our State—Then and Now."

9. Churchill demonstrates the power that labels can have in our society, saying that these labels cause "real pain and real suffering to real people" (paragraph 33). In a brief essay, reflect on the effects of labels that have been applied to you (by others or by yourself) and labels you have applied to others.

JAMES PROSEK
Introduction to Trout

*W*HAT WOULD COMPEL A YOUNG MAN *to travel across a continent just to catch, photograph, and then paint watercolor images of fish? James Prosek (b. 1975) offers some answers in the introduction to his cult classic* Trout *(1996), a collection of his watercolors published while he was still a student at Yale. Not surprisingly, Prosek's book was inspired by the work of another artist similarly interested in natural images, John James Audubon, famous for his massive folio* The Birds of America *(1827–38). Like Audubon, Prosek uses his art to convey what can only be described as his love for a natural object—"my celebration of the trout," as he describes it.*

This instinct to reproduce images of nature is at least as ancient as the cave drawings of Chauvet-Pont-d'Arc and Lascaux. And, surely, creating such images resembles what writers do when they use words to describe their worlds. Prosek combines both creative processes in "Introduction to Trout," *explaining in words how his enthusiasm for fishing led him to assemble his unique collection of images. Like his watercolors, his prose is direct, honest, and striking. Indeed, it was the honesty of Prosek's project that initially interested me. And in a chapter full of texts about visuals that falsify, manipulate, and complicate our world, I wanted to be sure to remember and honor images that delight us and make our lives richer.*

In addition to Trout, *Prosek has published* Joe and Me: An Education in Fishing and Friendship *(1997), an account of his relationship with a game warden who served as a mentor, and* The Complete Angler: A Connecticut Yankee Follows in the Footsteps of Walton *(1999), a book about his adventures on a Yale-funded fishing trip to England.* —J.R.

One of my greatest passions in life is fishing. For me it's more than a pastime or hobby; instead it is a way of life, and an escape. The environment of the stream is peaceful. The sound of the water over the rocks is soothing, and any sound of civilization is muffled by the trees. This solitude allows one to brush aside daily life and focus on the task at hand: to catch a fish. The brook, then, with all its colors and sounds, is an education, a place where I can learn about myself and other creatures as well.

The instructive nature of the trout stream is not forced upon its visitors, but held candidly by the water and the trees. The angler must make an effort to hear the stream's messages and see her beauty. I had learned superficially how to catch a trout—first with a worm and then by tying and casting flies—and when the trout would feed and on what type of insects. But my education really began once I'd spent enough time near my local stream that I could begin to understand her language. Only after I'd become comfortable with her modes of speech—winter silence, springtime growling roar, lazy summer trickling, and autumn calm—did I begin to understand that the stream was not only a place where I fished but also a living, breathing celebration of hardship and joy. My interest in the trout of North America grew out of this relationship with my home ponds and streams, which prepared me to explore the far corners of our beautiful continent and the personalities of innumerable kinds of trout.

It was my father who introduced me to nature and the security that she afforded, my father who first extended my hand to meet hers. His lifelong love of birds influenced me greatly, though I followed not birds but trout into nature's heart. My father's life and interests are the essential foundation of my own desires.

He and my uncle lived a carefree childhood in the heat and brilliant sun of coastal Brazil, where they were born. In the port city of Santos, they went to Catholic school in white uniforms and played in palm and lemon trees. Other than soccer, which consumed most free daylight hours in the streets of town, their untiring occupation was the hunting and capture of the sprightly songbirds that flitted from tree to tree in colors beyond imagination. If not testing their skills with slingshots, they would employ devices of live capture, collecting these vivid ornaments for the large cage on the veranda of their home. Here, shaded from the stifling heat, my father would sit and pore over his six treasured volumes of *The Arabian Nights* in Portuguese. Occasionally he'd pause to lift his head, dreamily caught in the melodious song of the caged birds. Their living colors drew his gaze, and before long he was enamored of them. These feathered spirits would become his life companions on whatever road he traveled, and though their songs and colors would vary as times passed and places changed, they would always be his guide.

When my father was twelve, his family left the lazy haze of Brazil on a   5 passenger ship bound for New York City. Both he and his brother longed for the days of sun and palm trees in which to climb, but at the same time they could not help marveling at their new environs and the wonder of their first winter storm. Yearning for a familiar sight or sound in such an unfamiliar place and season, my father found delight once more in birds. He sat by his window and watched them as they foraged in the falling snow.

Years later, after he and my mother married, he left his job as officer and navigator in the merchant marines. After some frustration at other jobs, he decided that teaching would be his profession and southwestern Connecticut his home. The birds, he often tells me, had led him to all good things. He chose the house in Connecticut not only because it was near the planetarium where he would teach children about stars, but also because of the bird sanctuary in the nearby town of Fairfield. His free time was spent with a pair of binoculars and a guidebook in the woods, where he taught himself the names and habits of all the local birds. After years of watching them, he found that his favorite birds were warblers—tiny and colorful phantoms that flitted from tree to tree, reminders of things he once knew but had never forgot. In my earliest years my father carried me on his shoulders down to the big red barn at the end of our street to watch the swallows as they chased insects and darted in and out of the barn tending their young. From this time it was certain that my father's love of birds and nature would soon be my own.

My initial interest in birds was not so much in wooded glens as in the pages of a book. For days on end I pored assiduously over John James Audubon's bird paintings of North America. The original edition of 1830 was called the Elephant Folio and displayed the birds in life size on 2½-by-3-foot sheets, with the name of the bird and the plant that provided its background at the bottom of the page. A smaller, modern edition spent more time on our living room table than in our local library. With my set of colored pencils and paper, I copied his feathered figures over and over.

Louis Agassiz Fuertes, an estimable bird portraitist and watercolorist, once remarked of Audubon's grand paintings that "it would be hard to estimate their effect upon me, but I am very sure that they were the most potent influence that was ever exerted on my youthful longings to do justice to the singular beauty of birds." I feel very much the same as Fuertes, and my fascination with the idea of capturing a living, ecstatically colorful creature within the pages of a book was born out of my love for both Audubon and Fuertes.

That the subject of my passion and painting would be trout was determined when, at about the age of nine, I was introduced to fishing by a school friend. On summer days I'd fish for bass in fits of dizzy rapture, the farm fields alive with the scent of wild rose, or I'd walk down to our town reservoirs in the evening and cast for smallmouth bass with topwater lures. I couldn't explain the desire to capture a large sunfish or pickerel with a live minnow, but I knew these were the settings in which I felt my time was best spent, in the company of lapping waves and the screeching hawk.

The world of the trout stream opened up to me as I began to pursue the more coveted local fish. Trout fishing carried with it a mystique to which I soon became attached. Trout dwelled in flowing water and were harder to see, given the heavy shade of hemlock and swamp maple; they were selective in their feeding, and there were optimum periods in which to catch them. They were the embodiment of what I held to be ideal.   10

I remember the day I began to paint them. Several years ago, one day in April, my father showed me a magazine article about a rare type of trout found only in eight small ponds in Maine. Called the blueback, it had been pushed to near extinction by man's encroachment on its habitat. Instantly intrigued, I searched the library for a volume on trout that was equivalent to Audubon's works on birds. Unable to find any suitable illustrations, I set out to do my own under the instruction of our great bird painters.

The paintings in this book are the fourth set I have completed. Each time I finished painting the seventy or so kinds of trout I wished to display in this book, I noticed an increase in quality from the first to the last. My skills improved with every painting, and I experimented with different mediums and grades of paper. I finally chose watercolor, because I thought it best captured the singular beauty of the fish.

In preparing to paint a trout, I use several devices. Over the years I have acquired some insanely hard-to-find old books written before trout were tampered with on a large scale, before they were decimated or hybridized. These descriptions are detailed, since they predate the color photograph. It is from such descriptions that I painted extinct species, like the yellowfin cutthroat, and I also use them to confirm photographs that friends and I have taken of specific fish. But the single most important source for these paintings is, of course, the color photograph. This is even more valuable than the actual specimen, because the brightness and the color of the fish fade shortly after it's removed from the water. The photos I've used were mostly of fish that were caught and released. By now I have covered thousands of miles in search of trout to photograph. In the case of the blueback, for example, my color photos are the only ones I've seen. I wouldn't be surprised if the same blueback I painted for this book is still swimming in Black Pond in Aroostook County, Maine.

Having seen several thousand trout and painted hundreds of them, I have found that each one has its own personality. By that I don't mean simply that every type, strain, form, variety, species, or subspecies is different, but that every *individual* trout is different. Not one trout has a spotting pattern that is duplicated in another. Each fish is distinct and unique. In fact, because of the trout's tendency for intense variation, it is sometimes difficult to identify a fish by species. I've caught the same wild brown trout from a small local stream four times, each time taking a picture before releasing it. At first I didn't realize it was the same fish, but discovered that indeed it was by holding the photos next to one another. I can now identify him streamside by the double spot just to the front left of his dorsal fin. The brown trout . . . lives in that same stream, in a pool about two miles farther north, and as I write this he is still alive, though he's become quite wary and I haven't caught him again.

Choosing which specimen to represent a species or strain of trout was quite difficult. The Yellowstone cutthroat, for instance, is brick red when spawning, though at other times of year it ranges from golden yellow to amber. I could easily have done twenty-five paintings for every one in this book, and each would look different. I often chose to represent a male fish in spawning colors, because that's the most colorful. Sometimes I've shown the trout in several stages of life. The brook trout painting is of a fish from a stream about a half-hour from my home; I thought it was the most beautiful brookie I'd ever seen, though of course they're all beautiful.

The trout of North America are as diverse as the regions they inhabit. Their native range extends from the Arctic Circle to the western coast of Mexico, less than one degree from the Tropic of Cancer. All trout are descendants of ocean relatives that permeated rivers and lakes during periods of glacial melt. Two types of trout exist: the true trout and the char. The former normally has dark spots on a light background, sometimes with red spots as well; the latter, light spots on a dark background. Also, char generally require colder waters and are confined to northern latitudes.

I've grouped the trout in this book in five sections: the char; the Apaches, Gilas, and Mexicans; the rainbows, redbands, and goldens; the cut-throats; brown trout and Atlantic salmon. All these are native to North America except the brown trout, which was introduced from Germany's Black Forest in 1883. The char are concentrated in the cold lakes and streams of our north country; the Mexicans, Apaches, and Gilas in the mountains of the southwest of our continent; the rainbows and redbands along the Pacific Coast from Baja California to Alaska. The goldens, ancient ancestors of the redband complex, evolved incredibly brilliant colors on the Kern Plateau in California. The cutthroats are found in the mountain west, and some coexist naturally with rainbows. And the Atlantic salmon call home the coastal rivers from New England through Canada.

All these fish, save the brown trout, existed in North America before the white man came, but things would never be the same after the first hatch-eries were established on the East Coast in the late 1800s. The reproduction of trout and careless distribution were nothing short of devastating to native trout. When trout were introduced to a stream, no thought was given to what kind of fish had been in there in the first place—resulting in much hy-bridization and mixing of species and subspecies. When rainbow trout native to the West Coast were stocked in Colorado mountain streams, they hy-bridized with the native cutthroat. When lake trout were stocked in Lake Sunapee, they hybridized with the Sunapee, and brown trout introduced to Northeast streams often nudged out native brook trout. Atlantic salmon stocked in the Rangeley Lakes wiped out the blueback, and when brook trout were introduced to the beautiful streams east of the continental divide in Colorado, the greenback cutthroat was wiped out.

Today it is common to catch trout where they don't "belong." Indeed, it is a rare event to catch a trout in its native stream. I've caught my biggest brook trout, some nineteen inches long, in a high mountain lake in Col-orado, far from its native New England streams. I catch egg-yolk-colored brown trout in my hometown creeks, not in the fabled chalk streams of the British Isles or the Black Forest. I've caught beautiful golden trout in the Wind River Range of Wyoming, the other side of the divide from their na-tive Kern Plateau, in the shadow of majestic Mount Whitney. I've caught wild rainbows in the Delaware River in New York State, not the McCloud River in California, where they first swam. I've caught lake trout below Jack-son Lake Dam in Wyoming, far from the Great Lakes where they once reigned. I've fished for steelhead in the tributaries of Lake Ontario, not the Deschutes River of Oregon or the Skeena of British Columbia.

Does it bother me that, in proportion to the number of days that I'm 20
fishing, I'm seldom pursuing a trout native to that stream? The idea that not
many people really know what they're fishing for pulls at a nerve inside me,
as does the fact that anglers in famous tail water streams, where cold water is
released from the bottom of a dam, often don't realize that the entire fishery is
fabricated. But the largest brown trout to come out of American waters was
in Arkansas's Little Red River, which surely never had a trout in it before.
We can't really reverse the incredible mixing that we've created in our haste
to spread the beauty of the trout, and my hope is, simply, to raise awareness
about which fish are native and which are not. The brown trout, though
non-native, is one of my favorites; he is wild, however, and after a hundred
years in our streams is almost as good as native. And since both my parents are
immigrants, I'm just as "foreign" as the brown trout.

A trout in its native stream is a very special thing and should be preserved above all other populations. But while it's of paramount importance to
maintain Paiute cutthroats in a desert stream in eastern California, it's no less
crucial that we understand "whirling disease"—a fatal affliction among non-
native rainbows in Montana's Madison River that could eventually devastate
entire fisheries throughout the West. If forced to choose between these two
projects, I'd be as confused as a brook trout in the Himalayas. But I do know
that people should realize where the amazing variety of our trout comes from.
And now that we know non-native fish can devastate native populations, we
should stop introducing them.

My purpose in this book is to expose people to the diversity of color,
form, and habits of the trout that swim in our waters. In the histories that
accompany the paintings, I describe where the trout live and some of the
struggles they've endured. As you leaf through the book, I hope you will admire the patterns and forms of the fish as much as I do. I hope they will engage you with their vitality. For me, the trout in its stream is the essence of
life—encompassing survival and beauty, death and birth. And I hope my celebration of the trout causes others to feel the same way.

QUESTIONING THE TEXT

1. Among the paintings of trout in Prosek's book are images of some extinct species. He bases his watercolors on the descriptions of these fish
   he finds in old books, noting "[t]hese descriptions are detailed, since
   they predate the color photograph." Consider the implications of that
   line (from paragraph 13). Then write a short essay in which you explore
   the ways that the recent explosion of images in popular media may be

changing our uses of language. For example, notice how often newspapers today rely on charts and illustrations, how image-heavy the World Wide Web is, and how TV relies on pulsing graphics and images in everything from news shows to music videos.

2. Can you identify in any way with the attraction Prosek feels to the pictures of birds in books by Audubon and Fuertes (paragraphs 7–8) and with his impulse to produce such images of his own? Have you ever experienced a similar obsession about something that led you to create, collect, or learn everything you could about it? Write a brief narrative about your experience.

MAKING CONNECTIONS

3. Prosek claims that fishing for trout provides him with a kind of education. In what ways might his learning relationship to nature resemble the connections Navajos feel between their land and culture? Read Alex Shoumatoff's "The Navajo Way" (p. 433) with that question in mind, and then write your answer in a paragraph or two.

4. Compare the relationship between father and son described by Prosek in this selection with that depicted by Fred Barnes in "Quantity Time" (p. 649). Write a brief essay exploring the different ways—direct and indirect—that parents influence their children.

JOINING THE CONVERSATION

5. Prosek has published his collection of paintings in part to draw attention to his concern for the survival of native species of trout. What set of images might you want to collect in order to advance a cause or principle you believe in? Write an introduction to your (hypothetical) collection of images, describing the project and explaining its rationale. For inspiration, you might search the library or Web for collections of photo essays to see what sorts of themes engage the interests of professional photographers.

6. Prosek is a painter and author just beginning his career. Working in a group, use the resources of your library and/or the Internet to find out as much as you can about him and about the reaction of critics to his images and prose. In a fully documented report, summarize your findings.

1   2   3

4   5   6

Turn the page and you will find a series of images beckoning you into conversation with them, beginning with one of America's best-known families, the Simpsons **(1)**. Following Homer and Marge's brood, the March 1998 cover of *Wired* represents Katy, a clone of sorts born in December 1999 **(2)**. A photograph taken by a college student captures the fatal 1970 confrontation between anti-Vietnam War student protesters and National Guardsmen at Ohio's Kent State University **(3)**. Next come two sports images: Michael Jordan—said to be the single best-known person in the world **(4)** —and fans of the Cleveland Indians celebrating their team's 1995 World Series win over the Atlanta Braves **(5)**. Finally the Web site for *The Blair Witch Project* plays on the difference between the imagined and the real by suggesting that the movie is a documentary based on actual events **(6)**. In each case, these pages present **images that call for your response** . . . .

WIRED

March 1998

My name is Katy.
I was born in 1999.
I am a clone.
My story is on page 146.

In October of 1994
three student filmakers disappeared
in the woods near Burkittsville, Maryland
while shooting a documentary...

A year later their footage was found.

THE BLAIR WITCH PROJECT

How much time do you spend interpreting and responding to images? How often do you stop to think critically about the images all around you? The preceding pages offer you an opportunity to reflect on these questions and to take special note of how you respond to images.

Questions for study and discussion . . . .

1. How does the use of color function in these images? What color(s) predominate, and why? What might the color represent or symbolize? How would changing the colors affect the impression each of these images creates?

2. Several of these images include written text. Look carefully at these pages and especially at the relationship between the images and the words. What would be lost if the words — or the central image — were removed? Are words and images equally necessary or not?

3. Each of these images seeks to make a strong statement or raise a question — or both. After studying them again, come up with at least two possible statements or questions implied by each of the images.

4. Which of these images makes the strongest, most lasting impression on you? What elements of the image, its composition, and its meaning account for that impression?

5. After dividing into small groups with one image assigned to each group, use the guidelines on pp. 8–9 to carry out a thorough analysis of the image assigned to your group. Prepare a brief oral report on your analysis to be presented to the entire class.

Questions for writing . . . .

6. Study the images that do not include words. Think about where the image might likely appear, who the primary audience is, and what the overall purpose of the image is. Then write a caption for each image and bring the captions to class for discussion.

7. Choose one of these images and use it and your analysis of it as evidence for a brief written argument (two or three pages at most) that "a picture is worth a thousand words."

8. Several of these images are related to readings in this text: the Cleveland Indians' fans and Ward Churchill's "Crimes against Humanity" (p. 497); clone Katy and Jeremy Rifkin's "Biotech Century" (p. 244); Michael Jordan and Henry Louis Gates Jr.'s "Net Worth" (p. 532). Choose one of these pairs and then read or reread the essay with the related image in mind, making notes on any connections or new ideas that come to mind. Then write a brief report for your class on the ways the two texts interacted in your latest reading: how did one affect your interpretation of the other, and why did it do so?

9. Working with one or two other students, gather a portfolio of three or four images outside of this book that you find particularly powerful. Then work together to analyze these images, identifying the elements responsible for their effectiveness (see pp. 8–9, 19–21 for guidelines for analysis). Finally, write a one-page analysis and a caption for each image. Use the portfolio to make a class presentation of 15 to 20 minutes.

10. Most images carry with them powerful but unstated cultural assumptions and values. Choose one of the black-and-white images in this book and study it very carefully, asking what it says about social, political, emotional, or other sets of values (does it, for example, focus on physical strength, on happiness, on material wealth, on family and friends, on individualism, on fun?) Then write a report to your class, using details from the image to support your findings.

NEIL POSTMAN
The Great Symbol Drain

NEIL POSTMAN *(b. 1931), a professor at New York University, is one of the most prolific writers on education, culture, and language in the United States. You can measure his intellectual range just by considering the titles of a few of his numerous books:* Teaching as a Subversive Activity *(1969),* Teaching as a Conserving Activity *(1979),* Amusing Ourselves to Death: Public Discourse in the Age of Show Business *(1985),* The End of Education *(1995). Concerned especially by the debased state of American popular culture, Postman believes that schools must deal more directly with the impact of television, technology, and the computer on the process of learning.*

In "The Great Symbol Drain," a chapter from Technopoly: The Surrender of Culture to Technology *(1992), Postman asks readers to consider how technology and advertising are corroding the very images that bind us together and give coherence to our lives. It may help you in reading Postman's chapter to know that he defines technopoly as "the deification of technology, which means that the culture seeks its authorization in technology, finds its satisfactions in technology, and takes its orders from technology."*

—J.R.

It is possible that, some day soon, an advertising man who must create a television commercial for a new California Chardonnay will have the following inspiration: Jesus is standing alone in a desert oasis. A gentle breeze flutters the leaves of the stately palms behind him. Soft Mideastern music caresses the air. Jesus holds in his hand a bottle of wine at which he gazes adoringly. Turning toward the camera, he says, "When I transformed water into wine at Cana, *this* is what I had in mind. Try it today. You'll become a believer."

If you think such a commercial is not possible in your lifetime, then consider this: As I write, there is an oft-seen commercial for Hebrew National frankfurters. It features a dapper-looking Uncle Sam in his traditional red, white, and blue outfit. While Uncle Sam assumes appropriate facial expressions, a voice-over describes the delicious and healthful frankfurters produced by Hebrew National. Toward the end of the commercial, the

It's happened! An auto company used the Last Supper in an ad campaign in France, provoking outrage from church and clergy. —J.R.

I'm surprised that someone hasn't already made such a commercial. Anything—or anyone—can be used as a vehicle for advertising these days. —A.L.

513

voice stresses that Hebrew National frankfurters surpass federal standards for such products. Why? Because, the voice says as the camera shifts our point of view upward toward heaven, "We have to answer to a Higher Authority."

I will leave it to the reader to decide which is more incredible—Jesus being used to sell wine or God being used to sell frankfurters. Whichever you decide, you must keep in mind that neither the hypothetical commercial nor the real one is an example of blasphemy. They are much worse than that. Blasphemy is, after all, among the highest tributes that can be paid to the power of a symbol. The blasphemer takes symbols as seriously as the idolater, which is why the President of the United States (circa 1991) wishes to punish, through a constitutional amendment, desecrators of the American flag.

What we are talking about here is not blasphemy but trivialization, against which there can be no laws. In Technopoly,* the trivialization of significant cultural symbols is largely conducted by commercial enterprise. This occurs not because corporate America is greedy but because the adoration of technology pre-empts the adoration of anything else. Symbols that draw their meaning from traditional religious or national contexts must therefore be made impotent as quickly as possible—that is, drained of sacred or even serious connotations. The elevation of one god requires the demotion of another. "Thou shalt have no other gods before me" applies as well to a technological divinity as any other.

There are two intertwined reasons that make it possible to trivialize traditional symbols. The first, as neatly expressed by the social critic Jay Rosen, is that, although symbols, especially images, are endlessly repeatable, they are not inexhaustible. Second, the more frequently a significant symbol is used, the less potent is its meaning. This is a point stressed in Daniel Boorstin's* classic book *The Image,* published thirty

Am I missing something here? Postman leaps from what is "incredible" in sentence 1 to what is "blasphemy" in sentence 2. I'll watch to see if he makes the connection clear. —A.L.

I wonder whether the opposite is true in advertising: does a symbol actually gain its commercial power by being ubiquitous? Consider the Nike "swoosh," the golden arches, or the Ford blue oval. They seem almost like natural objects. —J.R.

If there "can be no laws" against the ethical breach caused by trivialization, what alternatives remain? Educational ones? —H.R.

I don't see why "elevation of one" requires "demotion of the other." Why can't both be elevated or demoted? —A.L.

If "symbols . . . are not inexhaustible," can new symbols be created? —H.R.

---

technopoly: Postman defines *technopoly* as "the deification of technology."

Daniel Boorstin (b. 1914): historian of the American experience and author of many works on history and culture, including *The Image: A Guide to Pseudo-events in America* (1971), *The Discoverers* (1983), and *The Seekers* (1998)

years ago.[1] In it, Boorstin describes the beginnings, in the mid-nineteenth century, of a "graphics revolution" that allowed the easy reproduction of visual images, thus providing the masses with continuous access to the symbols and icons of their culture. Through prints, lithographs, photographs, and, later, movies and television, religious and national symbols became commonplace, breeding indifference if not necessarily contempt. As if to answer those who believe that the emotional impact of a sacred image is always and ever the same, Boorstin reminds us that prior to the graphics revolution most people saw relatively few images. Paintings of Jesus or the Madonna, for example, would have been seen rarely outside churches. Paintings of great national leaders could be seen only in the homes of the wealthy or in government buildings. There were images to be seen in books, but books were expensive and spent most of their time on shelves. Images were not a conspicuous part of the environment, and their scarcity contributed toward their special power. When the scale of accessibility was altered, Boorstin argues, the experience of encountering an image necessarily changed; that is to say, it diminished in importance. One picture, we are told, is worth a thousand words. But a thousand pictures, especially if they are of the same object, may not be worth anything at all.

What Boorstin and Rosen direct our attention to is a common enough psychological principle. You may demonstrate this for yourself (if you have not at some time already done so) by saying any word, even a significant one, over and over again. Sooner than you expect, you will find that the word has been transformed into a meaningless sound, as repetition drains it of its symbolic value. Any male who has served in, let us say, the United States Army or spent time in a college dormitory has had this experience with what are called obscene words, especially the notorious four-letter word which I am loath to reproduce here. Words that you have been taught not

Not just accessibility to symbols but also the mentality of consumerism seem to be contributing to the demise of symbolic meaning. —H.R.

I tried doing just this—repeating the word "mirror" over and over again— and the word took on wild and wonderful new meanings. —A.L.

There may be a key difference between a picture as a work of art and an image as a cultural symbol: a work of art is powerful in itself, whereas an icon or symbol gains power from familiarity and repetition. —J.R.

---

[1]Although in some ways Boorstin's book is dated, to him and his book go credit for calling early attention to the effects of an image society.

to use and that normally evoke an embarrassed or disconcerted response, when used too often, are stripped of their power to shock, to embarrass, to call attention to a special frame of mind. They become only sounds, not symbols.

Moreover, the journey to meaninglessness of symbols is a function not only of the frequency with which they are invoked but of the indiscriminate contexts in which they are used. An obscenity, for example, can do its work best when it is reserved for situations that call forth anger, disgust, or hatred. When it is used as an adjective for every third noun in a sentence, irrespective of the emotional context, it is deprived of its magical effects and, indeed, of its entire point. This is what happens when Abraham Lincoln's image, or George Washington's, is used to announce linen sales on Presidents' Day, or Martin Luther King's birthday celebration is taken as an occasion for furniture discounts. It is what happens when Uncle Sam, God, or Jesus is employed as an agent of the profane world for an essentially trivial purpose.

In Texas, the symbol of the Lone Star appears on everything from jars of salsa to plastic glasses. Yet it affirms a sense of place not as evident in other states where I have lived. The image still means something. —J.R.

An argument is sometimes made that the promiscuous use of sacred or serious symbols by corporate America is a form of healthy irreverence. Irreverence, after all, is an antidote to excessive or artificial piety, and is especially necessary when piety is used as a political weapon. One might say that irreverence, not blasphemy, is the ultimate answer to idolatry, which is why most cultures have established means by which irreverence may be expressed—in the theater, in jokes, in song, in political rhetoric, even in holidays. The Jews, for example, use Purim as one day of the year on which they may turn a laughing face on piety itself.

Here's "blasphemy" again, this time offered as a possible answer to "idolatry." It seems like the latter is a reference to something earlier in the article—but it really isn't. What is Postman doing with the word blasphemy? —A.L.

Why is consumption such a dominant mentality? Once it takes hold of a society, can its influence be reversed? —H.R.

But there is nothing in the commercial exploitation of traditional symbols that suggests an excess of piety is itself a vice. Business is too serious a business for that, and in any case has no objection to piety, as long as it is directed toward the idea of consumption, which is never treated as a laughing matter. In using Uncle Sam or the flag or the American Eagle or images of presidents, in employing such names as Liberty Insurance, Freedom Transmission Repair, and Lincoln Savings and Loan, business does not offer us examples of irreverence. It is merely declaring the irrelevance, in Technopoly, of distinguishing between the sacred and the profane.

I am not here making a standard-brand critique of the excesses of capitalism. It is entirely possible to have a market economy that respects the seriousness of words and icons, and which disallows their use in trivial or silly contexts. In fact, during the period of greatest industrial growth in America—from roughly 1830 to the end of the nineteenth century—advertising did not play a major role in the economy, and such advertising as existed used straightforward language, without recourse to the exploitation of important cultural symbols. There was no such thing as an "advertising industry" until the early twentieth century, the ground being prepared for it by the Postal Act of March 3, 1879, which gave magazines low-cost mailing privileges. As a consequence, magazines emerged as the best available conduits for national advertising, and merchants used the opportunity to make the names of their companies important symbols of commercial excellence. When George Eastman invented the portable camera in 1888, he spent $25,000 advertising it in magazines. By 1895, "Kodak" and "camera" were synonymous, as to some extent they still are. Companies like Royal Baking Powder, Baker's Chocolate, Ivory Soap, and Gillette moved into a national market by advertising their products in magazines. Even magazines moved into a national market by advertising themselves in magazines, the most conspicuous example being *Ladies' Home Journal,* whose publisher, Cyrus H. K. Curtis, spent half a million dollars between 1883 and 1888 advertising his magazine in other magazines. By 1909, *Ladies' Home Journal* had a circulation of more than a million readers.

Curtis' enthusiasm for advertising notwithstanding, the most significant figure in mating advertising to the magazine was Frank Munsey, who upon his death in 1925 was eulogized by William Allen White* with the following words:

OK, I'm beginning to see a pattern in these pairs: blasphemy and idolatry; trivialization and elevation; sacred and profane. Postman is setting up a set of either-or arguments; let's see where that takes him. —A.L.

Some products—such as Hershey's Chocolate—were not advertised at all until relatively recently. —J.R.

He seems to be implying that an economic condition—"low-cost mailing privileges"—provided the impetus for businesses to exploit symbols through advertising. —H.R.

William Allen White (1868–1944): influential American journalist and longtime editor of the *Emporia* (Kansas) *Gazette*

"Frank Munsey contributed to the journalism of his day the talent of a meat packer, the morals of a money changer and the manners of an undertaker. He and his kind have about succeeded in transforming a once-noble profession into an 8% security. May he rest in trust." What was the sin of the malevolent Munsey? Simply, he made two discoveries. First, a large circulation could be achieved by selling a magazine for much less than it cost to produce it; second, huge profits could be made from the high volume of advertising that a large circulation would attract. In October 1893, Munsey took out an ad in the New York *Sun* announcing that *Munsey's Magazine* was cutting its price from 25 cents to 10 cents, and reducing a year's subscription from $3 to $1. The first 10-cent issue claimed a circulation of forty thousand; within four months, the circulation rose to two hundred thousand; two months later, it was five hundred thousand.

Munsey cannot, however, be blamed for another discovery, which for convenience's sake we may attribute to Procter and Gamble: that advertising is most effective when it is irrational. By irrational, I do not, of course, mean crazy. I mean that products could best be sold by exploiting the magical and even poetical powers of language and pictures. In 1892, Procter and Gamble invited the public to submit rhymes to advertise Ivory Soap. Four years later, H-O employed, for the first time, a picture of a baby in a high chair, the bowl of H-O cereal before him, his spoon in hand, his face ecstatic. By the turn of the century, advertisers no longer assumed that reason was the best instrument for the communication of commercial products and ideas. Advertising became one part depth psychology, one part aesthetic theory. In the process, a fundamental principle of capitalist ideology was rejected: namely, that the producer and consumer were engaged in a rational enterprise in which consumers made choices on the basis of a careful consideration of the quality of a product and their own self-interest. This, at least, is what Adam Smith had in mind. But today, the television commercial, for

Another binary pair: irrational and rational. I don't see these as opposites. Nor do I believe that people ever made decisions based solely on reason, as Postman suggests later in this paragraph. —A.L.

example, is rarely about the character of the products. It is about the character of the consumers of products. Images of movie stars and famous athletes, of serene lakes and macho fishing trips, of elegant dinners and romantic interludes, of happy families packing their station wagons for a picnic in the country—these tell nothing about the products being sold. But they tell everything about the fears, fancies, and dreams of those who might buy them. What the advertiser needs to know is not what is right about the product but what is wrong about the buyer. And so the balance of business expenditures shifts from product research to market research, which means orienting business away from making products of value and toward making consumers feel valuable. The business of business becomes pseudo-therapy; the consumer, a patient reassured by psychodramas.

What this means is that somewhere near the core of Technopoly is a vast industry with license to use all available symbols to further the interests of commerce, by devouring the psyches of consumers. Although estimates vary, a conservative guess is that the average American will have seen close to two million television commercials by age sixty-five. If we add to this the number of radio commercials, newspaper and magazine ads, and billboards, the extent of symbol overload and therefore symbol drain is unprecedented in human history. Of course, not all the images and words used have been cannibalized from serious or sacred contexts, and one must admit that as things stand at the moment it is quite unthinkable for the image of Jesus to be used to sell wine. At least not a chardonnay. On the other hand, his birthday is used as an occasion for commerce to exhaust nearly the entire repertoire of Christian symbology. The constraints are so few that we may call this a form of cultural rape, sanctioned by an ideology that gives boundless supremacy to technological progress and is indifferent to the unraveling of tradition.

In putting it this way, I mean to say that mass advertising is not the cause of the great symbol drain. Such cultural abuse could not have occurred

The imagery is so obscure in some ads these days that I can't always figure out what's being sold. Or what is being sold is pure style—with no substance at all.
—J.R.

This claim—that our psyches are being not just manipulated but also devoured— sounds pretty scary and a bit extreme.
—H.R.

Is Postman's irony directed at the advertising industry or consumers? Can trivialization be used to work against the industry, or does it only fuel it? —H.R.

This point, made repeatedly for at least the last twenty years, seems fairly accurate to me: advertisements are about the desires and fantasies of consumers. But it's not exactly new news! —A.L.

I've been wondering when the title would come into play. Postman has been preparing readers for the concept he names in his title by giving lots of examples. Here, he pulls those examples together under the concept of "the great symbol drain." —A.L.

without technologies to make it possible and a world-view to make it desirable. In the institutional form it has taken in the United States, advertising is a symptom of a world-view that sees tradition as an obstacle to its claims. There can, of course, be no functioning sense of tradition without a measure of respect for symbols. Tradition is, in fact, nothing but the acknowledgment of the authority of symbols and the relevance of the narratives that gave birth to them. With the erosion of symbols there follows a loss of narrative, which is one of the most debilitating consequences of Technopoly's power.

We may take as an example the field of education. In Technopoly, we improve the education of our youth by improving what are called "learning technologies." At the moment, it is considered necessary to introduce computers to the classroom, as it once was thought necessary to bring closed-circuit television and film to the classroom. To the question "Why should we do this?" the answer is: "To make learning more efficient and more interesting." Such an answer is considered entirely adequate, since in Technopoly efficiency and interest need no justification. It is, therefore, usually not noticed that this answer does not address the question "What is learning for?" "Efficiency and interest" is a technical answer, an answer about means, not ends; and it offers no pathway to a consideration of educational philosophy. Indeed, it blocks the way to such a consideration by beginning with the question of how we should proceed rather than with the question of why. It is probably not necessary to say that, by definition, there can be no education philosophy that does not address what learning is for. Confucius, Plato, Quintilian, Cicero, Comenius, Erasmus, Locke, Rousseau, Jefferson, Russell, Montessori, Whitehead, and Dewey—each believed that there was some transcendent political, spiritual, or social idea that must be advanced through education. Confucius advocated teaching "the Way" because in tradition he saw the best hope for social order. As our first systematic fascist, Plato wished education to produce philosopher kings. Cicero argued that education must free the student from the tyranny of the present. Jefferson

I hope Postman explains this intriguing point more clearly.   —H.R.

The answer Postman gives to his own question (why use technology in school?) is not the only possible reply. Other and better responses are available.   —J.R.

Yikes! Here, Postman makes an enormous leap— that the "draining" of symbols leads to the death of narratives, which are the key to tradition— and packs a huge argument into part of a paragraph. He'll have to offer a lot of evidence for me to accept this cause-effect leap. —A.L.

This education example does not provide evidence for Postman's earlier claim; I'm disappointed.   —A.L.

I see a common theme of freedom among the educational ideologies Postman mentions. How might the current emphasis on personal freedom relate to these earlier notions? To the erosion of symbols?
—H.R.

thought the purpose of education is to teach the young how to protect their liberties. Rousseau wished education to free the young from the unnatural constraints of a wicked and arbitrary social order. And among John Dewey's aims was to help the student function without certainty in a world of constant change and puzzling ambiguities.

Only in knowing something of the reasons why they advocated education can we make sense of the means they suggest. But to understand their reasons we must also understand the narratives that governed their view of the world. By narrative, I mean a story of human history that gives meaning to the past, explains the present, and provides guidance for the future. It is a story whose principles help a culture to organize its institutions, to develop ideals, and to find authority for its actions. At the risk of repetition, I must point out again that the source of the world's greatest narratives has been religion, as found, for example, in Genesis or the Bhagavad-Gita or the Koran. There are those who believe—as did the great historian Arnold Toynbee —that without a comprehensive religious narrative at its center a culture must decline. Perhaps. There are, after all, other sources—mythology, politics, philosophy, and science, for example—but it is certain that no culture can flourish without narratives of transcendent origin and power.

Even when I agree with a writer, I get suspicious when I encounter any statement that claims "it is certain . . ." My instinctive reaction is to search for an exception or a qualifier to the statement. —J.R.

This does not mean that the mere existence of such a narrative ensures a culture's stability and strength. There are destructive narratives. A narrative provides meaning, not necessarily survival—as, for example, the story provided by Adolf Hitler to the German nation in the 1930s. Drawing on sources in Teutonic mythology and resurrecting ancient and primitive symbolism, Hitler wove a tale of Aryan supremacy that lifted German spirits, gave point to their labors, eased their distress, and provided explicit ideals. The story glorified the past, elucidated the present, and foretold the future, which was to last a thousand years. The Third Reich lasted exactly twelve years.

It is not to my point to dwell on the reasons why the story of Aryan supremacy could not endure. The point is that cultures must have narratives

Many *narratives are and always have been destructive.* —A.L.

What happens when narratives abound but do not receive widespread respect? —H.R.

Here, Postman links narrative with meaning, setting up yet another binary: either we have narrative, meaning, life, or we have no narrative, no meaning, no life. I acknowledge the power of narratives to shape meaning and life, but I don't see the choice between narrative and non-narrative as simply as Postman seems to. —A.L.

and will find them where they will, even if they lead to catastrophe. The alternative is to live without meaning, the ultimate negation of life itself. It is also to the point to say that each narrative is given its form and its emotional texture through a cluster of symbols that call for respect and allegiance, even devotion. The United States Constitution, for example, is only in part a legal document, and, I should add, a small part. Democratic nations—England, for one—do not require a written constitution to ensure legal order and the protection of liberties. The importance of the American Constitution is largely in its function as a symbol of the story of our origins. It is our political equivalent of Genesis. To mock it, to ignore it, to circumvent it is to declare the irrelevance of the story of the United States as a moral light unto the world. In like fashion, the Statue of Liberty is the key symbol of the story of America as the natural home of the teeming masses, from anywhere, yearning to be free. There are, of course, several reasons why such stories lose their force. This book is, in fact, an attempt to describe one of them—i.e., how the growth of Technopoly has overwhelmed earlier, more meaningful stories. But in all cases, the trivialization of the symbols that express, support, and dramatize the story will accompany the decline. Symbol drain is both a symptom and a cause of a loss of narrative.

Is Postman saying there are no narratives in technopoly? It seems to me he has already demonstrated exactly the opposite. —A.L.

The educators I referred to above based their philosophies on narratives rich in symbols which they respected and which they understood to be integral to the stories they wanted education to reveal. It is, therefore, time to ask, What story does American education wish to tell now? In a growing Technopoly, what do we believe education is for? The answers are discouraging, and one of them can be inferred from any television commercial urging the young to stay in school. The commercial will either imply or state explicitly that education will help the persevering student to get a good job. And that's it. Well, not quite. There is also the idea that we educate ourselves to compete with the Japanese or the Germans in an economic struggle to be number one.

I agree with how Aristotle would answer this question about education: he said that learning is one of life's chief pleasures. —A.L.

The symbolic power of the Constitution was never clearer than during the presidential impeachment hearing and trial in 1998–99. Both sides invoked it as the arbiter of truth and responsibility, of right and wrong. —J.R.

As Postman notes, the fact that education leads to economic success is the sort of slick message TV ads can deliver in 30 seconds or less. More complex rationales for learning wouldn't fit the medium.   —J.R.

Neither of these purposes is, to say the least, grand or inspiring. The story each suggests is that the United States is not a culture but merely an economy, which is the last refuge of an exhausted philosophy of education. This belief, I might add, is precisely reflected in the President's Commission Report, *A Nation at Risk,** where you will find a definitive expression of the idea that education is an instrument of economic policy and of very little else.

We may get a sense of the desperation of the educator's search for a more gripping story by using the "television commercial test." Try to imagine what sort of appeals might be effectively made on a TV commercial to persuade parents to support schools. (Let us, to be fair, sidestep appeals that might be made directly to students themselves, since the youth of any era are disinclined to think schooling a good idea, whatever the reasons advanced for it. See the "Seven Ages of Man"* passage in *As You Like It.*)

Can you imagine, for example, what such a commercial would be like if Jefferson or John Dewey prepared it? "Your children are citizens in a democratic society," the commercial might say. "Their education will teach them how to be valuable citizens by refining their capacity for reasoned thought and strengthening their will to protect their liberties. As for their jobs and professions, that will be considered only at a 'late and convenient hour'" (to quote John Stuart Mill,* who would be pleased to associate himself with Jefferson's or Dewey's purpose). Is there anyone today who would find this a compelling motivation? Some, perhaps, but hardly enough to use it as the basis of a national program. John Locke's* commercial would, I imagine, be

---

A Nation at Risk (1983): report of the National Commission on Excellence in Education that called for reform of education in the United States because of dropping scores on standardized tests

"Seven Ages of Man": from William Shakespeare's *As You Like It*: "*the whining schoolboy, with his satchel / And shining morning face, creeping like snail / Unwillingly to school*" (AYL 2.7)

John Stuart Mill (1806–73): English philosopher and advocate of Utilitarianism

John Locke (1632–1704): English philosopher and author of *An Essay concerning Human Understanding* (1690)

even less appealing. "Your children must stay in school," he might say, "because there they will learn to make their bodies slaves of their minds. They will learn to control their impulses, and how to find satisfaction and even excitement in the life of the mind. Unless they accomplish this, they can be neither civilized nor literate." How many would applaud this mission? Indeed, whom could we use to speak such words—Barbara Bush?* Lee Iacocca?* Donald Trump?* Even the estimable Dr. Bill Cosby would hardly be convincing. The guffaws would resound from Maine to California.

In recent years, a valiant attempt has been made by some—for example, E. D. Hirsch, Jr.—to provide a comprehensive purpose to education. In his book *Cultural Literacy,* Hirsch defines literacy as the capacity to understand and use the words, dates, aphorisms, and names that form the basis of communication among the educated in our culture. Toward this end, he and some of his colleagues compiled a list that contains, according to them, the references essential to a culturally literate person in America. The first edition of the book (1987) included Norman Mailer but not Philip Roth, Bernard Malamud, Arthur Miller, or Tennessee Williams. It included Ginger Rogers but not Richard Rodgers, Carl Rogers, or Buck Rogers, let alone Fred Rogers. The second greatest home-run hitter of all time, Babe Ruth, was there, but not the greatest home-run hitter, Hank Aaron. The Marx Brothers were there, but not Orson Welles, Frank Capra, John Ford, or Steven Spielberg. Sarah Bernhardt was included, but not Leonard Bernstein. Rochester, New York, was on the list. Trenton, New Jersey, one of our most historic cities, was not. Hirsch included the Battle of the Bulge,* which pleased my brother, who fought in it in

Many have criticized the exclusivity and elitism of Hirsch's project, particularly this list of information deemed "essential" to one's "cultural literacy." —A.L.

Barbara Bush (b. 1925): much-respected wife of President George H. Bush

Lee Iacocca (b. 1924): flamboyant former auto executive and chair of Statue of Liberty–Ellis Island Centennial Commission

Donald Trump (b. 1946): renowned financier and billionaire real estate developer

Norman Mailer . . . Battle of the Bulge: Postman lists people, places, and things that literate Americans might be expected to recognize.

1944. But my uncle who died in the Battle of the Coral Sea, in 1942, might have been disappointed to find that it didn't make the list.

To fill in the gaps, Hirsch has had to enlarge his list, so that there now exists a *Cultural Literacy Encyclopedia.* We may be sure that Hirsch will continue to expand his list until he reaches a point where a one-sentence directive will be all he needs to publish: "See the *Encyclopedia Americana* and *Webster's Third International.*"

It is, of course, an expected outcome of any education that students become acquainted with the important references of their culture. Even Rousseau,* who would have asked his students to read only one book, *Robinson Crusoe* (so that they would learn how to survive in the wild),* would probably have expected them to "pick up" the names and sayings and dates that made up the content of the educated conversation of their time. Nonetheless, Hirsch's proposal is inadequate for two reasons that reflect the inadequacies of Technopoly. The first . . . is that the present condition of technology-generated information is so long, varied, and dynamic that it is not possible to organize it into a coherent educational program. How do you include in the curriculum Rochester, New York, or Sarah Bernhardt* or Babe Ruth? Or the Marx Brothers? Where does Ginger Rogers go? Does she get included in the syllabus under a unit titled "Fred Astaire's Dancing Partners"? (In which case, we must include Cyd Charisse and, if I am not mistaken, Winston Churchill's daughter, Sarah.) Hirsch's encyclopedic list is not a solution but a description of the problem of information glut. It is therefore essentially incoherent. But it also confuses a consequence of education with a purpose. Hirsch attempted to answer the question "What is an

And the "information glut" has only gotten worse since Technopoly *was written. Thanks to the Internet, we now have access to more information than we can handle.* —J.R.

Rousseau: Jean-Jacques Rousseau (1712–78), French philosopher and thinker, author of *Emile; or, On Education* (1762)

Robinson Crusoe (1719–22): a novel about an island castaway by Daniel Defoe (1660–1731)

Rochester . . . Sarah Bernhardt: Postman offers more items from contemporary history and culture that educated people might be expected to know in Hirsch's view of education.

educated person?" He left unanswered the question "What is an education for?" Young men, for example, will learn how to make lay-up shots when they play basketball. To be able to make them is part of the definition of what good players are. But they do not play basketball for that purpose. There is usually a broader, deeper, and more meaningful reason for wanting to play—to assert their manhood, to please their fathers, to be acceptable to their peers, even for the sheer aesthetic pleasure of the game itself. What you have to do to be a success must be addressed only after you have found a reason to be successful. In Technopoly, this is very hard to do, and Hirsch simply sidestepped the question.

Postman has raised this question several times. I wonder if he'll attempt to answer it. —A.L.

Not so Allan Bloom.* In his book *The Closing of the American Mind,* he confronts the question by making a serious complaint against the academy. His complaint is that most American professors have lost their nerve. They have become moral relativists, incapable of providing their students with a clear understanding of what is right thought and proper behavior. Moreover, they are also intellectual relativists, refusing to defend their own culture and no longer committed to preserving and transmitting the best that has been thought and said.

Hirsch and Bloom (and Matthew Arnold, who Postman alludes to with "the best that has been thought and said") sidestep the question: the best according to—and for—whom? —A.L.

Bloom's solution is that we go back to the basics of Western thought. He does not care if students know who Ginger Rogers and Groucho Marx* are. He wants us to teach our students what Plato, Aristotle, Cicero, Saint Augustine,* and other luminaries have had to say on the great ethical and epistemological questions. He believes that by acquainting themselves with great books our students will acquire a moral and intellectual foundation that will give meaning and texture to their lives. Though there is nothing especially original in this, Bloom is a serious education philosopher, which is to say, unlike Hirsch, he is a moralist who understands that Tech-

This suggestion is misleading— Great Books don't really give meaning; they guide us to meaning. —H.R.

Allan Bloom (1930–92): American educator and professor of philosophy and political science at the University of Chicago

Ginger Rogers and Groucho Marx: film stars

Plato . . . Augustine: major philosophers and thinkers

nopoly is a malevolent force requiring opposition. But he has not found many supporters.

Those who reject Bloom's idea have offered several arguments against it. The first is that such a purpose for education is elitist: the mass of students would not find the great story of Western civilization inspiring, are too deeply alienated from the past to find it so, and would therefore have difficulty connecting the "best that has been thought and said" to their own struggles to find meaning in their lives. A second argument, coming from what is called a "leftist" perspective, is even more discouraging. In a sense, it offers a definition of what is meant by elitism. It asserts that the "story of Western civilization" is a partial, biased, and even oppressive one. It is not the story of blacks, American Indians, Hispanics, women, homosexuals—of any people who are not white heterosexual males of Judeo-Christian heritage. This claim denies that there is or can be a national culture, a narrative of organizing power and inspiring symbols which all citizens can identify with and draw sustenance from. If this is true, it means nothing less than that our national symbols have been drained of their power to unite, and that education must become a tribal affair; that is, each subculture must find its own story and symbols, and use them as the moral basis of education.

Standing somewhat apart from these arguments are, of course, religious educators, such as those in Catholic schools, who strive to maintain another traditional view—that learning is done for the greater glory of God and, more particularly, to prepare the young to embrace intelligently and gracefully the moral directives of the church. Whether or not such a purpose can be achieved in Technopoly is questionable, as many religious educators will acknowledge.

I will reserve for the . . . final chapter [of *Technopoly*] my own view of the struggle to find a purpose for education. . . . But here it must be said that the struggle itself is a sign that our repertoire of significant national, religious, and mythological symbols has been seriously drained of its potency.

Now I'm really getting tired of these pairs of supposed opposites: either we're all united under one "narrative of organizing power" or we're part of a "tribal affair," divided into many separate subcultures. I think there can be multiple narratives and that we, as citizens, can move among them. —A.L.

The tribalism Postman describes has become a driving force in American education as the nation's shared story and images have lost their resonance. Whether technology is the cause of these developments is another matter. —J.R.

"We are living at a time," Irving Howe* has written, "when all the once regnant world systems that have sustained (also distorted) Western intellectual life, from theologies to ideologies, are taken to be in severe collapse. This leads to a mood of skepticism, an agnosticism of judgment, sometimes a world-weary nihilism in which even the most conventional minds begin to question both distinctions of value and the value of distinctions."[2]

Into this void comes the Technopoly story, with its emphasis on progress without limits, rights without responsibilities, and technology without cost. The Technopoly story is without a moral center. It puts in its place efficiency, interest, and economic advance. It promises heaven on earth through the conveniences of technological progress. It casts aside all traditional narratives and symbols that suggest stability and orderliness, and tells, instead, of a life of skills, technical expertise, and the ecstasy of consumption. Its purpose is to produce functionaries for an ongoing Technopoly. It answers Bloom by saying that the story of Western civilization is irrelevant; it answers the political left by saying there is indeed a common culture whose name is Technopoly and whose key symbol is now the computer, toward which there must be neither irreverence nor blasphemy. It even answers Hirsch by saying that there are items on his list that, if thought about too deeply and taken too seriously, will interfere with the progress of technology.

I grant that it is somewhat unfair to expect educators, by themselves, to locate stories that would reaffirm our national culture. Such narratives must come to them, to some degree, from the political sphere. If our politics is symbolically impoverished, it is difficult to imagine how teachers can provide a weighty purpose to education. I am writing this chapter during the fourth week of the war against Iraq;* the rhetoric accompanying the onset

This is a very depressing scenario, and yet there are symbols here aplenty. I'm beginning to wonder if the "symbol drain" is as responsible for the rise of technopoly as Postman believes it to be. —A.L.

Does the image Postman draws of our times seem accurate? Technopoly does seem like an apt symbol at the beginning of a new millennium. —J.R.

Irving Howe (1920–93): noted American literary critic and professor of English at Hunter College of the City University of New York

[2]*The New Republic,* February 18, 1991, p. 42.

war against Iraq: The Allied attack on Iraq began on January 16–17, 1991.

of the war is still fresh in mind. It began with the President's calling Americans to arms for the sake of their "life-style." This was followed by the Secretary of State's request that they fight to protect their jobs. Then came the appeal—at a late and convenient hour, as it were—to thwart the "naked aggression" of a little "Hitler." I do not say here that going to war was unjustified. My point is that, with the Cold War at an end, our political leaders now struggle, as never before, to find a vital narrative and accompanying symbols that would awaken a national spirit and a sense of resolve. The citizens themselves struggle as well. Having drained many of their traditional symbols of serious meaning, they resort, somewhat pitifully, to sporting yellow ribbons as a means of symbolizing their fealty to a cause. After the war, the yellow ribbons will fade from sight, but the question of who we are and what we represent will remain. Is it possible that the only symbol left to use will be an F-15 fighter plane guided by an advanced computer system?

Afterwords

The subtitle of Postman's book, The Surrender of Culture to Technology, *provides a key to my response to this reading. While I appreciate much of Postman's work and am grateful for his trenchant critiques of contemporary culture, I find myself resisting one major premise of "The Great Symbol Drain"—that technology is somehow outside of culture, or that technology is capable of usurping and transforming culture. Certainly, technologies have always played a role in constituting culture: think of the role of writing, one of the Western world's oldest technologies, in shaping recorded history, for example. But to see the influence as one-way seems overly simple to me. In addition, I am not a big fan of the type of* either-or *arguments that characterize much of Postman's piece (as I note in my annotations).*

With that said, and in spite of what I see as overgeneralization and extremism, I think Postman makes some very important points. He is right that symbols play a great role in our personal, social, and national lives. Images—like words—can trivialize, mock, or hurt us; or they can heal, uplift, and inspire us. So his warning to take symbols and images very seriously seems important to me. I also agree that the ground of a symbol can be shifted so as to change its meaning in significant ways. Literary theorist Joseph Bentley has called this move, in poetry and prose, "semantic gravitation"—the strategy of taking a word or phrase that has strong positive meanings and systematically associating it with highly negative connotations. That is precisely what Postman is complaining about in terms of a "symbol drain"—the trivialization and "blaspheming" of unifying national and cultural images. More specifically, he sees technopoly as in the business of using all symbols available to it to further commercial interests, "devouring the psyches of consumers." Postman may be right. But I hold out some faith in our ability to resist these commercial images, to read them critically, and to analyze the motives that lie behind their use. Certainly, students and teachers face a major challenge: to be critical of the ways in which technopoly seeks to manipulate our desires through symbols and stories, and, perhaps even more important, to create new stories that can enrich our lives beyond the realm of "skills, technical expertise, and the ecstasy of consumption." —A.L.

Postman has an eerie ability to forecast the future. Writing in 1985, in Amusing Ourselves to Death, *he warned that the trivializing effects of television and technology would eventually undermine serious political discourse in the United States. Fifteen years later, we're now living in the dark shadows of his prophecy. We don't need primetime soap operas like* Melrose Place *anymore because the political news has become far racier and more entertaining. George Washington's cherry tree and Abraham Lincoln's top hat have been replaced by images we can't even begin to explain to children.*

As Postman was completing "The Great Symbol Drain" in 1992, he observed that political leaders, notably then-president George Bush, were struggling for words adequate to motivate Americans to support the Persian Gulf War. Why? Because all the older symbols of national spirit had been drained of their power. Today, as I write these words, the United States is again waging war, this time in the Balkans, and, once again, a president—Bill Clinton—is struggling to invent a "vital narrative" that makes sense of this latest campaign. But just as Postman had foreseen, no symbols are able to rally American sentiment in support of this foreign adventure. Even Congress is wavering.

Postman doubts that we can ever recover those lost symbols and stories of American unity that served us so well before the Vietnam era. But he is also pretty confident—and probably correct—that our blind faith in technology is not going to sustain us either. It's ultimately an empty narrative, vacuous, and morally bankrupt. Yet is there a story potent enough to displace the myth of technopoly? It may take a prophet to point the way. —J.R.

I think part of the problem Postman calls "technopoly" is that people are searching for something to fill an emptiness left by the trivialization of ideologies. Technology and consumerism have shifted the focus from broad concepts of culture and society to those of the individual, creating an obsession with inner health and worth. It's discomforting to think what a mess this has made of our society. The question is not whether resistance is an option or a necessity—it is, of course, the latter—but how to combat the influence of technopoly. I think Postman is right in saying that the burden of this problem cannot fall fully on educators, though they may play an important role in the struggle.

Although I find this selection interesting and agree with much of what Postman says about the effects of symbols, overall I consider his argument too pessimistic. It seems to me that certain symbols are still held sacred by many people, myself included. —H.R.

QUESTIONING THE TEXT

1. Postman provides several examples of advertisements in which religious images and symbols have been trivialized. Working in a group, list additional examples of images or icons sacred to a particular religion or a

people (for instance, to Native Americans) that have been abused in advertisements. Then, working independently, write an essay in which you examine your reaction to these commercials. Is the practice as harmful as Postman suggests on pp. 513–14, or do you have a different reaction to these advertising techniques?

2. Do images and words lose their power by repetition, as Postman claims? Conduct a survey of your campus environment. What dominant symbols are used by your college or university? By local organizations and the surrounding community? How often do you notice these images or symbols? In what circumstances do they have power and when do they become like images of George Washington in advertisements for Presidents' Day sales? Report your findings in a short paper.

MAKING CONNECTIONS

3. In what ways does Postman's critique of the use of computers in education parallel that of Todd Oppenheimer in "The Computer Delusion" (p. 255)? Read the two selections side by side, looking for common threads in the authors' analyses of technology in the classroom. Why do you agree or disagree with the authors? Put your response in the form of an opinion piece—one that might appear in a special edition of your campus newspaper devoted to computers on campus.

4. According to Postman, cultures cannot survive without powerful narratives that explain their pasts and direct their futures. Is it possible that the great narrative for technopoly might be *Frankenstein?* Review that selection by Mary Shelley (p. 231) and consider how Dr. Frankenstein's monster functions as a symbol for cultures that rely (too?) heavily on technology and science. Discuss the issue with your classmates.

JOINING THE CONVERSATION

5. Working in a group, discuss the implications of Postman's claim "that advertising is most effective when it is irrational" (p. 518). Consider especially the roles images play in advertising: are images themselves irrational or can they contribute to our deeper understanding of products or ideas? Using a carefully selected set of print or video advertisements as evidence, write an essay or create a Web site in response to Postman's statement.

6. The Constitution and the Statue of Liberty are, according to Postman, potent symbols of our shared national narrative. Write an essay in which you list and discuss other symbols or images that you believe are—or should be—a part of the story that gives meaning to the American experience.

HENRY LOUIS GATES JR.
Net Worth

I SAT DOWN, CLOSED MY EYES, *and tried to think of images that seemed most pervasive in our society. Michael Jordan's was the one that came to me first, and in "Net Worth," Henry Louis Gates Jr. (b. 1950) offers at least partial explanation for my response. About the megastar, who retired from the National Basketball Association not long after this essay was published, Gates says, ". . . Jordan's status as an international symbol of America . . . — and the sense that we have that he's ours — has become one of those things that constitute our identity as Americans. . . ."*

Named by Time *in 1997 as one of "the 25 Most Influential Americans," Gates is W. E. B. Du Bois Professor of Humanities at Harvard University, where he chairs the much-publicized W. E. B. Du Bois Institute for Afro-American Research. He comes to his subject with an extensive career as a critic of literature and culture in numerous books, including* The Signifying Monkey: A Theory of Afro-American Literary Criticism *(1988) and* Speaking of Race, Speaking of Sex: Hate Speech, Civil Rights, and Civil Liberties *(1994). He also lectures at universities nationwide and frequently appears on major television programs devoted to educational and social issues. In recent years, Gates has published a number of essays in the* New Yorker, *including "Net Worth" in June 1998, as well as interviews with the famous and powerful (Elizabeth Dole, General Colin Powell, Harry Belafonte).*

This essay seemed to me a fine selection for a chapter on images. Gates agrees that "Jordan's job is his image, in that being Michael Jordan has become his principal line of work." In addition, Gates offers an analysis of the complex relationship among star, brand name, and consumer — one that leaves me thinking hard about the ways in which I am a part of the images that surround and affect my experience of the world.

—A.L.

When do you know for sure? Basketball fans still talk about "the shot" — the sixteen-footer that a University of North Carolina freshman named Michael Jordan sank in 1982. With seconds left on the clock, Jordan scored the decisive basket against Georgetown, secured the NCAA* crown, and put himself, in his own words, "on the basketball map." David Falk, whom one would be tempted to call the Michael Jordan of sports agents if he weren't Michael Jordan's sports agent, tells about witnessing a similarly prophetic moment in Jordan's career. In 1985, Jordan, a coltish twenty-two, was holding a press conference in Chicago to announce an endorsement deal

---

NCAA: National Collegiate Athletic Association

he'd signed with the Coca-Cola Company. But those were not ordinary times, for New Coke had recently been introduced and a cola Kulturkampf was seething. "Which Coke do *you* like—New Coke or regular Coke?" a reporter threw at him.

Even now, in the recounting, Falk wants to make sure I get the full picture: an inexperienced young player, the cameras, the microphones, the blazing lights—and his future as a pitchman in the balance. "And Michael instantly responded, 'Coke is Coke. They both taste great.'" As the sportscasters say, nothing but net.

No one could have faulted Jordan had he made a different play—had he plumped for New Coke, and tried to justify the choice without slighting its precursor. "I mean, for me, I would have probably picked one and tried to explain why," Falk says intently. You can tell that the moment is part of his own personal highlights reel: the lights, the cameras, the question, the sudden clutch in his gut, and, finally, Jordan's soaring, effortless dunk. "What a great answer!" Falk exclaims. "He just has amazing instincts." If you're Falk, that's when you know.

Après Coke, le déluge. Edible cake decorations, golf-club covers, shower curtains, pot holders, aprons, rulers, kitchen towels, sleeping bags, canteens, insulated travel mugs, napkins, tablecloths, popcorn tins, foam furniture, first-aid kits, gift wrap, memo pads, book bags, pencil sharpeners, erasers, buttons, key chains, wallet cards, magnets, ring binders, tissue holders, diaries, address books, envelopes, flashlights, kites, toothbrush holders, wastebaskets, Sony and Sega play stations, pinball games, soap dishes, walkie-talkies, curtains, acrylic juice cups, gum, cookies, bandages, and comforters: this isn't a list of all the commodities that Jordan has endorsed, but it's the beginning of such a list. The economist Tyler Cowen, who has compiled a far longer list than this one, has approvingly noted that these endorsements represent a very simple form of mutualism: "It helps sell their product, and it makes Michael Jordan more famous."

Two forces contend for the soul of contemporary America, playing out   5 a sociohistorical version of King Kong versus Godzilla, only with better special effects. On the one hand, there's the growth of what has been termed "winner-take-all" markets, visible in every economic and cultural realm but epitomized by the star system of the NBA.* On the other hand, there's the growth of market micro-segmentation—the fragmentation of culture into ever narrower niches, from the proliferation of cable channels to the supposed balkanization of the canon. For at least the past decade, the struggle has been ceaseless, dug-in, brutal. Corporate behemoths meet and merge; then, buffeted by shareholder capitalism, spin off divisions like whirling nebulae. Twenty thousand new consumer products were introduced in this country last year; ninety per cent of them will fail. And so the battle continues. A

NBA: National Basketball Association

bulletin from the front: Michael Jordan—the ultimate winner-take-all celebrity—is gaining the upper hand.

"Forget the endorsements and the swoosh* and the dollar sign," Steve Wulf wrote in *Time* last year. "They just get in the way, like some beaded curtain that keeps us from truly appreciating what we have"—to wit, "the greatest athlete in the history of American sports." An uplifting sentiment, but you might just as fairly stand it on its head. The man's grandeur on the court—the dunks, the jump shots, the steals, the midair acrobatics—has tended to obscure another historic achievement: Michael Jordan has become the greatest corporate pitchman of all time. As a twentieth-century sports hero, he has plausible competition from Babe Ruth and Muhammad Ali; as an agent of brand equity, he is without peer.

The first thing you notice when you sit down with Michael Jordan is how very much like Michael Jordan he is. The resemblance is uncanny, and not incidental to his success. He's handsome and dark-skinned, with those three horizontal creases in his forehead which really become visible when he's at the free-throw line, glistening with sweat and glowering at the basket. His baritone is the one you've heard on a thousand commercials. But, more than that, the manner—direct and artless—is familiar. ("He can't really act," Falk was quoted as saying shortly before the Jordan vehicle *Space Jam** had its theatrical release, and it occurs to me only now that Falk was reassuring us, not warning us.) Jordan, who is self-aware without being self-conscious, recognizes that the alchemy of image requires realness, which in turn requires exposure, albeit controlled exposure.

"I know that it's got some coloring to it, and you are only going to see certain portions that they want you to see," Jordan says of his public persona. "But still, when I come in contact with people, I think they see me being a genuine person. And I get along with everybody. I'm a people person, yet I understand the game of corporate America and what they try to project."

We're sitting quietly in his private suite off the second-floor dining room of an establishment called Michael Jordan's Restaurant, on North LaSalle Street, in downtown Chicago. The most noticeable object here is an eleven-by-fourteen-inch photograph of his father, the late James Jordan.* Otherwise, the suite is sedate and muted, with cream-colored walls, a couple of tan leather sofas, and a marble dining table. Michael Jordan is across from me, sipping a cup of coffee, nibbling on fruit salad, and occasionally lifting up a piece of flatware, tilting it this way and that.

---

swoosh: symbol of Nike, a manufacturer of sports footwear and accessories

Space Jam: 1996 live-action/animated film featuring Michael Jordan and the Looney Tunes characters, including Daffy Duck, Porky Pig, and Elmer Fudd

James Jordan: James Jordan was murdered while he slept in his car on July 23, 1993. Two men were convicted of the crime.

Jordan was exaggerating when he said he got along with everybody. He   10
minces few words as he speaks about two of his previous coaches at Chicago:
Stan Albeck, who he feels was tolerant of mediocrity ("very laid-back—do
your job and then go out and party"), and Doug Collins, who was loyal to management but not to his players ("'*Fuck* Doug Collins' was the conversation on
the court"). Still, when it comes to elements that affect his and his team's performance, you wouldn't expect the most competitive member of the NBA to
display an attitude of live-and-let-live. Jordan has been equally acerbic toward
teammates who he feels have not pulled their weight. The person who continues to elicit Jordan's special loathing, though, is Jerry Krause, the general manager of the Chicago Bulls and thus Jordan's putative boss.

"I was a piece of meat to him," Jordan says, recounting one of their
many disputes. "He felt he could control me, because I had so much value to
him. But he didn't realize that I had value to myself: I was independent, and I
understood what I was."

Considered even as a piece of meat, Jordan need make no apologies. At
six feet six, he weighs almost twenty pounds more than he did when he
started his pro career—the result of a strenuous regimen of upper-body
weight training. The man is both hulking and suave, and it's easy to see why
he has become a totem of black masculinity; he makes Bill Cosby look like
Uncle Ben. He's dressed casually today: jeans, a beige T-shirt, and the familiar
gold earring, an adornment that seemed faintly daring and piratical when he
first adopted it, ten years ago. He does not generally push the limits of the acceptable. He may banter about condoms—he'll never endorse them, he has
said, because "they're too small!"—but he seldom edges past PG-13. This is a
guy who listens to Toni Braxton and Anita Baker, not to Ice Cube or the
WuTang Clan. He has a sense of being at ease with himself—a low center of
gravity, so to speak, despite his prowess at the vertical game. Relaxed and polite, he discusses his television advertisements with the same combination of
detachment and animation with which he discusses the game.

A Nike spot that Jordan is particularly proud of aired in 1997; in it, he
gives a recitation of missed shots and lost games, concluding, "I've failed over
and over and over again in my life. And that is why I succeed." Fade to the
Air Jordan logo. "I had to fight the agency about it, because they had wanted
to have me work with Oliver Stone* on a commercial," he says, making a
faint snorting sound, "and Oliver Stone was going to go through that process
of trying to figure out why my game is my game. And I said, 'Oliver Stone
don't know shit about basketball. Why don't you just show the actual situation? Let the people see exactly what's happened over the twelve years of my
career.' The idea is to tell young kids, 'Don't be afraid to fail, because a lot of

---

Oliver Stone (b. 1946): Controversial film director, writer, and producer. His works include *Born on the Fourth of July* (1989) and *JFK* (1991).

people have to fail to be successful—these are the many times that I've failed but yet I've been successful.' Let them know that it isn't always good for the people up top. I mean, they have bad things happen to them."

If one of those bad things is being stuck with a general manager like Krause, another, it seems, is being stuck with a team owner like the Chicago real-estate developer Jerry Reinsdorf. Jordan tells me about the meeting with Reinsdorf when his Bulls contract for the 1997–98 season—a one-year retainer worth thirty-odd million dollars—was agreed upon: "We shook hands. But one comment stuck with me as we left, and I lost total respect for him when he said it: 'At some point in time, I know I'm going to regret what we just did.'" For the previous eight years, Jordan had been saddled with a contract that had early on failed to keep pace with the escalating NBA marketplace. So the comment wasn't exactly sporting. Now Jordan gives me a meaningful look. "And I'm saying, All these years where you knew I was underpaid and you been making money and your organization's moved from a fifteen-million-dollar business when you bought it to a two-hundred-million-dollar business—all those years have just gone down the drain because *you have for once paid me my value*. And you *regretted* that! That hit me so deep inside—that sense of greed, of disrespect for me."

Since this kind of friction is commonplace in the NBA, it's easy to   15
miss how strange the whole situation is. After all, Jordan, considered strictly as an athlete, is the Second Coming, and Reinsdorf, considered strictly as a mogul, is a second-rater. It's as if Pat Robertson* were making Jesus punch a time card.

And all this is aside from Jordan's role as culture hero. A Plutarchian progression of biographies have mounted the best-seller list, chronicling the securely working-class childhood in Wilmington, North Carolina (father a foreman at a General Electric plant; mother in customer relations for the United Carolina Bank); the traumatic early failure (as a high-school sophomore, he was cut from the varsity team); his taste of greatness as a Tar Heel,* under the tutelage of Coach Dean Smith;* his début with the Chicago Bulls and the galvanizing effect he had upon the team and upon the sport in general. Later accounts describe the 1993 murder of his father, and his subsequent decision to leave basketball for minor-league baseball; the jubilation that marked his return to the Bulls in 1995; the ten scoring titles, five MVP* titles, and five championships over the past seven seasons. These things have been inscribed on the national memory like the battles of the Revolutionary War. For this is someone who over the past several years has been mentioned in an average of a hundred newspaper and magazine stories a day.

Pat Robertson (b. 1930): American evangelist
Tar Heel: an athlete for the University of North Carolina
Dean Smith (b. 1931): NCAA Hall of Fame basketball coach
MVP: most valuable player

Jordan, for his part, analyzes his celebrity so coolly that he might as well be marking up a playbook with "X"s and "O"s. "It could easily be a matter of timing, where society was looking for something positive," he says. "It could easily be a sport that was gradually bursting out into global awareness at a time when I was at the top. And then there's the connections that I've had with corporate America since I started with Coca-Cola and then went to Nike, which has gone totally global." He breaks off. "I really, really can't give you a sufficient answer."

Maybe not, but he's made a good start, as David Stern would agree. David Stern must himself be accounted a factor in Jordan's success: he has been the commissioner of the National Basketball Association for the past fourteen years, and brought a financially troubled and scandal-plagued organization to the land of milk and honey. A shortish man with a head of graying hair, Stern is tough and funny, and a self-professed worrier. (Commending the virtues of institutionalized anxiety, he tells me, "That's why it's good to have a Jewish organization. You worry *constantly*." True, the NBA has its share of tsuris* these days, but it's the kind you get when you've been all too successful: such troubles we should all have.) The rise of Jordan and the rise of the NBA have been propelled by many of the same trends, and Stern delineates them as well as anyone. "You wind up with a marketing revolution, a television and cable revolution, at a time when our league is also growing in stature," he says. However talented such players as Wilt Chamberlain and Bill Russell were, he points out, the numbers who watched them were minuscule relative to the numbers who watch NBA games today. When Stern started out, there were no regional sports channels; now those channels have fifty-five million subscribers. It's the difference between a vaudeville stage and a modern cineplex.

Then, there's the Jordan factor. "Here was a very handsome, friendly, eminently decent human being," Stern says, "who is the kind of person you'd like to have as a friend, and who just happens to be the most fiercely competitive athlete of his time and the best basketball player perhaps ever." Falk captures that quality in a nice formula: Jordan, he says, is "at once credible and incredible"—a down-to-earth guy who defies gravity on the court.

The guy on the court is the Michael Jordan who, in a game some thought 20
might be his last in Madison Square Garden, drove the baseline, did a one-eighty in midair, then flipped the ball backward over his head and into the basket. During the game, he'd put on his original Air Jordans—a pair he wore back in 1984—and he played vintage Air Jordan ball. And even when he's acting his age (he now tends toward artful outside fadeaways rather than the banging inside game of his youth), it only underscores his technical mastery. At one point

---

tsuris: Yiddish word meaning "troubles"

in the second game of the playoffs against the Pacers last week, Jordan nearly lost his footing, then, as he stumbled, launched a high arcing shot to the basket. Nobody who has watched his sheerly kinetic presence on the court has to wonder why every Bulls game since November 20, 1987, has been sold out. Or why a huge bronze statue of him . . . looms near an entrance to Chicago's United Center. Still, athletic pre-ëminence alone doesn't explain why Jordan is a walking brand, and the most recognizable one on the planet.

An inherent feature of what marketers call a "powerbrand," to be sure, is that this very status comes to seem inevitable and natural: we take it for granted that Michael Jordan is Michael Jordan because he's Michael Jordan. And yet neither his athleticism nor his affability suffices to explain his global ubiquity. Nor are conventional theories about celebrity endorsement much help. For decades, research in the subject focussed on attributes like "credibility" and "attractiveness," but by the eighties the inadequacies of those models were obvious. In the heyday of *The Cosby Show,* the credible and attractive Bill Cosby did wonders for Coca-Cola and Kodak. Then E. F. Hutton* signed him up, with disastrous results. John Houseman* triumphed at Smith Barney* but bombed at McDonald's. A more sophisticated account—such as one introduced in the late eighties by the anthropologist and marketing theorist Grant McCracken—would register the fact that there were kinds as well as degrees of credibility and attractiveness. Fame wasn't fungible. Different celebrities were repositories of different values and associations: Sigourney Weaver* didn't *mean* the same thing as Loni Anderson.* "Celebrities 'own' their meanings because they have created them on the public stage by dint of intense and repeated performance," McCracken declared. Yet meaning still travelled in one direction, from the celebrity to the product, and on to the consumer. "Thus does meaning circulate in the consumer society," McCracken concluded.

Look closer. David Falk, back in the eighties, had intuitively grasped something that was still eluding many business-school profs—the way "branding" can be a reciprocal process. Falk had no equity in Nike or McDonald's or Coca-Cola or Chevrolet. He had equity in Michael Jordan. The corporations wanted Jordan to leverage their brands; Falk would use their brands to leverage Jordan.

"I think that my role in managing Michael's image is one of the most misunderstood aspects of sports marketing," David Falk says. "There is a faction that feels that we have ridden on Michael's coattails as he has taken us

---

E. F. Hutton: an investment firm

John Houseman (1902–88): a distinguished American actor

Smith Barney: an investment firm

Sigourney Weaver (b. 1949): an actress who has played the action hero in films such as *Alien* (1979) and *Aliens* (1986)

Loni Anderson (b. 1945): an actress who has played stereotypical "blonde" roles

along on a joyride through the world of sports marketing for the last thirteen years. There are others who think that I'm Dr. Frankenstein and I cooked up this formula in my laboratory to make Michael the marketing king of the century. And both are really wide of the mark."

David Falk, now forty-seven, is tall and bald (albeit not so tall and bald as his most celebrated client), and, with his Zegna suits* and StarTac phone,* he has become a fixture at the NBA's draft night, where he gets to exercise his skills at coaxing, cosseting, and cudgelling in rapid succession. His position in professional sports is essentially the position that Michael Ovitz* once enjoyed in Hollywood, though his style is bristlier and more confrontational. After earning degrees in economics and law, he spent most of his career at the large sports-management firm ProServ. He split in 1992 to start his own agency, FAME, and, unlike Jerry Maguire,* he took all his clients with him. Just the other week, Falk sold his company to SFX Broadcasting for an estimated hundred million dollars, though he's promised to stay on as chairman and CEO.

"Protect your assets" is one of Falk's guiding rules, "assets" being the operative word. For what is perhaps the central relationship in Jordan's career has never been a bond of sentiment. To their credit, the two do not pretend otherwise. Jordan speaks of Falk in terms that are businesslike but not brusque—as someone who can be a son of a bitch ("an asshole" is Jordan's precise designation) but *his* son of a bitch.

Falk's positioning of his client started with an appreciation of how wonderfully American he was. "It was clear when you met him that he grew up in a close-knit family," Falk says. "His parents, James and Doloris, had been very, very close to their children, had great family values—they were disciplined, respectful, pretty much color-blind. And obviously, based on his style of play—and also based upon his tremendous success in the Olympics in Los Angeles in 1984—we felt that he represented something as all-American as apple pie. So the game plan was to get involved with all-American companies, like McDonald's and Coke and Chevrolet. Which we did."

The way Falk recounts the struggle to get Jordan "into the system," you might think he was talking about integrating the lunch counters at Woolworth's. "It took favors and arm-twisting," he says. Even then, the first deals with McDonald's were for local markets, in Chicago and North Carolina; they involved modest sums, and a lot of skepticism about whether a broad-based nonathletic brand could really be boosted by a black athlete—and a team athlete at that.

25

Zegna suits: a suit by fashion designer Ermenegildo Zegna
StarTac phone: a cellular phone manufactured by Motorola
Michael Ovitz (b. 1946): influential entertainment executive
Jerry Maguire: a character in a 1996 film by the same name; Maguire was a sports agent played by actor Tom Cruise

"In tennis or golf or boxing, the mystique is the individual," Falk says, "whereas, no matter how great Bill Russell or Bob Cousy was, it was the Celtic dynasty—it was always institutional. Michael changed all that. Single-handed. Today, when the NBA markets the teams, it says, Come watch Penny Hardaway and the Orlando Magic, come watch Grant Hill and the Detroit Pistons. Ten years ago, the NBA resisted doing that. It was just that Michael's force was so overwhelming. Basketball will never be an individual sport, but it's become a hybrid."

It was in Jordan's rookie year that Falk took his client shoe-shopping. "Instead of asking for offers I asked all the shoe companies to make a presentation to us and explain what they would do to market Michael," Falk recounts. An ailing sneaker company called Nike turned out to be the keenest suitor. "But still they refused to call it the Michael Jordan line," Falk says. "That's when I came up with the idea of calling the shoe Air Jordan, as a compromise between Michael Jordan and Nike." The result was then the largest basketball endorsement deal ever—worth about $2.5 million over five years, plus royalties. Falk insisted that the company spend at least a million dollars on promotion, and so guarantee his client that measure of commercial exposure. Nike insisted on an out clause if sales didn't take off. In fact, Air Jordan revenues reached a hundred and thirty million dollars by the end of the first year, and Nike happily spent several million dollars to promote the line. It was the most successful sneaker launch in history. The lesson wasn't lost on the national marketing executives at McDonald's and at Coca-Cola.

It is easy to lose sight of McDonald's and Coca-Cola as the cultural 30 promontories they are, in the way that it is hard to take in the Empire State Building from its base. They are the planet's two most successful brands, as ubiquitous as the ground underfoot—or the buildings overhead—and sometimes as unnoticeable. In tandem, they elevated Jordan far beyond his peers, and not just through visibility alone. A recent study by four experimental psychologists published in the *Journal of Personality and Social Psychology* employs the term "spontaneous trait transference," but you might as well call it the Michael Jordan Effect. Over time, speakers are seen as themselves possessing the qualities that they describe in others.

The basic notion is hardly new: it's what underlies talk about basking in reflected glory, or the urge to kill the messenger. Even so, the strength of such "trait transference" is startling. For instance, in the recent study participants were shown a videotape of a man talking about an acquaintance who was cruel to animals. In follow-up surveys, they associated that specific trait with the communicator: *he* was viewed as cruel to animals. And the effect was equally strong when the participants were told what was going on—when they knew that the "interview" might have been scripted. Even when you eliminate rational warrant for the inference, people still make the association: somehow we can't *not*. It is, the researchers conclude, a "relatively mindless" process, and one that may powerfully affect our impression even of those well known to us.

Yet the literature on the effect of endorsements upon the perception of brands has notably ignored the effect of brands upon the perception of their endorsers. Redoubtable though Jordan is, you might wonder whether his singular and singularly American charisma doesn't derive in part from the venerable magic of history's most powerful consumer brands. Dismiss Coke as mere sugared water if you like, but, culturally speaking, it's a powerful concoction, and in ways that go beyond its core values of permanence ("Always Coca-Cola") and authenticity ("The Real Thing"). The Coca-Cola Company conducts regular consumer surveys to determine how the beverage scores on more than a dozen value attributes, which have included "young," "modern," "warm," and "friendly." The tracking polls are keyed to a compensatory strategy: when the scores in a particular value wane, advertisements are designed to bolster them. Yet over the six years of Jordan's association with the product (he was lured over to Gatorade in 1991) the more powerful trait transference surely went from brand to spokesperson—from the attributes to their communicator. Who seems more modern, warm, and friendly than Jordan? Who seems more enduring (Always Michael Jordan) and authentic (The Real Thing)? And the same mechanism applies to his early association with McDonald's. Consider those core attributes of being reliable, fast, wholesome, American, and family-minded. Did somebody say Michael Jordan?

Fame, not water, is the universal solvent. What to do with the fact that the voice and the face of American corporate capitalism belong to an African-American—a very dark and very male one at that? Various critics have offered conjectures about the phenomenon, but it may be that David Falk sums it up best. "Celebrities aren't black," he tells me patiently, in the way one might make an observation about heat regulation in reptiles. "People don't look at Michael as being black. They accept that he's different because he's a celebrity. I'm not saying it to be derogatory. People who are exclusive and discriminatory don't look at those people as being black." Without ever playing the "raceless" card—without ever pretending to be anything other than what he was, a black kid from the South—Jordan has made race a nonissue. Talk about your fadeaway.

You can't assess the marketing of Michael without taking the measure of his own business savvy. Executives at Nike will tell you that Jordan has a knack for taking charge of any meeting at which he is present. He has clearly learned a lot from sorcerers like Falk—and Stern—but he is no longer an apprentice. To an unusual degree, he has helped shape his "creatives." Working with Tinker Hatfield, a senior designer at Nike, he has even been involved in styling his athletic footwear. All of which is to say that Jordan is, in a very nineteen-nineties way, both talent and suit. His partners know that he is sensitive to matters of dignity and does not care for every transaction to be commercial; but they also know that he can be wonderfully hard-core where matters of money are concerned. Indeed, the Falk relationship has lasted partly because Falk has been exquisitely attuned to this quality.

"For the first four or five years, Michael really kept me at arm's length," Falk says, "which only increases my admiration for him, because he *shouldn't* have trusted me." How, then, did Falk win Jordan's trust? By strategic sacrifices, he'll tell you, with the confidence of a chess master who knows when to forfeit a piece for a positional advantage. In 1988, Falk negotiated Jordan's second contract, which (though its eight-year duration ultimately proved a bane) was then the most lucrative ever in basketball. Afterward, Falk presented Jordan with a bill—the standard sports agent's fee, which is four per cent of the client's salary. Falk recalls that Jordan wasn't pleased: "He said immediately, 'I think it's too high,' and he offered to pay roughly half of what I had proposed." Falk agreed, but then went even further: he told Jordan that he was going to reduce the agency's marketing fee—the percentage, usually around twenty per cent, that it took on a player's marketing and endorsement deals—by a quarter. Falk recounts, "When he left, my partner said to me, 'He told you he was happy with the marketing—why on earth would you propose that?' I said, 'Because, as the market continues to escalate, one day he's gonna feel that it's too high, and I'd rather offer it to him voluntarily, as a gesture of good faith.' And from that day on we've never discussed fees again." This way, as Falk figured the angles, he himself benefited from "the good will of Michael's knowing that it was voluntary, as opposed to his putting a gun to your head one day and saying, 'I want to pay half.'" Agents—even one as brilliant, innovative, and aggressive as David Falk—are replaceable. A client like Michael Jordan is not.

Which is why, two years ago, when Jordan starred in *Space Jam,* Falk took a deep breath and made the same move. "I waived all my producing fees on the movie," he says, and you know that it must have felt like passing a kidney stone. "Since I was the executive producer of the movie, I got a very substantial fee. And I talked to different people who said, 'You're crazy. We have to explain to Michael that in Hollywood whether you got a dollar or ten million dollars to be executive producer of the movie wouldn't affect how much he made as an actor by one penny.' I said, 'I understand that, and you understand that, but I know he's not comfortable with it.' He just didn't feel it was appropriate for me to be involved on two or three different levels. He never *asked* me to do it. I went to him one day and just told him, 'I want you to know, I've earned *x* and I'm going to give it back to you.' And he was very appreciative of that. That's really what he wanted me to do."

This is the kind of thing you do when you value and protect your assets. Jordan got flak in the late eighties when, frustrated by the Bulls' poor performance in the playoffs, he took to calling his teammates "my supporting cast," but that's pretty much the way Falk sees things. He says, "You could almost have a lottery and take all the players in the league and say, 'O.K.,

Michael, you need eleven players. Take any four centers, any four forwards, and any three guards.' And you'd have a pretty damn good team."

I start to protest. "But you wouldn't have the Bulls and their dynasty."

"I think that's overrated," Falk says breezily. "Truthfully. I think you take Michael away and I think they're a very average team." Spoken, we can agree, like a man who secured his client a thirty-odd-million-dollar contract for the current season. Nothing but net worth.

Not all Jordan's relationships involve commercial transactions, of 40 course, and if he's been buoyed by his business ties he's been both protected and grounded by his personal ones. It's a significant fact about him that he has never surrounded himself with a gangsta-style posse — that his closest friend is a sixty-one-year-old black guy named Gus Lett, who used to work for him as a security consultant, and who somehow reminds him of a fellow who is no longer around, his father. Like James Jordan, Gus is an Air Force veteran and is almost exactly the age James would have been had he lived; he's also a man who worked long hours for many years, as an officer in the Chicago Police Department. When I finally met him, I was reminded of guys who used to hang out at my local black barbershop: this was the kind of fellow who knew how to drink bourbon and play bid whist at the same time, who taught his kids to do the right thing and call their elders "Ma'am" and "Sir." Dressed in jeans and a cap, Gus came across as both earthy and down-to-earth, well versed in sports but not obsessed with them, and quietly, vigilantly protective of Jordan. They became friends in 1985, when Jordan was limping around with a broken foot and Gus was working as a security guard at the Chicago Stadium. Gus used to help the young player with his bags as he negotiated the stairs, and somehow the two clicked. How close are Jordan and Gus? Jordan gave the man his championship rings.

Jordan became almost misty when he described the friendship. "Gus is very smart, very intelligent, but yet our rapport together is always joking and kidding," he told me. "And we can't do anything without hanging together. If it's going to the riverboat, he goes. I would never — I feel awkward telling him how much I love him, but yet . . . he knows." For the first time, Jordan's speech was halting. "And it's reciprocal, I can feel it. It's so unique where honestly my best, best friend is sixty-some years old and we share so much now. I can see it's like my father has come back and is living through this guy." Jordan's gaze drifted over to the large photograph of his father, who was killed in the summer of 1993, the victim of a roadside robbery in North Carolina. "It's God's way of telling me that I've gotta make some mature decisions without the support system of a father," he has said of his father's death, and yet he has also sought to re-create such a support system. "I trust Gus," Jordan said softly. "I know he's watching out for me, no matter what."

It has been a blow to him that, just recently, Gus was found to have metastatic lung cancer, and has had to undergo chemotherapy. Over the past several weeks, Jordan has been paying him regular visits, and has made sure that he receives the best possible treatment. "He's got my back," Jordan has always said of Gus. Those guys have each other's back.

"Michael's just a Southern guy," Juanita Jordan, his wife of eight years, tells me. "The night before a big game in the playoffs, he'll sit down and write out a list of names of the people that he has to remember to give tickets to. I find it amazing that he still does that. And he's always welcoming people to the house. His friends—friends he's known since North Carolina—are always there hanging out." She sounds faintly exasperated on this score, and makes it clear that she has had to establish certain boundaries. She grew up on the South Side of Chicago, and her husband's country ways are still slightly foreign to her. "It used to be that they'd just show up. I'd open the door and say 'Yes?' 'Oh, Michael didn't tell you?' 'No, he didn't. What do you want?' And meanwhile the cab's pulling off." A tight smile: "So now they call."

Juanita, who is four years older than her husband, is a poised, attractive, light-skinned woman, who has grown accustomed to the glare of publicity, though not inured to it. She's had a stint writing a column for a Chicago gazette, and recently returned to school, taking courses in journalism at Northwestern University. A lot of her time these days is spent helping to set up the M & J Endowment Fund, which will support community endeavors like shelters for battered women. And a lot of her time is spent raising their three children: Jeffrey, who is nine; Marcus, who is seven; and Jasmine, who is five. They're a photogenic family, though for the most part Michael has sensibly protected them from the klieg lights. Even so, being married to fame—having a husband you can see more easily on the tube than in the flesh—has been a curious experience. "In the early days of our relationship, I almost felt I wasn't part of his life: I was watching this celebrity person, and it was really kind of surreal," she told me. "In the beginning, the children would also be mesmerized by his appearance on the television set, almost thinking, What's he doing in there? But now when one of Daddy's commercials comes on, they'll just say, 'Oh, there's Daddy again,' and go on about their business." Not that turning the TV off would make much difference; these kids live in a world festooned with their father's image.

Michael Jordan has, indeed, been called a human billboard, but he's 45 acutely conscious of the fact that a billboard can be defaced. There are ironies here. Basketball is the most naked of team sports. Jordan has conjectured that he and other players tend to overdress off the court because they must wear so little on the court. Unlike other players, though, he never changes when reporters are patrolling the locker rooms. He will not risk being pictured—by word or image—in a state of undress; and surely it isn't much for even the world's most famous man to ask that his privates not be made public. There's a larger sense, too, in which Jordan doesn't wish to be caught undressed. He who lives by the image may also perish by it. In the fall of 1990, James

Worthy, Jordan's old college teammate and a power forward with the Los Angeles Lakers, was arrested in Houston on charges of solicitation when two call girls he hired turned out to be undercover policewomen; the episode received widespread and undue attention, along with many predictable jests about double-teaming. Among the athletic elect, schadenfreude vies with an even stronger emotion: there but for the grace of God. (One of the oldest NBA jokes: "What's the toughest thing about going on the road?" "Not smiling when you kiss your wife goodbye.") Jordan has said that being caught in a scandal that would taint his image is one of the things he dreads most.

It's an anxiety that his corporate clientele undoubtedly share. David Aaker, who is the author of *Building Strong Brands,* and is a marketing professor at Berkeley, says, "There's a big advantage in having a Pillsbury Doughboy or a Betty Crocker, because at least you know they won't take drugs." Or accumulate large gambling debts to convicted felons, which proved to be Jordan's principal indiscretion. In the early nineties, checks of his amounting to more than a hundred thousand dollars turned up in the possession of some unsavory characters, apparently as a result of high-stakes golf and poker games. Falk told reporters that his client had got hustled; Jordan told them that he was "no Pete Rose"; and Jordan's father told them, reasonably, "The amounts of money to me and you would have been astronomical. But with the kind of money he's making it's peanuts." Then a onetime golf partner wrote a book — tackily entitled *Michael & Me: Our Gambling Addiction . . . My Cry for Help!"* — claiming that Jordan had lost more than a million dollars in bets to him. Jordan was known to be fiercely competitive; now he was known to be a man who would bet on anything.

Not good. But not that bad, either. The betting was confined to recreational pursuits, golf and poker, and, though the stakes were high, Jordan's father was right to point out that they weren't anything he couldn't handle. As a rule of thumb, an indiscretion is truly damaging only if it is discordant with your perceived character: thus teen idols should be discouraged from cruising the men's rooms in public parks, and children's-television actors from getting off in adult-movie theatres. In this case, though, the picture of Jordan as a man possessed to win — in any endeavor — wasn't inconsistent with his demonic presence driving the lane. Besides, the misdeeds were, in nature, nonvenal, nonsexual, and nonviolent. Most fans figured he was much more the better for being a little bad.

Jordan, you could even argue, is as much at risk from his corporate clients as they are from him. It must have been discomfiting when, in the summer of 1990, Jesse Jackson's Operation PUSH* announced a boycott

---

PUSH: People United to Save Humanity, an organization founded in 1971 by Reverend Jesse Jackson (b. 1941) to expand educational and employment opportunities for the disadvantaged

against Nike, charging that the company was taking from the black community without giving back to it. It must have been discomfiting when subsequent controversies arose over Nike's use of low-paid overseas labor. But Jordan has handled the situations with considerable skill, chastising neither the
company nor its critics. To be sure, that nimbleness in sidestepping political
controversy has itself come under attack. The football legend Jim Brown—
speaking at President Clinton's town meeting on race and sports in April—
was only the latest activist to complain that Jordan had failed to use his visibility for social or political causes. Falk says, "Michael is definitely apolitical,"
and he means it as a recommendation. Others say it as a rebuke.

But should athletes be required to serve as political spokesmen? Jesse
Jackson, who likes to say that his role is to be the social conscience of the
mighty ("Whether Michael or the President," he says, in a significant pair-
ing), urges a sensible division of labor. "Why is it expected of a ballplayer or a
boxer to be an astute sociopolitical analyst?" he asks. "That is not what they
are really qualified to do. They move from city to city, and they're on the
road six months a year, and they're not in the best position to be social inter-
preters. Michael has not succumbed to that temptation."

This could sound like a backhanded compliment, but I'm not sure   50
Jackson means it that way. "You're saying he has sense enough to keep his
mouth shut?"

"And that is a great contribution," Jackson replies smoothly. "Besides,
the issue of trading with Indonesia without regard to human rights or child
labor is fundamentally a matter that United States trade policy must address. It
isn't right to shift the burden to him because he's a high-profile salesman."

Jordan has never sacrificed himself to a political cause in the way that
Muhammad Ali did, but he isn't apolitical, either, in the way that Falk makes
out. First, he's not afraid to admit some mildly partisan allegiances. ("I told
Colin Powell I would be right next to him, supporting him.") But, more than
that, he does have a strong social conscience, as was clear when I asked him
about the predominance of blacks in sports. "To be honest, I think it's a
curse," Jordan said. He was talking about the odds—the simple fact that to
practice hoops instead of hitting the books is like spending food money on
the lottery. "Doctors, lawyers, dentists will be practicing for thirty years, but
our window of opportunity is, at the most, eight years," he went on. "That's
a heck of a risk. And we're our own worst problem in terms of the marketing
and projecting"—of burnishing the mystique of the black athlete as opposed
to that of the black professional. Jordan has not occupied the crow's nest of
popular culture so long as to have forgotten how powerful the perch is. Or
how precarious.

Everyone on top lives with a morbid consciousness that fame—heat,
stardom, sociocultural *fit*—is a waterwheel. The rule obtains in the political
and the recreational realms alike: there is, as it were, a physiognomy of for-

tune, and sooner or later it alters. Robert Coover,* in one of his early novel-las, writes about a political fixer who, back when he was a congressman, had the sagacity to foresee his own electoral defeat against a "young tight-lipped challenger":

> You see, I am blessed—or damned, as you will—with puffy pink lips. They helped me to win my seat in the House of Representatives, just as later they helped me to lose it. My short stature, round belly, smooth pink scalp, anonymous name, and occasionally irascible temper no doubt contributed, but mainly it was the fat lips. By thrusting the lower one forward, I was able to project a marvelous complexion of self-righteous anger, a kind of holy Bible-belting zeal for judgment, which comple-mented nicely the central issue, so-called, of my winning campaign: an attack on my incumbent opponent's corruption. That wonderful pout did me little service, however, in defending myself against the same at-tacks two years later. Of course, there were many factors, many vectors, but the fat lips were decisive.

And there you have it. One day the star wakes up, and those projectile Gaultier breastplates aren't doing it anymore; the masses want a toothy, vir-ginal, choir-girl Whitney Houston, not the platinum-haired, sexually adven-turous material girl.* Fandom starts out like a love affair: no detail about the object of desire is too trivial to be of interest, and tabloid reams are filled with personal minutiae. But in time there comes a phase when the object, al-though prized, is taken for granted; then a measure of boredom sets in; and then you agree to see other people.

So the real question, as Jordan correctly maintains, is how the Jordan 55 mystique has lasted as long as it has. "Each and every year, I've been expect-ing it—the drop-off," Jordan says. "Just from human nature, from seeing someone's name in lights for so many years that everyone gets tired of hearing about that person. When you see something consistent all the time, you start to say, 'Well, wait, where's the change? Where is the next person? Where is the next phenomenon?' But it's not happening. And I don't really know why, or how long it's going to last."

In this respect, Jordan's core product—shoes—may be a useful augury. Nike, in the years since its original alliance with Jordan, has become the Mi-crosoft of the sneaker, accounting for more than forty per cent of the three hundred and fifty million pairs of sneakers that Americans bought last year. But now sneaker sales are in general starting to ebb. To Nike's distress, "brown shoes"—as non-sneakers are known in the trade—are gaining among its customers. In March, Nike announced that its 1998 earnings had declined by seventy per cent, and that it had laid off sixteen hundred

---

Robert Coover (b. 1932): American writer
Gaultier breastplates . . . material girl: an allusion to the career of pop star Madonna

employees. Jordan's imminent retirement is likely to show up on the bottom line, too: this has been clear since he spent that sabbatical, courtesy of Jerry Reinsdorf, playing minor-league baseball. "We didn't sell enough baseball shoes to make up for what we lost in basketball shoes," Phil Knight, Nike's charismatic chairman and CEO, says dryly.

Part of Nike's problem may be the overfamiliarity of its distinctive, high-impact advertising. Jordan's sneaker spots have come in every imaginable cinematic style, but during most of the past decade the campaigns produced by the ad agency Wieden & Kennedy, under the creative director Jim Riswold, set the tone: the play of silvery chiaroscuro, the beautiful black-and-white camerawork, the edgy message and understated product sell. What Josef von Sternberg was to Marlene Dietrich or what Scorsese was to De Niro, Wieden & Kennedy* has been to Jordan. Its ads depicted him as an object of allure, a mascot of urban manhood—supple, smooth, commanding, powerful, and hip. A stunning achievement, by any yardstick, but has it overtaken its sell-by date? Joanne DeLuca, a market researcher at Sputnik, has concluded that the deification of unreal athletes is losing its lustre, and that the "hard-edged 'win-at-all-costs' message" is beginning "to turn off younger consumers." More worrisome is the growing sense of backlash against the Air Jordan dynasty, against the hegemony of Nike generally, and even against what some people are cattily calling the swooshtika.

Has Jordan been overexposed? Phil Knight* has made no secret of his concern that Jordan's value to Nike was attenuated by his other endorsements. Nike may own the "jumpman" logo—an icon of Jordan jumping toward an unseen basket—but it doesn't own Jordan's visage. His endorsements for other companies may have helped entrench the brand that is Michael Jordan but lessened the specialness of his association with Nike. "If you were teaching a course in marketing, that wouldn't be the way to do it," Knight told me, adding quickly, "But he has overcome all those mistakes by his greatness." It's possible to be less sanguine about this situation. The advertiser's main enemy, of course, is what the industry calls "clutter," which is to say other people's ads. You hear estimates that the average consumer encounters almost three thousand marketing messages a day. Not a few of those messages bear the countenance of Michael Jordan. A koan for Madison Avenue: What do you do when you are your own clutter?

Jordan's counsellors grapple with these issues. After a few years of an endorsement spree, they halved the number of his corporate affiliations and increasingly emphasized long-term deals: since 1989, Jordan hasn't made a deal shorter

---

Josef von Sternberg . . . Wieden & Kennedy: Gates compares Jordan's relationship to his ad agency to that between famous actors and directors

Phil Knight (b. 1938): founder (in 1972) and chair of Nike, Inc.

than ten years. In general, Falk has been imposing discipline upon his client's endorsement range, restricting his principal product associations to Nike, Quaker Oats, Rayovac, Sara Lee, Bijan (Michael Jordan Cologne was the top-selling new fragrance in its début year), Wilson, CBS SportsLine, and WorldCom. Last year, Jordan's income was estimated to have been in excess of seventy million dollars.

Jordan's price tag not only reflects his extraordinary utility as an endorser; it may even contribute to it. There's a school of thought that says the cost of advertising must be considered part of the *content* of the advertising—that the key message of lots of ad campaigns is "Look how much we're spending on this ad campaign!" Marshall McLuhan* didn't get it quite right: the medium isn't the message; the moola is the message. And the value of the celebrity endorsement? According to the economist Mark Hertzendorf, a big problem with ad campaigns is that consumers are unlikely to see all of an advertiser's commercials, and so might not be properly impressed by its lavishness—a lavishness that implies its expectation of strong sales, which, in turn, implies the excellence of its product. The solution is to pack more price information into every spot; and you can do that by featuring a celebrity endorsement, since viewers know that such endorsements cost big. ("For example, a consumer who views one commercial containing an endorsement by Jerry Seinfeld can immediately conclude that the firm is spending millions of dollars on advertising," Hertzendorf observes.) The fact that Jordan is the winner-take-all pitchman—the one whose services are known to be the priciest—means that, whatever the product is, he can be relied upon to send a message about a generous ad budget, and so about company confidence.

Falk has long had an intuitive grasp of the Hertzendorf effect—he knew it would be *good* for Gatorade to cough up eighteen million dollars for the privilege of being guzzled by the greatest—but his latest brainstorm is to generate "marketing synergies" among Jordan's client corporations. "We're trying to intermarry his companies," Falk tells me. "For instance, since his next-to-last deal was with the telephone company WorldCom, we're trying to get as many of his existing companies to pick up WorldCom for their long-distance carrier and business carrier as possible." So far, it's unclear that any of them have done so, corporations being an even harder sell than consumers.

Still, Falk gets points for innovation. He likes to speak of himself as an artist, and his clients as canvases. The paint is pretty much dry on the Jordan landscape. "Most of my work for Michael is finished," he says, sounding almost elegiac. "It's not like he's looking for a lot more deals."

Truth to tell, it's hard to stay entirely unmoved on the subject of Jordan's retirement. From a fan's perspective, that's because the game will have

Marshall McLuhan (1911–80): professor of English at the University of Toronto and writer on communication; author of *The Medium Is the Massage* (1967)

lost its greatest and most exciting player—a man who, at the advanced age of thirty-five, is the highest scorer in the NBA this season. From Falk's perspective, it's because—Joe Namath and those Noxzema commercials notwithstanding—the record concerning the commercial longevity of retired athletes is not altogether encouraging. All the same, Juanita Jordan tells me, "once he retires, the companies that he endorses products for are going to pick up a lot of his time—I think he really wants to sink his teeth into the Brand Jordan concept with Nike, and to follow through with the commitments he has made to the major companies he is endorsing." Hence Falk's mantra: "Being a basketball player has become his job, but it's not his image." And yet you might say that Jordan's job *is* his image, in that being Michael Jordan has become his principal line of work.

Which means that Jordan has become a prisoner of repute. His livelihood as an endorser amounts to a gilded captivity, because his currency is his character. And it is so very hard to be so very good. He has summed up his relationship with Charles Barkley, the trash-talking forward of the Houston Rockets, as "a sort of good-son, bad-son thing," where "Charles gets to say all the things I'd like to say." And, though Jordan isn't so close to the Bulls' own enfant terrible, Dennis Rodman—he's recently made it clear how much his patience has been taxed by him—he views Rodman's bad-as-I-wanna-be act with some wistfulness. We're talking about what happened to Dennis Rodman years ago, when, the story goes, he came home to find out that his wife was sleeping with Vinnie Johnson, then Rodman's teammate on the Detroit Pistons. "It flipped him out," Jordan says. "It changed him. It changed his whole persona, his personality toward his teammates." He's referring to Rodman's now trademark combination of introversion and flamboyance. I tend to be skeptical about the lore of formative moments, but what strikes me is how fraternal Jordan sounds. Again, there's a sort of division of labor, with Rodman's freakishness helping to secure Jordan's normality. Jordan says, "I think he's a good person at heart. Like most people, he's found a niche to make a living."

Like most people, but not like Jordan. His burdens come from being the very opposite of a niche player. For one thing, the work of exposure, of supporting a global brand, presents clear-cut logistical problems for maintaining something resembling a private life. Jordan figures that it's been a decade since he has been able to go outside without getting mobbed, and says that he "can't wait till it changes." The media frenzy has its own troughs and peaks. In the speculation-filled days before his official return to basketball in the spring of 1995, the paparazzi would do things like tape over the card reader on the players' parking lot, hoping that Jordan would have to get out of his car and expose himself to their cameras. Of necessity, Jordan has become adept at setting limits: "I've come to grips, saying, 'Leave me alone, this is my family time, this is my private time.' And there are a lot of assholes who don't understand that. I can really get harsh if I feel you're infringing way past the niceness that I try to show you." He speaks softly, but you can hear the steel.

There are various people who help protect him, and sometimes become part of his extended family. As we're winding things up at North LaSalle Street, Jordan tells me about George Koehler, his friend and driver: "When I first came to Chicago, thirteen years ago, I didn't know one soul, and the Bulls didn't pick me up. I'm getting off the plane, and I run into this guy. He has his own limousine company, and his passenger didn't show up. So he comes over to me and gives me a ride."

At some point during the account, George Koehler himself makes an appearance, and is affably assured by Jordan that he's been telling me lies about him. For both of them, in a manner that's typically American and male, the vocabulary of intimacy is insult.

"Did you charge him?" I ask Koehler.

"Yeah," Jordan puts in, "he *over*charged me, I tell you."

"I didn't overcharge him." Koehler sulks.   70

"He ripped me off then," Jordan says, "and he's been ripping me off ever since."

"Actually, he gave me a huge tip," Koehler says, brightening at the memory. "I told him twenty-five bucks, he gave me fifty bucks and said, 'Keep the change.'"

"So I'm down here looking around and I'm scared as shit," Jordan says. "I don't know where the hell I'm going in a city that I've never been to. But he watched out for me."

"I'm paying for it now," George says.

"And he watches out for me now," Jordan says. Maybe it sounds a little 75 earnest, so he adds, "By lying. Being a pain in the ass."

In *The Frenzy of Renown,* a classic study of fame and its history, Leo Braudy writes that seasoned spectators "look not for style so much as sincerity," and that, traditionally, it was "the sports stars who most significantly handled the problem of public exposure because at their best they represented an unself-conscious perfection of the body, displayed for the pleasure of their fans. Here was fame unsullied by the alloy of history, language, or any mediation but the body's own." Jordan has rewritten the rules. In one magical package, Michael Jordan is both Muhammad Ali and Mister Clean, Willie Mays and the Marlboro Man. But if America's powerbrands helped insure Jordan's status as an international symbol of America, Jordan—and the sense we have that he's *ours*—has become one of those things that constitute our identity as Americans, as citizens of the winner-take-all society. Trait transference isn't a one-stop affair. And the work of what we call globalization, and what the rest of the world knows as Americanization, is never done. Michael Jordan, putting on his game face, says, "My father told me, 'If you're going to die, son, don't die with no bullets in your gun.' And I live by that."

When I venture beyond the quiet of Jordan's suite and into his restaurant, I feel oddly reassured by the loud carnival of Jordan iconography: huge posters, enormous murals, rows and rows of framed magazine covers, cascades of photographs—an empire of signs. The bar-and-grill on the first floor is dominated by a twenty-foot-by-six-foot video screen where customers can watch Jordan's greatest moments over and over and over again. It's a spectacle of kitsch—and, yes, of utter physical transcendence. Gazing for a spell at the highlights loop, I feel somehow uplifted by the procession of fadeaways, jump shots, dunks, fakeouts, double-pumps, alley-oops, layups. They also serve who only stand and cheer.

QUESTIONING THE TEXT

1. Early in the essay (paragraph 4), Gates includes a lengthy list of products endorsed by Michael Jordan. Why do you think Gates uses the list at this point? What are its intended effects? What effect does it have on you as a reader? Jot down notes in response to these questions and bring them to class for discussion.

2. Gates argues that "'branding' can be a reciprocal process" (paragraph 22); that is, the celebrity image and the brand image help sell each other. Working with a classmate, note the evidence Gates offers throughout the essay in support of this claim. Does his argument hold for other celebrities and brands? Brainstorm this question together. Then write a brief group report to your class explaining your answer and giving evidence to support it.

3. Consider how Gates uses adjectives (for example, "coltish" in paragraph 1) to paint a picture of Jordan in this essay. Working with two class-mates, make a list of all the adjectives Gates uses to describe his subject. What picture of Jordan emerges from your list of adjectives? What do the adjectives suggest about Gates's view of and attitude toward Jordan?

MAKING CONNECTIONS

4. In "'By Means of the Visible': A Picture's Worth" (p. 473), Mitchell Stephens claims that "[c]ertain pictures can put most sentences to shame. But this is as far as I'm willing to go in making the case for still images." Review Stephens's essay alongside Gates's piece, looking for evidence of how Gates might respond to Stephens's claim. Would Gates be likely to agree? Why, or why not?

5. John Updike opens "The Mystery of Mickey Mouse" (p. 489) with a very short sentence: "It's all in the ears." Use this technique to write a new opening sentence for Gates's essay: "It's all _____." Then ex-plain in a paragraph why you think your sentence would be an effective opening for "Net Worth."

6. Look at the photograph of Jordan in the color insert. In what ways does it support the image of Jordan that Gates creates here?

JOINING THE CONVERSATION

7. Choose a brand-name image that you feel especially attracted to or repelled by and then collect as many examples of it as you can from print ads, billboards, television spots, Web sites, and so on. Study your examples carefully. What is used to sell the brand-name image? What values are suggested by or associated with the image? What kinds of appeals does it rely on? (You might review the guidelines for reading visuals in Chapter 1, p. 8.) Write a brief critical analysis of the image based on your findings.

8. David Falk, Jordan's "image" manager, tells Gates that some people "think that I'm Dr. Frankenstein and [that] I cooked up this formula in my laboratory to make Michael the marketing king of the century" (paragraph 23). How do you respond to Falk's analogy? Do you see Jordan as the monster and Falk as the Dr. Frankenstein who created him? In what sense might the analogy hold—and in what sense might it be flawed? Address these questions in a brief exploratory essay.

KENNETH BROWER
Photography in the Age of Falsification

KENNETH BROWER *(b. 1944) has been thinking and writing about nature nearly all his life. As the son of David Brower, founder of Friends of the Earth and past director of Sierra Club, Brower knew from childhood many major figures in the early environmental movement, including noted artists and photographers. He began editing books about nature and the environment even before his graduation from college. Brower's own books include* With Their Islands around Them *(1974),* Wake of the Whale *(1979),* A Song for Satawal *(1983),* Yosemite: An American Treasure *(1990),* Realms of the Sea *(1991), and* American Legacy: Our National Forests *(1997).*

In the following essay, originally published in the Atlantic Monthly *(May 1998), Brower takes a close look at an emerging controversy: should the goals of photography be honesty and accuracy—or should digital manipulation of photographs go unchallenged? Brower explores several perspectives on the issue of "digital photofakery," giving detailed examples of images that are "pure" and others that are digitally altered in dramatic ways. In the bargain, he raises many questions about the relationship between images and reality, and about the role we (as viewers and participants) play in determining that relationship.*

I chose this essay because I've long admired Brower's writing and because the questions he raises about how—and why—to distinguish between appearance and reality are as old as Western history but nonetheless still pressing today. —A.L.

PRESTIDIGITATION

Thirty years ago, in the age before the cruise ships came, I spent four months in the Galápagos Islands with the photographer Eliot Porter. The Galápagos were wilder, less-visited islands then. They had yet to become the most photographed archipelago on earth. Porter was making the pictures, and I was gathering notes, for the first volume in what would become a vast library, that ponderous collection of large-format Galápagos books now decorating coffee tables everywhere. Porter, our first great master of nature photography in color, was then sixty-four, the grand old man of his art. I was twenty-one, just beginning a career that was to be spent in large part outdoors in the company of nature photographers. Among my duties in the Galápagos were helping to lug Porter's 4×5 camera and tripod up volcanoes, rowing dories in through surf, and hunting meat, like Robinson Crusoe, on various islands with our guide's old bolt-action .22. It was one of the best times of my life.

Accompanying our expedition was Tad Nichols, a former Disney cameraman, and in the islands we crossed paths with the British nature photographer Alan Root, then just beginning his own remarkable career. In the Galápagos I had my first opportunity to study the habits of cameramen in the wild.

Anchored off Santiago Island one evening, over a dinner of feral goat, the photographers grew expansive and the talk turned to nature fakery. Porter was a purist. He believed in shooting straight. He admitted to having occasionally moved a stone or feather or piece of driftwood to improve one of his compositions, but he was generally opposed to this sort of manipulation, and he grew uneasy talking about it. Root and Nichols came from a more pragmatic, rough-and-tumble school of commercial nature photography. Root told us the story of a *Life* cover a colleague had done. The image had begun in the mind of one of the magazine's editors. By a kind of redactional clairvoyance this editor, seated comfortably at his desk in Manhattan, had seen it all clearly: leopard and its kill in thorn tree, branches framing a setting sun. The photographer set off in quest of this vision, traveling the East African savanna for weeks with a captive leopard, killing antelopes, draping the carcasses in the branches of various thorn trees, and cajoling the leopard to lie proudly on the "kill," a tableau that the photographer shot against a succession of setting suns. Tad Nichols laughed ruefully yet appreciatively. He told the story of his own work on Disney's *The Living Desert,* most of which was filmed on ersatz dunes built on a vast sound-stage table. Root countered with a story of some clever photoduplicity, the details of which I have since forgotten. Nichols came back with a tale of how Disney's minions bulldozed lemmings off cliffs for the famous lemming-suicide sequence.

And so it went, confession piling on confession. Both Root and Nichols affected a sad cynicism about the unseemly things they were called upon to do, but underneath, clearly, was a grifter's glee at various con jobs well executed—and under *that,* if I am not mistaken, was a soupçon of genuine shame. At twenty-one, I was scarcely weaned from the Disney nature documentaries. I particularly remember one revelation of how Uncle Walt's men had fabricated the hawk-kills-flying-squirrel episode. (Assistant grip stands on tall stepladder with pouch of flying squirrels. Grip tosses squirrels—unpaid rodent extras—skyward one by one, as in skeet shoot, until trained hawk, after dozens of misses, finally gets it right.)

Photofakery, then, is nothing new. The first attempts at it no doubt followed shortly upon Daguerre's initial success with his camera obscura. But photography of late has entered a brave new epoch. No photographer today would bother cruising the bush with trained leopards to fake a sunset shot. Anyone with Adobe Photoshop ($589 when I last checked; $599 with a scanner thrown in) could find a perfectly adequate leopard in the zoo, digitally edit out the bars of the cage, tree the cat with subtle movements of mouse, bloodlessly procure a dead antelope (if his computer held any in files), and then set the whole collage against a virtual setting sun. Indeed, he could tree

5

his leopard against the rings of Saturn if he was so inclined. A leopard can't change his spots, but the modern photographer can easily do it for him. With some of the applications now available to filmmakers, the photographer could arrange for the leopard to lose a fight with John Wayne, or to dance with Fred Astaire, who has been shown dancing with a vacuum cleaner in a recent television commercial.

"In a strict sense photography can never be abstract, for the camera is incapable of synthetic integration," Ansel Adams wrote in 1932. Synthetic integration, unimaginable sixty-five years ago by one of the art's great technicians, is now full upon us. The old magic is fast becoming a kind of prestidigitation.

More and more digitally doctored images are appearing in the media. The trend alarms a number of photographers. It worries certain editors, and it worries me. I am troubled not only as a colleague—a nonfiction writer whose text often runs alongside photographs of wild lands and wildlife—but also as a casual student of the history of nature photography, an admirer of the art, and a friend of many who practice it. I have shared tents and blinds and small boats and even the mouthpieces of scuba regulators with these people. I love them for their hardiness, their courage, and their constant griping about the weather, sticky shutters, leaky housings, bad strobes, native customs, the myopia of photo editors, and the intransigence of wild animals. I am always impressed by their skill at improvisation in the field. I admire—to a certain extent—their ingenuity. But it is clear to me that the photographer's work philosophy is not always congruent with the expectations of those of us who view the work. Too few photographers, I think, appreciate how directly the new technology aims at the heart of the credibility that distinguishes this art form from others.

The controversy over digital manipulation has been simmering for some time. It first surfaced in 1982, when *National Geographic* ran a computer-altered photo of the Pyramids at Giza on its cover. To the traditional adjustments of reality that the photographer had already made—shooting with a telephoto lens to exaggerate the scale of the Pyramids and persuading three camel riders to pass a second time before those great tombs—the magazine's editors added a new one: digitally moving the camels backward a few paces.

In 1991 the board of directors of the National Press Photographers Association (NPPA), noting that emerging electronic technology enabled "the manipulation of the content of an image in such a way that the change is virtually undetectable," adopted a statement of principle: "As journalists we believe the guiding principle of our profession is accuracy; therefore, we believe it is wrong to alter the content of a photograph in any way that deceives the public."

The North American Nature Photography Association has yet to agree   10 on any principle so strong. Many NANPA members feel that they have a poetic license broader than the one issued to their cousins, the photojournalists of the NPPA. Still, at the first Annual Nature Photography Forum, held by NANPA in 1994, the ethics session was dominated by fierce debate on the issues of nature photography in commercial game farms and of digital manipulation. Tom Mangelsen, a wildlife photographer from Jackson, Wyoming, lamented the new trends and tallied the damage they had caused the profession: the loss of incentive to compete in the wild, the loss of the sense of adventure, the loss of pride in one's work, and the loss of the public's respect for wildlife photography.

Art Wolfe, a nature photographer based in Seattle, was the first in the crowd to respond. "We're living in an age of back-swinging toward conservative ethics," Wolfe said. "Whenever I hear the word 'ethics,' it raises the hair on the back of my neck. The point here is that we all have different standards. I certainly don't want to be told by somebody else what I should be doing."

The debate intensified in 1996, when exposés in the *Denver Post* and the *Seattle Post-Intelligencer* revealed how Wolfe's 1994 book *Migrations* had been fabricated. In about a third of the book's images the wildlife—caribou, zebra, geese, greater sandhill cranes—had been digitally enhanced, and some had been digitally cloned and multiplied.

"Nature photographs are generally accepted as and trusted to be straightforward records of what the photographer witnessed and recorded on film in a single instant," the photographer Gary Braasch wrote in a letter to the NANPA ethics committee in June of 1996, as the debate over *Migrations* fulminated in the camera magazines. "This is an acceptance hallowed by years of communication among photographers, editors, publishers, and viewers."

The fact is that this acceptance has often been "hallowed" in the breach. As the advocates of digital doctoring like to point out, the old boys faked it too.

Recently I checked my recollections of Eliot Porter with John 15 Rohrbach, the associate curator of photographs at the Amon Carter Museum, in Fort Worth, and the custodian of the Eliot Porter collection there. Rohrbach confirmed my impression that Porter did not believe in setups but was sometimes tempted. He corroborated my sense that Porter was uneasy discussing the matter. "We actually have a picture of him hacking away at a cactus to get a picture of a roadrunner nest," Rohrbach said. "Paul Strand was even more adamant that no retouching at all should occur. But there are prints where Strand drew in manholes or etched out people to balance his compositions."

In his first years of printing his most famous photograph, *Moonrise, Hernandez, New Mexico, 1941,* Ansel Adams, in his words, "allowed some random clouds in the upper sky area to show." They always annoyed him, and in the 1970s he arranged in the darkroom for those clouds to evaporate. In his celebrated *Winter Sunrise, the Sierra Nevada from Lone Pine, California,* Adams deleted from the dark foothills of the middle ground the big "LP" that the little town's high school students had laid out in whitewashed stones.

This image of the Sierra at sunrise—distant horse grazing beneath a horizon of bare aspens in sunlight; dark, unblemished foothills in shadow; and finally the bright, jagged cordillera of the Sierra in sunlight—opens *This Is the American Earth,* the first volume of the "exhibit-format series" that my father, David Brower, began in 1960 at the Sierra Club. Under my father's editorship the series eventually grew to thirty volumes, thirteen of which I wrote or edited. As a fourteen-year old, well before my father thought to press me into service, I watched *This Is the American Earth* come together at Adams's house in San Francisco. The creative excitement among the three principal contributors—Adams, my father, and Nancy Newhall, the author of the text—was a wonderful thing to behold until the martinis kicked in, always derailing Newhall first. I remember the print of *Lone Pine* on Adams's table. I have a vague recollection that the photographer was less than proud of having excised the "LP." My father recalls otherwise—that Adams simply thought the town's initials messed up his picture and he wanted them out of there.

In 1964, taking a kind of sabbatical after my freshman year at Berkeley, I assembled my first exhibit-format book, a photo essay on California's Big Sur coast. Early in the editing I worked for two weeks out of Adams's new house in Carmel Highlands. By day I collected the work of the several photographic geniuses resident along that shore. By night, back at Adams's house, I watched the maestro "dodge and burn" in his darkroom. To dodge—to withhold light from an area of the print for a timed period in the developing process—was once considered, as the term suggests, somewhat underhanded, but it had long since become accepted practice. The same was true of burning, or concentrating light on an area of the print. Adams's darkroom, then just two years old, was state-of-the-art. He had designed it to produce mural-size prints. The enlarging camera was huge, like a Brownie from Brobdingnag. The bellows on the thing would have worked for Vulcan at his forge. Mounted on rails, the camera faced a rail-mounted easel holding the print paper. Adams wore a blue apron that protected everything but the turquoise-and silver clasp of his string tie. Working over the nascent print, Adams would aim his great deviant beak at it appraisingly. (He had broken his nose when he was four years old, in the San Francisco quake of 1906, which had thrown him against a garden wall. In crushing his septum, the great earthquake was also responsible, I have always assumed, for the strange adenoidal quality of his voice.) His fingers, gnarled by arthritis, would hold the dodging wand. Making little incantatory circles with the wand over the area he wanted lightened, he would laugh his crazy, nasal, Mephistophelian laugh.

It was all white magic, I can't help thinking. The small adjustments to reality that occurred in Ansel Adams's darkroom, if crimes at all, were misdemeanors. That photographs should be "straightforward records of what the photographer witnessed and recorded on film in a single instant" still seems a worthy ideal, despite the fact that some of our greatest have stretched and jiggered it. Many fine principles are hallowed in the breach. This does not mean that they exert no influence, or that we should dispense with them entirely. . . .

A Flock of Golden Retrievers

Among photographers, opinion on digital manipulation seems to fall 20
into either of two schools, the principal spokesmen for which are Galen
Rowell and Art Wolfe, who have both been collaborators of mine. These
men are energetic in a force-of-nature way, tireless travelers, prodigiously
productive. Neither is a photographer so much as a little but prolific photographic industry, producing books, prints, postcards, and advertising images.

Mountain Light Photography, Galen and Barbara Rowell's shop, is a converted warehouse in Emeryville, California, not far from the shore of San Francisco Bay. When I visited recently, I was greeted at the door by Khumbu, the
Rowells' fifteen-year-old golden retriever. Khumbu wore a bandanna around
his neck—a memento of a recent grooming visit to Dogs by Diane. The hair on
his head and face had gone completely gray since I had seen him last. The bandanna and the salon pampering it symbolized seemed an indignity to an old out-
doorsman like Khumbu, but he bore it cheerfully enough.

Mountain Light is bright and spacious inside, the white walls of the
first-floor lobby museum-lit and hung with an ever changing gallery of Rowell's prints. Waiting for the photographer to appear, I made a circuit of his
walls: *Sunset over Machu Picchu. Last Light on Horsetail Falls. Polar Bear Resting
against Its Mother.* I lingered before Rowell's most famous photograph, *Rainbow over the Potala Palace, Lhasa.* The rainbow strikes the palace dead center.
This would put the pot of gold in the throne room or the pantry of the
palace, formerly owned by Rowell's friend the Dalai Lama. On the evidence
of this photo, Tibetan Buddhism is the answer. The rainbow seemed much
brighter than in other prints of it I had seen. I gave it a hard look and then the
benefit of the doubt. I moved on. At *Cuernos del Paine at Dawn, Lago Pehoe,
Patagonia,* I paused again. For years I never quite believed this picture—the
febrile radiance of the yellow-flowering shrubs in the foreground, the im-
probable aquamarine of the glacial lake in the middle distance, the sheer
phantasmagoric granite towers of the "Horns" of Paine in the sky. Then, last
February, on an assignment to southern Chile, I found myself at dawn on the
shore of this very lake, and I saw that it was all true. I crossed the room to
Alaska Brown Bear, Katmai National Park. The bear is standing in the white
torrent of a cascade, a salmon poised in mid-leap just inches from its open
jaws. The shutter had arrested the fish forever in the instant before its demise.

Another brown bear was once on this wall, rearing to its full height and
roaring directly into the camera. This bear was an actor named Bart, a grizzly
everyman, the brown bear you see in all the movies and commercials requiring brown bears. When Bart was mounted here, roaring his signature roar,
Mountain Light's visitors all gravitated to him. How in God's name, everyone
asked Rowell, had he managed to take this photograph and survive? When
Rowell explained that the bear was an acquaintance and a thespian, he saw a
little light of admiration die in their eyes. It seemed to him that they now
looked differently at all his pictures. He retired Bart from the wall.

Rowell, appearing at the head of the stairway, invited me up to his projection room. Khumbu followed at my heels. Khumbu was named for the Everest region of Nepal, one of his master's favorite hangouts. The dog was a climber once, but now his ascent of the stairway was labored and slow.

In the photography workshops Rowell teaches, he must, he believes, do 25 more than impart technique. These days he needs to impart ethics as well. Even as images grow sharper with digital enhancement, the honest path grows murkier, and Rowell feels that students need guidance. Today's class was just Khumbu and me. Rowell loaded the carousel of his ethics lesson on the projector, closed the curtain at the door, and pressed the button. The first slide showed an Eadweard Muybridge sequence of running horses from 1872. This particular series had settled a $25,000 bet over whether all four hooves are ever off the ground at the same time. (They are.) The Muybridge was a relic of the day when the photograph was incontrovertible, prima facie evidence. The second slide showed a photograph doctored by Senator Joe Mc-Carthy to juxtapose one of his targets with some Communist or fellow traveler. Guilt by association is a dubious proposition to begin with. This was *fake* guilt by association. The McCarthy represented the photograph as hoax. Rowell pressed the button again.

Elephants. A herd on the move, its subgroups tinted in several colors.

"This picture is from Art Wolfe's book *Migrations*," Rowell said. "This is how it appeared in a story on digital manipulation in the *Denver Post.* They've color-coded the animals to show groups that are identical and have been cloned." He walked to the screen and began pointing. "This whole group of seven is this group of seven. Three of *these* seven, up here, are these three down here—which have been cloned yet again, right here. This one is this one is this one is this one. This pair is this pair, and this pair is this pair. Fifty-four elephants in a picture that originally had fifteen."

The Pyramids at Giza in the smoky light of evening. Three camels and their riders in the foreground.

"The famous *National Geographic* cover," Rowell said. "The Pyramids were moved in relation to the camel riders to make room for the logo. Originally the cover was to be a picture of mine of a Tibetan boy. They kicked it off because the Chinese Embassy objected. The Chinese said they wouldn't let *National Geographic* writers and photographers into Tibet again if they ran that picture on the cover. It was already at the printer's. When they decided to yank mine out, they needed an instant replacement. They chose this picture, which was a horizontal. In making it a vertical they reset the riders."

Zebras. A tapestry of stripes, the herd standing so close together that not a speck 30 *of ground or wildebeest or anything else non-zebraic shows in the frame.*

"This is a close-up of the cover of *Migrations*," Rowell said. He pointed to the face of a zebra just above the *t* in the book's title. Then he pointed to another zebra face just below the *e* in Art Wolfe's name. "Zebras have a 'fingerprint' in their patterns," he said. "These are different frames of the same zebra."

Cleft rock in silhouette against pale evening sky, with pink, ethereal cirrus above.
I recognized this photo as Rowell's own, one I had always admired: blackness versus brightness, earth versus sky, near versus far. Solidity of stone versus ethereality of vapor. "This picture was digitally altered on the cover of my book *Mountain Light*," Rowell said. "In order to make it fit the cover, they did two things—with my permission. They 'chopped and channeled' it, like an old hot-rod. They took a section of sky out, which moved the cloud down so they wouldn't have to crop it so much. I felt there was a very good rationale for doing it, and that it preserved the original image I had in mind."

Negative space has positive virtues in art. Whole essays have been written on the dynamic interval—the electric synapse—between God's outstretched finger and Adam's on the Sistine Chapel ceiling. I asked Rowell which he preferred of the intervals between the heaven and earth of his own picture. Without hesitation he answered that he liked his original cleft rock and cloud. "That's why I took it that way. But if I had just stepped back and bent down, I would have gotten a picture with the cloud a little lower. I thought that the alteration was a little bit on the edge, but okay."

Cheetahs. A mother cat reclining on grass, six cubs piled upon her.   35
This cheetah family portrait, according to Rowell, was an Art Wolfe composite of two zoo photographs, one of a mother and single cub, the other of five cubs. Wolfe had digitally removed a zoo fence from the background and reseeded the area with virtual grass. The image had drawn fire at a conference of the North American Nature Photography Association, where an editor from the World Wildlife Fund had objected to it. "The complaint," Rowell said, "was that cheetahs can't have six cubs. Art's defense is that the zoologists who declared this were wrong. Apparently the literature says they can have as many as eight. So Art says, 'Yep, it's good natural history. They can have up to eight.'"

Whether or not six or eight cubs made sense, something was wrong with the photograph. I could not quite put my finger on it. It might have been in the attention of the cats, which seemed divided in an unnatural way. (Two things of considerable and absolutely equal interest seemed to be approaching the group of felines from different directions.) It might have been in the calm of the mother. She did not look like a cheetah inundated by six cubs. She had the relaxed eyes of a mother of one—which was what she was. The more I looked at the picture, the more artificial it appeared.

"In summary," Rowell said, and he pushed the button to advance the carousel. *Bald eagle.* "Totally wild photo, no problem." *Bust of bald eagle, filling frame.* "Totally captive photo. No problem for a lot of markets. Federal Express. Post Office. That's my photo, but it's a captive eagle, and I wouldn't sell it for a story on wild eagles without putting 'captive' on my slide mount. Some people would." *Eagle soaring against snowy ridge.* "Here's a photo that I manipulated years ago. That was an eagle on a gray sky that I superimposed against a ridge of Mount McKinley—a 'sandwich.' I did it for a slide show about twenty years ago, set to music. I never put it out for publication. Now I wouldn't even create it. I feel it would compromise my work."

Polar bear. A rear view, the bear relaxing on its belly, facing away across a channel of open water and small icebergs.

"This photo, advertised here in an ad for Tony Stone Images, became 40 very controversial. National Geographic Online, representing the Discovery Channel and the Explorer TV series, bought this image from Tony Stone without passing it by the editorial side of the magazine. It appeared in a full-page ad in *National Geographic*. As soon as it was discovered, *National Geographic* pulled the ad. This is a bear in a zoo in Ohio, superimposed digitally against the Lemaire Channel, in Antarctica, where there are no polar bears."

The Arctic is named for its *arctos*, its bear. Its antipodes have never had one. The photograph had reversed the polarity of the planet. I laughed at the boldness, or perhaps it was the oversight, that allowed the photographer to fill this empty Antarctic niche. The bear was a hoax and an oxymoron, but it was funny. The setting, Lemaire Channel, could have fooled me—its icebergs looked Arctic enough. But again I was nagged by something wrong in the picture. The longer I looked at it, the more it seemed to fall apart.

The bear's stubby tail and the dark pads of its rear paws faced the camera. It lay completely oblivious of the cameraman behind. Polar bears are far-ranging predators with wonderful sensory equipment. They inhabit vast solitudes and always know when they have company. In all the photographs of wild polar bears that I have seen (save those taken at Churchill, a town in Manitoba, where

the bears are semihabituated to human beings), the bear's nose is elevated as he tries to get a whiff of the cameraman, or he is moving off uneasily. This supposed Antarctic bear was indifferent to the human being behind it, and that was not natural. The bear's backside and the hams of its legs were matted and stained yellow. The pattern looked peculiar. In sedentary periods wild polar bears are often tinted an attractive old-ivory yellow all over, by their urine, but here the yellow was localized. The bear had dyed itself, I suspected, by sitting for long periods in its urine, before its digital liberation from a concrete slab in Cincinnati and its transport to the wrong pole. Rowell himself had not noticed this pattern. "I think you're right," he said, staring at his screen. "You wouldn't see it like that by open water."

Earthrise. Whiteness of moon in foreground. Across the barren lunar terrain a message scrawled in longhand: "To Tony, I hope you can see this someday. Bill Anders, Apollo 8."

"This was taken by Colonel William Anders in 1968," Rowell said. "He held his Hasselblad up to the window and fired away." Rowell, an acquaintance of Anders's, had begged a copy for his son Tony, and the print had arrived with its dedication in longhand, along with a cover note: "Here's a picture your dad asked me to send you that I took on my last vacation."

Earth levitated for a while in the darkened room, against the blackness of 45
eternal space. Khumbu, the golden retriever gone gray, had no interest in
earthrise. For dogs, compelling terrestrial images are much closer under the
nose. Khumbu put his chin on my thigh and looked soulfully into my eyes for
attention. He was highly redolent of old dog, not a bad smell, and I scratched
him behind the ear. Khumbu's master, for his part, seemed hypnotized by the
image. "This is all about lifting the camera and taking a picture of what you see,"
he said finally. "It's different from a remote picture that you don't quite believe
in the same way because there was no human being there behind the camera."

Snapped robotically, NASA photos of earthrise, more detailed and tightly
composed, have been published, Rowell said. In his opinion, none has the
poetic power or has evoked the sentiment and acclaim that this one has—the
shutter tripped by a human finger. Rowell believes, along with many, that
Anders's earthrise is epochal, that it is the most important photograph in the
history of environmental awareness.

The colonel's earthrise reminded Rowell of the words of another colleague, the Dalai Lama. The two collaborated on the book *My Tibet*—photos
by Rowell, text by His Holiness. In 1987, at a symposium of neuroscientists,
psychologists, and artificial-intelligence experts, Rowell said, the Dalai Lama
was asked how Buddhists validate their perceptions. The scientists wondered,
among other things, whether Buddhists accept the existence of external phenomena apart from concepts already in place in their minds. The answer, the
Dalai Lama said, was in the Buddhist concept called Extremely Hidden Phenomena. "I know the earth to be a round bluish globe," he explained, "although I have never seen it and have not done any conclusive reasoning
about it. I know the earth is round by relying on the words of someone who
has seen it and proved it with photographs. First you must prove that the person is reliable by various reasonings—that there is no reason he should tell
lies with false photos. After this you understand that the earth is round, although you haven't seen it. This is called inference based upon belief. You
have to rely on a person who has already had this kind of experience and has
no reason to tell lies."

Rowell glanced at me to see if the aptness of this had sunk in. Then he
quoted another astronaut, Rusty Schweickart, who had followed Colonel Anders into space. "You are the sensing element for humanity," Schweickart reported on returning. "And that becomes a rather special responsibility." That
special responsibility, in Rowell's opinion, is shared by photographers, too.

Cranes taking wing in Africa. Above them an impala leaping.

"Final picture," Rowell said. "This is from Ernst Haas's *The Creation*. 50
The impala was in the middle of one of those high bounds. Back then, when
The Creation was published, this was just a wonderful serendipity. Now the
first thing somebody would think is 'Ah, how did he fake it?' And that's what
we've lost."

Downstairs, as Rowell and Khumbu herded me toward the door, we
paused at a computer monitor in the stockroom. Rowell asked an assistant to

call up a particular image for me. The assistant searched rank upon rank of icons. Each icon marked the file of a photograph. The assistant double-clicked on one, and the computer chattered faintly to itself, making its thousands of binary decisions. Then the image formed and clarified. It was a photograph of Khumbu cloned many times, in the manner of Art Wolfe's elephants. A formation of dozens of identical leaping Khumbus filled the sky, and a few Khumbus in the lead were alighting with a splash in a marsh. "This is called *Golden Retrievers Migrating South,*" Rowell said, grinning.

"He was more athletic then, wasn't he?" I said, laughing. "And he was more numerous."

This fabrication was a riposte to Wolfe, I understood, and yet, as a friend of Khumbu's, and as someone who had just lost his own sixteen-year-old dog to the indignities of age, I found I liked the picture. It was winningly surrealistic, like something by Magritte or Escher. The apotheosis and replication of Khumbu made Rowell's point nicely, and yet it was somehow stirring.

PACK OF WOLFES

In an average year, according to the jacket copy for *Migrations,* Art Wolfe visits all seven continents and shoots more than 2,000 rolls of film. Indeed, *Migrations* might have served as a fine title for Wolfe's autobiography, had he not used it already for his work on the movements of animals. Like Galen Rowell, Wolfe is at home anywhere on earth—in the cold of either pole or in African heat, in jungle or desert, taiga or tundra, under water or above. Whereas Rowell works in higher regions (he began as a climber, and mountain light still illuminates the core of his work), Wolfe has more experience down on the savannas and steppes. Like his predator namesake, Wolfe derives his bread and butter from following the herds. In his ubiquity with a camera, he seems almost to have cloned himself. He has become a whole pack of Wolfes. By his reckoning, he has taken a million photographs, and his files now amount to a Noah's ark of images. It is odd—or perhaps not odd at all—that Rowell and Wolfe, in many ways so similar, should find themselves champions of opposing views. When I caught up with Wolfe recently, between expeditions, we had not spoken for a couple of years, since comparing notes on a magazine story we did together on the island of Mauritius. I asked him about the digital imbroglio.

"Certainly I've been in the heart of the controversy," he told me. "But 55 I can't really, honestly think it's been bad for my career. It certainly brought a lot of attention to the work I was doing. I think any artist or photographer— or writer, for that matter—would want that. A lot of people have noticed *Migrations.* A lot of people gave it a lot of praise. It also, as you know, got up the ire of some of my colleagues. But not most of them. I think a lot of people understood what I was trying to do with that book.

"*Migrations* is historically an old book now. It was published four years ago, and that's ancient history in the world of photography. We formulated a very clear policy as a result of that book. Since then we've published another book, *In the Presence of Wolves,* with five digital illustrations that were labeled as such, and no one objected. So we figured out that people were upset less because we used the technology than because we did not always say we had. We are using the technology now in developing stock photography—photos or illustrations fed directly into the advertising market. We've completely backed away from doing digital illustrations that can look real, simply because once it's out of our hands, we lose our control of where it's used."

Last September, Wolfe attended an ethics conference hosted by the National Museum of Wildlife Art, in Jackson Hole, Wyoming. He and a number of other nature photographers—including Frans Lanting, Jim Blaylock, Nick Nichols, Chris Johns, and Tom Mangelsen—discussed the problems of digital manipulation and photography of captive animals. "We talked about where we thought photography was going," Wolfe said. "We came to a pretty clear understanding of where we felt it should go, and how it should go. We felt that whatever we agreed upon would probably become the standard in the industry in the years to come.

"About three years ago I led the industry in demanding from my agencies that they start labeling digital illustrations as such. They concurred and started labeling. Now most stock agencies around the world are following suit. I think the rest of the photographers at Jackson Hole thought that that was the most appropriate way of presenting the work. They also felt that digital enhancement—darkening of sky, say, and other things that had been done in the past by printing techniques in the darkroom—need not be labeled."

Wolfe laughed. "Out of the million photos I've done, less than two hundred have digital components. I'm still not using the technology all that often."

"Has the controversy spoiled your fun in using digital?" I asked.   60

"No, not at all. I remain unbowed. I was clear on where I was going to use it from the very, very beginning. I knew it was going to be controversial before we even had the book printed. But also, to this day I would be in a quandary as to how to identify the digital work in *Migrations*. It really ran the spectrum from very radical combinations of photos to very minuscule fixes, where maybe a single head in a flock of two hundred birds would be changed just to complete a pattern. I know of no symbols that show that great a range."

AGE OF MENDACITY

Mankind has lived through ages of stone, iron, bronze, exploration, enlightenment, the atom, space. Our own time is, as much as anything else, the Age of Falsification. The nip, the tuck, the face-lift, the silicone implant. The fascination with virtual reality in a world teeming with real realities. The vogue of the magical realists and their pale, nervous whimsy in a world absolutely ashimmer with real magic. The Michael Jordan shoe. The sound bite and the injury it can do not only to content but also to honesty in our political discourse. (Lincoln required three hours of oration just to warm up.) The blockbuster movie in which story line and plausibility are sacrificed to digital effects and Dolby Sound. (At the present rate of entropy, all cinema will soon be one continuous explosion.) Those "Do people care?" Chevron ads, which have now suckled a whole generation. White female blues singers singing on National Public Radio in exactly the style of old black men from the Mississippi Delta.

Nature, in contrast, is always true. Throughout most of its history photography has been a chronicle of real moments. That is what is so disheartening about Art Wolfe's computer-generated flocks and herds. Nature photography is one part of our culture where authenticity might make a stand. It is dispiriting to see its practitioners turn and go with the flow.

Photofakery is pernicious to natural history. Lemmings do not commit suicide, either individually or en masse from cliffs—Darwin and common sense forbid it. Yet thanks to Disney, several generations of Americans believe that lemmings do. Only elephants can pull off an authentic migration of elephants. A photographer may have spent his life observing elephants, and may believe that he knows their habits well, but when he begins cloning his own herds, error and falseness will inevitably creep in.

"Over the years, as I reviewed the material," Art Wolfe writes in the introduction to *Migrations,* "I often had to pass over photographs because in a picture of masses of animals invariably one would be wandering in the wrong direction, thereby disrupting the pattern I was trying to achieve. Today the ability to digitally alter this disruption is at hand." 65

Wandering in the wrong direction according to whom? Whose patterns is the nature photographer supposed to celebrate—nature's or his own? In the human herd that animal wandering in the wrong direction would be the Buddha, or Luther, or Einstein. We generally regard these rogues and erratics as among the more interesting features of the big picture, and human history cannot be related without reference to them. Animals turned in the wrong direction are a truth of nature. If anything, they *validate* the pattern, as exceptions that prove the rule. The accidental and the unpredictable are vital to art. Without those elements art becomes boring. Reversing the contrary animal is wrongheaded, not only journalistically but also artistically.

Photofakery is pernicious to conservation. Photographers—along with poets, painters, astronauts, reporters—are a sensing element for humanity. The public increasingly depends for much of its environmental awareness on photographic images from around the world. These images need to be true. Zoo cheetahs, when subjected to digital fertility treatments and freed on a virtual savanna, can spawn huge litters, but real African cheetahs are in desperate reproductive trouble, their populations reduced to the point that inbreeding and its genetic consequences threaten their survival.

Digital photofakery creates problems for photographers who choose to shoot straight. Manufactured serendipity is so much quicker and easier than the genuine kind.

Digital photofakery is likely to be pernicious also, in the long run, to the continued good will of photography's audience. Photography and the public have an unusual compact. "The camera does not lie" is a proposition that most of us know to be false yet we half believe anyway. This is a dynamic unique in the arts. The "willing suspension of disbelief" that Coleridge detected at the heart of poetic faith becomes in photographic faith a nearly automatic suspension. Once betrayed, this sort of uncomplicated belief goes quickly past willing to unwilling. Art Wolfe's *Migrations* is the perfect example. The book is briefly entertaining as a "Where's Waldo?" exercise. Finding the reduplicated zebras on the book's cover requires a close attention to stripes, forcing one to appreciate as never before the wonderful painting on zebras. But soon one is just searching for Waldo and ceases to see wildlife. Interest evaporates as the pages are turned. Halfway through I found I did not want to look at the pictures anymore. Wolfe's defense—that the book is not natural history but art—does not wash. The title is *Migrations*, the subject is wild animals on the march, the text is natural history. The point of the book is not the artful composition of the images but the multitudes in them. Those multitudes are inflated and fake.

In *Biographia Literaria,* along with his famous observation on the willing suspension of disbelief, Coleridge listed "the two cardinal points of poetry, the power of exciting the sympathy of the reader by a faithful adherence to the truth of nature, and the power of giving the interest of novelty by modifying colors of imagination." In the digital doctoring of photographs these two cardinal points have come into conflict.

THE SNOWS OF CHO OYU

On my living-room wall is a Galen Rowell print, *Evening on the Tingri Plain below Cho Oyu (26,750 feet), 1988.* A Tibetan woman leads a gray horse across a vast gravel plain, under icy peaks at the roof of the world. Bringing up the rear, in the long evening shadow cast by woman and horse, walks a small Tibetan boy. I know that this is a reduplicated moment, because years ago I asked Rowell about it. Rowell saw the woman lead her horse under Cho Oyu, but his camera was not ready. His local companion casually suggested that he could ask the woman to pass under Cho Oyu again—it was the companion's wife on her way home. This minimal degree of setup hardly amounts to deception, and I still love the photograph, but for me a few lumens of brightness have faded from the picture. Rowell does not notice any such dimming. He sees only the triumph of one of his more wonderful pictures. The hard work of making a photograph is not like the easy work of looking at one, and a little crevasse will probably always lie between maker and viewer. Photography's task in the digital age will be to ensure that the crevasse does not erode into a chasm.

When one is not obliged to make photographs, one can easily take a position purer than the snows of Cho Oyu. On the matter of digital manipulation I have arrived at a view more pristine than that held by any of the photographers I have interviewed.

Galen Rowell, champion of the anti-digitalists, showed me a photo book called *Brother Wolf,* on the cover of which the titular wolf peeks out from behind a tree trunk. This wolf art was not by Art Wolfe but by the wildlife photographer Jim Brandenberg. "Brandenberg freely admits that this image has been altered," Rowell said. "He softened out the left side of the picture, where the title would go, and he intensified the eye. He brought out the color and whiteness to make that eye stand out more. I think that's okay."

But is it okay? Is it honest photography? How is it different from airbrushing?

Rowell opened the book to a photo of a running wolf. "In an image 75 like this he edge-sharpened the nose. And I don't have a problem with that. I think that if you're tuning in an image with digital technique to look more like what you saw, to do what the camera couldn't quite do, to make something sharper so you could see it better, something that was really there in front of the camera, then all that's fine."

I suggested to Rowell that "tuning in an image to look more like what you saw" allowed abundant room for the photographer to fool himself, and us, about what he had really seen. Rowell agreed.

"But these are things you technically could have gotten," he said, "if you used faster film or owned a faster lens, and your technique was better."

I can sympathize. But shouldn't the photographer's solution be to select that faster film, buy that faster lens, improve that technique?

"It was something that was in front of the camera," Rowell went on, "rather than something that was added. That's a big difference. As a general rule, but not absolute, things that are added are a red flag, where things that are subtracted may not be."

This, too, seems a suspect principle. The reasoning strikes me as flawed 80 in an almost mathematical way. If addition should be forbidden, why not subtraction? In their aesthetic tastes Rowell may be a reductionist and Art Wolfe a productionist, but no general rule of ethics can be abstracted from this.

In my talk with the printmaker Joseph Holmes I mentioned Ansel Adams's *Winter Sunrise, the Sierra Nevada from Lone Pine, California,* and Adams's excision of the "LP" from the picture. Holmes laughed. "He usually wasn't able to delete it all that effectively," he said. "You can still see it in the image. But he was right. It was a gross scar on the scene. It's like you can

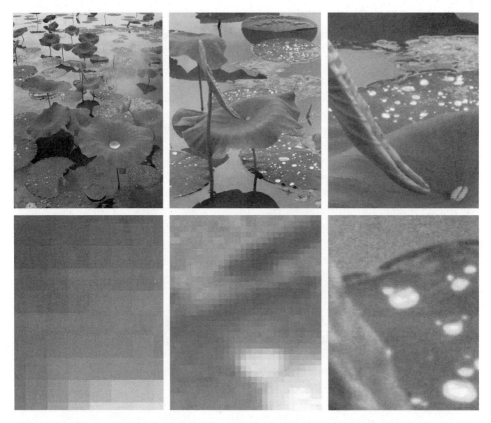

Clockwise from top left: Joseph Holmes's photograph *Lily pads, Reelfoot Lake, Tennessee, 1979*, with two hundred and eighty-five megabytes in the image. With each successive frame the magnification increases by a factor of four.

have the scene back in at least one reality. There was no point in spoiling it twice—first by spoiling this great landscape, and then spoiling the great picture of it, too."

When I asked Holmes if he had ever done digital manipulation that left him uncomfortable, he considered for a moment.

"The hardest decision I've had on a retouching job was whether to remove a really obvious road from a picture—a road that I always thought spoiled the way the scene looked. Taking out a less obvious road I don't have the slightest qualms about, but in the case of something really obvious, something recognizable—that's a problem. It's obvious to me, for example, that no recognizable landscape should be 'flopped.' Yosemite Valley you shouldn't flop. But if you have a picture of detailed vegetation, and it looks better backwards, you should reverse it. Because it doesn't make any difference to the natural history of the place. There's no left-rightness about the way the plants grow that would be misleading to a botanist. There's absolutely no reportage element in there of any value."

A one-lane road may be ripe for digital erasure, but a two-lane road is not? Logging road yes, interstate no? The rationale for the prohibition against flopping a famous landscape, I gather, is that if you flop it, the viewer might catch on. Is this the kind of relationship we want between photographer and audience? And who says that "left-rightness" has nothing to do with the way plants grow? Handedness is one of the enduring mysteries of life. If it manifests itself in molecules, perhaps it also manifests itself in trees.

"If I should pick up litter in a national park and thereby alter the land- 85 scape," Holmes said, "I would be just as happy to pick up litter in the virtual national park for the same reason exactly. If I don't want the national park to have litter in it, I'll pick it up."

He can pick it up if he wants, of course, but then what of the Buddhist doctrine of Extremely Hidden Phenomena? What of the photographer as sensing element for humanity?

A labeling system like the one settled on by the photographers and editors who convened at Jackson Hole last summer will help, but only marginally, I think. The labels will catch the attention of other photographers and editors, but will go largely unnoticed by the rest of us. I wish that the Jackson Hole gathering had included a *consumer* of photographs, not just producers. I find it odd that I, a word man, should be the one to point this out, but in photography the image is the thing—a photograph's essential existence is entirely separate from words and explanations. Art Wolfe published a disclaimer in *Migrations,* but nobody reads the text of photo books, particularly the introductions—as the author of many of them, I can testify to this. Bart, the brown bear who once roared on Galen Rowell's gallery wall, was identified in the caption as a trained bear, but few of the gallery visitors read the caption.

The photographer can insist till he's blue in the face that a given image is art, but the rest of us expect at least a measure of reportage there—and we are half the equation.

GROUP f/ 64

Early in its history photography was dismissed as a lesser art, or as no art at all. A photograph, critics said, was just a record of the external moment—a critique that the medium has never entirely escaped. Well into this century photographers found themselves apologetic about their work, and many were drawn to the abnegation of pictorialism. The Pictorialists produced blurred, symbolic, "poetic" prints in an effort to be painterly. The style was in vogue until the 1930s, with intermittent reinventions afterward. In 1932 a group of seven West Coast photographers, among them Ansel Adams, Imogen Cunningham, and Edward Weston, found themselves united in their distaste for the vapid ethic and misty look of pictorialism. One evening in Berkeley, at the house of a member of the group, Willard Van Dyke, the seven debated what they should call themselves. An eighth photographer, a visiting neophyte named Preston Holder, suggested "US 256," which was then a designation for one of the smaller lens stops—a constricted aperture allowing for the clarity and depth of field favored by the group. Adams worried that as US 256 they might be mistaken for a federal highway, but he liked Holder's drift; he picked up a pencil and sketched out "$f/64$." The aperture $f/64$ corresponded to US 256 in a new marking system just introduced. The seven photographers liked the graphic elegance of the name—the flourish of the long descender on the f Adams drew. They became Group $f/64$. The members believed in straight photography, in "pure" photography—in what Adams called "clear images, smooth honest papers, and . . . the complete absence of affected imitation of other art forms." They held their first shows, and the public quickly saw, with $f/64$ clarity, that the group of seven had found a better path. Pictorialism withered, and straight photography flourished.

History is circular, and we have come, it seems, to a similar crossroads. 90 Digital technology now allows photographers complete freedom to rearrange reality according to their whims. This is what painters do. The computer has provided the new Pictorialists with capabilities the old Pictorialists never dreamed of, and in so doing has presented all photography, nature photography in particular, with both a wonderful new toy and a crisis. I believe we need a new Group $f/64$. It could start small, as before—just a cell of believers committed to clarity and depth of field in images *and* ethics. The original Group $f/64$ believed that photography should encourage and celebrate its differences from painting, and so would the new. The members would just say no to prestidigitation. The Group $f/64$ of the 1930s was burdened, in Ansel Adams's words, with none of "the formal rituals of procedure, incorporations, or any of the limiting restrictions of artistic secret societies." He wrote, "We have issued no stony manifesto (such as the Surrealists did some years ago); we have stated in works and words what we consider straight photography to be, and we expect and welcome any fresh point of view." The new group would be similarly flexible. If I were a photographer, that is the bunch I would join.

One of the seven founders of Group $f/64$, John Paul Edwards, had been a prominent Pictorialist before going over to the other side. "The greatest aesthetic beauty, the fullest power of expression, the real worth of the medium, lies in its pure form," he wrote in *Camera Craft,* a magazine of the time, explaining his defection. "Witness the vogues which have in turn intrigued the worker: the soft-focus lens, carbon, carbro, gum, bromoil transfer, faint gray monotone printing, or its counterpoint, stygian blackness . . . they seemed so important at the time, and are now almost forgotten."

If the revolution goes as I've imagined it, to this list of forgotten vogues we will soon add digital duplicity. The decisive moment celebrated in Henri

Cartier-Bresson's epochal photo book *The Decisive Moment* will compress again to a very brief period of time, not the decisive hours and days spent at the computer screen by the prestidigitators. The eye, and not artifice, will have to solve the intimidating problem at the core of photographic art—the creation of an image that no one has seen before. Photographers will wander the world more like the Zen archers we imagine them to be, with just thirty-six chances per roll.

QUESTIONING THE TEXT

1. Two of the illustrations from Brower's essay are reprinted here, one a drawing by Istvan Banyai (pp. 562–563) and the other a series of photographs by Joseph Holmes (p. 570). Take a close look at these illustrations and then, in one paragraph for each, explain what they add to Brower's argument.

2. Brower announces a major theme in paragraph 7, noting that he is troubled that more and more "digitally doctored images are appearing in the media." He then spends the next few sentences talking about his respect for photographers. Why do you think Brower includes this information? How does he want readers to view him, and why? How does the "ethos" or character he builds here affect your reading of his article? Make brief notes in response to these questions and bring them to class for discussion.

MAKING CONNECTIONS

3. Would Plato (p. 467) be as troubled as Brower is by the proliferation of "fake" photos? In a brief journal entry, explain the similarities you see between Plato's and Brower's arguments.

4. James Prosek (p. 506) also writes in this chapter about nature and about his attempts to capture certain images of nature in his paintings. How do you think Prosek would respond to Brower's argument against digitally altered photographs? What evidence can you find in Prosek's selection that indicates his thinking on the accuracy of representations?

JOINING THE CONVERSATION

5. Brower argues that nature photography might be expected to insist on authenticity. Review Brower's essay, looking carefully for the evidence he offers in support of his claim. Then write a letter of response to Brower, explaining why you do or do not agree with him.

6. Brower finds fault with photographers who alter photographs of nature, arguing that "[t]he accidental and the unpredictable are vital to art" (paragraph 66). Working alone or with a classmate, test out this claim by choosing an art form you admire—a kind of music, painting, architecture, or dance, for example. Gather a number of good examples of the art form and study them, looking for the "accidental" or "unpredictable" and especially for the ways they contribute to the power of the art. Write a brief report of your findings and bring it to class for sharing and discussion.

7. Using the information in Brower's article, try your hand at writing an allegory that would capture Brower's argument metaphorically, as Plato's "Allegory of the Cave" (p. 467) captures his philosophy of the real versus the merely apparent. You may choose to work with one or two classmates on this assignment.

LINDA S. WATTS
Review of Inside the Mouse

How few readers of the following book review, I wonder, will not have grown up on Disney cartoons and movies or visited Disney theme parks? More important still, what are your experiences with Disney characters and the happy-go-lucky Disney image? Your answers to these questions will undoubtedly inform your reading of the following selection by Linda S. Watts, a book review of Inside the Mouse: Work and Play at Disney World *(1995). Watts (b. 1960), Professor of English at Drake University, earned her B.A. from the University of Delaware and her M.A. and Ph.D. in American Studies from Yale. Author of* Rapture Untold: Gender, Mysticism, and the "Moment of Recognition" in Works by Gertrude Stein *(1996), she has strong interests in nineteenth- and twentieth-century American literature, culture, and visual arts as well as in women's and African American studies.*

Watts's review first appeared in a 1997 issue of Radical Teacher, *a journal known for its left-leaning views on teaching and learning. Given her audience of educators, Watts sets her review in the context of a need to teach critical thinking (see especially paragraph 3) and includes a bibliography intended for further reading. I chose this review for several reasons. First, as a long-time advocate of collaboration and collaborative writing, I was intrigued by a book edited not by an individual person but by a collaborative group, Duke University's Project on Disney. In addition, because many students are asked to write critical book reviews, providing an example for discussion and criticism seemed valuable. Finally, my own long history of trying to avoid visiting a Disney theme park at all costs has made me curious about "the parks," as well as about the worldwide power of Disney images.* —A.L.

He kept a private apartment in the core of the Anaheim park, just above the Fire Station in Disneyland's Town Square, but it is a nearby location that fascinates me: "The Walt Disney Story." In the entry hall to another of Disneyland's attractions, "Great Moments with Mr. Lincoln," visitors get to glimpse a full-scale replica of Walt Disney's offices at the Disney Studios, a tribute to the man behind the mouse. In a bustling park where virtually everything moves, talks, sings, and dances insistently, it is a curiously still exhibit. The sealed office, left empty to honor its lost steward, is a further ironic scene at a location where hard work is rendered invisible, and work of any ordinary kind is often concealed altogether. The only workers a visitor sees in the parks assume the guise of play rather than labor, and the public is invited to see Disney staff as "cast members," people who are performing rather than working. They become somehow part of the attractions in a magic kingdom whose subjects never have to confront the park as a workplace.

If you have ever visited one of the Disney theme parks, though, you have likely wondered at the labor—both seen and unseen—necessary to maintain these fanciful environments. How and when are the grounds tended so painstakingly? How are the signs of high traffic erased from public facilities? What keeps employees ("cast members") so poised, meticulously groomed, and endlessly cheerful?

As educators, we seldom find an experience that our students so widely share as contact with the "Disney Way," whether from vacations, films, or acquaintance with icons such as Mickey Mouse. This familiarity (although admittedly not uniform or universal) creates an opportunity to engage students in critical thinking about both the social construction of pleasure and the work that makes this leisure possible.

In recent years, there has been an explosion of scholarship on Disney enterprises (see bibliography). Of these materials, many take a critical view of their subject, and a number of these items would be suitable for critical pedagogy concerning issues raised through Disney ventures, such as entrepreneurial and corporate capitalism, consumer culture, and cultural imperialism.

Of particular interest are those studies calling attention to the workplace   5
issues surrounding labor at Disney theme parks (primarily at California's Disneyland and Florida's Disney World). The best of these works appears to be *Inside the Mouse,* a jointly authored volume, published by "The Project on Disney" (a group whose members are Karen Klugman, Jane Kuenz, Shelton Waldrep, and Susan Willis). In "The Problem with Pleasure," Susan Willis opens the volume with a discussion of how the project got underway and how collaboration became a necessary feature of both its research and statement. Willis asks what it is we like about Disney, why we like it, and what that implies about us. In her other essays for *Inside the Mouse* ("The Family Vacation" and "Public Use/Private State"), Willis remarks the ways in which families negotiate interpersonal as well as commercial expectations while visiting the Disney parks. Shelton Waldrep examines the attraction narratives and architectural statements that characterize Disney theme parks, especially Disney World and EPCOT. Jane Kuenz's "It's a Small World after All" looks at how visitors to Disney World use and value the Florida park, but it is her second chapter, "Working at the Rat," that deserves special note. It is also the chapter apt to prove most shocking to readers (especially to students who regard Disney with nostalgia for their childhoods) as Kuenz exposes the circumstances surrounding employment at Disney World (disparaged by some around Orlando as "the rat").

As many know, Disney workers begin their training at Disneyland/Disney World University, where they receive three days of instruction about safety, deportment, protocol, and Disney philosophy. As part of this preparation for their "roles" at Disney, new workers learn the approved terms for Disney use. When describing their place of business, for instance, they are told never to call it an "amusement park," only and simply "the park." There are no customers at Disney parks, only guests. There are no uniforms, only costumes.

However, in the spirit of the book's search for what Karen Klugman calls the "alternative ride"—strategies by which paid workers or paying guests use their critical faculties to participate in the magic of Disney on their own terms, Kuenz probes the ways in which (through language, affect, and conduct) Disney workers find alternatives to utter compliance. Take, for instance, some of the slang used by Disney cast members:

- *The Rat:* Disney World
- *Spieler:* scripted cast member (high status)
- *Foxes:* plainclothes detectives watching guests; wearing cameras and dressing like tourists, they curtail shoplifting
- *Shoppers:* plainclothes detectives watching cast members; by sampling attractions and services unannounced, they monitor that things are being done the "Disney Way"
- *Brazilian:* problem guest or one who treats workers as non-human
- *Friendly Force:* a cast member's way of dealing with problem guests while still performing their roles (tugging too hard on a seat belt on a ride, etc.)

While Kuenz's research is also replete with stories of exploitation of part-timers, complaints of surveillance, capricious dismissals for small infractions of personal appearance codes, insider promotion paths, and the like, she also manages to find ways in which workers at Disney claim a creative space for their lived identities. One such example is the "family," as cast members know the sizable population of gay and lesbian workers at Disney.

Over all, though, the picture is one of a highly controlled "smile factory," as one employee termed it, where surplus visibility and relentless supervision sometimes outweigh the satisfaction of maintaining a standard of service once summoned years ago by whispers that "Walt's in the park." Upon Disney's passing, workers (old and new) were directed that now "Walt is always in the park." His legacy is as demanding as it is rich, and one should not be deceived by the quiet museum-like quality of the Disney office replica. It is said that before his death in 1966, Walt Disney used growth projections and building/renovation timetables to record his time-specific reminders, urgings, and messages for regular staff meetings through the 1980s. Whether our students identify with park patrons or employees, *Inside the Mouse* goes a long way toward informing the rhetoric surrounding the "happiest place on earth."

SELECTED BIBLIOGRAPHY

Bell, Elizabeth, Lynda Haas, and Laura Sells, eds., *From Mouse to Mermaid: The Politics of Film, Gender, and Culture.* Bloomington: Indiana University Press, 1995.

Brannen, Mary Yoko, "'Bwana Mickey': Constructing Cultural Consumption at Tokyo Disneyland," in Amy Kaplan and Donald E. Pease, eds., *Cultures of United States Imperialism*. Durham: Duke University Press, 1993.

Bukatman, Scott, "There's Always Tomorrowland: Disney and the Hypercinematic Experience." *October* 57 (Summer 1991): 55–78.

Burton, Julianne, "Don (Juanito) Duck and the Imperial-Patriarchal Unconscious: Disney Studios, the Good Neighbor Policy, and the Packaging of Latin America," in Andrew Parker, ed., *Nationalisms and Sexualities*. New York: Routledge, 1992.

Dorfman, Ariel, and Armant Mattelart, *How to Read Donald Duck: Imperialist Ideology in the Disney Comic*. Trans. David Kunzle. New York: International Generation, 1984.

Eliot, Marc, *Walt Disney, Hollywood's Dark Prince*. Carol/Birch, Lane Press, 1993.

Fjellman, Stephen M., *Vinyl Leaves: Walt Disney World and America*. Boulder: Westview Press, 1992.

Gottdiener, Mark, "Disneyland: A Utopian Urban Space," *Urban Life* 11 (2): 139–192.

Marin, Louis, "Disneyland: A Degenerate Utopia," in Robert Con Davis and Ronald Schleifer, eds., *Contemporary Literary Criticism: Literary and Cultural Studies*. Third Edition. New York: Longman, 1994, 283–295.

Mosley, Leonard, *Disney's World*. Stein and Day, 1985.

Smoodin, Erin, ed., *Disney Discourse: Producing the Magic Kingdom*. New York: Routledge, 1994.

Sorkin, Michael, "See You in Disneyland," *Design Quarterly* (Winter 1992): 5–13.

van Maanen, John, "The Smile Factory," in Peter Frost, ed., *Reframing Organizational Culture*. Sage, 1991.

Wallace, Mike, "Mickey Mouse History: Portraying the Past at Disney World," *Radical History Review* 32 (1985): 33–57.

Wilson, Alexander, "The Betrayal of the Future: Walt Disney's EPCOT Center." *Socialist Review* 84 (1985): 41–53.

Wilson, Alexander, *The Culture of Nature: Popular Landscapes from Disney to Chernobyl*. Toronto: Between the Lines Press, 1991.

Willis, Susan, "Fantasia: Walt Disney's Los Angeles Suite," *Diacritics* 17: 83–96.

Willis, Susan, ed., *South Atlantic Quarterly* [The World According to Disney] 92:1 (Winter 1993).

Zukin, Sharon, "Disney World: The Power of Facade/The Facade of Power," *Landscapes of Power*. Los Angeles: University of California Press, 1991.

QUESTIONING THE TEXT

1. Watts begins her review with "He kept a private apartment in the core of the Anaheim park," an unusual opening perhaps, especially because readers must infer who "He" is. Did you assume "He" was Walt Disney right away, or did you suspend your judgment until later? Look carefully at the opening paragraph. What focus or thesis emerges from it, and how does that focus help to hold the paragraph together? Finally, in what ways does the paragraph forecast what the review will focus on?

2. What is Watts's attitude toward the book she reviews? Is she an advocate, a harsh critic, evenhandedly critical, or some other mix? Working with a classmate, discuss this question and then reread the review. Finally, draw up a list of examples that illustrate what you take to be Watts's attitude.

MAKING CONNECTIONS

3. Read Watts's book review with John Updike's "The Mystery of Mickey Mouse" (p. 489) in mind. How might Updike review *Inside the Mouse*? Write a letter to the Project on Disney, making some of the points and asking some of the questions Updike might have.

4. In "Introduction to *Trout*" (p. 506), James Prosek says: "For me, the trout in its stream is the image of life—encompassing survival and beauty, death and birth." Think for a while about how Prosek might react to Disney theme parks. Then write two sentences modeled on the one above—one you think Prosek might write about the essence of Disney and one you think the CEO of Disney might write. Finally, write your own sentence about the essence of Disney. Bring all the sentences to class for discussion.

JOINING THE CONVERSATION

5. Working with two classmates, write a critical review of *Inside the Mouse* or of one of the books listed in Watts's bibliography. You may decide that all three of you will read the entire book or you may decide to

divide it up, reading individual parts of the book and then "teaching" that part to the others. Your job is to identify the major themes, points, and/or theses of the book and then to take a critical perspective on the text—that is, to establish your own stance in relation to it. Keep your review to roughly the same length as Watts's and assume you are writing it for your class. Prepare the review using a heading like the one Watts uses and putting your name and institutional affiliation at the end.

6. If you have ever visited a Disney theme park, spend some time reflecting on that experience and especially on the images that are most vivid in your memory. Looking back after considering the "underside" of working at Disney, do you remember anything that might have been related to working conditions? Then take half an hour or so to prepare a journal entry on "My Experience with Disney." Consider adding a subtitle that would say something about the nature of that experience.

7. For several days (at least three), keep a list of every image or reference associated with Disney characters, cartoons, movies, or parks you come across. Note down as well *where* the reference appears. Then analyze your list. What images predominate? What kinds of places do the references appear in and where do they *never* appear? What can you conclude about the presence or power of Disney images in your everyday life? Write a one-page report on your findings and bring it to class for discussion.

OTHER READINGS

Berger, John. *Ways of Seeing*. New York: Viking, 1973. A series of essays—some verbal, some purely pictorial—that explore contradictory and multiple ways of seeing images, often in terms of gender or sexuality. A classic text on this subject.

Douglas, Susan J. *Where the Girls Are: Growing up Female with the Mass Media*. New York: Times Books, 1995. A witty analysis of the effects mass media images have had on women in the twentieth century.

Halberstam, David. *Playing for Keeps*. New York: Random, 1999. Portrays Michael Jordan, one of the most written about athletes of the 1990s and yet arguably one of the least known, with balance, insight, and keen analysis.

McLuhan, Marshall. *The Medium Is the Massage*. New York: Random, 1967. A classic text offering a very early argument for the reformative influence of electronic technology on our lives. Full of provocative images and text that refuse to stay "in bounds," this is a book to be seen, not read about.

Norman, Geoffrey. "A Portrait of the Angler as a Young Man." *Men's Journal* Sept. 1997: 62–65. A look at the life and work of artist and writer James Prosek.

Postman, Neil. *Amusing Ourselves to Death: Public Discourse in the Age of Show Business*. New York: Penguin, 1984. Argues that television and other electronic media are corrupting public discourse.

Saunders, Dave. *The World's Best Advertising Photography*. London: Batsford, 1994. Some startling images from advertisements produced worldwide.

Updike, John. "Lost Art." *The Best American Essays, 1998*. Boston: Houghton 1998. 239–45. An intimate glimpse into the craft of cartooning.

ELECTRONIC RESOURCES

http://www.webring.org/cgi-bin/webring?ring=thais;list
Links to 117 sites related to Disney and Mickey Mouse.

http://www.nike.com/
A Web site set up by the Nike Corporation.

http://www.snap.com/directory/category/0,16,-26584,00.html
Lists several dozen photo essays. Check other search engines for similar listings.

http://www.stars.com/Vlib/Providers/Images_and_Icons.html
Lists collections of images, icons, and graphics available on the internet.

Look carefully at the photograph on the preceding page of a family living room. What is the central focus of this photo? ■ What about it suggests when it was taken? ■ What do the details of decoration and dress add to (or how do they detract from) the overall effect of the photograph? ■ What values does it implicitly express and/or support? ■ What impression do you think the photographer sought to create through this photo? ■ Does this impression differ from your own impression of it and, if so, in what ways?

8

At Home:
The Places I Come From

Well, college is supposed to be broadening, he muses, and there's no doubt he'll get broadened this year with a roommate like Cedric.

RON SUSKIND, *A Hope in the Unseen*

I remember early morning fogs in Georgia, not so dramatic as California ones, but magical too because out of the Southern fog of memory tramps my dark father, smiling and large, glowing with rootedness, and talking of hound dogs, biscuits and coons.

ALICE WALKER, *The Place Where I Was Born*

Sometimes I feel like I'm frozen in time, caught in a nightmare of a hot October afternoon when everything changed because my mother stopped living.

BARBARA SMITH, *Home*

Most statistics tell us breast cancer is genetic, hereditary, with rising percentages attached to fatty diets, childlessness, or becoming pregnant after thirty. What they don't say is living in Utah may be the greatest hazard of all.

TERRY TEMPEST WILLIAMS, *The Clan of One-Breasted Women*

Just as no patient would have designed today's system of health care, so no child would have chosen today's culture of divorce.

BARBARA DAFOE WHITEHEAD, *The Making of a Divorce Culture*

In a 1990 *Newsweek* poll, 42 percent predicted that the family would be worse in ten years and exactly the same percentage predicted that it would be better.

STEPHANIE COONTZ, *The Way We Wish We Were*

The long-term care facility . . . I work for is owned by a corporation that owns nursing homes throughout the country. Giving corporations like this control over the quality of medical care is handing over control to the fox.

JILL FRAWLEY, *Inside the Home*

Fatherhood isn't brain surgery. I say this in defiance of the new conventional wisdom that being a father is breathtakingly difficult. . . .

FRED BARNES, *Quantity Time*

If you're expecting overnight guests, tie a bath towel, hand towel, and washcloth together with a ribbon and set it at the end of each guest's bed.

Ask Martha: Guest Towels

The idea is to impress others, not warm the house.

Tom Connor and Jim Downey, *Well-Stacked Logs*

To read Martha Stewart is to know that there is no corner of your domestic life that cannot be beautified or improved under careful tutelage, none that should not be colonized by the rhetoric and the discipline of quality control.

Margaret Talbot, *Les Très Riches Heures de Martha Stewart*

Grandpa's flowers are scattered
down the line of tombstones, decorating
the graves of his wife, his children

Ed Madden, *Family Cemetery, near Hickory Ridge, Arkansas*

Introduction

CONSIDER FOR A MOMENT some well-known phrases that feature the word *home:* "home is where the heart is," for example, or "there's no place like home"; "home, sweet home"; "the home of the brave"; "you can't go home again." These phrases suggest that "home" is a place of comfort or solace, or at least "where the heart is." They capture what might be described as an American ideal of "home": a place where you can be safe and secure and living among those who care unconditionally for you.

In one of the most famous opening passages in literature, however, Leo Tolstoy complicates such an ideal vision of home: "Happy families are all alike," he says, but "every unhappy family is unhappy in its own way" (*Anna Karenina*). Tolstoy's sentence suggests what most of us know already in our bones: homes can be sites not only of comfort and solace but of pain and bitter unhappiness as well. In addition, one person's happy home is another person's disaster; what may look like a peaceful, loving home from one perspective may look just the opposite from another.

As the selections in this chapter will illustrate, what is "home" to one person may well be a "shelter" or a "poisoned land" or a place that exists only in the imagination to another. And whatever your own individual experience has been, you have certainly had some experience with the concept of "home." In fact, you have probably had multiple experiences with homes of various kinds, and some of these experiences may contradict or conflict with one another. This chapter may provide a timely opportunity, then, to consider the various places, people, or concepts you have known as "home" and to explore your own thinking about them.

Before you begin reading, you might want to consider these questions:

- What places could be categorized as "home" for you?
- What are some of the positive and/or negative qualities you associate with "home"?
- What kind of home would you most like to be part of? What problems might keep you from having the home and family you desire?
- How is "home" represented in the media? How is the word used in music and in the titles of films and TV and radio shows? You may want to brainstorm these questions with two or three classmates and bring your list to class for discussion.

• • •

RON SUSKIND
A Hope in the Unseen

RON SUSKIND'S A Hope in the Unseen: An American Odyssey from the Inner City to the Ivy League *(1998) tells the true story of Cedric Jennings, an African American youth from an inner-city school in Washington, D.C., who makes his way to an Ivy League college. His academic commitment and success mark him as an outsider at Frank W. Ballou Senior High, where he is taunted and ridiculed by classmates who don't understand his aspirations. While at Brown University Cedric finds academic support, but he encounters prejudices of a different sort among much more privileged students to whom his race, poverty, and religious upbringing are a mystery.*

The differences between Cedric and his friends at Brown, particularly his room-mate Rob, are not just metaphorical. To underscore the contrast between their worlds, I have juxtaposed two passages from A Hope in the Unseen *in the following selection: the first is from an early chapter describing Cedric at home in the Washington, D.C., apartment he shared with his mother, and the second is from a much later chapter intro-ducing Cedric's college roommate. As you'll see, the two young men try to negotiate their differences, not entirely successfully, within a space familiar to many students across the country—a dormitory room.*

Suskind, a journalist, won a Pulitzer Prize in 1995 for two Wall Street Jour-nal *articles he wrote about Cedric Jennings's high school years.* A Hope in the Un-seen *represents the continuation of that story, one that has inspired many readers. De-scribing the experience of writing about Cedric in a* NEA Today *online forum (November 11, 1998), Suskind observes that "[k]ids—all kids—are naturally hope-ful and, like any living thing, they bend toward the light. A teacher who can see through the eyes of a student will find clues about where to shine that light." That sounds like good advice for everyone.*   —J.R.

Apartment 307 on the third floor of the blond brick High View apart-ments at 1635 V Street, Southeast, is empty, dark, and warm at 6:04 P.M., when Cedric unlocks the door. There hasn't always been heat, with overdue bills and whatnot, and he always appreciates the warmth, especially after the long walk from the Anacostia bus and subway station in the icy dusk wind.

He slips out of his coat and backpack and goes from room to room turning on lights, something he's done since he was a small kid, coming home alone to apartments and tiptoeing, with a lump in his throat, to check if in-truders were lurking inside closets and under beds.

It's not a very big place—two bedrooms, a small bathroom, a kitch-enette, and an attached living and dining room—but it's one of the better apartments that he and his mother, Barbara, have lived in. He's even got his own bedroom in the far back corner.

He flips on the switch. It's like a bear's winter cave of strewn matter—a thick padding of clothes, magazines, rubber-soled shoes, books, loose papers, and more clothes.

Cedric turns on his beloved Sharp Trinitron, a 19-inch color TV that   5
his mother rented for him in ninth grade from a nearby Rent-a-Center (just paid off a month ago at an astonishing total price of nearly $1,500) and flops onto the bed. Like his proclivity for spying on street hustlers, the TV is a vital element of Cedric's secondhand life. He loves the tube, especially the racy, exhibitionist afternoon talk shows, which he watches for a few minutes tonight before turning to the local news—the lead story about a shooting not far from here—and then flipping to *The Flintstones,* a favorite.

He hears the thump of a door slamming.

"Lavar, you home?" comes the voice—calling him, as his mother always has, by his middle name—but he doesn't get up, figuring she'll wander back. In a moment, Barbara Jennings, hands on hips, is standing in the doorway.

In the sixteen and a half years since Cedric's birth, Barbara Jennings has been on a path of sacrifice and piety that has taken her far from the light-hearted haughtiness of her earlier self—the woman with a blonde wig, leather miniskirt, white knee-high boots, and a taste for malt liquor. Cedric has seen pictures of that skinny young thing, a striking girl with a quick smile who, as he has discerned from his mother's infrequent recollections, searched for love and found mostly trouble.

She stopped searching long ago. Barbara is a churchwoman now. On weekdays she works in a data input job at the Department of Agriculture, where she has been for almost eleven years, and splits the rest of her time between a church in a rough section of Washington north of the Capitol dome and this small, messy apartment.

Cedric looks her up and down and smiles thinly. Today, like most days,   10
she has opted for a black dress and sensible shoes, an outfit most appropriate to her general mood, needs, and heavier frame. But her features—her small-ish nose and pretty, wide-set eyes—have held up well, even at forty-seven and without makeup.

"I thought you would have made dinner by now," she says, slipping a thin chain with her dangling Department of Agriculture photo ID from around her neck. "How long you been home?"

"Only a couple of minutes," Cedric says, turning back to the tube. "What we got to eat?"

"I don't know, whatever's in there," she says curtly before disappearing into her room to change out of her work clothes. Taking his cue, Cedric moves into the kitchen and begins breaking up ground beef into a frying pan. He pours in a can of navy beans, some oil, chopped onions, some pepper, salt,

a little paprika, and other condiments. He does this without complaint or enthusiasm — it's what he does most nights — and soon there are two heaping
plates of steaming hash.

"Hey, it's ready and all," he calls around a short breakwall behind the
stove to Barbara, who's sitting in a bathrobe on the white living room couch
watching TV.

Usually, he takes his plate to his room and she eats on the low, wide living   15
room coffee table — each sitting in front of their own TV. Tonight, though, she
clears away newspapers and unopened bills from the dining room table.

"I haven't talked to you in ages, it seems," she says softly as they sit
down to eat.

"I've been around," he says, grateful for her attentions. "Just been a lot
going on — at school and whatever."

So it ends up being a night that they talk. It happens every couple of
weeks. It's not needed more than that, Cedric figures. He knows that his
mom wants to give him his space, now that he's sixteen and, by his reckoning, almost grown up, so she doesn't bother him in his room, where he
spends most of his time. Maybe too much time, she tells him sometimes, but
it's the only place he feels he has any privacy. After all, it's not as if he goes
out late on weekend nights with friends, like most kids at school. Inside his
room is the only place he can really relax.

He describes last week's assembly, about his not going, and she shakes
her head dismissively. "What did I tell you? Before you know it, you'll be
leaving them all behind. Just pay them no mind."

"Okay, okay," he says, "but what if I get rejected by MIT? That'd kill me."   20
Barbara heeds this more carefully. It was she, after all, who found a description of
the program in a scholarship book that someone gave to her at the office.

"You can't be worrying about MIT, Lavar. Just pray about it. If God
has meant it to happen, it will." She looks up between bites and sees he's not
convinced. "Look, your grades are perfect, your recommendations are good.
What can they not like?"

"Yeah, I guess," he concedes.

"What's the point of getting down on yourself?" she says. "People will
see that you're special."

He nods, letting her words sink in, and they eat for a while in silence —
just the two of them, the way it has been for years. Barbara's two older girls,
Cedric's half-sisters, are twenty-six and thirty-one and long gone, leaving
mother and son to rely on each other in more ways than they can count.

Through years of ups and downs — times when he was certain that he   25
was unworthy of success or love or any reasonable hope of getting something
better — her faith in him has been his savior. It always amazes him. Having
finished dinner quickly, he watches her clean her plate contentedly, and he
shakes his head. She's just rock solid certain that he's going to MIT. Who
knows, he wonders as he busses their plates and begins washing the dishes.
Maybe she's right.

Both return to their customary evening routines—Barbara back to the couch and her sitcoms while Cedric dries and puts away the dishes and silverware. Quieter now, with the sink water not running, he hears what sound like pops from outside, almost certainly gunshots. He looks over at his mother sitting by the window but she doesn't react, so he begins wiping down the kitchen counters.

Gunshots are part of the background score here. Listen on most nights and a few pops are audible. The corner nearest the house—16th and V—is among the worst half-dozen or so spots in the city for crack cocaine dealing. The corner a block north—16th and U—is, of late, the very worst. There has been lots of shooting on both corners recently, but still they're open all night, and the traffic of buyers on 16th remains strong and steady in all weather.

Cedric knows that the surrounding mayhem is not something he and his mother need to talk much about. Still, it's always there, ionizing the air in the apartment, lending it some extra gravity, which, Cedric told his mother a couple of weeks ago, gives him "a little something to push against."

Cedric hangs up the wet dish towel on a drawer handle and strides toward the short hallway leading to his room. He glances quickly at Barbara as he passes and realizes that the TV is on but she's no longer watching it. Her eyes are on him.

He stops. "What you looking at?"   30

She pauses as though she's trying to remember something. "What did I once tell you?" she asks finally, in a tentative voice.

"Ma, what are you talking about, talking crazy?"

"What did I once tell you, Lavar?"

"I don't know. You tell me lots of things."

She stands, tying her robe closed, and slowly points a finger at him,   35 buying an extra moment to get the words from Scripture just so: "The race," she says with a satisfied smile, "goes not to the swift nor the strong, but he who endureth until the end."

Oh yes, that's a good one, Cedric agrees, and nods. Hasn't heard that one in a while. "Thank you, Jesus," he says to her with a wry smile as he makes his way toward the back bedroom. Stopping at the threshold, he turns and calls back: "But it wouldn't be so terrible to be all swift and strong—just once in a while—and let some other people do all the enduring."

Barbara, sunk back into the couch, can't help but laugh. . . .

• • •

Rob Burton opens the door, delighted to see that the room is empty. It's Saturday, early afternoon, and he's ready for a little down time. He played soccer for a while on the green near Andrews dorm in the late morning, and, with lunch now in his belly, he's feeling whipped. It was a late night of partying last night—drinking beer mostly, cruising around the campus, and then talking until all hours on the third floor with some of these new guys.

Flopping on his unmade bed, he remembers that one of them—a guy named Billy who got 5's, highest you can get, on all of his achievement tests—said he went to a private Catholic school in Baltimore.

Just like me, Rob thinks. Head propped on his pillow, he admires his 40 corner lair. Got it just so. On the wall to his left are two glossy photos he tacked up yesterday. The nearest one is of him dancing, sweaty and close, with his girlfriend at his high school prom. He starred at the school, a private Catholic academy in Marblehead, his senior year—newspaper editor, varsity tennis and soccer player, second in the class. And a cute girlfriend, too. He broke it off with her this summer, and it's just as well, he realizes now, that he doesn't have an HTH (home town honey) like some of the guys. It would make things so complicated. He looks at the other photo, also a prom shot, of him and his best buddy in a drunken tuxedoed hug, and laughs. What a nut. Got to send him an e-mail later today, he thinks.

His mind wanders back to beloved Marblehead, a sumptuous seaside exurb of Boston where he could drink a bit, do some experimenting with his girlfriend in the back seat of his car, and then set off on his path to college and beyond. Rob's father is an obstetrician; his mother is a longtime emergency room doctor turned occupational physician. There was never any question about whether he would use his quick mind and good manners to excel. It was assumed in everything that cosseted him. His house is a stunning five-bedroom clapboard colonial, ten minutes from the blue Atlantic.

He misses it, but not terribly. He feels a sense of closure about it all after another excellent summer running a skiff at the Marblehead Yacht Club, hanging with his buddies, and going on a few trips with the folks. Sure, there was a sense that an era of his life was coming to an end. But it was time, no doubt, to take the next step.

He rolls onto his side, figuring he'll catch some sleep, and looks just to the left of his pillow at his favorite recent *Rolling Stone* cover—neatly taped up—a shot of Sting, all blond ease, gazing off remotely and effortlessly, very cool.

He lies there for a while, finds he doesn't really feel like napping, and sits up. Resting gently on top of his canvas bookbag, which is teetering on the edge of his desk right near the bed, is a letter home he started writing two days ago.

He snatches it, seeing if maybe he feels like finishing it.   45

"Dear Mom and Dad,
    This is my first letter, one of many I can guarantee. It's August 31st, Thursday. I've been here approximately 24 hours and I'm beginning to slowly realize I'm here. I'm slowly touching down to earth.
    All is going well. After saying good-bye to Mom, I returned to my room to find Cedric and his mom unpacking. We are getting along well, although our tastes in music couldn't be more different. . . ."

Cedric. He pushes a pile of his sweaty clothes from this morning's soccer game away with his foot and puts the letter down on a cleared spot of floor. Well, college is supposed to be broadening, he muses, and there's no doubt he'll get broadened this year with a roommate like Cedric. But it'll work out. Casual and nonconfrontational, upbeat and accommodating, Rob can get along with anyone—it's a point of pride for him. If people are reasonable and open-minded, conflict always dissolves. Even if they just agree to disagree, at least they will have agreed on something. Not that he won't be challenged when it comes to Cedric. He's never really been close to a black guy, barely known any. The few encounters he's had were characterized by caution, by him feeling like he was walking on eggshells, not wanting to offend, inadvertently, with an inappropriate tone or casual remark. Last night with the guys, when all the talk shifted to roommates, Rob said to everyone it was going fine. There's a lot of interest in Cedric from the other kids, him being a black city kid and all. Everyone agreed that none of them had spent too much time with a person like that and, God knows, there aren't all that many of them here at Brown.

He looks across the room at the empty bed, at the hospital corners and fluffed pillows, everything in order, like a fortress. It seems like he and Cedric couldn't be more different, he thinks, looking at his mess of socks and papers and empty juice bottles. Different, it seems, in every way.

He grabs a pen, bent on finishing the letter. It's dated two days ago, he should get it done.   50

The door opens.

"Hey, Rob."

"Oh, hi, Cedric," Rob says, looking up from the notebook on his lap with the letter on top. "Where you been?"

"Lunch."

"Yeah, me too," Rob says, wondering if Cedric saw him there and thought that Rob might have snubbed him because they didn't sit together. "I didn't see you."

"Oh, no. I had to go to the corner and get a sandwich. I lost my temporary ID. I'm just living off this money my mom gave me. It's baaaaad. I can't eat on my meal plan. It's like I don't exist." Rob commiserates and says   55
he'll steal stuff for Cedric from the cafeteria if he wants.

Cedric putters around for a bit, hopping over to his chair and looking at some scheduling forms on his desk, while Rob turns back to the letter, not making much headway.

"Do you like mopping floors?" Cedric asks, after a bit.

"No, I don't *think* so," Rob says mawkishly, thinking it's some sort of joke.

"I just want to take a mop to it once a week, just to keep this place clean," Cedric says.

"Sure, you can do that if you want," Rob says, not thinking until a mo-   60
ment later that Cedric might have been hoping for more participation.

"You know, Rob, your feet smell bad."

"Oh come on, they do not."

"Do too! Man, walking around in your bare feet . . . that's disgusting."

Rob, accustomed to cut grass, thick pile carpets, and clean beach sand, has no idea what he's talking about. "Cedric, everyone walks barefoot."

"Maybe where you're from," Cedric says, raising his eyebrows. "Not where I'm from."

Cedric sits on his bed and turns on the TV, flipping the channels, look-   65
ing for something to watch. Rob doesn't watch much TV and told Cedric that the first day. Now, with the noise, he can't seem to concentrate on the letter.

Instead, he grabs a novel he's been reading over the summer and flops on his bed, trying to ignore the blare. After a while, he drops the book and decides to see whom he can find to hang out with up on the third floor. He'll let Cedric enjoy the company of his TV.

"I'm outta here," he says to no one in particular as the door slams. For the first time, he notices how nice his bare feet feel on the hallway carpet. . . .

QUESTIONING THE TEXT

1. In what ways does the matter of bare feet in the dorm room embody basic differences between the home environments Cedric and Rob have experienced? List some of those differences and explore the implications of Cedric's complaint: "Rob, your feet smell bad" (paragraph 60).

2. Describing Cedric's apartment, Suskind notes that "[g]unshots are part of the background score here" (paragraph 27). Think about the noises at the place you currently think of as home. Would a stranger learn as much about your home from those sounds as readers discover about Cedric's life from the report of those gunshots? Why, or why not?

3. Television seems to play a major role in Cedric's life, both at his home and in his dormitory room. What comfort might TV offer a young man living in a hostile or an alien environment? Evaluate the part TV plays—if any—in your home life.

MAKING CONNECTIONS

4. Mothers play an important role in both Suskind's piece and bell hooks's "Keeping Close to Home" (p. 93). Review both selections and then describe the relationships that the two young scholars—bell and Cedric—have with their mothers. To what extent do these mothers represent "home"?

5. Just for the fun of it, read Dave Barry's "Guys vs. Men" (p. 372). Then, using a humorous slant like Barry's, rewrite and expand the conversa-

tion between Cedric and Rob on the matter of smelly feet. Or write a new version of the scene, based on a roommate problem you have experienced.

6. According to Shelby Steele in "The Recoloring of Campus Life" (p. 72), "black people make white people feel guilty." Does Suskind's description of Rob support Steele's claim, or is the relationship between Rob and Cedric more complex? Discuss the issue both in class and in a position paper that explores relationships between different groups on your campus.

JOINING THE CONVERSATION

7. Can a dormitory really be a home? Write a brief argument of definition in which you explore and answer this question, drawing on your own experiences and the issues raised by *A Hope in the Unseen* or any other readings in this chapter.

8. Although Cedric is ultimately not admitted to the Massachusetts Institute of Technology (MIT), he receives a scholarship to Brown University, confirming his mother's faith in him. In an article brief enough to serve as an op-ed piece in your local newspaper, explore the roles that home and family play in directing the ambitions and hopes of young people.

ALICE WALKER
The Place Where I Was Born

ALICE WALKER *(b. 1944), perhaps best known for her Pulitzer Prize-winning 1982 novel* The Color Purple, *is a writer of distinction in many areas, including poetry and short stories as well as other novels (*The Third Life of Grange Copeland, *1970;* The Temple of My Familiar, *1989;* Possessing the Secret of Joy, *1992;* By the Light of My Father's Smile, *1998) and essays (*In Search of Our Mothers' Gardens, *1983;* The Same River Twice, *1996;* Anything We Love Can Be Saved: A Writer's Activism, *1998). After attending Spelman College and graduating from Sarah Lawrence in 1965, Walker moved to Mississippi and taught at Jackson State College while working as a civil rights activist during one of the most harrowing times in our nation's history. Her personal courage during those years is reflected in the actions of many of her fictional characters, as is her commitment to celebrating the lives and achievements of African American women.*

In the following brief prose poem (the opening of Walker's 1991 volume of poetry, Her Blue Body Everything We Knew*), Walker, one of eight children of Georgia sharecroppers Willie Lee and Minnie T. Walker, speaks evocatively of the "land of my birth," the "small rounded hills" and "big leaf poplar" and pines of middle Georgia that for her speak of home.*

I debated a long time with myself before choosing this selection, for I was tempted by many other pieces of Alice Walker's writing, particularly her powerful essay "Looking for Zora [Neale Hurston]," which describes another kind of homecoming. In the end, I was drawn to this less well-known piece, partly because it mixes the genres of poetry and prose, partly because I too grew up in the South and counted Brer Rabbit a friend, and partly because I hoped it would spark some very fond memories in you.

—A.L.

I am a displaced person. I sit here on a swing on the deck of my house in Northern California admiring how the fog has turned the valley below into a lake. For hours nothing will be visible below me except this large expanse of vapor; then slowly, as the sun rises and gains in intensity, the fog will start to curl up and begin its slow rolling drift toward the ocean. People here call it the dragon; and, indeed, a dragon is what it looks like, puffing and coiling, winged, flaring and in places thin and discreet, as it races before the sun, back to its ocean coast den. Mornings I sit here in awe and great peace. The mountains across the valley come and go in the mist; the redwoods and firs, oaks and giant bays appear as clumpish spires, enigmatic shapes of green, like the stone forests one sees in Chinese paintings of Guilin.*

It is incredibly beautiful where I live. Not fancy at all, or exclusive. But from where I sit on my deck I can look down on the backs of hawks, and the wide, satiny wings of turkey vultures glistening in the sun become my present connection to ancient Egyptian Africa. The pond is so still below me that the trees reflected in it seem, from this distance, to be painted in its depths.

All this: the beauty, the quiet, the cleanliness, the peace, is what I love. I realize how lucky I am to have found it here. And yet, there are days when my view of the mountains and redwoods makes me nostalgic for small rounded hills easily walked over, and for the look of big leaf poplar and the scent of pine.

I am nostalgic for the land of my birth, the land I left forever when I was thirteen—moving first to the town of Eatonton,* and then, at seventeen, to the city of Atlanta.

I cried one day as I talked to a friend about a tree I loved as a child. A tree that had sheltered my father on his long cold walk to school each morning: it was midway between his house and the school and because there was a large cavity in its trunk, a fire could be made inside it. During my childhood, in a tiny, overcrowded house in a tiny dell below it, I looked up at it frequently and felt reassured by its age, its generosity despite its years of brutalization (the fires, I knew, had to hurt), and its tall, old-growth pine nobility. When it was struck by lightning and killed, and then was cut down and made into firewood, I grieved as if it had been a person. Secretly. Because who among the members of my family would not have laughed at my grief?

I have felt entirely fortunate to have had this companion, and even today remember it with gratitude. But why the tears? my friend wanted to know. And it suddenly dawned on me that perhaps it *was* sad that it was a tree and not a member of my family to whom I was so emotionally close.

> O, landscape of my birth
> because you were so good to me as I grew
> I could not bear to lose you.
> O, landscape of my birth
> because when I lost you, a part of my soul died.   5
> O, landscape of my birth
> because to save myself I pretended it was *you*
> who died.
> You that now did not exist
> because I could not see you.   10

Guilin: a city in China (Kweilin or Kueilin) characterized by its mountains
Eatonton: the town in which Walker attended high school

But O, landscape of my birth
now I can confess how I have lied.
   Now I can confess the sorrow
of my heart
      as the tears flow   15
and I see again with memory's bright eye
my dearest companion cut down
and can bear to resee myself
so lonely and so small
there in the sunny meadows   20
and shaded woods
of childhood
where my crushed spirit
and stricken heart
ran in circles   25
looking for a friend.

Soon I will have known fifty summers.
Perhaps that is why
my heart
an imprisoned tree   30
so long clutched tight
inside its core
insists
on shedding
like iron leaves   35
the bars
from its cell.

You flow into me.
And like the Aborigine or Bushperson or Cherokee
who braves everything   40
to stumble home to die
no matter that cowboys
are herding cattle where the ancestors slept
I return to you, my earliest love.

Weeping in recognition at the first trees   45
I ever saw, the first hills I ever climbed and rested my
unbearable cares
upon, the first rivers I ever dreamed myself across,
the first pebbles I ever lifted up, warm from the sun, and put
into   50
my mouth.

O landscape of my birth
you have never been far from my heart.
It is *I* who have been far.
    If you will take me back   55
    Know that I
    Am yours.

As a child I assumed I would always have the middle Georgia landscape to live in, as Brer Rabbit,* a native also, and relative, had his brier patch. It was not to be. The pain of racist oppression, and its consequence, economic impoverishment, drove me to the four corners of the earth in search of justice and peace, and work that affirmed my whole being. I have come to rest here, weary from travel, on a deck—not a Southern front porch—overlooking another world.

I am content; and yet, I wonder what my life would have been like if I had been able to stay home?

I remember early morning fogs in Georgia, not so dramatic as California ones, but magical too because out of the Southern fog of memory tramps my dark father, smiling and large, glowing with rootedness, and talking of hound dogs, biscuits and coons. And my equally rooted mother bustles around the corner of our house preparing to start a wash, the fire under the black wash pot extending a circle of warmth in which I, a grave-eyed child, stand. There is my sister Ruth, beautiful to me and dressed elegantly for high school in gray felt skirt and rhinestone brooch, hurrying up the road to catch the yellow school bus which glows like a large glow worm in the early morning fog.

QUESTIONING THE TEXT

1. Walker writes of a tree she "loved as a child." What about this tree is comforting and lovable—and sad? What in the natural world do you love most? Does this element "make up" for something else in any way?

2. Reread Walker's poem. What is the "lie" she has told? Discuss this question with one or two classmates.

3. Note the details of Walker's life that A.L. highlights in her introduction. Why do you think A.L. chose these specifics? How does she want readers to view Walker?

Brer Rabbit: from African legend, a trickster figure popularized in the Uncle Remus stories by Joel Chandler Harris (1848–1908), also born in the country near Eatonton, Georgia

MAKING CONNECTIONS

4. Look carefully at the descriptions of "home" included in this essay and in those by Ron Suskind (p. 588) and Terry Tempest Williams (p. 607). In what ways do they reveal similar attitudes toward "home," and in what ways do they differ? Which description of "home" is most compelling to you, and why? If you keep a reading log, answer these questions there. If not, respond in a paragraph for class discussion.

5. Which other essays in this chapter speak indirectly of "displaced persons"? How are their definitions of *displaced* similar or different? Try your hand at writing a definition of this term.

JOINING THE CONVERSATION

6. Working with two or three classmates, prepare an introduction to Alice Walker. Gather biographical information, and perhaps read two or three other works by Walker. You might watch *The Color Purple,* available on video, and check out Walker's writings about the making of that film. Pool your information, and select from it material for a 20-minute class presentation—"Introducing Alice Walker." (You may have gathered enough information for a more intensive research project on Walker. If so, talk with your instructor about pursuing such a project.)

7. Write your own brief essay titled "The Place Where I Was Born." If you wish, include a poem as Walker does in her essay.

BARBARA SMITH
Home

BARBARA SMITH's "Home" presents home not as a specific, physical place but rather as a location in the mind or heart, somewhere outside of time and space that signals rest and, most of all, acceptance. In the essay, the narrator thinks about the place she grew up, the house she had to sell when "all the women who'd raised" her were dead. Yet these women and that place exist in her memory, and she yearns to return, to share her history with her aunt and mother and grandmother. Most of all, she wants to introduce them to her partner, Leila, and to hear her aunt say "Your friend's so nice and down to earth. She's like one of us."

This is an essay about love and about loss, about living after the death of the family, and about the need to create new families, even if they can visit "home" only in our memories. Smith (b. 1946) writes out of long-standing exploration of these and similar issues. Cofounder of Kitchen Table: Women of Color Press, she has published four collections of essays, including Home Girls: A Black Feminist Anthology *(1983), in which "Home" first appeared. In this and other essays, Smith explores the relationships between African American women, the differences that lesbianism makes, and the call for inclusion of such differences within mainstream African American culture. I chose "Home" because it speaks directly, and positively, to a need many in our society face: how to create a family and a home when the traditional options seem unavailable.*   —A.L.

I can't sleep. I am sitting at an open window, staring at the dark sky and the barely visible nighttime gardens. Three days ago we came here to clean and paint this apartment in the new city we're moving to. Each night I wake up, shoulders aching, haunted by unfamiliarity. Come to this window. Let the fresh air and settled look of neighborhood backyards calm me until exhaustion pulls me back to bed.

Just now it was a dream that woke me. One of my dreams.

I am at home with Aunt LaRue and I am getting ready to leave. We are in the bedroom packing. I'm anxious, wonder if she can feel a change in me. It's been so long since I've seen her. She says she has a present for me and starts pulling out dozens of beautiful vests and laying them on the bed. I am ecstatic. I think, "She knows. She knows about me and it's all right." I feel relieved. But then I wake up, forgetting for a minute where I am or what has happened until I smell the heavy air, see Leila asleep beside me. The dream was so alive.

I felt as if I'd been there. Home. The house where I grew up. But it's been years since then. When Aunt LaRue died, I had to sell the house. My

601

mother, my grandmother, all the women who'd raised me were already dead, so I never go back.

I can't explain how it feels sometimes to miss them. My childish desire   5
to see a face that I'm not going to see. The need for certitude that glimpsing a
profile, seeing a head bent in some ordinary task would bring. To know that
home existed. Of course I know they're gone, that I won't see them again,
but there are times when my family is so real to me, at least my missing them
is so real and thorough, I feel like I have to do something, I don't know what.
Usually I dream.

Since we got here, I think of home even more. Like today when we
were working, I found a radio station that played swing. . . .

Every so often one of us sings a few lines of a song. I say, "Imagine. It's 1945,
the War's over, you've come back, and we're fixing up our swell new place."

Leila laughs. "You're so crazy. You can bet whoever lived here in 1945
wasn't colored or two women either."

"How do you know? Maybe they got together when their husbands
went overseas and then decided they didn't need the boys after all. My aunt
was always telling me about living with this friend of hers, Garnet, during the
War and how much fun they had and how she was so gorgeous."

Leila raises her eyebrows and says, "Honey, you're hopeless. You didn't   10
have a chance hearing stories like that. You had to grow up funny. But you
know my mother is always messing with my mind too, talking about her girlfriends this and her girlfriends that. I think they're all closet cases."

"Probably," I answer. We go on working, the music playing in the
background. I keep thinking about Aunt LaRue. In the early fifties she and
her husband practically built from scratch the old house they had bought for
all of us to live in. She did everything he did. More, actually. When he left a
few years later she did "his" work and hers too, not to mention going to her
job every day. It took the rest of her life to pay off the mortgage.

I want to talk to her. I imagine picking up the phone.

Hi Aunt LaRue. Ahunh. Leila and I got here on Monday. She's fine.
The apartment's a disaster area, but we're getting it together. . . .

Leila is asking me where the hammer is and the conversation in my
head stops. I'm here smoothing plaster, inhaling paint. On the radio Nat King
Cole is singing "When I Marry Sweet Lorraine." Leila goes into the other
room to work. All afternoon I daydream I'm talking with my aunt. This
move has filled me up with questions. I want to tell someone who knew me
long ago what we're doing. I want her to know where I am.

Every week or so Leila talks to her mother. It's hard to overhear them. I
try not to think about it, try to feel neutral and act like it's just a normal occurrence, calling home. After battling for years, Leila and her mother are very close.
Once she told me, "Everything I know is about my family." I couldn't say anything, thought, "So what do I know?" Not even the most basic things like, what

my father was like and why Aunt Rosa never got married. My family, like most, was great at keeping secrets. But I'd always planned when I got older and they couldn't treat me like a kid to ask questions and find out. Aunt LaRue died suddenly, a year after I'd been out of college and then it was too late to ask a thing.

For lack of information I imagine things about them. One day a few   15 weeks ago when I was packing, going through some of Aunt LaRue's papers, I found a bankbook that belonged to both my mother and Aunt LaRue. They had opened the account in 1946, a few months before I was born and it had been closed ten years later, a few months after my mother died. The pages of figures showed that there had never been more than $200 in it. Seeing their two names together, their signatures side by side in dark ink, I got a rush of longing. My mother touched this, held it in her hands. I have some things that belonged to Aunt LaRue, dishes and stuff that I use around the house, even the letters she wrote to me when I was in college. But Mommy died so long ago, I have almost nothing that belonged to her.

I see them the day they open the account. Two young Black women, one of them pregnant, their shoulders square in forties dresses, walking into the cavernous downtown bank. I wonder what they talk about on the bus ride downtown. Or maybe my mother comes alone on the bus and meets Aunt LaRue at work. How does my mother feel? Maybe she senses me kicking inside her as they wait in line. As they leave she tells my aunt, touching her stomach, "I'm afraid." My aunt takes her hand.

I wonder what they were to each other, specifically. What their voices might have sounded like talking as I played in the next room. I know they loved each other, seemed like friends, but I don't have the details. I could feel my aunt missing my mother all through my childhood. I remember the way her voice sounded whenever she said her name. Sometimes I'd do something that reminded her of my mother and she would laugh, remember a story, and say I was just like Hilda. She never pretended that she didn't miss her. I guess a lot of how they loved each other, my aunt gave to me.

But I wonder how someone can know me if they can't know my family, if there's no current information to tell. Never to say to a friend, a lover, "I talked to my mother yesterday and she said. . . ." Nothing to tell. Just a blank where all that is supposed to be. Sometimes I feel like I'm frozen in time, caught in a nightmare of a hot October afternoon when everything changed because my mother stopped living.

Most of my friends have such passionate, complicated relationships with their mothers. Since they don't get married and dragged off into other families, they don't have to automatically cut their ties, be grown-up heterosexuals. I think their mothers help them to be Lesbians. I'm not saying that their mothers necessarily approve, but that they usually keep on loving their daughters because they're flesh and blood, even if they are "queer." I envy my friends. I'd like to have a woman on my side who brought me here. Yes, I know it's not that simple, that I tend to romanticize, that it can be hell especially about coming out. But I still want what they have, what they take for granted. I always imagine with my aunt, it would have been all right.

Maybe I shouldn't talk about this. Even when Leila says she wants to hear about my family and how it was for me growing up, I think sometimes she really doesn't. At least she doesn't want to hear about the death part. Like everyone, a part of her is terrified of her mother dying. So secretly I think she only wants to know from me that it can be all right, that it's not so bad, that it won't hurt as much. My mother died when I was nine. My father had left long before. My aunt took care of me after that. I can't prove to Leila or anybody that losing them did not shatter my life at the time, that on some level I still don't deal with this daily, that my life remains altered by it. I can only say that I lived through it.

The deaths in your life are very private. Maybe I'm waiting for my friends to catch up, so our conversations aren't so one-sided. I want to talk like equals.

More than anything, I wish Leila and I could go there, home. That I could make the reality of my life now and where I came from touch. If we could go, we would get off the bus that stops a block from the house. Leila and I would cross 130th Street and walk up Abell. At the corner of 132nd I would point to it, the third house from the corner. It would still be white and there would be a border of portulaca gleaming like rice paper along the walk. We would climb the porch steps and Leila would admire the black and gray striped awnings hanging over the up and downstairs porches.

The front door would be open and I would lead the way up the narrow stairs to the second floor. Aunt LaRue would be in the kitchen. Before I would see her, I'd call her name.

She'd be so glad to see me and to meet Leila. At first she'd be a little formal with Leila, shy. But gradually all of us would relax. I'd put a record on the hi-fi and Ella would sing in the background. Aunt LaRue would offer us "a little wine" or some gin and tonics. I'd show Leila the house and Aunt LaRue's flowers in the back. Maybe we'd go around the neighborhood, walk the same sidewalks I did so many years ago. For dinner we'd have rolled roast and end up talking till late at night.

Before we'd go to bed, Aunt LaRue would follow me into the bathroom and tell me again, shyly, "Your friend's so nice and down to earth. She's like one of us." I'd tell Leila what she'd said, and then we'd sleep in the room I slept in all the while I was growing up.

Sometimes with Leila, it's like that. With her it can be like family. Until I knew her, I thought it wasn't possible to have that with another woman, at least not for me. But I think we were raised the same way. To be decent, respectful girls. They taught us to work. And to rebel.

Just after we met, Leila and her roommate were giving a party. That afternoon her roommate left and didn't come back for hours so I ended up helping Leila get things ready. As we cleaned and shopped and cooked, it hit me that almost without talking, we agreed on what needed to be done. After years of having to explain, for instance, why I bothered to own an iron, it felt like a revelation. We had something in common, knew how to live in a house like people, not just to camp.

When we first started living together I would get déjà vu, waves of feelings that I hadn't had since I'd lived in that other place, home. Once Leila was in the bathroom and I glimpsed her through the door bending over the tub, her breasts dropping as she reached to turn off the water. It was familiar. The steady comfort of a woman moving through the house.

I don't want to lose that moving here. This new place is like a cave. The poverty of the people who lived here before is trapped in the very walls. Harder than cleaning and painting is altering that sadness.

Tonight we made love here for the first time. It was almost midnight 30 when we stopped working, showered and fell aching into the makeshift bed. When I started to give Leila a single kiss, her mouth caught mine and held me there. Desire surprised me, but then I realized how much everything in me wanted touch. Sometimes our bodies follow each other without will, with no thought of now I'll put my hand here, my mouth there. Tonight there was no strategy, just need and having. Falling into sleep, holding her, I thought, "Now there is something here I know." It calmed me.

But I have been afraid. Afraid of need, of loving someone who can leave. The fear makes me silent, then gradually it closes my heart. It can take days to get beneath whatever haunts me, my spirit weakening like a candle sputtering in some place without air, underground. And Leila has her own nightmare, her own habits of denial. But we get through. Even when I'm most scared, I knew when I first met her that it would be all right to love her, that whatever happened we would emerge from this not broken. It would not be about betrayal. Loving doesn't terrify me. Loss does. The women I need literally disappearing from the face of the earth. It has already happened.

I am sitting at a table by a window. The sky is almost light. My past has left few signs. It only lives through words inside of me.

I get up and walk down the hall to the bathroom. If I can't get back to sleep, I'll never have the strength to work another fourteen hour day. In the bedroom I take off my robe and lie down beside Leila. She turns in her sleep and reaches toward me. "Where were you?" she asks, eyes still closed.

I answer without thinking, "Home."

QUESTIONING THE TEXT

1. The narrator of "Home" says, "Most of my friends have such passionate, complicated relationships with their mothers" (paragraph 19). What in the text describes the relationship the narrator has with her mother?

With Aunt LaRue? In what ways do her relationships with them seem "passionate" and "complicated"?

2. Near the end of the essay, the narrator states, "Loving doesn't terrify me. Loss does." Write a page or two in which you reflect on this statement and your response to it. If you keep a reading log, write your responses there.

3. In the opening of her introduction, A.L. gives her reading of how Barbara Smith presents "home." Do you agree with A.L.'s statement? Why, or why not?

MAKING CONNECTIONS

4. Alice Walker (p. 596) calls herself a "displaced person." Compare Walker's essay with Smith's "Home." In what ways is each writer "displaced" from home? In a brief (one- or two-page) essay, reflect on the different ways in which one can be "displaced," using examples from these two selections to support your points.

5. Ed Madden's poem "Family Cemetery" (p. 668) gives readers a scene of "home" after death. Try your hand at writing a brief poem called "Family Cemetery" from Smith's perspective, and people it with members of her family as they are evoked in "Home."

JOINING THE CONVERSATION

6. Freewrite for 15 to 20 minutes, jotting down every association you have with "home." Look through your list, highlighting the most interesting or evocative items. Then freewrite again, starting with the items you highlighted and writing down everything they bring to mind. When you have enough material, write an essay in which you define "home."

7. Imagine a conversation among Barbara Smith, Terry Tempest Williams (p. 607), Barbara Dafoe Whitehead (p. 619), and Fred Barnes (p. 649) on what an ideal home should be. Working with three classmates, write an exchange among these four writers that would compare and contrast their likely views on "home." Each student might take primary responsibility for one author.

TERRY TEMPEST WILLIAMS
The Clan of One-Breasted Women

IT IS CURRENTLY A CLICHÉ *to say that we live on a small planet—and perhaps a dying one as well. For all we hear of "Mother Earth," this parent of us all has not fared well at our hands. Witness the destruction of ancient forests; the death of rivers, lakes, even oceans; the filth of much city air; the disappearing species. The growing awareness of just how small and crowded—and necessary—the earth is may be at least partially responsible for an outpouring of work called "nature writing" or "environmental literature." Rachel Carson arguably sounded the alarm first, in the riveting opening of her 1963 classic explication of the effects of pesticides,* Silent Spring. *Carson has now been joined by dozens of other distinguished writers, from Aldo Leopold to Barry Lopez and Leslie Marmon Silko—and Terry Tempest Williams.*

Terry Tempest Williams (b. 1955) was born, raised, and educated in Utah, earning her master's degree in environmental education at the University of Utah. Naturalist-in-residence at the Utah Museum of Natural History, Williams, as the following essay suggests, is also a powerful teller of stories in which she attempts to bring the earth to our attention and to convince us that "there is no separation between our bodies and the body of the earth."

In "The Clan of One-Breasted Women," the epilogue of her 1991 book Refuge: An Unnatural History of Family and Place, *she explores the human connection to the earth in relation to the lives of women in her family who have died from or are living with cancer. If we poison Mother Earth, our home, she asks, will our own mothers (and we as well) not also be poisoned? This is a poignant question for me, since my mother and aunt also died of breast cancer. The latest figures from the National Institutes of Health, in fact, tell us that one in seven women in the United States today will contract such a cancer, and though medical researchers have identified some of the genetic bases of breast cancer, they have found no cure. These figures suggest that the issues Williams raises about the "home" represented by the earth and by our own bodies will touch every reader of this book, either directly or indirectly.* —A.L.

The title fooled me. On my first reading some years ago, unaware of who Terry Tempest Williams was

I belong to a Clan of One-Breasted Women. My mother, my grandmothers, and six aunts have all had mastectomies. Seven are dead. The two who survive have just completed rounds of chemotherapy and radiation.

607

I've had my own problems: two biopsies for breast cancer and a small tumor between my ribs diagnosed as a "borderline malignancy."

This is my family history.

Most statistics tell us breast cancer is genetic, hereditary, with rising percentages attached to fatty diets, childlessness, or becoming pregnant after thirty. What they don't say is living in Utah may be the greatest hazard of all.

We are a Mormon family with roots in Utah since 1847. The "word of wisdom" in my family aligned us with good foods—no coffee, no tea, to-bacco, or alcohol. For the most part, our women were finished having their babies by the time they were thirty. And only one faced breast cancer prior to 1960. Traditionally, as a group of people, Mor-mons have a low rate of cancer.

Is our family a cultural anomaly? The truth is, we didn't think about it. Those who did, usually the men, simply said, "bad genes." The women's attitude was stoic. Cancer was part of life. On Feb-ruary 16, 1971, the eve of my mother's surgery, I accidentally picked up the telephone and overheard her ask my grandmother what she could expect.

"Diane, it is one of the most spiritual experi-ences you will ever encounter."

I quietly put down the receiver.

Two days later, my father took my brothers and me to the hospital to visit her. She met us in the lobby in a wheelchair. No bandages were visible. I'll never forget her radiance, the way she held her-self in a purple velvet robe, and how she gathered us around her.

"Children, I am fine. I want you to know I felt the arms of God around me."

We believed her. My father cried. Our mother, his wife, was thirty-eight years old.

A little over a year after Mother's death, Dad and I were having dinner together. He had just returned from St. George, where the Tempest Company was completing the gas lines that would service south-ern Utah. He spoke of his love for the country, the sandstoned landscape, bare-boned and beautiful. He had just finished hiking the Kolob trail in Zion National Park. We got caught up in reminiscing, re-calling with fondness our walk up Angel's Landing on his fiftieth birthday and the years our family had vacationed there.

Over dessert, I shared a recurring dream of mine. I told my father that for years, as long as I could re-member, I saw this flash of light in the night in the desert—that this image had so permeated my being that I could not venture south without seeing it again, on the horizon, illuminating buttes and mesas.

"You did see it," he said.

"Saw what?"

"The bomb. The cloud. We were driving home from Riverside, California. You were sitting on Diane's lap. She was pregnant. In fact, I remember the day, September 7, 1957. We had just gotten out of the Service. We were driving north, past Las Vegas. It was an hour or so before dawn, when this explosion went off. We not only heard it, but felt it. I thought the oil tanker in front of us had blown up. We pulled over and suddenly, rising from the desert floor, we saw it, clearly, this golden-stemmed cloud, the mushroom. The sky seemed to vibrate with an eerie pink glow. Within a few minutes, a light ash was raining on the car."

I stared at my father.

"I thought you knew that," he said. "It was a common occurrence in the fifties."

It was at this moment that I realized the deceit I had been living under. Children growing up in the American Southwest, drinking contaminated milk from contaminated cows, even from the contami-nated breasts of their mothers, my mother—mem-bers, years later, of the Clan of One-Breasted Women.

It is a well-known story in the Desert West, "The Day We Bombed Utah," or more accurately, the years we bombed Utah: above ground atomic testing in Nevada took place from January 27, 1951 through July 11, 1962. Not only were the winds blowing north covering "low-use segments of the population" with fallout and leaving sheep dead in their tracks, but the climate was right. The United

In my memory of the 1950s, the "mushroom cloud" blooms, a source of fear and pride. Like Plato's hemlock, "the bomb" was both poison and cure. —A.L.

The shift from the "light," the "golden-stemmed cloud," the "pink glow," and "light ash" to "contami-nated" land and milk becomes ex-plicitly a "deceit." —A.L.

What does Williams mean by "deceit"? Could she, as late as the 1970s, have been unaware of nuclear testing that she claims, in the next paragraph, was a "well-known story"? —J.R.

Her characterization of the 1950s is grossly simplified, reducing a complex and difficult period to crude stereotypes. —J.R.

Her narrative here is inadequate too, using three quotations to speak for decades of controversy. —J.R.

States of the 1950s was red, white, and blue. The Korean War was raging. McCarthyism was rampant. Ike was it, and the cold war was hot. If you were against nuclear testing, you were for a communist regime.

Much has been written about this "American nuclear tragedy." Public health was secondary to national security. The Atomic Energy Commissioner, Thomas Murray, said, "Gentlemen, we must not let anything interfere with this series of tests, nothing."

Again and again, the American public was told by its government, in spite of burns, blisters, and nausea, "It has been found that the tests may be conducted with adequate assurance of safety under conditions prevailing at the bombing reservations." Assuaging public fears was simply a matter of public relations. "Your best action," an Atomic Energy Commission booklet read, "is not to be worried about fallout." A news release typical of the times stated, "We find no basis for concluding that harm to any individual has resulted from radioactive fallout."

On August 30, 1979, during Jimmy Carter's presidency, a suit was filed, *Irene Allen v. The United States of America.* Mrs. Allen's case was the first on an alphabetical list of twenty-four test cases, representative of nearly twelve hundred plaintiffs seeking compensation from the United States government for cancers caused by nuclear testing in Nevada.

Irene Allen lived in Hurricane, Utah. She was the mother of five children and had been widowed twice. Her first husband, with their two oldest boys, had watched the tests from the roof of the local high school. He died of leukemia in 1956. Her second husband died of pancreatic cancer in 1978.

In a town meeting conducted by Utah Senator Orrin Hatch, shortly before the suit was filed, Mrs. Allen said, "I am not blaming the government, I want you to know that, Senator Hatch. But I thought if my testimony could help in any way so this wouldn't happen again to any of the generations coming up after us . . . I am happy to be here this day to bear testimony of this."

I do not recall questioning the need for nuclear testing until much later in the 1960s. Williams makes me want to study the times more carefully and see if any stories of "burns, blisters, and nausea" were being told. —A.L.

The decision not to blame others seems an important part not only of Mormon culture as Williams presents it but of

God-fearing people. This is just one story in an anthology of thousands.

On May 10, 1984, Judge Bruce S. Jenkins handed down his opinion. Ten of the plaintiffs were awarded damages. It was the first time a federal court had determined that nuclear tests had been the cause of cancers. For the remaining fourteen test cases, the proof of causation was not sufficient. In spite of the split decision, it was considered a landmark ruling. It was not to remain so for long.

In April 1987, the Tenth Circuit Court of Appeals overturned Judge Jenkins's ruling on the ground that the United States was protected from suit by the legal doctrine of sovereign immunity, a centuries-old idea from England in the days of absolute monarchs.

In January 1988, the Supreme Court refused to review the Appeals Court decision. To our court system it does not matter whether the United States government was irresponsible, whether it lied to its citizens, or even that citizens died from the fallout of nuclear testing. What matters is that our government is immune: "The King can do no wrong."

In Mormon culture, authority is respected, obedience is revered, and independent thinking is not. I was taught as a young girl not to "make waves" or "rock the boat."

"Just let it go," Mother would say. "You know how you feel, that's what counts."

For many years, I have done just that—listened, observed, and quietly formed my own opinions, in a culture that rarely asks questions because it has all the answers. But one by one, I have watched the women in my family die common, heroic deaths. We sat in waiting rooms hoping for good news, but always receiving the bad. I cared for them, bathed their scarred bodies, and kept their secrets. I watched beautiful women become bald as Cytoxan, cisplatin, and Adriamycin were injected into their veins. I held their foreheads as they vomited greenblack bile, and I shot them with morphine when the pain became inhuman. In the end, I witnessed their last peaceful breaths, becoming a midwife to the rebirth of their souls.

Williams's own strategy. She has testified before Congress on these issues; I'd like to read that testimony. —A.L.

Her treatment of sovereign immunity—like her discussion of Cold War nuclear terror—seems dismissive. —J.R.

This section is hardest for me to read. Her descriptions, vivid and hurtful as they are, pale in comparison with real-life experiences with these deaths. —A.L.

Although this evokes strong feelings in the reader, it seems a little too graphic. —J.G.R.

The price of obedience has become too high.

The fear and inability to question authority that ultimately killed rural communities in Utah during atmospheric testing of atomic weapons is the same fear I saw in my mother's body. Sheep. Dead sheep. The evidence is buried.

The paragraph would be more powerful without the phrase "But I can't prove they didn't." Citing evidence from her own experience might work better than raising the prickly matter of proving causality. —J.R.

I cannot prove that my mother, Diane Dixon Tempest, or my grandmothers, Lettie Romney Dixon and Kathryn Blackett Tempest, along with my aunts developed cancer from nuclear fallout in Utah. But I can't prove they didn't.

Exact causation is notoriously difficult to prove in almost any case. Perhaps our legal system needs to admit other kinds of proof? —A.L.

My father's memory was correct. The September blast we drove through in 1957 was part of Operation Plumbbob, one of the most intensive series of bomb tests to be initiated. The flash of light in the night in the desert, which I had always thought was a dream, developed into a family nightmare. It took fourteen years, from 1957 to 1971, for cancer to manifest in my mother—the same time Howard L. Andrews, an authority in radioactive fallout at the National Institutes of Health, says radiation cancer requires to become evident. The more I learn about what it means to be a "downwinder," the more questions I drown in.

What I do know, however, is that as a Mormon woman of the fifth generation of Latter-day Saints, I must question everything, even if it means losing my faith, even if it means becoming a member of a border tribe among my own people. Tolerating blind obedience in the name of patriotism or religion ultimately takes our lives.

As I recall from the 1950s, religious groups were often in the forefront of "Ban the Bomb" movements. —J.R.

When the Atomic Energy Commission described the country north of the Nevada Test Site as "virtually uninhabited desert terrain," my family and the birds at Great Salt Lake were some of the "virtual uninhabitants."

Where do we draw the line? When can we feel civil disobedience is justified, even demanded? These are questions Williams—like Gandhi, Thoreau, King—asks us to consider. —A.L.

A second "dream" is introduced into the essay. Like the first dream, I wonder if this one is somehow related to a real event. —A.L.

One night, I dreamed women from all over the world circled a blazing fire in the desert. They spoke of change, how they hold the moon in their bellies and wax and wane with its phases. They mocked the presumption of even-tempered beings and made promises that they would never fear the witch inside themselves. The women danced wildly as sparks broke away from the flames and entered the night sky as stars.

And they sang a song given to them by Shoshone grandmothers:

Ah ne nah, nah	Consider the rabbits
nin nah nah—	How gently they walk on the earth—
ah ne nah, nah	Consider the rabbits
nin nah nah—	How gently they walk on the earth—
Nyaga mutzi	We remember them
oh ne nay—	We can walk gently also—
Nyaga mutzi	We remember them
oh ne nay—	We can walk gently also—

The little I know of Native American cultures suggests that the reverence for the earth that Williams draws on here is a powerful force. —A.L.

I read this section as a dream vision of the sort common among mystical poets imagining alternative worlds. —J.R

The women danced and drummed and sang for weeks, preparing themselves for what was to come. They would reclaim the desert for the sake of their children, for the sake of the land.

A few miles downwind from the fire circle, bombs were being tested. Rabbits felt the tremors. Their soft leather pads on paws and feet recognized the shaking sands, while the roots of mesquite and sage were smoldering. Rocks were hot from the inside out and dust devils hummed unnaturally. And each time there was another nuclear test, ravens watched the desert heave. Stretch marks appeared. The land was losing its muscle.

Here amid the images of death and destruction is an image of life—the "stretch marks" commonly experienced by women after giving birth. Williams seems to be returning to the earlier juxtaposition of life/death images. —A.L.

The women couldn't bear it any longer. They were mothers. They had suffered labor pains but always under the promise of birth. The red hot pains beneath the desert promised death only, as each bomb became a stillborn. A contract had been made and broken between human beings and the land. A new contract was being drawn by the women, who understood the fate of the earth as their own.

Under the cover of darkness, ten women slipped under a barbed-wire fence and entered the contaminated country. They were trespassing. They walked toward the town of Mercury, in moonlight, taking their cues from coyote, kit fox, antelope squirrel, and quail. They moved quietly and deliberately through the maze of Joshua trees. When a hint of daylight appeared they rested, drinking tea and sharing their rations of food. The women closed their eyes. The time had come to protest with the heart, that to deny one's genealogy with the earth was to commit treason against one's soul.

At dawn, the women draped themselves in mylar, wrapping long streamers of silver plastic around their arms to blow in the breeze. They wore clear masks, that became the faces of humanity. And when they arrived at the edge of Mercury, they carried all the butterflies of a summer day in their wombs. They paused to allow their courage to settle.

The town that forbids pregnant women and children to enter because of radiation risks was asleep. The women moved through the streets as winged messengers, twirling around each other in slow motion, peeking inside homes and watching the easy sleep of men and women. They were astonished by such stillness and periodically would utter a shrill note or low cry just to verify life.

The residents finally awoke to these strange apparitions. Some simply stared. Others called authorities, and in time, the women were apprehended by wary soldiers dressed in desert fatigues. They were taken to a white, square building on the other edge of Mercury. When asked who they were and why they were there, the women replied, "We are mothers and we have come to reclaim the desert for our children."

The soldiers arrested them. As the ten women were blindfolded and handcuffed, they began singing:

> *You can't forbid us everything*
> *You can't forbid us to think—*
> *You can't forbid our tears to flow*
> *And you can't stop the songs that we sing.*

The women continued to sing louder and louder, until they heard the voices of their sisters moving across the mesa:

> *Ah ne nah, nah*
> *nin nah nah—*
> *Ah ne nah, nah*
> *nin nah nah—*

Are these the same Mormon women she said didn't drink tea at the beginning of this story? —J.G.R.

It is unclear if this is still a dream or if it really happened. —J.G.R.

Nyaga mutzi
oh ne nay—
Nyaga mutzi
oh ne nay—

"Call for reinforcements," one soldier said.

"We have," interrupted one woman, "we have—and you have no idea of our numbers."

I crossed the line at the Nevada Test Site and was arrested with nine other Utahns for trespassing on military lands. They are still conducting nuclear tests in the desert. Ours was an act of civil disobedience. But as I walked toward the town of Mercury, it was more than a gesture of peace. It was a gesture on behalf of the Clan of One-Breasted Women.

As one officer cinched the handcuffs around my wrists, another frisked my body. She found a pen and a pad of paper tucked inside my left boot.

"And these?" she asked sternly.

"Weapons," I replied.

Our eyes met. I smiled. She pulled the leg of my trousers back over my boot.

"Step forward, please," she said as she took my arm.

We were booked under an afternoon sun and bused to Tonopah, Nevada. It was a two-hour ride. This was familiar country. The Joshua trees standing their ground had been named by my ancestors, who believed they looked like prophets pointing west to the Promised Land. These were the same trees that bloomed each spring, flowers appearing like white flames in the Mojave. And I recalled a full moon in May, when Mother and I had walked among them, flushing out mourning doves and owls.

The bus stopped short of town. We were released.

The officials thought it was a cruel joke to leave us stranded in the desert with no way to get home. What they didn't realize was that we were home, soul-centered and strong, women who recognized the sweet smell of sage as fuel for our spirits.

Marginal notes:

Williams exhibits the moral certitude common in the American tradition of civil disobedience, justifying crusades such as the civil rights and right-to-life movements. —J.R.

Williams's pen and paper weapons—can they ever be a match for guns and bombs? In the past, they have proved more than equal. —A.L.

So here is the actual equivalent of the dream, the point at which Williams answers her own questions about civil disobedience with personal action gesturing toward peace and "on behalf of the Clan of One-Breasted Women." —A.L.

I'm surprised by the positive tone of the conclusion. It suggests that Williams hopes that the land will prevail, and that the "sweet smell of sage" can help women continue to bring forth life. —A.L.

Afterwords

I take Terry Tempest Williams's piece to be operating on at least three levels. First, she is writing out her own grief at the pain and loss suffered by her mother, grandmothers, and six aunts, seven of whom had died of breast cancer at the time of this writing. Second, she is raising serious concerns about specific national policies that may well have left great parts of Utah and other western states toxic and extremely hazardous to human health. And third, she is offering an allegory about personal responsibility and civil disobedience, about the dual nature of scientific "advances," and about the need to protect and to celebrate the earth, our mutual home. Williams is not writing a traditional academic "argument," in which she sets up building blocks of "proof" to support her. Instead, she is weaving several strands and stories here, trying to evoke not assent or capitulation but response—and responsibility—in her readers.

I agree with J.R. that citizens in a democracy will always have to face up to the hard decisions involved in "real-world struggles" such as the threat of the bomb. But I also believe that citizens need—and deserve—information about the hard choices leaders may be making. If we choose to trade a certain number of lives in order to deploy a weapon, let us at least know that we have made the choice. If we choose to damage the earth, and the earth's ability to regenerate itself, in order to pursue nuclear dominance, let us at least know what we are doing—and what the possible as well as the real consequences will be. Let us reject silence as well as the fear that too much knowing may cause in us. —A.L.

Certainly one appreciates the injury Terry Tempest Williams must feel at the unwillingness of the government to compensate Utah's civilian victims of nuclear testing. But I find her earth-mother visions off-putting and inappropriate. The Cold War that prompted the nuclear tests that likely destroyed much of her family was not a shaman's vision but a real-world struggle that ultimately liberated a quarter of the world's population. The threat of the bomb, the horrible power that Williams herself witnessed, tempered the ambitions of dictators cruel as Stalin and foolhardy as Mao—and probably spared us all a third world war. Home-front victims of this struggle, the members of Williams's family, obviously deserve remembrance, apology, and whatever compensation may give them slender comfort now. But I don't find any special wisdom in Terry Tempest Williams's essay—only a poetic but unfocused anger. —J.R.

Williams writes with a clear voice of her undeniable pain, suffering, and frustration. Her sincerity gives her story a tough edge. It is so honest that I am uncomfortable reading it.

I have one question, though: what about the men in her family? She never mentions any of the men getting cancer. Although she tells of her father witnessing a number of blasts, he is apparently alive. Are men immune from this radiation? No, since she gives an example of Irene Allen who lost two husbands to cancers supposedly from the effects of nuclear radiation. How can she be sure that the breast cancer is not heredi-

tary, if both Tempest men and women were equally exposed to the explosions but only the women have a history of cancer, and then of breast cancer only? I do not mean to suggest that her suffering could be any less than it is, but her perspective may be clouded by a severe personal bias. She may be giving the U.S. government a little too much blame and unlucky genes not enough. —J.G.R.

QUESTIONING THE TEXT

1. Williams says that she "cannot prove that my mother . . . or my grand-mothers . . . along with my aunts developed cancer from nuclear fallout in Utah. But I can't prove they didn't." What strategies and pieces of evidence does Williams use to support her strong hunch that there is a relationship between the nuclear testing and the rate of cancer-related deaths?

2. Images of birth run alongside those of death in this essay. Reread the essay, highlighting all the images that have to do with birth. Then write an entry in your reading log (if you are keeping one) in which you reflect on how they add to the point Williams wants to make.

3. Why might Williams have decided to include her dream in this essay? How does it relate or speak to the section that immediately follows it?

4. What use does A.L. make of the metaphor "mother" in her introduction? How effective do you find the metaphor?

MAKING CONNECTIONS

5. Compare the role played by the earth in Williams's essay to its role in Ed Madden's "Family Cemetery, near Hickory Ridge, Arkansas" (p. 668). What does the natural world seem to signify for the family gathered for a funeral in Madden's poem? What has happened to the earth in Williams's piece? Reflect upon these differences in a paragraph or a reading log entry.

6. Both Williams and Barbara Dafoe Whitehead (p. 619) raise important questions about responsibility. What *is* a citizen's responsibility in the face of the kinds of urgent social and environmental problems they describe? Meet with two or three classmates to discuss how Whitehead and Williams might respond to this question. Then, working as a group or as individuals, write an essay about what a citizen's responsibility should be on a particular topic: nuclear testing and fallout, divorce, teen pregnancy, or any issue in which you feel citizens, yourself included, have much at stake.

JOINING THE CONVERSATION

7. Look into the environmental history of your city, region, or state, searching for issues of concern about the quality of water or air, for example. Then freewrite for half an hour or so about the issues that most concern you. What environmental hazards might you have encountered while you were growing up? Or was your region completely safe from contaminants? After you choose a topic and determine your stance on it, write a letter to the editor of your hometown newspaper raising the issues that concern you.

8. Williams describes a dream that in some ways turns out to be closely related to a real-life experience. How have your dreams been related to either predream or postdream real-life occurrences? In a brief essay, explore the relationships between "dream life" and "real life." If you keep a reading log, answer this question there.

9. Williams describes an act of civil disobedience in which she and other women took part. Spend some time thinking about your position on civil disobedience: when it is justified, when you would take such actions, when you would not take them, and so on. You might read about other acts of civil disobedience, such as those of Henry David Thoreau, Mahatma Gandhi, Martin Luther King Jr., or Rosa Parks. Then write a position paper explaining where you stand on the issue of civil disobedience and supporting your position with examples from your own, and others', experiences.

BARBARA DAFOE WHITEHEAD
The Making of a Divorce Culture

Growing up in the 1950s, *I knew only one classmate whose parents were divorced. In my tight ethnic neighborhood, stable two-parent families were the rule, and divorce was something observed only occasionally on the silver screen. In fact, families breaking up seemed very much a Hollywood phenomenon — what stars like Elizabeth Taylor and Frank Sinatra did to keep the tabloids focused on their careers. But Hollywood soon rubbed off on the rest of us.*

Within a generation, we've come to accept divorce as almost normal. But normal *here simply means that divorces now happen all the time, not that the pain of separation they cause has become easier to endure, especially for children. For me, that point was made most forcefully the first time I taught this "Home" chapter in an earlier edition of* The Presence of Others. *In class discussions, we explored all sorts of family concerns — from the changing role of fathers to conditions in nursing homes — but we had skirted one burning issue that emerged spontaneously as the theme of more than half the papers the unit produced. In draft after searing draft, my students detailed their personal and inevitably painful experiences with divorce. As we reviewed the drafts in subsequent class sessions, the writers often turned to each other for understanding and support as they recounted their feelings of hurt and betrayal. Clearly, for many students today, divorce has become a central event in their lives, shaping their views and attitudes toward family, commitment, and relationships with members of the opposite sex.*

Although it has recently become fashionable to talk about the normalcy of single parenthood and other nontraditional family arrangements, Barbara Dafoe Whitehead (b. 1944) argues that the willingness of American culture to accept divorce is genuinely new. A registered Democrat, Whitehead first came to public attention with an article she published in the Atlantic Monthly *with the now-famous title "Dan Quayle Was Right" (April 1993). In the piece, Whitehead, wielding numerous studies and statistics, argued that then-vice president Quayle had correctly identified a major problem in American society when he attacked TV sitcom mom Murphy Brown for celebrating single parenthood. The argument of Whitehead's influential piece evolved into her* The Divorce Culture *(1997), a book-length study of the causes and consequences of soaring divorce rates in America. "The Making of a Divorce Culture" is the introduction to Whitehead's book. Married and the mother of three children, Whitehead has a Ph.D. from the University of Chicago.* —J.R.

Divorce is now part of everyday American life. It is embedded in our laws and institutions, our manners and mores, our movies and television shows, our novels and children's storybooks, and our closest and most important relationships. Indeed, divorce has become so pervasive that many people naturally assume it has seeped into the social and cultural mainstream over a long period of time. Yet this is not the case. Divorce has become an American way of life only as the result of recent and revolutionary change.

The entire history of American divorce can be divided into two periods, one evolutionary and the other revolutionary. For most of the nation's history, divorce was a rare occurrence and an insignificant feature of family and social relationships. In the first sixty years of the twentieth century, divorce became more common, but it was hardly commonplace. In 1960, the divorce rate stood at a still relatively modest level of nine per one thousand married couples. After 1960, however, the rate accelerated at a dazzling pace. It doubled in roughly a decade and continued its upward climb until the early 1980s, when it stabilized at the highest level among advanced Western societies. As a consequence of this sharp and sustained rise, divorce moved from the margins to the mainstream of American life in the space of three decades.

Ideas are important in revolutions, yet surprisingly little attention has been devoted to the ideas that gave impetus to the divorce revolution. Of the scores of books on divorce published in recent decades, most focus on its legal, demographic, economic, or (especially) psychological dimensions. Few, if any, deal fully with its intellectual origins. Yet trying to comprehend the divorce revolution and its consequences without some sense of its ideological origins, is like trying to understand the American Revolution without taking into account the thinking of John Locke, Thomas Jefferson, or Thomas Paine. This more recent revolution, like the revolution of our nation's founding, has its roots in a distinctive set of ideas and claims.

This book [*The Divorce Culture*] is about the ideas behind the divorce revolution and how these ideas have shaped a culture of divorce. The making of a divorce culture has involved three overlapping changes: first, the emergence and widespread diffusion of a historically new and distinctive set of ideas about divorce in the last third of the twentieth century; second, the migration of divorce from a minor place within a system governed by marriage to a freestanding place as a major institution governing family relationships; and third, a widespread shift in thinking about the obligations of marriage and parenthood.

Beginning in the late 1950s, Americans began to change their ideas   5
about the individual's obligations to family and society. Broadly described, this change was away from an ethic of obligation to others and toward an obligation to self. I do not mean that people suddenly abandoned all responsibilities to others, but rather that they became more acutely conscious of their responsibility to attend to their own individual needs and interests. At least as important as the moral obligation to look after others, the new thinking suggested, was the moral obligation to look after oneself.

This ethical shift had a profound impact on ideas about the nature and purpose of the family. In the American tradition, the marketplace and the public square have represented the realms of life devoted to the pursuit of individual interest, choice, and freedom, while the family has been the realm defined by voluntary commitment, duty, and self-sacrifice. With the greater emphasis on individual satisfaction in family relationships, however, family well-being became subject to a new metric. More than in the past, satisfaction in this sphere came to be based on subjective judgments about the content and quality of individual happiness rather than on such objective measures as level of income, material nurture and support, or boosting children onto a higher rung on the socioeconomic ladder. People began to judge the strength and "health" of family bonds according to their capacity to promote individual fulfillment and personal growth. As a result, the conception of the family's role and place in the society began to change. The family began to lose its separate place and distinctive identity as the realm of duty, service, and sacrifice. Once the domain of the obligated self, the family was increasingly viewed as yet another domain for the expression of the unfettered self.

These broad changes figured centrally in creating a new conception of divorce which gained influential adherents and spread broadly and swiftly throughout the society—a conception that represented a radical departure from earlier notions. Once regarded mainly as a social, legal, and family event in which there were other stakeholders, divorce now became an event closely linked to the pursuit of individual satisfactions, opportunities, and growth.

The new conception of divorce drew upon some of the oldest, and most resonant, themes in the American political tradition. The nation, after all, was founded as the result of a political divorce, and revolutionary thinkers explicitly adduced a parallel between the dissolution of marital bonds and the dissolution of political bonds. In political as well as marital relationships, they argued, bonds of obligation were established voluntarily on the basis of mutual affection and regard. Once such bonds turned cold and oppressive, peoples, like individuals, had the right to dissolve them and to form more perfect unions.

In the new conception of divorce, this strain of eighteenth-century political thought mingled with a strain of twentieth-century psychotherapeutic thought. Divorce was not only an individual right but also a psychological resource. The dissolution of marriage offered the chance to make oneself over from the inside out, to refurbish and express the inner self, and to acquire certain valuable psychological assets and competencies, such as initiative, assertiveness, and a stronger and better self-image.

The conception of divorce as both an individual right and an inner experience merged with and reinforced the new ethic of obligation to the self. In family relationships, one had an obligation to be attentive to one's own feelings and to work toward improving the quality of one's inner life. This ethical imperative completed the rationale for a sense of individual entitlement to divorce. Increasingly, mainstream America saw the legal dissolution of marriage as a matter of individual choice, in which there were no other stakeholders or larger social interests. This conception of divorce strongly argued for removing the social, legal, and moral impediments to the free exercise of the individual right to divorce. 10

Traditionally, one major impediment to divorce was the presence of children in the family. According to well-established popular belief, dependent children had a stake in their parents' marriage and suffered hardship as a result of the dissolution of the marriage. Because children were vulnerable and dependent, parents had a moral obligation to place their children's interests in the marital partnership above their own individual satisfactions. This notion was swiftly abandoned after the 1960s. Influential voices in the society, including child-welfare professionals, claimed that the happiness of individual parents, rather than an intact marriage, was the key determinant of children's family well-being. If divorce could make one or both parents happier, then it was likely to improve the well-being of children as well.

In the following decades, the new conception of divorce spread through the law, therapy, etiquette, the social sciences, popular advice literature, and religion. Concerns that had dominated earlier thinking on divorce were now dismissed as old-fashioned and excessively moralistic. Divorce would not harm children but would lead to greater happiness for children and their single parents. It would not damage the institution of marriage but would make possible better marriages and happier individuals. Divorce would not damage the social fabric by diminishing children's life chances but would strengthen the social fabric by improving the quality of affective bonds between parents and children, whatever form the structural arrangements of their families might happen to take.

As the sense of divorce as an individual freedom and entitlement grew, the sense of concern about divorce as a social problem diminished. Earlier in the century, each time the divorce rate increased sharply, it had inspired widespread public concern and debate about the harmful impact of divorce on families and the society. But in the last third of the century, as the divorce rate rose to once unthinkable levels, public anxiety about it all but vanished. At the very moment when divorce had its most profound impact on the society, weakening the institution of marriage, revolutionizing the structure of families and reorganizing parent-child relationships, it ceased to be a source of concern or debate.

The lack of attention to divorce became particularly striking after the 1980s, as a politically polarized debate over the state of the American family took shape. On one side, conservatives pointed to abortion, illegitimacy, and homosexuality as forces destroying the family. On the other, liberals cited domestic violence, economic insecurity, and inadequate public supports as the key problems afflicting the family. But politicians on both sides had almost nothing to say about divorce. Republicans did not want to alienate their upscale constituents or their libertarian wing, both of whom tended to favor easy divorce, nor did they want to call attention to the divorces among their own leadership. Democrats did not want to anger their large constituency among women who saw easy divorce as a hard-won freedom and prerogative, nor did they wish to seem unsympathetic to single mothers. Thus, except for bipartisan calls to get tougher with deadbeat dads, both Republicans and Democrats avoided the issue of divorce and its consequences as far too politically risky.

But the failure to address divorce carried a price. It allowed the middle   15
class to view family breakdown as a "them" problem rather than an "us"
problem. Divorce was not like illegitimacy or welfare dependency, many
claimed. It was a matter of individual choice, imposing few, if any, costs or
consequences on others. Thus, mainstream America could cling to the comfortable illusion that the nation's family problems had to do with the behavior
of unwed teenage mothers or poor women on welfare rather than with the
instability of marriage and family life within its own ranks.

Nonetheless, after thirty years of persistently high levels of divorce, this
illusion, though still politically attractive, is increasingly difficult to sustain in
the face of a growing body of experience and evidence. To begin with, divorce has indeed hurt children. It has created economic insecurity and disadvantage for many children who would not otherwise be economically vulnerable. It has led to more fragile and unstable family households. It has caused a
mass exodus of fathers from children's households and, all too often, from
their lives. It has reduced the levels of parental time and money invested in
children. In sum, it has changed the very nature of American childhood. Just
as no patient would have designed today's system of health care, so no child
would have chosen today's culture of divorce.

Divorce figures prominently in the altered economic fortunes of middle-
class families. Although the economic crisis of the middle class is usually described
as a problem caused by global economic changes, changing patterns in education
and earnings, and ruthless corporate downsizing, it owes more to divorce than is
commonly acknowledged. Indeed, recent data suggest that marriage may be a
more important economic resource than a college degree. According to an
analysis of 1994 income patterns, the median income of married-parent households whose heads have only a high school diploma is ten percent higher than the
median income of college-educated single-parent households.[1] Parents who are
college graduates *and* married form the new economic elite among families with
children. Consequently, those who are concerned about what the downsizing of
corporations is doing to workers should also be concerned about what the downsizing of families through divorce is doing to parents and children.

Widespread divorce depletes social capital as well. Scholars tell us that
strong and durable family and social bonds generate certain "goods" and

---

[1]An analysis of income data provided by The Northeastern University Center for Labor
Market Studies shows the following distribution by education and marital status:

Median Incomes for U.S. Families with Children, 1994

Education of Household Head	Married Couple Families	Single Parent Families
College Graduate	$71,263	$36,006
High School Graduate	$40,098	$14,698

Based on 1994 Current Population Statistics. Families with one or more children under 18. Age of household head: 22–62.

services, including money, mutual assistance, information, caregiving, protection, and sponsorship. Because such bonds endure over time, they accumulate and form a pool of social capital which can be drawn down upon, when needed, over the entire course of a life. An elderly couple, married for fifty years, is likely to enjoy a substantial body of social and emotional capital, generated through their long-lasting marriage, which they can draw upon in caring for each other and for themselves as they age. Similarly, children who grow up in stable, two-parent married households are the beneficiaries of the social and emotional capital accumulated over time as a result of an enduring marriage bond. As many parents know, children continue to depend on these resources well into young adulthood. But as family bonds become increasingly fragile and vulnerable to disruption, they become less permanent and thus less capable of generating such forms of help, financial resources, and mutual support. In short, divorce consumes social capital and weakens the social fabric. At the very time that sweeping socioeconomic changes are mandating greater investment of social capital in children, widespread divorce is reducing the pool of social capital. As the new economic and social conditions raise the hurdles of child-rearing higher, divorce digs potholes in the tracks.

It should be stressed that this book is not intended as a brief against divorce as such. We must assume that divorce is necessary as a remedy for irretrievably broken marriages, especially those that are marred by severe abuse such as chronic infidelity, drug addiction, or physical violence. Nor is its argument directed against those who are divorced. It assumes that divorce is difficult, painful, and often unwanted by at least one spouse, and that divorcing couples require compassion and support from family, friends, and their religious communities. Nor should this book be taken as an appeal for a return to an earlier era of American family life. The media routinely portray the debate over the family as one between nostalgists and realists, between those who want to turn back the clock to the fifties and those who want to march bravely and resolutely forward into the new century. But this is a lazy and misguided approach, driven more by the easy availability of archival photos and footage from 1950s television sitcoms than by careful consideration of the substance of competing arguments.

More fundamentally, this approach overlooks the key issue. And that 20
issue is not how today's families might stack up against those of an earlier era; indeed, no reliable empirical data for such a comparison exist. In an age of diverse family structures, the heart of the matter is what kinds of contemporary family arrangements have the greatest capacity to promote children's well-being, and how we can ensure that more children have the advantages of growing up in such families.

In the past year or so, there has been growing recognition of the personal and social costs of three decades of widespread divorce. A public debate has finally emerged. Within this debate, there are two separate and overlapping discussions.

The first centers on a set of specific proposals that are intended to lessen the harmful impact of divorce on children: a federal system of child-support collection, tougher child-support enforcement, mandatory counseling for divorcing parents, and reform of no-fault divorce laws in the states. What is striking about this discussion is its narrow focus on public policy, particularly on changes in the system of no-fault divorce. In this, as in so many other crucial discussions involving social and moral questions, the most vocal and visible participants come from the world of government policy, electoral politics, and issue advocacy. The media, which are tongue-tied unless they can speak in the language of left-right politics, reinforce this situation. And the public is offered needlessly polarized arguments that hang on a flat yes-or-no response to this or that individual policy measure. All too often, this discussion of divorce poses what *Washington Post* columnist E. J. Dionne aptly describes as false choices.

Notably missing is a serious consideration of the broader moral assumptions and empirical claims that define our divorce culture. Divorce touches on classic questions in American public philosophy — on the nature of our most important human and social bonds, the duties and obligations imposed by bonds we voluntarily elect, the "just causes" for the dissolution of those bonds, and the differences between obligations volunteered and those that must be coerced. Without consideration of such questions, the effort to change behavior by changing a few public policies is likely to founder.

The second and complementary discussion does try to place divorce within a larger philosophical framework. Its proponents have looked at the decline in the well-being of the nation's children as the occasion to call for a collective sense of commitment by all Americans to all of America's children. They pose the challenging question: "What are Americans willing to do 'for the sake of *all* children'?" But while this is surely an important question, it addresses only half of the problem of declining commitment. The other half has to do with how we answer the question: "What are individual parents obliged to do 'for the sake of their own children'?"

Renewing a *social* ethic of commitment to children is an urgent goal, but   25
it cannot be detached from the goal of strengthening the *individual* ethic of commitment to children. The state of one affects the standing of the other. A society that protects the rights of parents to easy, unilateral divorce, and flatly rejects the idea that parents should strive to preserve a marriage "for the sake of the children," faces a problem when it comes to the question of public sacrifice "for the sake of the children." To put it plainly, many of the ideas we have come to believe and vigorously defend about adult prerogatives and freedoms in family life are undermining the foundations of altruism and support for children.

With each passing year, the culture of divorce becomes more deeply entrenched. American children are routinely schooled in divorce. Mr. Rogers teaches toddlers about divorce. An entire children's literature is devoted to divorce. Family movies and videos for children feature divorced families. *Mrs. Doubtfire,* originally a children's book about divorce and then a hit movie, is aggressively marketed as a holiday video for kids. Of course, these books and movies are designed to help children deal with the social reality and psychological trauma of divorce. But they also carry an unmistakable message about the impermanence and unreliability of family bonds. Like romantic love, the children's storybooks say, family love comes and goes. Daddies disappear. Mommies find new boyfriends. Mommies' boyfriends leave. Grandparents go away. Even pets must be left behind.

More significantly, in a society where nearly half of all children are likely to experience parental divorce, family breakup becomes a defining event of American childhood itself. Many children today know nothing but divorce in their family lives. And although children from divorced families often say they want to avoid divorce if they marry, young adults whose parents divorced are more likely to get divorced themselves and to bear children outside of marriage than young adults from stable married-parent families.

Precisely because the culture of divorce has generational momentum, this book [*The Divorce Culture*] offers no easy optimism about the prospects for change. But neither does it counsel passive resignation or acceptance of the culture's relentless advance. What it does offer is a critique of the ideas behind current divorce trends. Its argument is directed against the ideas about divorce that have gained ascendancy, won our support, and lodged in our consciousness as "proven" and incontrovertible. It challenges the popular idea of divorce as an individual right and freedom to be exercised in the pursuit of individual goods and satisfactions, without due regard for other stakeholders in the marital partnership, especially children. This may be a fragile and inadequate response to a profoundly consequential set of changes, but it seeks the abandonment of ideas that have misled us and failed our children.

In a larger sense, this book is both an appreciation and a criticism of what is peculiarly American about divorce. Divorce has spread throughout advanced Western societies at roughly the same pace and over roughly the same period of time. Yet nowhere else has divorce been so deeply imbued with the larger themes of a nation's political traditions. Nowhere has divorce so fully reflected the spirit and susceptibilities of a people who share an extravagant faith in the power of the individual and in the power of positive thinking. Divorce in America is not unique, but what we have made of divorce is uniquely American. In exploring the cultural roots of divorce, therefore, we look at ourselves, at what is best and worst in our traditions, what is visionary and what is blind, and how the two are sometimes tragically commingled and confused.

QUESTIONING THE TEXT

1. Whitehead claims in the opening sentence that "[d]ivorce is now part of everyday American life." What evidence can you point to—from popular culture, American society, or your own experience—to support *or* refute that claim?

2. Arguing that the increasing divorce rate is due, in part, to a shift in the way marriage is viewed, Whitehead says Americans have moved from an ethic of obligation within families to an ethic of self-fulfillment. Working in a group, explore these abstractions and try to give them a more concrete shape. When does a family member act according to an ethic of obligation and when according to an ethic of self-fulfillment? How compatible are these different views of the family?

MAKING CONNECTIONS

3. Whitehead mentions a "goal of strengthening the *individual* ethic of commitment to children" (paragraph 25). In a brief essay, explore this notion more fully, using the selections by Ron Suskind (p. 588) and Fred Barnes (p. 649) to furnish examples of such parental commitment. If appropriate, draw on examples from your own experience as well.

4. Read "The Rules about the Rules" (p. 157), from Stephen L. Carter's book *Integrity,* paying special attention to the three criteria Carter uses to define an act of integrity. Then write an essay in which you explore when and/or whether a divorce can fit that definition.

JOINING THE CONVERSATION

5. Whitehead disputes the popular argument that children are better off when divorce "make[s] one or both parents happier" (paragraph 11), suggesting that many contemporary problems can be traced to broken families. Write an essay exploring the consequences of divorce for children. For support, draw on library materials, your personal experience, and, possibly, firsthand information gathered through interviews.

6. Whitehead largely dismisses a series of public policy proposals "intended to lessen the harmful impact of divorce on children: a federal system of child-support collection, tougher child-support enforcement, mandatory counseling for divorcing parents, and reform of no-fault divorce laws in the states" (paragraph 22). Working in a group, discuss these and other options for making divorce less devastating for children, as well as ideas for making families more stable and successful. Then write a proposal paper on your own explaining one such idea. Your proposal need not endorse Whitehead's ideas about the causes or consequences of divorce.

STEPHANIE COONTZ
The Way We Wish We Were

*A*MERICANS PAY A HIGH PRICE *for their nostalgia about "traditional" families and homes, argues Stephanie Coontz in* The Way We Never Were: American Families and the Nostalgia Trap *(1992). In Coontz's view, as her title suggests, the good old days so many people long for never actually existed, and the futile effort to restore them keeps Americans from seeking realistic ways to enhance family life at the dawn of the twenty-first century.*

In the following chapter from her book, Coontz (b. 1944), Professor of History and Family Studies at Evergreen State College in Washington, traces changes in American family life and values from colonial times to the present, in each case emphasizing the complexity of family relationships; the shifting influence of social, political, and economic changes on families; and the often careless use of statistical data to make shaky claims about families. The impact of Coontz's work has been substantial: she has served as a consultant for many government and community agencies interested in children and families. Her most recent books, The Way We Really Are: Coming to Terms with America's Changing Families *(1997) and* American Families: A Multicultural Reader *(1998), continue to provide rich and complex explorations of the meaning of family life in the United States.*

I chose this selection in part because recent discussions in my classes tend to support Coontz's claim that students' key images of the "traditional family" are often related to television representations of family life. In addition, I quite like the title of her chapter: "The Way We Wish We Were." Where home and family are concerned, my guess is that such wishes are widely divergent—and that they will be fascinating to discuss.
                                                                                    —A.L.

When I begin teaching a course on family history, I often ask my students to write down ideas that spring to mind when they think of the "traditional family." Their lists always include several images. One is of extended families in which all members worked together, grandparents were an integral part of family life, children learned responsibility and the work ethic from their elders, and there were clear lines of authority based on respect for age. Another is of nuclear families in which nurturing mothers sheltered children from premature exposure to sex, financial worries, or other adult concerns, while fathers taught adolescents not to sacrifice their education by going to work too early. Still another image gives pride of place to the couple relationship. In traditional families, my students write—half derisively, half wistfully—men and women remained chaste until marriage, at which time they extricated themselves from competing obligations to kin and neighbors and committed themselves wholly to the marital relationship, experiencing an all-encompassing intimacy that our more crowded modern life seems to preclude. As one freshman wrote: "They truly respected the marriage vowels"; I assume she meant *I-O-U*.

Such visions of past family life exert a powerful emotional pull on most Americans, and with good reason, given the fragility of many modern commitments. The problem is not only that these visions bear a suspicious resemblance to reruns of old television series, but also that the scripts of different shows have been mixed up: June Cleaver suddenly has a Grandpa Walton dispensing advice in her kitchen; Donna Stone, vacuuming the living room in her inevitable pearls and high heels, is no longer married to a busy modern pediatrician but to a small-town sheriff who, like Andy Taylor* of *The Andy Griffith Show,* solves community problems through informal, old-fashioned common sense.

Like most visions of a "golden age," the "traditional family" my students describe evaporates on closer examination. It is an ahistorical amalgam of structures, values, and behaviors that never coexisted in the same time and place. The notion that traditional families fostered intense intimacy between husbands and wives while creating mothers who were totally available to their children, for example, is an idea that combines some characteristics of the white, middle-class family in the mid-nineteenth century and some of a rival family ideal first articulated in the 1920s. The first family revolved emotionally around the mother-child axis, leaving the husband-wife relationship stilted and formal. The second focused on an eroticized couple relationship, demanding that mothers curb emotional "overinvestment" in their children. The hybrid idea that a woman can be fully absorbed with her youngsters while simultaneously maintaining passionate sexual excitement with her husband was a 1950s invention that drove thousands of women to therapists, tranquilizers, or alcohol when they actually tried to live up to it.

Similarly, an extended family in which all members work together under the top-down authority of the household elder operates very differently from a nuclear family in which husband and wife are envisioned as friends who patiently devise ways to let the children learn by trial and error. Children who worked in family enterprises seldom had time for the extracurricular activities that Wally and the Beaver* recounted to their parents over the dinner table; often, they did not even go to school full-time. Mothers who did home production generally relegated child care to older children or servants; they did not suspend work to savor a baby's first steps or discuss with their husband how to facilitate a grade-schooler's "self-esteem." Such families emphasized formality, obedience to authority, and "the way it's always been" in their childrearing.

June Cleaver . . . Andy Taylor: Characters in various family-oriented television series. June Cleaver played a housewife in *Leave It to Beaver;* Donna Stone was a housewife in *The Donna Reed Show;* Andy Taylor was the sheriff of Mayberry in *The Andy Griffith Show.*

Wally and the Beaver: brothers in the television sitcom *Leave It to Beaver*

Nuclear families, by contrast, have tended to pride themselves on the   5
"modernity" of parent–child relations, diluting the authority of grandparents,
denigrating "old-fashioned" ideas about childraising, and resisting the "inter-
ference" of relatives. It is difficult to imagine the Cleavers or the college-
educated title figure of *Father Knows Best* letting grandparents, maiden aunts,
or in-laws have a major voice in childrearing decisions. Indeed, the kind of
family exemplified by the Cleavers . . . represented a conscious *rejection* of the
Waltons' model.

The Elusive Traditional Family

Whenever people propose that we go back to the traditional family, I
always suggest that they pick a ballpark date for the family they have in mind.
Once pinned down, they are invariably unwilling to accept the package deal
that comes with their chosen model. Some people, for example, admire the
discipline of colonial families, which were certainly not much troubled by divorce or fragmenting individualism. But colonial families were hardly stable:
High mortality rates meant that the average length of marriage was less than a
dozen years. One-third to one-half of all children lost at least one parent before the age of twenty-one; in the South, more than half of all children aged
thirteen or under had lost at least one parent.[1]

While there are a few modern Americans who would like to return to the
strict patriarchal authority of colonial days, in which disobedience by women
and children was considered a small form of treason, these individuals would
doubtless be horrified by other aspects of colonial families, such as their failure
to protect children from knowledge of sexuality. Eighteenth-century spelling
and grammar books routinely used *fornication* as an example of a four-syllable
word, and preachers detailed sexual offenses in astonishingly explicit terms. Sexual conversations between men and women, even in front of children, were remarkably frank. It is worth contrasting this colonial candor to the climate in
1991, when the Department of Health and Human Services was forced to can-
cel a proposed survey of teenagers' sexual practices after some groups charged
that such knowledge might "inadvertently" encourage more sex.[2]

---

[1]Philip Greven, *Four Generations: Population, Land, and Family in Colonial Andover, Massachusetts* (Ithaca, N.Y.: Cornell University Press, 1970); Vivian Fox and Martin Quit, *Loving, Parenting, and Dying: The Family Cycle in England and America, Past and Present* (New York: Psy-
chohistory Press, 1980), p. 401.

[2]John Demos, *A Little Commonwealth: Family Life in Plymouth Colony* (New York: Ox-
ford University Press, 1970), p. 108; Mary Ryan, *Cradle of the Middle Class: The Family in Oneida
County, New York, 1790–1865* (New York: Cambridge University Press, 1981), pp. 33, 38–39;
Carroll Smith-Rosenberg, *Disorderly Conduct: Visions of Gender in Victorian America* (New York:
Oxford University Press, 1985), p. 24.

Other people searching for an ideal traditional family might pick the more sentimental and gentle Victorian family, which arose in the 1830s and 1840s as household production gave way to wage work and professional occupations outside the home. A new division of labor by age and sex emerged among the middle class. Women's roles were redefined in terms of domesticity rather than production, men were labeled "breadwinners" (a masculine identity unheard of in colonial days), children were said to need time to play, and gentle maternal guidance supplanted the patriarchal authoritarianism of the past.

But the middle-class Victorian family depended for its existence on the multiplication of other families who were too poor and powerless to retreat into their own little oases and who therefore had to provision the oases of others. Childhood was prolonged for the nineteenth-century middle class only because it was drastically foreshortened for other sectors of the population. The spread of textile mills, for example, freed middle-class women from the most time-consuming of their former chores, making cloth. But the raw materials for these mills were produced by slave labor. Slave children were not exempt from field labor unless they were infants, and even then their mothers were not allowed time off to nurture them. Frederick Douglass* could not remember seeing his mother until he was seven.[3]

Domesticity was also not an option for the white families who worked   10 twelve hours a day in Northern factories and workshops transforming slave-picked cotton into ready-made clothing. By 1820, "half the workers in many factories were boys and girls who had not reached their eleventh birthday." Rhode Island investigators found "little half-clothed children" making their way to the textile mills before dawn. In 1845, shoemaking families and makers of artificial flowers worked fifteen to eighteen hours a day, according to the New York *Daily Tribune*.[4]

Within the home, prior to the diffusion of household technology at the end of the century, house cleaning and food preparation remained mammoth tasks. Middle-class women were able to shift more time into childrearing in this period only by hiring domestic help. Between 1800 and 1850, the proportion of servants to white households doubled, to about one in nine. Some servants were poverty-stricken mothers who had to board or bind out their own children. Employers found such workers tended to be "distracted," however; they usually preferred young girls. In his study of Buffalo, New

---

Frederick Douglass (1817–95): Son of a slave mother and white father, Douglass became an abolitionist leader and eloquent advocate for human rights.

[3]Frederick Douglass, *My Bondage and My Freedom* (New York: Dover, 1968), p. 48.

[4]David Roediger and Philip Foner, *Our Own Time: A History of American Labor and the Working Day* (London: Greenwood, 1989), p. 9; Norman Ware, *The Industrial Worker, 1840–1860* (New York: Quadrangle, 1964), p. 5; Barbara Wertheimer, *We Were There: The Story of Working Women in America* (New York: Pantheon, 1977), p. 91; Sean Wilentz, *Chants Democratic: New York City and the Rise of the Working Class, 1788–1850* (New York: Oxford University Press, 1984), p. 126.

York, in the 1850s, historian Lawrence Glasco found that Irish and German girls often went into service at the age of eleven or twelve.[5]

For every nineteenth-century middle-class family that protected its wife and child within the family circle, then, there was an Irish or a German girl scrubbing floors in that middle-class home, a Welsh boy mining coal to keep the home-baked goodies warm, a black girl doing the family laundry, a black mother and child picking cotton to be made into clothes for the family, and a Jewish or an Italian daughter in a sweatshop making "ladies" dresses or artificial flowers for the family to purchase.

Furthermore, people who lived in these periods were seldom as enamored of their family arrangements as modern nostalgia might suggest. Colonial Americans lamented "the great neglect in many parents and masters in training up their children" and expressed the "greatest trouble and grief about the rising generation." No sooner did Victorian middle-class families begin to withdraw their children from the work world than observers began to worry that children were becoming *too* sheltered. By 1851, the Reverend Horace Bushnell spoke for many in bemoaning the passing of the traditional days of household production, when the whole family was "harnessed, all together, into the producing process, young and old, male and female, from the boy who rode the plough-horse to the grandmother knitting under her spectacles."[6]

The late nineteenth century saw a modest but significant growth of extended families and a substantial increase in the number of families who were "harnessed" together in household production. Extended families have never been the norm in America; the highest figure for extended-family households ever recorded in American history is 20 percent. Contrary to the popular myth that industrialization destroyed "traditional" extended families, this high point occurred between 1850 and 1885, during the most intensive period of early industrialization. Many of these extended families, and most "producing" families of the time, depended on the labor of children; they were held together by dire necessity and sometimes by brute force.[7]

---

[5]Faye Dudden, *Serving Women: Household Service in Nineteenth-Century America* (Middletown, Conn.: Wesleyan University Press, 1983), p. 206; Susan Strasser, *Never Done: A History of American Housework* (New York: Pantheon, 1982); Lawrence Glasco, "The Life Cycles and Household Structure of American Ethnic Groups, in *A Heritage of Her Own: Toward a New Social History of American Women,* ed. Nancy Cott and Elizabeth Pleck (New York: Simon & Schuster, 1979), pp. 281, 285.

[6]Robert Bremmer et al., eds., *Children and Youth in America: A Documentary History* (Cambridge: Harvard University Press, 1970), vol. 1, p. 39; Barbara Cross, *Horace Bushnell: Minister to a Changing America* (Chicago: University of Chicago Press, 1958); Ann Douglas, *The Feminization of American Culture* (New York: Knopf, 1977), p. 52.

[7]Peter Laslett, "Characteristics of the Western Family Over Time," in *Family Life and Illicit Love in Earlier Generations,* ed. Peter Laslett (New York: Cambridge University Press, 1977); William Goode, *World Revolution and Family Patterns* (New York: Free Press, 1963); Michael Anderson, *Family Structure in Nineteenth-Century Lancashire* (Cambridge, England: Cambridge University Press, 1971); Tamara Hareven, ed., *Transitions: The Family and the Life Course in Historical*

There was a significant increase in child labor during the last third of the   15
nineteenth century. Some children worked at home in crowded tenement
sweatshops that produced cigars or women's clothing. Reformer Helen
Campbell found one house where "nearly thirty children of all ages and sizes,
babies predominating, rolled in the tobacco which covered the floor and was
piled in every direction."[8] Many producing households resembled the one
described by Mary Van Kleeck of the Russell Sage Foundation in 1913:

> In a tenement on MacDougal Street lives a family of seven—grand-
> mother, father, mother and four children aged four years, three years,
> two years and one month respectively. All excepting the father and the
> two babies make violets. The three year old girl picks apart the petals; her
> sister, aged four years, separates the stems, dipping an end of each into
> paste spread on a piece of board on the kitchen table; and the mother and
> grandmother slip the petals up the stems.[9]

Where children worked outside the home, conditions were no better.
In 1900, 120,000 children worked in Pennsylvania mines and factories; most
of them had started work by age eleven. In Scranton, a third of the girls between the ages of thirteen and sixteen worked in the silk mills in 1904. In
New York, Boston, and Chicago, teenagers worked long hours in textile factories and frequently died in fires or industrial accidents. Children made up
23.7 percent of the 36,415 workers in southern textile mills around the turn
of the century. When reformer Marie Van Vorse took a job at one in 1903,
she found children as young as six or seven working twelve-hour shifts. At
the end of the day, she reported: "They are usually beyond speech. They fall
asleep at the tables, on the stairs; they are carried to bed and there laid down
as they are, unwashed, undressed; and the inanimate bundles of rags so lie
until the mill summons them with its imperious cry before sunrise."[10]

Perspective (New York: Academic Press, 1978); Tamara Hareven, "The Dynamics of Kin in an In-
dustrial Community," in *Turning Points: Historical and Sociological Essays on the Family,* ed. John
Demos and S. S. Boocock (Chicago: University of Chicago Press, 1978); Linda Gordon, *Heroes of
Their Own Lives: The Politics and History of Family Violence, 1800–1960* (New York, Viking, 1988).

[8]Helen Campbell, *Prisoners of Poverty: Women Wage Workers, Their Trades and Their Lives*
(Westport, Conn.: Greenwood Press, 1970), p. 206.

[9]Rosalyn Baxandall, Linda Gordon, and Susan Reverby, eds., *America's Working Women*
(New York: Random House, 1976), p. 162.

[10]Rose Schneiderman, *All For One* (New York: P. S. Eriksson, 1967); John Bodnar, "So-
cialization and Adaptation: Immigrant Families in Scranton," in *Growing Up in America: Historical
Experiences,* ed. Harvey Graff (Detroit: Wayne State Press, 1987), pp. 391–92; Robert and Helen
Lynd, *Middletown: A Study in Modern American Culture* (New York: Harcourt Brace Jovanovich,
1956), p. 31; Barbara Wertheimer, *We Were There: The Story of Working Women in America* (New
York: Pantheon, 1977), pp. 336–43; Francesco Cordasco, *Jacob Riis Revisited: Poverty and the
Slum in Another Era* (Garden City, N.Y.: Doubleday, 1968); Campbell, *Prisoners of Poverty* and
Women Wage-Earners (Boston: Arnoff, 1893); Lynn Weiner, *From Working Girl to Working
Mother: The Female Labor Force in the United States, 1829–1980* (Chapel Hill: University of North
Carolina Press, 1985), p. 92.

By the end of the nineteenth century, shocked by the conditions in urban tenements and by the sight of young children working full-time at home or earning money out on the streets, middle-class reformers put aside nostalgia for "harnessed" family production and elevated the antebellum model once more, blaming immigrants for introducing such "un-American" family values as child labor. Reformers advocated adoption of a "true American" family—a restricted, exclusive nuclear unit in which women and children were divorced from the world of work.

In the late 1920s and early 1930s, however, the wheel turned yet again, as social theorists noted the independence and isolation of the nuclear family with renewed anxiety. The influential Chicago School of sociology believed that immigration and urbanization had weakened the traditional family by destroying kinship and community networks. Although sociologists welcomed the increased democracy of "companionate marriage," they worried about the rootlessness of nuclear families and the breakdown of older solidarities. By the time of the Great Depression, some observers even saw a silver lining in economic hardship, since it revived the economic functions and social importance of kin and family ties. With housing starts down by more than 90 percent, approximately one-sixth of urban families had to "double up" in apartments. The incidence of three-generation households increased, while recreational interactions outside the home were cut back or confined to the kinship network. One newspaper opined: "Many a family that has lost its car has found its soul."[11]

Depression families evoke nostalgia in some contemporary observers, because they tended to create "dependability and domestic inclination" among girls and "maturity in the management of money" among boys. But, in many cases, such responsibility was inseparable from "a corrosive and disabling poverty that shattered the hopes and dreams of . . . young parents and twisted the lives of those who were 'stuck together' in it." Men withdrew from family life or turned violent; women exhausted themselves trying to "take up the slack" both financially and emotionally, or they belittled their husbands as failures; and children gave up their dreams of education to work at dead-end jobs.[12]

---

[11]For examples of the analysis of the Chicago School, see Ernest Burgess and Harvey Locke, *The Family: From Institution to Companionship* (New York: American Book Company, 1945); Ernest Mowrer, *The Family: Its Organization and Disorganization* (Chicago: University of Chicago Press, 1932); W. I. Thomas and F. Znaniecki, *The Polish Peasant in Europe and America*, 5 vols. (Boston: Dover Publications, 1918–20). On families in the Depression, see Steven Mintz and Susan Kellogg, *Domestic Revolutions: A Social History of American Family Life* (New York: Free Press, 1988), pp. 133–49, quote on p. 136.

[12]Glen Elder, Jr., *Children of the Great Depression: Social Change in Life Experience* (Chicago: University of Chicago Press, 1974), pp. 64–82; Lillian Rubin, *Worlds of Pain: Life in the Working-Class Family* (New York: Basic Books, 1976), p. 23; Edward Robb Ellis, *A Nation in Torment: The Great American Depression, 1929–1939* (New York: Coward McCann, 1970); Ruth Milkman, "Women's Work and the Economic Crisis," in *A Heritage of Her Own: Toward a New Social History of American Women,* ed. Nancy Cott and Elizabeth Pleck (New York: Simon & Schuster, 1979), pp. 507–41.

From the hardships of the Great Depression and the Second World War   20
and the euphoria of the postwar economic recovery came a new kind of
family ideal that still enters our homes in *Leave It to Beaver* and *Donna Reed* reruns. . . . [T]he 1950s were no more a "golden age" of the family than any
other period in American history. . . . I will argue that our recurring search
for a traditional family model denies the diversity of family life, both past and
present, and leads to false generalizations about the past as well as wildly exaggerated claims about the present and the future.

The Complexities of Assessing Family Trends

If it is hard to find a satisfactory model of the traditional family, it is also
hard to make global judgments about how families have changed and whether
they are getting better or worse. Some generalizations about the past are pure
myth. Whatever the merit of recurring complaints about the "rootlessness" of
modern life, for instance, families are *not* more mobile and transient than they
used to be. In most nineteenth-century cities, both large and small, more than
50 percent—and often up to 75 percent—of the residents in any given year
were no longer there ten years later. People born in the twentieth century are
much more likely to live near their birthplace than were people born in the
nineteenth century.[13]

This is not to say, of course, that mobility did not have different effects
then than it does now. In the nineteenth century, claims historian Thomas
Bender, people moved from community to community, taking advantage . . .
of nonfamilial networks and institutions that integrated them into new work
and social relations. In the late twentieth century, people move from job to
job, following a career path that shuffles them from one single-family home
to another and does not link them to neighborly networks beyond the family.
But this change is in our community ties, not in our family ones.[14]

A related myth is that modern Americans have lost touch with
extended-kinship networks or have let parent-child bonds lapse. In fact, more
Americans than ever before have grandparents alive, and there is good evidence that ties between grandparents and grandchildren have become
stronger over the past fifty years. In the late 1970s, researchers returned to the

---

[13]Rudy Ray Seward, *The American Family: A Demographic History* (Beverly Hills: Sage,
1978); Kenneth Winkle, *The Politics of Community: Migration and Politics in Antebellum Ohio*
(New York: Cambridge University Press, 1988); Michael Weber, *Social Change in an Industrial
Town: Patterns of Progress in Warren, Pennsylvania, from the Civil War to World War I* (University
Park: Pennsylvania State University Press, 1976), pp. 138–48; Stephen Thernstrom, *Poverty and
Progress* (Cambridge: Harvard University Press, 1964).

[14]Thomas Bender, *Community and Social Change in America* (New Brunswick: Rutgers
University Press, 1978).

"Middletown" studied by sociologists Robert and Helen Lynd in the 1920s and found that most people there maintained closer extended-family networks than in earlier times. There had been some decline in the family's control over the daily lives of youth, especially females, but "the expressive/emotional function of the family" was "more important for Middletown students of 1977 than it was in 1924." More recent research shows that visits with relatives did *not* decline between the 1950s and the late 1980s.[15]

Today 54 percent of adults see a parent, and 68 percent talk on the phone with a parent, at least once a week. Fully 90 percent of Americans describe their relationship with their mother as close, and 78 percent say their relationship with their grandparents is close. And for all the family disruption of divorce, most modern children live with at least *one* parent. As late as 1940, 10 percent of American children did not live with either parent, compared to only one in twenty-five today.[16]

What about the supposed eclipse of marriage? Neither the rising age of   25
those who marry nor the frequency of divorce necessarily means that marriage is becoming a less prominent institution than it was in earlier days. Ninety percent of men and women eventually marry, more than 70 percent of divorced men and women remarry, and fewer people remain single for their entire lives today than at the turn of the century. One author even suggests that the availability of divorce in the second half of the twentieth century has allowed some women to try marriage who would formerly have remained single all their lives. Others argue that the rate of hidden marital separation in the late nineteenth century was not much less than the rate of visible separation today.[17]

Studies of marital satisfaction reveal that more couples reported their marriages to be happy in the late 1970s than did so in 1957, while couples in their second marriages believe them to be much happier than their first ones. Some commentators conclude that marriage is becoming less permanent but more satisfying. Others wonder, however, whether there is a vicious circle in our country, where no one even tries to sustain a relationship. Between the

---

[15]Edward Kain, *The Myth of Family Decline: Understanding Families in a World of Rapid Social Change* (Lexington, Mass.: D. C. Heath, 1990), pp. 10, 37; Theodore Caplow, "The Sociological Myth of Family Decline," *The Tocqueville Review* 3 (1981): 366; Howard Bahr, "Changes in Family Life in Middletown, 1924–77," *Public Opinion Quarterly* 44 (1980): 51.

[16]*American Demographics,* February 1990; Dennis Orthner, "The Family in Transition," in *Rebuilding the Nest: A New Commitment to the American Family,* ed. David Blankenhorn, Steven Bayme, and Jean Bethke Elshtain (Milwaukee: Family Service America, 1990), pp. 95–97; Sar Levitan and Richard Belous, *What's Happening to the American Family?* (Baltimore: Johns Hopkins University Press, 1981), p. 63.

[17]Daniel Kallgren, "Women Out of Marriage: Work and Residence Patterns of Never Married American Women, 1900–1980" (Paper presented at Social Science History Association Conference, Minneapolis, Minn., October 1990), p. 8; Richard Sennett, *Families Against the City: Middle Class Homes in Industrial Chicago, 1872–1890* (Cambridge: Harvard University Press, 1984), pp. 114–15.

late 1970s and late 1980s, moreover, reported marital happiness did decline slightly in the United States. Some authors see this as reflecting our decreasing appreciation of marriage, although others suggest that it reflects unrealistically high expectations of love in a culture that denies people safe, culturally approved ways of getting used to marriage or cultivating other relationships to meet some of the needs that we currently load onto the couple alone.[18]

Part of the problem in making simple generalizations about what is happening to marriage is that there has been a polarization of experiences. Marriages are much more likely to be ended by divorce today, but marriages that do last are described by their participants as happier than those in the past and are far more likely to confer such happiness over many years. It is important to remember that the 50 percent divorce rate estimates are calculated in terms of a forty-year period and that many marriages in the past were terminated well before that date by the death of one partner. Historian Lawrence Stone suggests that divorce has become "a functional substitute for death" in the modern world. At the end of the 1970s, the rise in divorce rates seemed to overtake the fall in death rates, but the slight decline in divorce rates since then means that "a couple marrying today is more likely to celebrate a fortieth wedding anniversary than were couples around the turn of the century."[19]

A similar polarization allows some observers to argue that fathers are deserting their children, while others celebrate the new commitment of fathers to childrearing. Both viewpoints are right. Sociologist Frank Furstenberg comments on the emergence of a "good dad–bad dad complex": Many fathers spend more time with their children than ever before and feel more free to be affectionate with them; others, however, feel more free simply to walk out on their families. According to 1981 statistics, 42 percent of the children whose father had left the marriage had not seen him in the past year. Yet studies show steadily increasing involvement of fathers with their children as long as they are in the home.[20]

---

[18]Mary Jo Bane, *Here to Stay: American Families in the Twentieth Century* (New York: Basic Books, 1976); Stephen Nock, *Sociology of the Family* (Englewood Cliffs, N.J.: Prentice Hall, 1987); Kain, *Myth of Family Decline,* pp. 71, 74–75; Joseph Veroff, Elizabeth Douvan, and Richard Kulka, *The Inner American: A Self Portrait from 1957 to 1976* (New York: Basic Books, 1981); Norval Glenn, "The Recent Trend in Marital Success in the United States," *Journal of Marriage and the Family* 53 (1991); Tracy Cabot, *Marrying Later, Marrying Smarter* (New York: McGraw-Hill, 1990); Judith Brown, *Sanctions and Sanctuary: Cultural Perspectives on the Beating of Wives* (Boulder, Colo.: Westview Press, 1991); Maxine Baca Zinn and Stanley Eitzen, *Diversity in American Families* (New York: Harper & Row, 1987).

[19]Dorrian Apple Sweetser, "Broken Homes: Stable Risk, Changing Reason, Changing Forms," *Journal of Marriage and the Family* (August 1985); Lawrence Stone, "The Road to Polygamy," *New York Review of Books,* 2 March 1989, p. 13; Arlene Skolnick, *Embattled Paradise: The American Family in an Age of Uncertainty* (New York: Basic Books, 1991), p. 156.

[20]Frank Furstenberg, Jr., "Good Dads–Bad Dads: Two Faces of Fatherhood," in *The Changing American Family and Public Policy,* ed. Andrew Cherlin (Washington, D.C.: Urban Institute Press, 1988); Joseph Pleck, "The Contemporary Man," in *Handbook of Counseling and Psychotherapy,* ed. Murray Scher et al. (Beverly Hills: Sage, 1987).

These kinds of ambiguities should make us leery of hard-and-fast pronouncements about what's happening to the American family. In many cases,
we simply don't know precisely what our figures actually mean. For example,
the proportion of youngsters receiving psychological assistance rose by 80 percent between 1981 and 1988. Does that mean they are getting more sick or receiving more help, or is it some complex combination of the two? Child abuse
reports increased by 225 percent between 1976 and 1987. Does this represent an
actual increase in rates of abuse or a heightened consciousness about the problem? During the same period, parents' self-reports about very severe violence
toward their children declined 47 percent. Does this represent a real improvement in their behavior or a decreasing willingness to admit to such acts?[21]

Assessing the direction of family change is further complicated because   30
many contemporary trends represent a reversal of developments that were
themselves rather recent. The expectation that the family should be the main
source of personal fulfillment, for example, was not traditional in the eighteenth and nineteenth centuries. . . . Prior to the 1900s, the family festivities
that now fill us with such nostalgia for "the good old days" (and cause such
heartbreak when they go poorly) were "relatively undeveloped." Civic festivals and Fourth of July parades were more important occasions for celebration
and strong emotion than family holidays, such as Thanksgiving. Christmas
"seems to have been more a time for attending parties and dances than for
celebrating family solidarity." Only in the twentieth century did the family
come to be the center of festive attention and emotional intensity.[22]

Today, such emotional investment in the family may be waning again.
This could be interpreted as a reestablishment of balance between family life
and other social ties; on the other hand, such a trend may have different results today than in earlier times, because in many cases the extrafamilial institutions and customs that used to socialize individuals and provide them with a
range of emotional alternatives to family life no longer exist.

In other cases, close analysis of statistics showing a deterioration in family well-being supposedly caused by abandonment of tradition suggests a more
complicated train of events. Children's health, for example, improved dramatically in the 1960s and 1970s, a period of extensive family transformation.
It ceased to improve, and even slid backward, in the 1980s, when innovative
social programs designed to relieve families of some "traditional" responsibilities were repealed. While infant mortality rates fell by 4.7 percent a year dur-

---

[21]National Commission on Children, *Beyond Rhetoric: A New Agenda for Children and
Families* (Washington, D.C.: GPO, 1991), p. 34; Richard Gelles and Jon Conte, "Domestic Violence and Sexual Abuse of Children," in *Contemporary Families: Looking Forward, Looking Back,*
ed. Alan Booth (Minneapolis: National Council on Family Relations, 1991), p. 328.

[22]Arlene Skolnick, "The American Family: The Paradox of Perfection," *The Wilson
Quarterly* (Summer 1980); Barbara Laslett, "Family Membership: Past and Present," *Social Prob-
lems* 25 (1978); Theodore Caplow et al., *Middletown Families: Fifty Years of Change and Continuity*
(Minneapolis: University of Minnesota Press, 1982), p. 225.

ing the 1970s, the rate of decline decreased in the 1980s, and in both 1988 and 1989, infant mortality rates did not show a statistically significant decline. Similarly, the proportion of low-birth-weight babies fell during the 1970s but stayed steady during the 1980s, and had even increased slightly as of 1988. Child poverty is lower today than it was in the "traditional" 1950s but much higher than it was in the nontraditional late 1960s.[23]

WILD CLAIMS AND PHONY FORECASTS

Lack of perspective on where families have come from and how their evolution connects to other social trends tends to encourage contradictory claims and wild exaggerations about where families are going. One category of generalizations seems to be a product of wishful thinking. As of 1988, nearly half of all families with children had both parents in the work force. The two-parent family in which only the father worked for wages represented just 25 percent of all families with children, down from 44 percent in 1975. For people overwhelmed by the difficulties of adjusting work and schools to the realities of working moms, it has been tempting to discern a "return to tradition" and hope the problems will go away. Thus in 1991, we saw a flurry of media reports that the number of women in the work force was headed down: "More Choose to Stay Home with Children" proclaimed the headlines; "More Women Opting for Chance to Watch Their Children Grow."[24]

The cause of all this commotion? The percentage of women aged twenty-five to thirty-four who were employed dropped from 74 percent to 72.8 percent between January 1990 and January 1991. However, there was an exactly equal decline in the percentage of men in the work force during the same period, and for both sexes the explanation was the same. "The dip is the recession," explained Judy Waldrop, research editor at *American Demographics* magazine, to anyone who bothered to listen. In fact, the proportion of *mothers* who worked increased slightly during the same period.[25]

This is not to say that parents, especially mothers, are happy with the   35 pressures of balancing work and family life. Poll after poll reveals that both men and women feel starved for time. The percentage of women who say they would prefer to stay home with their children if they could afford to do so rose from 33 percent in 1986 to 56 percent in 1990. Other polls show that

---

[23]*The State of America's Children, 1991* (Washington, D.C.: Children's Defense Fund, 1991), pp. 55–63; *Seattle Post-Intelligencer,* 19 April 1991; National Commission on Children, *Beyond Rhetoric,* p. 32; *Washington Post National Weekly Edition,* 13–19 May 1991; James Wetzel, *American Youth: A Statistical Snapshot* (Washington, D.C.: William T. Grant Foundation, August 1989), pp. 12–14.

[24]*USA Today,* 12 May 1991, p. 1A; Richard Morin, "Myth of the Drop Out Mom," *Washington Post,* 14 July 1991; Christine Reinhardt, "Trend Check," *Working Woman,* October 1991, p. 34; Howard Hayghe, "Family Members in the Work Force," *Monthly Labor Review* 113 (1990).

[25]Morin, "Myth of the Drop Out Mom"; Reinhardt, "Trend Check," p. 34.

even larger majorities of women would trade a day's pay for an extra day off. But, above all, what these polls reveal is women's growing dissatisfaction with the failure of employers, schools, and government to pioneer arrangements that make it possible to combine work and family life. They do not suggest that women are actually going to stop working, or that this would be women's preferred solution to their stresses. The polls did not ask, for example, how *long* women would like to take off work, and failed to take account of the large majority of mothers who report that they would miss their work if they did manage to take time off. Working mothers are here to stay, and we will not meet the challenge this poses for family life by inventing an imaginary trend to define the problem out of existence.

At another extreme is the kind of generalization that taps into our worst fears. One example of this is found in the almost daily reporting of cases of child molestation or kidnapping by sexual predators. The highlighting of such cases, drawn from every corner of the country, helps disguise how rare these cases actually are when compared to crimes committed within the family.

A well-publicized instance of the cataclysmic predictions that get made when family trends are taken out of historical context is the famous *Newsweek* contention that a single woman of forty has a better chance of being killed by a terrorist than of finding a husband. It is true that the proportion of never-married women under age forty has increased substantially since the 1950s, but it is also true that the proportion has *decreased* dramatically among women over that age. A woman over thirty-five has a *better* chance to marry today than she did in the 1950s. In the past twelve years, first-time marriages have increased almost 40 percent for women aged thirty-five to thirty-nine. A single woman aged forty to forty-four still has a 24 percent probability of marriage, while 15 percent of women in their late forties will marry. These figures would undoubtedly be higher if many women over forty did not simply pass up opportunities that a more desperate generation might have snatched.[26]

Yet another example of the exaggeration that pervades many analyses of modern families is the widely quoted contention that "parents today spend 40 percent less time with their children than did parents in 1965." Again, of course, part of the problem is where researchers are measuring from. A comparative study of Muncie, Indiana, for example, found that parents spent much more time with their children in the mid-1970s than did parents in the mid-1920s. But another problem is keeping the categories consistent. Trying to track down the source of the 40 percent decline figure, I called demographer John P. Robinson, whose studies on time formed the basis of this claim. Robinson's

---

[26]"Too Late for Prince Charming," *Newsweek*, 2 June 1986, p. 55; John Modell, *Into One's Own: From Youth to Adulthood in the United States, 1920–1975* (Berkeley: University of California Press, 1989), p. 249; Barbara Lovenheim, *Beating the Marriage Odds: When You Are Smart, Single, and Over 35* (New York: William Morrow, 1990), pp. 26–27; *U.S. News & World Report*, 29 January 1990, p. 50; *New York Times*, 7 June 1991.

data, however, show that parents today spend about the same amount of time caring for children as they did in 1965. If the total amount of time devoted to children is less, he suggested, I might want to check how many fewer children there are today. In 1970, the average family had 1.34 children under the age of eighteen; in 1990, the average family had only .96 children under age eighteen—a decrease of 28.4 percent. In other words, most of the decline in the total amount of time parents spend with children is because of the decline in the number of children they have to spend time with![27]

Now I am not trying to say that the residual amount of decrease is not serious, or that it may not become worse, given the trends in women's employment. Robinson's data show that working mothers spend substantially less time in primary child-care activities than do nonemployed mothers (though they also tend to have fewer children); more than 40 percent of working mothers report feeling "trapped" by their daily routines; many routinely sacrifice sleep in order to meet the demands of work and family. Even so, a majority believe they are *not* giving enough time to their children. It is also true that children may benefit merely from having their parents available, even though the parents may not be spending time with them.

But there is no reason to assume the worst. Americans have actually gained   40
free time since 1965, despite an increase in work hours, largely as a result of a decline in housework and an increasing tendency to fit some personal requirements and errands into the work day. And according to a recent Gallup poll, most modern mothers think they are doing a better job of communicating with their children (though a worse job of house cleaning) than did their own mothers and that they put a higher value on spending time with their family than did their mothers.[28]

NEGOTIATING THROUGH THE EXTREMES

Most people react to these conflicting claims and contradictory trends with understandable confusion. They know that family ties remain central to their own lives, but they are constantly hearing about people who seem to have *no*

---

[27]William Mattox, Jr., "The Parent Trap," *Policy Review* (Winter 1991): 6, 8; Sylvia Ann Hewlett, "Running Hard Just to Keep Up," *Time* (Fall 1990), and *When the Bough Breaks: The Cost of Neglecting Our Children* (New York: Basic Books, 1991), p. 73; Richard Whitmore, "Education Decline Linked with Erosion of Family," *The Olympian*, 1 October 1991; John Robinson, "Caring for Kids," *American Demographics,* July 1989, p. 52; "Household and Family Characteristics: March 1990 and 1989," *Current Population Reports,* series P-20, no. 447, table A-1. I am indebted to George Hough, Executive Policy Analyst, Office of Financial Management, Washington State, for finding these figures and helping me with the calculations.

[28]John Robinson, "Time for Work," *American Demographics,* April 1989, p. 68, and "Time's Up," *American Demographics,* July 1989, p. 34; Trish Hall, "Time on Your Hands? You May Have More Than You Think," *New York Times,* 3 July 1991, pp. C1, C7; Gannett News Service Wire Report, 27 August 1991.

family feeling. Thus, at the same time as Americans report high levels of satisfaction with their *own* families, they express a pervasive fear that other people's families are falling apart. In a typical recent poll, for example, 71 percent of respondents said they were "very satisfied" with their own family life, but more than half rated the overall quality of family life as negative: I'm okay; you're not."[29]

This seemingly schizophrenic approach does not reflect an essentially intolerant attitude. People worry about families, and to the extent that they associate modern social ills with changes in family life, they are ambivalent about innovations. Voters often defeat measures to grant unmarried couples, whether heterosexual or homosexual, the same rights as married ones. In polls, however, most Americans support tolerance for gay and lesbian relationships. Although two-thirds of respondents to one national poll said they wanted "more traditional standards of family life," the same percentage rejected the idea that "women should return to their traditional role." Still larger majorities support women's right to work, including their right to use child care, even when they worry about relying on day-care centers too much. In a 1990 *Newsweek* poll, 42 percent predicted that the family would be worse in ten years and exactly the same percentage predicted that it would be better. Although 87 percent of people polled in 1987 said they had "old-fashioned ideas about family and marriage," only 22 percent of the people polled in 1989 defined a family solely in terms of blood, marriage, or adoption. Seventy-four percent declared, instead, that family is any group whose members love and care for one another.[30]

These conflicted responses do not mean that people are hopelessly confused. Instead, they reflect people's gut-level understanding that the "crisis of the family" is more complex than is often asserted by political demagogues or others with an ax to grind. In popular commentary, the received wisdom is to "keep it simple." I know one television reporter who refuses to air an interview with anyone who uses the phrase "on the other hand." But my experience in discussing these issues with both the general public and specialists in the field is that people are hungry to get beyond oversimplifications. They don't want to be told that everything is fine in families or that if the economy improved and the government mandated parental leave, everything would be fine. But they don't believe that every hard-won victory for women's rights and personal liberty has been destructive of social bonds and that the only way to find a sense of community is to go back to some sketchily defined "traditional" family that clearly involves denying the validity of any alternative familial and personal choices.

---

[29] *New York Times,* 10 October 1989, p. A18.

[30] E. J. Dionne, Jr., *Why Americans Hate Politics* (New York: Simon & Schuster, 1991), pp. 110, 115, 325; *The Olympian,* 11 October 1989; *New York Times,* 10 October 1989; *Time,* 20 November 1989; *Seattle Post-Intelligencer,* 12 October 1990; Jerold Footlick, "What Happened to the Family?" *Newsweek Special Issue,* Winter/Spring 1990, p. 18.

Americans understand that along with welcome changes have come difficult new problems; uneasy with simplistic answers, they are willing to consider more nuanced analyses of family gains and losses during the past few decades. Indeed, argues political reporter E. J. Dionne, they are *desperate* to engage in such analyses.[31] Few Americans are satisfied with liberal and feminist accounts that blame all modern family dilemmas on structural inequalities, ignoring the moral crisis of commitment and obligation in our society. Yet neither are they convinced that "in the final analysis," as David Blankenhorn of the Institute for American Values puts it, "the problem is not the system. The problem is us."[32]

Despite humane intentions, an overemphasis on personal responsibility 45 for strengthening family values encourages a way of thinking that leads to moralizing rather than mobilizing for concrete reforms. While values are important to Americans, most do not support the sort of scapegoating that occurs when all family problems are blamed on "bad values." Most of us are painfully aware that there is no clear way of separating "family values" from "the system." Our values may make a difference in the way we respond to the challenges posed by economic and political institutions, but those institutions also reinforce certain values and extinguish others. The problem is not to berate people for abandoning past family values, nor to exhort them to adopt better values in the future—the problem is to build the institutions and social support networks that allow people to act on their best values rather than on their worst ones. We need to get past abstract nostalgia for traditional family values and develop a clearer sense of how past families actually worked and what the different consequences of various family behaviors and values have been. Good history and responsible social policy should help people incorporate the full complexity and the tradeoffs of family change into their analyses and thus into action. Mythmaking does not accomplish this end.

QUESTIONING THE TEXT

1. Coontz is highly critical of some researchers' careless or deceptive use of statistics to make "wild claims and phony forecasts" about families. Look closely at the author's use of statistical evidence. Does Coontz use statistics in a fully explained and evenhanded way? Explain the reasons for your answer.

2. How might Coontz describe the way *she* wishes families were defined? Discuss this question with a classmate and then reread the selection, taking notes on the underlying assumptions Coontz makes about

---

[31]Dionne, *Why Americans Hate Politics.*
[32]David Blankenhorn, "Does Grandmother Know Best?" *Family Affairs* 3 (1990): 13, 16.

families—traditional or otherwise. Bring your notes to class for a discussion of "where the author is coming from" in this selection.

MAKING CONNECTIONS

3. Read Barbara Dafoe Whitehead's "The Making of a Divorce Culture" (p. 619), keeping Coontz's views on divorce in mind. Then write a two- to three-page essay comparing and contrasting the two writers' positions on divorce, and explaining which one you find more persuasive.

4. Read back through Coontz's piece, listing all the evidence you can find in support of the argument Fred Barnes makes in "Quantity Time" (p. 649). Bring your list to class for discussion.

JOINING THE CONVERSATION

5. Coontz says her students' visions of traditional family life "bear a suspicious resemblance to reruns of old television series" except that "the scripts of different shows have been mixed up" (paragraph 2). Working with a classmate, choose a television series, either current or rerun, that features a family/home, and watch and videotape as many episodes as you can within a week or so. Take notes during and after the episodes, jotting down the family members' characteristics, the roles they play, the values they represent, the kind of home they live in, and any other observations you make about the TV family. Compare your notes with your classmate's, noting any discrepancies and resolving them, if possible. Then, with your partner, prepare a 15-minute presentation (about seven pages of double-spaced text with accompanying video) on "The American Family as Represented in [name of TV series]."

6. After freewriting or brainstorming about your own family experience, write a journal entry exploring how your experience matches up with or differs from any of the family paradigms Coontz describes. If you keep a reading log, write the entry there.

7. Imagine that you are asked to prepare a one- to two-page description of "a typical American family" to be placed in a time capsule marked for opening in 2150. Write the description; then ask several classmates to read and respond to it. With their feedback in mind, write a brief analysis of your description of the typical family, noting where you overgeneralize, leave out counterexamples, or use terms that may be unfamiliar to readers of the twenty-second century, for example. Bring your description and your analysis of it to class for discussion.

JILL FRAWLEY
Inside the Home

*J*ILL F*RAWLEY, a registered nurse and advocate for patients, left the employment of the nursing home she describes in this article. Originally published in the politically leftist* Mother Jones *magazine in 1991, "Inside the Home" demonstrates in graphic detail why she left and, in so doing, exposes the "big lie" told by institutions such as the one she worked for: "long-term care facilities" owned by big corporations care little or nothing for the patients whose money supports them or for the employees who do their bidding.*

I chose this essay because—in spite of the designation "nursing home"—I had never considered the word "home" to include such institutions. In fact, asked to list dozens of places that might count as "home," I would have failed to include facilities such as the one Frawley describes. And yet I have friends whose parents are even now in such homes. How, then, to explain my omission? Perhaps, I have reflected since reading Frawley's essay, because my silent neglect of such "homes" is part of the big lie she speaks of. Perhaps by ignoring them I bear some responsibility for the many nursing homes that are insufferable and insupportable.

Perhaps I should think more carefully about what is and is not designated as a "home." And perhaps I should think more carefully when big corporations call themselves "families." Are they families I want to support or belong to? Are the homes they provide ones I'd want to inhabit? Now read "Inside the Home." —A.L.

I'm just one little nurse, in one little "care facility." Each shift I work, I carry in my soul a very big lie. I leave my job, and there aren't enough showers in the world to wash away my rage, my frustration, my impotence.

The long-term-care facility (nursing home) I work for is owned by a corporation that owns nursing homes throughout the country. Giving corporations like this control over the quality of medical care is handing over control to the fox. Every chicken in the coop knows there is no hope—only the ticking away of a life devoid of dignity or even minimal respect.

I watch the videos they show to new employees during "orientation." Smiling people spout corporate policy and speak of "guest relations." They tell us we are special; we are going to participate in a rewarding job. Elderly people in the video are dressed nicely; they are coherent and grateful for the help the staff member has time to give. We sign the attendance sheet: We saw it; now we know what "guest relations" means. It means to act in front of the families so that they think everything is okay.

The truth is ugly; I confess it in a burst of desperation. The elderly lie in feces and urine because there is only one aide for thirty patients. Eventually, they get changed abruptly—too fast, too harshly. They cry out in confused terror. Doors are closed to "protect their privacy"—but really so no one will see. The covers get flung back. It's evening bed check. The old person is shoved from one side of the bed to the other. He tries to protest; he thinks something bad is happening. Whip out the soiled underpad, wipe him, throw the covers over him . . . on to the next body.

No time for mouth care; sometimes no time for showers; never time to hold someone's hand even for a moment. Aides feed the helpless two spoonfuls of pureed stuff, dripping down chins; no time to wait for them to swallow. It gets charted: "Resident didn't eat much tonight." She loses weight; she gets more frail as each day passes. The food is so bad I can't begin to describe it. The cook is young and doesn't care much; if I complain, he gets mad. One resident asks me for a cup of hot water so she can use the instant soup in her drawer. She can't eat the cold, badly cooked stuff that is on her tray. Slow starvation is hard to get used to.

Why is there only one aide on these halls night after night? Most employees don't stay. They can't stand being flung into jobs that are too hard, too horrid, for too little money. The ones that do stay have given up complaining. They shut their eyes and ears and do the best they can. They have children to support, no education, are caught by life in such a way that quitting would intensify their own suffering and not alleviate anyone else's.

We're always short-staffed. We know it's to save money. One tired aide does a double shift, straining to do a job it takes two people to do correctly. I guess when you make four dollars and something an hour, it takes working double shifts (that's sixteen hours) to make enough to live on. Tired people get impatient, make mistakes, take shortcuts. A nurse calls in sick. That means one nurse does three halls. One nurse to pass out medicines for eighty residents.

Patients are dropped or fall. My coworkers agree that it's a widespread practice to chart this to avoid problems. Every incident report I have ever seen states that the patient or resident was "found on the floor" or appeared to have bruises or skin tears of "unknown" origin. When there's no time to turn the bedridden every two hours, skin breaks down and ulcers develop. The elderly get skin tears and bruises because they are fragile, but also because there is no time to handle them gently. Again, we chart carefully so there is no blame. We let our old ones die for many reasons. Sometimes it is because of sickness; sometimes it is from neglect.

The admissions director is a nice lady. She lives uneasily with her task. She tells anxious families not to worry, that the facility will be like a second home to their relative. She tells them what they want to hear. The families go away determined to believe everything will be fine. Secretly, they are relieved that they won't have to deal with dementia, incontinence, or the total dependency of a senile elder.

The silence is ominous in the evening. Nothing to do; no place to go. The residents sit and wait for death. The staff is ground down in despair and hopelessness. The guys at corporate headquarters must be patting each other on the back about the profits they're making.

It got bad at the place I work. Too many unhappy people; too much barely controlled anger always close to erupting. A corporate spokesperson was sent from headquarters to listen to grievances. He listened, this quiet, intelligent man who had been to our facility before. I asked some of my fellow workers why they weren't going to speak out. "It doesn't do any good," was the response. "He's been coming for three or four years. Nothing changes." I went; I spoke out; they were right. Nothing changes.

The elderly suffer quietly. They are afraid they will be punished if they speak up for themselves. Most of them can't speak for themselves. They just want to escape this hell. I do too. They need a place to stay; I need a job. We're trapped.

I am one little nurse, in one little care facility, living with this terrible secret. If they knew I was telling on them, I wouldn't have a job. What about my rent? What about my needs? But I need to tell. I confess to my participation in these crimes. I can't keep this secret any longer.

If you have an elderly relative in a facility:

1. Visit at odd hours.
2. Visit at mealtime.
3. Don't believe what the staff tells you.
4. Ask questions.
5. Don't worry if small items are missing. Petty theft is not serious. Abuse is.
6. Make sure your relative is clean.
7. Notice if your relative is losing weight.
8. Check your relative's skin for bruises.
9. Let "them" know you are watching.
10. Be polite to staff, but raise hell with the administrator or the director of nursing. Though they are just employees and will tell you what you want to hear, it's worth a try.
11. Contact local ombudsmen if you can't get results. If that doesn't work, contact the state regulatory agency.
12. Complain to headquarters or whoever owns the facility.
13. Don't allow yourself to be blackmailed by veiled threats of being forced to move your relative.
14. Don't give up; wear them down.

QUESTIONING THE TEXT

1. What does Frawley mean by the "big lie"? Write out a brief definition of this "big lie."

2. What is Frawley's attitude toward her employers? Toward her patients? Toward herself? Point to places in the essay that reveal these attitudes to you.

3. Look back at the questions A.L. poses at the end of her introduction to this reading. Are they rhetorical questions, or does she intend for you to answer them? How do you know?

MAKING CONNECTIONS

4. Review this chapter's essays, poems, and opening illustration (p. 583) and then list all the places in them that fall under the category *home*. What do all these places have in common? Try to write a definition of *home* that accommodates all these places.

5. Imagine a conversation among Frawley, Ron Suskind (p. 588), and Barbara Smith (p. 601) on the definition and importance of *home*. Write out a page or so of that conversation.

JOINING THE CONVERSATION

6. Think for a while about the work you now do or have done. What about that work made you feel good about what you were doing? Did anything about it seem like a "big lie"? What, if anything, filled you with frustration? Based on your exploration of these questions, write a brief position paper on "how I feel about the work I do (or have done)."

7. Working with several classmates, do some research on nursing homes in your area. How are they regulated? Who owns them? How much does it cost to stay in them? Who works there, and how are such people licensed or certified? Have each member of your group visit one nursing home, taking notes on the facility and its atmosphere and, if possible, talking with people who work there as well as with people who live there. Pool your notes and prepare a written or oral report for your class on whether your research does or does not support Frawley's picture of nursing homes.

FRED BARNES
Quantity Time

AMERICAN POP CULTURE *has been tough on fathers. For every model television dad like* Father Knows Best's *Jim Anderson, viewers have been offered dozens of Archie Bunkers, Al Bundys, George Jeffersons, and Homer Simpsons—men whose parenting skills fall to the right of reptilian. Even the relatively benign sitcom dads portrayed by such comedians as Tim Allen (*Home Improvement*) or Ray Romano (*Everyone Loves Raymond*) are not much better than amiable bunglers, helpless without their unerring wives. Today, a television series entitled* Father Knows Best *could only be a satire or a parody.*

Men may, in fact, have done their part to earn the reputations that TV ruthlessly mimics. After all, we don't typically hear complaints about deadbeat moms. *Still, a torrent of negative TV images, week after week, must be eroding whatever remains of paternal self-respect. Even competent fathers must sometimes feel the urge today to destroy appliances, guzzle Rolling Rock, and scratch themselves in public—if only to seem like the real men they see on TV. Or, as an alternative, they might simply surrender to all the new-age media hype about a kinder, gentler "new fatherhood." In this modern-day fable, insensitive, cloddish sperm donors learn from Oprah Winfrey to become as caring as Rosie O'Donnell.*

In "Quantity Time," Fred Barnes (b. 1943) steers a middle course between these crude stereotypes of male behavior. Hanging out for a weekend with his eight-year-old son, he learns a practical lesson about fatherhood: time spent with the kids is what counts. Barnes is, after all, a busy man—exactly the sort liable to sacrifice parental duties for work. After a decade at the New Republic, *he is now the executive editor of the* Weekly Standard, *a journal of conservative political opinion. Appearing regularly on news shows such as the* McLaughlin Group, Crossfire, *and the* Beltway Boys, *Barnes is among the talking heads who practically define the Washington media. "Quantity Time" originally appeared in the* New Republic *(12 July 1993).*

—J.R.

Fatherhood isn't brain surgery. I say this in defiance of the new conventional wisdom that being a father is breathtakingly difficult, that it creates tough dilemmas and causes enormous stress and that fathers need a strategy, a plan, a vision, for carrying out their duties. I don't think so. Most men I know have an instinct for fatherhood that was triggered the day their first child was born. They instantly recognized the number one requirement of fatherhood: be there. Woody Allen may be a lousy father, but his rule for life applies to being a father. Yep, 90 percent of fatherhood is just showing up. Of course, millions of fathers don't show up at all because of divorce, out-of-

wedlock births, and so on. And the absence of fathers has awful consequences. But that's a social problem, quite different from the personal crisis
fathers supposedly face in their day-to-day interaction with their children.

Forget quality time. You can't plan magic moments or bonding or
epiphanies in dealing with kids. What matters is quantity time. Judging from my
own experience—four kids—children crave prolonged attention, preferably
undivided. They want whole days and nights of it. Knowing this, I opted for an
adventure in quantity time with my son, Freddy, in mid-June. He's eight. I took
him with me for a weekend at The Balsams, an elegant old resort hotel in
Dixville Notch, New Hampshire. All I had to do was give a speech Saturday
morning (I was a last-minute substitute for David Gergen) to a group of Maine
and Vermont bankers and their spouses. The rest of my time was Freddy's. The
only dilemma I faced was figuring out what to do with him while I spoke. He's
about as eager to listen to me hold forth on politics as President Clinton is to hear
another question from Brit Hume.* Since Freddy refused to participate in the
hotel's program for kids, there was only one solution. I paid him off. I gave him
$10 in quarters, hoping that would keep him busy for ninety minutes playing
video games. It worked only too well. When I came to get him later he'd spent
the money and was playing pool with an older kid named Zack. "Dad," he said,
"what'd you come so soon for?"

I had no strategy for how we'd spend our time or what we'd talk about.
We would play it by ear, by instinct. The hotel is situated beside a lake stocked
with trout, so fishing seemed logical. "We're men, aren't we?" Freddy said. We
got life jackets, a rowboat, oars, and two fly rods and headed for the middle of
the lake. I rowed, and Freddy accused me of splashing him as I rowed. Sad to
say, my knowledge of fly fishing consisted of having seen the movie *A River
Runs through It,** and that turned out to be insufficient. Fly fishing, like golf, is
hard. By the time we'd casted a few times, the boat had floated back to the shore,
and I had to stop fishing and row again. This process repeated itself a few times.
After a half-hour, Freddy said, "Dad, we'll never catch a fish." I told him he was
wrong, that if we stuck to it for a while more, we'd catch something. He was
right. The fishing episode produced no moments of deep father-son rapport,
only a shared sense of relief that the two young women who were fly fishing at
the same time didn't catch anything either.

Basketball was better. Freddy showed me everything he'd learned earlier
that week at basketball camp. We pretended to be the Bulls and the Suns.
Hiking was better still. When we returned, it was time for dinner. Freddy and
I were signed up to attend the bankers' formal banquet. I was worried that he
would be bored and bad. Instead, I experienced two of the blessings of father-

---

Brit Hume: conservative journalist likely to ask the liberal president difficult questions
A River Runs through It: 1992 film by Robert Redford (b. 1937), based on a story by
Norman Maclean

hood (these apply also to motherhood). One is that people are unusually nice when you're with your children. When Freddy balked at prime rib, the waitress brought him a burger and fries. The other joy is when your kid unexpectedly displays his best behavior in public. Freddy acted like Little Lord Fauntleroy.* He sat still, responded to everyone who talked to him, didn't once call anyone a "butthead," his favorite epithet. He got restless after roughly an hour. So I gave him $3 to play video games.

During the weekend, I managed to resolve what *Time,* in its June 28 cover story ("Fatherhood: The guilt, the joy, the fear, the fun . . ."), suggests are the two great dilemmas of modern fatherhood. You know, choosing between work and family and deciding whether to be a New Father or an Old Father. This was no big deal. In fact, it's a false choice, one most fathers don't really have to make. The weekend itself combined work and family. Nothing extraordinary there. Fathers balance work and family all the time. You go to work, but if your child is doing something eventful, or needs your immediate help, then you take off. (Those, that is, who have the luxury of skipping out of work when they choose.) You never get credit for being there with your kid. But you get blame—and suffer remorse—if you aren't. Only once have I ever been forced to make a conscious choice between work and family. It occurred when my daughter Grace had a weekday soccer game and her mother was away. I thought: I have so much to do I can't leave work at 4:00 P.M. But I did. Grace scored four goals, her best game ever.

As for new fatherhood—more nurturing and soft-edged, less rigid and aloof—you don't have to embrace it or reject it. You adopt the parts you're comfortable with and forget the rest. I never believed I'd find it thrilling to be in the delivery room to see my child being born. I was wrong. *Time* says that "it is still the mother who carries her child's life around in her head." Like many fathers, I try to keep track of what my kids are doing every day. But I can't be a second mother to them. Men, my friends anyway, aren't good at that. Robert Griswold, in *Fatherhood in America,* complains that American culture "lacks any coherent and unified vision of what fathers and fatherhood should be." He's right, but so what? That's a problem of our culture and its need to put a theory behind things that work in practice. Fathers get along fine without such a vision.

As the banquet was ending, Freddy returned from the game room, ready for attention. We went outside to reconnoiter the eighteen-hole putting green, where we intended to play the next morning. The sky was amazingly clear, the stars glistening like they never do through the haze over Washington. A couple from Camden, Maine, spent thirty minutes talking to

Little Lord Fauntleroy: the well-behaved little hero of Frances Eliza Hodgson Burnett's novel of the same name, published in 1886

Freddy and me. The wife took Freddy aside and pointed out the big Dipper to him. He was ecstatic. "I couldn't see it before," he said. The husband talked about other wonders in the sky. Freddy was enthralled. As we walked back to our room, he said, "That man really knew a lot." It was 10:00 P.M., time for bed. Freddy jumped under the covers and insisted we sleep in the same bed. "Dad, Dad, there's so much I want to tell you," he said. Before he could remember exactly what, he was fast asleep.

QUESTIONING THE TEXT

1. Decide whether your father or a father figure in your life fits the stereo-type of "old father" or "new father" briefly described in "Quantity Time." To find out more about this distinction, review the *Time* article (28 June 1993) Barnes mentions in paragraph 5.

2. J.R.'s introduction to Barnes's article includes references to a number of names and images drawn from popular culture. List the people and im-ages mentioned in the first two paragraphs of the introduction. Then, working with a small group, discuss the assumptions J.R. has made about his audience. Which items in the list make a clear point about fa-therhood? Which did you puzzle over? If members of your group were to rewrite the introduction, what names and images might you use in-stead of Jim Anderson, Archie Bunker, and so on?

MAKING CONNECTIONS

3. In "Introduction to *Trout*" (p. 506), James Prosek explains how he ac-quired his love of nature through his father's passion for birds. In "Quantity Time," Fred Barnes and his son actually go trout fishing, though neither has a life-changing experience or catches any fish. Still, it seems that parent-child moments can be important and memorable for both parties. Write a brief narrative recounting a similar memorable time you have shared with a family member.

4. In "The Mind of Man" (p. 120), David Thomas cites research that sug-gests that boys are inclined to be more rambunctious and active than girls, especially in the preteen years. How do you think Barnes's week-end would have been different—if at all—were he traveling with a daughter of the same age? How does Barnes keep his eight-year-old son occupied while he gives a speech, and do you think a mother might have handled the situation differently? Why, or why not?

JOINING THE CONVERSATION

5. How are fathers portrayed on television today? To find out, choose a specific TV network, designate a period of time for viewing (such as three nights of prime-time shows), and keep a record of all the fathers who appear on the network's programs. Since you can't study every aspect of fatherhood, you might first want to create a scale or checklist of specific criteria for evaluating or characterizing their parenting. Then report your findings in a brief essay. To increase the size of the TV sample you study, you may want to do this assignment with the help of a small group, with each participant watching a different network.

6. Barnes makes a simple claim about fatherhood: quantity is more important than quality when it comes to spending time with kids. Write an essay in which you explore his argument, drawing from your own experiences as a child, parent, or person otherwise involved with children.

Ask Martha: Guest Towels

Ever wondered how to make your bed properly? How to serve bread and butter in the most elegant way? How to make a fabric-covered mousepad for your computer desk? Just ask former model and stockbroker Martha Stewart (b. 1941), and you can get the answers to these and every other imaginable question on homemaking, gardening, or entertaining. The Martha Stewart Web site, which seems to be updated almost constantly, offers an overview of her domain. I checked in recently to see what Martha was doing on her television show. In the "Ask Martha" section, I found the following question and answer. So if you've ever wondered how to set out guest towels properly in your bathroom, read on.

Stewart's advice is so detailed and demanding (to serve bread and butter, for instance, you should "set a warm roll on every guest's bread plate" along with an individual pat of molded butter placed carefully "on top of scented geranium leaves, bay leaves, or nasturtium leaves") that it is easily parodied, as it is regularly by Saturday Night Live's *Ana Gasteyer, for instance. One of a trilogy of parodies orchestrated by Tom Connor and Jim Downey,* Is Martha Stuart Living?, *includes a page on how to achieve the perfectly made bed à la Martha: "I soak rotating sets of 700-point, South Sea Island, pima-cotton sheets overnight in a mixture of starch derived from imported Irish new potatoes and a light, glue-based fixative from one of my herd of Appaloosas, bred exclusively for this purpose. When dry, these sheets will hold a crease all night long." (For another excerpt from Connor and Downey's parody, see p. 656.)*

Millions of people find Martha Stewart inspiring, a force for order, calm, tranquillity, and civility; others find her ridiculous—and only out to make a buck. What's your take on Stewart?
—A.L.

ASK MARTHA: GUEST TOWELS

What is the proper way to set guest towels out in the bathroom (both cloth and paper)? My guests often skip the guest towels and use the bath towels instead.

Jay Baxter, Los Angeles
(At Roger's Gardens, in Corona del Mar, CA)

To encourage your guests to use your guest towels, the key is to make it obvious that the towels are for use and not just for show. Stack or roll up a generous number of hand towels (you can also use dish towels or washcloths), and set them out in a basket or tin. You can also fold them and lay them on the edge of the sink or bathtub. Paper towels are also an option: Look for good, substantial ones that feel almost like cloth at party-supply stores.

654

If you're using cloth towels, be sure to set out a receptacle such as a basket or enamel bucket into which guests can throw the towels they've used. Martha usually places a towel into the basket before the party so that guests know to follow suit.

If you're expecting overnight guests, tie a bath towel, hand towel, and washcloth together with a ribbon and set it at the end of each guest's bed.

QUESTIONING THE TEXT

1. Who answers the question posed by Jay Baxter? Read the answer again and then decide whether you think the respondent is Martha Stewart or one of her staff.

MAKING CONNECTIONS

2. Read the parody of Stewart by Tom Connor and Jim Downey (p. 656). What qualities have they exaggerated? What do the photographs by J. Barry O'Rourke add to the humor?

3. Note that the second paragraph advises putting a (presumably used) towel in a basket so that guests will know what they are to do with the towels they use. With this advice in mind, read Margaret Talbot's essay about Stewart (p. 657) and then consider what this advice suggests about the people Martha is advising. In what ways does the "Guest Towels" example from Stewart's Web site support or fail to support Talbot's claim that "large numbers of Americans have lost confidence in their own judgment about the most ordinary things"?

JOINING THE CONVERSATION

4. How popular is Martha Stewart among your friends, relatives, and acquaintances? Conduct an informal survey to find out. How many know of Stewart's publications, TV show, or other ventures? How many are fans? How many watch her show or read her magazine on a regular basis? Write up a brief report of your findings and bring it to class for discussion.

TOM CONNOR and JIM DOWNEY
Well-Stacked Logs

*I*F YOU'VE EVER HAD THE URGE *to poke fun at someone by taking one or more of their characteristics and exaggerating them to absurd proportions, you'll recognize that impulse in Tom Connor and Jim Downey's 1995 parody of Martha Stewart's enormously successful and influential magazine,* Martha Stewart Living. *In* Is Martha Stuart Living? *(note the deliberate misspelling), Connor and Downey produced a glossy, 8½ × 11-inch magazine that looks at first glance very much like the subject of its amusement. Then the twists and turns of exaggeration begin, yielding a very funny product. In the passage that follows, the faux Martha gives advice on how to stack wood — but not in order to preserve it for use during the winter.* —A.L.

Anyone can fell a tree, haul it home, chop it up, split the logs and toss them onto a pile. But a well-designed log pile is truly a thing of beauty. Try stacking wood in a variety of ways, starting with the three patterns shown above. Try not to use the logs. The idea is to impress others, not warm the house. If the winter is cold and you must use them, take logs from the least successful and attractive pile first.

IN RESPONSE

1. Try your hand at writing a parody of Martha Stewart. If you are not already familiar with her, begin by visiting her Web site, watching her TV show, or looking at issues of *Martha Stewart Living*. Then choose one aspect of her work you want to parody — a recipe or gardening tip, for instance — and list all the characteristics of it you can identify. Practice exaggerating those characteristics or linking them in bizarrely unexpected ways. Finally, write your parody, keeping it fairly short in order to sustain its humor and including a visual illustration if possible.

MARGARET TALBOT
Les Très Riches Heures de Martha Stewart

MARGARET TALBOT *(b. 1961) wrote the following essay for the* New Republic, *where she is now a contributing editor. She says that she particularly enjoyed completing this assignment, perhaps because she was pregnant at the time and thus "thinking a lot about the perils and pleasures of domesticity." "Les Très Riches Heures de Martha Stewart" explores the perils and pleasures and meaning of what Talbot calls "the cult of Martha"—the 1.5 million magazine subscribers and literally countless television viewers and other consumers who seem charmed, instructed, even calmed by the Stewart persona of perfection.*

Certainly Stewart—with her amazingly complicated recipes and grossly time-consuming household "tips"—makes an easy target, as the many parodies of her attest (see "Other Readings" at the end of this chapter for a list of some of these parodies as well as for the Martha Stewart Web site address). Her very ubiquity probably plays a part as well in calling forth a certain amount of ridicule: last December my local newspaper announced—on page one—that it would initiate "Martha-Free Days" in which the editors pledged that nothing at all regarding the "DragonLady of Domesticity" would appear in its pages.

Yet as Talbot's essay demonstrates, there's more to the Martha phenomenon than meets the eye—or the dust cloth. Beyond the rigidly shaped beauties of Martha Stewart Living *lie questions about what homemaking should be, about anxieties for graces lost or threatened, about fears of failure, about a lack of judgment and of knowing how to live our lives. Whether you are a Martha Stewart fan or foe—or an indifferent bystander—Talbot prompts you to ask, "What does the cult of Martha mean [and] . . . what have we done, exactly, to deserve her?" and, in turn, to examine your own lifestyle and the values it represents.* —A.L.

Every age gets the household goddess it deserves. The '60s had Julia Child, the sophisticated French chef who proved as permissive as Dr. Spock. She may have proselytized for a refined foreign cuisine from her perch at a Boston PBS station, but she was always an anti-snob, vowing to "take a lot of the la dee dah out of French cooking." With her madras shirts and her penumbra of curls, her 6'2" frame and her whinny of a voice, she exuded an air of Cambridge eccentricity—faintly bohemian and a little tatty, like a yellowing travel poster. She was messy and forgiving. When Julia dropped an egg or collapsed a soufflé, she shrugged and laughed. "You are alone in the kitchen, nobody can see you, and cooking is meant to be fun," she reminded her viewers. She wielded lethal-looking kitchen knives with campy abandon, dipped her fingers into crème anglaise and wiped her chocolate-smeared hands on an apron tied carelessly at her waist. For Child was also something of a sensualist, a celebrant of appetite as much as a pedant of cooking.

In the '90s, and probably well into the next century, we have Martha Stewart, corporate overachiever turned domestic superachiever, Mildred Pierce in earth-toned Armani. Martha is the anti-Julia. Consider the extent of their respective powers. At the height of her success, Child could boast a clutch of bestselling cookbooks and a *gemütlich* TV show shot on a single set. At what may or may not be the height of her success, here's what Stewart can claim: a 5-year-old magazine, *Martha Stewart Living,* with a circulation that has leapt to 1.5 million; a popular cable TV show, also called *Martha Stewart Living* and filmed at her luscious Connecticut and East Hampton estates; a dozen wildly successful gardening, cooking and lifestyle books; a mail-order business, Martha-by-Mail; a nationally syndicated newspaper column, "Ask Martha"; a regular Wednesday slot on the *Today* show; a line of $110-a-gallon paints in colors inspired by the eggs her Araucana hens lay; plans to invade cyberspace*—in short, an empire.

Julia limited herself to cooking lessons, with the quiet implication that cooking was a kind of synecdoche for the rest of bourgeois existence; but Martha's parish is vaster, her field is all of life. Her expertise, as she recently explained to *Mediaweek* magazine, covers, quite simply, "Beautiful soups and how to make them, beautiful houses and how to build them, beautiful children and how to raise them." (From soups to little nuts.) She presides, in fact, over a phenomenon that, in other realms, is quite familiar in American society and culture: a cult, devoted to her name and image.

In the distance between these two cynosures of domestic life lies a question: What does the cult of Martha mean? Or, to put it another way, what have we done, exactly, to deserve her?

If you have read the paper or turned on the television in the last year or   5 so, you have probably caught a glimpse of the WASPy good looks, the affectless demeanor, the nacreous perfection of her world. You may even know the outlines of her story. Middle-class girl from a Polish-American family in Nutley, New Jersey, works her way through Barnard in the early '60s, modeling on the side. She becomes a stockbroker, a self-described workaholic and insomniac who by the '70s is making six figures on Wall Street, and who then boldly trades it all in . . . for life as a workaholic, insomniac evangelist for domesticity whose business now generates some $200 million in profits a year. (She herself, according to the *Wall Street Journal,* makes a salary of $400,000 a year from Time Inc., which generously supplements this figure with a $40,000 a year clothing allowance and other candies.) You may even have admired her magazine, with its art-book production values and spare design, every kitchen utensil photographed like an Imogen Cunningham nude, every

---

plans to invade cyberspace: You can view her beachhead at <http://www.marthastewart.com/>.

plum or pepper rendered with the loving detail of an eighteenth-century botanical drawing, every page a gentle exhalation of High Class.

What you may not quite realize, if you have not delved deeper into Stewart's oeuvre, is the ambition of her design for living—the absurd, self-parodic dream of it. To read Martha Stewart is to know that there is no corner of your domestic life that cannot be beautified or improved under careful tutelage, none that should not be colonized by the rhetoric and the discipline of quality control. Work full time though you may, care for your family though you must, convenience should never be your watchword in what Stewart likes to call, in her own twee coinage, "homekeeping." Convenience is the enemy of excellence. "We do not pretend that these are 'convenience' foods," she writes loftily of the bread and preserves recipes in a 1991 issue of the magazine. "Some take days to make. But they are recipes that will produce the very best results, and we know that is what you want." Martha is a kitchen-sink idealist. She scorns utility in the name of beauty. But her idealism, of course, extends no further than surface appearances, which makes it a very particular form of idealism indeed.

To spend any length of time in Martha-land is to realize that it is not enough to serve your guests homemade pumpkin soup as a first course. You must present it in hollowed-out, hand-gilded pumpkins as well. It will not do to serve an Easter ham unless you have baked it in a roasting pan lined with, of all things, "tender, young, organically-grown grass that has not yet been cut." And, when serving a "casual" lobster and corn dinner al fresco, you really ought to fashion dozens of cunning little bamboo brushes tied with raffia and adorned with a chive so that each of your guests may butter their corn with something pretty.

To be a Martha fan (or more precisely, a Martha adept) is to understand that a terracotta pot is just a terracotta pot until you have "aged" it, painstakingly rubbing yogurt into its dampened sides, then smearing it with plant food or "something you found in the woods" and patiently standing by while the mold sprouts. It is to think that maybe you could do this *kind* of thing, anyway—start a garden, say, in your scruffy backyard—and then to be brought up short by Martha's enumeration, in *Martha Stewart's Gardening,* of forty-nine "essential" gardening tools. These range from a "polesaw" to a "corn fiber broom" to three different kinds of pruning shears, one of which—the "loppers"—Martha says she has in three different sizes. You have, perhaps, a trowel. But then Martha's garden is a daunting thing to contemplate, what with its topiary mazes and state-of-the-art chicken coop; its "antique" flowers and geometric herb garden. It's half USDA* station, half Sissinghurst.* And you cannot imagine making anything remotely like it at your own house, not without legions of artisans and laborers and graduate students in landscape design, and a pot of money that perhaps you'll unearth when you dig up the yard.

USDA: United States Department of Agriculture
Sissinghurst: a lush English garden designed by Vita Sackville-West in the 1930s

In *The Culture of Narcissism,* Christopher Lasch describes the ways in which pleasure, in our age, has taken on "the qualities of work," allowing our leisure-time activities to be measured by the same standards of accomplishment that rule the workplace. It is a phenomenon that he memorably characterizes as "the invasion of play by the rhetoric of achievement." For Lasch, writing in the early '70s, the proliferation of sex-advice manuals offered a particularly poignant example. Today, though, you might just as easily point to the hundreds of products and texts, from unctuous home-furnishings catalogs to upscale "shelter" magazines to self-help books like *Meditations for Women Who Do Too Much,* that tell us exactly how to "nest" and "cocoon" and "nurture," how to "center" and "retreat," and how to measure our success at these eminently private pursuits. Just as late-nineteenth-century marketers and experts promised to bring Americans back in touch with the nature from which modern industrial life had alienated them, so today's "shelter" experts—the word is revealingly primal—promise to reconnect us with a similarly mystified home. The bourgeois home as lost paradise, retrievable through careful instruction.

Martha Stewart is the apotheosis of this particular cult of expertise, and its   10 most resourceful entrepreneur. She imagines projects of which we would never have thought—gathering dewy grass for our Easter ham, say—and makes us feel the pressing need for training in them. And she exploits, brilliantly, a certain estrangement from home that many working women feel these days. For women who are working longer and longer hours at more and more demanding jobs, it's easy to think of home as the place where chaos reigns and their own competence is called into doubt: easy to regard the office, by comparison, as the bulwark of order. It is a reversal, of course, of the hoary concept of home as a refuge from the tempests of the marketplace. But these days, as the female executives in a recent study attested, the priority they most often let slide is housekeeping: they'll abide disorder at home that they wouldn't or couldn't abide at the office. No working couple's home is the oasis of tranquility and Italian marble countertops that Marthaism seems to promise. But could it be? Should it be? Stewart plucks expertly at that chord of doubt.

In an era when it is not at all uncommon to be cut off from the traditional sources of motherwit and household lore—when many of us live far from the families into which we were born and have started our own families too late to benefit from the guidance of living parents or grandparents—domestic pedants like Martha Stewart rightly sense a big vacuum to fill. Stewart's books are saturated with nostalgia for lost tradition* and old moldings, for her childhood in Nutley and for her mother's homemade preserves. In the magazine, her "Remembering" column pines moralistically for a simpler era, when beach vacations meant no television or video games, just dig-

---

nostalgia for lost tradition: See Stephanie Coontz's "The Way We Wish We Were" (p. 628), paragraphs 11–13, for a perspective on such nostalgia.

ging for clams and napping in hammocks. Yet Stewart's message is that such simplicity can only be achieved now through strenuous effort and a flood of advice. We might be able to put on a picnic or a dinner party without her help, she seems to tell us, but we wouldn't do it properly, beautifully, in the spirit of excellence that we expect of ourselves at work.

It may be that Stewart's special appeal is to women who wouldn't want to take their mother's word anyway, to baby-boomer daughters who figure that their sensibilities are just too different from their stay-at-home moms', who can't throw themselves into housekeeping without thinking of their kitchen as a catering business and their backyards as a garden show. In fact, relatively few of Martha's fans are housewives—72 percent of the subscribers to *Martha Stewart Living* are employed outside the home as managers or professionals—and many of them profess to admire her precisely because she isn't one, either. As one such Martha acolyte, an account executive at a Christian radio station, effused on the Internet: "[Stewart] is my favorite independent woman and what an entrepreneur! She's got her own television show, magazine, books and even her own brand of latex paint. . . . Martha is a feisty woman who settles for nothing less than perfection."

For women such as these, the didactic faux-maternalism of Martha Stewart seems the perfect answer. She may dispense the kind of homekeeping advice that a mother would, but she does so in tones too chill and exacting to sound "maternal," singling out, for example, those "who will always be too lazy" to do her projects. She makes housekeeping safe for the professional woman by professionalizing housekeeping. And you never forget that Stewart is herself a mogul, even when she's baking rhubarb crisp and telling you, in her Shakeresque mantra, that "It's a Good Thing."

It is tempting to see the Martha cult purely as a symptom of anti-feminist backlash. Though she may not directly admonish women to abandon careers for hearth and home, Stewart certainly exalts a way of life that puts hearth and home at its center, one that would be virtually impossible to achieve without *somebody's* full-time devotion. (Camille Paglia has praised her as "someone who has done a tremendous service for ordinary women—women who identify with the roles of wife, mother, and homemaker.") Besides, in those alarming moments when Stewart slips into the social critic's mode, she can sound a wee bit like Phyllis Schlafly*—less punitive and more patrician, maybe, but just as smug about the moral uplift of a well-ordered home. Her philosophy of cultivating your own walled garden while the world outside is condemned to squalor bears the hallmarks of Reagan's America—it would not be overreading to call it a variety of conservatism. "Amid the horrors of genocidal war in Bosnia and Rwanda, the AIDS epidemic and increasing crime in many cities," Stewart writes

---

Phyllis Schlafly (b. 1924): founder of the Eagle Forum and advocate for traditional family values

in a recent column, "there are those of us who desire positive reinforcement of some very basic tenets of good living." And those would be? "Good food, gardening, crafts, entertaining and home improvement." (Hollow out the pumpkins, they're starving in Rwanda.)

Yet it would, in the end, be too simplistic to regard her as a tool of the   15 feminine mystique, or as some sort of spokesmodel for full-time mommies. For one thing, there is nothing especially June Cleaverish,* or even motherly, about Stewart. She has taken a drubbing, in fact, for looking more convincing as a businesswoman than a dispenser of milk and cookies. (Remember the apocryphal tale that had Martha flattening a crate of baby chicks while backing out of a driveway in her Mercedes?) Her habitual prickliness and Scotchguard perfectionism are more like the badges of the striving good girl, still cut to the quick by her classmates' razzing when she asked for extra homework.

Despite the ritual obeisance that Martha pays to Family, moreover, she is not remotely interested in the messy contingencies of family life. In the enchanted world of Turkey Hill, there are no husbands (Stewart was divorced from hers in 1990), only loyal craftsmen, who clip hedges and force dogwood with self-effacing dedication. Children she makes use of as accessories, much like Parisian women deploy little dogs. The books and especially the magazine are often graced with photographic spreads of parties and teas where children pale as waxen angels somberly disport themselves, their fair hair shaped into tasteful blunt cuts, their slight figures clad in storybook velvet or lace. "If I had to choose one essential element for the success of an Easter brunch," she writes rather menacingly in her 1994 *Menus for Entertaining,* "it would be children." The homemade Halloween costumes modeled by wee lads and lasses in an October 1991 issue of *Martha Stewart Living* do look gorgeous—the Caravaggio colors, the themes drawn from nature. But it's kind of hard to imagine a 5-year-old boy happily agreeing to go as an acorn this year, instead of say, Batman. And why should he? In Marthaland, his boyhood would almost certainly be overridden in the name of taste.

If Stewart is a throwback, it's not so much to the 1950s as to the 1850s, when the doctrine of separate spheres did allow married or widowed women of the upper classes a kind of power—unchallenged dominion over the day-to-day functioning of the home and its servants, in exchange for ceding the public realm to men. At Turkey Hill, Stewart is the undisputed chatelaine, micromanaging her estate in splendid isolation. (This hermetic pastoral is slightly marred, of course, by the presence of cameras.) Here the domestic arts have become ends in themselves, unmoored from family values and indeed from family.

Stewart's peculiar brand of didacticism has another nineteenth-century precedent—in the domestic science or home economics movement. The do-

---

June Cleaverish: June Cleaver was the stay-at-home mother in the television situation comedy *Leave It to Beaver.*

mestic scientists' favorite recipes—"wholesome" concoctions of condensed milk and canned fruit, rivers of white sauce—would never have passed Martha's muster; but their commitment to painstakingly elegant presentation, their concern with the look of food even more than its taste, sound a lot like Stewart's. And, more importantly, so does their underlying philosophy. They emerged out of a tradition: the American preference for food writing of the prescriptive, not the descriptive, kind, for food books that told you, in M. F. K. Fisher's* formulation, not about eating but about what to eat. But they took this spirit much further. Like Stewart, these brisk professional women of the 1880s and '90s believed that true culinary literacy could not be handed down or casually absorbed; it had to be carefully taught. (One of the movement's accomplishments, if it can be called that, was the home ec curriculum.)

Like Stewart, the domestic scientists were not bent on liberating intelligent women from housework. Their objective was to raise housework to a level worthy of intelligent women. They wished to apply rational method to the chaos and the drudgery of housework and, in so doing, to earn it the respect accorded men's stuff like science and business. Neither instinct, nor intuition, nor mother's rough-hewn words of advice would have a place in the scientifically managed home of the future. As Laura Shapiro observes in *Perfection Salad,* her lively and perceptive history of domestic science, the ideal new housewife was supposed to project, above all, "self-sufficiency, self-control, and a perfectly bland façade." Sound familiar?

It is in their understanding of gender roles, however, that the doyennes   20
of home ec most closely prefigure Marthaism. Like Stewart, they cannot be classified either as feminists or traditionalists. Their model housewife was a pseudo-professional with little time for sublimating her ego to her husband's or tenderly ministering to his needs. She was more like a factory supervisor than either the Victorian angel of the home or what Shapiro calls the courtesan type, the postwar housewife who was supposed to zip through her chores so she could gussy herself up for her husband. In Martha's world, too, the managerial and aesthetic challenges of "homekeeping" always take priority, and their intricacy and ambition command a respect that mere wifely duties never could. Her husbandless hauteur is rich with the self-satisfaction of financial and emotional independence.

In the end, Stewart's fantasies have as much to do with class as with gender. The professional women who read her books might find themselves longing for a breadwinner, but a lifestyle this beautiful is easier to come by if you've never needed a breadwinner in the first place. Stewart's books are a dreamy advertisement for independent wealth—or, more accurately, for its facsimile. You may not have a posh pedigree, but with a little effort (okay, a lot) you can adopt its trappings. After all, Martha wasn't born to wealth

---

M. F. K. Fisher (1908–92): distinguished food writer and author of *The Art of Eating* (1954)

either, but now she attends the weddings of people with names like Charles Booth-Clibborn (she went to his in London, the magazine tells us) and caters them for couples named Sissy and Kelsey (see her *Wedding Planner,* in which their yacht is decorated with a "Just Married" sign).

She is not an American aristocrat, but she plays one on TV. And you can play one, too, at least in your own home. Insist on cultivating only those particular yellow plums you tasted in the Dordogne,* buy your copper cleaner only at Delherin* in Paris, host lawn parties where guests come "attired in the garden dress of the Victorian era," and you begin to simulate the luster of lineage. Some of Stewart's status-augmenting suggestions must strike even her most faithful fans as ridiculous. For showers held after the baby is born, Martha "likes presenting the infant with engraved calling cards that the child can then slip into thank you notes and such for years to come." What a great idea. Maybe your baby can gum them for a while first, thoughtfully imprinting them with his signature drool.

The book that best exemplifies her class-consciousness is *Martha Stewart's New Old House,* a step-by-step account of refurbishing a Federal-style farmhouse in Westport, Connecticut. Like all her books, it contains many, many pictures of Martha; here she's frequently shown supervising the work of plasterers, carpenters and other "seemingly taciturn men." *New Old House* establishes Stewart's ideal audience: a demographic niche occupied by the kind of people who, like her, can afford to do their kitchen countertops in "mottled, gray-green, hand-honed slate from New York state, especially cut" for them. The cost of all this (and believe me, countertops are only the beginning) goes unmentioned. If you have to ask, maybe you're not a Martha kind of person after all.

In fact, Stewart never seems all that concerned with reassuring her readers of their ability to afford such luxuries or their right to enjoy them. She's more concerned with establishing her own claims. Her reasoning seems to go something like this: the houses that she buys and renovates belong to wealthy families who passed them down through generations. But these families did not properly care for their patrimony. The widowed Bulkeley sisters, erstwhile owners of Turkey Hill, had let the estate fall "into great disrepair. All the farms and outbuildings were gone. . . . The fields around had been sold off by the sisters in 2-acre building lots; suburbia encroached." The owner of the eponymous New Old House was a retired librarian named Miss Adams who "had little interest in the house other than as a roof over her head. Clearly a frugal spirit, she had no plans to restore the house, and she lived there until she could no longer cope with the maintenance and upkeep of the place. The house was in dire need of attention, and since no other family member wanted to assume re-

---

Dordogne: An agricultural region of southwestern France. For another perspective on the social advantages of specialized French agricultural produce, see David Brooks, "Conscientious Consumption" (p. 200).

Delherin: J. Delherin in Paris deals in restaurant supplies.

sponsibility, Miss Adams reluctantly decided to sell her family home. I wanted very much to save the Adams house, to put it to rights, to return its history to it, to make it livable once again."

25

It's a saga with overtones of Jamesian comedy: a family with bloodlines but no money is simultaneously rescued and eclipsed by an energetic upstart with money but no bloodlines. The important difference—besides the fact that Martha is marrying the house, not the son—is that she also has taste. And it's taste, far more than money, she implies, that gives her the right to these splendid, neglected piles of brick. Unlike the "frugal" Misses Bulkeley, she will keep suburbia at bay; unlike the careless Miss Adams, she would never resort to "hideous rugs" in (yuck) shades of brown. They don't understand their own houses; she does, and so she *deserves* to own their houses. But leave it to Martha to get all snippy about these people's aesthetic oversights while quietly celebrating their reversion to type. They're useful to her, and not only because their indifference to decor bolsters her claim to their property. Like the pumpkin pine floors and original fixtures, these quaintly cheeseparing New Englanders denote the property's authenticity.

The fantasy of vaulting into the upper crust that Martha Stewart fulfilled, and now piques in her readers, is about more than just money, of course. Among other things, it's about time, and the luxurious plenitude of it. Living the Martha way would mean enjoying a surfeit of that scarce commodity, cooking and crafting at the artisanal pace her projects require. Trouble is, none of us overworked Americans has time to spare these days—and least of all the upscale professional women whom Stewart targets. Martha herself seemed to acknowledge this when she told *Inside Media* that she attracts at least two classes of true believers: the "Be-Marthas," who have enough money and manic devotion to follow many of her lifestyle techniques, and the "Do-Marthas," who "are a little bit envious" and "don't have as much money as the Be-Marthas."

To those fulsome categories, you could surely add the "watch Marthas" or the "read Marthas," people who might consider, say, making their own rabbit-shaped wire topiary forms, but only consider it, who mostly just indulge in the fantasy of doing so, if only they had the time. There is something undeniably soothing about watching Martha at her absurdly time-consuming labors. A female "media executive" explained the appeal to Barbara Lippert in *New York* magazine: "I never liked Martha Stewart until I started watching her on Sunday mornings. I turn on the TV, and I'm in my pajamas, still in this place between sleep and reality. And she's showing you how to roll your tablecloths in parchment paper. She's like a character when she does her crafts. It reminds me of watching Mr. Green Jeans on Captain Kangaroo. I remember he had a shoebox he took out that was filled with craft things. There would be a close-up on his hands with his buffed nails. And then he would show you how to cut an oaktag with a scissor, or when he folded paper, he'd say: 'There you go, boys and girls,' and it was very quiet. It's like she brings out this great meditative focus and calm."

The show does seem strikingly unfrenetic. Unlike just about everything else on TV, including the *Our Home* show, which follows it on Lifetime, it eschews Kathy Lee-type banter, perky music, swooping studio shots and jittery handheld cameras. Instead there's just Martha, alone in her garden or kitchen, her teacherly tones blending with birdsong, her recipes cued to the seasons. Whimsical recorder music pipes along over the credits. Martha's crisply ironed denim shirts, pearl earrings, and honey-toned highlights bespeak the fabulousness of Connecticut. Her hands move slowly, deliberately over her yellow roses or her Depression glasses. Martha is a Puritan who prepares "sinful" foods—few of her recipes are low-fat or especially health-conscious—that are redeemed by the prodigious labors, the molasses afternoons, involved in serving them. (She preys upon our guilt about overindulgence, then hints at how to assuage it.) Here at Turkey Hill, time is as logy as a honey-sated bumblebee. Here on Lifetime, the cable channel aimed at baby-boom women, Martha's stately show floats along in a sea of stalker movies, Thighmaster commercials and "Weddings of a Lifetime" segments, and by comparison, I have to say, she looks rather dignified. Would that we all had these *très riches heures*.

But if we had the hours, if we had the circumstances, wouldn't we want to fill them with something of our own, with a domestic grace of our own devising? Well, maybe not anymore. For taste is no longer an expression of individuality. It is, more often, an instrument of conformism, a way to assure ourselves that we're living by the right codes, dictated or sanctioned by experts. Martha Stewart's "expertise" is really nothing but another name for the perplexity of her cowed consumers. A lifestyle cult as all-encompassing as hers could thrive only at a time when large numbers of Americans have lost confidence in their own judgment about the most ordinary things. For this reason, *Martha Stewart Living* isn't really living at all.

QUESTIONING THE TEXT

1. Talbot's title, "Les Très Riches Heures de Martha Stewart," alludes to a kind of book—a "book of hours"—that was handmade for wealthy people in medieval Europe and used as a guide in private religious devotions. Why do you think Talbot chooses this title? What does the allusion suggest about the connections between such books and Martha Stewart's world, including those who consult her magazine, books, and TV programs?

2. Although the topic of Talbot's essay may seem fairly light, the argument of "Les Très Riches Heures de Martha Stewart" is quite complex and serious, especially in its concluding pages, where Talbot escalates her attack on Stewart. Working with two or three classmates, write a 300-word summary of the essay—one that clearly states Talbot's key argu-

ments against what she describes as "Marthaism" (paragraph 10). Compare the summary your team composes with those prepared by other groups in the class. Then discuss any important differences in your summaries.

MAKING CONNECTIONS

3. Which selection in this chapter other than the two previous ones has the most resonance with Martha Stewart's world? Look carefully through the chapter and then write a response to this question, explaining the reasons for your choice. Bring your response to class for discussion.

4. According to Talbot (paragraph 3), Martha Stewart presides over a cult "devoted to her name and image." Read the selection by Neil Postman (p. 513) with this question in mind: is Stewart participating in what Postman calls "technopoly" and "the great symbol drain"? Working with a classmate, explore this question, making a list of the evidence that supports the answer you give. Bring your list to class for discussion.

5. How do you imagine Martha Stewart might respond to Talbot's analysis of her and to parodies like Tom Connor and Jim Downey's "Well-Stacked Logs" (p. 656)? Think about this question as you reread these two pieces and the passage from Stewart's Web site (p. 654). Then work with a classmate to write a brief dialogue (no more than two or three pages) from an imaginary talk show featuring Stewart, Connor, Downey, and Talbot.

JOINING THE CONVERSATION

6. Talbot claims that "Stewart's books are a dreamy advertisement for independent wealth—or, more accurately, for its facsimile" (paragraph 21). Investigate her claim by consulting library sources, reading issues of *Martha Stewart Living,* visiting the Martha Stewart Web site, watching her TV show, and so on. Take careful notes on your findings and then write a response to Talbot's claim, explaining how your research supports, challenges, or perhaps complicates the claim.

ED MADDEN
Family Cemetery,
near Hickory Ridge, Arkansas

WE FEEL THE TOUCH *of our extended families at important moments of transition: birth, graduation, marriage, death. Anyone with a large clan knows, however, that such occasions can bring out the worst in people. Cousins grown a lanky foot taller in the last year may trade blows (or gossip) at a wedding; at a baptism, aunts from different sides of the family will quarrel over the choice of godparents; and otherwise dutiful children will spend a holiday reunion silently coveting Grandpa's power tools, wondering who will inherit them when the old man finally crosses the bar.*

Yet at such thresholds, we need our families too and look for support from these people who knew us from our birth, who share our rambling gait, conspicuous nose, and deepest memories.

In the following poem Ed Madden writes about one such family time. Madden (b. 1963) is a poet and an assistant professor at the University of South Carolina. He grew up on a rice and soybean farm in northeast Arkansas. His interests range from theology and feminist theory to pop culture and Elvis Presley, and his poems have appeared in College English, Christianity and Literature, *and elsewhere.*   — J.R.

I

Redwing blackbirds shout
themselves hoarse from the oaks
of the cemetery. A crop–duster drones
above a nearby ricefield. The long

caravan of cars that left the church   5
is still arriving, the dust drifting
in waves that coat the dull green rows
of grain sorghum and soybeans, dust

still hanging in air hot
with the smell of Arkansas honeysuckle   10
and vetch and the sweet maroon
ferment of funeral roses.

II

I breathe deeply: the summer
grass rich at the verge of brown,
freshly mown, the musty, almost acrid   15
earth of this sandy hillside,

piled by the grave. These things
must be remembered, like the daffodils
in solemn yellow spurts that marked
my grandma's death, standing in silent   20

clusters of mourning at the cemetery,
dotting her yard like relatives, nodding,
touching, like cousins laughing, flaring
their bright lives against the grey spring wind.

III

Grandpa's flowers are scattered   25
down the line of tombstones, decorating
the graves of his wife, his children;
it seems the office of aunts to gather

the blooms, to drape these odd dots
and splashes, against brown earth, grey stone.   30
We the men, the sons and grandsons,
take the shovels in groups of three,

marking our ties with the thuds that fill
the grave: it is love, it is something
of God. And there must be a word   35
to fill the hole it creates.

IN RESPONSE

1. Read "Family Cemetery" alongside Alice Walker's piece (p. 596), and
   respond with a paragraph on your own definition of *family*. If you keep
   a reading log, write the paragraph there.

2. Examine the role that nature plays in "Family Cemetery." In a short analysis, explain your reaction to the sights, sounds, and smells in this poem.

3. In a group, share your experience of a family moment that you might turn into a poem.

OTHER READINGS

Ehrlich, Gretel. "Home Is How Many Places." *Islands, the Universe, Home.* New York: Viking, 1991. A mix of Chumash Indian history and personal narrative, this essay recounts the author's trip to the Santa Barbara Channel Islands.

Garr, Evan. "Is Going Home Possible?" *The American Enterprise* May/June 1998: 50–51. Defends "home-by-choice" mothers.

Hoagland, Edward. "A Peaceable Kingdom." *The Best American Essays 1998.* Eds. Cynthia Ozick and Robert Atwan. New York: Houghton, 1998. 157–62. Describes an idyllic country home.

Kidder, Tracy. *Home Town.* New York: Random, 1999. A portrait of life in Northampton, Massachusetts, at the end of the twentieth century.

Newman, Zoe. "The Hermeneutics of Martha." *Harper's Magazine* May 1998: 33. An examination of Martha Stewart as a trademark and archetype of white femininity and immigrant dreams.

Rushdie, Salman. *The Wizard of Oz.* London: BFI, 1992. An analysis of the classic film and a reflection on what it means to desire home.

Switzer, Ellen. *Anyplace but Here: Young, Alone, and Homeless.* Boston: Atheneum, 1992. A study based on numerous interviews with young people living on the streets.

Walker, Alice. "Home." *Anything We Love Can Be Saved.* New York: Random, 1997. 71–73. A short reflection that locates "home" for the author in the presence of family.

ELECTRONIC RESOURCES

http://www.marthastewart.com/nav/index.asp
Visit Martha's online site and see for yourself.

http://www.salon1999.com/sneaks/sneakpeeks970108.html
Leora Tanenbaum reviews Barbara Dafoe Whitehead's *The Divorce Culture* and suggests additional material on the subject.

http://www.afa.net/main.htm
The American Family Association defends traditional family values, particularly against assaults in entertainment media.

http://www.fathers.com/
The National Center for Fathering offers fathers advice for improving their parenting skills.

Look carefully at the photograph on the preceding page of a woman working out. What is the effect of the placement of the woman in the picture, and of the angle at which the picture is taken? ■ What does the background of the photo add to the overall impression it creates? ■ What do you think is the attitude of the photographer toward the subject of the photo— and what clues in the photo lead you to that conclusion? ■ What might this photograph imply about the relationship between work and working out?

Work:
As Poor Richard Says . . .

9

We are taxed twice as much by our idleness, three times as much by our pride, and four times as much by our folly; and from these taxes the commissioners cannot ease or deliver us by allowing an abatement.

BENJAMIN FRANKLIN, *The Way to Wealth*

My first job was to jump off a burning ship into salt water with dangerous tides. I lived.

MERIDEL LESUEUR, *Women and Work*

"We want to work. We are trying hard to work. . . ." We are worth something even if our ships have come in and set sail again without us.

JULIA CARLISLE AND FLORENCE HOFF, *Young, Privileged, and Unemployed*

I was materialistic to the core: I loved money; I loved the idea of money; I even liked novels about the rich and movies about how the poor became rich. I liked everything about money except the prospect of buckling down and making it.

ARTHUR KRYSTAL, *Who Speaks for the Lazy?*

More lectures eventually lead us to the "sales orientation," a frighteningly brief twenty-five minutes in length, nearly devoid of specifics. . . . I go to sleep at night wondering when we will receive instructions on how to sell these cars.

REILLY BRENNAN, *Would You Buy a Car from This Man?*

Do they go to work each morning because they love the challenge of creation and wouldn't switch vocations even if they were offered marginally higher pay?

ROBERT A. LUTZ, *The Primary Purpose of Business Is Not to Make Money*

. . . southern black work traditions taught us the importance of working with integrity irrespective of the task.

BELL HOOKS, *Work Makes Life Sweet*

. . . in all the lengthy analyses of what's wrong with American education, I have not heard employment by students being blamed.

WALTER S. MINOT, *Students Who Push Burgers*

The work of the world is common as mud.

MARGE PIERCY, *To Be of Use*

Introduction

THE UNITED STATES OF AMERICA declared its independence from Great Britain in 1776, the same year that the Scottish philosopher Adam Smith (1723–90) published what would become the classic work on capitalism, *The Wealth of Nations*. The conjunction of events proved to be auspicious: nowhere on earth would the principles of free market capitalism be more enthusiastically applied than in the nation assembled from Britain's thirteen rebellious colonies. The revolutionaries in New York, Virginia, and Massachusetts fought not only for political liberty but also for the freedom to buy and sell in competitive world markets. At the time of the War of Independence, American entrepreneurs, schooled in the economic wisdom of Benjamin Franklin's Poor Richard, had already set into motion economic forces that would make the United States affluent and powerful.

The American Revolution also coincided with the dawn of the industrial revolution. Within a century after the shots fired at Lexington and Concord, powerful new machines capable of doing many times the work of manual laborers had transformed the economic structure of the nation. Processes as different as weaving, mining, and reaping would be successfully mechanized, reducing the cost of goods and making them available to more people. And the new industries would generate yet more capital, leading to still more entrepreneurship, investment, and development. It seemed that a formula for enduring prosperity had been discovered.

But the convergence of industrialism and capitalism also brought suffering. Human labor became a commodity measurable by the hour and subject to market forces. People looking for employment abandoned the countryside to crowd into urban slums with high crime and poor sanitation. Disease was rampant. Workers, many of them mere children, faced grueling days in dangerous factories and mines, earning meager wages that they then often had to spend in company stores. Mills and foundries brutalized the landscape, darkening the skies and fouling the rivers.

In England, conditions like these moved Karl Marx to write *Das Kapital* (vol. 1, 1867), in which he condemned laissez-faire capitalism, predicted its demise, and imagined a utopian socialist alternative: communism. For more than a century afterward, capitalists and communists struggled worldwide for economic and military supremacy—the United States and western Europe as the major proponents of free markets and entrepreneurship, and the Soviet Union, China, and eastern Europe as the advocates of socialism.

Socialism lost. Today, serious arguments for Marxist economics are still being made only perhaps in China, in Cuba, and in American universities. Overcoming industrialism's initial ills, capitalist countries offered their citizens vastly greater wealth and liberty than authoritarian Marxist regimes could. Labor unions and numerous reform movements in the West, too, had helped quash monopolies and increase membership in the dominant middle class. Yet all is not perfect. Far from it.

In this chapter we explore some of the economic problems and opportunities that Americans still face today—a subject both vast and complicated. Some of our selections examine the nature of American economic thinking; others look at the ways Americans actually work in or are excluded from the economic mainstream. At times, we can only point to areas for more reading and exploration. This is one chapter we know will raise many questions and provoke lengthy debates.

Following are some questions that you may want to think about as you read this chapter:

- How do Americans feel about work?

- Have the economic values of Americans changed? What major questions of economics divide people or political parties in the United States?

- What rights do workers have to a job? For what reasons may employers exclude someone from employment?

- Is the United States managing prosperity well?

- What is the mission of business?

- Do we put too much emphasis on work? Do Americans fear leisure?

• • •

BENJAMIN FRANKLIN
The Way to Wealth

T*HE* MAXIMS OR APHORISMS *that Benjamin Franklin (1704–90) recorded in* Poor Richard's Almanac *(first issue, 1733) have become part of American folk culture. There's probably not an American alive who wasn't introduced in preschool to Franklin's advice on waking early or hoarding change:*

> *Early to bed, and early to rise, makes a man healthy, wealthy, and wise.*

> *A penny saved is a penny earned.*

Because such adages are short and amusing, we're apt to dismiss them as childish stuff. Why, then, do they and many other sayings from Franklin's "The Way to Wealth" persist in our memories?

Perhaps common sense and thrift never go out of style. The adages Father Abraham doles out in the essay Franklin wrote to mark the twenty-fifth anniversary of Poor Richard's Almanac *still ring true to many readers eager to get ahead. To his credit, Franklin's advice was as stern and honest in 1758 as it is today: you get rich not by manipulating stock funds or light-footing your way through real estate deals, but by working hard, spending little, saving a lot, and borrowing nothing.*

How deeply embedded in the American psyche are attitudes typified by Poor Richard's *maxims? It is hard to say. Benjamin Franklin's fictional character reveals a disturbing mistrust of leisure. Serious writers have even described Franklin — an aggressive, hardheaded, and penurious genius — as the very embodiment of America's defining Protestant ethic. I think old Ben still makes us feel guilty every time we reach for the MasterCard.*

In "The Way to Wealth," Franklin's persona of Poor Richard is at an auction where he hears Father Abraham repeat the most famous maxims from Poor Richard's Almanac. *This framing device allows Richard (a.k.a. Franklin) to comment on his own wisdom without seeming to praise himself too much.* —J.R.

PREFACE TO POOR RICHARD IMPROVED

Courteous Reader,

I have heard that nothing gives an author so great pleasure, as to find his works respectfully quoted by other learned authors. This pleasure I have seldom enjoyed; for though I have been, if I may say it without vanity, an eminent author of almanacs annually now a full quarter of a century, my brother authors in the same way, for what reason I know not, have ever been very sparing in their applauses, and no other author has taken the least notice of me, so that did not my writings produce me some solid pudding, the great deficiency of praise would have quite discouraged me.

I concluded at length, that the people were the best judges of my merit; for they buy my works; and besides, in my rambles, where I am not personally known, I have frequently heard one or other of my adages repeated, with "as Poor Richard says" at the end on 't; this gave me some satisfaction, as it showed not only that my instructions were regarded, but discovered likewise some respect for my authority; and I own, that to encourage the practice of remembering and repeating those wise sentences, I have sometimes quoted myself with great gravity.

Judge, then, how much I must have been gratified by an incident I am going to relate to you. I stopped my horse lately where a great number of people were collected at a vendue* of merchant goods. The hour of sale not being come, they were conversing on the badness of the times and one of the company called to a plain clean old man, with white locks, "Pray, Father Abraham, what think you of the times? Won't these heavy taxes quite ruin the country? How shall we be ever able to pay them? What would you advise us to?" Father Abraham stood up, and replied, "If you'd have my advice, I'll give it you in short, for a *word to the wise is enough, and many words won't fill a bushel,* as Poor Richard says." They joined in desiring him to speak his mind, and gathering round him, he proceeded as follows:

"Friends," says he, "and neighbors, the taxes are indeed very heavy, and if those laid on by the government were the only ones we had to pay, we might more easily discharge them; but we have many others, and much more grievous to some of us. We are taxed twice as much by our idleness, three times as much by our pride, and four times as much by our folly; and from these taxes the commissioners cannot ease or deliver us by allowing an abatement. However, let us hearken to good advice, and something may be done for us; *God helps them that help themselves,* as Poor Richard says, in his Almanack of 1733.

"It would be thought a hard government that should tax its people one-   5 tenth part of their time, to be employed in its service. But idleness taxes many of us much more, if we reckon all that is spent in absolute sloth, or doing of nothing, with that which is spent in idle employments or amusements, that amount to nothing. Sloth, by bringing on diseases, absolutely shortens life. *Sloth, like rust, consumes faster than labor wears; while the used key is always bright,* as Poor Richard says. *But dost thou love life, then do not squander time, for that's the stuff life is made of,* as Poor Richard says. How much more than is necessary do we spend in sleep, forgetting that *the sleeping fox catches no poultry* and that *there will be sleeping enough in the grave,* as Poor Richard says.

"*If time be of all things the most precious, wasting time must be,* as Poor Richard says, *the greatest prodigality;* since, as he elsewhere tells us, *lost time is never found again; and what we call time enough, always proves little enough:* let us

---

vendue: a sale

then up and be doing, and doing to the purpose; so by diligence shall we do more with less perplexity. *Sloth makes all things difficult, but industry all easy,* as Poor Richard says; *and he that riseth late must trot all day, and shall scarce overtake his business at night;* while *laziness travels so slowly, that poverty soon overtakes him,* as we read in Poor Richard, who adds, *drive thy business, let not that drive thee,* and *early to bed, and early to rise, makes a man healthy, wealthy, and wise.*

"So what signifies wishing and hoping for better times. We may make these times better, if we bestir ourselves. *Industry need not wish,* as Poor Richard says, *and he that lives upon hope will die fasting. There are no gains without pains; then help hands, for I have no lands,* or if I have, they are smartly taxed. And, as Poor Richard likewise observes, *he that hath a trade hath an estate; and he that hath a calling, hath an office of profit and honor;* but then the trade must be worked at, and the calling well followed, or neither the estate nor the office will enable us to pay our taxes. If we are industrious, we shall never starve, for, as Poor Richard says, *at the workingman's house hunger looks in, but dares not enter.* Nor will the bailiff or the constable enter, for *industry pays debts, while despair increaseth them,* says Poor Richard. What though you have found no treasure, nor has any rich relation left you a legacy, *diligence is the mother of goodluck,* as Poor Richard says, and *God gives all things to industry. Then plow deep, while sluggards sleep, and you shall have corn to sell and to keep,* says Poor Dick. Work while it is called today, for you know not how much you may be hindered tomorrow, which makes Poor Richard say, *one today is worth two tomorrows,* and farther, *have you somewhat to do tomorrow, do it today.* If you were a servant, would you not be ashamed that a good master should catch you idle? Are you then your own master, *be ashamed to catch yourself idle,* as Poor Dick says. When there is so much to be done for yourself, your family, your country, and your gracious king, be up by peep of day; *let not the sun look down and say, inglorious here he lies.* Handle your tools without mittens; remember that *the cat in gloves catches no mice,* as Poor Richard says. 'Tis true there is much to be done, and perhaps you are weak-handed, but stick to it steadily; and you will see great effects, for *constant dropping wears away stones,* and *by diligence and patience the mouse ate in two the cable;* and *little strokes fell great oaks,* as Poor Richard says in his Almanack, the year I cannot just now remember.

"Methinks I hear some of you say, 'must a man afford himself no leisure?' I will tell thee, my friend, what Poor Richard says, *employ thy time well, if thou meanest to gain leisure; and, since thou art not sure of a minute, throw not away an hour.* Leisure is time for doing something useful; this leisure the diligent man will obtain, but the lazy man never; so that, as Poor Richard says *a life of leisure and a life of laziness are two things.* Do you imagine that sloth will afford you more comfort than labor? No, for as Poor Richard says, *trouble springs from idleness, and grievous toil from needless ease. Many without labor, would live by their wits only, but they break for want of stock.* Whereas industry gives comfort, and plenty, and respect: *fly pleasures, and they'll follow you. The diligent spinner has a large shift,** and now I have a

---

a large shift: change of clothing, wardrobe

sheep and a cow, everybody bids me good morrow; all which is well said by Poor Richard.

"But with our industry, we must likewise be steady, settled, and careful, and oversee our own affairs with our own eyes, and not trust too much to others; for, as Poor Richard says

> *I never saw an oft-removed tree,*
> *Nor yet an oft-removed family,*
> *That throve so well as those that settled be.*

And again, *three removes* is as bad as a fire;* and again, *keep thy shop, and thy shop will keep thee;* and again, *if you would have your business done, go; if not, send.* And again,

> *He that by the plough would thrive,*
> *Himself must either hold or drive.*

And again, *the eye of a master will do more work than both his hands;* and again, *want of care does us more damage than want of knowledge;* and again, *not to oversee workmen is to leave them your purse open.* Trusting too much to others' care is the ruin of many; for, as the Almanack says, *in the affairs of this world, men are saved, not by faith, but by the want of it;* but a man's own care is profitable; for, saith Poor Dick, *learning is to the studious,* and *riches to the careful,* as well as *power to the bold,* and *heaven to the virtuous,* and farther, *if you would have a faithful servant, and one that you like, serve yourself.* And again, he adviseth to circumspection and care, even in the smallest matters, because sometimes *a little neglect may breed great mischief;* adding, *for want of a nail the shoe was lost; for want of a shoe the horse was lost; and for want of a horse the rider was lost, being overtaken and slain by the enemy; all for want of care about a horseshoe nail.*

"So much for industry, my friends, and attention to one's own business; but to these we must add frugality, if we would make our industry more certainly successful. A man may, if he knows not how to save as he gets, keep his nose all his life to the grindstone, and die not worth a groat* at last. A *fat kitchen makes a lean will,* as Poor Richard says; and

> *Many estates are spent in the getting,*
> *Since women for tea forsook spinning and knitting,*
> *And men for punch forsook hewing and splitting.*

If you would be wealthy, says he, in another Almanack, *think of saving as well as of getting: the Indies have not made Spain rich, because her outgoes are greater than her incomes.*

"Away then with your expensive follies, and you will not then have so much cause to complain of hard times, heavy taxes, and chargeable families; for, as Poor Dick says,

---

removes: moves
groat: a coin of small value

Women and wine, game and deceit,
Make the wealth small and the wants great.

And farther, *what maintains one vice would bring up two children.* You may think perhaps, that a little tea, or a little punch now and then, diet a little more costly, clothes a little finer, and a little entertainment now and then, can be no great matter; but remember what Poor Richard says, *many a little makes a mickle,** and farther, *Beware of little expenses; a small leak will sink a great ship;* and again, *who dainties love shall beggars prove;* and moreover, *fools make feasts, and wise men eat them.*

"Here you are all got together at this vendue of fineries and knicknacks. You call them goods; but if you do not take care, they will prove evils to some of you. You expect they will be sold cheap, and perhaps they may for less than they cost; but if you have no occasion for them, they must be dear to you. Remember what Poor Richard says; *buy what thou hast no need of, and ere long thou shalt sell thy necessaries.* And again, *at a great pennyworth pause a while:* he means, that perhaps the cheapness is apparent only, and not real; or the bargain, by straightening thee in thy business, may do thee more harm than good. For in another place he says, *many have been ruined by buying good penny-worths.* Again, Poor Richard says, *'tis foolish to lay out money in a purchase of re-pentance;* and yet this folly is practiced every day at vendues, for want of mind-ing the Almanack. *Wise men,* as Poor Dick says, *learn by others' harms, fools scarcely by their own;* but *felix quem faciunt aliena pericula cautum.** Many a one, for the sake of finery on the back, have gone with a hungry belly, and half-starved their families. *Silks and satins, scarlet and velvets,* as Poor Richard says, *put out the kitchen fire.*

"These are not the necessaries of life; they can scarcely be called the conveniences; and yet only because they look pretty, how many want to have them! The artificial wants of mankind thus become more numerous than the natural; and, as Poor Dick says, *for one poor person, there are an hundred indigent.* By these, and other extravagancies, the genteel are reduced to poverty, and forced to borrow of those whom they formerly despised, but who through industry and frugality have maintained their standing; in which case it appears plainly, that *a plowman on his legs is higher than a gentleman on his knees,* as Poor Richard says. Perhaps they have had a small estate left them, which they knew not the getting of; they think, ''Tis day, and will never be night'; that a little to be spent out of so much is not worth minding; *a child and a fool,* as Poor Richard says, *imagine twenty shillings and twenty years can never be spent* but, *always taking out of the meal-tub, and never putting in, soon comes to the bot-tom;* as Poor Dick says, *when the well's dry, they know the worth of water.* But this they might have known before, if they had taken his advice; *if you would know*

---

mickle: a great deal
felix . . . cautum: the Latin version of the previous saying

the value of money, go and try to borrow some; for, he that goes a-borrowing goes a-sorrowing; and indeed so does he that lends to such people, when he goes to get it in again. Poor Dick farther advises, and says,

> *Fond pride of dress is sure a very curse;*
> *E'er fancy you consult, consult your purse.*

And again, *pride is as loud a beggar as want, and a great deal more saucy.* When you have bought one fine thing, you must buy ten more, that your appearance may be all of a piece; but Poor Dick says, *'tis easier to suppress the first desire, than to satisfy all that follow it.* And 'tis as truly folly for the poor to ape the rich, as for the frog to swell, in order to equal the ox.

> *Great estates may venture more,*
> *But little boats should keep near shore.*

'Tis, however, a folly soon punished; for *pride that dines on vanity sups on contempt,* as Poor Richard says. And in another place, *pride breakfasted with plenty, dined with poverty, and supped with infamy.* And after all, of what use is this pride of appearance, for which so much is risked, so much is suffered? It cannot promote health, or ease pain; it makes no increase of merit in the person, it creates envy, it hastens misfortune.

> *What is a butterfly? At best*
> *He's but a caterpillar dressed*
> *The gaudy fop's his picture just,*

as Poor Richard says.

"But what madness must it be to run in debt for these superfluities! We   15
are offered, by the terms of this vendue, *six months' credit;* and that perhaps has induced some of us to attend it, because we cannot spare the ready money, and hope now to be fine without it. But, ah, think what you do when you run in debt; you give to another power over your liberty. If you cannot pay at the time, you will be ashamed to see your creditor; you will be in fear when you speak to him; you will make poor pitiful sneaking excuses, and by degrees come to lose your veracity, and sink into base downright lying; for, as Poor Richard says, *the second vice is lying, the first is running in debt.* And again, to the same purpose, *lying rides upon debt's back.* Whereas a free-born Englishman ought not to be ashamed or afraid to see or speak to any man living. But poverty often deprives a man of all spirit and virtue: *'tis hard for an empty bag to stand upright,* as Poor Richard truly says.

"What would you think of that prince, or that government, who should issue an edict forbidding you to dress like a gentleman or a gentlewoman, on pain of imprisonment or servitude? Would you not say, that you were free, have a right to dress as you please, and that such an edict would be a breach of your privileges, and such a government tyrannical? And yet you are about to put yourself under that tyranny, when you run in debt for such dress! Your creditor has authority at his pleasure to deprive you of your liberty, by confining you in gaol* for life, or to sell you for a servant, if you should not be able to pay him! When you have got your bargain, you may, perhaps, think little of payment; but *creditors,* Poor Richard tells us, *have better memories than debtors;* and in another place says, *creditors are a superstitious sect, great observers of set days and times.* The day comes round before you are aware, and the demand is made before you are prepared to satisfy it, or if you bear your debt in mind, the term which at first seemed so long, will, as it lessens, appear extremely short. Time will seem to have added wings to his heels as well as shoulders. *Those have a short Lent,* said Poor Richard, *who owe money to be paid at Easter.* Then since, as he says, *The borrower is a slave to the lender, and the debtor to the creditor,* disdain the chain, preserve your freedom; and maintain your independency: be industrious and free; be frugal and free. At present, perhaps, you may think yourself in thriving circumstances, and that you can bear a little extravagance without injury; but,

> *For age and want, save while you may;*
> *No morning sun lasts a whole day,*

as Poor Richard says. Gain may be temporary and uncertain, but ever while you live, expense is constant and entire; and *'tis easier to build two chimneys than to keep one in fuel,* as Poor Richard says. So, *rather go to bed supperless than rise in debt.*

> *Get what you can, and what you get hold;*
> *'Tis the stone that will turn all your lead into gold,*

as Poor Richard says. And when you have got the philosopher's stone,* sure you will no longer complain of bad times, or the difficulty of paying taxes.

"This doctrine, my friends, is reason and wisdom; but after all, do not depend too much upon your own industry, and frugality, and prudence, though excellent things, for they may all be blasted without the blessing of heaven; and therefore, ask that blessing humbly, and be not uncharitable to those that at present seem to want it, but comfort and help them. Remember, Job* suffered, and was afterwards prosperous.

"And now to conclude, *experience keeps a dear school, but fools will learn in no other, and scarce in that;* for it is true, *we may give advice, but we cannot give conduct,* as Poor Richard says: however, remember this, *they that won't be counseled, can't be helped,* as Poor Richard says: and farther, that, *if you will not hear reason, she'll surely rap your knuckles."*

---

gaol: jail
philosopher's stone: an alchemical object capable of turning crude metals into gold
Job: a figure in the Old Testament sorely tested by God

Thus the old gentleman ended his harangue. The people heard it, and approved the doctrine, and immediately practiced the contrary, just as if it had been a common sermon; for the vendue opened, and they began to buy extravagantly, notwithstanding his cautions and their own fear of taxes. I found the good man had thoroughly studied my almanacs, and digested all I had dropped on these topics during the course of five and twenty years. The frequent mention he made of me must have tired any one else, but my vanity was wonderfully delighted with it, though I was conscious that not a tenth part of the wisdom was my own, which he ascribed to me, but rather the gleanings I had made of the sense of all ages and nations. However, I resolved to be the better for the echo of it; and though I had at first determined to buy stuff for a new coat, I went away resolved to wear my old one a little longer. Reader, if thou wilt do the same, thy profit will be as great as mine. I am, as ever, thine to serve thee,

Richard Saunders
July 7, 1757

QUESTIONING THE TEXT

1. Which of the aphorisms Franklin repeats would you regard as outdated today? Why? Explain in a paragraph.

2. Based on this selection, what role do you think Franklin expects government to play in the lives of people? Explain.

3. Do you disagree with any assumptions or assertions in J.R.'s introduction? If so, which ones and why?

MAKING CONNECTIONS

4. Read Franklin's "The Way to Wealth" alongside Robert A. Lutz's "The Primary Purpose of Business Is Not to Make Money" (p. 712), annotating the Lutz selection from Poor Richard's point of view. Does Poor Richard's perspective offer any insights on contemporary problems? Why, or why not?

5. In "Conscientious Consumption" (p. 200), David Brooks describes a contemporary economic ethic much different from the one recommended by Franklin's Poor Richard. Read "Conscientious Consumption" and then write a short essay in which you compare Poor Richard's aphorisms with the rules of economic behavior offered by Brooks.

JOINING THE CONVERSATION

6. Have American values strayed from the path charted by Franklin's Poor Richard, or are Americans still influenced by the attitudes toward getting and spending described here? Write a short dialogue between Poor Richard and a contemporary figure — Peter J. Gomes (p. 205), Jeremy Rifkin (p. 244), or Bill Gates, for example.

7. What is Poor Richard's attitude toward debt? Would such an attitude today hurt or help the U.S. economy? Explain your answer in a short letter to the editor that quotes Poor Richard at least once.

8. Could a family or individual today live normally and comfortably according to Franklin's philosophy? What problems might arise? In an essay, describe what a life lived according to Poor Richard's advice might be like.

9. Try your hand at writing a few aphorisms that Poor Richard might recommend to Americans in the 2000s, and bring them in to class for discussion.

MERIDEL LESUEUR
Women and Work

Meridel LeSueur *(1900–96) wrote all her life in the service of those too-often-invisible Americans who do the work of our world. LeSueur—a writer who held many other jobs, including actress, stuntwoman, and labor organizer—was a fascinating figure. From her earliest essays in the 1920s, her writings offer an unromanticized and vivid picture of twentieth-century work and workers (especially women), and she was well known as an author during the 1930s and 1940s. Her association with labor organizations and with communism, however, brought down the wrath of Senator Joseph McCarthy and his cohorts. Blacklisted in the 1950s, LeSueur had great difficulty publishing her work during the next thirty years, although the last two decades of her life were kinder to her. LeSueur reported doing the "best writing" of her life at ninety-four and rejoiced at the new audience she found among the American Indian, Chicano/a, and women's movements.*

LeSueur's books and essays speak to all people who know what it is to work, and especially to those who do the work of writing. In the brief autobiographical essay that follows, she reflects on what work meant in her life, on the work she was allowed (and not allowed) to do, and on the 140 notebooks of writing she accumulated over the years—one hard-working woman's "letter to the world." I chose this selection because LeSueur's work and life demonstrate how one can live through the worst deprivations, the worst economic depressions, and still find meaningful work. I also chose this piece because it's inspirational to see someone writing and thinking and publishing right to the end of a long and truly remarkable life. "Women and Work" originally appeared in a 1994 collection of essays by the same title edited by Maureen R. Michelson.

—A.L.

When I was 10 years old in 1910 I knew my two brothers could be anything they wanted. I knew I could be a wife and mother, a teacher, a nurse or a whore. And without an education, I could not be a nurse or teacher and we were very poor. Women could be china painters, quiltmakers, embroiderers. They often wrote secretly. Even read certain books secretly. My mother tried to go to college and women could not take math or history, only the domestic sciences.

I began to write down what I heard, sitting under the quilting frames. I tried to listen to these imprisoned and silenced women. I had a passion to be witness and recorder of the hidden, submerged, and silent women. I did not want to be a writer; I did not know a woman writer; I did not read a woman writer. It was a thick, heavy silence and I began to take down what I heard.

My Gramma hated my writing. "We have tried to hide what has happened to us," she said, "and now you are going to tell it." "I am. I am going to tell it," I cried, and I began a long howl and cry that finally found its voice in the women's movement, as it is called. A book I wrote in 1930, cruelly criticized by male editors, was not published until 1975. My audience was women, who now wanted to talk, bear witness.

I made my living working in factories, writing for the labor movement. A good thing for a writer to keep close to life, to the happening, and I have lived in the most brutal century of two world wars, millions killed and exploited, and now the atom bomb and the global struggle.

I went to the International Women's Conference in Nairobi at 85 years   5
old to see the thousands of women now bearing their own witness and I read my poem *Solidarity,* which I wrote for the Vietnamese Women's Union, and it was translated at once into Swahili as I read it. A great climax to my life. I believe this is the most enlightened moment I have seen in history and rooted in my life's passion to bear witness to the common struggle, the heroic people rising out of the violence, all becoming visible and alive.

My struggle was never alone, always with others. This makes my life bright with comradeship, marches with banners, tribal courage, and warmth. Remember, I didn't vote 'til I was 19 in 1919. Women only came into the offices after the first World War. Every young man I knew in high school never returned. The fathers and husbands had been killed. A terrible reaction set in after that bloody war to consolidate patriarchal money and power. The twenties were a terrible sinking into the Depression.

My mother, wanting to be an actress, sent me to dramatic school. I tried to fulfill her desires. The theater then was developing actresses who exploited the sexist feminine, and males who had to be John Waynes. The plays were also made for this image of sexism. Coming from the prairies, I played *Lady Windermere's Fan* by Oscar Wilde, learning to walk and use a fan and speak British. I didn't cotton to that at all. I went to Hollywood where again, your career was based on sexism, the female stereotypes. You had to go every morning to the hiring hall and show your legs and teeth and get a job for the day signing a contract that if you were killed or injured the company would not be responsible. Many extras were killed. You were a dime a dozen and the studios were flooded with the beautiful prairie girls from the Midwest. It was a meat market and developed one of the greatest prostitute rings in Los Angeles, San Francisco, Seattle, and Las Vegas.

My first job was to jump off a burning ship into salt water with dangerous tides. I lived. You could make $25 a day, an enormous sum, and I could save it and hole in and write for a few months. So I began to write about the open market on women; cheap labor of women, oppression and silencing and bartering of women. Also, fighting in the unions and housing. In the Depression, women were not on any list. There were no soup kitchens for women.

Also, there was the danger of sterilization. Groups of women were netted and taken to women's prisons and might be sterilized by morning. There was a theory that the only solution to the Depression was sterilization of the workers. It began to be known Hitler had the same idea.

In desperation, I think, I boldly had two children at the beginning of the Depression. You couldn't get any other kind of life, and you might give birth to friends and allies. I had two girls, who all my life, have been just that.

I became a correspondent from the Middle West, reporting on the 10 farmers' struggles, the third party, all that was happening. I wrote for several national magazines and began to have stories in *American Mercury,* and university quarterlies, and writings about my children were sold to the women's magazines. So I began to make a modest living at writing, which was wonderful. I became known as a witness, as I wanted to be. I became well known for two pieces: *Corn Village,* about the small town; and, I *Was Marching,* about the '34 teamsters' strike.

I feel we must be deeply rooted in the tribal family and in the social community. This is becoming a strong and beautiful force now in our societies. Women speaking out boldly, going to jail for peace and sanctuary, defending the children against hunger. We still get half of what men get. But as I saw in Nairobi the struggle of women is now global. My Gramma and mother are not any more silenced and alone. Writing has become with women not a concealment, but an illumination. We are not alone. The hundreds of women writers now who speak for us to a large audience.

This makes me write more than I ever did. I have 140 notebooks, my letter to the world, published some day for a new woman I dreamed of. I have 24 great grandchildren who have freedoms I could only dream of. One granddaughter is raising five children herself. Another has two sons. They are not alone; that's the point. They live in collectives and work in social fields with women and children. They have an independence I never had, a boldness and a communal life and support.

I am writing as I never wrote before. I have three books, besides my notebooks, to "finish." I call it getting in my crop before the frost! It is my best writing, I believe . . . I have learned to bear witness with love and compassion and warm readers to whom I am truthful. And they return my witness, so women rise from the darkness singing together, not the small and tortured chorus of my grandmothers, but millions becoming visible and singing.

QUESTIONING THE TEXT

1. LeSueur speaks of "female stereotypes." Reread her essay, highlighting every example of such stereotypes. How much evidence does LeSueur marshal to illustrate these stereotypes? Discuss these examples.

2. LeSueur calls Hollywood and the film industry a "meat market." What evidence does she give to support this analogy? Does the analogy still hold today? What evidence can you offer to support or refute it?

MAKING CONNECTIONS

3. Look through all the selections in this chapter and decide which writer LeSueur has the most in common with, as well as which writer she would probably disagree with most strongly. In an entry in your journal or reading log, explore these similarities and differences, and weigh in with your own ideas as well. Which of these writers do you have most in common with, and why?

4. Review Benjamin Franklin's "The Way to Wealth" (p. 678) and then try writing a few Poor Richard–like maxims as LeSueur might pen them. Bring the maxims to class for discussion.

JOINING THE CONVERSATION

5. Working with two or three classmates, draw up some questions you would like to ask people who are now in their eighties or nineties about their experiences with work. Start with your own grandparents or great-grandparents, or those of your friends. If possible, find three or four additional men and women to interview, perhaps through the American Association of Retired Persons or an assisted-living group in your community. Together, write a brief report for your class on your interviewees' experiences with work.

6. Spend some time thinking about the kind of work you most want to do. Then write an exploration of your knowledge and feelings about such work, including an examination of both positive and negative points. If you keep a reading log, explore this issue there.

JULIA CARLISLE and FLORENCE HOFF
Young, Privileged, and Unemployed

WHAT COUNTS AS WORK? *Answers to this question vary radically over time and from culture to culture. Some people think of their real work as that which they do when not on the job—as is the case with many serious writers and many "volunteer" workers. Some people think that housework counts as real. Others disagree. And in an age of information, when much of the work that earns a living is sedentary, spent with a keyboard and computer screen, many people think of "working out" as an important, even necessary, form of work.*

The issues raised by asking What counts as work? *are addressed squarely in the following article and letter, published in April 1991 in the* New York Times. *The first half of this selection is the brief news article in which Julia Carlisle, recently laid off by CBS News, speaks of "life without a job" and of the "absurd" work she and others like her must do while they look for "real" work. In the responding letter to the editor, Florence Hoff, a housewife, mother, and unemployed clerical worker, scathingly chastises those who have learned too late that "there is no entitlement in life" and points out that the jobs Carlisle labels "absurd" are currently held by a group of people apparently dismissed as unimportant.*

I chose these pieces because seldom have I come across an exchange that captures so succinctly what is at stake in our definitions of work. I find myself in sympathy with both writers. How about you?   —A.L.

We are young, urban and professional. We are literate, respectable, intelligent and charming. But foremost and above all, we know what it's like to be unemployed.

Forced into dishonesty to survive, we have bounced checks to keep ourselves in oxford shirts and Ann Taylor dresses. But we have no solid ground. Our parents continue to help. Our grandparents send an occasional check. Some of us have trust funds, but the majority do not.

Our parents must wonder, "My child turned 18, then 21, got the right to vote and to drink, graduated from college, found work, then was out of work—and we're still providing the support." And we think the same. "I've done what I had to do, passed my rites of passage and yet, how demeaning, having to go back to my parents for financial support." And that's when we're lucky.

Love, well, there is love. We have loved and lost. We may even have loved and won. But there is little time for love—the kind that comes out with the cherry blossoms—when you're unemployed. Love is a simple lifeline, a desperate clinging to a shoulder as we tabulate taxes we cannot pay.

The rent, the car payments and the American Express bill are all figured under the glare of a light bulb, in tears and shouting in rushes of frustration at the only thing we have, the one we "love."

Yes, we read the *New York Times* and the *Wall Street Journal* and the   5 *Washington Post.* We watched *60 Minutes, Cheers* and the evening news. We read more than we did before—the latest Vintage or Penguin Contemporaries paperbacks.

But the days have been filled with the bureaucracy of life without a job. Unemployment clerks brusquely said that we'd better not risk the full sum of our unemployment checks by earning too much in a part-time job. "Honey," one told us, "Just sit back and draw out those payments."

Shocked, we insisted: "We want to work. We are trying hard to work. We have found a little something that could become permanent." We expect rewards for our efforts and recognition. We are worth something even if our ships have come in and set sail again without us.

We have been confined to our homes more evenings than not. Our spacious studios quickly turned into dorm rooms for two. Still, occasionally, unable to help ourselves, we have gone out to dinner, pretending it's easy and natural. But we wonder if the people around us knew. The $50 bill came, and suddenly we realized that a frozen pizza at home could have caused the same pain.

The work we have to do while "looking" is almost absurd. The television producer became a typist for a home foreclosure agency. The secretary became a baby sitter. The former manager of a lucrative downtown courier service, a man with a new house and boat, went mad caring for his three young children. But, while drinking just a little more often, he gained a new appreciation of his wife who went back to work, trying to sell real estate. The chef became a consultant training waiters and catering birthday parties.

Without a doubt, we are our work. We had it, we made it and we lost   10 it. We worked hard and we feel we deserved something. But we've learned an awful, preposterous truth—that we are expendable. We have been told, in so many ways, that our stature and charm and intelligence are unwanted or are not enough. Our companies' budgets dictated that, talent aside, we were no longer needed. Who could possibly believe it?

JULIA CARLISLE

To the Editor:

So the young and privileged (Julia Carlisle in the "Voices of the New Generation" series, Op-Ed, April 4) are learning what we of the working classes have always understood too well: there is no entitlement in life.

We have always taken the jobs you label "absurd." Our mothers are the women who clean your mothers' houses, iron the clothes. Our fathers work on the BMW's, on the Lincoln Town Cars. Our sisters type your insurance policies in the factorylike setting of back offices. Our brothers are in the Marine Corps.

We are the polite and patient voice on the 24-hour 800 customer service number when you call to complain that you cannot pay your credit card bill. We are the people who work Sundays at the mall; the people who mind your children while you pursue your meaningful careers.

We do not have meaningful careers. We left school at 17. There was no money for college; we were not among the brilliant few who could win one of the increasingly scarce scholarships. Our parents were on short time themselves.

We are not without our dreams, our longings. We too find eight hours a   15
day seated in a tiny cubicle doing machine transcription demeaning to the human spirit, but we are glad at this time to have a job with a decent company that pays benefits.

We too entered a changed world where well-paying factory jobs had all but disappeared, where the bargaining powers of unions had melted away.

FLORENCE HOFF
San Francisco, April 4, 1991

Afterwords

To the Editor:

I have some sympathy with both Carlisle and Hoff, who write from very different perspectives about changes in the job market and in the nature of work.

Carlisle writes out of her own privileged experience, as one who has learned that work should offer not only challenges but some fulfillment as well. In this sense, work and self-worth are closely linked, as indeed they are for many in a country where strangers typically begin a conversation with "What do you do?" or "What is your work?" Hoff writes out of her experience as well, as one who has not been privileged and who has lived with work not as a means of fulfillment and self-definition but as a means of survival. In this sense, work is what one does in order to be allowed, in other venues, to pursue fulfillment, perhaps in family relations, in religion, in music or sport or art. Both writers, as Hoff says, have "entered a changed world."

But what is the nature of the current "changed world" of work? That is the question that devils me and many of my students. How will work be defined in the twenty-first century? Might work include things we now undervalue (and consequently do not pay much for), such as the work described by Hoff or jobs in elder and child care? Might it include those jobs we now tend to lump under "community service" or "volunteer work"? More to the point, might we need to redefine work in order for there to be enough work—of any kind—to go around? Who will—and who won't—have access to which kinds of work? Even more to the point, as a teacher I wonder how we can best prepare for redefined work and for lives that can be enriched, rather than impoverished, by that work.

These are questions I'd like to hear Carlisle and Hoff—as well as our leaders of government, industry, and community—discuss and then address through action.   —A.L.

To the Editor:

John Henry Newman (p. 46) suggests that among the qualities of mind a liberal education ought to cultivate are "freedom, equitableness, calmness, moderation, and wisdom." Julia Carlisle's education, whatever it entailed, seems to have given her only a sense of entitlement, one that inclines her to imagine happiness in terms of status and objects— "oxford shirts and Ann Taylor dresses."

In the long history of humankind, few people have lived lives as comfortable and protected as Ms. Carlisle's, even in her semi-employed state. They haven't had checks to bounce, Vintage paperbacks to read, fifty-dollar dinners to bemoan. They couldn't get out most nights, fall in love at cherry blossom time, or bask in the warmth of paid-in-full American Express accounts. Rather simply, they worked in the sweat of their brows till they returned to the ground. Bummer, hey, Ms. Carlisle, freelance TV and radio news writer?

Florence Hoff, in her response to Ms. Carlisle, demonstrates a calmer and more moderate view of reality—despite her lack of a college education. She understands that people in less-than-glamorous jobs need dreams too, but they must often accept the daily grind Carlisle thinks beneath her for no reason other than that she's been bred to expect better. I only wish for the sake of Hoff and millions of other laborers that our society spoke more often about the dignity of work. We've practically lost our vocabulary for discussing blue-collar jobs. Our popular culture is especially inept when it comes to working people, often depicting them as beer-guzzling, overweight, plaid-shirted rubes. We prefer to celebrate exactly the kind of urban up-and-comers that Carlisle hoped to be. No wonder Julia feels let down and Hoff envious.   —J.R.

To the Editor:

As a college student, I have difficulty ignoring the instability of the "real world." Many of Carlisle's fears lurk in the back of minds of students all over the country. The prospect of succeeding in school and then graduating only to find no opportunities for employment is a real concern for many in colleges and universities today. We have been taught that hard work and dedication to studies are the keys to a bright future, but as Carlisle points out, securing a degree does not always guarantee a job. So many companies have been forced into cutbacks that the jobs simply do not exist anymore. It is also growing increasingly difficult to become an entrepreneur, evident in the number of small hometown businesses that are folding under the market pressure of corporate giants. Where are we supposed to look for encouragement? Carlisle is not alone in her feelings of instability.

Several of Carlisle's described actions may make her audience skeptical of her true level of need. It seems incredible, considering her lack of funds, that Carlisle speaks of bouncing checks to maintain a seemingly extravagant lifestyle. I was brought up to do without if the money simply was not there, so Carlisle's practices of knowingly going farther into debt seem ridiculous. Going out for dinner when pizza at home was more financially responsible is perhaps Carlisle's way of trying to ignore the pain of unem-

ployment. However, the Florence Hoffs of America cannot afford to take those kinds of risks. Hoff, able to accept what Carlisle refers to as "absurd" positions, possesses a more realistic view of the world. Carlisle needs to realize that those "absurd" jobs provide character-building experiences that would make her (and her contemporaries) more marketable to possible employment opportunities.

It is painful to realize how many others are competing for jobs in your line of business. Earning a degree is not enough anymore: we must now prove that we have what it takes to perform well in any setting; we all have personal dreams and goals that we must sometimes put on the back burner in exchange for more realistic options. No matter how hard we work, sometimes setbacks are unavoidable. We may feel we have "earned" a good place in society, but unfortunately the world does not always respond as we would like it to. The key is persistence and the will not to give in to the pressures and stresses of everyday life. —T.E.

QUESTIONING THE TEXT

1. Look carefully at the concrete language used in both the article and the letter—the "oxford shirts" and "Ann Taylor dresses" mentioned by Carlisle, for example, and the "Lincoln Town Cars" mentioned by Hoff. What do such specific details add to each piece? Do they make one writer more persuasive than the other? Why, or why not?

2. Using the information provided in this selection, write a definition of *work* for each writer. Then write a definition of your own. Bring all three to class to compare with others.

3. Given what she says in her introduction, how do you think A.L. defines *work*?

MAKING CONNECTIONS

4. What advice might Arthur Krystal (p. 697) give to Carlisle and Hoff about what counts as work? Would his advice be the same or different for each writer? Read Krystal's essay and then imagine a brief exchange among these three writers, making notes on the major points each speaker would likely address in the exchange.

5. Working in a group, prepare a talk show presentation for your class. The program will address the question What counts as work? and feature Meridel LeSueur (p. 687), Julia Carlisle, Florence Hoff, and bell hooks (p. 717) as guest speakers, as well as a talk show host. Write up the host's introduction and a list of three questions that he or she will ask the participants; then compose the answers the guests will give. Bring your talk show material to class and be ready to perform it.

JOINING THE CONVERSATION

6. Write your own letter to the editor in response to Carlisle's article. Like Hoff, you may choose to disagree and to criticize her. Or you may write out of agreement and appreciation. Bring your letter to class for discussion.

7. What experiences, institutions, or other background influences do you think helped create Carlisle's and Hoff's very different attitudes toward work? Choose one of the writers, and freewrite for a while on where you think her attitudes come from. Then turn the spotlight on yourself. Where do you get your attitude toward and definition of *work*? From movies and television? From family? From a place of worship? From school? Bring your reflections to class and discuss them with two or three classmates. Then write an essay on "Influences That Have Shaped My View of Work."

ARTHUR KRYSTAL
Who Speaks for the Lazy?

ARTHUR KRYSTAL *(b. 1947) takes on the task of answering his title question by drawing on his own intimate experience with a lifetime of laziness. But laziness, under Krystal's somewhat doleful gaze, is far from simple, having philosophical, psychological, even possible genetic underpinnings. In addition, as a subject, laziness can be the cause of work—as in Krystal's writing of this essay, which appeared in the* New Yorker *(April 26, 1999) and no doubt landed the author a substantial fee.*

In a world seemingly run by workaholics who "relax" after hours by throwing themselves relentlessly into the secondary work of keeping fit (how many miles did you run today?), with the workweek getting longer instead of shorter, with the trend toward combining work with everything, including school, perhaps we need a little sympathy for laziness, for the sheer "disinclination to work." I might as well admit, however, that I read Krystal's essay with some mix of amusement and horror. I can't imagine anything more boring than experiencing the vegetative state Krystal describes as ultimate laziness: when "prying the cap off a Schlitz" is seen as "a good day's work." But my old-fashioned Protestant work ethic is showing. What's your own laziness quotient? Read Krystal's essay to see how you stack up among the truly imaginative lords of laziness. —A.L.

For a white American male, in good health and in possession of an advanced degree from an Ivy League school, I have, over the past twenty-five years, made a ridiculously small amount of money. And when I say small I mean *small.* Until five years ago, my best year netted me a little more than sixteen thousand dollars, and most years my annual income after taxes fluctuated between eight and ten thousand. Really. Being a writer only partially explains this woeful fiscal history. The real question is not so much how I've managed to survive but why I have accepted living in humble circumstances when my tastes are anything but. It's a question that friends, for whom my way of life has often been a subject of rueful and hilarious conversation, have speculated on. Here are some of the answers they've come up with: came of age in the sixties; never came of age; has an aversion to authority; has a structural anomaly of the brain; lost his mother when he was ten; was an only child; was an only child of parents who survived the war in Europe; read too many books at too early an age; found a really cheap, rent-stabilized apartment; is generally a moody, shiftless, self-absorbed individual.

Not making a lot of money says something about a man in a society where financial success is equated with acumen, resourcefulness, and social standing. Aside from those who enter professions in which money is not the

The author relished everything about money except working for it.

main consideration—teaching, say, or diplomacy, or documentary filmmaking—the nonmoneyed are thought to lack the confidence or wherewithal to make the big bucks. There is an assumption that a feeling of ineligibility keeps us from realizing the earning potential both in ourselves and in the marketplace. It is, of course, just this entrepreneurial inner child that self-help books mean to awaken. True or not, success American-style is seen to be a matter of gumption, of get-up-and-go: economic hardship isn't about race or class, it's about character. Want money? Follow the appropriate twelve-step program, demonstrate the requisite stick-to-itiveness, and—badda badda bing—you're rolling in it.

Although it would be nice to say that the absence of a portfolio in my case suggested a well-developed ego, an indifference to the world's approval,

I'm afraid that emotional immaturity as well as financial shortsightedness are nearer the mark. When I was in my twenties, it didn't matter that other men my age earned eighty grand a year while I survived on eight. I was healthy, strong, O.K.-looking, with a good head of hair (never discount male vanity as consolation for practically anything). There'd be time, I thought, to remedy matters. And let's be clear: I did not disdain the dollar. I was no ascetic, and my spiritual itch was more than satisfied by reading Hermann Hesse.* In truth, I was materialistic to the core: I loved money; I loved the idea of money; I even liked novels about the rich and movies about how the poor became rich. I liked everything about money except the prospect of buckling down and making it.

My father used to say that I became a writer so that I wouldn't have to work. Most writers will snort at this: what is writing *but* work? He had a point, though. The thought of being bound and defined by work that didn't interest me sent shivers down my spine. The solution was a string of part-time jobs that I could blow off whenever I wanted to—until I made it as a writer. Between 1971 and 1981, I drove a cab, hefted sacks of grain in an animal-feed warehouse, served time as a night watchman in a run-down hotel, lifted boxes on and off a conveyor belt, tutored philosophy, worked construction, loaded and unloaded trucks for UPS, and hauled freight along the Louisville-Cincinnati-Lexington triangle. None of these jobs paid more than four dollars an hour, and until 1992 I had no bank account: no checking, no savings. Also no car, no credit cards, no cashmere socks. Sometimes I moved from one city to another simply because I had a chance to house-sit or because a friend offered to put me up. I don't defend, and I most certainly don't recommend, this way of life. It may, in fact, no longer be feasible, given today's success-oriented ethos and the way prices have risen. In the mid-seventies, a quart of milk cost thirty cents in Boston; a carton of cigarettes, two dollars in South Carolina; filet mignon, four dollars a pound in Kentucky. One of the best Chambertins I ever drank set me back seventeen dollars in New Jersey.

Looking back, my peripatetic, hand-to-mouth existence puzzles more   5 than it embarrasses me. Why did I settle for so little when I wanted so much more? And yet at the time it seemed like the life I should lead. Not because I wanted to be a writer (it wasn't as if the words to "Vissi d'arte"* filled my head) but because I saw myself—and this is where it does get a little embarrassing— in the light of books I had read as a teen-ager. I was great for poets and poetry and for whatever seemed fantastic, romantic, and tragic in books. I didn't exactly identify with Marlowe, Coleridge, Byron, Keats, Poe, Baudelaire, Rimbaud, and Pushkin,* but their examples did make me feel that hewing to the straight and narrow would somehow be disloyal to their own fervid imaginings.

Hermann Hesse (1877–1962): German novelist

"Vissi d'arte": "I live for art," the beginning of an aria from the opera *Tosca*, by Giacomo Puccini (1858–1924)

Marlowe . . . Pushkin: major writers and poets

One of the dangers of reading the right books at the wrong age is the tendency to confuse the creator with the creation. Since Des Esseintes, Pechorin, Stavrogin, Julien Sorel, Maldoror, and the Corsair* could have been given shape only by men very much like themselves, I decided around the age of fourteen to become a blasé voluptuary, a weary adventurer who travelled the world over, conquering women and boredom. This foolishness didn't last long, but for a time words and expressions like "anomie," "ennui," "spleen," "melancholy," and "alienated consciousness" made it difficult for me to think practically about the future.

But to say that I avoided long-term employment merely out of some misguided application of literature to life (where Emma Bovary* sought liaisons, I sought leisure) would be preposterous. I never wanted to work. Even as a kid, I thought working for money, whether I needed it or not, was a bad trade-off. In 1960, planted in front of an old RCA console, I warmed to the ersatz beatnik Maynard G. Krebs, on "The Many Loves of Dobie Gillis," who on hearing the word "work" would involuntarily yelp "Work!" as if an angry bee had suddenly dived into view. I didn't want to be Maynard G. Krebs, but then I didn't want to be much of anything. That annoying question kids have to contend with—"What do you want to be when you grow up?"—left me stupefied.

Not that I didn't have ambition. I had plans: I was going to write big, fat novels and make potloads of money. But what good is ambition without energy? It's nothing more than daydreaming. Novels demand drive and Trollope-like commitment.* Naturally, I wasn't up to it, although I did manage to become a regular contributor to various publications. Yet even as a recognized member of a guild I was a spectacular non-go-getter. You would not have seen my shining face at conferences, panel discussions, readings, parties, or wherever else editors, agents, and publishers showed up. Networking and self-promotion, the hallmarks of literary aspirants, demand hustle, and hustling, among other things, means moving briskly. I stayed home. I wrote about books, literary trends, academic criticism. And though I occasionally took on an assignment to write about boxing or business (experience obviously not required), my earnings pretty much stayed on an even keel. I wrote book reviews for the *money*.

Some men are born lazy, some acquire laziness, some have laziness thrust upon them. But, however gained, laziness remains ill-gotten. Because we make a virtue of what is necessary, the precept of work is like a com-

---

Des Esseintes . . . the Corsair: heroic, defiant, or decadent characters in literary works

Emma Bovary: Heroine of *Madame Bovary,* novel by Gustave Flaubert (1821–80). Influenced by her reading of romantic novels, she pursues adulterous love affairs to disastrous effect.

Trollope-like commitment: Anthony Trollope (1815–82), an English novelist, was known to compose regularly 1,000 words per hour.

mandment sans stone tablet. It's man's nature to work; without work, people tend to wilt. On the other hand, some people droop by design. Look at small children: not all are animated tykes scampering about the playground; there are always one or two likely to sit by themselves, ruminating on the fact that they have ten fingers and toes instead of nine or eleven. They are the suspect ones, the nascent lazy, and, left to their own devices, will probably not metamorphose into the movers and shakers of their generation.

Although laziness in its simplest terms is the disinclination to work, the   10 condition is not reducible to a simple formula. For most of recorded history, laziness was thought to arise from the natural confluence of mind and body. The lazy suffered from melancholia, or an excess of black bile (carried by the blood to the brain), which in extreme cases kept them from finding solace in spiritual devotion. Those in whom the spirit failed to move or to be moved were afflicted with acedia—a condition that the early Church fathers felt deserved a measure of compassion, along with the usual tsk–tsking. But as the world grew older, and time got tangled up with the idea of progress, work, or busyness, rather than piety, took on antonymic meaning where laziness was concerned. By the late Middle Ages, acedia had come to include the notion of worldly sloth. And who was responsible for sloth? You were. Sloth didn't just slide into the world along with your squalling body; you had to seek it out and embrace it.

As a secular sin, laziness reached its apogee during the Industrial Revolution, when any sign of malingering was seen as a threat to the capitalist order. If you didn't work, you didn't produce, and if you didn't produce you were a parasite; you were, my friend, subversive. Don't get me wrong: I'm not defending the lazy. All I'm saying is that the subject makes people take extreme views. When Boswell suggested that "we grow weary when idle," the otherwise sensible Dr. Johnson* remonstrated, "That is, sir, because others being busy, we want company; but if we were idle, there would be no growing weary; we should all entertain one another." Is he kidding? The man obviously never hung out with the deadbeat crowd I used to know, for whom prying the cap off a Schlitz was a good day's work. Most people disdain the lazy not only because they serve no useful purpose but because their own metabolisms and circadian rhythms seem to recognize those whose own systems are out of sinc. The lazy are different from you and me. I mean, of course, just you.

Medically, however, I'm fine. Two blood tests, years apart, revealed no bacterial parasites or high concentrations of viral antibodies, or any other noxious agents that could account for my usual indolence. No toxins in the air, no food groups, no glowing chunks of kryptonite rob me of my powers. Nor, when I look around, can I lay the blame on the sixties, or on my being an

---

Boswell . . . Dr. Johnson: Essayist James Boswell (1740–95) was the biographer of English man of letters Samuel Johnson (1709–84).

only child, or on my retreating into books at a tender age, or, for that matter, on family history. Although the early death of a parent so constricts the heart that it can never regain its original shape, plenty of children suffer loss and sadness and go on to lead busy, productive lives.

Sometimes the only good explanation for the arc life takes is that a person has only so much spring in his step, that one is born to travel only so far. And, while most of us want to get to the top, not all of us are willing to make the climb. My father wasn't entirely mistaken in claiming that I turned to writing in order to avoid work. Let's face it, some boys and girls become writers because the only workplace they're willing to visit is the one inside their heads. And even then it's a tough commute, since the same urge that leads them to write may also keep them from doing their work. That general discontent with the world which is at the bottom of all writing tends to pull writers down, deplete them of initiative, and make them wonder if it's worth doing at all. This applies as well to writers who churn out prose at a ferocious clip as it does to those of us who, like Bartleby,* prefer not to. The trick is to turn that urge to one's advantage. "I write of melancholy, by being busy to avoid melancholy," wrote the industrious Robert Burton.*

Likewise, writers who know themselves to be lazy conscientiously and routinely meet their inertia head-on. Profound laziness is not so much about doing nothing as it is about the strain of doing practically *anything*. Lazy people can accomplish things, thank you very much. We have our paroxysms of activity, the occasional eruptions of busyness and bursts of productivity. Walter Benjamin,* for instance, acknowledged that he had entered "the world under the sign of Saturn—the star of the slowest revolution, the planet of detours and delays," yet the man's formidable essays didn't, as they say, write themselves. Our first essayist, Montaigne,* also professed to have a wide streak of laziness, and Cyril Connolly,* whose journal *Horizon* helped keep English letters afloat during the Second World War, gloated, "Others merely live; I vegetate."

But vegetation among writers and thinkers takes peculiar forms. Someone who sits and conjures up names and explanations for characters or subatomic particles cannot be said to be doing nothing. A world of difference exists between a valetudinarian fused to his bed and Max Beerbohm,* who never voluntarily went out for a walk, because "it stops the brain." Still, the standard, hackneyed conception of laziness prevails. "Doomed as I was to a 15

Bartleby: the lead character in Herman Melville's short story "Bartleby the Scrivener" (1856), famous for his repeated remark, "I would prefer not to"

Robert Burton (1577–1640): author of *The Anatomy of Melancholy* (1621)

Walter Benjamin (1892–1940): influential German critic and essayist

Montaigne: Michel Eyquem, Seigneur de Montaigne (1533–92); French writer, author of *Essais* (first edition 1580)

Cyril Connolly (1903–74): English critic and editor

Max Beerbohm (1872–1956): English essayist and parodist

life of perpetual idleness, I did absolutely nothing," says the landscape painter in Chekhov's story* "The House with an Attic." "I spent hours looking out of the window at the sky, the birds, the avenues, read everything that was brought to me from the post, and slept. Sometimes I left the house and went for walks till late at night." Yes, yes, we've heard all this before. Don't be fooled: there's no uniformity about the lazy. Energetic people may all be alike, but the lazy cruise along at their own varying rates of speed. Some bite the bullet and go off to jobs; some stay home while their more energetic spouses tackle the workaday world; some really do watch the grass grow, or, its millennial equivalent, daytime television.

There is something preëmptive about laziness, something that smacks of a decision to refuse all offers even before they're put on the table. The lazy don't come to the table. And I think there is a philosophical component in this resistance. At bottom, laziness is negation, turning one's back on what others neutrally, cheerfully, or resignedly go to meet. The truly lazy—the ones who cannot bring themselves to greet and meet, to scheme and struggle, to interact on a daily basis with others—are, in effect, refusing to affix their signatures to the social contract. Given that success hinges on understanding, using, and occasionally subverting the social contract, the lazy don't stand a chance.

The secret to failure is far more elusive than the secret to success. Lagging behind when one could have advanced isn't just about laziness; it's about all the things that psychoanalysis takes a rather serious view of—the absence of love, coping with anger, rationalizing failure, the reluctance to supersede or replace one's father. Heavy stuff, and perhaps true, but the acknowledgment of which never put a dime in my pocket. Laziness just is. It's like being freckled or color-blind. Indeed, when the world was younger, intelligent people believed they had no choice in the matter of who was naughty or nice, passive or active. Hippocrates' theory of "temperament," which anchored Western medicine for two millennia, put some muscle behind varieties of human behavior. Well, not muscle exactly—more like four cardinal humors, whose relative proportion in the blood determined personality and moods. The Church fathers were on the right track; only the messenger and the manner of delivery were wrong. It's not black bile that causes Oblomov-like symptoms* but a certain kind of electro-chemical activity in the left frontal lobe of the brain, or whatever. The point is, everyone enters the world predisposed physiologically to think and feel in certain ways.

Happenstance also has its place; I don't deny that. But do any two people react identically to the same stimuli? The event that jump-starts one

---

Chekhov's story: Anton Chekhov (1860–1904), Russian writer
Oblomov-like symptoms: Oblomov, a passive Russian noble described in a novel of the same name by Ivan Goncharov (1812–91), spent most of his time in bed.

person's psyche does not necessarily have the same effect on another's. It's one thing to concede that certain tendencies can be reinforced or weakened by experience; it is quite another to think that some event during my formative years, which might have occurred but didn't, would have had me sharing a bucket of KFC with Bill Gates, or loping down a runway in Milan wearing a spiffy outfit by Valentino. In short, there's no contradiction in thinking that temperament defines you and thinking that you're still in charge of your life: temperament is the gas, but you've got a foot on the pedal.

Because of some elusive sequence of recombinant DNA and early experiences, I always knew I'd write things. I also knew I was an incurable lazybones. This accounts, in my case, for the odd tension between writing and laziness which Samuel Beckett describes to a T: "There is nothing to express, nothing with which to express, nothing from which to express, no power to express, no desire to express, together with the obligation to express." As a solid constituent of the couchant class, I can say that the obligation to express does not weigh heavily. Still, I have my moments—moments when I feel like addressing the fading shimmer of my own skin. I want answers. Or, more precisely, one big answer. In a sense, life is like an examination that has only one question—the one that asks why you're taking the exam in the first place. Having been instructed to "fill in the blank" (an aptly phrased command), you ponder, and then wonder if perhaps the truest answer is no answer at all. But in the end, because there is, after all, plenty of time to reflect and you do want to leave the room, you hunker down and fill in the blank. My own response is hardly profound or incisive: I'm taking the exam because I like writing sentences, and because—well, what else do I have to do?

As for the laziness that moves with me wherever I go, I have finally   20
found a way to make it "work" for me. Lassitude, aloofness, low-grade depression, coupled with a healthy respect for money, have gradually steered me to the obvious vocation. Yes, dear reader, I have become a screenwriter.

QUESTIONING THE TEXT

1. How does Krystal define *laziness*? By his own definition, is he truly lazy? Gather evidence from the essay to support your answers to these questions.

2. The illustration that accompanies this essay (p. 698) carries a reference to the author and to one of the points he makes. What other captions could effectively go with this illustration? Create several possible appropriate captions and bring them to class for discussion.

3. Krystal ends his essay by revealing how he has finally made laziness "work" for him: he has "become a screenwriter." Is Krystal being ironic or satiric here? Reread the essay with this question in mind and then

write a one-paragraph explanation or elaboration of this final paragraph, exploring (in humorous terms if you want) what Krystal's meaning may be.

MAKING CONNECTIONS

4. Both Krystal and bell hooks (p. 717) talk about the way in which success in work has been measured in terms of the amount of money earned. In what ways are their attitudes toward this traditional linking of success with money similar? In what ways do their attitudes differ? Which view seems most persuasive to you, and why?

5. Imagine a brief correspondence between Benjamin Franklin (p. 678) and Arthur Krystal, in which Krystal offers advice on how to avoid work and Franklin counters with advice on how to cure laziness. Write a rough draft of their exchange. Then, after reading the exchange aloud to two or three classmates and getting feedback, revise the exchange. Finally, write a paragraph or two explaining which side of the conversation you find most effective—and why.

JOINING THE CONVERSATION

6. Write an extended definition of *laziness,* including a well-developed analogy and one or two metaphors. You may want to review the guidelines for writing definitions on p. 23. Bring the definition to class for discussion and reading aloud.

7. Use the resources of your library and the Internet to explore the literary and political concept of *Oblomovism,* briefly alluded to by Krystal. Keywords for your search might include *Oblomov, Ivan Goncharov,* and the term *superfluous man.* Are there any contemporary equivalents of Oblomovism you can identify—the couch potato or the slacker, for example? Give examples of these types and then write a short essay discussing how indolent people are portrayed today in literature, film, or popular culture.

REILLY BRENNAN
Would You Buy a Car from This Man?

GOOFY JOBS ARE PART OF GROWING UP. *Sooner or later, almost everyone has a workplace experience that provides material for years of storytelling. Lots of students learn the nine-to-five grind for the first time standing behind the counter at a Burger King or waiting tables at an Olive Garden. I spent two offbeat summers between college terms as a gardener at Cedar Point, a huge amusement complex in Sandusky, Ohio, now famous for its roller coasters.*

But how goofy is it to be a sales representative for a major auto company while you're still in college? I'm not talking about sweeping the linoleum at an established dealership, either. No, I mean being the person classmates in a dorm might consult to order up a fully equipped Daewoo Lanos, Nubira, or — if their parents bought Intel a decade ago — Leganza. What's a Daewoo? That's part of the story Reilly Brennan tells in "Would You Buy a Car from This Man?"

Brennan was a nineteen-year-old motor gopher for Automobile *(talk about an ideal college job!) when an editor suggested that the magazine investigate Daewoo's innovative marketing scheme from the inside by having the University of Michigan sophomore pose as a potential "campus advisor" for the South Korean automobile manufacturer. Soon, Brennan was on his way to South Korea to learn about the Daewoo empire and the products he might be selling in Ann Arbor. Brennan's article about his experience, subsequently published in* Automobile *(February 1999), is a humorous narrative of one possible alternative to flippin' burgers.* — J.R.

Korean Airlines Flight 017—
Any other successful company might think that a major financial crisis, a weak national presence in the car industry, and a risky, college-kid-based marketing plan would doom the launch of a South Korean automobile company in the United States, the world's most demanding market. However, Daewoo, a company founded by a guy who will freely admit his ideas are crazy, is attempting to prove the majority of America's media wrong.

Kim Woo-Choong is the crazy man in question, almost deified by his employees and celebrated by his country's people. I have just spent a week flying and driving all over South Korea. The idea for this trip occurred during 1998's early summer months, when associate editor Eddie Alterman and I — motor gopher and intrepid nineteen-year-old University of Michigan sophomore — discussed the notion of my joining the Daewoo Campus Advisor (DCA) program on an incognito basis. As one of the 2000 students in the program last summer, I would fly to South Korea and see how the company would train us ragamuffin American undergrads, an aggregate upon which Daewoo is betting all its chips.

That's right. Daewoo's total U.S. marketing strategy is based on college students selling its cars. Don't ask me.

Day One: After a debacle with a delayed plane out of Detroit, I find myself   5
on a different carrier, headed to Seoul the long way, via New York and Anchorage. I arrive irritated but fresh, due to an abundance of hot Asiana Airlines towels.

Along with two other latecomers to the DCA program, I am whooshed

The author, posing with the only woman in South Korea who gave him any time.

via a Hyundai taxi through Seoul's congested streets to the city's southern village towns. Eventually, I'll disembark in rural Yong-In, at Daewoo's Management Development Center, a gigantic training center that would make a perfect religious compound in southern Texas. My group of about 100 students—a mixture of nearly half Korean-Americans and randomly assorted Yanks—is just one of about twenty different crews that Daewoo will bring to Korea during the summer. Later on I learn one reason for the large Korean-American contingent—Daewoo offered open-ended plane tickets to all DCAs, encouraging extra-long stays to visit relatives in Korea. One DCA even finagled a one-week trip to Manila, on Daewoo's nickel, before the return flight to the United States.

A day consisting of tedious lectures from the Daewoo staff, each one basically recapitulating Daewoo's history and deifying Chairman Kim, who seems to wield more power in South Korea than the country's president, is happily broken up by an honest meal in the compound's cafeteria. I opt for large helpings of *bool go gi,* a personal favorite consisting of steak and vegetables, and the soybean-based *den jang* soup. A small side of *kimchi,* a spicy cabbage concoction, was the good kick I needed to hop out of my fourteen-hour jet lag. *Duk,* a gummy rice cake ball, was an ample dessert, and my favorite beverage on the trip, bottled water, washed it down.

While the majority of my fellow DCAs were undergrads about my age, many others were older than I expected, with a few nearing Ralph Furley in years and appearance—few Chrissy Snows, though. One bright note: They gave us each a backpack, a mesh hat, and two navy golf shirts emblazoned with the Daewoo logo. You haven't seen attitude until you witness twenty-year-old girls from Los Angeles being told they have to wear mesh hats.

More lectures eventually lead us to the "sales orientation," a frighteningly brief twenty-five minutes in length, nearly devoid of specifics and presented by a less than enthusiastic marketing manager. I go to sleep at night wondering when we will receive instructions on how to sell these cars.

Day Two: I wake at 5:30 A.M., pack, and shower, drying off with the provided doily-sized bath towel. A long day of bus travel to Kunsan, a west coast port city on the Yellow Sea, is characterized by hourly stops at several open markets, which are the closest you'll get to truck stops in Korea. It was here that fellow DCA Samantha Son, a native-born Korean and current student at the University of Illinois, introduced me to Bong Bong. What sounds like the makings of an interesting morning is actually a non-carbonated grape beverage that attempts to convince the drinker that real chunks of grapes really do taste good coming out of an aluminum can.

Daewoo's Kunsan Plant, the facility that produces all three types of the Nubira model (sedan, hatchback, and wagon), is our destination. We are given a tour of every production process in the plant, but it is somewhat lonely, as 97 percent of the factory is automated—the highest such percentage in the world. Up to 300,000 units can be produced here per year, and since Kunsan is located on the coast, the cars are driven directly from the factory to waiting Daewoo-built ships.

10

After the tour, we are given a few hours to romp around in some real, live Daewoo cars at Kunsan's test track. With visions of screaming e-brake turns in the Nubira wagon and corner-limit tests in the Lanos hatchback, I am a bit disappointed when we are introduced to an expanse of asphalt with as many dramatic turns as a Korean how-to-polka video. Twice as much time is spent listening to someone explaining the rules of the track as actually driving the cars. Drive time amounts to a scant sixty minutes and is chaperoned so tightly that most DCAs don't even get a chance to drive all three models: the Lanos, the Nubira, and the Leganza. What is skimped on drive time is definitely made up, before and after the test drive, with explanations about all the great technology that goes into these elusive machines. No fewer than seven times do I hear a Daewoo engineer say that Porsche assisted in the development of the Lanos's suspension. After our group's test drive, I overhear one DCA swear he could feel the Porscheness of the Lanos he had driven down the track's glorified driveway. Yeah, sure.

Day Three: I wake early and eat a quick breakfast of sautéed rice and scrambled eggs before catching a short Korean Airlines flight to Kimhae. We eventually find ourselves touring Daewoo's Okpo Shipyard, which is located on the island of Okpo off Korea's southeast coast. Daewoo is spending a lot of money on each student for this program. A rumored $4500 per student covers just the trip to South Korea (okay, Daewoo has an affiliation with Korean Airlines), and no DCA has any real obligation to sell a car or do anything for the company once he or she gets back to the States. However, if a DCA should decide to take part in the program, the company provides the student with a new car for ninety days, a chance to buy their test car initially at a 50 percent discount, and cash incentives ranging from $300 to $500 for each car sold. I begin to wonder what the IMF* thinks of this program.

The Okpo Shipyard that we tour is another egregious example of the company's mammoth size and power. Trumpeting the largest multipurpose heavy industrial base in the world, the Okpo Shipyard covers 1.55 square miles. And just for kicks, Daewoo's 900-ton Goliath crane is in the *Guinness Book of Records*. Keeping 100 American college students enthralled with a shipyard is like keeping Ron Jeremy* in a chastity belt, so it is with great pleasure that we move on to our next site, the Daewoo Motor complex at Changwon. They pump out 240,000 units a year here, but the cars they make—the Tico, the Matiz, the Labo, and the Damas—won't cross U.S. borders. On this day, production results are probably a little shy of expectations, since we walk right down on the factory floor, inches from workers who are installing new seats in Matizes and instrument panels in Ticos. Distracting Changwon's workers isn't tough, especially when you're with a handful of girls from Los Angeles with their mesh hats on.

IMF: International Monetary Fund
Ron Jeremy (b. 1953): a performer in adult films

The day's biggest surprise, and some say the trip's most memorable mo-   15
ment, comes after the tour of the factory, when we get to ride in a K200A1 or a
K1FV, our choice—military tanks, of course. A smiley Changwon employee
narrates the thirty-minute tank demonstration while his compadres race about
in the moat, climb the steep grade, and take to the high-speed bank. Later on, I
climb inside the K200A1, pop my head out one of the gunner holes, and let the
wind tug on my cheeks as the driver takes the diesel beast up to 60 mph around
the test oval. Now this . . . I could sell this! A K200A1? I'd sell more tanks than
Corvette Vicki does cars. As hard as I tried, I couldn't figure out how my riding
in a tank could help Daewoo sell cars in America, but hey, it sure was a hoot.

Day Four: Waking up in Kyongju's swanky Hilton Hotel is not a bad
way to start a day for a young kid from Detroit. Another of Daewoo's myriad
possessions, the Hilton is located in the palm of an eccentric Korean city, one
that has three universities and numerous nightclubs ripe for a hundred obnoxious Americans to devour.

But first, our day starts not with cars but with morning bus travel to sleepy
Gumi, where Daewoo's electronics plant is located. Once again, our group is
waved at as if we are a hundred David E. Davis, Jr.'s* instead of a hundred college kids. Of course, the now-ubiquitous factory floor tour ensues. After curious observation from one keen DCA, our amiable tour guide, Sun Young Lee,
informs us that Daewoo not only makes its own televisions in the Gumi Plant,
but it also produces some units that sell under a different name: Sony.

That Nubira test drive is becoming a fading memory.

An early return back to the Hilton makes possible a night of mischief in
Kyongju, and thankfully most of the group answers the call. Later on in the
evening, hoards of us abandon our geeky Daewoo garb for the confines of the
Havana nightclub in, ahem, the Hyundai Hotel.

Day Five: Farewell, Kyongju.   20

Alone, with the friendly staff of Korean Airlines looking over me on my
flight back to the States, it is remarkable to recall how little time was spent on
the raw discussion of brilliant marketing schemes, slick sales techniques, or
even basic car data. I did leave with a souvenir binder of Nubira photos,
though. Now what are we supposed to do? Daewoo never gave us, the Campus Advisors, a feeling of weighty responsibility. A bit strange, I thought, because what exactly will Daewoo do if I fail?

One Month Later: Back in Ann Arbor, I get word that Kim Woo-
Choong is coming to speak to the University of Michigan Business School.
Finally, I get a peek at the guy.

After his talk, I carefully position myself next to him as he walks out of the
building. As I attempt to introduce myself, a pushy bodyguard knocks me into
the man, and as an unconscious reaction I find my right arm draped around the
shoulder of the chairman and founder of one of the world's most powerful com-

---

David E. Davis Jr.: editor of *Automobile* magazine

panies. I casually offer up one of the two Korean phrases in my repertoire, *"Annyong haseyo."* Chairman Kim smiles, says hello, and offers me a Winston. Perfectly, there we stand, outside my university, on the heels of a trip that took me to his country, courtesy of his company. I have my arm around the guy, and he's puffing a Winston. And all I want him to do is admit that this program is the weirdest, the riskiest, and possibly the most disastrous thing he could do for Daewoo. "Of course the idea is crazy," he says. "But I know it will work."

QUESTIONING THE TEXT

1. Underscore or list the allusions and expressions in Brennan's article that mark the writer as a college undergraduate. What parts of the piece might an older person find puzzling? How would you characterize the tone of the article? Formal? Informal? Colloquial?

2. How does Brennan organize this account of his trip to Korea and subsequent events? Do you find the narrative clear? Why, or why not? How else might he have organized the piece?

3. What are the implications of the title of Brennan's article: "Would You Buy a Car from This Man?" How does the accompanying photograph on p. 707 (of Brennan with his arm around a Korean Airlines flight attendant) influence your reading of the title?

MAKING CONNECTIONS

4. Brennan ends his article by quoting Daewoo Chairman Kim Woo-Choong: "'Of course the idea is crazy,' he says [of his plan to use American college students to market his company's cars]. 'But I know it will work.'" Based on your own experiences as a consumer, would you argue that Kim is displaying the sort of risk-taking right-brain thinking that Robert A. Lutz praises in "The Primary Purpose of Business Is Not to Make Money" (p. 712)? Would you be hesitant to buy a car from a college student? Read Lutz's piece with these questions in mind.

5. Examine Brennan's essay side by side with two other selections by college-aged writers in this collection: Wendy Shalit's "The Future of Modesty" (p. 214) and James Prosek's "Introduction to *Trout*" (p. 506). What similarities in theme or style can you point to? What in particular marks these pieces as the work of young writers?

JOINING THE CONVERSATION

6. Write a brief narrative about any job or job training you have had. Like Brennan, use your narrative to tell the story and convey your judgment of the experience.

ROBERT A. LUTZ

The Primary Purpose of Business Is Not to Make Money

For some readers, it's enough just to say that the Dodge Viper is Bob Lutz's baby. But others may want to know that Lutz played a leading role in transforming the Chrysler Corporation, a U.S. auto manufacturer once famous for its clunky sedans and scrapes with bankruptcy, into an organization dynamic enough to attract the attention of Germany's prestigious Daimler-Benz, the oldest auto company in the world. The two firms merged in 1999 to become DaimlerChrysler, a powerful player on the international automobile market.

Behind this success story lies a passion for work. Lutz and the executives working with him at Chrysler Corporation shared a visceral love for the products they designed and manufactured. They reorganized the way cars were created by establishing cooperative "platform teams" that got engineers, designers, and assembly-line workers talking to each other. More important, they decided to build cars they wanted to drive themselves, not designs dictated by bean counters. No rational company as low on cash as Chrysler was in the early 1990s should have built the Viper, but the 400-horsepower V-10 sports car restored the corporate spirit and reputation—and earned the company $100 million in free publicity.

Robert A. Lutz defends his unusual business philosophies in Guts: The Seven Laws of Business That Made Chrysler the World's Hottest Car Company *(1998), from which the following selection is taken. In "The Primary Purpose of Business Is Not to Make Money," Lutz explains "Law 2," one of the most provocative of his seven laws. Work, if Lutz is right, is not about labor and money only. It can be about creativity and passion as well.* —J.R.

"*Not make money?* That's ridiculous," you say. And of course you're right. A business must make money. What I mean to suggest with this Law, however, is that companies that *do* make a lot of money almost never have as their goal "making a lot of money."

They tend to be run by enthusiasts who, in the normal course of gratifying their *own* tastes and curiosities, come up with products or services so startling, so compelling, and so exciting that customers practically rip their trouser pockets reaching for their wallets.

Robert McNamara (I don't think I'm letting any cats out of the bag here) was not such a man. When he was president of Ford, he reportedly arrived in the office one Monday morning with some calculations he had jotted on the back of an envelope during church. These specified the financial performance he expected could be had from a new car of such and such a weight and size. He told his designers to get busy on it. "Gee, Mr. McNamara," they asked, "what should the car look like?" That didn't matter, said McNamara, so long as it met his financial stipulations.

People of this stripe regard product as nothing more than a conduit: In one end they pour as little money as they can get away with; out of the other end they expect a munificent return.

Business doesn't work like this. Great profits are produced only one   5 way—by great products. And great products derive from enthusiasm turned loose, which is a fair description of how we at Chrysler arrived at the original Viper concept car—the kind of machine that sets car buffs drooling, but that hardly anyone ever sees outside auto shows.

. . . I'm frequently asked—especially by the Japanese, who worship research—what process of market analysis led us to Viper's design. There was none. I'd love to say we did a careful survey and found that a huge segment of the American (and European and Japanese and Middle Eastern) public was just dying for a $50,000 car with no door handles, no real top, no windows, a big gas-guzzler tax, no factory air, no C/D player, no automatic transmission, a steering column borrowed from the Jeep Cherokee, room for barely two people, and next to no luggage space. But we didn't *do* a survey.

We just decided it might be nice, for a change, to let our most impassioned car buffs design a car to suit *their* tastes.

The result is a beautiful example of what can happen when the whole brain is engaged. The car owed its birth to an act of almost pure, spontaneous creativity: the proverbial "eureka!" or "aha!" when a designer is smitten by inspiration. That was quickly followed, however, by more than a little left-brained analysis: Could we actually *build* the car? How much would it cost? How badly might the expenditure imperil Chrysler's finances if the experiment went wrong? What price could we sell it for? Who'd buy it? How many buyers might there be? All left-brained questions—all highly necessary!

Was our primary goal with Viper to make money? No. It was to see if we could, in one fell swoop, design and build the world's most unique and desirable sports car. As the car's cult has grown, Chrysler has indeed made money on it. But Viper's role in *rehabilitating Chrysler's image* has been the car's far more valuable contribution. In a stroke, Viper erased two of the three words everyone had grown thoroughly sick of hearing: "stodgy old Chrysler." Now Chrysler wasn't stodgy. It was the company with the breakthrough product.

It's hard to predict with certainty which products will succeed. Indeed,   10 some of the most unlikely ones become the biggest hits. The very same idea that causes a Mr. McNamara nothing but a derisive chuckle may, when it gets to market, sell better than he or anyone else could have predicted. Look at *Cigar Aficionado* magazine.

In case you are not acquainted with this sterling publication, it is dedicated to the proposition that cigars, cigar smoking, cigar bands, cigar humidors, cigar cutters, women who like the smell of cigars, and all adjuncts to and appurtenances of cigars are either good, very good, or better.

Now that a large segment of the U.S. public has rediscovered (rekindled?) an affection for cigars, this proposition may not seem revolutionary. Yet in 1991, when the *Aficionado* was but a smoky gleam in the eye of its publisher, Marvin Shanken, the idea of a pro-cigar magazine seemed outrageous if not daft. Shanken might as well have been singing the praises of cholera. "Health Nazis" were then at their most puissant.

It was Shanken's peculiarity, however, to love cigars. And it was his genius to apprehend that huddled masses of would-be libertines were chafing under Healthdom's iron heel. He decided he would offer them a pro-smoking, pro-drinking, pro-steak-eating magazine whose ethic might be expressed as, "Eh, so what if it kills you—*live a little.*" He published the first issue with his own money, and the rest, as they say, is publishing history. *Cigar Aficionado* caught fire.

So popular have cigars become that retailers have experienced shortages. Some have imposed rationing—only-three-to-a-customer-type limits on how many cigars a customer may buy of certain heavily sought-after brands. I myself have experienced sticker shock. As demand has driven prices skyward, I have seen the cost of one of my favorite cigars, La Gloria Cubana (of course, I smoke only the U.S.-legal ones!), waft upward from a not unreasonable $1.75 to $2.25, then $4, then $5 and then all the way up to as high as $14!

All of which proves what? That great products are unpredictable. That   15 most, in their infancy, seem indefensible (at least to left-brained people). That the best are expressions of quirky tastes and squirrelly passions, irreducible to neat formulas on the backs of envelopes. Tom Peters states succinctly: "Whether we're talking about art, science, or Apple computers, the signature products and services of our time will continue to come from some kinky mind somewhere." It's fine (necessary!) to test the brainchildren of that kinky mind for soundness, strength, and viability, just as Chrysler subjected Viper to a cost and sales analysis. But these ideas must not be dismissed out of hand simply because, on first hearing, they *sound* batty. Dismiss them, in fact, and you risk parboiling a golden-egg-laying goose.

Forbes magazine, during a recent ebb in Disney's business, asked, "When did the magic start to ooze from the Magic Kingdom?"

Box office returns for the company's animated features, it seemed, had fallen steadily since the release of *The Lion King. Forbes* fingered Disney's "battalions of MBAs [who] too often win over the more creative types." Every time creatives suggested a premise they thought might make for a hit, they were asked: How can you prove that? (One can imagine the meetings: Why *seven* dwarves, exactly? Wouldn't six be cheaper? Wouldn't 1,000 be bigger box office? Can't we get a computer analysis of dwarf configurations?) Yet, concluded *Forbes* sagely, "The computer hasn't been invented—and probably never will be—that can predict how many tickets a movie will sell."

You usually can tell how well a company understands Law 2 by seeing how they go about formulating a five-year business plan: Do they start with the numbers (e.g., so much investment will generate so much return)? Worse, do they start with a specific return, then figure their way back to the minimum amount of money they think they'll have to invest in order to attain it?

Or do they instead start with a passionate, all-consuming vision of an idiosyncratic product or service? Do they themselves find the idea for it exciting? Do they go to work each morning because they love the challenge of creation and wouldn't switch vocations even if they were offered marginally higher pay? If so, then hock your kid's retainer and buy stock in this second company! It's certain to outperform the first in every way, including profits.

Much of business devolves, it's true, to a mastery of disciplines and sci- 20
ence. Running a successful restaurant requires an understanding of food science. Making movies takes accounting. But technical proficiency by itself is not enough—especially today, when competitors are apt to be every bit as adept as you. To make money, a business must generate products that *demand* attention—ones so compelling that they push the consumer's "gotta have it" button, rather than the one marked "hmmm, that's nice."

To get such products, foster a corporate culture where right-brained visionaries feel safe suggesting "gotta have it" ideas. Then, only after giving your enthusiasts a respectful hearing should you ask the necessary left-brained questions.

QUESTIONING THE TEXT

1. Lutz makes several mentions of left- and right-brained people or analyses. What's the purported difference between left- and right-brained thinking? If you're not sure, do some research to find out. Does the distinction strike you as valid? Why, or why not?

2. Read up on Robert McNamara, the automobile executive Lutz characterizes as the consummate financial technician. What vehicles did he create? What was his management philosophy? What role did he go on to play in American history?

MAKING CONNECTIONS

3. The Viper sports car described by Lutz probably falls on the "guy" side of the fence if examined according to the scheme Dave Barry offers in "Guys vs. Men" (p. 372). How then does it make good business sense to produce such a product? Analyze its appeal by reviewing the Barry

piece and then pushing beyond the "Guys vs. Men" framework. Can you identify other "off-the-wall" products that appeal to people viscerally?

4. The critics James Q. Wilson describes in "Cars and Their Enemies" (p. 303) would, of course, not embrace Lutz's gas-guzzling Dodge Viper. How might Lutz defend such a product as beneficial to society? Working in a group, write a dialogue between Lutz and car critics on this issue.

JOINING THE CONVERSATION

5. Lutz suggests that both the Viper and *Cigar Aficionado* magazine are products that appeal to pent-up emotional demands in consumers. Working in a group, design a product or service you think might have similar reach. Begin by identifying markets, consumers, or desires currently ignored by corporations, schools, or other institutions. Then write a group essay explaining what your new product or service is and how you expect to sell it.

6. In an exploratory essay, study the dynamics of your work situation, asking what role, if any, passion and creativity currently play. Would the work be "better" if managers and workers were more right-brained? Or is the situation out of control and in need of some left-brain discipline? Your work situation can include the classroom.

BELL HOOKS
Work Makes Life Sweet

Do PEOPLE WORK TO LIVE OR LIVE TO WORK—*or some combination of the two? In "Work Makes Life Sweet," from* Sisters of the Yam: Black Women and Self-Recovery *(1993) , bell hooks (b. 1952) takes a look at the working traditions of African American women, noting that "[t]he vast majority of black women in the United States know in girlhood that [they] will be workers." She also considers the different circumstances that allow work to be "sweet" or that ensure that it will be sour—alienating and unsatisfying. In sum, she says the majority of black women she has talked with do not enjoy their work—and she goes on to offer reasons for such dissatisfaction as well as a way to "unlearn" conventional thinking about work so that it will once again have the capacity to make life sweet.*

For hooks, the work of writing seems sweet indeed, as evidenced by her publication of seventeen books in under twenty years. Yet she often remarks on the ways in which her need to work for a living—accompanied by fears of poverty or joblessness—have interfered with her ability to live for the work of her writing. And for this work she is often criticized—for writing without extensive footnotes and bibliography, for not being "intellectual" enough, for writing about the same subjects (especially the intersection of class, race, and gender), even for writing too much. To these criticisms, hooks generally turns a deaf ear, saying "I'm playful, anybody who hangs with me knows that, but I am also a dead-serious intellectual woman who is on the job."

Most recently on the job in her new Remembered Rapture: The Writer at Work *(1999), hooks offers her latest ideas on the work of writing and on her passion for that work. What work, I wonder, do you have a passion for? In what ways does that work make your life sweet?*

—A.L.

"Work makes life sweet!" I often heard this phrase growing up, mainly from old black folks who did not have jobs in the traditional sense of the word. They were usually self-employed, living off the land, selling fishing worms, picking up an odd job here and there. They were people who had a passion for work. They took pride in a job done well. My Aunt Margaret took in ironing. Folks brought her clothes from miles around because she was such an expert. That was in the days when using starch was common and she knew how to do an excellent job. Watching her iron with skill and grace was like watching a ballerina dance. Like all the other black girls raised in the fifties that I knew, it was clear to me that I would be a working woman. Even though our mother stayed home, raising her seven children, we saw her constantly at work, washing, ironing, cleaning, and cooking (she is an incredible cook). And she never allowed her six girls to imagine we would not be working women. No, she let us know that we would work and be proud to work.   **717**

The vast majority of black women in the United States know in girl-hood that we will be workers. Despite sexist and racist stereotypes about black women living off welfare, most black women who receive welfare have been in the workforce. In *Hard Times Cotton Mill Girls,** one can read about black women who went to work in the cotton mills, usually leaving farm labor or domestic service. Katie Geneva Cannon* remembers: "It was always assumed that we would work. Work was a given in life, almost like breathing and sleeping. I'm always surprised when I hear people talking about some-body taking care of them, because we always knew that we were going to work." Like older generations of southern black women, we were taught not only that we would be workers, but that there was no "shame" in doing any honest job. The black women around us who worked as maids, who stripped tobacco when it was the season, were accorded dignity and respect. We learned in our black churches and in our schools that it "was not what you did, but how you did it" that mattered.

A philosophy of work that emphasizes commitment to any task was useful to black people living in a racist society that for so many years made only certain jobs (usually service work or other labor deemed "undesirable") available to us. Just as many Buddhist traditions teach that any task becomes sacred when we do it mindfully and with care, southern black work traditions taught us the importance of working with integrity irrespective of the task. Yet these attitudes towards work did not blind anyone to the reality that racism made it difficult to work for white people. It took "gumption" to work with integrity in settings where white folks were disrespectful and downright hateful. And it was obvious to me as a child that the black people who were saying "work makes life sweet" were the folks who did not work for whites, who did what they wanted to do. For example, those who sold fishing worms were usually folks who loved to fish. Clearly there was a mean-ingful connection between positive thinking about work and those who did the work that they had chosen.

Most of us did not enter the workforce thinking of work in terms of finding a "calling" or a vocation. Instead, we thought of work as a way to make money. Many of us started our work lives early and we worked to ac-quire money to buy necessities. Some of us worked to buy school books or needed or desired clothing. Despite the emphasis on "right livelihood" that was present in our life growing up, my sisters and I were more inclined to think of work in relation to doing what you needed to do to get money to buy what you wanted. In general, we have had unsatisfying work lives. Ironi-cally, Mama entered the paid workforce very late, after we were all raised,

---

Hard Times Cotton Mill Girls: an oral history of life in southern textile mills, compiled by Victoria Byerly (b. 1949), a former mill worker

Katie Geneva Cannon: The first black woman ordained a Presbyterian minister. She worked with Victoria Byerly, author of *Hard Times Cotton Mill Girls.*

working for the school system and at times in domestic service, yet there are ways in which she has found work outside the home more rewarding than any of her children. The black women I talked with about work tended to see jobs primarily as a means to an end, as a way to make money to provide for material needs. Since so many working black women often have dependents, whether children or other relatives, they enter the workforce with the realistic conviction that they need to make money for survival purposes. This attitude coupled with the reality of a job market that remains deeply shaped by racism and sexism means that as black women we often end up working jobs that we do not like. Many of us feel that we do not have a lot of options. Of the women I interviewed, the ones who saw themselves as having options tended to have the highest levels of education. Yet nearly all the black women I spoke with agreed that they would always choose to work, even if they did not need to. It was only a very few young black females, teenagers and folks in their early twenties, who talked with me about fantasy lives where they would be taken care of by someone else.

Speaking with young black women who rely on welfare benefits to survive economically, I found that overall they wanted to work. However, they are acutely aware of the difference between a job and a fulfilling vocation. Most of them felt that it would not be a sign of progress for them to "get off welfare" and work low-paying jobs, in situations that could be stressful or dehumanizing. Individuals receiving welfare who are trying to develop skills, to attend school or college, often find that they are treated with much greater hostility by social-service workers than if they were just sitting at home watching television. One woman seeking assistance was told by an angry white woman worker, "welfare is not going to pay for you to get your B.A." This young woman had been making many personal sacrifices to try and develop skills and educational resources that would enable her to be gainfully employed and she was constantly disappointed by the level of resentment toward her whenever she needed to deal with social services.

Through the years, in my own working life, I have noticed that many black women do not like or enjoy their work. The vast majority of women I talked to . . . agreed that they were not satisfied with their working lives even though they see themselves as performing well on the job. That is why I talk so much about work-related stress in [*Remembered Rapture*]. It is practically impossible to maintain a spirit of emotional well-being if one is daily doing work that is unsatisfying, that causes intense stress, and that gives little satisfaction. Again and again, I found that many black women I interviewed had far superior skills than the jobs they were performing called for but were held back because of their "lack of education," or in some cases, "necessary experience." This routinely prevented them from moving upward. While they performed their jobs well, they felt added tension generated in the work environment by supervisors who often saw them as "too uppity" or by their own struggle to maintain interest in their assigned tasks. One white-woman administrator shared that the clearly overly skilled black woman who works as an administrative assistant in her office was resented by white male "bosses" who felt that she did not have the proper attitude of a "subordinate." When I spoke to this woman she acknowledged not liking her job, stating that her lack of education and the urgent need to raise children and send them to college had prevented her from working towards a chosen career. She holds to the dream that she will return to school and someday gain the necessary education that will give her access to the career she desires and deserves. Work is so often a source of pain and frustration.

Learning how to think about work and our job choices from the standpoint of "right livelihood" enhances black female well-being. Our self-recovery is fundamentally linked to experiencing that quality of "work that makes life sweet." In one of my favorite self-help books, Marsha Sinetar's *Do What You Love, the Money Will Follow,* the author defines right livelihood as a concept initially coming from the teachings of Buddha which emphasized "work consciously chosen, done with full awareness and care, and leading to enlightenment." This is an attitude toward work that our society does not promote, and it especially does not encourage black females to think of work in this way. As Sinetar notes:

> Right Livelihood, in both its ancient and its contemporary sense, embodies self-expression, commitment, mindfulness, and conscious choice. Finding and doing work of this sort is predicated upon high self-esteem and self-trust, since only those who like themselves, who subjectively feel they are trustworthy and deserving dare to choose on behalf of what is right and true for them. When the powerful quality of conscious choice is present in our work, we can be enormously productive. When we consciously choose to do work we enjoy, not only can we get things done, we can get them done well and be intrinsically rewarded for our effort.

Black women need to learn about "right livelihood." Even though I had been raised in a world where elderly black people had this wisdom, I was more socialized by the get-ahead generation that felt how much money you were making was more important than what you did to make that money. We have difficult choices ahead.

As black females collectively develop greater self-esteem, a greater sense of entitlement, we will learn from one another's example how to practice right livelihood. Of the black women I interviewed the individuals who enjoyed their work the most felt they were realizing a particular vocation or calling. C.J. (now almost forty) recalls that generations of her family were college-educated. She was taught to choose work that would be linked with the political desire to enhance the overall well-being of black people. C.J. says, "I went to college with a mission and a passion to have my work be about African-Americans. The spirit of mission came to me from my family, who taught us that you don't just work to get money, you work to create meaning for yourself and other people." With this philosophy as a guiding standpoint, she has always had a satisfying work life.

When one of my sisters, a welfare recipient, decided to return to college, I encouraged her to try and recall her childhood vocational dreams and to allow herself adult dreams, so that she would not be pushed into preparing for a job that holds no interest for her. Many of us must work hard to unlearn the socialization that teaches us that we should just be lucky to get any old job. We can begin to think about our work lives in terms of vocation and calling. One black woman I interviewed, who has worked as a housewife for many years, began to experience agoraphobia. Struggling to regain her emotional well-being, she saw a therapist, against the will of her family. In this therapeutic setting, she received affirmation for her desire to finish her undergraduate degree and continue in a graduate program. She found that finishing a master's and becoming a college teacher gave her enormous satisfaction. Yet this achievement was not fully appreciated by her husband. A worker in a factory, whose job is long and tedious, he was jealous of her newfound excitement about work. Since her work brings her in touch with the public, it yields rewards unlike any he can hope to receive from his job. Although she has encouraged him to go back to school (one of his unfulfilled goals), he is reluctant. Despite these relational tensions, she has found that "loving" her work has helped her attend to and transform previous feelings of low self-esteem.

A few of the black women I interviewed claimed to be doing work 10 they liked but complained bitterly about their jobs, particularly where they must make decisions that affect the work lives of other people. One woman had been involved in a decisionmaking process that required her to take a stance that would leave another person jobless. Though many of her peers were proud of the way she handled this difficult decision, her response was to feel "victimized." Indeed, she kept referring to herself as "battered." This response troubled me for it seemed to bespeak a contradiction many women experience in positions of power. Though we may like the status of a power position and wielding power, we may still want to see ourselves as "victims" in the process, especially if we must act in ways that "good girls, dutiful daughters" have been taught are "bad."

I suggested to the women I interviewed that they had chosen particular careers that involved "playing hard ball" yet they seemed to be undermining the value of their choices and the excellence of their work by complaining that they had to get their hands dirty and suffer some bruises. I shared with them my sense that if you choose to play hardball then you should be prepared for the bruises and not be devastated when they occur. In some ways it seemed to me these black women wanted to be "equals" in a man's world while they simultaneously wanted to be treated like fragile "ladies." Had they been able to assume full responsibility for their career choices, they would have enjoyed their work more and been able to reward themselves for jobs well done. In some cases it seemed that the individuals were addicted to being martyrs. They wanted to control everything, to be the person "in power" but also resented the position. These individuals, like those I describe in the chapter on stress, seemed not to know when to set boundaries or that work duties could be shared. They frequently over-extended themselves. When we over-extend ourselves in work settings, pushing ourselves to the breaking point, we rarely feel positive about tasks even if we are performing them well.

Since many people rely on powerful black women in jobs (unwittingly turning us into "mammies" who will bear all the burdens—and there are certainly those among us who take pride in this role), we can easily become tragically over-extended. I noticed that a number of us (myself included) talk about starting off in careers that we really "loved" but over-working to the point of "burn-out" so that the pleasure we initially found dissipated. I remember finding a self-help book that listed twelve symptoms of "burn-out," encouraging readers to go down the list and check those that described their experience. At the end, it said, "If you checked three or more of these boxes, chances are you are probably suffering from burn-out." I found I had checked all twelve! That let me know it was time for a change. Yet changing was not easy. When you do something and you do it well, it is hard to take a break, or to confront the reality that I had to face, which was that I really didn't want to be doing the job I was doing even though I did it well. In retrospect it occurred to me that it takes a lot more energy to do a job well when you really do not want to be doing it. This work is often more tiring. And maybe that extra energy would be better spent in the search for one's true vocation or calling.

In my case, I have always wanted to be a writer. And even though I have become just that and I love this work, my obsessive fears about "not being poor" have made it difficult for me to take time away from my other career, teaching and lecturing, to "just write." Susan Jeffers' book, *Feel the Fear and Do It Anyway,* has helped me to finally reach the point in my life where I can take time to "just write." Like many black women who do not come from privileged class backgrounds, who do not have family we can rely on to help if the financial going gets rough (we in fact are usually the people who are relied on), it feels very frightening to think about letting go of financial security, even for a short time, to do work one loves but may not pay the bills. In my case, even though I had worked with a self-created financial program aimed at bringing me to a point in life when I could focus solely on writing, I still found it hard to take time away. It was then that I had to tap into my deep fears of ending up poor and counter them with messages that affirm my ability to take care of myself economically irrespective of the circumstance. These fears are not irrational (though certainly mine were a bit extreme). In the last few years, I have witnessed several family members go from working as professionals to unemployment and various degrees of homelessness. Their experiences highlighted the reality that it is risky to be without secure employment and yet they also indicated that one could survive, even start all over again if need be.

My sister V. quit a job that allowed her to use excellent skills because she had major conflicts with her immediate supervisor. She quit because the level of on-the-job stress had become hazardous to her mental well-being. She quit confident that she would find a job in a few months. When that did not happen, she was stunned. It had not occurred to her that she would find it practically impossible to find work in the area she most wanted to live in. Confronting racism, sexism, and a host of other unclear responses, months passed and she has not found another job. It has changed her whole life. While material survival has been difficult, she is learning more about what really matters to her in life. She is learning about "right livelihood." The grace and skill with which she has confronted her circumstance has been a wonderful example for me. With therapy, with the help of friends and loved ones, she is discovering the work she would really like to do and no longer feels the need to have a high-paying, high-status job. And she has learned more about what it means to take risks.

In *Do What You Love, the Money Will Follow,* Sinetar cautions those of   15
us who have not been risk-takers to go slowly, to practice, to begin by taking small risks, and to plan carefully. Because I have planned carefully, I am able to finally take a year's leave from my teaching job without pay. During this time, I want to see if I enjoy working solely as a writer and if I can support myself. I want to see if (like those old-time black folks I talk about at the start of the essay) doing solely the work I feel most "called" to do will enhance my joy in living. For the past few months, I have been "just writing" and indeed, so far, I feel it is "work that makes life sweet."

The historical legacy of black women shows that we have worked hard, long, and well, yet rarely been paid what we deserve. We rarely get the recognition we deserve. However, even in the midst of domination, individual black women have found their calling, and do the work they are best suited for. Onnie Lee Logan, the Alabama midwife who tells her story in *Motherwit,* never went to high school or college, never made a lot of money in her working life, but listened to her inner voice and found her calling. Logan shares:

> I let God work the plan on my life and I am satisfied at what has happened to me in my life. The sun wasn't shinin' every time and moon wasn't either. I was in the snow and the rain at night by my lonely self. . . . There had been many dreary nights but I didn't look at em as dreary nights. I had my mind on where I was going and what I was going for.
>
> Whatever I've done, I've done as well as I could and beyond. . . . I'm satisfied at what has happened in my life. Perfectly satisfied at what my life has done for me. I was a good midwife. One of the best as they say. This book was the last thing I had planned to do until God said well

done. I consider myself—in fact if I leave tomorrow—I've lived my life and I've lived it well.

The life stories of black women like Onnie Logan remind us that "right livelihood" can be found irrespective of our class position, or the level of our education.

To know the work we are "called" to do in this world, we must know ourselves. The practice of "right livelihood" invites us to become more fully aware of our reality, of the labor we do and of the way we do it. Now that I have chosen my writing more fully than at any other moment of my life, the work itself feels more joyous. I feel my whole being affirmed in the act of writing. As black women unlearn the conventional thinking about work—which views money and/or status as more important than the work we do or the way we feel about that work—we will find our way back to those moments celebrated by our ancestors, when work was a passion. We will know again that "work makes life sweet."

QUESTIONING THE TEXT

1. hooks takes the term "right livelihood" from Marsha Sinetar's *Do What You Love, the Money Will Follow.*" Look at the way hooks defines this term and at the passages she quotes from Sinetar's book. Then list the people mentioned in hooks's essay who successfully practice "right livelihood." What do they have in common?

2. According to hooks, under what circumstances can "work make life sweet"? Do you accept the conditions she offers? Might there be other circumstances in which work could make someone's life sweet? After thinking carefully about your responses to these questions, write a paragraph arguing for or against hooks's claims.

MAKING CONNECTIONS

3. Read hooks's essay alongside the selection by Julia Carlisle and Florence Hoff (p. 691). Then, working with a classmate, consider how hooks might respond to both Carlisle's and Hoff's views on work. Write up a dialogue in which one of you gives hooks's response to Carlisle and the other gives hooks's response to Hoff.

4. Read Kenneth Brower's description of the work of photographers in "Photography in the Age of Falsification" (p. 554). Would Brower agree with hooks's definition of the kind of work that makes life sweet? Why, or why not?

JOINING THE CONVERSATION

5. In paragraph 6, hooks claims "[i]t is practically impossible to maintain a spirit of emotional well-being if one is daily doing work that is unsatisfying. . . ." Does this statement reflect your firsthand experience of work? Write a journal entry describing your work experience and explaining why it does or does not support hooks's claim. If you keep a reading log, write the entry there.

6. Imagine that you are applying for the job of your dreams, one that would indeed make your life sweet. Write a job announcement or advertisement for the position and bring it to class for discussion. Be prepared to explain your reasons for wanting this job as well as the ways you are—and are not—currently prepared for it.

7. Working with one or two classmates, discuss this slight revision of hooks's title: "Schoolwork Makes Life Sweet." Decide what conditions would need to exist for this statement to be accurate. Then, working together, write up a catalog description of the kind of schoolwork guaranteed to make life sweet. You may decide to take a humorous approach to this topic.

WALTER S. MINOT
Students Who Push Burgers

F OR ALMOST A GENERATION NOW, *the media have been examining the steady move-*
ment of women into the job market. But as Walter S. Minot observes in the following
selection, there's been relatively little comment on a related phenomenon: the growing
numbers of college students who also work full time (or nearly so), even while they
struggle to carry regular course loads. Students with jobs are, of course, nothing new—
especially at two-year schools where people routinely hold 40-hour-a-week employment
while taking classes. But most of those students rarely take more than one or two
courses each term.

As a teacher, I regret the academic opportunities that working students miss when
they hustle off to evening jobs. No arts performances, student activities, or guest lectures
for them. When they can, they squeeze in their assignments and reading during breaks.
But the course work suffers and learning becomes an ordeal. I worry, too, about their
physical well-being: I no longer take it personally when a red-eyed student slumps at a
desk or falls asleep in class. Chances are that he or she spent most of the previous
evening bussing tables or tending bar.

Part of the problem is that college has gotten so expensive that many students
can't afford not to work. Despite ample college loans, many students have little cash left
for living after taking care of tuition, fees, rent, books, computers, clothes, and food.
And most students do want to live a little higher up the ladder these days than previous
generations did. Gotta have that killer stereo, the Jeep, the Tag Heuer watch, and the
latest batch of music CDs. Oddly, if Minot is right, this grueling work ethic is acquired
not in college but in high school. And I think Minot, an English teacher himself, hits
uncomfortably close to the mark in his diagnosis—to judge by all the huffing and puff-
ing his essay evokes from my students. Minot clearly touches a nerve in "Students
Who Push Burgers," originally published in the Christian Science Monitor *(No-*
vember 22, 1988).
— J.R.

A college freshman squirms anxiously on a chair in my office, his eyes
avoiding mine, those of his English professor, as he explains that he hasn't finished his paper, which was due two days ago. "I just haven't had the time,"
he says.

"Are you carrying a heavy course load?"

"Fifteen hours," he says—a normal load.

"Are you working a lot?"

"No, sir, not much. About 30 hours a week." 5

"That's a lot. Do you have to work that much?"

"Yeah, I have to pay for my car."

"Do you really need a car?"

"Yeah, I need it to get to work."

This student isn't unusual. Indeed, he probably typifies today's college   10
and high school students. Yet in all the lengthy analyses of what's wrong with
American education, I have not heard employment by students being blamed.

I have heard drugs blamed and television—that universal scapegoat. I
have heard elaborate theories about the decline of the family, of religion, and
of authority, as well as other sociological theories. But nobody blames student
employment. The world seems to have accepted the part-time job as a normal
feature of adolescence. A parochial school in my town even had a day to
honor students who held regular jobs, and parents often endorse this employment by claiming that it teaches kids the value of the dollar.

But such employment is a major cause of educational decline. To argue
my case, I will rely on memories of my own high school days and contrast
them with what I see today. Though I do have some statistical evidence, my
argument depends on what anyone over 40 can test through memory and direct observation.

When I was in high school in the 1950s, students seldom held jobs.
Some of us babysat, shoveled snow, mowed lawns, and delivered papers, and
some of us got jobs in department stores around Christmas. But most of us
had no regular source of income other than the generosity of our parents.

The only kids who worked regularly were poor. They worked to help
their families. If I remember correctly, only about five people in my class of
170 held jobs. That was in a working-class town in New England. As for the
rest of us, our parents believed that going to school and helping around the
house were our work.

In contrast, in 1986 my daughter was one of the few students among ju-   15
niors and seniors who didn't work. According to Bureau of Labor statistics,
more than 40 percent of high school students were working in 1980, but sociologist Ellen Greenberger and Laurence Steinberg in "When Teenagers
Work" came up with estimates of more than 70 percent working in 1986,
though I suspect that the figure may be even higher now.

My daughter, however, did not work; her parents wouldn't let her. Interestingly, some of the students in her class implied that she had an unfair advantage over them in the classroom. They were probably right, for while she
was home studying they were pushing burgers, waiting on tables, or selling
dresses 20 hours a week. Working students have little time for homework.

I attended a public high school, while she attended a Roman Catholic
preparatory school whose students were mainly middle class. By the standards
of my day, her classmates did not "have to" work. Yet many of them were
working 20 to 30 hours a week. Why?

They worked so that they could spend $60 to $100 a week on designer
jeans, rock concerts, stereo and video systems, and, of course, cars. They were
living lives of luxury, buying items on which their parents refused to throw

hard-earned money away. Though the parent would not buy such tripe for their kids, the parents somehow convinced themselves that the kids were learning the value of money. Yet, according to Ms. Greenberger and Mr. Steinberg, only about a quarter of those students saved money for college or other long-term goals.

How students spend their money is their business, not mine. But as a teacher, I have witnessed the effects of employment. I know that students who work all evening aren't ready for studying when they get home from work. Moreover, because they work so hard and have ready cash, they feel that they deserve to have fun—instead of spending all their free time studying.

Thus, by the time they get to college, most students look upon studies as   20 a spare-time activity. A survey at Pennsylvania State University showed that most freshmen believed they could maintain a B average by studying about 20 hours a week. (I can remember when college guidebooks advised two to three hours of studying for every hour in class—30 to 45 hours a week.)

Clearly individual students will pay the price for lack of adequate time studying, but the problem goes beyond the individual. It extends to schools and colleges that are finding it difficult to demand quantity or quality of work from students.

Perhaps the reason American education has declined so markedly is because America has raised a generation of part-time students. And perhaps our economy will continue to decline as full-time students from Japan and Europe continue to out-perform our part-time students.

QUESTIONING THE TEXT

1. Minot claims that more than 70 percent of high school students in the United States have jobs. Conduct an in-class survey to test the accuracy of this observation. Also gather some statistics on college students: what percentages of the students in your writing class currently work part time, full time, or not at all?

2. Not many years ago, it was unusual for college students—especially those in their first or second year—to have cars on campus. How many students in your writing class have their own car? Is a car absolutely necessary for most students? Write an essay exploring these questions.

MAKING CONNECTIONS

3. In "The Idea of a University" (p. 46), John Henry Newman champions a well-rounded education, one that prepares students for all occasions in life. Do you think that working while in school contributes to or de-

tracts from the ideal of a liberal education? Discuss the question in a group and then, working independently, write a position paper in which you take a side on the issue.

4. Does the number of students working while in school contribute to campus problems with cheating? Review Mark Clayton's "A Whole Lot of Cheatin' Going On" (p. 185) and then write an essay examining cause-effect relationships between cheating and work. Might there be any? Why, or why not?

JOINING THE CONVERSATION

5. Write a critical analysis of Minot's essay based on your own experiences as a student who has or has not worked while in school. Be specific in citing Minot's claims and the cause-effect relationships he draws upon.

MARGE PIERCY
To Be of Use

Marge Piercy (b. 1936) is remarkable by any standard: she is the author of over two dozen books of poetry (including The Moon Is Always Female *[1980] and* Mars and Her Children *[1992]) and fiction (including* Going Down Fast *[1969],* Woman on the Edge of Time *[1976],* Fly Away Home *[1984], and* He, She, and It *[1991]); a political activist (she helped organize Students for a Democratic Society in the 1960s); an ardent feminist; and a constant social critic. Piercy writes with passion and power that are hard to ignore. Often, her passion for justice and equity as well as for what she calls "work that is real" is born of hard experience. The child of often poor and working-class parents, Piercy (who is white and Jewish) grew up in a predominantly African American section of Detroit, where she learned firsthand about what she calls "the indifference of the rich, racism . . . the working-class pitted against itself." The first member of her family to attend college, she won a scholarship and graduated from the University of Michigan; she has contributed her prolific collection of manuscripts to its graduate library.*

Many of Piercy's poems get their power from a kind of pent-up rage that explodes on the page in front of her readers. In fact, I first got to know her work through just such poems, a number of which (like "Barbie Doll," which appeared in the first edition of this book) haunt me still. But Piercy can be hopeful, even celebratory, as well. And in the following poem from To Be of Use *(1973), she is both, defining in vivid images and rhythmic cadences "work that is real." This is one of only four poems I carry with me always.* —A.L.

> The people I love the best
> jump into work head first
> without dallying in the shallows
> and swim off with sure strokes almost out of sight.
> They seem to become natives of that element, 5
> the black sleek heads of seals
> bouncing like half-submerged balls.
>
> I love people who harness themselves, an ox to a heavy cart,
> who pull like water buffalo, with massive patience,
> who strain in the mud and the muck to move things forward, 10
> who do what has to be done, again and again.
>
> I want to be with people who submerge
> in the task, who go into the fields to harvest

and work in a row and pass the bags along,
who stand in the line and haul in their places,   15
who are not parlor generals and field deserters
but move in a common rhythm
when the food must come in or the fire be put out.

The work of the world is common as mud.
Botched, it smears the hands, crumbles to dust.   20
But the thing worth doing well done
has a shape that satisfies, clean and evident.
Greek amphoras for wine or oil,
Hopi vases that held corn, are put in museums
but you know they were made to be used.   25
The pitcher cries for water to carry
and a person for work that is real.

IN RESPONSE

1. Piercy says work that is worth doing "has a shape that satisfies, clean and evident." Think for a while about examples you could give of such work. Reflect on them and on your relationship to and feelings about them in a journal entry. If you keep a reading log, record your responses there.

2. Try your hand at adding a stanza to this poem, after the second stanza. Begin with the words "I love people who . . ." Bring your stanza to class to share with others.

3. Which writers in this chapter might Piercy see as doing "work that is real"? In a brief exploratory essay, give reasons for your choices.

OTHER READINGS

Baida, Peter. *Poor Richard's Legacy: American Business Values from Benjamin Franklin to Donald Trump.* New York: Morrow, 1990. Examines the history of American attitudes toward enterprise and labor.

Bridges, William. *Job Shift: How to Prosper in a Workplace without Jobs.* Reading, MA: Addison, 1994. Argues that although "good, steady jobs" are declining, people can rethink work. Includes a career guide for the twenty-first century.

Friedman, Milton. *Capitalism and Freedom.* Chicago: U of Chicago P, 1962. (With Rose D. Friedman). Classic defense of free enterprise.

Hochschild, Arlie. *The Second Shift: Working Parents and the Revolution at Home.* New York: Viking, 1989. Case studies that reveal the difficulties of balancing work inside and outside the home.

Michelson, Maureen R., ed. *Women and Work: In Their Own Words.* Troutdale, OR: NewSage, 1994. Includes short autobiographical stories by working women and essays on women's work in the 1990s.

Richmond, Lewis. *Work as a Spiritual Practice: A Practical Buddhist Approach to Inner Growth and Satisfaction on the Job.* New York: Broadway Books, 1999. Suggestions for becoming more aware, awake, and engaged in one's work life.

Shields, Cydney, and Leslie C. Shields. *Work, Sister, Work: How Black Women Can Get Ahead in Today's Business Environment.* New York: Simon, 1994. A guide, especially for African American women, for attaining career goals and navigating corporate culture.

Snyder, Gary. "On the Path, Off the Trail." *The Practice of the Wild.* San Francisco: North Point, 1990. Uses paths and trails as metaphors for work, claiming that skills and work are reflections of the order found in nature.

ELECTRONIC RESOURCES

http://www.cei.org/
Site of the Competitive Enterprise Institute, which champions free enterprise and opposes government regulation of businesses and workplaces.

http://www.4adodge.com/viper/frameset_viper.html
Presents the Dodge Viper, the car Robert Lutz describes in "The Primary Purpose of Business Is Not to Make Money."

http://www.dol.gov
Provides information about the Department of Labor.

http://www.womenswire.com/work
Provides links to resources for working women.

Acknowledgments (continued from p. iv)

Fred Barnes. "Me and My Cars." © 1992 The New Republic Inc. Reprinted by permission of *The New Republic*, June 1, 1992.

Dave Barry. "Guys vs. Men." From *Dave Barry's Complete Guide to Guys*. Copyright © 1995 by Dave Barry. Reprinted with the permission of Random House, Inc.

J. Michael Bishop. "Enemies of Promise." From *The Wilson Quarterly* (Summer 1995). Copyright © 1995 by J. Michael Bishop. Reprinted by permission of the author.

Anthony Brandt. "Do Kids Need Religion?" From *Parenting* (December 1987). Copyright © 1987 by Anthony Brandt. Reprinted by permission of the author.

Reilly Brennan. "Would You Buy a Car from This Man?" From *Automobile* magazine, February 1999. Reprinted by permission.

David Brooks. "Conscientious Consumption." From *The New Yorker*, November 23, 1998. Reprinted by permission of David Brooks.

Gwendolyn Brooks. "We Real Cool." From *Blacks* by Gwendolyn Brooks. Copyright © 1991 by Gwendolyn Brooks. Published by Third World Press, Chicago, Ill. Reprinted by permission of the author.

Kenneth Brower. "Photography in the Age of Falsification." From *The Atlantic Monthly*, May 1998. Copyright © 1998 by Kenneth Brower. Reprinted by permission of the author.

Stephen L. Carter. "The Rules about the Rules." From *Integrity* by Stephen L. Carter. Copyright © 1996 by Stephen L. Carter. Reprinted by permission of Basic Books, a member of Perseus Books L.L.C.

Ward Churchill. "Crimes against Humanity." From *Z Magazine*, March 1993. Copyright © 1993 by Ward Churchill. Reprinted by permission of the author.

Mark Clayton. "A Whole Lot of Cheatin' Going On." Copyright © 1999 The Christian Science Publishing Society. Reproduced with permission. All rights reserved.

Stephanie Coontz. "The Way We Wish We Were." From *The Way We Never Were* by Stephanie Coontz. © 1992 by Stephanie Coontz. Reprinted by permission of Basic Books, a member of Perseus Books, L.L.C.

Joan Didion. "On Morality." From *Slouching Towards Bethlehem* by Joan Didion. Copyright © 1968 and copyright renewed © 1996 by Joan Didion. Reprinted by permission of Farrar, Straus, & Giroux, L.L.C.

Bruce Feiler. "Gone Country." From *The New Republic*, February 5, 1996, pp. 19–24. © Bruce Feiler. Reprinted by permission of the author. Song excerpts courtesy of respective publishers.

Jill Frawley. "Inside the Home." From *Mother Jones* (1991). Copyright © 1991 by Foundation for National Progress. Reprinted with the permission of *Mother Jones*.

Henry Louis Gates Jr. "Net Worth." Originally published in *The New Yorker*, June 1, 1998. Copyright © 1998 by Henry Louis Gates Jr. Reprinted with permission of the author.

Carol Gilligan. "Concepts of Self and Morality." From *In a Different Voice* by Carol Gilligan. Copyright © 1982, 1993 by Carol Gilligan. Reprinted by permission of Harvard University Press, Cambridge, Mass.

Reverend Peter J. Gomes. "Civic Virtue and the Character of Followership: A New Take on an Old Hope." The Reverend Professor Peter J. Gomes, *Plummer Professor of Christian Morals and Pusey Minister in The Memorial Church, Harvard University*, is Preacher to Harvard University. All rights reserved.

Jeffrey Hart. "How to Get a College Education." From *National Review*, September 30, 1996, pp. 34–40. © 1996 by National Review, Inc., 215 Lexington Ave., New York, NY 10016. Reprinted by permission.

bell hooks. "Work Makes Life Sweet." From *Sisters of the Yam*, pp. 41–52. Copyright © 1993 by bell hooks. "Keeping Close to Home, Class and Education" from *Talking Back*, pp. 73–83. Copyright © 1989 by bell hooks. Reprinted by permission of South End Press.

Langston Hughes. "Theme for English B." From *The Collected Poems of Langston Hughes*, edited by Arnold Rampersad and David Roessel. Copyright © 1926 and renewed 1958 by Langston Hughes. Reprinted with the permission of Alfred A. Knopf, Inc.

Zora Neale Hurston. "How It Feels to Be Colored Me." From *The World Tomorrow* 11 (May 1928). Copyright © 1929 by Zora Neale Hurston. Renewed © 1956 by John C. Hurston. Later published in *I Love Myself When I'm Laughing,* edited by Alice Walker. New York: Feminist Press (1973).

Martin Luther King Jr. "Letter from Birmingham Jail." Copyright © 1963 by Martin Luther King Jr. Copyright renewed 1991 by Coretta Scott King. Reprinted by arrangement with The Heirs to the Estate of Martin Luther King Jr., c/o Writers House, Inc. as agent for the proprietor.

Robert D. King. "Should English Be the Law?" © 1997 Robert D. King. First published in *The Atlantic Monthly,* April 1997. Reprinted by permission of the author.

Maxine Hong Kingston. "No Name Woman." From *The Woman Warrior* by Maxine Hong Kingston. Copyright © 1975 by Maxine Hong Kingston. Reprinted with the permission of Alfred A. Knopf, Inc.

Georgina Kleege. "Call It Blindness." From *The Yale Review* 82, no. 2, April 1994. Copyright © 1994 by Georgina Kleege. Reprinted with the permission of the author.

Arthur Krystal. "Who Speaks for the Lazy?" From *The New Yorker,* April 26 and May 3, 1999. Copyright © 1999 by Arthur Krystal. Reprinted by permission of the author.

Meridel LeSueur. Excerpt from *Women and Work: In Their Own Words* by Maureen R. Michelson, ed. Copyright © 1994 by Maureen R. Michelson. Reprinted with permission of New Sage Press.

Robert A. Lutz. "The Primary Purpose of Business Is Not to Make Money." From *GUTS: The Seven Laws of Business That Made Chrysler the World's Hottest Car Company.* Copyright © 1998. Reprinted by permission of John Wiley & Company, Inc.

Ed Madden. "Family Cemetery, near Hickory Ridge, Arkansas." Reprinted with permission of the author.

Emily Martin. "The Body at War." Excerpt from *Flexible Bodies* by Emily Martin. Copyright © 1994 by Emily Martin. Reprinted by permission of Beacon Press, Boston.

Walter S. Minot. "Students Who Push Burgers." Reprinted by permission of the author.

Kathleen Norris. "Little Girls in Church." From *Little Girls in Church* by Kathleen Norris. © 1995. Reprinted by permission of The University of Pittsburgh Press.

Todd Oppenheimer. "The Computer Delusion." Originally published in *The Atlantic Monthly,* July 1997, pp. 42–62. Copyright © 1997 by Todd Oppenheimer. Permission granted by The Rhoda Weyr Agency, New York.

Marge Piercy. "To Be of Use." From *Circles on the Water* by Marge Piercy. Copyright © 1982 by Marge Piercy. Reprinted with the permission of Alfred A. Knopf, Inc.

Neil Postman. "The Great Symbol Drain." From *Technopoly* by Neil Postman. Copyright © 1993 by Neil Postman. Reprinted by permission of Alfred A. Knopf, Inc.

James Prosek. "Trout." From *Trout* by James Prosek. Copyright © 1996 by James Prosek. Reprinted by permission of Alfred A. Knopf, Inc.

Adrienne Rich. "What Does a Woman Need to Know?" From *Blood, Bread, and Poetry: Selected Prose 1979–1985* by Adrienne Rich. Copyright © 1986 by Adrienne Rich. Reprinted by permission of the author and W.W. Norton & Company, Inc.

Jeremy Rifkin. "Biotech Century." Excerpt from *Biotech Century: Harnessing the Gene and Remaking the World* by Jeremy Rifkin. Copyright © 1998 by Jeremy Rifkin. Reprinted by permission of Penguin Putnam.

Mike Rose. "Lives on the Boundary." From "Crossing Boundaries" in *Lives on the Boundary: The Struggles and Achievements of America's Underprepared* by Mike Rose. Copyright © 1989 by Mike Rose. Reprinted with the permission of The Free Press, a Division of Simon & Schuster, Inc.

Pamela Samuelson. "The Digital Rights War." From *The Wilson Quarterly,* Autumn 1998, pp. 48–53. © Pamela Samuelson, 1998. Reprinted by permission of the author.

Wendy Shalit. Abridgment of Chapter 12, "Beyond Maturity," pp. 231–38, in *A Return to Modesty: Discovering the Lost Virtue* by Wendy Shalit. Copyright © 1999 by Wendy Shalit. Reprinted by permission of the author and The Free Press, a Division of Simon & Schuster.

Alex Shoumatoff. "The Navajo Way." From *Men's Journal,* November 1998. © 1998 by Men's Journal Company, L.P. Reprinted by permission. All rights reserved.

Barbara Smith. "Home." From *Home Girls: A Black Feminist Anthology* by Barbara Smith, ed. Copyright © 1983 by Barbara Smith. Reprinted with permission of the author.

Jon Spayde. "Learning in the Key of Life." From *Utne Reader*, May/June 1998. Reprinted by permission of the author.

Shelby Steele. "The Recoloring of Campus Life." From *The Content of Our Character* by Shelby Steele. Copyright © 1990 by Shelby Steele. Reprinted by permission of St. Martin's Press, L.L.C.

Mitchell Stephens. "By Means of the Visible." From *The Rise of the Image, The Fall of the Word* by Mitchell Stephens. Copyright © 1998 by Mitchell Stephens. Used by permission of Oxford University Press, Inc.

Andrew Sullivan. "What Are Homosexuals For?" From *Virtually Normal: An Argument about Homosexuality* by Andrew Sullivan. Copyright © 1995 by Andrew Sullivan. Reprinted with the permission of Alfred A. Knopf, Inc.

Ron Suskind. Excerpt from *A Hope in the Unseen* by Ron Suskind. Copyright © 1998 by Ron Suskind. Used by permission of Broadway Books, a division of Random House, Inc.

Margaret Talbot. "Les Très Riches Heures de Martha Stewart." Reprinted by permission of *The New Republic*, May 13, 1996. © 1996 The New Republic, Inc.

David Thomas. "The Mind of Man." Excerpt from *Not Guilty* by David Thomas. Copyright © 1993 by David Thomas. Reprinted by permission.

Sherry Turkle. "Who *Am* We?" From *Wired*, January 1996. Copyright © 1996 by Sherry Turkle. Reprinted by permission of the author.

John Updike. "The Mystery of Mickey Mouse." From *The Art of Mickey Mouse*, edited by Craig Yoe and Janet Morra-Yoe. Introduction by John Updike. Copyright © 1991 The Walt Disney Company. Introduction copyright © John Updike. Published by Hyperion. Reprinted by permission.

Alice Walker. "My Heart Has Reopened to You." From *Her Blue Body: Everything We Know, Earthling Poems 1965–1990.* Copyright © 1991 by Alice Walker. Reprinted by permission of Harcourt, Inc.

Linda Watts. Review of *Inside the Mouse: Work and Play at Disneyworld.* From "Teaching Notes" in *Radical Teacher 50* (1997): 43–44. Reprinted by permission of Radical Teacher.

Barbara Dafoe Whitehead. "The Making of a Divorce Culture." From *The Divorce Culture* by Barbara Dafoe Whitehead. Copyright © 1996 by Barbara Dafoe Whitehead. Reprinted by permission of Alfred A. Knopf, Inc.

Terry Tempest Williams. "The Clan of One-Breasted Women." From *Refuge: An Unnatural History of Family and Place* by Terry Tempest Williams. Originally published in *Northern Lights*, January 1990. Copyright © 1990 by Terry Tempest Williams. Reprinted by permission of Pantheon Books, a division of Random House, Inc.

Edward O. Wilson. "The Biological Basis of Morality." From *Consilience* by Edward O. Wilson. Copyright © 1998 by Edward O. Wilson. Reprinted by permission of Alfred A. Knopf, Inc., a Division of Random House, Inc.

James Q. Wilson. "Cars and Their Enemies." Reprinted from *Commentary*, July 1997, by permission of the author and the publisher. All rights reserved.

W. B. Yeats. "The Second Coming." From *The Poems of W. B. Yeats*, a New Edition, by Richard J. Finneran, editor. Copyright © 1924 by Macmillan Publishing Company. Renewed 1952 by Bertha Georgie Yeats. Reprinted with the permission of Simon & Schuster, Inc.

Cover Photo Acknowledgments

Wendy Shalit: © Susan Shacter/Corbis Outline; *Maxine Hong Kingston:* Tony Barboza/Ken Barboza Associates; *Dave Barry:* Michael Ferguson/Globe Photos; *Michael Jordan:* Allsport USA; *bell hooks:* Rose Hartman/Globe Photos; *James Prosek:* Michael Marsland/Yale University Office of Public Affairs; *Martha Stewart:* © Matthew Jordan Smith/Corbis Outline.

Chapter Opener Photos

Chapter 3: Student photo page from *A Student Prospectus*, courtesy of the University of Chicago; *Chapter 4:* Corbis-Bettmann; *Chapter 5:* Henry Groskinsky/Life Magazine; *Chapter 6:* David de Lossy/ The Image Bank; *Chapter 7:* AP/Wide World Photos; *Chapter 8:* © FPG International LLC; *Chapter 9:* © FPG International LLC.

Color Insert

(1) Archive Photos; (2) "My Name Is Katy," *Wired,* March 1998 cover. Copyright © 1999 The Conde Nast Publications, Inc. All rights reserved. Used with permission. Photo, courtesy Eric Tucker Photography and Ford Models, Los Angeles, CA; (3) AP/Wide World Photos; (4) Allsport USA/All rights reserved; (5) AP/Wide World Photos; (6) © 1999 Artisan Pictures Inc. All Rights Reserved.

Chapter Photos

Chapter 3: University "Mission" Web sites: **p. 52** © 1998 by the Regents of the University of Minnesota. **53** Moorehouse College. **54** The Evergreen State College. **55** California State University, Monterey Bay. **56** Thomas Aquinas College, Santa Paula, California. Reprinted by permission. **59** Anthony Karlic. © 1998. *Chapter 4:* **186** Courtesy Joe Rocco. **202** © The New Yorker Collection 1998 Michael Crawford from Cartoonbank.com. All rights reserved. *Chapter 5:* **246–47** Illustration by T. Majewski. **288** © 1988 Time, Inc. Reprinted by permission. **293** Copyright © 1989 John Benziger. Reprinted by permission. **295** From L. DeSchepper, *Peak Immunity,* 1989, pp. 15-16. Reprinted by permission. **296** From D. Cherry, "AIDS Virus," in *Risky Business,* 1988, p. 5. Reprinted by permission of the publisher and the San Francisco AIDS Foundation. *Chapter 6:* **410** Courtesy Mel Lindstrom Photography, Inc. **437** Gwendolen Cates/CPI. *Chapter 7:* **475–76** Danger symbol photo by Mitchell Stephens; Apple file-folder icon, courtesy of Apple Computer Inc.; Sistine ceiling, Corbis-Bettmann; NASA plaque (NASA). **562–63** © Istvan Banyai. **570** © Joseph Holmes 1999. *Chapter 8:* **656** Courtesy of Mimi Lipton, "Stacking Wood" (Thames & Hudson, 1993). *Chapter 9:* **698** © Peter Till. **707** Photo by Reilly Brennan. Reprinted by permission of *Automobile* magazine.

Acknowledging sources, 35

Advertisements, 8–9

"Ain't I a Woman?" (Truth), 347–48

"Allegory of the Cave" (Plato), 467–72

Analysis, 6–7, 19–21

Analysis, critical, 20–21
  assignments
    education, 91
    identities, 420
    images, 553, 579–80
    moralities, 190
    work, 711, 729
  readings
    "Allegory of the Cave" (Plato), 467–72
    "Enemies of Promise" (Bishop), 237–43
    "Letter from Birmingham Jail" (King),
      142–56
    "The Mind of Man" (Thomas), 120–25
    "Photography in the Age of Falsifica-
      tion" (Brower), 554–74

Analysis, rhetorical, 20
  assignments
    education, 91
  readings
    "The Body at War: Media Views of the
      Immune System" (Martin), 286–302
    "Crimes against Humanity" (Churchill),
      497–505
    "The Mystery of Mickey Mouse" (Up-
      dike), 489–96
    "Net Worth" (Gates), 532–53
    "Les Très Riches Heures de Martha
      Stewart" (Talbot), 657–67

Annotating, 6

Arendt, Hannah, 35

Argument, 21–22
  assignments
    education, 64, 92, 104, 118
    home, 595, 626, 644, 667
    identities, 348, 360, 421
    moralities, 213
    science and technology, 253, 314, 321
    work, 724

  readings
    "Biotech Century: Playing Ecological
      Roulette with Mother Nature's De-
      signs" (Rifkin), 244–54
    "Cars and Their Enemies" (Wilson),
      303–14
    "The Computer Delusion" (Oppen-
      heimer), 255–85
    "Crimes against Humanity" (Churchill),
      497–505
    "Enemies of Promise" (Bishop), 237–43
    "The Future of Modesty" (Shalit),
      214–21
    "Letter from Birmingham Jail" (King),
      142–56
    "The Recoloring of Campus Life"
      (Steele), 72–92
    "Should English Be the Law?" (King),
      409–21
    "What Are Homosexuals For?" (Sulli-
      van), 350–60
    "What Does a Woman Need to
      Know?" (Rich), 65–71

"Ask Martha: Guest Towels," 654–55

Assignment, considering the, 14

Audience, 14–15

Barnes, Fred, "Quantity Time," 649–53

Barry, Dave, "Guys vs. Men," 372–83

"Biological Basis of Morality, The"
  (Wilson), 322–40

"Biotech Century: Playing Ecological
  Roulette with Mother Nature's Designs" (Rifkin), 244–54

Bishop, J. Michael, "Enemies of Promise,"
  237–43

"Body at War, The: Media Views of the Immune System" (Martin), 286–302

Brainstorming, 22
  assignments
    education, 57, 119
    identities, 407, 457, 458, 461
    images, 472, 552

Brainstorming *(cont.)*
  assignments
    science and technology, 236, 253
Brandt, Anthony, "Do Kids Need Religion?"
    191–99
Brennan, Reilly, "Would You Buy a Car from
    This Man?" 706–11
Brooks, David, "Conscientious Consumption,"
    200–204
Brooks, Gwendolyn, "We Real Cool," 133–34
Brower, Kenneth, "Photography in the Age of
    Falsification," 554–74
"'By Means of the Visible': A Picture's Worth"
    (Stephens), 473–88

California State University, Monterey Bay, mis-
    sion statement, 55
"Call It Blindness" (Kleege), 389–408
Carlisle, Julia, "Young, Privileged, and Unem-
    ployed" (with Hoff), 691–96
"Cars and Their Enemies" (Wilson), 303–14
Carter, Stephen L., "The Rules about the
    Rules," 157–68
Charts, 8
Churchill, Ward, "Crimes against Humanity,"
    497–505
"Civic Virtue and the Character of Follower-
    ship" (Gomes), 205–13
"Clan of One-Breasted Women, The"
    (Williams), 607–18
Clayton, Mark, "A Whole Lot of Cheatin'
    Going On," 185–90
Collaboration, 35–36
Comparing and contrasting, 22–23
  assignments
    education, 91, 132
    home, 606, 644
    images, 505, 512
    moralities, 199, 203, 212
    science and technology, 236, 313
    work, 685
  readings
    "Allegory of the Cave" (Plato), 467–72
    "The Biological Basis of Morality" (Wil-
      son), 322–40
    "'By Means of the Visible': A Picture's
      Worth" (Stephens), 473–88
    "Cars and Their Enemies" (Wilson),
      303–14
    "Conscientious Consumption" (Brooks),
      200–204
    "Guys vs. Men" (Barry), 372–83

"How It Feels to Be Colored Me"
    (Hurston), 384–88
"Keeping Close to Home: Class and Edu-
    cation" (hooks), 93–104
"Lives on the Boundary" (Rose), 105–19
"The Mind of Man" (Thomas), 120–25
"Photography in the Age of Falsification"
    (Brower), 554–74
"The Recoloring of Campus Life" (Steele),
    72–92
"The Way We Wish We Were" (Coontz),
    628–44
"Computer Delusion, The" (Oppenheimer),
    255–85
"Concepts of Self and Morality" (Gilligan),
    169–78
Connor, Tom, "Well-Stacked Logs" (with
    Downey), 656
"Conscientious Consumption" (Brooks),
    200–204
Coontz, Stephanie, "The Way We Wish We
    Were," 628–44
"Crimes against Humanity" (Churchill),
    497–505
Critical analysis, 20–21
Critical reading
  defined, 1–2
  determining whether you are a critical reader,
    3–5
  how to become a more critical
    reader, 5–7
  of online texts, 4, 9–10
  reasons for, 2–3
  saying *yes, no,* and *maybe* and, 2
  of visual texts, 8–9
  writing and, 10–11
Critical response essay, sample, 37–40

Definition, 23–24
  assignments
    education, 64, 104
    home, 595, 600, 606, 627, 647, 648, 669
    identities, 383
    moralities, 156, 168, 177, 199
    science and technology, 302, 320, 339
    work, 695, 704, 705, 724
  readings
    "Ain't I a Woman" (Truth), 347–48
    "Call It Blindness" (Kleege), 389–408
    "Concepts of Self and Morality" (Gilligan),
      169–78
    "Guys vs. Men" (Barry), 372–83

"Learning in the Key of Life" (Spayde),
58–64
"On Morality" (Didion), 179–84
"The Rules about the Rules" (Carter),
157–68
"Who Speaks for the Lazy?" (Krystal),
697–705
Description, 24
assignments
education, 91, 118
identities, 359, 388, 408, 421, 440,
458, 460
images, 487
work, 686, 725
readings
"A Hope in the Unseen" (Suskind),
588–95
"Home" (Smith), 601–6
"How It Feels to Be Colored Me"
(Hurston), 384–88
"Introduction to *Trout*" (Prosek), 506–12
"Lives on the Boundary" (Rose), 105–19
Mission statements (various colleges),
51–57
"The Navajo Way" (Shoumatoff), 433–40
"Net Worth" (Gates), 532–53
"The Place Where I Was Born" (Walker),
596–600
Dialogue, 24–25
assignments
education, 71
home, 606
identities, 360, 388, 408, 457
images, 472
moralities, 190, 221
work, 686, 695, 716, 724
readings
"Allegory of the Cave" (Plato), 467–72
"A Hope in the Unseen" (Suskind),
588–95
"The Way to Wealth" (Franklin), 678–86
Didion, Joan, "On Morality," 179–84
"Digital Rights War, The" (Samuelson), 315–21
"Do Kids Need Religion?" (Brandt), 191–99
Downey, Jim, "Well-Stacked Logs" (with
Connor), 656
Drafting, 16
Drawings, 8–9

Editing, 18
Editorials and op-ed pieces
assignments
education, 71

home, 595
moralities, 184
science and technology, 314
Education, 43–136
"How to Get a College Education" (Hart),
126–32
"The Idea of a University" (Newman), 46–50
"Keeping Close to Home: Class and Educa-
tion" (hooks), 93–104
"Learning in the Key of Life" (Spayde), 58–64
"Lives on the Boundary" (Rose), 105–19
"The Mind of Man" (Thomas), 120–25
Mission statements from the University of
Minnesota; Morehouse College; The
Evergreen State College; California State
University, Monterey Bay; and Thomas
Aquinas College, 51–57
"The Recoloring of Campus Life" (Steele),
72–91
"We Real Cool" (Brooks), 133–34
"What Does a Woman Need to Know?"
(Rich), 65–71
"Enemies of Promise" (Bishop), 237–43
Evaluation
assignments
education, 50
home, 594
images, 488
moralities, 213, 220
science and technology, 243, 313
readings
"The Computer Delusion" (Oppen-
heimer), 255–85
"Crimes against Humanity" (Churchill),
497–505
"Enemies of Promise" (Bishop), 237–43
"How to Get a College Education" (Hart),
126–32
"Inside the Home" (Frawley), 645–48
"Net Worth" (Gates), 532–53
"The Primary Purpose of Business Is Not
to Make Money" (Lutz), 712–16
"The Recoloring of Campus Life" (Steele),
72–92
"Les Très Riches Heures de Martha
Stewart" (Talbot), 657–67
"We Real Cool" (Brooks), 133
"What Does a Woman Need to Know?"
(Rich), 65–71
of sources, 32–33
writing an, 25
Evergreen State College mission
statement, 54

Exploratory writing, 25–26
  assignments
    education, 50, 132
    home, 627, 653
    identities, 360, 421, 432, 440
    images, 471, 487–88, 496, 511, 553
    moralities, 168, 178, 184, 203, 212, 221
    science and technology, 235, 253, 314
    work, 705, 716, 728, 731
  readings
    "Allegory of the Cave" (Plato), 467–72
    "The Biological Basis of Morality"
      (Wilson), 322–40
    "Call It Blindness" (Kleege), 389–408
    "Civic Virtue and the Character of Follow-
      ership" (Gomes), 205–13
    "The Clan of One-Breasted Women"
      (Williams), 607–18
    "Do Kids Need Religion?" (Brandt), 191–99
    "Home" (Smith), 601–6
    "How It Feels to Be Colored Me"
      (Hurston), 384–88
    "The Idea of a University" (Newman), 46
    "Keeping Close to Home" Class and Edu-
      cation" (hooks), 93–104
    "Learning in the Key of Life" (Spayde),
      58–64
    "On Morality" (Didion), 179–84
    "Photography in the Age of Falsification"
      (Brower), 554–74
    "Quantity Time" (Barnes), 649–53
    "What Are Homosexuals For?" (Sullivan),
      350–60
    "What Does a Woman Need to Know?"
      (Rich), 65–71
    "Who Speaks for the Lazy?" (Krystal),
      697–705

"Family Cemetery, near Hickory Ridge,
    Arkansas" (Madden), 668–70
Feedback, 17
Feiler, Bruce, "Gone Country," 422–32
Final version, 18–19
"Frankenstein" (Shelley), 231–36
Franklin, Benjamin, "The Way to Wealth,"
    678–86
Frawley, Jill, "Inside the Home," 645–48
Freewriting, 26
  assignments
    education, 91, 103, 125, 132
    home, 618
    identities, 371, 439
    science and technology, 236, 243, 285
"Future of Modesty, The" (Shalit), 214–21

Gates, Henry Louis Jr., "Net Worth," 532–53
Gilligan, Carol, "Concepts of Self and Moral-
    ity," 169–78
Gomes, Peter J., "Civic Virtue and the Charac-
    ter of Followership," 205–13
"Gone Country" (Feiler), 422–32
Graphs, 8
"Great Symbol Drain, The" (Postman), 513–32
"Guys vs. Men" (Barry), 372–83

Hart, Jeffrey, "How to Get a College Educa-
    tion," 126–32
Hoff, Florence, "Young, Privileged, and Unem-
    ployed" (with Carlisle), 691–96
Home, 585–672
    "Ask Martha: Guest Towels," 654–55
    "The Clan of One-Breasted Women"
      (Williams), 607–18
    "Family Cemetery, near Hickory Ridge,
      Arkansas" (Madden), 668–70
    "Home" (Smith), 601–6
    "A Hope in the Unseen" (Suskind), 588–95
    "Inside the Home" (Frawley), 645–48
    "The Making of a Divorce Culture"
      (Whitehead), 619–27
    "The Place Where I Was Born" (Walker),
      596
    "Quantity Time" (Barnes), 649–53
    "Les Très Riches Heures de Martha Stewart"
      (Talbot), 657–67
    "The Way We Wish We Were" (Coontz),
      628–44
    "Well-Stacked Logs" (Connor and Downey),
      656
"Home" (Smith), 601–6
hooks, bell
    "Keeping Close to Home: Class and Educa-
      tion," 93–104
    "Work Makes Life Sweet," 717–25
"Hope in the Unseen, A" (Suskind), 588–95
"How to Get a College Education" (Hart),
    126–32
"How It Feels to Be Colored Me" (Hurston),
    384–88
Hughes, Langston, "Theme for English B,"
    459–61
Hurston, Zora Neale, "How It Feels to Be Col-
    ored Me," 384–88

"Idea of a University, The" (Newman), 46
Ideas, generating, 15–16
Identities, 344–462
    "Ain't I a Woman?" (Truth), 347–48
    "Call It Blindness" (Kleege), 389–408

"Gone Country" (Feiler), 422–32
"Guys vs. Men" (Barry), 372–83
"How It Feels to Be Colored Me" (Hurston), 384–88
"The Navajo Way" (Shoumatoff), 433–40
"No Name Woman" (Kingston), 361–71
"Should English Be the Law?" (King), 409–21
"Theme for English B" (Hughes), 459–61
"What Are Homosexuals For?" (Sullivan), 350–60
"Who Am We?" (Turkle), 442–58
Images, 465–581
    "Allegory of the Cave" (Plato), 467–72
    "'By Means of the Visible': A Picture's Worth" (Stephens), 473–88
    "Crimes against Humanity" (Churchill), 497–505
    "The Great Symbol Drain" (Postman), 513–32
    "Introduction to *Trout*" (Prosek), 506–12
    "The Mystery of Mickey Mouse" (Updike), 489
    "Net Worth" (Gates), 533–53
    "Photography in the Age of Falsification" (Brower), 554–74
    "Review of *Inside the Mouse*" (Watts), 575–80
Incorporating sources, 35
"Inside the Home" (Frawley), 645–48
Interviewing, 27
    assignments
        home, 627
        identities, 371
        moralities, 177, 189, 190
        work, 690
    readings
        "Concepts of Self and Morality" (Gilligan), 169–78
        "The Recoloring of Campus Life" (Steele), 72–92
        "Work Makes Life Sweet" (hooks), 717–25
"Introduction to *Trout*" (Prosek), 506–12

"Keeping Close to Home: Class and Education" (hooks), 93–104
King, Martin Luther Jr., "Letter from Birmingham Jail," 142–56
King, Robert D., "Should English Be the Law?" 409–21
Kingston, Maxine Hong, "No Name Woman," 361–71
Kleege, Georgina, "Call It Blindness," 389–408
Krystal, Arthur, "Who Speaks for the Lazy?" 697–705

"Learning in the Key of Life" (Spayde), 58–64
LeSueur, Meridel, "Women and Work," 687–90
"Letter from Birmingham Jail" (King), 142–56
Letters to the editor, 27–28
    assignments
        home, 618
        moralities, 221
        work, 686, 696
    readings
        "Young, Privileged, and Unemployed" (Carlisle and Hoff), 691–96
Listserv, writing to a, 28–29
"Little Girls in Church" (Norris), 222–24
"Lives on the Boundary" (Rose), 105–19
Lutz, Robert A., "The Primary Purpose of Business Is Not to Make Money," 712–16

Madden, Ed, "Family Cemetery, near Hickory Ridge, Arkansas," 668–70
"Making of a Divorce Culture, The" (Whitehead), 619–27
Martin, Emily, "The Body at War: Media Views of the Immune System," 286–302
"Mind of Man, The" (Thomas), 120–25
Minot, Walter S., "Students Who Push Burgers," 726–29
Mission statements, 51–57
Moralities, 139–226
    "Civic Virtue and the Character of Followership" (Gomes), 205–13
    "Concepts of Self and Morality" (Gilligan), 169–78
    "Conscientious Consumption" (Brooks), 200–204
    "Do Kids Need Religion?" (Brandt), 191
    "The Future of Modesty" (Shalit), 214–21
    "Letter from Birmingham Jail" (King), 142–56
    "Little Girls in Church" (Norris), 222–24
    "On Morality" (Didion), 179–84
    "The Rules about the Rules" (Carter), 157
    "A Whole Lot of Cheatin' Going On" (Clayton), 185–90
Morehouse College mission statement, 53
"Mystery of Mickey Mouse, The" (Updike), 489–96

Narration, 28
    assignments
        education, 125
        home, 652
        images, 512

Narration
  assignments *(cont.)*
    moralities, 221
    science and technology, 321
    work, 711
  readings
    "The Clan of One-Breasted Women"
      (Williams), 607–18
    "Frankenstein" (Shelley), 231–36
    "Home" (Smith), 601–6
    "A Hope in the Unseen" (Suskind), 588–95
    "Introduction to *Trout*" (Prosek), 506–12
    "Keeping Close to Home: Class and Edu-
      cation" (hooks), 93–104
    "Lives on the Boundary" (Rose), 105–19
    "Quantity Time" (Barnes), 649–53
    "Women and Work" (LeSueur), 687–90
    "Would You Buy a Car from This Man?"
      (Brennan), 706–11
"Navajo Way, The" (Shoumatoff), 433–40
"Net Worth" (Gates), 532–53
Newman, John Henry, "The Idea of a Univer-
  sity," 46
"No Name Woman" (Kingston), 361–71
Norris, Kathleen, "Little Girls in Church," 222–24

Online forum, writing to an, 28–29
  assignments
    images, 496
  readings
    "Who Am We?" (Turkle), 442–58
    "A Whole Lot of Cheatin' Going On"
      (Clayton), 185–90
Online texts, critical reading of, 4, 9–10
"On Morality" (Didion), 179–84
Oppenheimer, Todd, "The Computer Delusion," 255–85

Paraphrasing, 33–34
Parody, 29–30
  assignments
    education, 57
    home, 667
    science and technology, 236, 321
  readings
    "Conscientious Consumption" (Brooks),
      200–204
    "Guys vs. Men" (Barry), 372–83
    "Well-Stacked Logs" (Connor and
      Downey), 656
Photographs, 8–9
"Photography in the Age of Falsification"
  (Brower), 554–74

Piercy, Marge, "To Be of Use," 730–31
"Place Where I Was Born, The" (Walker),
  596–600
Planning, 16
Plato, "Allegory of the Cave," 467–72
Poetry assignments
  education, 118, 134
  home, 600, 606, 670
  moralities, 183, 224
  work, 731
Position papers, 30–31
  assignments, 50
    education, 132
    home, 618, 648
    identities, 348, 431
    moralities, 190, 199
    science and technology, 236, 321
    work, 729
  readings
    "Ain't I a Woman?" (Truth), 347–48
    "Biotech Century: Playing Ecological
      Roulette with Mother Nature's Designs"
      (Rifkin), 244–54
    "How to Get a College Education" (Hart),
      126–32
    "Keeping Close to Home: Class and Edu-
      cation" (hooks), 93–104
    "Letter from Birmingham Jail" (King),
      142–56
    "Lives on the Boundary" (Rose), 105–19
    Mission statements (various colleges), 51–57
    "Photography in the Age of Falsification"
      (Brower), 554–74
Postman, Neil, "The Great Symbol Drain,"
  513–32
Previewing, 5–6
"Primary Purpose of Business Is Not to Make
  Money, The" (Lutz), 712–16
Proposing solutions, 31
  assignments
    home, 627
    science and technology, 243
  readings
    "The Biological Basis of Morality"
      (Wilson), 322–40
    "Cars and Their Enemies" (Wilson), 303–14
    "Civic Virtue and the Character of Follow-
      ership" (Gomes), 205–13
    "How to Get a College Education" (Hart),
      126–32
    "The Idea of a University" (Newman), 46
    "Letter from Birmingham Jail" (King),
      142–56

"Lives on the Boundary" (Rose), 105–19
"The Mind of Man" (Thomas), 120–25
"The Primary Purpose of Business Is Not to Make Money" (Lutz), 712–16
Prosek, James, "Introduction to *Trout*," 506–12
Purpose, 14–15

"Quantity Time" (Barnes), 649–53
Quoting sources, 33, 34

Reading habits, examining your, 3–5
Reading logs, 31–32
    assignments
        education, 49, 104, 118, 134
        home, 600, 606, 617, 618, 669
        identities, 359, 383
        images, 472
        moralities, 199
        work, 690, 725, 731
"Recoloring of Campus Life, The" (Steele), 72–92
Reporting, 32
    assignments
        education, 92, 125
        home, 648, 653, 656
        identities, 371, 440
        images, 472, 488, 532, 552, 574, 580
        moralities, 156, 178, 190
        science and technology, 243, 253
        work, 690
    readings
        "The Body at War: Media Views of the Immune System" (Martin), 286–302
        "Call It Blindness" (Kleege), 389–408
        "Concepts of Self and Morality" (Gilligan), 169–78
        "The Digital Rights War" (Samuelson), 315–21
        "Gone Country" (Feiler), 422–32
        "Lives on the Boundary" (Rose), 105–19
        "The Making of a Divorce Culture" (Whitehead), 619–27
        "The Recoloring of Campus Life" (Steele), 72–92
        "The Way We Wish We Were" (Coontz), 628–44
        "Who Am We?" (Turkle), 442–58
        "A Whole Lot of Cheatin' Going On" (Clayton), 185–90
    See also Research papers
Rereading, 7
    assignments
        education, 49

Research papers
    assignments
        home, 648
        images, 505, 512
        science and technology, 236, 254, 302, 314, 321
    See also Reporting
Responding, 7
    assignments
        education, 131, 134
        home, 606
        identities, 348, 383, 407, 458
        images, 495, 532, 553, 574
        moralities, 221
        science and technology, 253, 254, 285
"Review of *Inside the Mouse*" (Watts), 575–80
Revising, 17–18
Rhetorical analysis, 20
Rich, Adrienne, "What Does a Woman Need to Know?" 65–71
Rifkin, Jeremy, "Biotech Century: Playing Ecological Roulette with Mother Nature's Designs," 244–54
Rose, Mike, "Lives on the Boundary," 105–19
"Rules about the Rules, The" (Carter), 157–68

Samuelson, Pamela, "The Digital Rights War," 315–21
Science and technology, 229–341
    "The Biological Basis of Morality" (Wilson), 322–40
    "Biotech Century: Playing Ecological Roulette with Mother Nature's Designs" (Rifkin), 244–54
    "The Body at War: Media Views of the Immune System" (Martin), 286–302
    "Cars and Their Enemies" (Wilson), 303–14
    "The Computer Delusion" (Oppenheimer), 255–85
    "The Digital Rights War" (Samuelson), 315–21
    "Enemies of Promise" (Bishop), 237–43
    "Frankenstein" (Shelley), 231
Shalit, Wendy, "The Future of Modesty," 214–21
Shelley, Mary, "Frankenstein," 231–36
"Should English Be the Law?" (King), 409–21
Shoumatoff, Alex, "The Navajo Way," 433–40
Smith, Barbara, "Home," 601–6
Sources, 32–35
Spayde, Jon, "Learning in the Key of Life," 58–64

Steele, Shelby, "The Recoloring of Campus Life," 72–92

Stephens, Mitchell, "'By Means of the Visible': A Picture's Worth," 473–88

"Students Who Push Burgers" (Minot), 726–29

Sullivan, Andrew, "What Are Homosexuals For?" 350–60

Summarizing, 6, 34
  assignments
    education, 119
    home, 666–67
    images, 488, 504
    moralities, 220
    science and technology, 243, 253, 313

Suskind, Ron, "A Hope in the Unseen," 588–95

Tables, 8

Talbot, Margaret, "Les Très Riches Heures de Martha Stewart," 657–67

"Theme for English B" (Hughes), 459–61

Thomas, David, "The Mind of Man," 120–25

Thomas Aquinas College mission statement, 56

"To Be of Use" (Piercy), 730–31

"Très Riches Heures de Martha Stewart, Les" (Talbot), 657–67

Truth, Sojourner, "Ain't I a Woman?" 347–48

Turkle, Sherry, "Who Am We?" 442–58

University of Minnesota mission statement, 52

Updike, John, "The Mystery of Mickey Mouse," 489–96

Visual texts, critical reading of, 8–9

Walker, Alice, "The Place Where I Was Born," 596–600

Watts, Linda S., "Review of Inside the Mouse," 575–80

"Way to Wealth, The" (Franklin), 678–86

"Way We Wish We Were, The" (Coontz), 628–44

"Well-Stacked Logs" (Connor and Downey), 656

"We Real Cool" (Brooks), 133

"What Are Homosexuals For?" (Sullivan), 350–60

"What Does a Woman Need to Know?" (Rich), 65–71

Whitehead, Barbara Dafoe, "The Making of a Divorce Culture," 619–27

"Who Am We?" (Turkle), 442–58

"Whole Lot of Cheatin' Going On, A" (Clayton), 185–90

"Who Speaks for the Lazy?" (Krystal), 697–705

Williams, Terry Tempest, "The Clan of One-Breasted Women," 607–18

Wilson, Edward O., "The Biological Basis of Morality," 322–40

Wilson, James Q., "Cars and Their Enemies," 303–14

"Women and Work" (LeSueur), 687–90

Work, 674–732
  "The Primary Purpose of Business Is Not to Make Money" (Lutz), 712–16
  "Students Who Push Burgers" (Minot), 726–29
  "To Be of Use" (Piercy), 730–31
  "The Way to Wealth" (Franklin), 678–86
  "Who Speaks for the Lazy?" (Krystal), 697–705
  "Women and Work" (LeSueur), 687–90
  "Work Makes Life Sweet" (hooks), 717–25
  "Would You Buy a Car from This Man?" (Brennan), 706–11
  "Young, Privileged, and Unemployed" (Carlisle and Hoff), 691–96

"Work Makes Life Sweet" (hooks), 717–25

"Would You Buy a Car from This Man?" (Brennan), 706–11

Writing (writing process)
  assignment, 14
  critical reading and, 10
  drafting, 16
  editing, 18
  effective, 14–16
  feedback and, 17
  final version, 18–19
  generating ideas and making plans for, 15–16
  to learn, 13–14
  purpose and audience of, 14–15
  revising, 17–18

"Young, Privileged, and Unemployed" (Carlisle and Hoff), 691–96